The Encyclopedia of Middle Grades Education

The Encyclopedia of Middle Grades Education

edited by

Vincent A. Anfara, Jr.
The University of Tennessee

Gayle Andrews
The University of Georgia

Steven B. Mertens
University of Illinois

NMSA

National Middle School Association
Westerville, Ohio

INFORMATION AGE
PUBLISHING

Greenwich, Connecticut • www.infoagepub.com

BP53

Library of Congress Cataloging-in-Publication Data

The encyclopedia of middle grades education / edited by Vincent A. Anfara,
Jr., Gayle Andrews, Steven B. Mertens.
   p. cm.
 Includes bibliographical references and index.
 ISBN 1-59311-172-X (pbk.) — ISBN 1-59311-173-8 (hardcover)
 1. Middle school education—Encyclopedias. I. Anfara, Vincent A. II.
Andrews, Gayle. III. Mertens, Steven B.
 LB1623.E53 2005
 373.23603—dc22
                                        2005029312

Printed in the United States of America

11/14/07

Contents

List of Anchor Essays

Middle Level Education: A Personal History
John H. Lounsbury and Gordon F. Vars

Academically Excellent Curriculum, Instruction, and Assessment
P. Elizabeth Pate

The Challenge of Middle School Equity
Nancy M. Doda

Creating Developmentally Responsive Middle Level Schools
Gert Nesin and Edward N. Brazee

Leadership in the Middle Level School
Ronald D. Williamson and J. Howard Johnston

The Professional Preparation of Middle Level Teachers and Principals
C. Kenneth McEwin, Thomas S. Dickinson, and Vincent A. Anfara, Jr

Middle Grades Education: Back to the Future
Gayle Andrews

List of Entries

Contributors

Maud Abeel
Academy for Educational Development

Patrick Akos
*The University of North Carolina
Chapel Hill*

Elizabeth Albright
The University of Tennessee

Nancy Ames
Educational Development Center, Inc.

Gayle Andrews
The University of Georgia

Vincent A. Anfara, Jr.
The University of Tennessee

Joanne M. Arhar
Kent State University

Merritt M. Arnold
The University of Georgia

Lynne M. Bailey
The University of North Carolina Charlotte

Robert Balfanz
Talent Development Middle Schools

Dana L. Bickmore
The University of Georgia

Betty Shockley Bisplinghoff
The University of Georgia

Bethany K. Black
Missouri State University

Rhonda Black
University of Hawaii, Manoa

Barbara R. Blackburn
Winthrop University

Gena Bramlett-Guignon
Association of Illinois Middle-Level Schools

Michael J. Brannigan
*Queensbury Middle School,
Queensbury, NY*

Edward N. Brazee
University of Maine

Shari L. Britner
Bradley University

Cynthia G. Brown
Center for American Progress

Alison Buehler
The University of Tennessee

Peggy H. Burke
Central Michigan University

Cathy Carter
The University of Georgia

Loyce Caruthers
University of Missouri, Kansas City

Micki M. Caskey
Portland State University

Leslie S. Cook
University of North Carolina, Charlotte

Sondra S. Cooney
Southern Regional Education Board

Cecelia P. Daniels
Success for All Foundation, Inc.

Erika D. Daniels
California State University, San Marcos

Paul Deering
University of Hawaii, Manoa

Barbara S. DeHart
Lilly Endowment Inc.

Thomas S. Dickinson
DePauw University

Nancy Doda
National Louis University

Thomas O. Erb
DePauw University

L. Mickey Fenzel
Loyola College in Maryland

Christine Finnan
College of Charleston

Angela G. Fiske
The University of Georgia

Janis D. Flint-Ferguson
Gordon College

Nancy Flowers
CPRD, University of Illinois

Patrick K. Freer
Georgia State University

Dan French
Center for Collaborative Education

Paul S. George
The University of Florida

Matthew D. Goodman
University of Missouri

Jennifer S. Goodwin
Teachers College, Columbia University

Melanie W. Greene
Appalachian State University

Christy Guilfoyle
*Association for Supervision and
Curriculum Development*

Katherine B. Harmon
Missouri State University

John A. Harrison
*Southern Forum to Accelerate
Middle-Grades Reform*

Kimberly J. Hartman
The University of North Carolina Charlotte

Mary Henton
National Middle School Association

Glenda Y. Hernández
Montgomery College, Maryland

Elaine R. Homestead
McConnell Middle School, Grayson, GA

David Hough
Missouri State University

Gail Ingwalson
University of North Dakota

Alecia Youngblood Jackson
Appalachian State University

Virginia M. Jagla
National-Louis University

Karen Embry Jenlink
St. Edward's University

David W. Johnson
University of Minnesota

Roger T. Johnson
University of Minnesota

J. Howard Johnston
University of South Florida

Shelly Kale
The Galef Institute

Deborah Kasak
*National Forum to Accelerate
Middle-Grades Reform*

Louise Kennelly
New American Schools

Emily Lin
University of Nevada, Las Vegas

Richard Lipka
Pittsburg State University

Joan Lipsitz
MDC, Inc.

John H. Lounsbury
Georgia College and State University

Douglas J. Mac Iver
Talent Development Middle Schools

Monica Martinez
KnowledgeWorks Foundation

C. Kenneth McEwin
Appalachian State University

Margaret J. McLaughlin
University of Maryland

Steven B. Mertens
CPRD, University of Illinois

Jim Miller
California Department of Education

Hayes Mizell
National Staff Development Council

Patrick Montesano
Academy for Educational Development

Mike Muir
University of Maine at Farmington

Peter F. Mulhall
CPRD, University of Illinois

P. Maureen Musser
Willamette University

John Myers
University of West Georgia

John Nori
*National Association of
Secondary School Princiaps*

Gert Nesin
University of Maine, Orono

Kris Kaiser Olson
Parents for Public Schools

P. Elizabeth Pate
The University of Texas at San Antonio

Sara Davis Powell
College of Charleston

Donna D. Price
University of Houston

Cheryl Riggins
*National Association of Elementary
School Principals*

Kathleen Roney
The University of North Carolina Wilmington

Lea Williams Rose
Academy for Educational Development

Steven M. Ross
The University of Memphis

Allen Ruby
Talent Development Middle Schools

Leah Rugen
Center for Collaborative Education

Betsy Rymes
The University of Georgia

Vicki L. Schmitt
University of Kansas

Deb Schrock
Association of Illinois Middle-Level Schools

Nick Scott
University of Maine at Farmington

Michele Jean Sims
University of Alabama at Birmingham

Tracy W. Smith
Appalachian State University

Bryan Sorohan
Brenau University

Sandra L. Stacki
Hofstra University

Cody Stephens
CPRD, University of Illinois

Allan Sterbinsky
The University of Memphis

David B. Strahan
Western Carolina University

John H. Swaim
Otterbein College

Shirley Theriot
University of Texas, Arlington

Katherine F. Thompson
The University of Georgia

Nicole L. Thompson
Mississippi State University

Sue C. Thompson
University of Missouri, Kansas City

Reese H. Todd
Texas Tech University

Carol Ann Tomlinson
University of Virginia

Jerry Valentine
University of Missouri

Thomas M. Van Soelen
City Schools of Decatur, GA

Gordon F. Vars
Kent State University (Retired)

Hersh C. Waxman
University of Houston

Holly Wess
University of Maine at Farmington

Barbara L. Whinery
University of Northern Colorado

Ronald D. Williamson
Eastern Michigan University

Gretchen Wolfram
Lilly Endowment Inc.

About the Editors

Gayle Andrews is assistant professor and middle school program coordinator at The University of Georgia. A graduate of the University of North Carolina at Chapel Hill, she served as national director of Carnegie Corporation of New York's Middle Grade School State Policy Initiative. With Anthony Jackson, she is coauthor (under the name "Davis") of *Turning Points 2000: Educating Adolescents in the 21st Century*. She also serves on National Middle School Association's Research Advisory Board, the board of directors of the National Forum to Accelerate Middle-Grades Reform, and as a council member for the American Educational Research Association's Middle Level Education Research Special Interest Group.

Vincent A. Anfara, Jr is associate professor and program coordinator of educational administration and supervision at The University of Tennessee. He has written over 40 articles and edited/authored eight books focused on middle grades issues. He is the editor of the book series, *The Handbook of Research on Middle Level Education*. Additionally, he is the chair of the National Middle School Association's Research Advisory Board and the past-president of the American Educational Research Association's special interest group, Middle Level Education Research. Before entering the professorate, he worked in both middle and high schools for 18 years.

Steven B. Mertens is a senior research scientist at the Center for Prevention Research and Development (CPRD) at the University of Illinois. For the past decade he has served as the project director for the design, research, and evaluation of several large-scale evaluations of comprehensive middle-grades reform efforts, including Michigan Middle Start, Mid South Middle Start, and Turning Points. He and his colleagues have published numerous articles and reports addressing varying aspects of middle-grades school reform and improvement. Currently he serves as a member of National Forum to Accelerate Middle-Grades Reform, NMSA's Research Advisory Board, and Council Member for AERA's Middle Level Education Research Special Interest Group.

Preface

The Encyclopedia of Middle Grades Education, more than 2 years in the making, has filled a recognized void. This unique publication provides the first authoritative set of definitions and descriptions of all the elements, features, and characteristics that comprise the middle level concept. Anchored by several major essays, it also chronicles the history and development of the middle level movement and the philosophical foundations of the movement.

This major work represents the outstanding commitment of the various writers as well as its editors, Dr. Vincent Anfara, Dr. Gayle Andrews, and Dr. Steven Mertens. All authors are recognized middle level leaders, researchers, and practitioners. Representatives of various professional organizations including the National Middle School Association, National Association of Secondary School Principals, National Forum to Accelerate Middle Grades Reform, Association of Illinois Middle Schools, and the Academy of Educational Development have shared their vision and knowledge of middle level education so that a definitive middle level resource could be readily available.

As the first-ever encyclopedia covering middle level education topics, its significance is readily apparent. Every superintendent, middle level principal, and other stated middle level leaders should have a copy on their desks. Policymakers at the local, state, and national level should also use this as a key resource. Likewise, every college and university preparing middle level teachers, counselors, and administrators should provide copies of the encyclopedia in its library.

Educating young adolescents is a complex undertaking and one that deserves our best efforts and total commitment if we are to successfully implement what research, cumulative practice, and common sense tell us is needed. At this particular point in time, we find ourselves engaged in a renewed debate regarding the implementation of the middle level concept and this encyclopedia will bring greater understanding and consistency of interpretation to middle level practices as efforts are made to improve education at this critically important time in the lives of 10- through 14-year-olds.

Middle level educators have been leaders in recent school reform and research-based initiatives. Accepted middle level practices such as interdisciplinary teaming, adult advocacy, and the creation of small and personalized learning communities are currently being recommended as needed reform initiatives in the high schools. But much more still needs to be done at the middle level itself if we are to meet our goal of ensuring an academically challenging education that is developmentally appropriate for every young adolescent.

Therefore, National Middle School Association welcomes the publication of this new resource and is proud to be a copublisher of it. This encyclopedia will bring clarity to the field and serve as a vital resource by both policymakers and practitioners who are committed to implementing successful schools for young adolescents.

Sue Swaim
Executive Director
National Middle School Association

Introduction

The landscape of American education changed dramatically in the 1960s as the need to reform the junior high school evolved into a call for the creation of the middle school. In 1965, the National Education Association (NEA) defined the middle school as "the school which stands academically between elementary and high school, is housed separately, and offers at least three years of schooling beginning with either grade five or six" (p. 5). Later, in its first position paper, *This We Believe*, National Middle School Association (NMSA, 1982) extended that definition, which focused on grade level designation, to include consideration of the distinct developmental needs of young adolescents and to highlight important programmatic components such as interdisciplinary teams, flexible organizational structures, varied instructional strategies, exploratory curricula, comprehensive advising and counseling, and educators knowledgeable about and committed to middle school students.

The foundations of the middle school were built by a myriad of funders, researchers, and advocates, including the National Middle School Association, the National Association of Secondary School Principals (NASSP), the National Association of Elementary School Principals (NAESP), the Association for Supervision and Curriculum Development (ASCD), Carnegie Corporation of New York, the Edna McConnell Clark Foundation, the W. K. Kellogg Foundation, Lilly Endowment, Inc., the Middle Level Education Research Special Interest Group of the American Educational Research Association, and the National Forum to Accelerate Middle-Grades Reform. Several of these participants in the development of the middle school movement issued seminal reports such as, *The Middle School We Need* (ASCD, 1975), *This We Believe* (NMSA, 1982, 1995, 2003), *An Agenda for Excellence in Middle Level Education* (NASSP, 1985), and *Turning Points: Preparing American Youth for the 21st Cen-*

tury (Carnegie Council on Adolescent Development, 1989), and the National Forum's vision statement describing high-performing middle grades schools (National Forum to Accelerate Middle-Grades Reform, 1998). Influential individuals included, among others, William Alexander, Donald Eichhorn, Paul George, Joan Lipsitz, John Lounsbury, Ken McEwin, Nancy Doda, Conrad Toepfer, and Gordon Vars. Eventually, *Turning Points 2000: Educating Adolescents in the 21st Century* (Jackson & Davis, 2000), follow-up to the landmark 1989 report, was published. What is most striking is the fact that from these vastly different reports a very consistent set of principles emerged that have become the foundations of the middle school (or middle grades) movement. We define the middle school or middle grades movement as the long-running series of efforts to improve schooling for young adolescents, those students between the ages of 10 and 15.

Since the mid-twentieth century the number of middle schools, as defined by grade configuration and adopted name, has grown significantly. In 1993-1994, there were 80,740 public schools in the United States, about 15% of them middle schools. The number of middle schools increased from 9,086 to 11,712 between 1987-1988 and 1993-1994, while the number of elementary and secondary schools remained about the same. The growth occurred almost solely in schools with Grades 6–8. Of some 41.6 million students in public schools in 1993-1994, 6.8 million were enrolled in middle schools (see Alt & Choy, 2000).

In 1989, in its seminal publication, *Turning Points*, the Carnegie Task Force on the Education of Young Adolescents noted that "young adolescents face significant turning points" (Carnegie Council on Adolescent Development, p. 8). In 2005, middle grades schools find themselves faced with similar challenges. We would be negligent not to admit that middle grades schools are on the defensive and that many school systems, especially large urban districts, have returned to K–8 grade configurations with the hope that grade configuration is the deciding factor in the quality of schools for young adolescents. Those attacking middle grades schools generally cite data that show a decline in academic performance for students in Grade 8 (e.g., Third International Mathematics and Science Study, Mid-Atlantic Eisnhower Consortium for Mathematics and Science Education, 1997). Little regard is paid to whether or not the "middle grades school" has adopted with any degree of fidelity the middle school concept, that set of consistent principles mentioned above, or simply changed the name above the schoolhouse door. We are not shy in admitting that we are strong proponents of the middle grades movement and that we believe that whatever grade configuration is in vogue, young adolescents (student between the ages of 10 and 15) must be educated in a manner that is academically excellent, developmentally appropriate, and socially equitable (National Forum to Accelerate Middle-Grades Reform, 1998).

This encyclopedia of middle grades education is the first of its kind. The idea for this resource was first discussed in Columbus, Ohio, in October of 2003. The editors of this encyclopedia, members of NMSA's Research Advisory Board, were meeting in Columbus as part of the National Middle School Association's All-Committee Weekend. The uniqueness of this project explains part of the attraction that would lead us to undertake a venture of this magnitude. The other alluring element of undertaking this project is rooted in the definition of "encyclopedia"—an "all-encompassing education." No one practitioner or researcher knows everything. Even experts must search for the exact meaning of some term, the importance of some person to the middle school movement, or review what research exists on a particular topic. In short, this encyclopedia brings together, in one place, authoritative essays and entries on virtually all middle grades topics.

While the appeal of this encyclopedia is evident for researchers, our hope is that it will also be useful to undergraduate and graduate students in middle grades teacher and administra-tor preparation programs, middle grades teachers and administrators, policymakers, and general readers (e.g., journalists) who want to understand more about middle grades schools and the young adolescents they serve.

As one quickly reviews the encyclopedia, it is evident that there are two major divisions of entries. The first division includes what we refer to as anchor essays. These seven essays cover the most important issues in middle level education, and the authors of these essays engage their readers in an extended explication of their topics. The other major division includes the A-Z entries. While in Columbus in 2003, we developed what we thought to be an exhaustive list of all possible entries. As the process unfolded, some entries were culled, some consolidated, and some added. In the spirit of the first encyclopedia, *l'Encyclopedie*, by Diderot and d'Alembert in 1751, we tried to examine everything that concerned the middle grades school. Although some things are undoubtedly not examined, it remains for our readers to tell us what they are.

Once the entry list was basically set, we began to contact potential contributors. We were amazed and gratified by the support for this publication that came from the community of middle grades researchers, practitioners, and policymakers. It was this support that solidified in us the belief that the time had come for an *Encyclopedia of Middle Grades Education* and that our efforts were not in vain.

It needs to be noted that some of these entries are approximately 2,000 words in length whereas others are approximately 500 words. Important people, organizations, and books were limited to 500 words, whereas important terms, concepts, and programmatic components were given a 2,000 word limit. We are confident that readers will find that these essays and entries are intelligently written by recognized experts in the field.

Altogether, there are 146 entries. Examples of excellent treatments of a whole host of topics abound in the following pages of these volumes. By assembling into one encyclopedia entries of various origins, we hope that readers will come to appreciate the rich heritage of middle grades education and the importance of this knowledge to all levels of the K-12 educational system. Many elementary schools already incorporate many of the programmatic components that are promoted for middle grades students. Additionally, in the most recent report, *Works in Progress: A Report on Middle and High School Improvement Programs* (The Comprehensive School Reform Quality Center, 2005), it is interesting to note the call for the introduction of advisory programs, thematic units, and team teaching into the reform of the American high school.

In addition to the contributors, there are others who are responsible for the success of this encyclopedia. A project of this magnitude would not have been possible without the support of members of the Middle Level Education Research Special Interest Group (MLER—SIG). The MLER—SIG is an affiliate of the American Educational Research Association (AERA) and is the largest organization of researchers who are dedicated to looking at issues related to middle grades education. Its membership is international in scope and can truly be counted on when a need arises. Alison Buehler, a doctoral student at The University of Tennessee, spent countless hours checking references and APA formatting. She has become an expert in finding volume and pages numbers for citations that were not always completely supplied by contributing authors. Finally, we want to thank George Johnson of Information Age Publishing for his willingness to support middle grades education and for his ability to recognize the importance of this project to the future of middle grades education.

REFERENCES

Alt M. N., & Choy, S. P. (2000). *In the middle: Characteristics of public schools with a focus on middle schools* (NCES 2000-312). Washington, DC: National Center for Education Statistics.

The Comprehensive School Reform Quality Center. (2005). *Works in progress: A report on middle and high school improvement programs*. Washington, DC: American Institutes for Research.

Association for Supervision and Curriculum Development. (1975). *The middle school we need*. Washington, DC: Author.

Carnegie Council on Adolescent Development. (1989). *Turning points: Preparing American youth for the 21st century*. The Report of the Task Force on Education of Young Adolescents. New York: Carnegie Corporation of New York.

Jackson, A. W., & Davis, G. A. (2000). *Turning points 2000: Educating adolescents in the 21st century*. New York: Teachers College Press.

Mid-Atlantic Eisenhower Consortium for Mathematics and Science Education. (1997). *A sourcebook of 8th-grade findings: TIMSS*. Philadelphia: Research for Better Schools.

National Association of Secondary School Principals Council on Middle Level Education. *(1985). An agenda for excellence at the middle level*. Reston, VA: Author.

National Education Association. (1965). *Middle schools*. Washington, DC: Author.

National Forum to Accelerate Middle-Grades Reform. (1998). *Vision statement of the National Forum to Accelerate Middle-Grades Reform*. Newton, MA: Education Development Center.

National Middle School Association. (1982). *This we believe*. Columbus, OH: Author.

National Middle School Association. (1995. *This we believe: Developmentally responsive middle level schools*. Columbus, OH: Author.

National Middle School Association. (2003). *This we believe: Successful schools for young adolescents*. Columbus, OH: Author.

Vincent A. Anfara, Jr.
The University of Tennessee

Gayle Andrews
The University of Georgia

Steven B. Mertens
Center for Prevention Research and Development, University of Illinois, Champaign

Middle Level Education
A Personal History

John H. Lounsbury
Gordon F. Vars

Note: What follows is a listing of important events and resources that chronicle the history of middle level education—as the authors have viewed and experienced it. They make no claim as to the historical validity of their listings and judgments about these events but offer them nevertheless as a way to identify the roots and trace the developments that comprise the history of middle level education in America.

Following military service in World War II, they both completed their preparation for teaching with John going to North Carolina to teach social studies and Gordon heading to Maryland to teach in a core curriculum. Their paths would cross a few years later at George Peabody College for Teachers at Vanderbilt University, beginning a productive, professional association that spans more than half a century.

1888 **The question, "Can school programs be shortened and enriched?" was raised.** Harvard President Charles W. Eliot posed this question in an address to the Department of Superintendence. This is generally recognized as the event that kicked off the movement to reorganize secondary education because it led to the appointment of several national committees and other activities that resulted in the creation of the junior high school and, several decades later, the middle school.

1894 **The Committee of Ten on Secondary School Studies.** Established in 1892 under the auspices of the National Education Association (NEA) with President Eliot as chairman, this influential committee, which was made up primarily of college administrators, not surprisingly advocated that high school subjects such as algebra should begin earlier and that elementary education be limited to 6 years—all to serve the needs of higher education.

1895 **Richmond, Indiana, establishes a seventh and eighth grade "intermediate school."** Was this the first junior high school? Apparently, it was an independent action not created to be a part of the not-yet-underway junior high school movement.

1899 **The Committee on College Entrance Requirements.** This NEA-established group supported the 6/6 elementary and secondary division but based it on the belief that "the seventh grade, rather than the ninth, is the natural turning point in the pupil's life, as the age of adolescence demands new methods and wiser direction." This report was the first to advance the idea of reorganization on some basis other than better college preparation.

1905 **G. Stanley Hall authored *Adolescence*.** This first major work on adolescence emphasized the extent of changes youth undergo and the difficulties they face. Hall used the term "storm and stress," a phrase that came to be commonly associated with adolescence. His ideas supported making changes in the schools when young people experience what Hall called, "a psychological second birth."

1907 **E.L. Thorndike's study, *The Elimination of Pupils from Schools*.** Thorndike's data revealed the extent of dropouts in 23 large cities and gave support to the need for changes in the school program. Additional studies by Leonard Ayres, *Laggards in Our Schools* (1909), and by George Strayer, *Age and Grade Census of Schools and Colleges* (1911) confirmed the extent of dropouts after Grade 5 and also reported on the high number of repeaters, called "left backs," in these grades. The economic impact of having so many pupils repeat a grade also became a justification for making changes in the way we educate young adolescents.

1909   **Indianola Junior High School.** This 6-8 school, located in Columbus, Ohio, is generally recognized as the first junior high school. A historical marker on the site claims it as the first.

1910   **Two "introductory high schools" introduced in Berkeley, California.** These 7-9 schools were established by Superintendent Frank Bunker who was an outspoken advocate and champion for reorganization.

1918   **Commission on the Reorganization of Secondary Education.** This was the most famous of the many early committees that dealt with the reorganization issue. Perhaps better known for its listing of the *Cardinal Principles of Secondary Education,* the commission's statements on reorganization had great influence on the infant junior high school movement. These sentences from the report are particularly pertinent:

> We, therefore, recommend a reorganization of the school system whereby the first six years shall be devoted to elementary education and the second six years to secondary education.
>
> The six years to be devoted to secondary education may well be divided into two periods. In the junior period emphasis should be placed upon the attempt to help the pupil explore his own aptitudes and to make at least provisional choice of the kinds of work to which he shall devote himself....
>
> In the junior high school there should be a gradual introduction of departmental instruction, some choice of subjects under guidance, promotion by subjects, prevocational courses, and a social organization that calls forth initiative and develops the sense of personal responsibility for the welfare of the group.

Note the degree to which these statements have a "middle school" flavor and that the recommendation on departmentalization was rarely followed. The Seven Cardinal Principles—really objectives—were important for their recognition that secondary education, now including grades 6 through 12, had responsibilities that went far beyond college preparation. This report is a landmark in American education.

1920   *The Junior High School.* Two books, each with this simple title, were published in 1920 by the movement's foremost leaders at that time, Thomas H. Briggs and Leonard V. Koos. Both volumes sought to define the fledgling institution and had considerable influence, although they failed to curb the dominance of high school organizational structures and practices as early junior high schools were made operational. The junior high school, as advocated by these and other early leaders, was indeed very similar to today's middle school concept—a reality seldom recognized.

John corresponded with and met Dr. Koos. The last book written by Koos, Junior High School Trends (1955), cites John's dissertation.

1927   *The Junior High School Curriculum.* The fifth yearbook of the Department of the Superintendence, National Education Association (NEA), involved hundreds of educators and included chapters on each of 10 separate subject areas as well as historical and status information. One chapter was titled "Shall the Junior High School Be Free from the Responsibility of Direct Preparation for College?" The improvement of college preparation, the objective that started the reorganization movement, was soon to become its first casualty as other justifications took hold.

1934   **The Eight-Year Study launched.** The Progressive Education Association began the most comprehensive, long-range, experimental research study on curriculum ever conducted. Although dealing mostly with high school, the study's work on curriculum was and still is germane to the middle level. The study's findings were published in 1943 in a series of five books. Unfortunately, America was then at war, and so the significant results never received the attention their importance warranted. The work of the experimental schools that participated in the study advanced collaborative teaching based on what was known about learning and the democratic way of life. The core curriculum, resource units, and summer institutes were among developments that grew out of this project.

In 1948 Gordon visited 19 secondary schools in Ohio, Indiana, Illinois, and Missouri to see if he really wanted to become a teacher. Six of those schools had participated in the Eight-Year Study. John and Gordon participated in the 1998 NMSA book, The Eight-Year Study Revisited (Lipka, Lounsbury, Toepfer, Vars, & Alessi).

1944 *Education for All American Youth.* This work of the Educational Policies Commission of NEA and American Association of School Administrators (AASA) was a fairly detailed elaboration of what 6 years of secondary education—grades 6-12—would look like in a city and in a rural area. Emphasized was a "common learnings" course. The book included the "Ten Imperative Needs of Youth," a frequently cited listing of the broader responsibilities of modern secondary education that echoed the Seven Cardinal Principles.

1944 *Adolescence.* This publication by the influential National Society for the Study of Education (NSSE) was an early attempt to compile and review studies of this age group that was now drawing increased attention.

1946 **The separate junior high school becomes majority practice.** By the late 1940s, the clearly predominant pattern of school organization in the United States involved having a junior high school apart from the senior high school. The need to build more schools following World War II helped to bring the junior high school movement to its apex even as it was coming under increased and well-founded criticism.

1947 *The Modern Junior High School* by William Gruhn and Harl Douglass, became something of a classic and helped keep the original intent of the junior high school alive. Its listing of the six functions of the junior high was widely quoted and remains valid today as the functions of any middle level institution. Revised editions were published in 1956 and in 1971.

Both Gordon and John had several opportunities to associate with one or both of these junior high leaders. In 1984, Gordon revisited the Gruhn and Douglass functions and looked for their expression in major middle school publications. This analysis appeared in Perspectives: Middle School Education 1964-1984, *developed and edited by John, in which prominent advocates reviewed the first 2 decades of the middle school movement.*

1947 *Reorganizing the High School Curriculum* by Harold Alberty was the most influential of several books dealing with the core curriculum written during the late 1940s and early 1950s. Alberty advocated that programs in Grades 7-12 be based on the characteristics and needs of adolescents and employ the core curriculum, a problem-centered block of time usually under the direction of one teacher.

Alberty had been director of the Ohio State University School. While completing a master's degree at Ohio State in 1948-49, Gordon took two courses with Alberty and spent many hours observing classes and interviewing the personnel at the school. Alberty was instrumental in Gordon's getting his first teaching position.

1952 **Illinois Junior High School Principals' Association Conferences.** By sponsoring a series of annual studies, conferences, and workshops, the Illinois Principals' Association, in conjunction with the Junior High School Association of Illinois, provided an early long-term effort to share and extend progressive thinking and practices.

1953 *The Junior High School: Today and Tomorrow* by Gertrude Noar still is a cogent argument for democratic and student-centered middle level education.

1953 **National Association for Core Curriculum.** Educators from 14 states and the District of Columbia gathered at the University of West Virginia "to consider the establishment of a National Council of Core Teachers." Included were prominent progressive educators such as Harold Alberty, Arno Bellack, Roland Faunce, Nelson Bossing, and Grace Wright from the United States Office of Education. Mrs. Wright's three national studies of core curriculum revealed that most core or "core like" programs were at the junior high school level (see, for example, Wright, 1952, 1958, 1963).

Gordon rode the bus all night from Nashville, Tennessee, to attend this meeting. In 1961 he became executive secretary/treasurer and editor of the association's quarterly newsletter, The Core Teacher, *a position he has maintained for over 50 years.*

1959 **Junior High School Project, Cornell University.** Supported by a grant from the Ford Foundation, this project, which continued through 1967, offered graduate-level preparation for junior high school teaching to undergraduates from noneducation fields. Its publications, such as *The Intellectual Responsibility of the Junior High School* (Johnson, 1962), and other professional activities promoted high quality middle level education.

Gordon was one of the four staff members and served as director for 1 year.

1960 *Recommendations for Education in the Junior High School Years.* This memorandum to school boards was written by Harvard President James B. Conant who had achieved considerable notoriety with his 1959 book *The American High School Today.* Recommendations in this brief treatise were supportive of conservative subject-centered programs. Most noted and quoted was his condemnation of junior high school marching bands and interscholastic athletics, in his view, prime examples of inappropriately replicating the senior high school. An interesting and somewhat critical analysis of Conant's Memorandum was done by Thomas Briggs (see 1920, 1960) and published in the special issue of *NASSP Bulletin* of November 1960 on "The Junior High School, Today and Tomorrow."

John appeared on a panel with Conant to discuss the report.

1961 *Modern Education for the Junior High School Years.* This book by William Van Til, Gordon Vars, and John Lounsbury provided a thorough examination of the history, status, and philosophy of junior high school education built around Van Til's argument that education must meet the needs of students, address social realities of the times, and promote democratic values. One section detailed the core curriculum in action. A revised edition of this work was published in 1967.

Gordon was a core teacher at the Peabody Demonstration School and John was William Van Til's graduate assistant. Van Til had been a core teacher at the Ohio State University School under Alberty in the 1930s. Gordon succeeded John as Van Til's graduate assistant in 1954. Both were greatly influenced by Van Til, who was their major professor and continued as a mentor throughout their subsequent careers.

1961 *The Junior High School We Need.* The Association for Supervision and Curriculum Development (ASCD) continued its interest in and support of the reorganization movement by publishing this small monograph developed by the association's Commission on Secondary Curriculum.

John joined the commission this year and developed the Shadow Study Project (see 1964) as a commission project.

1961 **Mt. Kisco conferences on the middle school.** Two conferences on the middle school convened at Mt. Kisco, New York, the site of an early middle school, to examine the purpose, spirit, and shape of the middle school. Included were such well-known educators as Robert Anderson and Jerome Bruner from Harvard and Lawrence Cremin from Teachers College. Publication of this report and descriptions of other "state of the art" buildings by Educational Facilities Laboratories (1962) helped shape perceptions of what a middle school should be.

1962 *Growth at Adolescence.* This book by J.M. Tanner, a respected English psychologist, detailed the earlier age at which young people now mature, a condition that supported a 6-8 intermediate unit rather than a 7-9 unit. Other studies appeared with similar conclusions, giving a clear biological basis for the middle school and also recognizing the social-emotional concerns of young adolescents.

1963 *Evaluative Criteria for Junior High Schools.* The National Study of Secondary School Evaluation (NSSE) published an adaptation of its nationally used high school accreditation instrument when some regional associations began accrediting junior high schools. In 1970, a completely new document, *Junior High School/Middle School Evaluative Criteria* was released. Just 9 years later, a revision, *Middle School/Junior High School Evaluative Criteria* was published. And finally, in 1999, a completely new document, *Evaluative Criteria for Middle Level Schools* was made available. Note how changes in the titles reflect advances in the middle level movement.

John was a member of the board of directors of NSSE for many years and was an active participant in the development of all but the first of these instruments.

1963 **William Alexander's "middle school" speech.** At the Tenth Annual Conference of School Administrators held at Cornell University, William Alexander made the speech in which he first used the term "middle school." As a result of his continuing advocacy of this middle school idea, Alexander is considered the Father of the Middle School.

Gordon was present and a presenter at this conference.

1964 *The Junior High School We Saw: One Day in the Eighth Grade.* This ASCD report by John Lounsbury and Jean Marani was the first of what ultimately turned out to be five national shadow studies that revealed what a school day was like for middle level students. Volunteers from across the country spent the same school day following randomly selected students and recording what each student was doing. The results of this "reality check" were perhaps more revealing than encouraging. The shadow study technique became a frequently used and highly effective activity in preservice education and in professional development. Twenty-four years later, NASSP published *Life in the Three Sixth Grades* by Lounsbury and J. Howard Johnston in 1988 and *Inside Grade Eight: From Apathy to Excitement* by Lounsbury and Donald Clark in 1990. The central lesson in these shadow studies was "the teacher makes the difference."

Gordon was an analyst for some of these studies.

1966 *The Middle School* by Donald Eichhorn, a founder of the middle school, was the first comprehensive treatment of both the philosophy and practice of this infant institution. Eichhorn introduced the term "transescence" as a label for this distinctive age cohort and advanced the idea of developmental or maturity grouping of students rather than age-grade grouping. These ideas had been tested in Fort Couch and Boyce Middle Schools in Upper St. Clair, Pennsylvania, under Eichhorn's direction. Because of its importance, this book was reissued by NMSA and NASSP in 1987.

1967 **The Toledo Conference** addressed various aspects of "the middle school idea" and featured William Alexander, Donald Eichhorn, Kaoru Yamamoto, and Gordon Vars. Gordon and Alexander presented quite different curriculum designs for the "emerging middle school."

Gordon's design was later published in the 1978 book by John and Gordon, A Curriculum for the Middle School Years.

1968 **Survey by Alexander reveals 1,101 middle schools.** Using the definition "schools having at least three but not more than five grades and including grades 6 and 7," this survey did not include any 2-year, 7-8 schools. It should be noted that Alexander was an early proponent of a 5-8 as well as a 6-8 middle school. Two years later a survey by Ronald Kealy (1971), using the same definition as Alexander, yielded a total of 2,298 middle schools, over half of them being 6-8 schools. The early appeal of the middle school idea is evidenced by this doubling in numbers in just 2 years.

1968 *The Emergent Middle School.* William Alexander was the lead author of this early middle school text (Alexander, Williams, Compton, Hynes, & Prescott, 1968). The authors make a strong case for the "new" middle school and offer recommendations concerning curriculum, instruction, and organization. The book was so well received, an expanded version was published the next year. Dissatisfaction with the way the junior high school evolved in practice had created a readiness for change, and the middle school idea offered a fresh start.

1969 *Common Learnings: Core and Interdisciplinary Team Approaches.* Edited by Gordon Vars, this book reasserted the value of the core approach for providing students with "common learnings," that is the fundamental concepts, skills, and values considered essential for any citizen. It also explored the relationship of core to other approaches and issues that were receiving attention at the time, such as team teaching, independent study, middle school, and "the culturally disadvantaged."

In putting this book together, Gordon called upon people he knew through the National Association for Core Curriculum. Expected to be a definitive work on core curriculum, it unfortunately never received wide circulation.

1969 **Council on the Emerging Adolescent Learner.** ASCD gave specific attention to the growing movement by establishing this council and supporting its working groups over the next 6 years. Members conducted workshops all over the country and developed a package of sound filmstrips. Donald Eichhorn and Conrad Toepfer were influential in this group.

1970 **Midwest Middle School Association organized.** School administrators from Ohio and Michigan and teacher educators from three colleges or universities met in Toledo to consider the need for an organization to promote the middle school. The next year MWMSA was formally organized "to promote the development and growth of the middle school as a distinct and necessary entity in the structure of American education."

Gordon was elected MWMSA's first president.

1972 **The Shoreham-Wading River Middle School** was organized under the imaginative leadership of Dennis Littky with the support of an enlightened board of education. This new middle school became a much visited and written about model of a progressive middle school. Ross Burkhardt, 1996 NMSA president, was a first hire and taught there until he retired in 2001.

1972 *FLAEMS: Florida's Emerging Middle Schools.* Paul George of the University of Florida launched this newsletter for middle level educators. By winter of that year, it claimed 6,000 readers and announced the formation of the Florida League of Middle Schools. The organization thrived, and by the fall of 1973, attracted more than 500 participants to its annual conference. Other state organizations soon followed, including the Michigan Association of Middle School Educators and the North Carolina Middle School Association.

1973 **National Middle School Association.** In an historic move, the only recently created Midwest Middle School Association declared itself the National Middle School Association. Conrad (Connie) Toepfer, Glenn Maynard, Gordon Vars, and Hal Gaddis played major roles in this bold move.

1973 *Transescence: The Journal of Emerging Adolescent Education.* Developed and maintained almost single handedly for more than 20 years by Conrad Toepfer, this journal provided a resource focused on the nature and needs of this age group at a time when there were few other materials available.

1973 **"What Research Says About the Middle School."** This article by Tom Gatewood in the December 1973 issue of *Educational Leadership*

recognized the reality that new middle schools were more often than not still junior high schools in programs and practices. In the early days of the middle school movement, the junior high school *in practice* was compared to the middle school *in theory* in a "junior high school vs. the middle school" scenario. This report helped the movement to grow beyond this false stage.

1974 **Number of middle schools reaches 3,723.** This survey, using the same definitions as previous surveys described above (see 1968), was conducted by Mary Compton (1976), one of Alexander's first students and an early NMSA leader. As before, 7-8 schools were not included although large numbers existed. The south and north central regions had the largest number of middle schools, and only the District of Columbia had none to report.

1974 **Lincoln Middle School.** Under the dynamic leadership of John Spindler, Lincoln Middle School was opened in Gainesville, Florida. Having studied with Alexander and George, Spindler started this new middle school in an old high school building and incorporated all of the characteristics of the middle school being advanced. The school gained national attention as an early model. Nancy Doda began her teaching career as an interdisciplinary team member here.

1974 **National Middle School Resource Center.** Established by Robert Malinka with a grant from the U.S. Office of Education, this center was a valuable clearinghouse for desperately sought materials dealing with the new middle school. Copies of schedules, school curriculum, advisory programs, and other related information were submitted, copied, and made available on request at no cost through this project, which ran for 11 years under the sponsorship of the Indianapolis Public Schools.

1974 **Alpha Program launched.** In 1967, a new school building designed to serve Grades 4-8 was opened in Shelburne, Vermont. Teacher Jim Reid began a program of self-selection by students. With the full support of founding principal, John Winton, a multiage team was started in 1974 and given the innocuous name of "Alpha." Carol Smith joined the team in 1975 and continued with it until her retirement in

2001. This highly successful Alpha team has been a prime example of the middle school concept fully implemented.

1975   *The Middle School We Need.* This report of the ASCD Working Group on the Emerging Adolescent Learner by Tom Gatewood and Charles Dilg sets forth a rationale for the middle school based on an analysis of physical, mental, intellectual, and personality development of middle level students.

1976   **National Middle School Leadership Seminar.** Organized by Paul George and cosponsored by the University of Florida, Alachua County Public Schools, the Florida League of Middle Schools, NMSA, ASCD, and the Kettering Foundation, this seminar was the first gathering of most, if not all, of the early middle school leaders. Over 300 educators from across the nation and several foreign countries came to Gainesville, Florida, for 3 days of intensive discussions heralding the coming heyday of workshops, conferences, and professional development activities supporting the middle school.

1977   *The Middle School: A Look Ahead.* National Middle School Association began its publication of books with this work edited by Paul George. The 14 contributors included the present authors and other early leaders. An amateurish effort in production and format, it nevertheless started NMSA on the road to becoming a major publisher of professional books.

1977   *Growing Up Forgotten: A Review of Research and Programs Concerning Early Adolescence.* In this report to the Ford Foundation, researcher Joan Lipsitz documented the inadequate attention to the needs of young adolescents by all institutions of society: schools, service institutions, families, voluntary youth-serving agencies, and the juvenile justice system. This book had considerable impact by bringing to the attention of both the public and profession how early adolescents were underserved in our society.

1978   **Center for Early Adolescence.** Under the leadership of Joan Lipsitz, this center was established at the University of North Carolina, Chapel Hill, with initial support from the Mary Reynolds Babcock and Ford Foundations. The center exerted considerable influence through its training, technical assistance, publications, and conferences. Particularly important was its work with government officials and policymakers, and its unprecedented refereed collection of the best resources related to young adolescents in their homes, schools, and communities. The center's newsletter, *Common Focus,* was widely shared. The center was closed in 1994, and its resources were acquired by the Search Institute.

1978   *A Curriculum for the Middle School Years.* In this small book, the present authors (Lounsbury, & Vars, 1978) outlined their conception of an ideal program based on three foundations: needs of the learner, expectations of society, and disciplines of knowledge and organized that ideal program into three components: core, continuous progress, and "variable" (physical education, electives, student activities, and exploratory courses).

Gordon implemented much of this model while serving as a teacher and middle school coordinator at the Kent State University School from 1966 to 1975.

1979   **NMSA Teacher Education Initiative.** At this year's annual conference, a group petitioned the board to appoint a committee to prepare a position statement on the preparation of middle school teachers. The committee's draft was accepted by the board and published in *Middle School Journal* (Committee on Teacher Education of NMSA, 1981). In 1986 NMSA published a more extensive position paper on teacher education, and a revised edition, *Professional Certification and Preparation for the Middle Level,* was published in 1991 under the leadership of Ken McEwin.

Gordon participated in these early efforts, serving with such distinguished colleagues as William Alexander, Chris Stevenson, Ken McEwin, and John Swaim. As editor of NMSA publications, John also played a role.

1980   *Toward Adolescence: The Middle School Years.* This National Society for the Study of Education Yearbook was the first and only NSSE volume devoted to early adolescence. The yearbook committee had planned to call the volume *Transescence,* but one of the most distinguished contributors would not accept use of that term. Mauritz Johnson, former director of the Cornell Junior High Project, was overall editor.

Gordon served on the planning committee and edited the section on the age group. In his prologue, he proposed that transescence could be defined as "beginning in biology and ending in sociology."

1980   The Center of Education for the Young Adolescent (CEYA). For more than 20 years, the small staff of this professional development center at the University of Wisconsin-Platteville has promoted quality middle level education. Thousands of middle level educators have benefited from its popular Summer Seminars, publications, and its large resource library. Illinois and Maine have also conducted highly regarded annual summer institutes over many years, following somewhat this early model.

John and Gordon both participated in the Summer Seminars and other CEYA programs. John was a staff member in several of the Illinois and Maine institutes.

1981   *The Exemplary Middle School,* by William Alexander and Paul George, elaborates on the conception of the middle school proposed in 1968 and cites numerous examples of middle schools implementing these features. Viewed as the definitive text on middle level education, this book is now in its third, expanded edition.

1982   *This We Believe.* National Middle School Association's first position statement almost never got published because of disagreements among members of the writing committee. Salvaged by John, it went on to become a very influential document. With a rationale based on characteristics and needs of the age group, the paper identified 10 essential elements of a "true" middle school.

Gordon was one of the committee members who developed the position statement.

1983   *A Nation At Risk.* This widely publicized report (National Commission on Excellence in Education, 1983) accused the public schools of failing to prepare young people for life and work in the competitive global economy. While not addressed specifically to middle level education, it reflected a "get tough with the schools" approach that has culminated in the No Child Left Behind Act (2002) and other legislation in subsequent years. Middle level education, with its emphasis on democratic processes and the characteristics and needs of students, has been especially vulnerable to conservative political initiatives.

1984   *Successful Schools for Young Adolescents.* This book of case studies of exemplary middle schools was written by Joan Lipsitz. Reprinted at least 12 times, it contains detailed and comprehensive descriptions of excellent middle schools in action, including Shoreham-Wading River Middle School.

1985   *An Agenda for Excellence at the Middle Level.* The Middle Level Council of the National Association of Secondary School Principals published this brief but strong statement developed, in part at least, as a response to *A Nation At Risk,* which was philosophically at odds with the middle school concept. The council, created in the early 1980s by George Melton, Associate Executive Director, presented "front-line conferences" in various parts of the country, developed other publications, a video, and otherwise exerted considerable influence, particularly with principals. The council included Conrad Toepfer as Chairman, Al Arth, J. Howard Johnston, and John Lounsbury for most of its existence.

George Melton had initiated use of the term "middle level education" in the early 1980s. It soon was universally accepted and served to breach the junior high school versus middle school dilemma and also took the focus off the school as an organizational entity.

1987   *Moving Into Adolescence: The Impact of Pubertal Change and School Context.* This scholarly, research-based book by Roberta Simmons and Dale Blyth highlighted the great differences between boys and girls and noted the long- and short-term negative effects of moving to an impersonal junior high school.

1987   First International Middle School Conference held in Brussels. Out of this grew the European League of Middle Schools, joining what in 2005 has become a tremendous network of 59 state and regional affiliates of NMSA.

John was a presenter at this and three subsequent European League conferences.

1987 Foundations support reform in urban middle schools. This year saw the launching of major efforts by two philanthropic foundations to reform middle level education in urban districts.

The Edna McConnell Clark Foundation focused first on a few schools in Baltimore, Louisville, Milwaukee, Oakland, and San Diego with Chattanooga and Jackson, Mississippi, later added. In 1995, the foundation shifted its focus to entire school systems that seemed committed to reforming all their middle schools and had the will and capacity to do so. Hayes Mizell, as director of these projects, was a strong voice promoting efforts to reform middle schools.

The Lilly Endowment's Middle Grades Improvement Program (MGIP), directed by Joan Lipsitz, was focused on Indiana and involved 64 middle grades schools in 16 urban school districts.

Both projects encountered huge obstacles to substantive reform in urban school districts. Joan Lipsitz, after her retirement from the Lilly Endowment, said that MGIP schools were, "for the most part, friendlier, warmer, more relaxed, and more respectful," but she expressed disappointment with academic outcomes. Unfortunately, economic and social realities in inner city schools too often reduced the effectiveness of these and other well-intentioned, privately funded interventions.

1987 Watershed program started. At Radnor Middle School in Wayne, Pennsylvania, seventh grade teachers Mark Springer and Ed Silcox boldly initiated a fully integrative learning program that became a prime example of what is possible when the barriers of subjects and periods are removed. The story of this educational odyssey has been recorded in *Watershed: A Successful Voyage Into Integrative Learning* (NMSA, 1994) by Mark Springer.

John claims that of the more than 100 books he has edited and produced, this is his favorite, combining excellent writing by the author, a most significant and engaging message, and creative formatting.

1988 NMSA becomes a constituent member of the National Council for Accreditation of Teacher Education (NCATE). Two years later, NMSA published the first edition of *NCATE-Approved Curriculum Guidelines* (see, for example, NMSA, 1988, 2001). These guidelines set high standards for middle level teacher preparation programs. Their acceptance by NCATE and the consequent portfolio review process conducted by NMSA continues to be a significant factor in improving the preparation of middle level educators.

1989 *Turning Points: Preparing American Youth for the 21st Century.* This report of the Task Force on Education of Young Adolescents of the Carnegie Corporation of New York brought the education of young adolescents to the attention of the general public in a new and forceful way. The report depicted the plight of 10- to 15-year-olds in inadequate schools. Its eight recommendations for improving schooling became a standard that hundreds of schools sought to implement.

1989 *Team Organization: Promise—Practices and Possibilities.* Published by NEA and written by Tom Erb and Nancy Doda, both students of Paul George, this early book on what became the distinguishing structure of middle schools had considerable impact.

1990 *A Middle School Curriculum: From Rhetoric to Reality.* This NMSA monograph, reprinted and expanded in 1993, summarizes the arguments of a most persuasive educator, James A. Beane, and shifted the focus of middle school concerns from organization to curriculum. Almost single-handedly he sparked a major revival of interest in curriculum integration, making some of the same arguments as early advocates of core curriculum. One outcome of this "new wave" was that more books on integrative curriculum were published between 1990 and 2000 than in any previous decade, even during the heyday of progressive education.

1994 NMSA establishes satellite office in Washington, D.C. As the association gained status as a major professional organization, a national presence became important. In the decade that followed, this move proved to have been a wise one as NMSA, under Executive Director Sue Swaim, became firmly established as the nationally recognized voice of middle level education.

1995 *This We Believe: Developmentally Responsive Middle Level Schools.* Changes in education and the maturation of middle level education called for a new edition. This second edition of NMSA's position paper was a completely new document developed by a 10-member committee that met, discussed intensively, and developed drafts. Well received, it went through many reprints as it gained recognition as the definitive statement on middle level education.

Gordon and John were members of this committee, and along with Ross Burkhardt, they comprised the smaller refining and writing committee.

1997 "Research on Middle Grades." This insert in the March *Phi Delta Kappan* (Felner, Jackson, Kasak, Mulhall, Brand, & Flowers, 1997) summed up more than a decade of efforts by philanthropic foundations and professional organizations to define and implement a comprehensive model of middle level education. Included was the long-awaited report of the Project on High Performance Learning Communities, often referred to as the "Felner Study," after the name of the principal investigator. This was a study of the relative effects of piecemeal versus comprehensive changes in middle level schools. In general, student achievement, mental health, and "socio/behavioral" functioning were greatest in schools where the most *Turning Points* recommendations were carried out and with the greatest intensity.

1997 Month of the Young Adolescent launched. With over 30 national cosponsors, NMSA initiated this annual event that has done much to call attention to the importance of young adolescents and the type of school program needed to serve them well. Since being established, it has expanded with many more national co-sponsors and activities.

1997 National Forum to Accelerate Middle-Grades Reform. This alliance of over 60 educators, researchers, national associations, and foundations was formed to promote the academic performance and healthy development of young adolescents. The forum developed out of a sense of urgency that middle school improvement had stalled. The forum's vision built on the concept that middle schools should be academically effective, developmentally responsive, and socially equitable and has helped to reframe national discourse about middle grades education. The Schools to Watch Program, now implemented in 11 states, has high-

lighted over 50 excellent middle schools that are fulfilling that vision.

2000 *Turning Points 2000: Educating Adolescents in the 21st Century.* This follow-up to the Carnegie Corporation's 1989 report is a thorough and comprehensive document that gives increased attention to the areas of curriculum and instruction. Anthony Jackson, the lead writer for the first report, and Gayle Davis (then Andrews) authored this volume of continuing importance to middle level education.

2001 9/11/01. Our world has changed dramatically since the terrorist attacks on the World Trade Center and the Pentagon. Not since the British invasions during the War of 1812 have people in the United States had to deal with a "war" on their own soil. Americans are feeling the perpetual anxiety under which millions of people around the world live every day. Now thousands of our citizens are facing death firsthand in Afghanistan, Iraq, and elsewhere.

What does this have to do with education? Among other things, it has created a climate of fear that inevitably affects learning. Neither students nor teachers can do their best work under such emotional stress. Second, the cost of America's wars drains already stretched financial resources. At the very time that young people need more personal services, schools are reducing guidance staffs, eliminating enrichment programs, and struggling just to maintain minimal programs. Curricula are stripped down. Proven desirable middle level practices such as interdisciplinary teaming, a rich variety of free choice activities, or even fundamental enrichment courses such as art, music, consumer science, and technology education are reduced or eliminated. As usual, conditions are the worst in communities and districts already dealing with poverty.

2001 No Child Left Behind. At a time when schools are struggling to deal with budget cuts, they have to deal with the No Child Left Behind Act with its unfunded mandates and almost impossible requirements. Demanding "adequate yearly progress" from all schools regardless of their resources and requiring all students to reach a uniform level of performance by a certain date fly in the face of reality. NCLB is a political solution to education's problems, but not an educational one. It reflects a mistaken belief that human beings can be bullied into learning if the punishment is sufficiently severe. Rather than cultivating a love of learning and encouraging young people to make full use of their unique gifts, students are being converted into joyless test-crammers. To some observers, NCLB has been deliberately designed to destroy public school education in favor of private, church-related, or corporate institutions. All this is especially destructive of the student-centered democratic conception of middle level education long advocated by these writers and embodied in public statements such as NMSA's *This We Believe* (2003).

2003 *This We Believe: Successful Schools for Young Adolescents.* Although only 7 years had passed since the second edition was published, significant events and public criticism of middle schools warranted a review of NMSA's position paper. Over 250 middle level educators were sent copies of the 1995 edition and invited to review it and offer suggestions for changes and additions. Suggestions received were reviewed by a representative committee of eight. Strong support for maintaining the advocacy of the second edition led to some elaboration and additions but no philosophical changes. Many drafts were considered by the committee, the board, and selected others. The final product contained an all new listing of the Characteristics of Young Adolescents completed by Peter Scales and an expanded Call to Action.

Also published at the same time, *Research and Resources in Support of This We Believe* (Anfara, Andrews, Hough, Mertens, Mizelle, & White, 2003) was the long-sought compilation of relevant research. It was prepared by NMSA's research committee under the leadership of Vincent Anfara.

John was a member of the revision committee, and along with Ed Brazee and Sue Swaim, a member of the subcommittee charged with final editing.

2004 **Middle schools gain new numerical predominance.** As of January 2004, according to Market Data Retrieval, there are 14,548 public middle schools and only 554 junior high schools of grades 7-9. The face of American education has indeed been remade twice through the reorganization movement that began about 1910 and continues to this day.

IN RETROSPECT

First, a closing caveat: We recognize fully that there are many other events or resources important to the advancement of middle level education that could have been cited. Our first drafts, in fact, included many others; but space limitations precluded their inclusion. So we offer a sincere apology to those many individuals and activities that should have been included.

THE CULTURAL CONTEXT

It is important to note that nearly all of our efforts have taken place within the public schools and colleges of the United States. Public education in this country, although presumably dedicated to preparing effective citizens for a democratic society, is primarily carried out by bureaucracies that are subject to the will and the whims of people as expressed through political processes. Education continues to be viewed by the general public as essentially transmission of information, with various special interests apt to protest if schools raise significant value questions or engage students in serious consideration of controversial issues. And, of course, the heavy hand of tradition always wields a powerful influence.

Americans also have a penchant for quick fixes, opting for short-term rather than long-term solutions to pressing social issues. Developing a quality middle level school, however, requires long-term commitment to the difficult and often stressful process of changing the way people, both young people and adults, think and do things. Moreover the middle school idea is complex, requiring simultaneous attention to the needs of students, the demands and expectations of society, and the understanding and practice of democratic processes. Like the human body, it does not function well unless all systems are working reasonably well: smoothly functioning teams, effective teacher guidance and advocacy, meaningful curriculum and competent academic instruction, harmonious relations among staff, students, families, and community, and so forth.

The limited progress in fully implementing the middle school concept is discouraging and frustrating to those of us committed to it, especially when we recognize its components are clearly in line with what is known about human growth and development and the accepted principles of learning—a claim that cannot be made for the test-driven methods currently being advocated. The middle school philosophy is backed by research, abundant examples of successful practice, and a rich history. Its validity has never been refuted, yet it struggles to gain wide acceptance. This condition calls to mind the astute comment made by someone who observed that the only thing wrong with religion was that it hadn't been practiced.

Nevertheless, we have faith in the middle school concept and are optimistic that eventually it will become common practice. The democratic, student-centered education it embodies is in keeping with the heart of America. And we continue to be inspired by the committed efforts of dedicated men and women who serve in our nation's classrooms. They continue to struggle against almost insurmountable obstacles to nourish and champion the precious gifts found in all children and youth.

ACHIEVEMENTS

In reviewing the 55 years that we have been involved with middle level education, we can identify several significant accomplishments.

1. The age of early adolescence has been recognized as a distinct developmental period. While still not fully understood in the minds of the general public and not evident in all scholarship and practice, there has been wide acceptance of the concept that youth, roughly between the ages of 10 and 15, comprise a special group.
2. A three-tiered organization of public education has been achieved. While not fully implemented in all states and districts, the old elementary-secondary pattern has largely given way to an elementary-middle-high school pattern. Although increasingly recognized in teacher preparation and certification or licensure, the middle level school continues to face challenges, such as the reversion to K-8 schools in several large cities.
3. The concept of teaming as a viable way to organize for instruction has gained wide acceptance. Once teaching was either done primarily in self-contained classrooms or in departmentalized situations. Now teaming in various forms has become standard in middle level education and is also being used in elementary and high schools.
4. The value of actively engaging students in their learning has been accepted as desirable even if not yet widely implemented. Soliciting and acting on student voice is now recognized as a valid way to improve student learning and is an acknowledged goal of many teachers.
5. Middle level education has kept alive and under active consideration the tenets of pro-gressive education that many had discarded even though they have never been proven to be invalid.
6. Research supportive of student-centered, democratic education advocated by progressive middle level educators accumulates. In addition, increasing numbers of ongoing examples prove by their effective practice that the middle school concept is valid.

Public education is under siege in America, however quietly and slowly. As champions of public education, we believe that our nation's success is due as much to this system as it is to her economic principles or abundant natural resources. The public schools have been the farm system for our democracy, nurturing it in a way no other institution can; we are concerned that our schools are no longer serving that function. They have become too utilitarian, too ready to serve special interests, and have lost in the process the common unifying vision that was so instrumental in creating and building them. America has moved rapidly toward becoming a selfish, competitive society that rewards success all too lavishly. Middle level education, however, with its acknowledged responsibility for preparing persons for active citizenship in a democracy and for acquiring appropriate personal attributes, is one clear force still working to bring about a better society. Its ultimate success is critical to the future of America.

REFERENCES

Alberty, H. (1947). *Reorganizing the high school curriculum.* New York: Macmillan.

Alexander, W. M. (1963, July). *The junior high school: A changing view.* Address to the tenth annual conference of School Administrators, Cornell University, Ithaca, NY.

Alexander, W. M. (1968). *A survey of organizational patterns of reorganized middle schools: Final report, USOE project 7-D-026.* Washington, DC, and Gainesville, FL: U.S. Department of Health, Education, and Welfare and University of Florida.

Alexander, W. M. (1995, January). The junior high school: A changing view. *Middle School Journal, 26*(3). (Reprinted from *Readings in curriculum,* by G. Hass & K. Wiles (Eds.), 1964, Boston, MA: Allyn & Bacon.)

Alexander, W. M., & George, P. S. (1981). *The exemplary middle school.* New York: Holt, Rinehart, and Winston.

Alexander, W. M., Williams, E., Compton, M., Hynes, V., & Prescott, D. (1967). *The emergent middle school.* New York: Holt, Rinehart and Winston.

Anfara, V. A., Andrews, P. G., Hough, D. L., Mertens, S. B., Mizelle, N. B., & White, G. (2003). *Research and resources in support of This We Believe.* Westerville, OH: National Middle School Association.

Ayres, L. (1909). *Laggards in our schools: A study of retardation and elimination in city school systems.* New York: Charities Publication Committee.

Beane, J. A. (1990). *A middle school curriculum: From rhetoric to reality.* Columbus, OH: National Middle School Association.

Briggs, T. H. (1920). *The junior high school.* Boston: Houghton Mifflin.

Briggs, T. H. (1960). The Conant report on junior high schools: Education in the junior high school years. *NASSP Bulletin, 44*(259), 13-20.

Carnegie Council on Adolescent Development. (1989). *Turning points: Preparing American youth for the 21st century.* Report of the Task Force on Education of Young Adolescents. New York: Carnegie Corporation of New York.

Commission on the Reorganization of Secondary Education. (1918). *Cardinal principles of secondary education.* Bulletin 1918, No. 35. Washington, DC: U.S. Department of the Interior, Bureau of Education.

Commission on Secondary Curriculum. (1961). *The junior high school we need: A report from the ASCD Commission on Secondary Curriculum.* Washington, DC: Association for Supervision and Curriculum Development.

Committee on College Entrance Requirments. (1899). *Journal of proceedings and addresses, Los Angeles, 1899.* Washington, DC: National Education Association.

Committee on Teacher Education of National Middle School Association. (1981). Preparing teachers for the middle grades: A position paper. *Middle School Journal, 12*(4), 17-19.

Compton, M. (1976). The middle school: A status report. *Middle School Journal, 7*(2), 3-5.

Conant, J. B. (1959). *The American high school today: A first report to interested citizens.* New York: McGraw-Hill.

Conant, J. B. (1960). *A memorandum to school boards: Recommendations for education in the junior high school years.* Princeton, NJ: Educational Testing Service.

Department of Superintendence. (1927). *The junior high school curriculum (Fifth yearbook).* Washington, DC: National Education Association.

Educational Facilities Laboratories. (1962). *Middle school: A report of two conferences at Mt. Kisco on the definition of its purpose, its spirit, and its hope.* New York: Author.

Educational Policies Commission. (1944). *Education for all American youth: A further look.* Washington, DC: National Education Association and American Association of School Administrators.

Eichhorn, D. H. (1966). *The middle school.* New York: Center for Applied Research in Education.

Eliot, C. (1888). *Shortening and enriching the grammar school course.* Address to the annual convention of the National Education Association.

Erb. T. O., & Doda, N. (1989). *Team organization: Promise—practices and possibilities.* Washington, DC: National Education Association.

Felner, R. D., Jackson, A. W., Kasak, D., Mulhall, P., Brand. S, & Flowers, N. (1997). The impact of school reform for the middle years: A longitudinal study of a network engaged in turning points-based comprehensive school transformation. *Phi Delta Kappan, 78*(7), 528-523, 541-550.

Gatewood, T. (1973, December). What research says about the middle school. *Educational Leadership, 31*(3), 221-224.

Gatewood, T. E., & Dilg, C. (1975). *The middle school we need.* Washington, DC: Association for Supervision and Curriculum Development.

George, P. S. (Ed.). (1977). *The middle school: A look ahead.* Fairborn, OH: National Middle School Association.

Gruhn, W. T., & Douglass, H. R. (1947). *The modern junior high school.* New York: Ronald Press.

Hall, G. S. (1905). *Adolescence.* New York: D. Appleton Century.

Jackson, A. W., & Davis, G. A. (2000). *Turning points 2000: Educating adolescents in the 21st century.* New York: Teachers College Press.

Johnson, M. (1962). *The intellectual responsibility of the junior high school: A statement of position by members of the staff of the Junior High School Project, Ford Foundation.* Ithaca, NY: Cornell University School of Education.

Johnson, M. (Ed.). (1980). *Toward adolescence: The middle school years.* Seventy-ninth yearbook of the National Society for the Study of Education. Chicago, IL: University of Chicago Press.

Kealy, R. P. (1971). The middle school movement. *The National Elementary Principal, 51*(3), 20-25.

Koos, L. V. (1920). *The junior high school.* New York: Harcourt, Brace, and Howe.

Koos, L. V. (1955). *Junior high school trends.* New York: Harper & Row.

Lipka, R. P., Lounsbury, J. H., Toepfer, Jr., C. F., Vars, G. F., Alessi, Jr., S. P., & Kridel, C. (1998). *The Eight-Year Study revisited.* Columbus, OH: National Middle School Association.

Lipsitz, J. (1977). *Growing up forgotten: A review of research and programs concerning early adolescence: A report to the Ford Foundation.* Lexington, MA: Lexington Books.

Lipsitz, J. (1984). *Successful schools for young adolescents.* New Brunswick, NJ: Transaction Books.

Lounsbury, J. H. (Ed.). (1984). *Perspectives: Middle school education, 1964-1984.* Columbus, OH: National Middle School Association.

Lounsbury, J. H., & Clark, D. C. (1990). *Inside grade eight: From apathy to excitement.* Reston, VA: National Association of Secondary School Principals.

Lounsbury, J. H., & Johnston, J. H. (1988). *Life in the three sixth grades.* Reston, VA: National Association of Secondary School Principals.

Lounsbury, J. H., & Marani, J. (1964). *The junior high school we saw: One day in the eighth grade.* Alexandria, VA: Association for Supervision and Curriculum Development.

Lounsbury, J. H., & Vars, G. F. (1978). *A curriculum for the middle school years.* New York: Harper & Row.

Middle Level Council. (1985). *An agenda for excellence at the middle level.* Reston, VA: National Association of Secondary School Principals.

National Commission on Excellence in Education. (1983, April 27). *An open letter to the American people: A nation at risk: The imperative for educational reform.* Washington, DC: U.S. Government Printing Office.

National Education Association. (1894). *Report of the committee of ten on secondary school studies.* New York: American Book.

National Middle School Association. (1982). *This we believe.* Columbus, OH: Author.

National Middle School Association. (1986, reprinted 1991). *Professional certification and preparation for the middle level: A position paper of National Middle School Association.* Columbus, OH: Author.

National Middle School Association. (1988). *NCATE-approved curriculum guidelines.* Columbus, OH: Author.

National Middle School Association. (1995). *This we believe: Developmentally responsive middle level schools.* Columbus, OH: Author.

National Middle School Association. (2001). *National Middle School Association/National Council for Accreditation of Teacher Education-Approved middle level teacher preparation standards.* Westerville, OH: Author. Retrieved August 24, 2003, from http://www.nmsa.org/services/teacher_prep/nmsastandards.htm

National Middle School Association. (2003). *This we believe: Successful schools for young adolescents.* Westerville, OH: Author.

National Society for the Study of Education. (1944). *Adolescence. Forty-third yearbook, Part I.* Chicago: University of Chicago Press.

National Study of School Evaluation. (1970). *Junior high school/middle school evaluation criteria.* Washington, DC: Author.

National Study of School Evaluation. (1979). *Middle school/junior high school evaluation criteria.* Arlington, VA: Author.

National Study of School Evaluation. (1999). *Evaluation criteria for middle level studies.* Falls Church, VA: Author.

National Study of Secondary School Evaluation. (1963). *Evaluative criteria for junior high schools.* Washington, DC: Author.

No Child Left Behind Act of 2001, Pub. L. No. 107-110, 115 Stat. 1425 (2002). Retrieved August 9, 2004, from http://www.ed.gov/offices/OESE/asst.html

Noar, G. (1953) *The junior high school: Today and tomorrow.* New York: Prentice-Hall.

Simmons, R. G., & Blyth, D. A. (1987). *Moving into adolescence: The impact of pubertal change and school context.* New York: A. de Gruyter.

Springer, M. (1987). *Watershed: A successful voyage into integrative learning.* Columbus, OH: National Middle School Association.

Strayer, G. D. (1911). *Age and grade census of schools and colleges.* Washington, DC: U.S. Government Printing Office.

Tanner, J. M. (1962). *Growth at adolescence, with a general consideration of the effects of hereditary and environmental factors upon growth and maturation from birth to maturity.* Springfield, IL: Blackwell Scientific Publications.

Thorndike, E. L. (1907). *The elimination of pupils from schools.* Washington, DC: U.S. Government Printing Office.

Van Til, W., Vars, G. F., & Lounsbury, J. H. (1961). *Modern education for the junior high school years.* Indianapolis, IN: Bobbs-Merrill.

Vars, G. F. (Ed.). (1969). *Common learnings: Core and interdisciplinary team approaches.* Scranton, PA: International Textbook.

Wright, G. S. (1952). *Core curriculum development: Problems and practices.* Office of Education, Bulletin 1952, No. 6. Washington, DC: U.S. Government Printing Office.

Wright, G. S. (1958). *Block-time classes and the core program.* Washington, DC: U.S. Government Printing Office.

Wright, G. S. (1963). *The core program: Unpublished research 1956-1962.* Washington, DC: U.S. Dept. of Health, Education, and Welfare, Office of Education.

Academically Excellent Curriculum, Instruction, and Assessment

P. Elizabeth Pate

Academically excellent curriculum, instruction, and assessment are not out of reach for today's middle schools. Integral to academically excellent curriculum, instruction, and assessment are teachers, students, content/standards, and school/community. When teachers reflect on their philosophy and values, examine their teaching style and preferences, consider their personality traits, and use this information when developing and delivering curriculum, instruction, and assessment, then academic excellence occurs. When professional judgment is used to make sound decisions regarding how to respect and address the cultural contexts, personal knowledge, and voices of each and every student in curriculum, instruction, and assessment, then academic excellence occurs. When school and district-level, state-mandated, and professional association standards are analyzed for clarity and purpose and developmentally appropriate content is identified, then academic excellence occurs. When the school (e.g., students, teachers, administrators, staff, parents) is true to its vision and mission, when the community (e.g., young and elderly, advantaged and disadvantaged) develops a sense of place, and when the school and the community work together for the betterment of each other, then academic excellence occurs.

Academically excellent curriculum, instruction, and assessment represent an accumulation of high standards, rigorous learning, and meaningful work occurring across time. In schools where academically excellent curriculum, instruction, and assessment are in place, students are being challenged, learning to work with others, and engaging actively in their own learning. Academically excellent curriculum, instruction, and assessment result in young adolescents becoming more responsible, self-directed, independent thinkers and see the value of their learning through its connections to the world outside the classroom. Academically excellent curriculum, instruction, and assessment result in students, teachers, schools, and communities becoming more reflective of, responsive to, and accountable for each other. With academically excellent curriculum, instruction, and assessment comes success—the continuous improvement (academic and otherwise) of students (Jackson & Davis, 2000; National Forum to Accelerate Middle-Grades Reform, 1998; National Middle School Association, 2003).

In a recent year-long research initiative focused on curriculum, instruction, and assessment, the author collaborated with a classroom teacher to collect data from a team of eighth grade students in their democratically run social studies classroom. Throughout this anchor essay, the voices of these eighth grade students will serve to represent middle grades students' ideas regarding curriculum, instruction, and assessment (Homestead & Pate, 2004).

ACADEMICALLY EXCELLENT CURRICULUM

Curriculum is sometimes thought of as a listing of subjects taught in schools (e.g., mathematics, language arts); planned and formal (e.g., courses of study and curriculum guides) or unplanned or *hidden* (e.g., implied values and attitudes, unwritten rules of behavior); those experiences that individuals require for full and authentic preparation in society (e.g., consensus building); or as all school experiences that students encounter (Ornstein & Hunkins, 1998). Regardless of how one views curriculum, it should be effective (e.g., uses complex tasks and essential questions); relevant (e.g., allows students to pursue answers to questions they have about themselves, content, and the world; promotes activities that are rich in personal meaning); challenging (e.g., enables students to assume control of their own learning); integrative (e.g., focuses on issues that cross subject boundaries); and exploratory (e.g., encourages self-discovery) (National Middle School Association, 2003).

At the heart of academically excellent curriculum is the student. Each young adolescent has unique and diverse cultural contexts and has accumulated 10-15 years of personal knowledge. Cultural contexts include, but are not limited to, geographic locations (e.g., country, state, region, town); cultural norms (e.g., eye contact, personal space, issues of power); school experiences (e.g., home, public, private, progressive, traditional); religion (e.g., Christian, Islamic, Jewish, atheistic, polytheistic); lifestyles (e.g., work, leisure, hobbies); personal, familial, and societal expectations (e.g., family size, marriage expectations); gender distinctions and expectations (e.g., chores, educational opportunity); race, ethnicity, and language (e.g., history, dialect); and socioeconomic class distinctions and expectations (Pate, Powell, Yaksic, & Navarro, 2001). Personal knowledge is familiarity with, awareness of, and understanding about such things as likes and dislikes, goals and aspirations, practical skills, and interests, needs, and concerns.

Academically excellent curriculum takes into account student voice. According to the voices of young adolescents, curriculum should be about *real life*. According to young adolescents, curriculum should be "more up to date with today's society," and "[confront] present and future issues." Students call for attention to issues such as racism, prejudice, teen pregnancy, child abuse, crime, violence, illegal drugs, diseases, missing children, and environmental problems. One student said curriculum should focus on "things that we the students care about and want to learn." Another said students should have "choice; [we should] be exposed to a lot of different topics and then we could choose from there. A student argued that curriculum should require students to use "logic—the students would be given a situation and asked what they would do," and "we should be [learning about] making responsible decisions and good choices," and one young adolescent asserted that middle grades students should learn about "things that affect our future and influence our choices" (Homestead & Pate, 2004).

Academically excellent curriculum requires a thorough understanding of content and standards. Content (subject matter) and standards (common subject matter criteria) are identified by school districts, state boards of education, content area councils (e.g., National Council of Teachers of English, National Council of Teachers of Mathematics) and content area associations (e.g., International Reading Association, National Science Teachers Association). Content and standards are generally presented in a scope (depth of knowledge) and sequence (order of learning) framework. Many standards are complex and often difficult to understand. To make them more understandable and therefore more usable, it is helpful to analyze each one and develop framing questions. For example, the Social Studies Grade Eight Texas Essential Knowledge and Skills (TEKS) History (b1B) reads The student is to understand traditional historical points of reference in U.S. history through 1877. The student is expected to apply absolute and relative chronology through the sequencing of significant individuals, events, and time periods (Texas Education Agency, 2005, §113.24). What exactly is the student required to learn? Why is it important to learn?

Students and/or teachers can analyze each content/standard and develop framing questions for clarity and purpose. What does *apply* mean? What does *absolute* mean? What does *relative* mean? What does *chronology* mean? What is meant by the phrase *absolute and relative chronology*? What is *sequencing*? What does *significant* mean? What is meant by the word *individual*? What does *event* mean? What is a *time period*? What makes an event, person, time period, and so forth significant? Who were the significant individuals in U.S. history through 1877? What were the significant events in U.S. history through 1877? What were the significant time periods in U.S. history through 1877? Using absolute and relative chronology, who were the significant individuals, what were the significant events, and what were the significant time periods in U.S. history through 1877? From a student's perspective, "Why should I know about these people, events, and time periods and their sequence in history?" This last question, the relevance question, is critical to address and frequently hard to answer. Unless there is a substantial reason, beyond preparing for a test, to take time out of a child's life to learn the standard, then it need not be taught. By breaking down each standard, developing framing questions, and sequencing the questions to determine order of learning, a teacher knows exactly what must be taught and a student knows exactly what is required and what must be learned.

CURRICULUM MODELS

With the framing questions as a basis of curriculum, appropriate curriculum model(s) must be determined. Curriculum models refer to the type, design, presentation, format, and intent of curriculum that, ideally, provide for academically excellent curriculum. Teachers should approach curriculum using a variety of models as determined by the needs of students, the beliefs and characteristics of the teacher, content and standards, and school and community expectations. Curriculum models often used in the middle grades include individualized (e.g., contracts, learning centers, Web-based), subject-centered, parallel, interdisciplinary and multidisciplinary, service-learning, and curriculum integration. A unit of study can incorporate one or even several curriculum models.

The primary focus of individualized curriculum is for individuals or small groups of students to work on activities designed to address a particular need or deepen understanding about concepts and topics. Individualized curriculum is designed by the teacher or a team of teachers, textbook companies, researchers, and, to a much lesser degree, by students.

Contracts

Contracts are independent studies allowing opportunities for decision making about goal, interest, assessment, and deadline. Contracts typically consist of contract requirements and agreements, grading procedures, and activities. A contract is entered into following the selection of a trade book to be read (e.g., *Because of Winn Dixie,* DiCamillo, 2000) or a concept to be investigated (e.g., decimals in mathematics) and identification of activities associated with the book or concept. Students first understand that a contract, which is a written and enforceable agreement between two or more parties, states the expectations of that agreement and is a binding document that typically cannot be changed. They also understand that some circumstances may necessitate a change requiring all parties—student, care-givers, and teacher—to negotiate new terms for the contract. Students select from a list of activities that address varied learning styles and multiple intelligences and have real-world applications. The selection and completion of activities, to the best of one's ability, determines the grade received. For example, for the concept contract, *Ratios,* students might choose the following activity: With another friend, take turns making baskets with a basketball in a basketball hoop. Each person should take 100 shots. Record how many baskets each of you made on a chart. Using a ratio, compare your two scores. Reduce your ratio and then write your ratio in words (example: "85 baskets out of 100"), in a fraction (85/100), using a colon (85:100), as a percentage (85%), and in decimal format (.85). For the tradebook contract on *How to Eat Fried Worms* (Rockwell, 1973), students might choose an activity that asks them to illustrate how earthworms move and document how fast they travel or they might choose the activity that requires them to research the benefits of earthworms to the soil and prepare a brochure. Contracts are appropriate for fostering independence, focusing on

student interest, accommodating different rates and styles of learning, involving families in the learning process, and integrating content areas. As just these two examples show, tradebook and concept contracts can draw from knowledge and skills in several different content areas.

Learning Centers

Learning centers are independent studies in which students, individually or in small groups, go to classroom areas or "stations" where they do structured or unstructured independent work on a given topic or subject. For example, for a 5-day learning center comparing and contrasting Halloween with Dia de los Muertos, students read about and discuss the two celebrations (days one and two), visit six stations over two days (Religion, Origin and History, Food, Customs, Vocabulary, Stories), and discuss, reflect, and assess on day five. For a learning center entitled *Immigration to America,* students spend 30 minutes at each of five stations across 3 days—Reasons for Immigration and Profile of an Immigrant; Ellis Island; Scrapbook of an Immigration Experience; Living Conditions of Urban Immigrants; and The Great Migration of African Americans. Day four is spent on sharing work, reflection, and assessment. With learning centers, students move around the room with a constant changes of pace, activities, and settings; learn skills of cooperation and teamwork; engage in a variety of activities designed to solidify learning and allow success; and engage in perspective taking.

Web-Based

Web-based curricula are independent studies allowing students to make decisions and investigate topics and issues as they interact with internet resources, research, and self-correcting materials. This curriculum consists of instruction, references, exercises, problems, and self-correcting materials. For example, the Royal Ontario Museum (ROM) has an interactive Website titled *Ancient Egypt Discovery Case.* Students are able to walk through an interactive timeline, make a mummy, use the hieroglyphic alphabet to write their names, visit the Egyptian Exhibit at the ROM in a virtual tour, take a quiz on ancient Egypt, and pose questions for an Egyptologist to answer online (ROM, 2005). Students and teachers from Pine River Middle School (PRMS), Michigan, created their own Web-based curriculum, *Ancient Egypt and the Seven Wonders,* incorporating activities from the Royal Ontario Museum Website as well as other interactive Web-based sites. The school's goal for the integration of technology was "to create a learning environment where students are successful and learn according to their abilities, while reinforcing and extending the middle school curriculum into areas of technology" (PRMS, n.d.). Web-based curriculum facilitates linkages to daily living; fosters motivation; and addresses various learning styles and ability levels.

Subject-Centered

Subject-centered curriculum, the most common curriculum model in use in schools today, focuses on one scholarly field (e.g., language arts, mathematics, science, or social studies) or branch of specialized inquiry (e.g., earth science, life science, physical science). Subject-centered curriculum is generally taught within a specific timeframe (e.g., 55 minutes, 90 minutes) within a school day. The primary focus of subject-centered curriculum is on mastering content from only one discipline area or branch of specialized inquiry within a discipline (e.g., biology within science). Content is learned using methods found within the discipline. For example, scientists use the scientific method; therefore, the scientific method is used in science classes. Generally, in subject-centered curriculum, the textbook is used as the primary and often sole source of information. Publishing companies generally produce textbooks addressing content standards.

Subject-centered curriculum is familiar to both students and parents, is readily available, and is standards friendly. If a teacher or school makes the decision to use primarily subject-centered curriculum, care must be taken to ensure that the text reflects the teachers' philosophies, values, teaching styles, and preferences; addresses students' cultural contexts, personal knowledge and voice; contains developmentally appropriate content; interprets relevant standards correctly; and reflects and addresses both the school's and the community's needs.

Parallel

Parallel or correlated curriculum is one in which teachers sequence their lessons to correspond to lessons in each other's disciplines. The focus of parallel curriculum is still on mastering content from one discipline area or branch of specialized inquiry, but there is an intentional attempt to sequence lessons on a topic in one discipline to correspond to lessons on the same topic in other subjects. For example, while students read *Across Five Aprils* (Hunt, 1993) in language arts they are simultaneously studying the Civil War in social studies. Or, students in a mathematics class will learn the meaning and uses of probability while they simultaneously investigate genetic outcomes involving dominant and recessive traits in their life science

class. Parallel curriculum is easy to plan, and students can generally identify the relationship between the two content areas.

Interdisciplinary and Multidisciplinary

Interdisciplinary and multidisciplinary curricula imply a series of interconnected lessons in several disciplines on a general topic or theme (Jacobs, 1989). The primary focus in interdisciplinary (language arts, mathematics, science, social studies) and multidisciplinary (language arts, mathematics, science, social studies, fine arts, physical education) curricula is on mastering content from the subjects involved. Interdisciplinary and multidisciplinary curricula are typically organized around issues (e.g., homelessness); topics (e.g., math mania); current events (e.g., presidential election); concepts (e.g., magnetism); or questions (e.g., Why are rain forests in jeopardy?). The emphasis may be heavier in one subject; lessons might last a day, a week, a year, or even multiple years; and interdisciplinary and/or multidisciplinary curriculum can be developed for one classroom, a team of students, or an entire school.

Interdisciplinary and multidisciplinary curricula include targeted efforts to make connections between subjects. Students are generally more motivated to learn the content if they are involved in making decisions about unit topics than if their voices are not heard.

Service-Learning

Service-learning is a philosophy and methodology involving the application of academic skills in solving or addressing real-life problems in the community. Service-learning can be teacher directed or democratic in nature. Components of service-learning include need, learning, students, collaborators, project activities, service, reflection, evaluation, and publicity. In the *Disaster Awareness and Action Campaign* (DAAC), 35 diverse, multiage (sixth, seventh, and eighth grade), and multiability level students with special needs, their teacher, interested educators, and community members collaborated to address the need for barrier island residents and visitors to develop their awareness of natural (e.g., hurricanes, tornadoes, tsunamis, water spouts, tropical storms, flooding) and man-made (e.g., chemical spills, refinery accidents, terrorist activities) disasters and to develop personal action plans. The "learning" aspect of the DAAC service-learning effort was achieved through collaborative inquiry including on-line and community-based research about barrier islands, natural and man-made disasters, community-building, and action planning. Participants in the DAAC service-learning effort

- Framed questions (e.g., what science content knowledge is important to know about natural disasters in order to develop effective action plans?);
- Designed plans for research (e.g., flow charts);
- Chose appropriate resources and inquiry tools (e.g., relevant Internet sites, experts);
- Investigated and learned appropriate state-mandated skills and content (e.g., note-taking, climatology);
- Collected, recorded, and analyzed data (e.g., scientific process);
- Interpreted findings and offered conclusions (e.g., perspective-taking, cause and effect);
- Considered and reflected on questions and then asked new questions (e.g., Do we need an action plan for each type of disaster or will one action plan work for all disasters?); and
- Shared interpretations and new learning during community presentations.

During the community presentations, students shared the charrettes (short, focused portfolios used for use in decision making and for documentation of learning) they had created for each disaster and provided disaster action plans, both English and Spanish versions, to community residents and visitors.

As a result of service-learning, students become active citizens while making contributions to society; student motivation and ownership increases; students have increased interactions with peers and community members; students apply their knowledge to address or solve community needs and concerns; and students value their learning.

Curriculum Integration

Curriculum integration "takes into account the particular views of young adolescents, the purpose of middle schools, the sources of the curriculum, the nature of learning, the contexts of knowledge and skill, and the organization of the curriculum" (Beane, 1993, p. 4). Central to curriculum integration is democracy. Students and teachers collaboratively make decisions about what to learn, how to learn, how to be assessed, and the importance of that learning. Students become teachers and teachers become learners. In curriculum integration, students are engaged in identifying significant problems or issues of social or personal concern, determining skills that are requisite, designing assessments, determining learning activities, and locating resources in order to

address problems or issues. Subject areas are important in helping to answer student-posed questions, understand issues, and solve problems, but subject areas are not *the* focus of integrated curriculum. Teachers and students together develop themes of study around student interests and concerns with mandated content and skills addressed within those themes. Themes might revolve around environmental problems, racial issues, societal needs, and personal concerns. In a unit on human and Civil Rights and responsibilities, students experienced curriculum integration as they examined the relationships between and among past, present, and future human and civil rights issues from the 1600s to the present (e.g., Salem Witch Trials, Industrial Revolution, Balkan Crisis). They acquired new knowledge by analyzing relevant information and engaging in critical thinking and group processing. Students demonstrated their knowledge on worksheets, through group presentations, during discussions, through the simulation of a peace conference, and while play-acting in a living history timeline (Pate, Homestead, & McGinnis, 1997).

Curriculum integration emphasizes process and product, provides opportunities for students to take risks and learn from mistakes, promotes problem posing and problem solving, includes goal setting and reflection, utilizes collaboration, and incorporates traditional and authentic assessment. In curriculum integration, students and teachers together can develop contracts, design learning centers, utilize interactive Websites, learn content-specific knowledge and skills, create interdisciplinary units, and engage in service-learning projects.

Academically excellent curriculum is aligned with nationally recognized standards; provides a coherent vision for what students should know and be able to do; is rigorous, nonrepetitive, and evolving; emphasizes deep understanding of important concepts; makes connections across the disciplines to reinforce important concepts; fosters development of essential skills; and provides opportunities for application of what has been learned to real-world problems (National Forum to Accelerate Middle-Grades Reform, 2003, ¶ 3).

ACADEMICALLY EXCELLENT INSTRUCTION

Intricately linked with academically excellent curriculum is instruction. Instruction is defined as the planned arrangement of experiences to help a learner develop understanding and to achieve a desirable change in behavior (Kellough & Kellough, 1999).

Instruction should be relevant to each student (e.g., needs, skill levels, abilities, learning styles, prior knowledge, viewpoint); pedagogically sound (e.g., dependent on learning objectives, developmentally appropriate, research-based); varied (e.g., field trips, debates, experiments, guest experts, discussions); exploratory (e.g., health, wellness, safety, sexuality, anger management, and conflict resolution); and engaging for both students and teachers (e.g., inclusive, democratic, collaborative and team oriented, authentic) (National Middle School Association, 2003). Academically excellent instruction addresses the cultural contexts and life knowledge of student scholars, as well as their voices.

According to the voices of young adolescents, academically excellent instruction should be about

- Opportunities for interacting with different people;
- Hands-on activities;
- Reading and discussion;
- Field trips and speakers;
- Interactive lessons;
- Simulations;
- Cooperative learning;
- Research;
- In-depth information about a subject or topic;
- Project work;
- Reflections;
- Presentations and demonstrations; and
- Choice (Homestead & Pate, 2004)

Their voices are strong—"Book work, dittos, and lectures are not doing the trick for us." One student both asked and answered his own question:

Who was that person that made up the idea of sitting a person down and filling them with information? Instead of sitting around classrooms and reading books about different subjects, we should be in the world. Life is an adventure. We should be a part of the adventure, not a bystander. We should have the right to learn from experience. (Homestead & Pate, 2004)

Academically excellent instruction should be linked to the contexts of the community (e.g., location, demographics, issues, collaboration or lack of); school (e.g., demographics, mission, vision); family (e.g., involvement or lack of, communication or lack of); and classroom (e.g., physical setup, students, team configuration, time parameters). Lesson plans, whether a teacher constructs them or they are coconstructed by students and their teacher(s), should incorporate a clear and attainable goal; target main ideas, concepts, and skills; address prior knowledge;

justify the importance and relevance of content to be learned; identify content and standards; fit within a curriculum continuum; be framed around a focus question; incorporate student involvement; use student-friendly terminology; provide for an audience for sharing student learning; identify procedures for starting and closing class and dismissing students; and incorporate a variety of teaching and learning strategies, activities, and assessments (formative and summative) specifically targeted given both the content and student needs.

A strategy is a plan or course of action selected in pursuit of a specific goal or objective. Students might use the strategies of chalk-talk, interviewing, and needs analysis to develop new solutions and insights. They might use logs of activities, note-taking, and charrettes to document and retain important facts, skills, and ideas. They might use inquiry, action plans, and critiques to help develop conceptual understanding, reasoning, and problem-solving processes. They might engage in demonstrations, jigsaw, and peer-tutoring to learn to relate to each other and learn from each during collaborative grouping. Lesson plans should also identify appropriate transition strategies; list all necessary resources; identify lesson extenders, accommodations, and modifications; anticipate explanations, clarifications, and classroom management dilemmas; and, incorporate opportunities for student feedback. Lesson plans should only be used class-to-class and year-to-year *if* modifications are made that address the different students and their varied needs in each situation.

Academically excellent instruction includes a range of challenging and engaging strategies and activities that are clearly related to the concepts and skills being taught; student access to exemplars of high quality work that meet the performance standard; and adequate time for extended projects, hands-on experiences, and inquiry-based learning (National Forum to Accelerate Middle-Grades Reform, 2003).

ACADEMICALLY EXCELLENT ASSESSMENT

Assessment is directly connected to academically excellent curriculum and instruction. Assessment is defined as the process of estimating a student's progress toward an objective for the purpose of using the information to help the student make further progress (National Middle School Association, 2003) or the relatively neutral process of finding out what students are learning or have learned as a result of instruction (Kellough & Kellough, 1999). Assessment includes all those activities, undertaken by teachers and/or their students in assessing themselves, that provide information to be used as feedback to modify teaching and learning activities. Assessment is also used to help teachers make instructional decisions, determine individual student needs, provide parents with feedback, and assign grades. Regardless of how one views assessment, it should be continuous and authentic; provide evidence of student success; help identify learning goals; give students the opportunity to be active participants in assessing and charting their individual growth, reflecting on their progress, and discovering their own strengths, weaknesses, interests, aptitudes, and personalities; and allow students to see their own accomplishments and develop a fair and realistic self-concept (National Middle School Association, 2003).

According to the voices of young adolescents, assessment should

> not just be about grades. People should come to school to learn. It should be like this because if people make bad grades they get stressed out and sometimes they give up on trying. They just give up and pretend it doesn't matter. If we could study interesting things and in interesting ways, we'd be learning no matter what. (Homestead & Pate, 2004)

TYPES OF ASSESSMENTS

Academically excellent assessment is a *combination* of formative and summative and traditional and alternative/authentic. Formative assessment is conducted throughout a unit of study and includes evidence to be used to adapt teaching to meet student needs. Summative assessment is conducted at the conclusion of a unit of study and includes evidence of learning across time (Black & William, 1998). Traditional assessments include short answer, essay, true/false, and matching and are often teacher made. When using traditional assessment, it is better to have frequent short tests rather than infrequent long ones, and new learning should be tested within a week. When using traditional assessment, ask students to identify troubling questions and then work through or discuss the problems as a class. Try to save 2 days for traditional assessments: one for giving the assessment and one for going over the assessment.

Short Answer

Short answer assessments typically have framed questions and short, precise answers are sought. Short answer questions typically focus on recall and usually address who, what, when, where, why, or how. An example of a short answer test question

would be: What event caused the United States to enter World War II?

Essay

Essay assessments require the student to answer a question, either in one paragraph (short answer essay) or in multiple paragraphs (long answer essay). Essay tests generally ask students to compare (e.g., Compare the causes of World War I with the causes of World War II); contrast (e.g., Contrast the Union army with the Confederate army); define (e.g., Define the poetry form of haiku); describe (e.g., Describe the writing process); discuss (e.g., Discuss the role of the legislative branch of government); evaluate (e.g., Evaluate the Constitution of the United States of America); explain (e.g., Explain the immediate effects of the atomic bomb on Hiroshima); identify (e.g., Identify the defenders of the Alamo); list (e.g., List the steps used in Polya's model of mathematical problem solving); outline (e.g., Outline the causes of the Revolutionary War); prove (e.g., Prove that Austin was not the original capital of Texas); relate (e.g., Relate the moon to the Earth); review (e.g., Review the role of the proofreader in editing a story); state (e.g., State the relationship between the moon and tidal action); summarize (e.g., Summarize the Articles of the Federation); or trace (e.g., Trace the early settlement of California) (Sebranek, Meyer, & Kemper, 1993).

True/False and Matching

True/false assessments have items that must be clearly true (e.g., Complete sentences include both a subject and a predicate) or clearly false (e.g., Squares have only three sides and two right angles) and present only one fact (e.g., Extroverts are outgoing) (Cooper, 1982).

Matching assessments provide two lists of items with the task of matching each item from one list with an item from the other list. A well-written set of matching items will illustrate some particular relationship between pairs of items (e.g., vocabulary terms and definitions, historical events and their dates, novels and their authors, tools and their uses, problems and their solutions, elements and their symbols, causes and their effects, drawings and their interpretations) from the two lists.

Multiple Choice

Multiple-choice items are used most frequently in traditional assessments. The stem introduces a problem or poses a question; distractors provide plausible but incorrect answers, while the *correct* alternative supplies the right answer. Multiple-choice items should: (1) present a single problem or question; (2) measure a learning outcome that can be tested by selecting a right or best answer from among several alternatives; (3) include alternatives that are terse, with most of the item's information occurring in the stem; (4) include alternatives that are very similar in wording, writing style, length, and so forth; (5) Include alternatives that follow logically and grammatically from the stem; and, (6) include distractors that are plausible but not correct (Cooper, 1982).

Alternative/Authentic Assessments

Student-friendly alternative/authentic assessments include multimedia projects, presentations, speeches, experiments, rubrics, reflections, charrettes, and portfolios. A rubric is a scaled checklist of criteria that clearly defines for the student and teacher what excellence looks like (Pate, Homestead, & McGinnis, 1997). Rubrics, whether collaboratively constructed or teacher constructed, are assessment strategies used to determine whether knowledge has been gained and how it is to be conveyed. Rubrics should have enough detail that no one has questions as to how well the activity was done. Communication (e.g., dialog, reflections, conferencing, questioning) helps students know how to effectively examine and communicate their evolving understanding. When communicating, either orally or in writing, with students, teachers should try not to elicit just an answer or response, rather, they should try to get the students to explain and justify their thought processes, reasoning, and logic and allow enough time for students to think, reflect, and consider carefully their responses.

Academically excellent assessment should address alternative approaches to documenting student learning, problem-solving strategies, and community involvement. Two such alternative approaches are portfolios and charrettes. Portfolios are intended to serve as a collection of work or learning across time. Student participation in the selection of portfolio pieces is important to ensure assessment is student-centered. A charrette is an illustrative portfolio documenting the efforts or progress toward solving or addressing a community issue, problem, or need. Charrettes, although a type of portfolio, typically focus on a specific topic and are used to provide guidance for decision makers. In the *B.R.O.A.D.—Being Responsible for Our Aquatic Life Downstream* service-learning project, eighth grade students researched 17 watershed issues, translated technical definitions into their own words, created drawings to illustrate the issues, created storyboards, and typed their charrettes. The charrettes were used to document their

learning and are now used as resources for others interested in learning about topics and issues related to watersheds.

There should be a known target in academically excellent assessment—a focus question, a problem, and so forth. Assessing growth in learning toward that target is what is important, not solely the assignment of a grade. When communicating with students about their work, whether on traditional or alternative/authentic assessments, provide clear and ideally, immediate feedback. Feedback is not just the giving of grades and marks. Feedback provides students with information about what they are doing well and what is needed to make work complete.

Academically excellent assessment includes a variety of authentic methods (e.g., exhibitions, projects, performance tasks, portfolios); fosters student responsibility (e.g., assessment of their own and others work, revision of work based on feedback); and allows for multiple opportunities to have extra help as needed and to succeed (National Forum to Accelerate Middle-Grades Reform, 2003). In academically excellent assessment, the goal is growth in learning, not necessarily getting the right answers all of the time.

CONCLUSION

Each middle grades school should have academically excellent curriculum, instruction, and assessment at the heart of efforts to ensure student success. When there are clear connections between the curriculum and teachers, students, schools, and communities, then academically excellent curriculum, instruction, and assessment in the middle grades is achievable. With a clear understanding of the intricacies of and relationships between curriculum, instruction, and assessment, academic excellence is attainable. With hard work, determination, and an understanding of what works for the education of young adolescents, academically excellent curriculum, instruction, and assessment can be in place in middle grades schools. Right now. Today.

REFERENCES

Beane, J. A. (1993). Research and evaluation for a "new" curriculum. *Research in Middle Level Education, 16*(2), 1-6.

Black, P., & William, D. (1998, October). Inside the black box: Raising standards through classroom assessment. *Phi Delta Kappan, 80*(2), 139-148.

Cooper, J. M. (1982). *Classroom teaching skills* (2nd ed.). Lexington, MA: Heath.

DiCamillo, K. (2000). *Because of Winn Dixie*. Cambridge, MA: Candlewick Press.

Homestead, E. R., & Pate, P. E. (2004). [Anecdotal notes and student reflections in eighth grade social studies classroom]. Unpublished raw data.

Hunt, I. (1993). *Across five Aprils.* Morristown, NJ: Silver Burdett Press.

Jackson, A. W., & Davis, G. A. (2000). *Turning points 2000: Educating adolescents in the 21st century.* New York: Teachers College Press.

Jacobs, H. H. (Ed.). (1989). *Interdisciplinary curriculum: Design and implementation.* Alexandria, VA: Association for Supervision and Curriculum Development.

Kellough, R. D., & Kellough, N. G. (1999). *Middle school teaching: A guide to methods and resources* (3rd ed.). Upper Saddle River, NJ: Prentice-Hall.

National Forum to Accelerate Middle-Grades Reform. (1998). *Vision statement of the National Forum to Accelerate Middle-Grades Reform.* Newton, MA: Education Development Center.

National Forum to Accelerate Middle-Grades Reform. (2003). *Schools to watch selection criteria.* Retrieved January 18, 2005, from http://www.mgforum.org

National Middle School Association. (2003). *This we believe: Successful schools for young adolescents.* Westerville, OH: Author.

Ornstein, A. C., & Hunkins, F. P. (1998). *Curriculum: Foundations, principles, and issues.* Toronto: Allyn & Bacon.

Pate, P. E., Homestead, E. R., & McGinnis, K. L. (1997). *Making curriculum integration work: Teachers, students, and the quest for coherent curriculum.* New York: Teachers College Press.

Pate, P. E., Powell, J. V., Yaksic, D., & Navarro, C. (2001). *Early and young adolescents in cultural contexts: Documenting our voices.* Unpublished manuscript, University of Georgia at Athens.

Pine River Middle School. (n.d.). *Ancient Egypt and the seven wonders.* Retrieved July 1, 2005, from http://www.pineriver.k12.mi.us/ms/lessonplans/lessonplans.html

Rockwell, T. (1973). *How to eat fried worms.* New York: Dell.

Royal Ontario Museum. (2005). *Ancient Egypt discovery case.* Retrieved July 1, 2005, from http://www.rom. on.ca/egypt/case/

Sebranek, P., Meyer, V., & Kemper, D. (1993). *Write source 2000: A guide to writing, thinking, & learning.* Burlington, WI: Write Source Educational Publishing House.

Texas Education Agency. (2005). *Texas essential knowledge and skills for social studies: Subchapter B: Middle school.* Retrieved March 1, 2005, from http://www.tea.state.tx.us/teks/

The Challenge of Middle School Equity

Nancy M. Doda

EQUITY IN THE MIDDLE SCHOOL

The goal of creating equitable middle grades schools is a noble and ambitious one. It includes a vision for schooling that is dedicated to eliminating any and all prevailing injustice that exists in American education and in American life. As William Ayers states, "If we take as our goal the education of all children—or even a gesture in that direction—our system is a failure. It is an unjust system. Our impulse to change must build, then, an opposition to this injustice" (2000, p. 7). So it is that efforts to advance equity in education should be considered in relation to the critical role schools play in developing a democratic society in which the lives of all people are enhanced, enriched, and improved. This agenda constitutes more than a hope for decent schools; it constitutes a hope for a more fair and just society and world.

Middle schools striving for equity must first examine this larger moral purpose. Do our middle schools advance pluralism and democracy? Do our middle schools empower all children, even those who come without the needed developmental assets? Do our middle schools give the best educational curriculum, teachers, and resources to every child? Are our middle schools places that value and embrace human variability? Will middle school education, as we know it, advance social justice for all? These are difficult questions to consider.

We have a rich national legacy, however, on which to build an agenda for equity. In 1837, Horace Mann first spearheaded the "common school" movement as his proposed radical and great equalizer for all Americans. In the present day, federal and state laws now affirm that every U.S. citizen has the right to a free, high quality public school education regardless of his or her race, ethnicity, religion, gender, age, disability, or social class (see, for example, the Equal Educational Opportunities Act, 1974).

Though riddled with contention and political debate, we have in this nation declared our obligation to protect children and to provide them with promising futures; not just some of them, but all of them. As Deborah Meier said, "The question is not, 'Is it possible to educate all children well?' but rather, 'Do we want to do it badly enough?'" (1995, p. 4). In the next generation of middle schools, this is indeed a question to be answered.

The middle school movement's illustrious history has centered for decades on the goal of creating "developmentally responsive" schools for young adolescents, fashioning educational practices that respond to the unique developmental characteristics of young adolescents, those ages 10 to 15 (National Middle School Association, 1995). As such, the middle school's unique identity has been aligned with the physical, social, and intellectual changes of young adolescence. In 1989, the Carnegie Council on Adolescent Development's Task Force on Education of Young Adolescents produced its seminal report, *Turning Points: Preparing American Youth for the 21st Century*, in which the authors articulated this rationale for middle grades reform: "There exists a volatile mismatch between the organization and curriculum of middle grades schools and the intellectual and interpersonal needs of young adolescents" (Carnegie Council on Adolescent Development, 1989, p. 32).

School reform based on young adolescent development alone, however, has not led to sufficient attention to equity (Gay, 1994b). Restructured middle grades schools have shifted from isolated teaching departments to collaborating teacher teams. Many middle schools have liberated their period-by-period schedule into larger, more flexible blocks of instructional time (McEwin, 1997). About 40% of the nation's middle level schools have infused adult support and attention into the middle school day, and others have sought to advance more active, student-centered curriculum and instruction (Galassi, Gulledge, & Cox, 1997). These changes have improved the learning experiences of our young adolescents and have indirectly enhanced equity, but they have not guaranteed that our middle schools are considerably more fair and equitable places (Dickinson, 2001).

In 1999, the National Forum to Accelerate Middle-Grades Reform created a set of criteria to identify high-performing middle grades schools. Based on the forum's crafted vision describing high-performing middle grades schools as "developmentally responsive, academically excellent, and socially equitable" (National Forum to Accelerate Middle-Grades Reform, 1998), the forum generated criteria to identify socially equitable schools:

- High-performing schools with middle grades are socially equitable, democratic, and fair. They provide every student with high-quality teachers, resources, learning opportunities, and support. They keep positive options open for all students.
- Faculty and administrators expect high-quality work from all students and are committed to helping each student produce it. Evidence of this commitment includes tutoring, mentoring, special adaptations, and other supports.
- Students may use many and varied approaches to achieve and demonstrate competence and mastery of standards.
- The school continually adapts curriculum, instruction, assessment, and scheduling to meet its students' diverse and changing needs.
- All students have equal access to valued knowledge in all school classes and activities.
- Students have on-going opportunities to learn about and appreciate their own and others' cultures. The school values knowledge from the diverse cultures represented in the school and our nation.
- Each child's voice is heard, acknowledged, and respected.
- The school welcomes and encourages the active participation of all its families.
- The school's reward system demonstrates that it values diversity, civility, service, and democratic citizenship.
- The faculty is culturally and linguistically diverse.
- The school's suspension rate is low and in proportion to the student population (National Forum to Accelerate Middle-Grades Reform, 2001).

While the criteria represent a seminal step for middle school equity, they still lack the capacity to clarify equity in ways that bridge the gap between rhetoric and reality. Misinformed interpretations of equity often occur. It is possible, for example, to have students "use many and varied approaches" to study content that is presented with bias. Or "keeping options open for students" could, in fact, translate into a conviction that certain children should not par-ticipate in a middle school's most accelerated curriculum offerings. Take the instance of a middle school that offers an accelerated program and advertises it as open to all kinds of learners. This may be viewed as keeping options open when in fact the majority of students who are compelled to enroll in that program, and who qualify, tend to be advantaged students who are supported by families and a history of school success. If acceleration provides students with a more intellectually stimulating learning experience, why would we exclude any child? Does this action not imply that the richest curriculum a school might offer is only suitable for some children? Most importantly such an approach to managing differences violates equity. There is considerable research to reveal that such accelerated options divide student populations along lines of economics and race (Ford, Harris, Tyson, & Trotman, 2002).

In the history of middle school education, the literature is replete with advocacy for the elimination of some inequitable practices that were troublesome in the junior high school, such as high school-like star systems, athletic cut policies, cheerleading try-outs, select music groups, and narrowly defined rewards and recognition programs (George, Stevenson, Thomason, & Beane, 1992). The mantra supporting these changes has been at the core of the middle school concept: that young adolescents benefit from exposure, exploration, opportunity, and inclusion (Jackson & Davis, 2000; National Middle School Association, 2003). Further, as some scholars and researchers have concluded, when a middle school employs a sort and select approach to extracurricular activities participation, it is potentially harming young adolescents and the school's culture and limiting young adolescents' future options (Elkind, 1984; Kohn, 1986). A thorough review of middle school theory and research, however, reveals that substantive equity discussions are rare, and discussions of race, social class, and gender are almost nonexistent. Do we realize the status of equity in America's middle schools?

THE COSTS OF INEQUITY

Young adolescence is both a period of enormous opportunity and enormous risk. In 1989, Carnegie Council on Adolescent Development's (CCAD) Task Force on Education of Young Adolescents presented this challenge to the middle grades educational community:

Depending on family circumstances, household income, language, neighborhood, or the color of their skin, some of these young adolescents receive the education and support they need to develop self-respect, an active mind, and a healthy body. They will emerge from their teen years as promising youth who will become the scientists and entrepreneurs, the educators and health care professionals, and the parents who will renew the nation. These are the thoughtful, responsible, caring, ethical, robust young people the Task Force envisions. To them, society can entrust the future of the country with confidence.

Under current conditions, however, far too many young people will not make the passage through early adolescence successfully. Their basic human needs—caring relationships with adults, guidance in facing sometimes overwhelming biological and psychological changes, the security of belonging to constructive peer groups, and the perception of future opportunity—go unmet at this critical stage of life. Millions of these young adolescents will never reach their full potential … early adolescence for these youth is a turning point towards a diminished future. (CCAD, 1989, p. 20)

The majority of young adolescents from diverse life circumstances enter the years of preadolescence with grand aspirations for themselves and their social and vocational futures (Ladson-Billings, 1994). The majority of them aspire to attend college (National Center for Educational Statistics, 1999), and many dream of professions in law, medicine, education, business, and government. For too many young people, as was noted above, these aspirations often diminish or even vanish completely during the middle school years as they find these dreams deferred in uninviting and discouraging school environments (Fullan, 2001; Goodlad, 1984).

The consequences of losing millions of young adolescents are grave and have enormous implications for our youth and, ultimately, the nation's economic and social welfare. When young people fall out of love with hopeful visions of their futures, when they enter schools that inadvertently create barriers to success, they can fall prey to many high-risk choices and behaviors that can wreak havoc with their development and capacity to learn and succeed in and out of school. For example, in 1998, approximately 50% of eighth graders had engaged in alcohol, illicit drug, and/or tobacco use. In spite of a recent decline in teenage sexual activity, (i.e., approaching 50%), the United States still has the highest incidence of teenage births among developed countries in the world (Annie E. Casey Foundation, 1998, p. 11). Many young adolescents choose to leave school, with a substantially higher dropout rate for minority, non-English speaking, and poor students (Levin, 1998).

In recent years, attention to equity in the middle school has been heightened by data suggesting flat academic gains among the nation's middle grades students (Haycock, 2001), and persistent differences in performance between poor and minority students and their White and upper-class peers (Bracey, 1999; Donahue, Voekl, Campbell, & Mazzeo, 1999; Gutman, Sameroff, & Eccles, 2002). Gutman et al. (2002) contend that African American children fall behind their White peers by as much as two grade levels by the end of middle school. Likewise, African American and Hispanic students are less likely than their White peers to enroll in postsecondary education and are even less likely to graduate from it (Anyon, 1997; Maruyama, 2003).

While this attention to equity has led to a number of questionable reform initiatives, it has gratefully illuminated and reconfirmed the disturbing gap in achievement among diverse populations of students. This has, in turn, nudged a reexamination of middle school practices with a critical eye on equity in school programs, practices, and pedagogy. Perhaps the most significant conclusion from the research is that middle schools in the United States still fail to educate all students equally well (Dickinson, 2001; Jackson & Davis, 2000). In fact, in spite of the middle school movement's long history of advocacy for all children, many middle schools remain entrenched in cultural patterns, practices, pedagogy, and beliefs that prohibit success for all learners (Wheelock, 1998).

THE KIND OF MIDDLE SCHOOLS WE NEED

Sociologists have long argued that schools mirror the social inequities in society and thus actually increase the gap between students who enter school with advantage and those who enter with less. How can this be reversed? If we are to have an equitable middle school experience for every child in America, what must be done?

ELIMINATION OF TRACKING AND ABILITY GROUPING

Closing the gap in achievement requires closing the gap in opportunity, and the first challenge for middle grades schools is to determine how opportunity is allocated or denied. The leading organizational arrangement of assigning students to classes based on notions of academic potential or ability can no longer be treated as benign as such assignments play a powerful role in shaping opportunity to learn. Nearly 89% of Americas' middle grades schools still employ some form of tracking and/or ability grouping as a means of managing student diversity (Braddock, 1990). This practice is based on the assumption that adaptation in student learning assignments happens best when these students are grouped together for instruction (Lounsbury & Clark, 1990). Regardless of the ongoing "tracking wars" (Loveless, 1999), this practice continues to compromise school equity (Oakes, 1990; Wheelock, 1992) by institutionalizing the perception that some students have what it takes to be successful while others do not (Wheelock, 1998, p. 91). These perceptions in turn influence curriculum, teacher expectations, and instruction, which ultimately shape students' learning and opportunities to grow.

Numerous and substantial studies (Braddock & Slavin, 1992; Goodlad, 1984; Morgan, 1977; Oakes, 1985; Rosenbaum, 1976) provide convincing proof that tracking perpetuates inequities along race, ethnic, and socioeconomic lines. Children of color and children of poverty are disproportionately assigned to lower academic tracks in which they are unintentionally fed a steady diet of low level, skill-based, cognitively undemanding tasks with instructional methods often chosen to sustain control rather than inspire engagement (Goodwin, 2000; Haberman, 1991; Singham, 1998). Similarly, African American, Native American, and low-income eighth graders are twice as likely as White or upper income students to be placed in remedial math courses taught by the least experienced teachers (McDonnell, Burnstein, Ormeth, Catterall, & Moody, 1990; National Center for Educational Statistics, 1999). Given that mathematics is deemed the contemporary great equalizer, this is a frightening finding with which to be reckoned (Oakes, 1990; Reese, Miller, Mazzeo, & Dossey, 1997). Moreover, Lipman's ethnography (1998) of middle grades schools revealed that many middle school teachers view their African American students and other less advantaged students as "at-risk," which led them to engage in pervasive labeling, lowering expectations, and offering those students less stimulating learning experiences. As Goodwin (2000) concludes

> When one examines the literature on teachers' interactions with their students, an implicit hierarchy emerges. It appears that European American boys benefit from the most positive teacher interactions, followed by European American girls, then girls of color, particularly African American girls, with African American and Latino boys following. (p. 2)

What is often overlooked in understanding the destructive nature of tracking is the powerful role class composition plays in determining the quality of classroom life. Many argue that best practices can happen with any group of students even if all of the low performing students are grouped together. That

assumption is on shaky ground. Classroom norms and teaching practices are inextricably linked to the student composition of those classes (Gamoran, 1986; Rosenbaum 1976). Teachers are not inherently evil and are not attempting to undermine student achievement. Rather, the classroom composition plays a powerful role in shaping teacher expectations, which are linked to chosen practices and student outcomes. The level of discourse, the degree of student freedom, the choices of literature, the nature of pedagogy, and so on, are all moderated by the class demographics (Morgan, 1997).

Class ability groupings are further destructive as they can reinforce mistaken beliefs that students have about themselves. Young adolescents labeled "honors" may actually shy away from challenge for fear of failing and thus losing that identity. Likewise, students placed in the low groups may also come to accept that low ability label as accurate. In racially diverse middle schools, where ability grouping contributes to in-school segregation and the majority of advanced students are White, African American, and Latino students are vulnerable to the steady loss of the confidence they need to be intellectually challenged (Wheelock, 1998).

Inclusive, Caring, Collaborative Cultures

Students' motivation to achieve in school depends on the school's capacity to insure that students feel they can belong in school and will benefit from it (Steele, 1997). It also depends on the school's ability to create a sense of safety for every kind of child and learner. For too many students, the norms of classroom life are unsafe in numerous ways. Instructional norms, for example, too often celebrate verbal skills, quick wit, fast answers, and on-the-spot knowledge. Such norms celebrate a very limited vision of intellectual activity and exacerbate inequities between and among students whose learning styles and cultural orientations differ. Equitable classrooms have altered norms that emphasize human variability, steady effort and improvement over quick wit and speed, with attention to thinking, personal relevance, understanding, redoing work, polishing products, and taking risks (Wheelock, 1998). Classroom norms should support success for all, allowing students to learn free of fear and anxiety about punitive outcomes (Caine & Caine, 1997). Instead, students should encounter norms that encourage accountability to the group, the class, themselves, the community and to quality itself (Newmann, Marks, & Gamoran, 1995). In one highly successful middle school setting—Radnor Middle School in Wayne, Pennsylvania—where two teachers and 45 students work in an integrated learning community and where letter grades have been abandoned and replaced with authentic assessment (e.g., student self-assessment, portfolios, and student-led parent conferences), an observing visitor asked a student to explain why every student in that team seemed to be working with such collaborative commitment to quality. One eighth-grade student responded, "It may seem hard to believe this but we don't want to let each other down."

For a learning setting of this sort to take shape, middle schools will have to become deeply caring and collaborative cultures in which every child feels known, understood, included, and valued. Exclusion is deadly for young adolescents. The single greatest complaint of students in middle and high schools is, "'They don't care' ... they feel alienated from their school work, separated from adults who try to teach them, and adrift in a world perceived as baffling and hostile" (Noddings, 1992, p. 2). Students express concern about their peer relationships, noting that they, too, are the source of considerable stress. In middle schools where the arrangement of classes, the daily schedule, and curriculum plans separate students in ways that accentuate social class, gender, and race differences, those arrangements are contributing to the isolation of certain groups of students, the potential escalation of hostility and bullying, and the failure to provide students with the equal chance to be welcomed members of the group. Dubois and Hirsch (1990) note that cross race friendships diminish in the middle school years, yet in middle schools that cultivate compassion and caring across diverse groups, inclusive relationships are more likely.

The contemporary emphasis on high-stakes testing and the heightened focus on test-driven accountability has many educators in low performing schools feeling pressed to shift attention away from relationships in order to make achievement gains. When relationships are undervalued, however, middle schools and classrooms become impersonal factories lacking the trust and intimacy needed to carry out powerful learning (Wehlage & Rutter, 1986). Moreover, teachers under the pressure of high-stakes rewards and sanctions may inadvertently sabotage the responsive relationships needed for meaningful learning (Jones & Whitford, 1997). It is unjust and disrespectful to tell our young people that we adults are trustworthy and then use our positions to create competitive, fear-based schools. Moreover, such school cultures advance the gap between students who are doing well and those who are not. Disengaged students who are especially vulnerable need to lean heavily on affiliations with teachers and peers in order to succeed. This is true, however, of all young adolescents,

and even many apparently successful students describe school conditions that undermine their sense of safety and well-being in school (Gay, 1994b; Pipher, 1996).

It is not surprising that many middle schools that have implemented advisory-type programs to enhance relationships have found the results disappointing (Gallessi et al., 1997). This is often so because an advisory program's affective goals run counter to the essence of a school's culture. As one middle school student queried during a focus group I conducted, "Do they really want us to like each other and work together or not?" Equity in classroom life depends on students living democratically in diverse learning communities. Moreover, it requires having adult help in learning the value of diversity in the community life. This means that all students, through democratic means, in any given classroom, will have to play an active part in shaping the life of that room. Unless every child is heard and taken seriously, truly caring cultures will remain a lofty ideal. Students must see that their ideas, questions, and concerns are valuable and worthy of use. They must also witness this respect being given freely to every kind of learner.

There is abundant evidence that students suffer in middle schools that allow interpersonal hostilities to exist. If students face encounters with prejudice, from teachers or peers, they are increasingly vulnerable to emotional stress and school failure (Resnick et al., 1997). These hostile encounters are more likely to occur in middle schools that have sorted and separated students into academic subgroups that inadvertently develop notions about themselves as members of that school. It is difficult to create cliques and to dispel them simultaneously. Interdisciplinary teams that attempt to become caring communities find this goal blocked because the internal academic tracking disallows these subgroups to interact in ways that support an equitable team community culture. Moreover, with attention so tightly fixed on high-stakes achievement, many teams dare not devote any class or team time to challenging these interpersonal barriers for fear of falling behind.

Effective and equitable middle grades schools are distinguished by a synergy of interconnected structures, programs, and practices that evoke higher levels of caring and connectedness (Strahan, Smith, McElrath, & Toole, 2001). Certainly, practices like looping, multiage grouping, team organization, flexible block scheduling, advisory-type programs, open enrollment athletics, and detracking all advance the equity agenda. It is clear, for example, that team planning and teaching arrangements provide teachers with the opportunity to view students through the diverse perspectives of several colleagues. This can create the cognitive dissonance needed to shift teachers' thinking about student capacity and potential (Doda, 1984). The aggressive and long-term use of recommended middle school structures is, of course, what ultimately yields results (Felner, Jackson, Kasak, Mulhall, Brand & Flowers, 1997).

ELIMINATING STUDENT DISENGAGEMENT: A NEW PEDAGOGY

Disengagement from learning is the key to our most dramatic school inequities. We leave students behind in America's middle schools because we fail to provide meaningful, relevant, and engaging learning experiences for all of our students. Many middle school students describe schoolwork as mediocre and boring. Only one in four middle school students report being excited about something they are learning in school (Farkus & Johnson, 1997; Lounsbury & Clark, 1990). O'Loughlin (1995) observed that 95% of the time students participate in passive learning environments where student voice is absent and where "transmission of information" teaching dominates. This is the very kind of teaching we know places the heaviest burden on our disenfranchised or struggling students.

Students from supportive home cultures who apply themselves to schoolwork will often confess they do so not because what they are learning is meaningful, relevant or useful to them, but rather because they have the support needed to tolerate the school game (Clinchy, 1997). Sadly, many of these students, whose grades reflect success, come to value completing work in compliance with regulations over the quality of the work itself (Haberman, 1997). Thus, even for our advantaged students, potential to grow in profoundly intellectual ways is compromised by the curriculum and instruction most encounter. As Michael Fullan concludes

> Only when schooling operates in a way that connects students relationally in a relevant, engaging, and worthwhile experience can substantial learning occur. That only a small proportion of students are so engaged is a measure of the seriousness of the problem. (Fullan, 2001, p. 152)

Middle school pedagogy must be transformed in substantive ways if we are to achieve the equity dream. First and foremost, our models of teaching and learning must guarantee that students have the right to be who they are (McDaniel, Necochea, Rios, Stowell, & Kritzer, 2001). Such a middle school would place students and their diverse development, lan-

guages, races, intelligences, disabilities, and cultures at the center of all educational planning. Students bring to school unique cognitive maps they must use to make sense of the world and what they encounter in school. They have no choice in this, since culture, class and language shape cognition. Hence, we have never had the right, nor can we afford to ask learners to unlearn their cognitive maps in order to succeed in school. Middle school classrooms must structure learning in ways that allow for many cognitive styles and for cultural congruence in what and how students learn (Huber & Pewewardy, 1990; Neito, 1992).

This perspective on social equity implies that different ways of knowing are not deficits or difficulties to be overcome, but assets to be engaged in the way that schools design learning. Traditional notions of intelligence would have to be abandoned and replaced with a notion of intelligence as an expandable and flexible attribute. In socially equitable middle grades schools, "smart" would no longer be used to describe a student's innate condition. Instead, it would be an attribute used to describe learning behaviors that are taught, developed, and nurtured. This shift in beliefs is enormously important in altering what students ultimately have the chance to learn.

In a study of student motivation, Henderson and Dweck (1990) found that what students believe about intelligence shapes their motivation to learn. Students who see intelligence as inborn associated their difficulty in completing challenging tasks with the lack of innate ability. Those who viewed intelligence as flexible and expandable were more likely to tie success or failure to their own efforts. Young adolescents' self-limiting beliefs are linked closely with the beliefs others hold about them. Consequently, if adults in the middle school view intelligence as fixed and innate rather than expandable and flexible, not only will they reinforce students' self-limiting beliefs, they will not hold the highest level of expectations for all of their students nor will they teach to make young people smart. Unfortunately, a considerable percentage of the middle school teaching community covet tacit assumptions about intelligence that reduce their expectations for certain kinds of students (Goodwin, 2000). Only when members of a school community can embrace a belief in their capacity to make learning happen for every child, in diverse classroom settings, can middle schools become equitable places for all learners.

Currently, most middle school classrooms are suited to best serve students who generally come from White, English-speaking, two-parent families (Gay, 1994a); with strengths in the two most celebrated of the intelligences—linguistic and mathematical (Gardner, 1993); and with the ability to sit still for 6 hours a day. Students who fall outside the lines of these conventional boundaries are at far greater risk of school failure. Often grouped together as less successful, they struggle to gain ground in classrooms characterized by perspectives and practices associated with what Martin Haberman (1997) called, "the pedagogy of poverty," the kind of teaching which relies heavily on giving information, textbook content, worksheets, paper and pencil tests, seatwork, and homework. Likewise, traditional means of assessment have a long history of disadvantaging girls, students of poverty, and members of visible racial and ethnic groups (Garcia & Pearson, 1994), yet they prevail in most middle schools.

Authentic pedagogy demands a shift from a narrow and closed conception of students and of learning to an expansive model of curriculum, instruction, and assessment. Such a model would reflect an image of every student as capable of significant learning; would focus instruction on developing skills for deeper understanding, including posing questions, gathering information, reasoning, synthesizing different perspectives, communicating conclusions, and applying new learning; and would engage students in studying real world issues and concerns (Beane, 1997; Wheelock, 1998; Zemelman, Daniels, & Hyde, 1993). This approach to instruction has been identified as responsible for marked student improvement across diverse student populations (Newmann & Wehlage, 1995).

While instructional change will be fundamental to creating equitable learning in the middle grades, the nature of the curriculum is equally fundamental. As Sonia Neito (1992) explains, "Children who are not in the dominant group have a hard time finding themselves or their communities in the books they read or the curriculum to which they are exposed" (p. 76).

When content does not reflect all children's lives or in fact distorts those lives, young adolescents cannot connect school with their known world. Liberating pedagogy alone is not sufficient. Studying distorted views of Native Americans in cooperative learning groups would not constitute a socially equitable setting for young adolescents. An equitable middle school classroom must allow every child meaningful entry points into the learning process.

The standards movement has articulated the "what" of curriculum in such a way as to potentially endanger democratic schooling in many states. If we truly aspire to achieve equity, middle schools must seek to eliminate curriculum models that fail to be democratic. Curriculum models that endorse specialized classes, set aside for only certain students, do not advance equity. They reflect the class roots of American education based on the historical vocational versus academic tracks.

Since 1993, when James Beane wrote the seminal middle school curriculum text, *From Rhetoric to Reality: A Middle School Curriculum*, the middle school community has been invited to rethink the curriculum. More recently, Beane (2004) further explained the relationship between curriculum and equity:

> In the interest of equity and developmental responsiveness, a middle school curriculum should emphasize a general education for all young adolescents. Put another way, what is offered in the school program would be intended for all students and all students would be involved in it....
>
> Young adolescents are not ready to make decisions about their futures, even though they may express early preferences or inclinations. Moreover, adults have a dismal record of predicting what those futures might be. To force young adolescents to make such decisions or, worse yet, to decide for them is one way in which some curriculum arrangements have been developmentally inappropriate for young adolescents.
>
> The move toward more specialized curriculum offerings based upon individual differences or interests has also been one of the main ways by which social and economic inequities have been sustained in the school. To understand this we need look no further than limited Algebra sections in the eighth grade in schools with diverse populations. Too often, such sections are disproportionately filled with social[ly] and economically privileged students. Moreover, including these tracked courses as well as specialized performing musical groups and other single section classes in the regular school schedule usually interferes with diversity in class and team groupings across the whole school, disrupting the general education curriculum, differentiating access to knowledge, and unfairly judging the future possibilities and aspirations of young adolescents. A moral and ethical middle school curriculum simply cannot allow these kinds of inequities. (pp. 52-53)

A new pedagogy for our next generation of middle schools needs to emerge from altered beliefs about the nature of our young people, altered beliefs about the nature of intelligence and learning, and altered views about the role of schooling in the lives of all Americans.

COLLABORATIVE PROFESSIONAL LEARNING COMMUNITIES

Building a culture that supports social equity demands that middle schools cultivate collegial professional communities committed to creating more compelling and equitable learning environments. Middle schools aspiring to reach all learners can no longer afford to sustain isolating professional cultures. A school's capacity to affect student learning is linked to its faculty's capacity to behave as a collective, reflective, learning community (Senge, Kleiner, Roberts, Ross, & Smith, 1994).

Cultivating this kind of culture is challenging as teachers have long labored in a professional culture that supports native ingenuity as the key to great teaching. Middle schools must redefine teaching as a collaborative profession and plan for teacher learning in ways that reflect this. Unless school cultures are dramatically collaborative, where teachers acknowledge and embrace their individual and collective responsibility to make learning happen for every child, the equity agenda will be compromised. Many middle schools have large signs boasting their commitment to "success for all," yet it is often precisely these schools that violate their ambitious agenda in subtle ways. Take, for example, high performing middle schools that tend to have a disproportionate number of minorities in their In School Suspension programs, or schools that have awards allocated and dispersed to the same small group of students on a repeat basis. Consider the many schools that still continue to employ high-school-like athletic cut policies, which can endanger students' identity development and sense of inclusion (McEwin & Dickinson, 1996). Likewise, consider the inordinate number of middle schools that still place their least experienced teachers with their most needy students in classes commissioned for remediation. In nearly all such examples, the roadblock was not in talent or dedication, but in beliefs about what schools should be seeking to do and for whom. These schools, and many others, have not yet imagined that it might be possible to create a general education middle school and curriculum in which there would be a place at the table for every child.

Transforming middle grades schools is a collective enterprise involving all educators, families, organizations, associations, and agencies that work on behalf of middle grades education. As Oakes and her colleagues (2000) observed in their study of 16 Turning Points schools

> As at most of the 16 schools we studied, many faculty members were solidly committed to the principles of racial equality and fairness, and they struggled with discrimination, inequality and injustice. …there were also schools that showed concern for gender fairness, and they questioned and challenged many of the commonly accepted "limits" that schools place on

special education students. They tried to change the curricula and structure to expand access, provide extra support when needed, and improve relations among diverse groups of children.

> Although the Turning Points reform approach was in many ways a "best case" example, it provided little support for the most difficult reform challenges the schools confronted…. As is usually the case, little attention was paid to the profound cultural and political challenges that lay at the heart of reform. (Oakes, Quartz, Ryan, & Lipton, 2000, pp. 571-574)

The challenges are enormous, yet middle school educators can get started immediately by examining their own beliefs. They can risk discussing the often "undiscussables" of how they see differences and how they define equity, struggling with fundamental moral issues at the heart of school reform. Never will America's middle school reform agenda be free from the venerable tensions in our society between the concern for the common good and concern for the individual liberties and private interests of its citizens. Such tensions will always play out in schools. In spite of such tensions, the modern middle school has made strides toward equity and must persevere (Wheelock, 1992). What matters most, however, in our equity reform work ahead is that we strive to become a socially conscious educational community. We can no longer afford to turn our backs on the subtle and overt inequities that have limited human potential for decades. It is time for middle level schools to act for equity so that we grow a more humane and fully democratic society that insures a quality life for every citizen in this nation.

REFERENCES

Annie E. Casey Foundation. (1998). *When teens have sex: Issues and trends.* Kids Count Special Report. Baltimore, MD: Author.

Anyon, J. (1997). *Ghetto schooling: A political economy of urban educational reform.* New York: Teachers College Press.

Ayers, W. (2000). Simple justice: Thinking about teaching and learning, equity, and the fight for small schools. In W. Ayers, M. Klonsky, & G. H. Lyon (Eds.), *A simple justice: The challenge of small schools* (pp. 1-8). New York: Teachers College Press.

Beane, J. A. (1993). *A middle school curriculum: From rhetoric to reality* (2nd ed.). Columbus, OH: National Middle School Association.

Beane, J. A. (1997). *Curriculum integration: Designing the core of democratic education.* New York: Teachers College Press.

Beane, J. A. (2004). Creating quality in the middle school curriculum. In S. Thompson (Ed.), *Reforming middle level education: Considerations for policymakers* (pp. 49-63). Greenwich, CT: Information Age.

Bracey, G. W. (1999). Research: Poverty and achievement. *Phi Delta Kappan, 81*(4), 330-331.

Braddock, J. H., II. (1990). Tracking in the middle grades: National patterns for grouping instruction. *Phi Delta Kappan, 71*(6), 445-449.

Braddock, J. H., II, & Slavin, R. E. (1992, September). *Why ability grouping must end: Achieving excellence and equity in American education.* Paper presented at Common Destiny Conference, Washington, DC.

Caine, R. N., & Caine, G. (1997). *Education on the edge of possibility.* Alexandria, VA: Association for Supervision and Curriculum Development.

Carnegie Council on Adolescent Development. (1989, June). *Turning points: Preparing American youth for the 21st century. The Report of the Task Force on Education of Young Adolescents.* New York: Carnegie Corporation of New York.

Clinchy, B. M. (1997). The standardization of the student. In E. Clinchy (Ed.). *Transforming public education: A new course for America's future.* New York: Teachers College Press.

Dickinson, T. S. (Ed.). (2001). Reinventing the middle school: A proposal to counter arrested development. In *Reinventing the middle school* (pp. 3-20). New York: Routledge Falmer.

Doda, N. M. (1984). *Teachers' perspectives and practices in two organizationally different middle schools.* Unpublished doctoral dissertation, The University of Florida, Gainesville.

Donahue, P. L., Voekl, K. E., Campbell, J. R., & Mazzeo, J. (1999). *The NAEP reading report card for the nation and the states (NCES 1999-500).* Washington, DC: U.S. Department of Education, Office of Educational Research and Improvement and the National Center for Educational Statistics.

Dubois, D. L., & Hirsch, B. J. (1990). School and neighborhood friendships of Blacks and Whites in early adolescence. *Child Development, 61,* 524-536.

Elkind, D. (1984). *All grown up & no place to go: Teenagers in crisis.* Reading, MA: Addison-Wesley.

Equal Educational Opportunities Act. (1974). Title 20, Chapter 39, Subchapter I, Part 2, United States Court, Section 1703(f). Retrieved July 7, 2005, from http://www.usdoj.gov/crt/cor/byagency/ed1703.htm

Farkus, S., & Johnson, J. (1990). *Kids these days: What Americans really think about the next generation.* New York: Public Agenda.

Felner, R. D., Jackson, A.W., Kasak, D., Mulhall, P., Brand, S., & Flowers, N. (1997). The impact of school reform for the middle years: Longitudinal study of a network engaged in Turning Points-based comprehensive school transformation. *Phi Delta Kappan, 78*(7), 528-532, 541-550.

Ford, D., Harris, J. H., Tyson, C. A., & Trotman, M. F. (2002). Beyond deficit thinking: Providing access for gifted African American students. *Roeper Review, 24*(2), 52-53.

Fullan, M. (2001*). The new meaning of educational change.* New York: Teachers College Press.

Gallassi, J. P., Gulledge, S. A., & Cox, N. D. (1997). Middle school advisories: Retrospect and prospect. *Review of Educational Research, 67*(3), 301-338.

Gamoran, A. (1986). Instructional and institutional effects of ability grouping. *Sociology of Education, 59*(4), 185-198.

Garcia, G. E., & Pearson, P. D. (1994). Assessment and diversity. *Review of Educational Research, 20,* 337-392.

Gardner, H. (1993). *Frames of mind: The theory of multiple intelligences.* New York: Basic Books.

Gay, G. (1994a). *At the essence of learning: Multicultural education.* West Lafayette, IN: Kappa Delta Pi.

Gay, G. (1994b). Coming of age ethnically: Teaching young adolescents of color. *Theory Into Practice, 33,* 149-155.

George, P., Stevenson, C., Thomason, J., & Beane, J. A. (1992). *The middle school and beyond.* Alexandria, VA: Association for Supervision and Curriculum Development.

Goodlad, J. (1984). *A place called school.* New York: McGraw Hill.

Goodwin, A. L. (2000, March). Education assessment: Honoring ways of knowing. *WEEA Digest,* 1-9.

Gutman, L. M., Sameroff, A. J., & Eccles, J. S. (2002). The academic achievement of African American students during early adolescence: An examination of multiple risk, promotive, and protective factors. *American Journal of Community Psychology, 30*(3), 367-369.

Haberman, M. (1991). The pedagogy of poverty versus good teaching. *Phi Delta Kappan, 72*(4), 290-294.

Haberman, M. (1997). Unemployment training: The ideology of non-work learned in urban schools. *Phi Delta Kappan, 78*(7), 499-503.

Haycock, K. (2001). Closing the achievement gap. *Educational Leadership, 58*(6), 6-11.

Henderson, V., & Dweck, C. (1990). Motivation and achievement. In. S. S. Feldman & G. R. Elliott (Eds.), *At the threshold: The developing adolescent.* Cambridge, MA: Harvard University Press.

Huber, T., & Pewewardy, C. (1990). *Maximizing learning for all students: A review of literature on learning modalities, cognitive styles, and approaches to meeting the needs of diverse learners.* (ERIC Document Reproduction Service No. ED 346082).

Jackson, A. W., & Davis, G. A. (2000). *Turning points 2000: Educating adolescents in the 21st century.* New York: Teachers College Press.

Jones, K., & Whitford, B. L. (1997, December). Kentucky's conflicting reform principles: High stakes school accountability and student performance. *Phi Delta Kappan, 79*(4), 276-287.

Kohn, A. (1986). *No contest: The case against competition: Why we lose in our race to win.* Boston, MA: Houghton Mifflin.

Ladson-Billings, G. (1994). *Dreamkeepers: Successful teachers of African American children.* San Francisco: Jossey-Bass.

Levin, H. M. (1998). Educational performance standards and the economy. *Educational Researcher, 27*(4), 4-10.

Lipman, R. (1998*). Race, class, and power in school restructuring.* Albany: State University of New York Press.

Lounsbury, J., & Clark, D. (1990) *Inside grade eight: From apathy to excitement.* Reston, VA: National Association of Secondary School Principals.

Loveless, T. (1999). *The tracking wars: State reform meets school policy.* Washington, DC: The Brookings Institution.

Maruyama, G. (2003). Disparities in educational opportunities and outcomes: What do we know and what can we do? *Journal of Social Forces, 59*(3), 653-655.

McDaniel, J. E., Necochea, J., Rios, F. A., Stowell, L. P., & Kritzer, C. (2001). The arc of equity in reinvented middle schools. In. T. S. Dickinson (Ed.), *Reinventing the middle school* (pp. 56-78). New York: Routledge Falmer.

McDonnell, L. M., Burnstein, L., Ormeth, T., Catterall, J., & Moody, D. (1990, June). *Discovering what schools really teach: Designing improved coursework indicators* (Report for Office of Educational Research and Improvement). Washington, DC: U.S. Department of Education.

McEwin, C. K. (1997). *Specialized middle level teacher preparation in the United States: A status report.* Boone, NC: Appalachian State University.

McEwin, C. K., & Dickinson, T. S. (1996). Placing young adolescents at risk in interscholastic sports programs. *Clearing House, 69*(4), 217-221.

Meier, D. (1995). *The power of their ideas: Lessons for America from a small suburban school in Harlem.* Boston: Beacon Press.

Morgan, E. P. (1997). *Inequality in classroom learning: Schooling and democratic citizenship.* New York: Praeger.

National Center for Educational Statistics. (1999, April). *National Educational Longitudinal Survey of 1988* (NELS:88). Washington DC: Office of Educational Research and Improvement. (NCES no. 91-460)

National Forum to Accelerate Middle-Grades Reform. (1998). *Vision statement of the National Forum to Accelerate Middle-Grades Reform.* Newton, MA: Education Development Center.

National Forum to Accelerate Middle-Grades Reform (2001). *Social equity.* Retrieved June 30, 2005, from http://www. schoolstowatch.org/criteria.equity.html

National Middle School Association. (1995). *This we believe: Developmentally responsive middle level schools.* Columbus, OH: Author.

National Middle School Association. (2003). *This we believe: Successful schools for young adolescents.* Columbus, OH: Author.

Neito, S. (1992). *Affirming diversity: The sociopolitical context of multicultural education.* White Plains, NY: Longman.

Newmann, F. M., Marks, H., & Gamoran, A. (1995). Authentic pedagogy: Standards that boost student performance. *Issues in Restructuring Schools, 8,* 1-11.

Newmann, F. M., & Wehlage, G. G. (1995). *Successful school restructuring: A report to the public and educators by the Center on Organization and Restructuring of Schools.* Madison, WI: Board of Regents of the University of Wisconsin System.

Noddings, N. (1992). *The challenge to care in schools.* New York: Teachers College Press.

Oakes, J. (1985). *Keeping track: How schools structure inequality.* New Haven, CT: Yale University Press.

Oakes, J. (1990). *Multiplying inequalities: The effects of race, social class, and tracking on opportunities to learn math and science.* (Report # R-3928-NSF). Santa Monica, CA: RAND.

Oakes, J., Quartz, K. H., Ryan, S., & Lipton, M. (2000). *Becoming good American schools: The struggle for civic virtue in education reform.* San Francisco: Jossey-Bass.

O'Loughlin, M. (1995). Daring the imagination: Unlocking voices of dissent and possibility in teaching. *Theory into Practice, 34*(2), 107-115.

Pipher, M. (1996). *The shelter of each other: Rebuilding our families.* New York: G. P. Putnam.

Reese, C. M., Miller, K. E., Mazzeo, J., & Dossey, J. A. (1997). *NAEP 1996 mathematics report card for the nation and the states.* Washington, DC: U.S. Department of Education, Office of Educational Research and Improvement, National Center for Educational Statistics.

Resnick, M. D., Barman, P. S., Blum, R. W., Bauman, K. E., Harris, K. M., Jones, J., Tabor, J., Bearing, T., Sieving, R., Shew, M., Ireland, M., Bearinger, L. H., & Udry, J. R. (1997). Protecting adolescents from harm: Findings from the National Longitudinal Study on Adolescent Health. *Journal of the American Medical Association, 278,* 823-832.

Rosenbaum, J. E. (!976). *Making inequality.* New York: Interscience.

Senge, P. M., Kleiner, A., Roberts, C., Ross, B. R., & Smith, B. J. (1994). *The fifth discipline field book: Strategies and tools for building a learning organization.* New York: Doubleday.

Singham, M. (1998). The canary in the mine: The achievement gap between Black and White students. *Phi Delta Kappan, 80*(1), 8-15.

Steele, C. M. (1997). A threat in the air: How stereotypes shape intellectual identity and performance. *American Psychologist, 52*(6), 613-629.

Strahan, D., Smith, T. W., McElrath, M., & Toole, C. M. (2001). Connecting caring and action: Teachers who create learning communities in their classrooms. In T. S. Dickinson (Ed.), *Reinventing the middle school* (pp. 96-116). New York: Routledge Falmer..

Wehlage, G. & Rutter, R. (1986). Dropping out: How much do schools contribute to the problem? *Teachers College Record, 87*(3), 374-392.

Wheelock, A. (1992). *Crossing the tracks: How "untracking" can save America's schools.* New York: New Press.

Wheelock, A. (1998). *Safe to be smart: Building a culture for standards-based reform in the middle grades.* Columbus, OH: National Middle School Association.

Zemelman, S., Daniels, H., & Hyde, A. (1993). *Best practice: New standards for teaching and learning in America's schools.* Portsmouth, NH: Heinemann.

Creating Developmentally Responsive Middle Level Schools

Gert Nesin
Edward N. Brazee

WHAT IS DEVELOPMENTAL RESPONSIVENESS?

What is developmental responsiveness? What do developmentally responsive middle level schools do? What are they responsive to and how are they responsive? These are essential questions in defining fully this fundamental aspect of the middle school concept.

Developmental responsiveness is the knowledge and ability to develop schools and programs that take into consideration the full range of the needs and characteristics of human growth and development, particularly the stages, tasks, or challenges that human beings negotiate from birth to adulthood. For middle level schools that means that every aspect of the school program—curriculum, instruction, assessment, organization, and grouping issues, for example—is influenced by what research tells us about young adolescent students' needs as a result of the unique changes they experience from ages 10 to 15 years. The concept of developmental responsiveness appears in most descriptions of schools for young adolescents (Eichhorn, 1966; George & Alexander, 2003: Jackson & Davis, 2000), and this concept is well recognized. However, it is also one of the most misunderstood concepts for educators and noneducators alike, due primarily to the *perception* that middle level schools have promoted development in all areas except academic achievement.

Early adolescent developmental-stage theorists such as Jean Piaget, Erik Erikson, Lawrence Kohlberg, and Robert Havighurst have contributed greatly to understanding this critical and unique period of transition known as adolescence (George & Alexander, 2003, p. 7). Havighurst (1972), like others, posed several specific stages or areas of development during these years that individuals need to master successfully in order to become healthy members of society.

Havighurst's eight tasks, which begin in early adolescence, include developing mature relations with age mates of both sexes; achieving a masculine or feminine role; learning about one's body and using it in healthy ways; gaining emotional independence from parents and other adults; preparing for marriage, family life, and a career; developing a set of values and an ethical framework as a guide; and striving for and achieving socially responsible behavior (Cobb, 2001, p. 7). While there is more emphasis now on continuous movement through such tasks rather than treating them as discrete stages, Havighurst's suggestions are helpful for envisioning how young adolescents prepare themselves for later ages.

Levinson's research (1978) supported the belief that successfully negotiating the transitions of early adolescence is critical to smooth and successful development in the next stage. Hence, a school that is developmentally responsive needs to provide an organization, programs, and services to meet the essential needs of young adolescents. In some schools, such responses have consisted of devising a schedule that gives young adolescents the time they need to learn or instituting an advisory program that provides one caring adult for each young adolescent. In other schools, developmental responsiveness is more a natural part of the school, where every decision made is in the best interests of young adolescents.

While a fundamental concept of middle level schools, developmental responsiveness has often been misunderstood, in spite of nearly universal agreement that developmental responsiveness should be a goal of every middle level school. There is some disagreement and confusion about whether this concept was actually a rationale for what would later be referred to as "the middle school concept," or simply a result of the implementation of middle school characteristics.

Still, this fundamental concept is widely acknowledged in "the middle school movement, which has sought to create educational institutions that recognize all we know about 10-to-15-year-olds and design programs accordingly" (Lounsbury, 1997). Responding to the period of early adolescence by understanding the biological, cognitive, and social changes is a central theme in middle level literature. In the early development of middle schools, such "signature programs" as interdisciplinary teams, block-of-time schedules, advisory programs, exploratory programs, and integrated curriculum were seen as developmentally responsive.

Meeting the needs of young adolescents has always been a rallying cry for the middle school movement. National Middle School Association's (NMSA) first release of its seminal position paper, *This We Believe* in 1982 (and since released in new revisions in 1995 and 2003) called for "a balanced curriculum based on the needs of young adolescents." Indeed, the ten components (e.g. positive school climate, full exploratory program, and more) were based on the needs of young adolescents. NMSA's most recent revision, *This We Believe: Successful Schools for Young Adolescents* (2003), reminds us that

> [F]or a middle school to be successful, their students must be successful; for students to be successful, the school's organization, curriculum, pedagogy, and programs must be based upon the developmental readiness, needs, and interests of young adolescents. This concept is at the heart of middle level education. (NMSA, 2003, p. 1)

Similarly, the vision of the National Forum to Accelerate Middle-Grades Reform is based on a three-pronged approach to improving middle level schools—academic excellence, social equity, and developmental responsiveness (National Forum to Accelerate Middle-Grades Reform, 1998). The National Forum's definition of developmental responsiveness (2001) includes such ideals as establishing personalized learning environments to support each student; teachers who use a wide variety of instructional strategies; a curriculum that is both socially significant and relevant to the personal needs of young adolescents, and; a school that provides opportunities for students to explore a rich array of topics and interests.

Finally, the original *Turning Points: Preparing American Youth for the 21st Century* found that

> [T]oo often … the main educational institution serving young adolescents—the middle grades school—falls short of meeting the educational and social needs of millions of students.… A volatile mismatch exists between the organization and curriculum of middle grades schools and the intellectual, emotional, and interpersonal needs of young adolescents. (Carnegie Council on Adolescent Development, 1989, p. 32)

As with the previous models mentioned, "much of the value and appeal of *Turning Points* thus lies in its portrayal of the middle grades school as a comprehensible system of interrelated elements, each of which is amenable to improvement" (Jackson & Davis, 2000, p. 3).

So, what does all of this mean? Simply stated, schools are developmentally responsive when their programs meet the physical, social, emotional, psychological, moral, and intellectual needs of their students.

WHY IS DEVELOPMENTAL RESPONSIVENESS NECESSARY TO STUDENT SUCCESS?

Once understood, developmental responsiveness gives us a framework for studying adolescent development. When schools concentrate solely on academic development, they may overlook the multiplicity of influences on young adolescents that affect their learning. We must remember that all of the elements of developmental responsiveness influence each other. Self-esteem influences learning; physical growth and how young adolescents feel about their physical development influences how and when they learn; students' cognitive development certainly influences learning.

It is also important to remember that what is often referred to as "academic" is not necessarily intellectual or particularly rigorous. When schools purport to focus on "academics," they may simply mean that time is spent teaching the traditional subjects of language arts, social studies, science, and mathematics. Another interpretation with regard to academics refers to a limited focus on reading and writing, usually teacher-directed, which severely limits opportunities for student thinking.

Developmental responsiveness means more than knowing why young adolescents think, act, speak, and respond as they do and much more than knowing the chemical and physical changes and the hormonal shifts occurring during this distinctive time of life. And, it is much more than recognizing the myriad social changes that occur between the ages of 10 and

15. It does mean, however, understanding and acting on the interconnections, what some call a multidisciplinary perspective (Steinberg, 1993, p. 4).

Schools and teachers are developmentally responsive when they know and act on the information available to them about various aspects of growth and development, particularly the notable characteristics of young adolescents in the physical, cognitive, moral, psychological, and social-emotional dimensions of development.

While most young adolescents in the United States will exhibit these characteristics to some degree, the relative importance of each characteristic can vary widely depending on each young adolescent. Gender, race, ethnicity, and other cultural influences; family and economic situations; learning and physical disabilities; a young adolescent's temperament; and qualities of his or her community or neighborhood are just some of the factors that work together to give their developmental dimensions and characteristics personal and social meaning (National Middle School Association, 2003).

Youth between the ages of 10 to 15 are characterized by their diversity as they move through the pubertal growth cycle at varying times and rates. Yet as a group they reflect important developmental characteristics that have major implications for parents, educators, and others who care for them and seek to promote their healthy growth and positive development. (National Middle School Association, 2003, p. 43)

We also know that young adolescents have a greater influence on their own development than they did earlier in their lives. Most if not all of the significant characteristics are the result of a give and take between the young adolescent and his or her ecology (National Middle School Association, 2003). The fundamental changes of adolescence—biological transitions, cognitive transitions, and social transitions—are critical to their later development. The contexts of adolescence—families, peer groups, schools, work, and leisure—all are significant influences on developmental responsiveness. Furthermore, the field of psychology also refers to the developmental concerns of adolescence—identity, autonomy, intimacy, sexuality, and achievement. Together, the fundamental changes, the contexts, and the developmental concerns give us a framework for understanding early adolescent development (Steinberg, 1993, p. 14).

George and Alexander (2003) note that "educators in exemplary middle schools can build developmentally responsive schools based on the knowledge educators currently possess about the nature and needs of this age group and the characteristics of schools that respond appropriately and effectively" (p. 30). The chief implication of our knowledge about middle school age learners is that they need a school focused sharply on their needs, and educators, with the help of researchers in related fields, must keep searching out these needs and the best means for their satisfaction.

Stevenson (2002) explains that, "It is vital that middle grades teachers serve a highly diverse constituency in ways that are responsive to the students' contextual and developmental circumstances" (p. 77). He describes five caveats about developmental responsiveness including

- Early adolescence is a growth period characterized by enormous change and variability among children;
- Individual schedules of change are idiosyncratic;
- Home, neighborhood, prevailing gender roles, and racial and ethnic identity influence development;
- The influences and effects of early adolescent experiences are long lasting; and
- Young adolescents thrive when their needs are being met (Stevenson, 2002, pp.76-78).

While the theory of the middle school is that it responds to the needs of its clientele—young adolescents—the junior high school also was concerned with developmental responsiveness. Smith (1925) described the junior high school as "a more suitable school for the adolescent age," when he noted,

The character of such a school—its subject matter, its methods, and in fact its whole atmosphere—it was pointed out, would be largely determined by the needs of adolescents and would, therefore, constitute a far more suitable educational environment for seventh and eighth grade pupils. (1925, p. 153)

Exemplary middle schools understand that young adolescents learn in very complex ways that reflect the many influences on their growth. If we expect our students to "meet high academic standards and use their minds well" (National Forum to Accelerate Middle-Grades Forum, 1998), we have to understand that academic success occurs best when students' other needs—physical, social, emotional—are also being met. The junior high school failed (Lounsbury, 1984) when it followed the senior high school model and concentrated solely on academic achievement. The middle school will likely meet the same fate if it does not understand the importance of recognizing the critical developmental factors that impact a student's learning.

NOT EVERYONE UNDERSTANDS DEVELOPMENTAL RESPONSIVENESS

Being developmentally responsive has always been misunderstood and for many critics of the middle school, being responsive means everything except being responsive to academic success. For some people, saying that a middle level school is developmentally responsive is a negative; they buy into the myth of middle schools as soft on academics with much time spent on building students' self-esteem. Unfortunately, a serious misreading of developmental responsiveness has caused such schools to be regarded as less than intellectually rigorous.

Dickinson rebuts this charge as he describes one of the most devastating elements of "arrested development"—when middle level schools do not follow through with the tenets of the middle school concept—is an image of middle schools that began in the 1960s and one that exists too often today. This image is the result of "the inability to balance the middle school as a good place for young adolescents to learn and grow with challenging and involving academic work in those good places" (2001, p. 8). But, he contends, nowhere did "the founders and early advocates of this movement ever speak, write, or intend that the school should be less than a positive place to be *and* a challenging and involving intellectual environment" (Dickinson, 2001, p. 8).

Jackson and Davis addressed the same issue in *Turning Points 2000: Educating Adolescents in the 21st Century* (2000) as they also acknowledged the primacy of intellectual development in middle level education:

> Let us be clear. The main purpose of middle grades education is to promote young adolescents' intellectual development. It is to enable every student to think creatively, to identify and solve meaningful problems, to communicate and work with others, and to develop the base of factual knowledge and skills that is the essential foundation for these "higher order" capacities. (Jackson & Davis, 2000, pp. 10-11)

Jackson and Davis were even blunter as they explained that asserting the primacy of intellectual development in middle grades education was

> necessary because critics of middle grades schools will otherwise continue to assert—wrongly—that middle grades educators do not believe their students are capable of significant intellectual achievement or that they believe it is more important to help students successfully traverse the emotional vicissitudes inherent in this developmental stage. (2000, p. 11)

It is curious that such a fundamental position; one that has played such a major role in the growth of the middle school concept is still so misunderstood. Perhaps this is not so surprising when one considers how the middle school concept, which runs counter to many traditional aspects of education, has been implemented consistently in too few schools.

Perhaps too, developmental responsiveness was interpreted to mean what others wanted it to mean. For some, this became the opportunity to turn general dissatisfaction with public schools into a new point of attack through narrowing the definition of developmental responsiveness by excluding a focus on academic success. As others have noted (Dickinson, 2001; Jackson & Davis, 2000; National Middle School Association, 1995), the focus on developmental responsiveness was never intended to de-emphasize academic achievement.

Another way of looking at developmental responsiveness was suggested by Beane (1999), who recommended that middle school advocates move away from developmental responsiveness as their defining slogan because focusing on developmental responsiveness leaves many people with the impression that middle schools are only concerned about what is going on in the lives of young adolescents. Beane argues, "perhaps now is the time for advocates to supplement their important talk about young people with some thought about what kinds of social purposes they think they should promote" (1999, p. 6). Beane continues to advocate for democratic schools, for if adults really care about young people as they say they do, then they would want schools that work against the inequities and injustices that detract from so many young lives (Apple & Beane, 1995; Beane, 1999; Sehr, 1997).

Today, middle level educators find themselves in a quandary. Instead of using the original concept of developmental responsiveness that included all aspects of students' growth and development *including* academic and intellectual, or broadening the concept to include a balanced and realistic view of young adolescents, we have moved from the perception that middle schools cared little for academic success to a singular focus on academic success as determined by a too-narrow definition—high test scores on high stakes tests. Unfortunately, "academic" is not always equated to intellectual, or even to learning. While students are spending more and more of their time on what some view as "academic tasks," in reality, these tasks are less and less oriented to meaningful, compelling, engaging, and deep learning.

Why has the middle level school been so closely aligned with the ideal of developmental responsiveness when elementary and senior high schools have not? Is it because the reality of dealing with young adolescents is so dramatic and compelling that to ignore the distinctive features of their development is nearly impossible, or is it because middle level educators were looking for a reasonable explanation for behavior, actions, and academic success, or the lack of it, in their students? Regardless of the reason, young adolescents have been well served by this often intense focus on developmental responsiveness.

If middle level schools are to succeed in meeting the lofty goals set for them by our society, they must reassert, and more importantly implement, a definition of developmental responsiveness that does not, in any way, exclude academic success.

In the balance of this essay, we will develop the concept of developmentally responsive schools, what they look like, and what students and teachers do in them.

WHAT DOES A DEVELOPMENTALLY RESPONSIVE MIDDLE SCHOOL LOOK LIKE?

Any school that serves any age cohort should be developmentally responsive. In order to be developmentally responsive, however, educators have to know exactly what that means. Schools that best serve young adolescents incorporate a variety of aspects that work together in creating an optimal learning environment.

Turning Points 2000: Educating Adolescents in the 21st Century (Jackson & Davis, 2000) and *This We Believe: Successful Schools for Young Adolescents* (National Middle School Association, 2003), recent defining publications in middle school education, suggest several vital elements to consider. Each work defines and organizes the characteristics differently, but a synthesis of the main elements from each includes standards-based curriculum that is meaningful to young adolescents; instruction that responds to the needs of young adolescents; varied assessments that promote quality learning; safe and supportive environments; collaboration between and among schools, parents, and communities; organizational structures that support relationships and learning; and specifically prepared educators. All of these elements combine as an organic whole to foster success—academic, emotional, physical, social, and moral—for all students. But what exactly does each of these elements look like?

CURRICULUM THAT IS MEANINGFUL TO YOUNG ADOLESCENTS AND GROUNDED IN CONCEPTS AND PRINCIPLES FROM ESTABLISHED STANDARDS

Curriculum is the most fundamental aspect of schools; it is what comprises all school learning—from math to reading, from relationships to life-long habits, from understanding oneself to understanding the world. The key to establishing developmental responsiveness is for students to learn deeply the concepts, principles, and skills required by standards in a context that they find valuable in helping them understand themselves and their world. It is only through personal meaning that deep learning will occur; to attempt academic excellence while ignoring relevance will be futile.

A meaningful curriculum helps students find answers to their questions. It uses math, science, social studies, language arts, fine arts, and other subjects to provide numerous ways of examining and understanding such complicated issues as poverty, health, culture, and personal development. Academic standards become a means to assist young adolescents in synthesizing information to develop personally meaningful, integrative answers to questions. But from where do these questions come?

As students approach and grow through early adolescence, they begin to see and comprehend the world for the first time. They notice that individuals and cultures are different, that justice does not always prevail, that there are more daily and long-term choices to be made than they had ever imagined. These young people constantly ask why, how, and what can be done. Educators have only to provide a safe forum and questions emerge—numerous and essential. Beane (1993) describes one effective process for finding and organizing students' questions into an integrative curriculum, but the task can be approached in many other ways. The vital core to all developmentally responsive approaches is keeping students and their questions, as well as questions that society poses for them, at the center of the curriculum. This will greatly increase the likelihood that students will connect to the curriculum, find relevance and meaning, and achieve deep and lasting learning.

INSTRUCTION THAT RESPONDS TO THE NEEDS, INTERESTS, AND LEARNING STYLES OF DIVERSE STUDENTS

Young adolescents are an extremely diverse group of students. In addition to the individual and cultural differences they bring to the classroom, they also vary tremendously on their path to development. We can see the diversity in their physical development: some eighth graders are small and could easily pass for 10-year-olds while others tower over adults and grow thick beards. Although not as visible, intellectual, social, emotional, and moral developmental patterns are just as varied and extensive. To complicate matters even more, development is not consistent from one characteristic to another, one day to another, or one task to another. Diversity is the primary hallmark of middle level students as John Lounsbury states:

> The middle level school differs in one important, but seldom-recognized, way from the elementary school and the high school. The elementary school is designed to serve children, and whether they are first graders or fourth graders, they are children. The high school serves a different developmental level, adolescence, and whether students are 10th graders or seniors, they are adolescents. The middle school, however, does not exist to serve a relatively homogeneous group but rather young adolescents who are distinguished by their diversity. We bring 10- to 14-year-olds together not because they are alike but because they are unalike. What they have in common is their lack of commonality as individuals, each at his or her own rate and timetable, as they each make the transition from childhood to adolescence. Schools traditionally operate on assumptions of likeness, yet the middle level school exists to serve diversity. And it is this reality that makes the education of young adolescents a particularly challenging but exciting calling. (J. Lounsbury, personal communication, December 2, 2004)

To deal with such tremendous diversity, middle school educators must use a variety of instructional methods that can simultaneously challenge and support every individual in every classroom. Effective differentiation becomes essential to student success, beginning with tasks that are accessible on a variety of levels. Consider, for example, the difference between two tasks, both dealing with World War II. The first task is to memorize the important battles of the war listed in a common textbook. The second task is to explain the causes and effects of the war.

In the first task, it is difficult to imagine effective ways to challenge students who quickly memorize the dates or ensure success for students who have trouble reading and memorizing. And the expected outcome is the same, whether written or shared orally.

The second task, however, allows a variety of student approaches. First, many different resources could be helpful and individuals could choose the ones that best fit their abilities, interests, and personal development. Students could read well-illustrated books and college texts, interview veterans and politi-

cians, view art and listen to music, listen to lectures and prepare presentations for others. Some students may understand the rudimentary causes and effects while others may be able to provide in-depth details and analysis. Every student could offer a very different (correct) answer presented in a very different form. The first task makes differentiation difficult and artificial, the second allows for a natural incorporation of individual differences.

When the task is decided, a variety of strategies can and should be used including, just to name some possibilities, lecture, labs, demonstrations, primary research, Internet and library research, large group discussion, small group tasks, and individual exploration. Young adolescents should be helped to make decisions about what kinds of activities and instruction will best serve learning for particular groups, individuals, and tasks. Through planning their own learning, young people develop the skills to become lifelong learners and also to become effective members of a diverse learning community. The goal is for each individual, through meaningful curriculum and effective instruction, to be "engaged in active learning" (National Middle School Association, 2003, p. 7), with "active" defined as intellectual engagement and not simply "hands-on" busy-ness.

SYSTEM OF VARIED ASSESSMENTS AND EVALUATIONS TO PROMOTE QUALITY LEARNING

Assessment and evaluation can be threatening to students and detrimental to learning, especially if evaluations emphasize competition and set an end to learning. For young adolescents who are beginning to define themselves as learners and human beings, it is especially critical that assessments provide valuable, specific feedback while minimizing the risk of failure and labeling. Equally as important is the opportunity for students to demonstrate their learning in various ways and at numerous times. High stakes tests as a single measure of success and learning runs completely contrary to the practice of effective assessment.

Effective assessment starts with goals that are clearly understood by students as well as teachers and, along with curriculum and instruction, may be developed collaboratively between teachers and students. Assessments should also be related, but not limited to, required standards. Clear goals define levels of quality to which a task may be completed, often in teacher and student generated rubrics. Each level must be clearly defined so that both students and teachers can easily and relatively objectively assess the level of learning evidenced. For example, one mathematics goal may be to construct graphs given a table of data. The first level of quality could be that the x- and y-axes are written on the graph and the data is plotted. The second level may be x- and y-axes are written and labeled correctly and the data is plotted correctly. The third level then might be the x- and y-axes are written and labeled correctly with units, the data is plotted correctly and the origin is labeled, along with a title for the graph. To make the goal clearer, students can look at examples of each kind of graph. Such descriptions focus directly on learning and quality rather than making the goal only to complete the task.

The next step of effective assessment is specific feedback. While engaged in learning activities, students and teachers should periodically compare their learning to the stated goals. In the example above, the teacher or the student could look at any particular graph and give feedback on the level of learning it shows, along with specific suggestions for further learning and improvement. Over time, several graphs, and given feedback and further instruction, every student should be able to improve and achieve the stated goals.

Some students may reach the third level on the first graph and sustain that, some students may need several tries to reach the third level, and many students will be somewhere in between. The number of tries or attempts required to reach the goal should be irrelevant. Students should neither be rewarded for learning more quickly nor punished for requiring more time and support.

Given clear goals and specific feedback, young adolescents can think about their learning and set individual goals to improve and advance it. Goals can be personal, social, and academic and can apply to individuals, small groups, or large groups. Because goals and feedback clarify learning, students can also communicate their learning with other students, teachers, and their parents or guardians.

If middle schools truly want every student to learn in the time and way he or she requires and schools incorporate a system of assessment to support that goal, students will be more willing to take risks to learn. This is especially critical for young adolescents who are deciding their academic abilities and futures based on the feedback they receive in school. Too often grading practices discourage further effort.

SAFE, CARING, SUPPORTIVE ENVIRONMENT

Effective curriculum, instruction, and assessment may mean little if the environment in which both educators and young people work does not provide safety, caring, and support. To have the greatest impact on learning, school communities must purposefully address this aspect of the learning environment across all areas of the school.

According to Maslow's hierarchy (Huitt, 2004), basic needs must be met before students can effectively engage in intellectual pursuits. Bullying, both verbal and physical, impedes students' ability to learn and their desire to attend school. Although it is other students who engage in this behavior, sometimes teachers unknowingly encourage such behavior by using sarcasm or showing favoritism. Especially during the middle school years, young people are particularly prone to participate in and be impacted by bullying because they are unsure of their own social status.

Educators have the responsibility to make school a safe place by helping students understand the consequences of the choices they make—as bullies, victims, and onlookers. They also have the responsibility to help students understand the importance of diversity and respecting individual, cultural, and sexual differences in order to create an atmosphere in which all students can best learn. It takes time to build caring learning communities, but it is time well spent, for it pays off in better academic learning. Learning to be a contributing member of a diverse community is an important goal of one's education.

Beyond physical safety, students need to know that they can find support at school. Young adolescents question daily who they are, where they belong, and what their learning potential might be. Students need support to find realistic and positive responses to those concerns. As schools raise the bar on academic achievement, they must also raise the level of support to ensure that every individual can clear that bar. In practice, this will mean extra time for some students to learn, adequate numbers of educators to provide expertise and time for both classroom teachers and individual students, and professional development to better prepare educators to differentiate instruction.

As part of taking care of basic needs, support also means guidance and health services readily available and accessible in school, as well as an emphasis on well-being. In addition, each student must know that he or she has at least one adult advocate in the school—someone who cares and checks in on a regular basis. Some schools achieve this through a formal advisory program while others choose to form small teams (2-3 teachers and 40-75 students) in which the teachers have few enough students so that they truly know each individual and his or her family. Multiage and looping teams in which teachers and students stay together for multiple years also help serve this purpose.

Educators and others sometimes incorrectly perceive young adolescents as cruel and self-serving. This sometimes happens in schools because they fail to teach students how to be kind and caring. If schools emphasize only the acquisition of information, that is exactly what students will learn. They will be less likely to learn subject matter in any lasting way, however, if they are not taught to be caring participants in supportive learning communities.

COLLABORATION BETWEEN AND AMONG SCHOOLS, PARENTS, AND COMMUNITIES TO SUPPORT STUDENT LEARNING

Students spend many hours beyond the classroom and many adults influence them, primarily family and community members. Research clearly shows that involvement of parents and other adults in students' lives is correlated with higher achievement, better behavior, and greater support of schools (National Middle School Association, 2003).

Involvement means much more than asking parents to help chaperone field trips, or asking the community to support a fundraiser. It implies an interaction of ideas and experiences centered on the learning of young people. Collaboration can take various forms, but the school must take the initiative in all cases.

Schools can conduct educational programs so that parents can better understand the development and behavior of their children. Teachers can create and maintain partnerships with parents and families through open meetings, e-mail, school Web sites, student-led conferences, and various written communication. Often students, with teacher guidance, can take part in or even lead these communication efforts. Families can share expertise about their students or other topics that the class is investigating. All of these are meaningful ways for families to become involved in their students' education and develop a positive relationship with teachers and the school.

Communities and young adolescents have a great deal to offer each other. Communities contain a wide variety of resources in a vast number of areas. Community organizations and agencies can provide programs and support outside of school hours and offer apprenticeships. Young people, in turn, have much to offer them. As they begin to perceive the world around them with new eyes, the idealism that middle school students have can indeed change the world. They enthusiastically participate in service-learning in which they apply academic knowledge and skills to

solving or addressing real-life problems in the community so that they are actually making a difference (Pate, this volume). When given opportunities, young adolescents indeed can positively change their communities.

Forming partnerships with parents and communities to best plan for the education of young adolescents in and out of school will improve their lives and learning.

ORGANIZATIONAL STRUCTURES THAT SUPPORT MEANINGFUL RELATIONSHIPS AND LEARNING

Organizational structures exist to serve the purposes of education in the school. Therefore, decisions about organization should follow, not precede, important decisions about curriculum, instruction, assessment, and relationships. Often schools make decisions about teaming and schedules first and then have to alter the more important elements to fit. What kind of organizational structures actually support the elements of curriculum, instruction, assessment, and relationships described above?

In all of the elements, effective implementation requires teachers who know students and their families well. Educators must know their students well enough to build meaningful curriculum around student needs and concerns; differentiate in heterogeneous classrooms; provide appropriate group and individual instruction; set specific goals and assess group and individual progress toward those goals; communicate student learning; build effective learning communities; and assist students in understanding themselves as learners and humans. Admittedly, an awfully tall order! It is only through integrating all of these elements that they can be achieved. Certain organizational features support the integration and achievement of these worthy goals.

Effective middle schools organize into teams. In the past those teams have generally consisted of 4-5 teachers, each teacher responsible for a core subject area and 100-125 students. Although teachers nobly attempt it, they cannot know 125 students and their families well, especially if they see any one student for only a period a day. Some schools mitigate the lack of time with individual students through multiage grouping, looping, and advisory programs.

Two- and three-person teacher teams, each working with 40-75 common students, have several advantages over larger teams, especially when used in combination with multiage grouping and looping. Teachers can get to know fewer students and families well and build meaningful relationships with and among students and families. On small teams, it becomes much easier to know and act on individuals' learning styles, challenges, and strengths. It is more effective to organize and document comprehensive student learning. Regular, in-depth conferences with students and parents become possible. Curriculum themes can be developed in collaboration with students in a reasonably sized group. Teachers also must necessarily take a larger and more integrated view of the curriculum since they can no longer be attached to just one subject area. The disadvantage, of course, is that teachers grounded in one subject have to expand their expertise.

Time is the key to working effectively with young adolescents. Schedules can open up and provide that time or constrict and limit it. Days filled with numerous 45-minute periods make it almost impossible to build relationships and learning. A more effective way to schedule is to provide teams with large blocks of time that they can schedule as needed day by day. A team may need several short periods of time one day for several minilessons and one huge block of time another day for extended research, a laboratory experiment, or to prepare for student-led conferences. With a large block of time for which they are responsible, a team can accommodate various instructional activities.

With the right organization, educators can implement the curriculum, instruction, assessment, and relationship-building most responsive to the needs of young adolescents. The organization should exist to best assist students to engage with learning and each other, not serve as a straight-jacket restricting efforts to do so.

EDUCATORS SPECIFICALLY PREPARED TO WORK WITH YOUNG ADOLESCENTS

Young adolescents are a unique group of students who are dealing with many developmental issues that can distract them from learning, if those issues are ignored or minimized, or those developmental issues can make learning fun, exciting, and meaningful. Educators who work with these young people must appreciate them in all their diversity and how they best learn. To ensure developmental responsiveness, educators need specific preparation coupled with middle level licensure as well as professional development aimed at teaching young adolescents.

Licensure essential for preparing expert middle school teachers should not overlap significantly with either elementary or secondary education. To teach in a middle grades school, educators will then have to be specifically prepared to do so. With middle school licensure, post-secondary institutions will have to follow the licensure mandate with programs that equip educators to teach young adolescents, at both the undergraduate and graduate levels. In K-8 preparation programs, the focus inevitably is often on the lower grades while secondary programs focus primarily on the senior high school grades. To gain a specific middle school focus will require a specific middle school licensure.

In addition to licensure, middle school teachers also need ongoing professional development dealing specifically with issues unique to the middle level, such as effective teaming, integrating curriculum, and young adolescent development. Even more general issues such as technology, differentiation, literacy, and assessment should look different in the middle level than at the elementary or secondary level. Middle school students are distinctive, so licensure and professional development should be distinctive as well.

ELEMENTS WORK TOGETHER

The elements described above—meaningful, standards-based curriculum; responsive instruction; varied assessments; safe, supportive environment; collaboration among schools, parents, and communities; supportive organizational structures; and specifically prepared educators—should not be taken as a checklist of separate characteristics. In this case, the whole is greater than the sum of the parts. For the elements to have optimal impact, they must work in concert.

For example, consider the element of meaningful, standards-based curriculum. To be meaningful, standards should help students address questions they have about themselves and the world. This requires students trusting each other and their teachers enough to share those questions and concerns and develop themes from them. It also requires time for teachers and students to plan and share as a group. The organization will have to provide the time to build the community and plan collaboratively. Instruction and assessment must follow both the spirit and the organization of the curriculum. None of this can happen without the support of specifically prepared educators. In just this one example, all of the elements have been included.

To be developmentally responsive, middle schools cannot choose one element and move ahead with it, ignoring the others. The elements are separated only for purposes of clarification and description. In practice, the elements interact and overlap and cannot be divided.

REFERENCES

Apple, M. & Beane, J. A. (Eds.). (1995). *Democratic schools.* Alexandria, VA: Association for Supervision and Curriculum Development.

Beane, J. A. (1993). *A middle school curriculum: From rhetoric to reality* (2nd ed.). Columbus, OH: National Middle School Association.

Beane, J. A. (1999). Middle schools under siege: Responding to the attack. *Middle School Journal, 30*(5), 3-6.

Carnegie Council on Adolescent Development. (1989, June). *Turning points: Preparing American youth for the 21st century* (Report of the Task Force on Education of Young Adolescents). New York: Carnegie Corporation of New York.

Cobb, N. (2001). *Adolescence: Continuity, change, and diversity* (4th ed.). Mountain View, CA: Mayfield.

Dickinson, T. S. (Ed.). (2001). *Reinventing the middle school.* New York: Routledge Falmer.

Eichhorn, D. (1966). *The middle school.* New York: Center for Applied Research in Education.

George, P. S., & Alexander, W. M. (2003). *The exemplary middle school* (3rd ed.). Belmont, CA: Wadsworth.

Havighurst, R. J. (1972). *Developmental tasks and education.* New York: David McKay.

Huitt, W. (2004). Maslow's hierarchy of needs. *Educational Psychology Interactive.* Retrieved December 12, 2004, from Valdosta State University Web site: http://chiron.valdosta.edu/whuitt/col/regsys/maslow.html.

Jackson, A. W., & Davis, G. A. (2000). *Turning points 2000: Educating adolescents in the 21st century.* New York: Teachers College Press.

Levinson, D. (1978). *Seasons of a man's life.* New York: Ballantine Books.

Lounsbury, J. H. (Ed.). (1984). *Perspectives: Middle school education, 1964–1984.* Columbus, OH: National Middle School Association.

Lounsbury, J. H. (1997). *Understanding and appreciating the wonder years.* Retrieved December 5, 2004, from http://www.nmsa.org/moya/moya_2004/related_lounsbury.htm

National Forum to Accelerate Middle-Grades Reform. (1998). *Vision statement of the National Forum to Accelerate Middle-Grades Reform.* Newton, MA: Education Development Center.

National Forum to Accelerate Middle-Grades Reform. (2001). *Developmental Responsiveness.* Retrieved November 15, 2004, from http://www.schoolstowatch.org/criteria.develp.html

National Middle School Association. (1982). *This we believe.* Columbus, OH: Author.

National Middle School Association. (1995). *This we believe: Developmentally responsive middle level schools.* Columbus, OH: Author.

National Middle School Association. (2003). *This we believe: Successful schools for young adolescents.* Westerville, OH: Author.

Sehr, D. (1997). *Education for public policy.* Albany: State University of New York Press.

Smith, W. A. (1925). *The junior high school.* New York: MacMillan.

Stevenson, C. (2002). *Teaching ten to fourteen year olds.* New York: Longman.

Steinberg, L. (1993). *Adolescence* (3rd ed.). New York: McGraw-Hill.

Leadership in the Middle Level School

Ronald D. Williamson
J. Howard Johnston

INTRODUCTION

Virtually every report recommending reforms in public education recognizes the critical role that leadership plays in nurturing and sustaining initiatives that improve the educational experiences of students (see, for example, Jackson & Davis, 2000; National Middle School Association, 2003). The evidence is clear. High-quality leadership is necessary for improved student achievement (Leithwood & Riehl, 2003; Valentine, Maher, Quinn, & Irvin, 1999).

A report prepared for the Edna McConnell Clark Foundation (Lewis, 1993) describing progress toward strengthening middle schools in five urban school districts stated that, when school reform was effective, principals "act as levers for change" (p. 114). Principals "balance time-consuming daily routines against whatever it takes to fulfill the vision the staff has agreed upon. They make time for change" (p. 114). It reported that "where systematic change is most visible, good leadership ripples through the system" (p. 111).

Despite the nearly universal acclaim for strong and effective leadership, there is no common vision of what leadership is or how it manifests itself. Therein lays the difficulty when discussing leadership. We know it when we experience it. We recognize it when it is absent. We appreciate its power to transform institutions such as schools and classrooms, yet we find it difficult to define. Cronin (1993) described leadership as "one of the most widely talked about subjects and at the same time one of the most elusive and puzzling" (p. 7).

Perhaps most important about leadership is that rather than being fixed and unchanging, when most effective, leadership is malleable, adapting itself in ways that reflect a deep understanding of the context and a reliance on certain bedrock principles, principles that reflect an unwavering commitment to improving the educational experiences of students.

Leadership has been described as a cauldron of competing interests vying for power and influence (Bolman & Deal, 2003). Nowhere is that milieu more dynamic than at the middle level. It is during the middle years that students develop in dramatic ways and parents and communities confront their own biases and stereotypes about middle level students. Leadership in a middle grades setting requires a deep commitment to serving middle grades students, but also to working with teachers, parents, and community members in complex ways often not required at other grade levels (Brown & Anfara, 2002; Valentine, Clark, Hackmann, & Petzko, 2004).

This anchor essay will explore this leadership milieu beginning with a brief discussion of contextual factors affecting the work of middle level leaders. This will be followed by an examination of several different views of leadership and their implications for leadership in middle level schools.

Finally, the anchor essay will examine what is known about the contemporary middle level leader. It will include a description of critical roles for all educational leaders, but particularly those serving in the middle grades. The transformation of the leadership role will be described including key points of leverage where middle level leaders can maximize their impact.

The emphasis throughout the anchor essay will be on discussing leadership in middle grades schools. Examples will draw primarily from the work of middle level leaders. However, the evidence is unclear about whether leadership in the middle grades differs from leadership at any other level. The authors suspect that effective leadership at any level incorporates each of the roles and functions described in this essay. What varies is the context in which that leadership occurs. For example, it is clear that effective middle level leaders understand the developmental needs of middle grades students. It is also clear that effective elementary school leaders understand the developmental needs of elementary students and a similar knowledge about older adolescents is present in effective high school leaders (National Association of Secondary School Principals, 1996).

CONTEXT FOR LEADERSHIP IN THE MIDDLE LEVEL SCHOOL

Middle level schools are shaped and influenced by a unique set of variables. It is during the middle grades that student development accelerates in unique and interesting ways. Not only do middle grades students experience significant changes in their own intellectual, social, emotional, and physical development but the range of developmental stages across the middle grades transcends almost every other age group (Cobb, 1992).

STUDENT DEVELOPMENT

Effective middle level leaders understand the significant ways that these developmental factors impact their work (Jackson & Davis, 2000). They also know that parents of middle level students grapple with the same developmental issues with their own children. This occasionally leads to tension between school and parent about the type of academic and social experiences offered for students (Johnston & Williamson, 1998; Williamson & Johnston, 1998).

ACCOUNTABILITY

Since the publication of *A Nation at Risk* (National Commission on Excellence in Education, 1983) the debate about accountability in schools has accelerated. More recently, the No Child Left Behind Act of 2001 (NCLB) (2002) has reignited the debate about appropriate accountability systems and altered the context for accountability in individual schools.

School systems and individual educators have been criticized for failing to recognize the institutional inequities in the prevailing educational system. Frequently the criticism was quite pointed—failure to believe all students can learn, failure to provide academically challenging educational experiences, failure to maintain high standards, and failure to adopt the structural changes necessary to assure high levels of achievement for every child (Beane, 1999).

Nowhere has the tension about educational accountability been more pronounced than at the middle level. Middle schools have been described as both "the last best hope of American youth" (Carnegie Council on Adolescent Development, 1989) and as "education's weak link" (Southern Regional Education Board, 1989).

Proponents of the middle school and its detractors have engaged in passionate debate about the merits of particular educational practices (see, for example, Beane, 1999; Williamson & Johnston, 1999; Yecke, 2003). These sharply differing perspectives helped create a yearning for earlier approaches to middle schooling (Arth et al., 2004).

MIDDLE LEVEL REFORM

Recognizing that unilateral action by individual advocacy organizations or by committed individuals was less effective than collaborative work, several foundations invited leading middle level researchers and advocates to participate in a series of discussions about the attributes of high-performing middle level schools. Out of these initial conversations, middle level researchers, practitioners, and other advocates created the National Forum to Accelerate Middle-Grades Reform.

The National Forum developed a research-based set of descriptors of high-performing middle schools oriented around the three areas of the National Forum's vision: academic excellence, developmental responsiveness, and social equity (National Forum to Accelerate Middle-Grades Reform, 1998, 2004a). Recognizing that, in addition to the descriptors, there was a need to identify schools that exemplified these practices, the National Forum launched an initiative called Schools to Watch (National Forum to Accelerate Middle-Grades Reform, 2004b). As a result of this work, approximately 55 schools across the nation have been identified as Schools to Watch, reflecting their progress toward achieving the National Forum's vision, and 11 states have state-level Schools to Watch programs. The complete list of descriptors is available at the National Forum's Schools to Watch Web site (http://www.schoolstowatch.org).

At the same time that a definition and descriptors of a high-performing middle school emerged, researchers conducted studies examining the connection between these characteristics and student learning. These empirical studies found that where a "high-fidelity" middle school program was implemented, there was a positive impact on student achievement and school climate (Balfanz & Mac Iver, 2000; Felner et al., 1997; Lee & Smith, 1993; Mertens & Flowers, 2003; Mertens, Flowers, & Mulhall, 1998).

This growing body of empirical research supporting many of the long-standing recommendations for sound middle level practice profoundly impacts the work of the school leader. As they advocate for sound middle level practices, they are empowered with research demonstrating the impact that those middle level practices can have on student learning.

IMPLICATIONS FOR LEADERSHIP

With the increased emphasis on accountability, the role of the school leader has also come under scrutiny. While nearly all reform proposals recognized the importance of sound and effective leadership, there was little agreement about what to expect from the leader.

Educational leaders face an increasingly complex work environment, characterized by difficult and often contentious issues. Adoption of curricular standards and accompanying accountability standards (NCLB, 2002), the changing demography of schools (National Center for Educational Statistics, 2002), the need for strengthened family and community support (Epstein, 2001), and the competition for resources from an aging electorate characterize the milieu in which school leaders work.

In responding to the demand for a different type of school leader, many preparation programs were modified. Some incorporated the knowledge, skills and dispositions advocated by national accrediting bodies (National Policy Board for Educational Administration, 2002). Others worked to identify the knowledge base reflective of contemporary school leadership (Murphy, 1999; Thomson, 1993) or built programs around teaching and learning as the core activities of schools (Achilles, 1998; Schneider, 1999).

Out of this changing context and from these varied and occasionally competing recommendations emerged one central emphasis: the role of the principal and the leadership practices a principal employs are critical to implementing the reforms necessary to positively impact student learning (Leithwood & Riehl, 2003; Valentine et al., 2004).

RESEARCH ON MIDDLE LEVEL LEADERSHIP

From the earliest writings on middle level schools, leadership was identified as a critical factor in the implementation of middle level programs (Alexander & George, 1981; Alexander et al., 1968; Lounsbury, 1991). As the middle school comes under renewed scrutiny, once again leadership is cited as essential to sustaining and invigorating the middle school model (Dickinson, 2001; Jackson & Davis, 2000; Valentine et al., 2004; Williamson & Johnston, 1999).

Only recently has research focused on middle level leaders. Most notable were a series of studies spon-

sored by the National Association of Secondary School Principals (NASSP) to, first, examine the junior-high school principalship (Rock & Hemphill, 1966) and later the middle level principalship (Keefe, Clark, Nickerson & Valentine, 1983; Keefe, Valentine, Clark & Irvin, 1994; Valentine, Clark, Nickerson & Keefe, 1981; Valentine, Clark, Irvin, Keefe & Melton, 1993) and most recently , research begun in 2000 (Valentine et al., 2002, 2004). These ongoing research efforts, known as the "decade studies," reported data about the status of middle level programs and the personal and professional characteristics of middle level leaders.

The most recent study, begun in 2000, reported on the characteristics of middle level schools and their leaders (Valentine et al., 2002). The second part of the study took an in-depth look at the leaders of 98 highly successful middle level schools (Valentine et al., 2004). These highly successful schools were selected from among those nominated by education leaders in each state based on criteria developed from the recommendations of *Turning Points: Preparing American Youth for the 21st Century* (Carnegie Council on Adolescent Development, 1989) and from *Turning Points 2000: Educating Adolescents in the 21st Century* (Jackson & Davis, 2000).

The current NASSP study (Valentine et al., 2004) compared principals in the 98 "highly effective" schools with principals in the larger national study (Valentine et al., 2002). With school demographics similar to those in the national sample, these 98 principals were more likely to possess a vision for their schools grounded in a commitment to the success of each individual student. The principals recognized the developmental issues embedded in middle level schooling and embraced the developmental differences as an opportunity to adopt and incorporate best middle level curricular and instructional practices.

Perhaps the most important feature that distinguished these principals was their impact on the culture and climate of their schools. The schools were characterized as places of continuous and collective learning. Collaboration across the school community between constituent groups was evident. The research team described it best when they reported, "the leaders of the highly successful schools have worked more effectively with their faculties and communities and collaboratively developed, maintained, and refined their exemplary schools" (Valentine et al., 2004, p. 53).

Much of the earlier literature on middle level leadership was not empirical but rather descriptive of characteristics or attributes that the writers believed important for middle level leaders. George and Grebing (1992) described a set of skills that would support the implementation of middle level teaming and shared decision-making. Other writers described the importance of understanding adolescent development (Eichhorn, 1966; George, 1990). Williamson (1991) described the multiple roles that middle level leaders must play, including inspirational leader, human resource developer, and change agent.

Brown and Anfara (2002) conducted a study of middle level principals in three eastern and south-eastern states. They investigated the leadership of principals in "developmentally responsive schools" (p. 14) using National Middle School Association's (NMSA) characteristics of developmentally responsive schools to guide the study (NMSA, 1995). They reported that the principals were "emotionally invested in their schools" (p. 24) and their leadership was responsive to the needs of students, faculty, staff, and community.

The Brown and Anfara study (2002) suggested a model of leadership they described as "developmentally responsive." They posited a three-dimensional model of responsiveness that included

(1) Responsiveness to the developmental needs of middle grades students, (2) responsiveness to the developmental needs of the faculty who support learning for middle grades students, and (3) responsiveness to the development of the middle school itself as a unique innovating entity. (p. 149)

The authors argued that the unique nature of the middle level school called for an inclusive and distributed leadership model. Central to the model was a developmentally responsive leader who "connected with students, their needs, and their current developmental circumstances" (p. 149).

While approaching the conception of middle level leadership from quite different perspectives, these writers (Brown & Anfara, 2002, 2003; George & Grebing, 1992; Valentine et al., 2002, 2004; Williamson, 1991) agreed on one theme. The role of the middle level leader is an evolving one—one grounded in three necessities. First, leaders need to enhance their capacity to work in an increasingly diverse school setting—diverse racially and ethnically, diverse socio-economically, and diverse in learning style and approach (National Center for Educational Statistics, 2002).

Second, middle level leaders need to create and sustain a work environment where the expectations for shared and collaborative leadership prevail. This includes distributed leadership within the school and within the greater school community (Murphy & Datnow, 2003; Spillane, Halverson, & Diamond, 2001).

Finally, middle level leaders must maintain a clear and persistent vision of the role and purpose of the middle level school and recognize the powerful role that middle level leaders play in improved student learning (Anfara & Waks, 2001; Clark & Clark, 2003; Cotton, 2003; Jackson & Davis, 2000; Waters, Marzano, & McNulty, 2003).

VIEWS OF LEADERSHIP

Ample research provides rich, detailed descriptions of the work of school leaders (Brown and Anfara, 2002; Valentine, Clark, Irvin, Keefe, & Melton, 1993; Valentine, et al., 2002, 2004) and the skills and predispositions required of them (DePree, 1989; Johnston & Markle, 1986; Mizell, 1994; Valentine, Trimble, & Whitaker, 1997). But the research reveals stark differences about what constitutes leadership.

Despite these differences, researchers agree about the importance of sound leadership (Clark & Clark, 2003; Cotton, 2003; Jackson & Davis, 2000; Mizell, 1994; Sergiovanni, 2001). Johnston and Markle (1986), in one of the earliest examinations of middle level leadership, described the importance of the principal:

Almost without exception, the major studies and reviews of school effectiveness, regardless of the operational definition of effectiveness that is employed or the theoretical orientations of the researchers, have identified the principal as a strong performer in achieving educational excellence. (p. 12)

The effective schools studies from the 1970s revealed that leadership was among the organizational characteristics of schools that impacted student outcomes (Austin, 1979; Brookover & Lezotte, 1977; Edmonds, 1979).

Edmonds (1979) studied urban schools that were instructionally effective for poor and minority children. The premise of the study was "that all children are eminently educable and that the behavior of the school is critical in determining the quality of that education" (p. 20). He identified five attributes of effective schools: strong instructional leadership, clear instructional goals, a safe and orderly school climate, high expectations for student success, and frequent monitoring of pupil progress.

The vital role of leadership in successful schools has been demonstrated repeatedly (Brookover & Lezotte, 1979; Brown & Anfara, 2002; Lipman, 1981; Murphy & Datnow, 2003; Sweeney, 1982; Useem, Christman, Gold, & Simon, 1997; Valentine et al., 1997). A synthesis of research on effective schools published by the Northwest Regional Educational

Laboratory (1984) found that, across all the studies reviewed, leadership was a critical component in school effectiveness.

Even with broad agreement about the importance of leadership, differences about the definition persist. An early critique of leadership cautioned against a simplistic look at the "pivotal role of the school principal" (Cuban, 1984, p. 145). Cuban described his concern:

> No study I have seen lays out empirically derived principal behaviors that produced the desired outcomes. Instead, there are recipe-like prescriptions stemming from personal experience, case studies of principals, or inferential leaps based upon theories or data drawn from other organizations. Thus, the connective tissue, the set of behaviors that principals engage in to develop a school climate that supports academic achievement—to gain staff commitment, to engender high expectations, to supervise individual teachers and the entire instructional program ... none of these complex, interacting behaviors has been linked in the literature to the production of higher test scores. (p. 145)

Several professional groups have also studied leadership. The National Association of Secondary School Principals (1985) identified 12 elements of leadership effectiveness. The elements included problem analysis, judgment, organizational ability, decisiveness, leadership, sensitivity, range of interests, personal motivation, educational values, stress tolerance, and oral and written communication skill.

In an effort to articulate a shared vision of the knowledge and skills needed by educational leaders, the National Policy Board for Educational Administration (NPBEA) identified 21 functional domains in which the school leader functions (Thomson, 1993). The NPBEA suggested that these domains "constitute the essential repertoire of knowledge and skills required of principals for practice" (p. xiii).

Sergiovanni (1992) suggested that then-current conceptions of leadership were lacking. He argued that prevalent school leadership models were too often based upon bureaucratic models, emphasizing knowledge and skill. What they neglected, he suggested, was moral authority as a basis for leadership. He proposed that incorporating a moral dimension within leadership necessitates development of shared values and a shared leadership model. He described the shift in the leadership function:

> The effectiveness of the leader lies in his ability to make activity meaningful for those in his role set—not to change behavior but to give others a sense of understanding what they are doing, and especially to articulate it so that they can communicate about the meaning of their behavior. (p. 140)

APPROACHES TO UNDERSTANDING LEADERSHIP

Early studies of leadership often begin with the work of Taylor (1911). Taylorism or Scientific Management suggested that economics were the motivator for human behavior and therefore, organizations should be based on a rational plan focused on efficiency and increased production. The role of the leader was to set organizational goals, establish performance standards, and control workers.

More recently other dimensions of human motivation have been studied. Research has focused on understanding human behavior and identifying and addressing the needs of workers as a means of motivation (Maslow, 1954; McGregor, 1965). Maslow postulated that human beings are motivated by an intrinsic desire for "self-actualization" once other needs are satisfied.

McGregor (1965) developed a set of management theories based on Mazlow's earlier work. McGregor's "Theory X and Theory Y" were based on certain assumptions regarding human nature. Theory X suggested that people find work distasteful and avoid work if possible and that most people were not interested in assuming responsibility, preferring instead to be directed. In contrast, McGregor's Theory Y suggested people find work to be as natural as play, are ambitious and creative and can be self-directed, achieving their own goals by directing their own efforts.

The leader operating under Theory X assumptions will attempt to structure, control and utilize external controls to manage employees. On the other hand, leaders predisposed toward Theory Y assumptions will structure tasks so that the potential of employees can be developed.

Others suggested that any study of leadership must consider the context in which the leader worked. Tannenbaum and Schmidt (1957) identified seven leader behaviors, each reflecting the complex interaction of forces existing between the leader, the follower, and the situation. The behaviors ranged from democratic and relationship oriented to authoritarian and task oriented. They suggested that leader behaviors exist on a continuum that reflects varying degrees of freedom for the follower (more democratic) and areas of authority for the leader (more autocratic) providing options for the leader based on the context of the situation.

McGregor (1965) and Tannenbaum and Schmidt (1957), as well as more contemporary models of leadership (Bolman & Deal, 2003; Hersey & Blanchard,

1993), reflect an appreciation for the importance of context in leadership behavior.

Situational leadership (Hersey & Blanchard, 1993) reflected an understanding that "leaders may ... not be effective unless they can adapt their leadership style to meet the demands of the environment" (p. 183). They suggested that leadership consists of the complex interrelationships between and among (a) guidance and direction provided by the leader; (b) the relationship reflected in socioemotional support provided by the leader; and (c) the readiness of followers in performing the task (p. 184).

The importance of followers is critical to the understanding of situational leadership. Hersey and Blanchard (1993) described the role of followers: "Followers in any situation are vital, not only because individually they accept or reject the leader, but because as a group they actually determine whatever personal power the leader may have" (p. 185). They suggested that leader behaviors are comprised of the interplay between task behavior, that is providing guidance, and relationship behavior, that is providing support.

Hersey and Blanchard (1993) also described the importance of leaders attending to the readiness of followers. To determine whether a leader's style is appropriate, they suggested looking at the results of the group's work. The leader can adjust his/her behavior to provide greater attention either to task or to support, based upon how the group is performing.

Yet another model for the study of leadership took into account the diverse and complex contexts in which the leader functions (Bolman & Deal, 2003). Drawing on the research on organizational development, Bolman and Deal described a model of leadership that includes four unique perspectives, or frames. The model included the structural frame built around the formal roles and relationships within an organization; the human resource frame built around the concept that organizations are comprised of people and those individuals possess all of the needs and feelings of human beings; the political frame reflecting competition for power and resources from varied interest groups; and the symbolic frame viewing organizations as cultures which can be best understood through their symbolic actions such as rituals, ceremonies, heroes, and myths (p. 16).

Bolman and Deal (2003) suggested that effective leaders understand each of the four frames and are able to integrate the frames into a unique leadership style. They described the importance of multiple frames for the work of leaders:

Like maps, frames are both windows on a territory and tools for navigation. Every tool has distinctive strengths and limitations. The right tool makes the job easier, but the wrong one just gets in the way. One or two tools may suffice for simple jobs, but not for more complex undertakings. (p. 13)

Sergiovanni (1996) questioned the usefulness of leadership models adapted from business. Rather than adopt theories from other fields, Sergiovanni suggested that school leadership must link leaders and followers "together by a consensual understanding" (p. 87) based on shared purposes and moral obligations. He described the need for school leaders to accept the role of steward and reflect a "personal commitment to 'do the right thing for our children'" (p. 96). Such a commitment, Sergiovanni stated, should "emphasize the building of authentic communities where values are rooted in the democratic Judeo-Christian traditions that define our nation and where values reflect our commitment to school purposes and ideals" (pp. 20-21).

CONSIDERATIONS FOR MIDDLE LEVEL LEADERS

Middle level leaders work in a complex environment. Demands for improved student performance often drive the debate about school programs and structure. Successful leaders understand this complexity and possess a set of skills that allow them to successfully both navigate and change the social context of schooling at their school.

ORGANIZATION, STRUCTURE, AND SOCIAL CONTEXT OF CHANGE

Researchers have come to appreciate the complexity of school reform. Cuban (1990), in a study of why reforms return again and again, suggested that they "return because policy makers fail to diagnose problems and promote correct solutions" (p. 3). This is exacerbated by the pressure placed on schools to align with public shifts in values driven by economic, social, and demographic changes.

Fullan and Miles (1992) studied the failure of reform efforts and concluded that reforms fail "because our attempts to solve problems are frequently superficial" (p. 747). They also suggested that reformers often do not understand the complexity of problems, misunderstand resistance to change, utilize symbols over substance, and allow successful reform efforts to atrophy.

Several suggestions for addressing these problems were provided by Fullan and Miles (1992). They argued that reformers must view their work as systemic—focusing on two separate but linked elements. First, reformers must be attentive to the "development and interrelationships of all the main components of the system simultaneously" (p. 751). Second, they must attend to developing a deeper understanding of the culture of the system.

Fullan and Miles (1992) argued that systemic reform goes beyond structure, policy, and regulations. It involves both restructuring of the organization and "reculturing" (Hargreaves, 1994).

ORGANIZATIONAL AND SOCIAL CONTEXT OF SCHOOLS

Schools are complex organizations, often envisioned in terms of their physical setting—a site and a building—or the courses and programs offered to students. However, they also comprise a network of social connections—student to student, student to teacher, and teacher to teacher. McLaughlin (1993) summarized the importance of the social setting for teachers: "This aspect of the workplace—the nature of the professional community that exists there—appears to be more critical than any other factor to the character of teaching and learning for teachers and their students" (p. 99).

In a study of the social context of schooling, Rowan (1995) described education administration "as the exercise of leadership in the context of formal, organizational arrangements explicitly chartered by society to produce learning through teaching" (p. 349).

Newmann, Rutter, and Smith (1989) explored the impact of ten organizational features in 353 public schools on three climate variables: teacher efficacy, sense of community, and expectations. They found that organizational features such as encouragement of innovation, teachers' knowledge of one another and one another's courses, the responsiveness of administrators, and teachers' willingness to help one another, had significant effects on teachers' work.

Several studies explored the relationship between organizational context and leadership. Oakes, Quartz, Gong, Guiton, & Lipton (1993) examined change initiatives in middle schools and identified three dimensions of reform: technical, normative, and political. The technical aspects included "the structures (e.g., arrangement of space, time, people, and materials), strategies (e.g., curricular, pedagogical, governance), and knowledge (e.g., adolescent development, teacher training) that are central to achieving the reform's goals" (p. 464).

The second dimension was normative. Oakes and her colleagues (1993) found that substantive reform required modifying "the norms of what constitutes a good middle school" (p. 468). Changing the technical aspects of a school also required modifying the norms. Without such change, the researchers argued, at best there will be only reluctant compliance with the new practices.

The third dimension of reform identified by Oakes et al. (1993) was political. This dimension included consideration of the redistribution of power and resources, the formation of new coalitions, as well as decision-making processes. As decision making moved closer to students through the implementation of interdisciplinary teams, it altered the political landscape thereby triggering political implications for those whose power and influence were eroded.

Social models of change, such as restructuring a middle level school, rely heavily upon consensus. Once a group has agreed on a vision, goal, or practice it can command great support (Williamson & Johnston, 1991). Reaching agreement on new norms can become the underpinning of a restructured middle level school. When accepted, new norms "redefine people's conception of middle school practice—these norms will demand that the old regularities be challenged in order to construct a radically new school culture" (Oakes et al., 1993, p. 471).

Oakes et al. (1993) suggested that leaders must consider the technical, normative, and political dimensions of change if they are to succeed in restructuring the middle level school. Successful change initiatives require a comprehensive examination of the factors that both support and impede change. Only through consideration of all aspects of reform efforts will leaders find their efforts successful.

CULTURE

The culture of a school is a powerful tool for shaping the behavior of those who work there and reflects the important values and underlying assumptions of that school. Understanding culture is critical for educational leaders (Deal & Peterson, 1990; Sergiovanni, 1990). In discussing the culture of schools, Deal (1987) described its importance:

Culture is a social invention created to give meaning to human endeavor. It provides stability, certainty, and predictability. People fear ambiguity and want assurance that they are in control of their surroundings. Culture imbues life with meaning and through symbols creates a sense of efficacy and control. (p. 7)

Schools face enormous pressure to reform their programs. Suggestions of reform introduce uncertainty and unpredictability into the lives of educators. As educational leaders launch reform initiatives, it is critical that they understand both the elements of organizational culture and strategies for embedding and refining cultural values.

The concept of organizational culture emerged from the early work of Deal and Kennedy (1982), Deal and Peterson (1990), and Schein (1984, 1985). Each contributed to an understanding of the interpersonal dynamics present in any organization.

Two key ideas emerged from Deal and Kennedy's work (1982): "A strong culture is a system of informal rules that spells out how people are to behave most of the time" (p. 15), and "a strong culture enables people to feel better about what they do, so they are more likely to work harder" (p. 16).

Schein conducted several studies of organizational culture (1984, 1985, 1990) and described the importance of culture as a tool to mold and shape organizations. Schein (1985) also studied the impact of founders on the culture of organizations. He described founders, those who have a new vision or new idea for a product, as key to how the organization embraces new initiatives. He identified tools that organizational leaders can use to embed and reinforce new norms and initiatives. They included

1. What leaders pay attention to, measure, and control;
2. Leader reactions to critical incidents and organizational crises;
3. Deliberate role modeling, teaching, and coaching by leaders;
4. Criteria for allocation of rewards and status; and
5. Criteria for recruitment, selection, promotion, retirement, and excommunication. (pp. 224-225)

The strategies described in this section have been identified as tools that leaders can use to shape the culture of their organization (Deal & Kennedy, 1982; Deal & Peterson, 1990; Schein, 1985). They are so important that Schein (1992) argued that "the only thing of real importance that leaders do is to create and manage culture and . . . the unique talent of leaders is their ability to understand and work with culture" (p. 5).

CULTURAL LEADERSHIP

Understanding culture and learning strategies to shape culture are critical to effective leadership. Ser-

giovanni (1987) discussed the value of cultural leadership.

> It is a pragmatic way to achieve coordinated effort toward school goals in a loosely connected world. Where management schemes fail to link together people and events in a way that provides for successful schooling, the leadership values are able to bond people together in a common cause. (p. 125)

A core responsibility of middle school leaders is providing leadership for the values of the organization. Sergiovanni stated the importance of cultural leadership: "Cultural leaders help to shape this culture, work to design ways and means to transmit this culture to others, but more important, they behave as guardians of the values that define the culture" (1987, p. 124).

Cunningham and Gresso (1993) studied leadership and found that while schools often focus reform efforts on structural change, that alone was not sufficient. School leaders must "focus on the culture of excellence and the structures will evolve to support that culture" (p. 24).

Other researchers also affirmed the importance of culture as a tool to achieve school reform. Sashkin (1993) suggested steps that a leader can take to impact the culture of his or her school. The first is to construct a vision of the ideal school. Second is turning that vision and cultural ideals into organizational reality, and third is to implement the vision through personal practice. These steps include effective use of communication, expressing the vision in unusual and exciting ways, being consistent in one's actions, and exhibiting and expressing respect for oneself and for others. Sashkin described the importance of these steps:

> Principals cannot simply be administrators (although effective administration is not unimportant or irrelevant); they must be culture-builders as well. Doing so is easier if the principal understands the critical functions of a school's culture—adapting, achieving, and coordinating—and the key values that support these functions. But more than understanding is needed. Effective school leaders must be able to conceive of a vision, a cultural ideal, for the school. They must be able to generate school wide support for this vision, by involving others in articulating a philosophy that summarizes the vision and by creating policies and programs that turn the philosophy (and the vision) into action. Finally, school leaders carry out their visions through their own specific behavioral practices. (p. 84)

The culture of a school is related to its effectiveness. School leaders who understand the concept of culture and the ways they can shape that culture in their schools are better positioned to lead reform efforts at their school. The power of culture to either inhibit or accelerate school reform should not be minimized.

CORE FUNCTIONS OF SCHOOL LEADERS

Much is known about how schools operate. Little is known about the leadership attributes that link most directly to personal and school success. Despite the idiosyncratic nature of the application of leadership, broad agreement has been reached about the core functions of the school leader. The model suggested by Sergiovanni (2001) reflects the complexity of leadership. At the core of their work, leaders are expected to supervise the instructional program by supervising teachers and modeling effective instructional practices. Beyond this core, leaders manage the culture, provide for day-to-day management, and hire and provide professional development for staff. Further, they work with staff, as well as parents and other external stakeholders, to develop and promote a shared vision. If that is not enough, they must also deal with both internal and external political demands and considerations.

In their study of middle level leadership, Brown and Anfara (2002) described seven different approaches to leadership originally suggested by Leithwood, Jantzi, & Steinbach (1999). They included instructional leadership (Hallinger & Murphy, 1985), transformational leadership (Burns, 1978), cultural leadership (Deal & Kennedy, 1982; Schein, 1985), moral leadership (Greenfield, 1991; Hodgkinson, 1991; Sergiovanni, 1996), participative leadership, managerial leadership, and contingent leadership (Hersey & Blanchard, 1993). They then suggested an eighth approach—developmentally responsive leadership (Brown & Anfara, 2002).

THE LEADER AS AN AGENT OF CHANGE

One theme permeates all of the literature on middle level leadership: the importance of the leader as one who understands effective middle level practices (Valentine et al., 2004) and who possesses the knowledge and skills to be an effective advocate for their adoption (Clark & Clark, 1994, 2004; Williamson & Johnston, 1991).

In 1994, Don and Sally Clark described a comprehensive approach to restructuring the middle level school. They identified two "crucial factors": "new

leadership roles for administrators and teachers" and "a school culture that promotes collegiality and participatory governance" (p. 177).

These two factors have indeed emerged as critical to middle level leadership. The recent NASSP study of "highly effective schools" at the middle level found that these schools were places where leaders recognized the power of distributed leadership and cultural connections (Valentine et al., 2004). They did so by strengthening the social connections within the school through fostering trust, communicating their expectations, and enforcing norms for sound practice.

These social connections are paramount in the middle grades because of the nearly universal recommendation that teachers and students work together in interdisciplinary teams (Valentine et al., 2002). Clark and Clark (1994) found that teams promote a "culture of collaboration" (p. 192). They are an important tool to focus faculty work on how to positively impact student learning.

The National Forum's Schools to Watch Program also identified schools described as "high-performing." The schools were recognized for their achievements based on the National Forum's indicators, which are organized around the concepts of academic excellence, developmental responsiveness, and social equity (National Forum to Accelerate Middle-Grades Reform, 2004a). The National Forum selected four national Schools to Watch and developed case studies of each of the schools (National Forum to Accelerate Middle-Grades Reform, 2004b). Analysis of the cases revealed that in each school the leader worked collaboratively with the faculty in support of a common vision of a strong academic experience for every student.

Clark and Clark (2004) examined both the Schools to Watch Program (National Forum to Accelerate Middle-Grades Reform, 2004a) and the NASSP "highly effective schools" study (Valentine et al, 2004), looking for common attributes. They identified three factors: "commitment to a vision, focus on learning, and building and sustaining relationships" (p. 50).

We find this analysis compelling and suggest that leaders of successful middle level schools are those that focus on the three factors identified by Clark and Clark (2004). We further suggest that these leaders are successful because they choose to do their work differently.

Building on the work of Schoen (1983), Costa and Garmston (1994), and Garmston and Wellman (1999), the work in these "high-performing" and "highly successful schools" was guided by a deep commitment to the success of every student anchored in an appreciation of the value of individual and group reflection.

The schools were characterized by their commitment to inquiry, inquiry about what worked and what didn't. They were comfortable challenging long-standing norms and practices. The leaders of these schools were supportive when faculty tried new practices, even when they were less than successful (National Forum to Accelerate Middle-Grades Reform, 2004a; Valentine et al., 2004).

These schools also used different tools to guide their practice. Analysis of the schools found that their commitment to student learning propelled them to gather and use data about the instructional program. Instructional walk-throughs (Richardson, 2001), student shadow studies (Lounsbury & Clark, 1990; Lounsbury & Johnston, 1988), whole faculty study groups (Murphy, 1995), and analysis of student work (Langer, Colton, & Goff, 2003; Lewis, 1998) were practices frequently used by the faculties of these schools.

CONCLUDING THOUGHTS

Researchers have suggested a number of roles for school leaders (Leithwood, Jantzi & Steinbach, 1999). One of those roles is that of transformational leader, described as a more comprehensive approach because it encompasses many of the other roles (Leithwood & Jantzi, 2000). We contend that successful leadership in the middle grades is about more than good management, more than instructional improvement, and more than political astuteness.

Effective middle level schools have leaders who are committed to transforming their schools. These transformations will result in schools becoming places where every student experiences success, where every student has access to a rigorous and challenging educational experience, where student development is understood and appreciated, and where the culture and climate is characterized by an unwavering commitment to social justice and equity (National Forum to Accelerate Middle-Grades Reform, 2004a).

The leadership model we discuss here is much more integrative than prior models. It reflects a fundamental belief in the power of leadership to positively impact the school community and student learning. It appreciates the dynamic context in which school leaders function and suggests that leadership skills are ever changing, not fixed and static.

REFERENCES

Achilles, C. (1998, Summer). *How long? The AASA professor,* 22(1). Retrieved December 8, 1999, from http://www.aasa.org/TAP/summer9804.htm

Alexander, W. M., & George, P. S. (1981). *The exemplary middle school.* New York: Holt, Rinehart, and Winston.

Alexander, W. M., Williams, E., Compton, M., Hines, V., Prescott, D., & Kealy, R. (1969). *The emergent middle school* (2nd ed.). New York: Holt, Rinehart, and Winston.

Anfara, V. A., Jr., & Waks, L. (2000). Resolving the tension between academic rigor and developmental responsiveness. *Middle School Journal, 32*(2), 46-51.

Arth, A., Ashford, A., Jenkins, J., Burns, J., Kane, T., Mitchell, K., Shepard, D., Toepfer, C., & Wheeler, K. (2004). Present imperfect. *Principal Leadership, 4*(8), 37-42.

Austin, G. R. (1979). Exemplary schools and the search for effectiveness. *Educational Leadership, 37*(2), 10-14.

Balfanz, R., & Mac Iver, D. J. (2000). Transforming high-poverty urban middle schools into strong learning institutions: Lessons from the first five years of the Talent Development Middle School. *Journal of Education for Students Placed at Risk, 5*(1/2), 137-158.

Beane, J. (1999). Middle schools under siege: Points of attack. *Middle School Journal, 30*(4), 3-9.

Bolman, L., & Deal, T. (2003). *Reframing organizations: Artistry, choice and leadership* (3rd ed.). San Francisco, CA: Jossey-Bass.

Brookover, W. B., & Lezotte, L. W. (1977). *Changes in school characteristics coincident with changes in student achievement.* East Lansing, MI: Michigan State University, College of Urban Development.

Brown, K., & Anfara, V. A., Jr. (2002). *From the desk of the middle school principal: Leadership responsive to the needs of young adolescents.* Lanham, MD: Scarecrow.

Brown, K., & Anfara, V. A., Jr. (2003). Paving the way for change: Visionary leadership in action at the middle level. *NASSP Bulletin, 87*(635), 16-33.

Burns, J. (1978). *Leadership.* New York: Harper and Row.

Carnegie Council on Adolescent Development (1989, June). *Turning points: Preparing American youth for the 21st century* (Report of the Task Force on Education of Young Adolescents). New York: Carnegie Corporation of New York.

Clark, S., & Clark, D. (1994). *Restructuring the middle level school: Implications for school leaders.* Albany: State University of New York Press.

Clark, S., & Clark, D. (2003). The middle school achievement project: Involving parents and community in school improvement. *Middle School Journal, 34*(3), 12-19.

Clark, S., & Clark, D. (2004). Principal leadership for developing and sustaining highly successful middle level schools. *Middle School Journal, 36*(2), 49-55.

Cobb, N. (1992). *Adolescence: Continuity, change, and diversity.* Mountain View, CA: Mayfield.

Costa, A., & Garmston, R. (1994). *Cognitive coaching: A foundation for renaissance schools.* Norwood, MA: Christopher-Gordon.

Cotton, K. (2003). *Principals and student achievement: What the research says.* Alexandria, VA: Association for Supervision and Student Achievement.

Cronin, T. E. (1993). Reflections on leadership. In W. E. Rosenbach & R. L. Taylor (Eds.), *Contemporary issues in leadership* (pp. 7-25). Boulder, CO: Westview Press.

Cuban, L. (1984). Transforming the frog into a prince: Effective schools research, policy, and practice at the district level. *Harvard Educational Review, 54*(2), 129-151.

Cuban, L. (1990). Reforming again, again, and again. *Educational Researcher, 9*(1), 3-13.

Cunningham, W., & Gresso, D. (1993). *Cultural leadership: The culture of excellence in education.* Boston: Allyn & Bacon.

Deal, T. (1987). The culture of schools. In R. Brandt (Ed.), *Leadership: Examining the elusive* (pp. 3-15). Alexandra, VA: Association for Supervision and Curriculum Development.

Deal, T., & Kennedy, A. (1982). *Corporate cultures: The rites and rituals of corporate life.* Reading, MA: Addison-Wesley.

Deal, T., & Peterson, K. (1990). *The principal's role in shaping school culture.* Washington, DC: U.S. Department of Education.

DePree, M. (1989). *Leadership is an art.* New York: Dell.

Dickinson, T. S. (Ed.) (2001). *Reinventing the middle school.* New York: Routledge Falmer.

Edmonds, R. (1979). Effective schools for the urban poor. *Educational Leadership, 37*(2), 15-27.

Eichhorn, D. (1996). *The middle school.* New York: The Center for Applied Research in Education.

Epstein, J. (2001). *School, family, and community partnerships: Preparing educators and improving schools.* Boulder, CO: Westview Press.

Felner, R., Jackson, A. W., Kasak, D., Mulhall, P., Brand, S., & Flowers, N. (1997). The impact of school reform for the middle years: A longitudinal study of a network engaged in *turning points*-based comprehensive school transformation. *Phi Delta Kappan, 78*(7), 528-532, 541-550.

Fullan, M., & Miles, M. (1992). Getting reform right: What works and what doesn't. *Phi Delta Kappan, 73*(10), 745-752.

Garmston, R., & Wellman, B. (1999). *The adaptive school: A sourcebook for developing collaborative groups.* Norwood, MA: Christopher-Gordon.

George, P. S. (1990). From junior high to middle school—Principals' perspectives. *NASSP Bulletin, 74*(253), 86-94.

George, P. S., & Grebing, W. (1992). Seven essential skills of middle level leadership. *Schools in the Middle, 1*(4), 3-11.

Greenfield, T. (1991). Re-forming and re-valuing educational administration: Whence and when cometh the phoenix? *Educational Management and Administration, 19*(4), 200-217.

Hallinger, P., & Murphy, J. (1985). Assessing the instructional management behavior of principals. *Elementary School Journal, 86*(2), 217-247.

Hargreaves, A. (1994). Restructuring restructuring: Postmodernity and the prospect for educational change. *Journal of Education Policy, 9*(1), 47-65.

Hersey, P., & Blanchard, K. (1993). *Management of organizational behavior* (6th ed.). Englewood Cliffs, NJ: Prentice Hall.

Hodgkinson, C. (1991). *Educational leadership: A moral art.* Albany: State University of New York Press.

Jackson, A. W., & Davis, G. A. (2000). *Turning points 2000: Educating adolescents in the 21st century.* New York: Teachers College Press.

Johnston, J. H., & Markle, G. (1986). *What research says to the middle level practitioner.* Columbus, OH: National Middle School Association.

Johnston, J. H., & Williamson, R. (1998). Listening to four communities: Parent and public concerns about middle level schools. *NASSP Bulletin, 82*(597), 44-52.

Keefe, J., Clark, D., Nickerson, N., & Valentine, J. (1983). *The middle level principalship: Volume II: The effective middle level principal.* Reston, VA: National Association of Secondary School Principals.

Keefe, J., Valentine, J., Clark, D., & Irvin, J. (1994). *Leadership in middle level education, Volume II: Leadership in successfully restructuring middle level schools.* Reston, VA: National Association of Secondary School Principals.

Langer, G., Colton, A., & Goff, L. (2003). *Collaborative analysis of student work: Improving teaching and learning.* Alexandria, VA: Association for Supervision and Curriculum Development.

Lee, V., & Smith, J. (1993, July). Effects of school restructuring on the achievement and engagement of middle-grade students. *Sociology of Education, 66*, 164-187.

Leithwood, K., & Jantzi, D. (2000). The effects of transformational leadership on organizational conditions and student engagement with school. *Journal of Educational Administration, 38*(2), 112-129.

Leithwood, K., Jantzi, D., & Steinbach, R. (1999). *Changing leadership for changing times.* Buckingham, England: Open University Press.

Leithwood, K., & Riehl, C. (2003, April). *What do we already know about successful school leadership.* Paper presented at the annual meeting of the American Educational Research Association, Chicago, IL.

Lewis, A. (1993). *Changing the odds: Middle school reform in progress, 1991-1993.* New York: Edna McConnell Clark Foundation.

Lewis, A. (1998). Student work: This focus for staff development leads to genuine collaboration. *Journal of Staff Development, 19*(4), 24-27.

Lipman, J. A. (1981). *Effective principal, effective school.* Reston, VA: National Association of Secondary School Principals.

Lounsbury, J. H. (1991). *As I see it.* Columbus, OH: National Middle School Association.

Lounsbury, J. H., & Clark, D. (1990). *Inside grade eight: From apathy to excitement.* Reston, VA: National Association of Secondary School Principals.

Lounsbury, J. H., & Johnston, J. H. (1988). *Life in the three sixth grades.* Reston, VA: National Association of Secondary School Principals.

Maslow, A. H. (1954). *Motivation and personality.* New York: Harper & Row.

McGregor, D. M. (1965). *The human side of enterprise.* New York: McGraw-Hill.

McLaughlin, M. W. (1993). What matters most in teachers' workplace context? In J. W. Little & M. W. McLaughlin (Eds.), *Teachers' work: Individuals, colleagues, and contexts* (pp. 79-103). New York: Teachers College Press.

Mertens, S., & Flowers, N. (2003). Middle school practices improve student achievement in high-poverty schools. *Middle School Journal, 35*(1), 33-43.

Mertens, S., Flowers, N., & Mulhall, P. (1998). *The middle start initiative, phase 1: A longitudinal analysis of Michigan middle-level schools.* Urbana: University of Illinois.

Mizell, M. H. (1994). *The new principal: Risk, reform and the quest for hard-core change.* New York: Edna McConnell Clark Foundation.

Murphy, C. (1995). Whole-faculty study groups: Doing the seemingly undoable. *Journal of Staff Development, 16*(3), 37-44.

Murphy, J. (1999, April). *The quest for a center: Notes on the state of the profession of educational leadership.* Paper presented at the annual conference of the American Educational Research Association, Montreal, PQ, Canada.

Murphy, J., & Datnow, A. (2003). Leadership lessons from comprehensive school reform designs. In J. Murphy & A. Datnow (Eds.). *Leadership lessons from comprehensive school reforms* (pp. 263-278). San Francisco: Jossey-Bass.

National Association of Secondary School Principals. (1985). *Performance-based preparation of principals.* Reston, VA: Author.

National Association of Secondary School Principals. (1996). *Breaking ranks: Changing an American institution.* Reston, VA: Author.

National Center for Educational Statistics. (2002). *Digest of education statistics, 2002.* Washington, DC: U.S. Department of Education, Office of Educational Research and Improvement.

National Commission on Excellence in Education. (1983, April 27). *An open letter to the American people: A nation at risk: The imperative for educational reform.* Washington, DC: U.S. Government Printing Office.

National Forum to Accelerate Middle-Grades Reform. (1998). *Vision statement of the National Forum to Accelerate Middle-Grades Reform.* Newton, MA: Education Development Center.

National Forum to Accelerate Middle-Grades Reform. (2004a). *What are schools to watch.* Retrieved November 1, 2004, from http://www.schoolstowatch.org/what/htm

National Forum to Accelerate Middle-Grades Reform. (2004b). *Our schools.* Retrieved November 1, 2004, from http://www.schoolstowatch/visit.htm

National Middle School Association. (1995). *This we believe: Developmentally responsive middle level schools.* Columbus, OH: Author.

National Middle School Association. (2003). *This we believe: Successful schools for young adolescents.* Columbus, OH: Author.

National Policy Board for Educational Administration. (2002). *Standards for advanced programs in educational leadership.* Washington, DC: Author.

Newmann, F., Rutter, R., & Smith, M. (1989). Organizational factors that affect school sense of efficacy, community, and expectations. *Sociology of Education, 62*(4), 221-238.

No Child Left Behind Act of 2001, Pub. L. No. 107-110, 115 Stat. 1425 (2002).

Northwest Regional Educational Laboratory. (1984). *Effective schooling practices: A research synthesis.* Portland, OR: Author.

Oakes, J., Quartz, K., Gong, J., Guiton, G., & Lipton, M. (1993). Creating middle schools: Technical, normative, and political considerations. *The Elementary School Journal, 93*(5), 461-480.

Richardson, J. (2001, October/November). Seeing through new eyes: Walk throughs offer new way to view schools. *Tools for Schools,* 1-3.

Rock, D., & Hemphill, J. (1966). *Report of the junior-high principalship.* Washington, DC: National Association of Secondary School Principals.

Rowan, B. (1995). Learning, teaching, and educational administration: Toward a research agenda. *Educational Administration Quarterly, 31*(3), 344-354.

Sashkin, M. (1993). The visionary principal: School leadership for the next century. In M. Sashkin & H. Walberg (Eds.), *Educational leadership and school culture* (pp. 77-88). Berkeley, CA: McCutchan.

Schein, E. (1984). Coming to a new awareness of organizational culture. *Sloan Management Review, 25*(2), 3-16.

Schein, E. (1985). *Organizational culture and leadership.* San Francisco: Jossey-Bass.

Schein, E. (1990). Organization culture. *American Psychologist, 45*(2), 109-119.

Schein, E. (1992). *Organizational culture and leadership* (2nd ed.). San Francisco: Jossey-Bass.

Schneider, J. (1999, February). *Improve the preparation of school leaders by eliminating the master's degree in educational administration.* Paper presented at the National Council of Professors of Educational Administration's Conference within a Conference at the Annual Meeting of the American Association of School Administrators, New Orleans, LA.

Schoen, D. (1983). *The reflective practitioner: How professionals think in action.* New York: Basic Books.

Sergiovanni, T. (1987). The theoretical basis for cultural leadership. In R. Brandt (Ed.), *Leadership: Examining the elusive* (pp. 116-129). Alexandria, VA: Association for Supervision and Curriculum Development.

Sergiovanni, T. (1992). *Moral leadership: Getting to the heart of school improvement.* San Francisco: Jossey-Bass.

Sergiovanni, T. (1996). *Leadership for the school house: How is it different? Why is it important?* San Francisco: Jossey-Bass.

Sergiovanni, T. (2001). *The principalship: A reflective practice perspective* (4th ed.). Boston: Allyn & Bacon.

Southern Regional Education Board. (1989). *Education's weak link: Student performance in the middle grades.* Atlanta, GA: Author.

Spillane, J., Halverson, R., & Diamond, J. (2001). Investigating school leadership practice: A distributed perspective. *Educational Researcher, 30*(3), 23-28.

Sweeney, J. (1982). Principals can provide instructional leadership—It takes commitment. *Education, 103*(2), 204-207.

Tannenbaum, R., & Schmidt, W. (1957). How to choose a leadership pattern. *Harvard Business Review, 36*(2), 95-101.

Taylor, F. (1911). *The principles of scientific management.* New York: Harper & Row.

Thomson, S. D. (1993). Professionalizing the principalship. *International Journal of Educational Reform, 2*(3), 296-299.

Useem, E., Christman, J., Gold, E., & Simon, E. (1997). Reforming alone: Barriers to organizational learning in urban school change initiatives. *Journal of Education of Students Placed at Risk, 2*(1) 55-78.

Valentine, J., Clark, D., Hackmann, D., & Petzko, V. (2002). *A national study of leadership in middle level schools: Volume I: A national study of middle level leaders and school programs.* Reston, VA: National Association of Secondary School Principals.

Valentine, J., Clark, D., Hackmann, D., & Petzko, V. (2004). *A national study of leadership in middle level schools: Volume II: Leadership for highly successful middle level schools.* Reston, VA: National Association of Secondary School Principals.

Valentine, J., Clark, D., Irvin, J., Keefe, J., & Melton, G. (1993). *Leadership in middle level education, Volume I: A national survey of middle level leaders and schools.* Reston, VA: National Association of Secondary School Principals.

Valentine, J., Clark, D., Nickerson, N., & Keefe, J. (1981). *The middle level principalship: Volume I: A survey of middle level principals and programs.* Reston, VA: National Association of Secondary School Principals.

Valentine, J., Maher, M., Quinn, D., & Irvin, J. (1999). The changing roles of effective middle level principals. *Middle School Journal, 30*(5), 53-56.

Valentine, J., Trimble, S., & Whitaker, T. (1997). The middle level principalship. In J. Irvin (Ed.), *What current research says to the middle level practitioner* (pp. 337-347). Columbus, OH: National Middle School Association.

Waters, J. T., Marzano, R. J., & McNulty, B. A. (2003). *Balanced leadership: What 30 years of research tells us about the effect of leadership on student achievement.* Aurora, CO: Mid-Continent Research for Education and Learning.

Williamson, R. (1991). Leadership at the middle level. In J. Capelluti & D. Stokes (Eds.), *Middle level education: Programs, policies, & practices* (pp. 36-41). Reston, VA: National Association of Secondary School Principals.

Williamson, R., & Johnston, J. H. (1991). *Planning for success: Successful implementation of middle level reorganization.* Reston, VA: National Association of Secondary School Principals.

Williamson, R., & Johnston, J. H. (1998). Responding to parent and public concerns about middle level schools. *NASSP Bulletin, 82*(599), 73-82.

Williamson, R., & Johnston, J. H. (1999). Challenging orthodoxy: An emerging agenda for middle level reform. *Middle School Journal, 30*(4), 10-17.

Yecke, C. (2003). *The war against excellence: The rising tide of mediocrity in America's middle schools.* Westport, CT: Praeger.

The Professional Preparation of Middle Level Teachers and Principals

C. Kenneth McEwin
Thomas S. Dickinson
Vincent A. Anfara, Jr.

MIDDLE LEVEL TEACHER PREPARATION

There is widespread consensus among researchers, educators, policymakers, and other stakeholders that the quality of teachers is one of the most salient school-related factors influencing student achievement (McCabe, 2004; Rice, 2003). However, much disagreement and spirited debate characterize discussions regarding what it means to be highly qualified and about the best way to prepare teachers for the nation's schools (Wilson, Floden, & Ferrini-Mundy, 2001). One of the most long-running debates focuses on whether teachers who teach young adolescents need specialized professional preparation to do so.

Historically, there has been little ambivalence among leading advocates of junior high schools and middle schools about the importance of specialized middle level teacher preparation. Middle level literature has included calls for such preparation for middle level teachers for more than 80 years (Alexander & McEwin, 1988; Curtis, 1972; Eichhorn, 1966; Floyd, 1932; Koos, 1927; McEwin, Dickinson, Erb, & Scales, 1995; McEwin, Dickinson, & Smith, 2003; National Forum to Accelerate Middle-Grades Reform, 2002; National Middle School Association, 2004).

Unfortunately, many policymakers, educators, state education agencies, and boards responsible for teacher licensure have been negligent in their responsibility to ensure that all young adolescents are taught by teachers who have the specialized knowledge, skills, and dispositions to be highly successful. The absence of mandatory specialized middle level teacher preparation and the licensure regulations that require and support middle level teacher preparation have perpetuated the practice of allowing almost anyone with any type of preparation to teach in the middle grades (McEwin, Dickinson & Smith, 2003).

ESSENTIAL TEACHER PREPARATION PROGRAM COMPONENTS

Middle level researchers and advocates share a strong consensus concerning what program components should be part of a specialized middle level teacher preparation program (Jackson & Davis, 2000; National Forum to Accelerate Middle-Grades Reform, 2002; National Middle School Association, 2001, 2004; McEwin, Dickinson & Hamilton, 2000; McEwin, Dickinson & Smith, 2003). The essential middle level teacher preparation program components described below represent only those that are unique to middle level teacher preparation programs and do not include program components common and essential to all teacher preparation programs (e.g., technology, diversity, educational foundations).

Young Adolescent Development

Specialized middle level teacher preparation programs include a major focus on providing prospective middle level teachers with multiple opportunities to obtain a comprehensive understanding of young adolescent development and the implications of that knowledge for effective teaching and learning. This comprehensive understanding provides a substantial basis upon which middle level teachers can build curriculum, assessment, and pedagogy. Effective middle level teacher preparation programs provide this knowledge through a variety of learning opportunities including the formal study of young adolescent development and the application of that knowledge through working directly with young adolescents in field-based experiences.

Middle School Philosophy and Organization

Middle level teacher preparation programs highlight middle level philosophy and organization. Study of middle level philosophy and organization typically includes, but is not limited to (a) the origins and development of middle level schools, (b) middle level philosophy, (c) effective middle level school organizational features and practices, (d) middle level trends and issues, and (e) other information that helps middle level teachers understand the rationale for and context of middle level schooling (McEwin, Dickinson & Smith, 2003, 2004). Middle level teacher candidates learn about the philosophical foundations of middle level education and the organizational structures that support middle level schooling and student learning through formal study and through experiences in middle level schools.

Middle School Curriculum

Middle level curriculum is a high priority program component in middle level teacher preparation programs. Study in this area requires in-depth knowledge of at least two subject areas and an emphasis on making curriculum "relevant, challenging, integrative and exploratory" (National Middle School Association, 2003, p. 7; NMSA, 2002). Prospective middle level teachers learn about middle level curriculum through both formal study and by working directly with the curriculum during field placements in middle level schools. Typical topics include past and present theorists of middle school curriculum and various curriculum designs, formats, and propositions important to the developing a deep understanding of that curriculum. Middle level teacher preparation programs emphasize how middle level curriculum can be designed to support and extend young adolescents' learning (McEwin & Dickinson, 1996).

Subject Matter Knowledge

Middle level teacher preparation programs typically include study in two subject areas (e.g., mathematics and science). Having content knowledge in two areas, rather than a single area, provides a solid academic foundation for effective middle level teaching and promotes an understanding of the connections and interrelationships among subject areas taught at the middle level.

The rationale for having two teaching fields includes, but is not limited to (a) teachers that teach on teams are knowledgeable in two disciplines, making it easier to integrate subject areas; (b) teachers are licensed to teach in two content areas, which provides flexibility in employment whether or not the teachers teach on teams; and (c) content knowledge in two broad teaching fields more accurately reflects the nature of middle level curriculum (e.g., science rather than just biology or physics). (McEwin et al., 2003, p. 16)

Middle School Planning, Teaching, and Assessment

Effective middle level teacher preparation programs provide middle level teacher candidates with many opportunities to learn how to plan for teaching, teach, and assess student work based on content knowledge and a comprehensive understanding of young adolescent development. Middle level teacher candidates learn a wide variety of teaching strategies and demonstrate the ability to apply these strategies effectively during internships and student teaching. Candidates also construct and employ assessment techniques ranging from traditional testing to authentic assessments, portfolios, exhibitions, and open-ended problems (McEwin et al., 2003).

Middle School Field Experiences

Early and continuing middle level field experiences are an additional essential component of effective middle level teacher preparation programs. These experiences provide a context for learning about young adolescents, middle level instruction, middle level organizational features, and other key elements of successful teaching and schooling. In their description of effective field experiences, Jackson and Davis (2000) point out, "High-quality field experiences provide a learning laboratory where prospective teachers can apply knowledge gained through university course work in settings where educational faculties (from schools and universities) can teach, supervise, and advise" (p. 100).

SPECIALIZED MIDDLE LEVEL TEACHER LICENSURE

The primary role of teacher licensure/certification agencies and professional practice boards is ensuring that all students are taught by highly qualified teachers who have the specialized knowledge, skills, and dispositions needed to be effective. This responsibility seems both reasonable and noble. Historically, however, considerable apathy and disagreement has surrounded the issue of whether middle level teachers need specialized professional preparation to work with young adolescents. "This disagreement, in combination with the neglect of the welfare of this sometimes unpopular age group, has resulted in malpractice on the part of many policy makers, educators, and other stakeholders" (McEwin et al., p. 115). Regrettably, in many states virtually anyone with any kind of degree or licensure, or no license at all, is permitted to teach young adolescents enrolled in the middle grades.

To address the problem of having large numbers of middle level teachers who have not had distinctive preparation for teaching young adolescents, states should adopt licensure regulations that require that preparation. Many successful model middle level teacher preparation programs exist, and national standards for middle level teacher preparation have been written by National Middle School Association (NMSA) and approved by the National Council for the Accreditation of Teacher Preparation (NMSA/NCATE, 2001). An encouraging trend is the adoption by several states of these national standards as state teacher preparation and licensure standards. However, in numerous states middle level teacher preparation and licensure continue to be low priorities. For example, although 44 states now have some form of middle level teacher license, certification, or endorsement, only 21 states require that middle level teachers hold these credentials to teach young adolescents (Gaskill, 2002).

THE CURRENT STATUS OF MIDDLE LEVEL TEACHER PREPARATION

In many ways, it is both the best and worst of times for middle level teacher preparation. On the positive side, advocacy for specialized middle level teacher preparation and licensure has reached unprecedented high levels. For example, position papers strongly supporting middle level teacher preparation are readily available (National Forum to Accelerate Middle-Grades Reform, 2002; National Middle School Association, 2004). The majority of teacher preparation programs in the nation now have middle level teacher preparation programs or at least some targeted middle level courses (McEwin, Dickinson & Swaim, 1996). The National Board for Professional Teaching Standards (NBPTS) has developed certification in five middle school areas (see http://www.nbpts.org), and several states have developed and implemented exemplary state-wide, rigorous requirements for middle level teachers (e.g., North Carolina, Ohio).

As previously mentioned, national standards for middle level teacher preparation have been written

by National Middle School Association (2001), and adopted by several states as state standards for teacher preparation and middle level teacher licensure. These standards are also part of the national accreditation process for teacher preparation units that seek accreditation through the National Council for Accreditation of Teacher Education (NCATE). The result of these and other encouraging accomplishments is that increasing numbers of young adolescents are being taught by teachers who wish to teach them and have the specialized knowledge, skills, and dispositions to be highly effective (McEwin et al., 2003, 2004; Mertens, Flowers & Mulhall, 2002).

On the negative side, however, is the present political climate that fails to recognize the importance and necessity of providing prospective and practicing teachers with the professional preparation they need to be highly successful. For example, the No Child Left Behind (NCLB) legislation (2002) and recent related initiatives from the United States Department of Education have emerged as major deterrents to having middle level teachers who have the specialized knowledge, skills, and dispositions to be highly effective. NCLB requirements for *highly qualified* middle school teachers entering the profession are limited almost exclusively to subject matter knowledge (U.S. Department of Education, 2004). Subject matter knowledge is certainly essential for effective teaching. However, there are many other areas of knowledge and skills that are crucial to the effective professional preparation of middle school teachers (McEwin et al., 2003, 2004).

The American Board for Certification of Teacher Excellence (ABCTE) provides an additional illustration of the deterioration of support for high quality professional preparation for teachers—including middle level teachers. Despite its misleading name, ABCTE identifies and certifies teachers who have not gone through traditional teacher preparation institutions and facilitates their entry into the teaching profession. This organization is yet another attempt to bypass professional preparation and staff the nation's schools with teachers who have little or no professional preparation or experience before they begin their careers. These kinds of efforts to undermine professional preparation, and the profession itself, are ominous and pose substantial short and long-term threats to the education of youth in the United States. Unfortunately, efforts such as NCLB and ABCTE are also frequently embraced by policy makers and others who are seeking short-term, inexpensive ways to cope with the growing teacher shortage problem.

CONCLUDING REMARKS ON THE PREPARATION OF MIDDLE LEVEL TEACHERS

It is both a time for celebration and concern for those responsible for the professional preparation of middle level teachers. Specialized middle level teacher preparation is more prominent and widespread than at any other time in history. Yet emerging challenges threaten to stall the momentum toward the goal that all teachers of young adolescents have specialized professional preparation that provides them with the knowledge, skills, and dispositions teachers need.

Despite challenges to success noted by the authors here and in other publications, the good news is that the potential to overcome these concerns is already present.

With the strong support of professional associations, advocacy groups, teachers, administrators, and other groups and individuals, advocacy and political action can overcome obstacles in the present political climate and educational environment. More than ever before, increasing numbers of stakeholders realize that to neglect the professional preparation of middle level teachers is to neglect the education and welfare of young adolescents. (McEwin et al., 2003, p. 21)

Courageous, concerted actions on the part of all those responsible for the education and welfare of young adolescents will be required to continue moving toward the goal of having competent, well prepared teachers in all middle grades classrooms. These efforts must be successful, for the future of young adolescents is at stake.

MIDDLE LEVEL PRINCIPAL PREPARATION

"Almost all educational reform reports have come to the conclusion that the nation cannot attain excellence in education without effective school leadership" (Crawford, 1998, p. 8). We know that effective principals (1) recognize teaching and learning as the main business of school, (2) communicate the school's mission and vision clearly and consistently to all constituents, (3) promote an atmosphere of trust and collaboration, and (4) emphasize professional development (see Bauck, 1987; George & Grebing, 1992; Weller, 1999). In describing a renewed interest in the role of the school principal, Olson (2000) wrote

After years of work on structural changes, standards and testing, and ways of holding students accountable, the education policy world has turned its attention to the people charged with making the system work.... But nowhere is the focus on the human ele-

ment in public education more prevalent than in the renewed recognition of the importance of strong and effective leadership. (p. 1)

In its position paper, *This We Believe: Successful Schools for Young Adolescents* (2003), the National Middle School Association also recognizes the need for "courageous, collaborative leadership" (see pp. 10-11).

Despite the consensus that leadership counts, deep philosophical and political disagreements remain about what kind of educational leaders are needed, what knowledge and skills they should possess, and how they should be professionally prepared. This debate is particularly strong in the realm of middle grades education and is intensified by research that points to the need for additional knowledge and skills (e.g., an understanding of the middle school concept, the nature of young adolescence) not considered necessary for all principals. Some of this research (see Felner et al., 1997) establishes powerful connections between fidelity to the middle school concept and improved student academic and socioemotional performance.

In short, if middle grades principals are to promote and sustain quality middle grades schools they must possess basis skills and knowledge in school administration, and they must also have a firm understanding of middle school philosophy, organizational structure, and instructional practices. In addition to dealing with instructional leadership, participatory decision-making, school improvement planning, school-based budgeting, financial management, and a host of other issues, middle grades principals must be knowledgeable about young adolescents and what components or structures (e.g., teaming, advisory, exploratories) have been deemed essential for the "good" middle school (see, for example, Jackson & Davis, 2000; National Forum to Accelerate Middle-Grades Reform, 1998; NMSA, 2003).

Currently, few middle grades principals are prepared specifically to work with young adolescents. Most have not received any formal preparation in the instructional and organizational needs of a middle school. Many do not understand young adolescents' developmental needs and the relationship of those needs to teaching, learning, and the everyday functioning of a middle grades school. Gaskill (2002) reported that only seven states have special certification programs for middle grades principals. These include Alaska, Kentucky, Massachusetts, Missouri, Nebraska, Ohio, and Oklahoma. Only five of the seven require a middle level credential. While the number of states that have recognized the need to have middle level administrative licensure is low, the picture becomes bleaker when one investigates the content of educational administration programs in these seven states. In most instances, these states only require an internship (field-based experience) in a middle school setting. A few of the seven states call for an additional course or two that focus on the educational issues related to young adolescents.

Currently, the trend at the state level is to offer pre-K-12 administrative licensure. As educational administration programs are designed to address the needs of schools and students across this tremendous grade span, there is little hope that any of the levels of schooling (elementary, middle, or high) will receive the attention they need and deserve. Political pressure to offer alternative routes to administrative licensure is working its way into most state departments of education as well. Potentially, the effects of these typically less rigorous alternative routes on the performance of middle level principals and the achievement of middle grades students could be devastating.

As a result of the recent indictments against middle schools (see Bradley, 1998; Bradley & Manzo, 2000; Yecke, 2003) and the heightened focus on school administrators, three major policy considerations have emerged. These include (1) strengthening the preservice preparation of aspiring principals by enhancing certification requirements and formal academic work, (2) improving the process of selecting principals, and (3) enriching and increasing the professional development opportunities for practicing middle level principals. The remainder of this anchor essay focuses on the first of these policy issues. This discussion begins by looking at performance standards for school administrators and concludes by focusing on university-based preparation programs. Policy recommendations are offered.

PERFORMANCE STANDARDS FOR ADMINISTRATORS

Many professional organizations have developed performance standards that are meant to govern the preservice preparation and everyday work of school administrators. These organizations include the American Association of School Administrators (AASA), the National Policy Board for Educational Administration (NPBEA), the National Association of Elementary School Principals (NAESP), and the Interstate School Leadership Licensure Consortium (ISLLC) (Council of Chief State School Officers, 1996).

ISLLC standards have been widely adopted by states across the nation and successful completion of an examination, the School Leaders Licensure Assessment (SLLA), has become part of most states' mandated process of obtaining administrative licensure.

The ISLLC standards apply to all levels of the principalship, pre-K-12, and focus on a principal's knowledge, skills, and dispositions related to the school's mission and vision, culture, and learning environment. These standards also focus on the principal's ability to understand and influence the larger political, social, economic, and cultural context of the school and to work collaboratively in an ethical manner with all constituents. (For a PDF version of the ISLLC Standards, please refer to http://www.ccsso.org/publications).

Most national organizations that focus on school administrators direct little attention to the middle grades, though the National Association of Secondary School Principals (NASSP) and the National Association of Elementary School Principals (NAESP) offer notable exceptions. NASSP has supported research resulting in a multiphase, multivolume series highlighting middle level leadership (see, for example, Keefe, Clark, Nickerson, & Valentine, 1983; Keefe, Valentine, Clark, & Irvin, 1994; Valentine, Clark, Hackmann, & Petzko, 2002, 2004).

In 1986 (revised 1991 and 1997) the National Association of Elementary School Principals (NAESP) published *Elementary and Middle School Proficiencies for Principals*. NAESP recognized that middle level schools are extremely complex organizations that require a wide range of leadership proficiencies. While NAESP notes that it is unrealistic to expect every principal to possess all of the proficiencies cited in the report, they contend that an outstanding principal is characterized by 96 proficiencies. For example, NAESP argues that an outstanding principal (1) involves the school community in identifying and accomplishing the school's mission; (2) recognizes the individual needs and contributions of all staff and students; (3) applies effective interpersonal skills; (4) conducts needs assessments; (5) advances the profession through participation in professional organizations; (6) uses active listening skills; (7) works to build consensus; (8) understands group dynamics; (9) maintains a visible presence in the classrooms; (10) engages the staff in the study of effective teaching practices; and (11) uses effective strategies to deal with political forces that affect the school (NAESP, 1997, p. 3).

In addition to these proficiencies, NAESP also identified four prerequisites for success as an elementary and middle level leader. These prerequisites include (1) an advanced understanding of teaching and learning processes; (2) a thorough understanding of child growth and development; (3) a broad base of knowledge, including a solid background in the liberal arts; and (4) a sincere commitment to educational equity and excellence. While it is encouraging to see

NAESP's attention to middle schools, the connections between their standards and the characteristics and programmatic components of a successful middle school (see NMSA, 2003) are extremely weak.

MIDDLE LEVEL PRINCIPAL PREPARATION

The purpose of most educational administration programs is to prepare school leaders with the knowledge, skills, and commitment to ensure student success, including increasing the level of academic expectations and performance for all students. But the efficacy of graduate preparation in educational administration is relatively unstudied. In 1997, Haller, Brent, and McNamara noted that "overall, our reading of the limited literature on this subject suggests that there is little evidence that graduate training increases the effectiveness of school managers" (p. 224).

According to the research of Anfara, Brown, Mills, Hartman, and Mahar (2000) and Brown, Anfara, Hartman, Mahar, and Mills (2001), formal preparation did not heavily influence the acquisition of essential skills for a group of 72 middle grades principals. During interviews for the research, several principals commented about this. Here are five representative comments:

Principal: My preparation program was a whole lot of theory and not much practical application.

Principal: I don't know how much you really learn from courses. I have two masters' degrees in education and I'm not really certain how much one learns from being in a university classroom, reading all the research.

Principal: I think people need to get out and need the opportunity to see what the job is all about. When I was in training there wasn't any of that.

Principal: The training I got in college did not really address or get into middle school at all.

Principal: The hardest thing I learned on the job was that I needed to learn more. I needed to learn what the kids were all about and what techniques worked with them.

According to Scales (1992), preparation that enables prospective middle level educators to "understand early adolescent development but not to be responsive to it" (p. 65) is futile. While his comment was directed toward teachers, it applies just as well to principals.

Because practicing principals perceived a deficiency in their overall leadership preparation, Anfara et al. (2000) and Brown et al. (2001) explored princi-

pals' feelings about the added dimension of working in a middle school. Foremost, the middle level principals viewed the middle school as distinctive. Most of those interviewed in these studies noted "It's pretty much a whole different animal."

The results of a national survey conducted by DeMedio and Mazur-Stewart (1990) regarding educators' attitudes toward middle level certification "support the belief that those preparing to teach middle grade students need special middle grade preparation and appropriate middle grade certification" (p. 70). While the middle level principals in the Anfara et al. and Brown et al. studies were not able to reach a consensus regarding this notion of middle level certification/licensure for administrators, they were able to voice a common concern surrounding the lack of practical middle level preparation.

The reform literature (Jackson & Davis, 2000; NMSA, 2003) contends that effective middle level principals support and promote the establishment of structures that address the developmental needs of young adolescents, such as advisory programs, exploratories, teaming of teachers, transition programs, and flexible scheduling. The respondents in the Anfara et al. (2000) and Brown et al. (2001) studies reported that "you kind of learn by practice at this level." The principals who were interviewed did indicate that middle level principals are seeking better preparation and professional development specifically geared to effectively leading a middle school. They are requesting specific preparation dedicated to the concept of structuring educational programs to meet the unique developmental needs of young adolescents. Middle level principals are searching for opportunities to learn about themselves and their particular leadership styles as these relate to middle schools.

The respondents offered two major preservice suggestions for institutions of higher education: (1) prepare middle grades leaders in a supportive cohort style, and (2) provide real, meaningful middle school internships for prospective administrators. Once they begin their work in middle schools, the principals in these studies suggest that professional associations take a more active role in providing professional growth opportunities.

ESSENTIAL PRINCIPAL PREPARATION PROGRAM COMPONENTS

Very little attention has been given to the essential ingredients of a program to prepare middle level principals. The current trend to offer all-encompassing, pre-K-12 administrative certification/licensure has allowed and encouraged this neglect. As noted earlier, only seven states have some form of middle level administrative licensure. Common to all seven of these licensure programs is the internship or field-based experience in a middle school. With no degree of consistency across these seven states, some programs require a course in "The Middle School," and possibly courses in middle school curricular issues and adolescent psychology. In a policy brief written for the Middle Level Education Research Special Interest Group (MLER-SIG) of the American Educational Research Association, Anfara and Valentine (2003) identify the following competencies as essential for middle level preparation programs: (1) the unique needs and characteristics of young adolescents; (2) age-appropriate programs and practices used to promote the learning of young adolescents; (3) developmentally appropriate curriculum, instruction, and assessment; (4) middle school history and philosophy;

and (5) the qualities and characteristics of effective middle level teachers.

CONCLUDING REMARKS ON THE PREPARATION OF MIDDLE LEVEL PRINCIPALS

Educational administration preparation programs have begun to acknowledge the immense shift in the principal's role in recent years. That said, courses need to be designed specifically for prospective administrators desiring to work in middle grades schools. State departments of education need to acknowledge the necessity for specific middle level licensure. Additionally, studies need to be conducted that reveal the effects and unintended consequences of the generic certification/licensure that has become so widespread. Alternative routes to certification need to be very carefully approached. Anfara and Valentine (2003) offer the following policy recommendations: (1) states should establish mandatory requirements

Table 1.   The Evolution of Middle Grades Principal Preparation Programs

Generalized Components of Current Preparation Programs	Recommended Practices to Prepare Middle Level Leaders
Generally no distinction among preparation for elementary, middle, and secondary principalship	Preparation programs with specific courses focused on the middle level and its uniqueness; Extended middle school internships/field experiences
Early adolescence as a developmental period viewed as not important to the development of programs, curriculum, instruction, or assessment	"Developmental appropriateness" used as a template in the development of all components and functioning of a middle school
Recognizes content as a need and curriculum as "what is"	Understands and applies the components of integrated curriculum, small learning communities, team teaching, flexible/block scheduling, advisory programs, etc.; Awareness of the need to address both cognitive and affective domains of the learner
Uncoupling of administration from teaching and learning	Reconnecting administration to teaching and learning through instructional leadership
Pre-service principals "trained" to be aware of the trends in education and to respond to needs	Establishes the principal as a life-long learner; Emphasizes the central role that in-service and professional organizations provide; Emphasizes the importance of the principal as "risk-taker"
Train to manage and efficiently administer a school	Prepare principals to be collaborative in their approach to leading; Principals able to deal with ambiguity and uncertainty
Maintenance of organizational infrastructure	Development of human resources
Excellence as a "state of being"	Excellence as a "state of becoming"

for future middle level administrators as incentive for both colleges/universities and individuals to pursue specialization in middle level administration; (2) states should require current middle level principals who have not had specialized middle level preparation to engage in graduate coursework or professional development; (3) colleges and universities should establish preparation programs that allow for specialized coursework and internships in middle level schools for future principals and graduate coursework for current principals who have not had specialized preparation; and (4) school districts and schools should require expertise in middle level issues as prerequisite to being hired as a middle level administrator (see http://www.middlelevel.pdx.edu/Policy% 20Brief_Principals.pdf).

Significant shifts in the principal's role require shifts in the accent and focus of administrative preparation programs (see Table 1). Issues of concern to middle level principals have become increasingly complex. Principals who are serious about reforming their middle grades schools face a daunting challenge. In many respects, the demands on principals are similar to those on teachers who are attempting to become facilitators of students' learning and thus rethinking their conceptions of content, pedagogy, and assessment.

If, indeed, educational excellence is inextricably linked to effective school leadership, there is much to be gained from studying the experiences of middle school leaders as they relate to administrators' preservice preparation. More specifically, given the virtual absence of research specific to middle level principals, we need more research that provides us insights into these individuals as they live out their professional lives in schools. Issues related to the preparation of aspiring principals have become multifaceted, and schools have become very complex organizations. The challenges we face in middle schools are great. Unless we confront them, we cannot expect the current indictments of a "less than rigorous curriculum" and "poor student academic performance" (see Bradley, 1998; Bradley & Manzo, 2000) to disappear. Middle school reform will remain rhetoric with the only change occurring in the name above the schoolhouse door.

REFERENCES

Alexander, W. M., & McEwin, C. K. (1988). *Preparing to teach at the middle level.* Columbus, OH: National Middle School Association.

Anfara, V. A., Jr., Brown, K. M., Mills, R., Hartman, K., & Mahar, R. J. (2001). Middle level leadership for the 21st century: Principals' views on essential skills and knowledge: Implications for successful preparation. In V. A. Anfara, Jr. (Ed.), *The handbook of research in middle level education* (pp. 183-214). Greenwich, CT: Information Age.

Anfara, V. A., Jr., & Valentine, J. (2003). *Middle-level principal preparation and licensure: A policy brief of the Middle Level Education Research Special Interest Group.* Retrieved September 10, 2004, from http://www.middlelevel.pdx.edu/ Policy %20Brief_Principals.pdf

Bauck, J. (1987). Characteristics of the effective middle school principal. *NASSP Bulletin, 71*(500), 90-92.

Bradley, A. (1998). Muddle in the middle. *Education Week, 17*(31), 38-42.

Bradley, A., & Manzo, K. (2000, October 4). The weak link. (Special Report). *Education Week, 49*(2), 3-8.

Brown, K. M., Anfara, V. A., Jr., Hartman, K. J., Mahar, R. J., Mills, R. (2001, April). *Professional development of middle level principals: Pushing the reform forward.* Paper presented to the annual meeting of the American Educational Research Association. Seattle, WA.

Council of Chief State School Officers. (1996). *Interstate School Leaders Licensure Consortium: Standards of school leaders.* Washington, DC: Author.

Crawford, J. (1998). Changes in administrative licensure: 1991-1996. *UCEA Review, 39*(3), 8-10.

Curtis, T. E. (1972). Preparing teachers for middle and junior high schools. *NASSP Bulletin, 56*(364), 61-70.

DeMedio, D., & Mazur-Stewart, M. (1990). Attitudes toward middle grades certification: A national survey. *NASSP Bulletin, 74*(525), 64-70.

Eichhorn, D. H. (1966). *The middle school.* New York: The Center for Applied Research in Education.

Felner, R., Jackson, A. W., Kasak, D., Mulhall, P., Brand. S., & Flowers, N. (1997). The impact of school reform for the middle grades: Longitudinal study of a network engaged in turning points-based comprehensive school transformation. In R. Takanishi & D. Hamburg (Eds.), *Preparing adolescents for the twenty-first century: Challenges facing Europe and the United States* (pp. 38-69). Cambridge, UK: Cambridge University Press.

Floyd, O. R. (1932). *The preparation of junior high school teachers.* U.S. Office of Education Bulletin 20, Washington, DC: U.S. Government Printing Office.

Gaskill, P. E. (2002). Progress in the certification of middle level personnel. *Middle School Journal, 33*(5), 33-40.

George, P., & Grebing, W. (1992). Seven essential skills of middle level leadership. *Schools in the Middle, 1*(4), 3-11.

Haller, E., Brent, B., & McNamara, J. (1997). Does graduate training in educational administration improve America's schools? *Phi Delta Kappan, 79*(3), 222-227.

Jackson, A. W., & Davis, G. A. (2000). *Turning points 2000: Educating adolescents in the 21st century.* New York: Teachers College Press.

Keefe, J., Clark, D., Nickerson, N., & Valentine, J. (1983). *The middle level principalship: Vol. II. The effective middle level principal.* Reston, VA: National Association of Secondary School Principals.

Keefe, J., Valentine, J., Clark, D., & Irvin, J. (1994). *Leadership in middle level education: Vol. II. Leadership in successfully restructuring middle level schools.* Reston, VA: National Association of Secondary School Principals.

Koos, L. V. (1927). *The junior high school.* Boston: Ginn and Company.

McCabe, M. (2004). *Teacher quality.* Retrieved September 3, 2004, from http://www.edweek.org/context/topics/issuespage.cfm?id=50

McEwin, C. K., & Dickinson, T. S. (1996). *Forgotten youth, forgotten teachers: Transformation of the professional preparation of teachers of young adolescents* (Background paper prepared for the Middle Grade School State Policy Initiative). New York: Carnegie Corporation of New York.

McEwin, C. K., Dickinson, T. S., Erb, T. O., & Scales, P. C. (1995). *A vision of excellence: Organizing principles for middle grades teacher preparation.* Westerville, OH: National Middle School Association.

McEwin, C. K., Dickinson, T. S., & Hamilton, H. (2000). National board certified teachers' views regarding specialized middle level teacher preparation. *The Clearing House, 73*(4), 211-213.

McEwin, C. K., Dickinson, T. S., & Smith, T. W. (2003). Middle level teacher preparation: Status, progress, and challenges. In P. G. Andrews & V. A. Anfara (Eds.), *Leaders for a movement: Professional preparation and development of middle level teachers and administrators* (pp. 3-26). Greenwich, CT: Information Age.

McEwin, C. K., Dickinson, T. S., & Smith, T. W. (2004). The role of teacher preparation, licensure, and retention in creating high performing middle schools. In S. Thompson (Ed.), *Reforming middle level education: Considerations for policymakers* (pp. 109-129). Greenwich, CT: Information Age.

McEwin, C. K., Dickinson, T. S., & Swaim, J. H. (1996). *Specialized middle level teacher preparation programs in the United States: A status report* (Working paper). Boone, NC: Appalachian State University.

Mertens, S. B., Flowers, N., & Mulhall, P. (2002). The relationship between middle-grades teacher certification and teaching practices. In V. A. Anfara & S. L. Stacki (Eds.), *Middle school curriculum, instruction, and assessment* (pp. 119-138). Greenwich, CT: Information Age.

National Association of Elementary School Principals. (1997). *Elementary & middle school proficiencies of principals* (3rd ed.). Alexandria, VA: Author.

National Forum to Accelerate Middle-Grades Reform. (1998). *Vision statement of the National Forum to Accelerate Middle-Grades Reform.* Newton, MA: Education Development Center.

National Forum to Accelerate Middle-Grades Reform. (2002). *Policy statement: Teacher preparation, licensure, and recruitment.* Newton, MA: Education Development Center. Retrieved August 11, 2004, from http://www.mgforum.org

National Middle School Association. (2001). *National Middle School Association/National Council for Accreditation of Teacher Education-Approved middle level teacher preparation standards.* Westerville, OH: Author. Retrieved August 24, 2003, from http://www.nmsa.org/services/teacher_prep/nmsastandards.htm

National Middle School Association. (2002). *Position paper on curriculum integration.* Retrieved September 26, 2004, from http://www.nmsa.org/news/positionpapers/integrativecurriculum.htm

National Middle School Association. (2003). *This we believe: Successful schools for young adolescents.* Columbus, OH: Author.

National Middle School Association. (2004). *National Middle School Association's position statement on professional preparation of middle level teachers.* Westerville, OH: Author. Retrieved August 5, 2004, from http://www.nmsa.org/news/middlelevelteachers.htm

No Child Left Behind Act of 2001, Pub. L. No. 107-110, 115 Stat. 1425 (2002). Retrieved August 9, 2004, from http://www.ed.gov/offices/OESE/asst.html

Olson, L. (2000). Policy focus converges on leadership: Several major new efforts under way. *Education Week, 31*(5), 490-510.

Rice, J. K. (2003). *Teacher quality: Understanding the effectiveness of teacher attributes.* Washington, DC: Economic Policy Institute.

Scales, P. (1992). *Windows of opportunity: Improving middle grades teacher preparation.* Carrboro, NC: Center for Early Adolescence.

U.S. Department of Education. (2004). *Improving teacher quality state grants.* Academic Improvement and Teacher Quality Programs. Retrieved July 6, 2005, from http://www.ed.gov/programs/teacherqual/guidance.pdf

Valentine, J., Clark, D., Hackmann, D., & Petzko, V. (2002). *A national study of leadership in middle level schools: Vol. 1. A national study of middle level leaders and school programs.* Reston, VA: National Association of Secondary School Principals.

Valentine, J., Clark, D., Hackmann, D., & Petzko, V. (2004). *A national study of leadership in middle level schools: Vol. 2. Leadership for highly successful middle level schools.* Reston, VA: National Association of Secondary School Principals.

Weller, L. (1999). *Quality middle school leadership: Eleven central skill areas.* Lancaster, PA: Technomic.

Wilson, S. M., Floden, R. E., & Ferrini-Mundy, J. (2001). *Teacher preparation research: Current knowledge, gaps, and recommendations* (Document R-01-3). Seattle: University of Washington: Center for the Study of Teaching and Policy.

Yecke, C. P. (2003). *The war against excellence: The rising tide of mediocrity in America's middle schools.* Westport, CT: Praeger.

Middle Grades Education
Back to the Future

Gayle Andrews

You remember the movie, right? Marty McFly, played by Michael J. Fox in his heyday, is the teenager who returns to his parents' high school days to save his own and his family's present and future. Christopher Lloyd plays the mad scientist, complete with lab coat and halo of wild white hair, who turns a DeLorean car into a transport to the past … and back to the future. Lessons learned from his expedition into the past inform Marty's understanding of his parents as adults, and give him a sense of the past's reverberations into the future.

What does that have to do with middle grades schools? Well, sometimes you have to go back to the past to understand the present and to get back to the future you imagine. Middle grades schools have a long and checkered history, a history explored in greater depth by two of the fathers of the middle school movement, John H. Lounsbury and Gordon F. Vars, in another anchor essay in this volume: "Middle Level Education: A Personal History." I will hit the highlights of that history, much as Marty McFly skims the surface of his parents' high school days, drawing the connections to the present and the possible future of improving schooling for young adolescents. Sadly, this adventure doesn't come with the keys to a DeLorean, nor a satisfying lightning strike of change, but it hopefully will provide some fuel for thought as I try to point middle grades schooling back to the future we advocates have envisioned for decades.

YESTERDAY, TODAY, AND TOMORROW

Much of the history of middle grades schooling echoes into the present and the future. As an example, early in the twentieth century, advocates for improving young adolescents' schooling described the need to strengthen academics in the middle grades, respond to young adolescents' needs and characteristics, and provide equitable opportunities for all students to succeed (Briggs, 1920; Gruhn & Douglass, 1947; Koos, 1920; Montgomery, 1940). Very late in that same century, another group of advocates concerned about the quality of schooling for young adolescents called for high-performing middle grades schools that are "academically excellent, developmentally responsive, and socially equitable" (National Forum to Accelerate Middle-Grades Reform, 1998). Those echoes are pretty loud. In "Teaching in Middle Schools," Beane and Brodhagen (2001) describe the importance of studying the middle school's past:

> Teaching cannot be separated from the social and institutional context within which it takes place, and the context cannot be fully understood without some historical grounding. Thus, it is important to begin a review of research on teaching at a particular level with a statement of the origins and evolution of education at that level. This approach is especially the case with regard to middle schools, for it is in the early years of the junior high school movement that we find the roots of the expectations of what that institution is intended to do. (p. 1157)

This section briefly describes past efforts to improve schooling for young adolescents, outlining the aims of the reformers who strived to make middle grades schools better, the echoes into the present, and the influences that affected, and in some cases continue to affect, their success in making a difference.

PAST AS PROLOGUE: COLLEGE PREP, TRACKS, CARNEGIE UNITS, STANDARDS, AND CORE

College Preparation

It is a bit disconcerting to be reminded that the efforts to improve schooling for young adolescents, those ages 10 to 15, have been going on for well over 100 years. Charles Eliot, then president of Harvard University, was the first to complain publicly about the quality of schooling for young adolescents in his 1888 speech to the National Education Association (NEA), *Shortening and Enriching the Grammar School*

Course. Concern for his own beloved higher education motivated Eliot to focus on the middle grades, Grades 7 and 8, which were then upper elementary grades. Eliot wanted incoming freshmen to be better prepared for college-level work, and he wanted to lower the average age of students entering college. To accomplish his goals, Eliot proposed, as his speech's title implies, shortening the amount of time students spent on "elementary" subjects, like reading and writing, and introducing college preparatory coursework in grades 7 and 8. (See also National Education Association, 1894, 1895.) Eliot's suggestions would serve as the impetus for a new institution, the junior high school.

Eliot's focus on the middle grades as training ground for secondary and post-secondary education foreshadows much of the rhetoric surrounding middle grades education today, from the best intentioned activists calling for increased academic rigor so more young people will have the opportunity to pursue post-secondary education (e.g., the College Board, U.S. Department of Education's (2005) GEAR-UP program) to those who may be the worst intentioned, critics who want middle grades schools to focus on academics so that schools prepare the elite for their rightful place in the world to the exclusion of the masses (e.g., Yecke, 2003).

Tracks

In addition to better preparing students for college, introducing college preparatory work earlier in the secondary curriculum served another purpose, one the social efficiency experts (e.g., Dutton & Snedden, 1912) of the early twentieth century found particularly appealing: sorting and selecting American youth into tracks, typically either academic or vocational, beginning as early as the seventh grade (Beane & Brodhagen, 2001). For efficiency's sake, the argument went, students' time and the education system's resources could be better spent if it was clear early on whether a student was destined for a white collar or a blue one. Yecke and her ilk represent today's reverberations of this elitist argument cloaked in efficiency language.

The notion of schooling as destiny was, and is, made manifest in a common practice in America's middle grades schools: ability grouping or tracking. Ability grouping literally means assigning a student to groups or courses based on the student's perceived ability or achievement level. Tracking takes ability grouping a step further by placing students in sets of courses that serve as tracks: academic (read: college preparatory), vocational, or remedial. Since its inception, the middle grades school has served as an efficient sorting machine, taking in young adolescents in large numbers and turning out older adolescents on track for college, or a blue-collar vocation, or, in the case of the student perpetually assigned to remedial classes, on track for a lifelong struggle to survive. In her anchor essay in this volume, "The Challenge of Middle School Equity," Nancy Doda points out, "The leading organizational arrangement of assigning students to classes based on notions of academic potential or ability can no longer be treated as benign as such assignments play a powerful role in shaping opportunity to learn."

Carnegie Units and Tracking Redux

Tracking seemed appropriate, even necessary, to the academic elites who first proposed changing education for young adolescents. Charles Eliot of Harvard, Woodrow Wilson of Princeton, and Arthur Hadley of Yale, who served as trustees for the Carnegie Foundation for the Advancement of Teaching (CFAT), "were determined to reform from the top down, beginning with the colleges, a system of schooling that they regarded as chaotic and ineffective" (Tyack & Cuban, 1995, p. 91).

Along with other leaders from academia who served as trustees for the Foundation, these university presidents sealed the fate of generations of middle grades students when they defined college entrance requirements in Carnegie units. Henry Pritchett, then-president of the foundation, defined a Carnegie unit as "a course of five periods weekly throughout an academic year" (Carnegie Foundation for the Advancement of Teaching, 1906, p. 38), with each period typically lasting 50-60 minutes. The trustees recommended that colleges require students to accumulate 14 Carnegie units prior to admission (CFAT, 1906, 1907). For example, for acceptance into college a graduating high school senior would need evidence he (and it was always a "he" at this point) had accumulated four units in English, which translated into four years of "seat time" in an English course that met five days a week for an average of 50 minutes per day; four units of mathematics; three units of science; two units of history; and two units of foreign language, preferably including Latin or Greek.

To ensure their elite students met the college entrance requirements, high schools offered college preparatory classes in all the required subjects, classes that were not open to any and all, but only to the few. In a study of the influences on the evolution of the junior high school, Davis explained the impact of the Carnegie unit:

The Carnegie unit's standardization of instruction, though gradual, had a lasting impact on both high schools and junior highs. Since the criteria included four years of high school preparation based on Carnegie units, the units started to accumulate in ninth grade. Most junior high schools included the crucial ninth grade and adopted 45- to 60-minute periods for the ninth graders. For simplicity's sake if nothing else, junior high schools tended to adopt the ninth grade's unit-driven, 50-minute period schedule for the lower grades, too. If it looks like a high school and schedules classes like a high school, it is probably pretty close to being a high school. (1996, p. 27)

The schedule wasn't the only thing that the junior high adopted from the Carnegie unit mentality. The notion of serving the cream of the crop, the group of students who needed to be enrolled in the "right" college preparatory classes to ensure their attainment of those precious Carnegie units and success in higher education, reinforced the "efficient" pattern of tracking students based on perceived ability. And, as Perlstein and Tobin (1988) pointed out, it was probably inevitable that the criteria the junior high used for sorting students into tracks reflected society's class system. Research on grouping practices in modern middle grades schools reveal a similar blueprint, with minority and economically disadvantaged students overrepresented in the lower tracks (see, for example, Oakes, 1985) and an expansion of the achievement gap because students in lower tracks are expected to have lower abilities and little chance of moving "up" (Tucker & Codding, 1998).

In their most recent survey of middle grades school administrators for the National Association of Secondary School Principals, Valentine and his colleagues found that 85% of the middle grades schools they surveyed had ability grouping (Valentine, Clark, Hackmann, & Petzko, 2002, p. 90). The researchers also confirmed that this percentage is actually creeping upward over time, demonstrating an increase from a similar study Valentine and his colleagues conducted in 1992 (Valentine, Clark, Irvin, Keefe, & Melton, 1993).

Standards

Harvard President Charles Eliot chaired the NEA's Committee on Secondary School Studies, more commonly known as the Committee of Ten (NEA, 1894). In another presage of the current focus on the content and the quality of the curriculum, the Committee of Ten focused its energies on analyzing the curriculum in American secondary schools, concentrating on how well (or not) the course of study prepared students for the university. As part of their analysis process, the Committee of Ten convened nine conferences, each focused on a separate subject and each invested in strengthening that subject's position in the secondary school curriculum. The Committee of Ten's 1894 report suggested lengthening and intensifying the course of study in every academic discipline they reviewed, including history, mathematics, English, science, and Latin.

Understandably, national content organizations are similarly vested in strengthening their respective disciplines' position in the curriculum landscape. The curriculum standards that the content organizations published in the 1990s, like the Committee of Ten's subject-focused conferences, reflect a subject-centric perspective. If one stacked up every set of content standards and/or curriculum guides produced by the content associations in the last 15 years, the resulting pile would measure in feet, not inches. As a general rule, each content area association calls for more, not less, attention to its discipline. (For more on the curriculum standards developed in the 1990s, see, for example, Task Force of the National Council of the Social Studies, 1994).

However, as Thomas Dickinson pointed out in his treatise on the "arrested development" of middle schools, content organizations have failed to focus on the middle grades:

> To a large extent it is understandable why the national content organizations should look at the middle school level as nothing more than an extension of the secondary school. This was their basic position on the junior high school throughout its history. Wasn't the middle school just the junior high school updated somewhat? (Dickinson, 2001, p. 12)

Core/Integrated Curriculum

As Elizabeth Pate describes in her anchor essay, "Academically Excellent Curriculum, Instruction, and Assessment," the separate-subject curriculum model dominates the landscape in middle grades schools. Academics, that is university professors, laid the foundation for that dominance in 1894 with the Committee of Ten conferences, and academics challenged that foundation in the progressive movement that began in the 1930s and resonates in middle grades education to this day. Progressives argued for a core curriculum, one that blurred, even erased, the lines between subjects and instead focused on problems and issues that crossed all the boundaries. As modern-day progressive James Beane pointed out, progressive forebear Colonel Francis Parker was calling for a problem and issue-centered curriculum before the start of the twentieth century (1997, p. 22). John Dewey picked up the thread in his work, calling for a curriculum that considered "the experiences of the child and social issues" (Beane, 1997, p. 22). As Beane did in his landmark work on curriculum, *Curriculum Integration: Designing the Core of Democratic Education* (1997), I will quote John Dewey's explanation of the natural connections between the curriculum and real life:

> All studies grow out of relations in the one great common world. When the child lives in varied but concrete and active relationship to this common world, his studies are naturally unified. It will no longer be a problem to correlate studies. The teacher will not have to resort to all sorts of devices to weave a little arithmetic into the history lesson, and the like. Relate the school to life, and all studies are of necessity correlated. (Dewey, 1900/1915, p. 32).

Many leaders in the middle school movement took up the call for a curriculum that blurred subject boundaries and made genuine connections to the real world. Gordon Vars has had a leadership role in the National Association for Core Curriculum (NACC) for more than 50 years, and his friend and colleague, John Lounsbury, has been writing about the need for integrative, exploratory curriculum for young adolescents for decades (see, for example, the collection of many of Lounsbury's essays and columns, *As I See It*, 1991). A hundred years after Dewey's words, Dickinson described the 1990s as the decade when middle grades curriculum took center stage:

> When James A. Beane's work on integrated curriculum burst on the middle school scene in the 1990s, the middle school concept had at last its own distinctive curriculum. The clarion call of Beane's work brought forth an outpouring of related efforts by other curriculum theorists as well as practitioners who had been practicing this approach, often for years, in disconnected enclaves around the country (Arnold, 1993; Dickinson, 1993; Pate, Homestead, and McGinnis, 1997; Stevenson and Carr, 1993). This outpouring of theory, applications, and stories of practitioners engaged in integrated curriculum work made the early 1990s seem, to many of us, a golden age of curriculum. (2001, p. 11)

Much has changed since those halcyon days of a decade ago, with the national and federal focus on separate-subject content standards often viewed as an insurmountable obstacle to integrated curriculum. However, researchers and practitioners across the country continue to demonstrate that a curriculum organized around middle grades students' concerns about themselves and the world can, as Dewey pointed out, quite naturally address all the content, standards-driven or otherwise, that students need. For stories of curriculum integration in action in the age of standards, see, for example, *The Story of the Alpha Project* (Kuntz, 2004), *Watershed: A Successful Voyage Into Integrative Learning* (Springer, 1994), *Integrative Studies in the Middle Grades: Dancing Through Walls* (Stevenson & Carr, 1993), and *Making Integrated Curriculum Work: Teachers, Students, and the Quest for Coherent Curriculum* (Pate, Homestead, & McGinnis, 1997).

RESPONDING TO ADOLESCENT DEVELOPMENT: CHILD-CENTERED AND DIFFERENTIATED

G. Stanley Hall's work (1905) is the most famous of the psychological studies in the early twentieth century that drew attention to early adolescence as a distinct phase of human development, a phase Hall described as characterized by "storm and stress." That depiction of turbulence has become the stereotype of young people between the ages of 10 and 15: moody, contentious, self-focused, and overwhelmed by the rapid pace of change in their bodies, relationships, and perceptions of themselves and the world (Jackson & Andrews, 2004). The attention to the age group's developmental tasks and challenges has driven a call for "developmental responsiveness" in middle grades schools that is evident in the writings of both junior high school advocates (e.g., Briggs, 1920; Gruhn & Douglass, 1947; Koos, 1920, 1927) and middle school advocates (e.g., Dorman, 1985; Lipsitz, 1977; Lounsbury, 1991; Stevenson, 1992).

When schools are developmentally responsive—i.e., designed to support young adolescents in meeting the challenges of their cognitive, social, emotional, physical, and moral development—then middle grades students can easily demonstrate that they represent so much more than a stereotype. In their anchor essay in this volume, "Creating Developmentally Responsive Middle Level Schools," Gert Nesin and Ed Brazee offer a comprehensive model for developmentally responsive middle grades schools, drawing on the latest research on adolescent development and the best educational practice.

Developmental responsiveness and progressivism go hand in hand; both center on students. Junior high school advocates like Leonard Koos called for a child-centered approach in line with the progressive vision of John Dewey. Nearly 80 years ago, Koos said, "Equalization of educational opportunity cannot be achieved without adjustment to individual differences" (1927, p. 62). In her widely quoted book on differentiating instruction in mixed ability classrooms, Carol Ann Tomlinson, one of today's most outspoken proponents of child-centeredness, described teachers as "diagnosticians, prescribing the best possible instruction for their students" (1999, p. 2). In differentiating instruction,

> Teachers can adjust content, process, or product to match their students' levels of readiness, interests, or learning profiles. Although it sounds like a very complicated chemistry experiment, which could blow up if done incorrectly, the underlying idea of differentiation is quite simple: work *with* students' variability instead of ignoring it. (Jackson & Davis, 2000, p. 78)

RELATIONSHIPS AND TEAMS

In their milestone work, *The Modern Junior High School*, Gruhn and Douglass (1947) outlined the ideal functions of the junior high school. They said that junior high school educators should provide guidance to their students, pointing them toward "intelligent" vocational and educational decisions and helping them with the transitions and adjustments typical of young adolescence (1947, p. 60). Their inclusion of guidance in the list of the ideal functions of the junior high school both reflected the child-centeredness of the progressives and expanded upon it, drawing attention to relationships as a basis for learning. Relationships matter for children's learning, from the relationships between infants and their parents (e.g., Watson, Battistich, & Solomon, 1997) to relationships between teachers and students within a school community (e.g., Goodenow, 1993). Through relationships, adults and students convey their expectations of one another, their caring (or the lack thereof) for one another, and their support for each other's successes and empathy for one another's challenges.

Interdisciplinary teams, done well, exemplify relationships as the basis for teaching and learning. Though the roots of interdisciplinary teaming go back at least until the 1960s, systematic research on its benefits did not really get underway until the late 1980s (Arhar, 1997). Once begun in earnest, research on teaming has flourished (e.g., Arhar, 1990; Dickinson & Erb, 1997; Flowers, Mertens, & Mulhall, 1999, 2000; Warren & Muth, 1995).

PREPARING MIDDLE GRADES EDUCATORS

In their anchor essay, "The Professional Preparation of Middle Level Teachers and Principals," Ken McEwin, Tom Dickinson, and Vincent Anfara point out the long tenure of the call for specialized preparation for middle grades educators:

Historically, there has been little ambivalence among leading advocates of junior high schools and middle schools about the importance of specialized middle level teacher preparation. Middle level literature has included calls for such preparation for middle level teachers for more than 80 years (Alexander & McEwin, 1988; Curtis, 1972; Eichhorn, 1966; Floyd, 1932; Jackson & Davis, 2000; Koos, 1927; McEwin, Dickinson, Erb, & Scales, 1995; McEwin, Dickinson, & Smith, 2003; National Forum to Accelerate Middle-Grades Reform, 2002; National Middle School Association, 2003).

Despite the apparent unanimity, both current and historic, among advocates for improved schooling for young adolescents, specialized preparation for middle grades teachers is not nearly widespread enough, and specialized preparation for middle grades administrators is practically nonexistent. Dickinson (2001) contended that the absence of specially prepared educators likely spelled the demise of the junior high school:

> One of the primary failures of the junior high school, the original school in the middle, was its failure to establish teacher education programs to educate professionals for this new school. This failure, coupled with the failure to influence licensure, contributed mightily to its demise. Without a supply of teachers prepared specifically to teach at this level, schools were forced to implement the new ideas of the junior high school with staff who were trained for teaching other students. (2001, p. 6)

Dickinson (2001) also argued that the lack of teacher and administrator preparation programs and licensure that focus on the middle grades has contributed to the "arrested development" of middle schools, and he posited that, without significant change, the absence of specialized preparation and certification would also spell doom for the middle school.

In fact, the latest data on the status of specialized middle grades preparation can make the glass seem half empty or half full. Twenty-one states, less than half, require middle grades teachers to hold a specialized credential or endorsement to teach young adolescents, with some states requiring as little as one course to qualify. Remarkably, only seven states offer any specialized preparation for middle grades administrators, with just five of the seven requiring a distinctive credential for middle grades principals (Gaskill, 2002). On the half full side of the equation, however, 44 states offer some specialized coursework for prospective middle grades teachers, and the trend has been heading upward for several years. Though specialized preparation and distinctive middle grades certification are not required in most states, the last decade has seen considerable growth in the number of states recognizing that preparation for middle grades teaching should be specialized (McEwin, Dickinson, & Smith, 2003).

Why aren't requirements for specialized middle grades preparation and licensure more widespread? Middle grades certification has taken some side roads in the name of compromise, and those tangents have too often led into the wilderness. One of the most common detours involves offering middle grades certification/licensure that overlaps, often significantly, with licensure for elementary and high school teachers. This overlap in state licensure (e.g., K-5, 4-8, 6-12), which quite obviously indicates that specialized preparation is not really necessary for teaching young adolescents, tends to undermine targeted preparation programs. Middle level endorsements have also proven to be trips down the primrose path in many states. Jackson and Davis (2000) call endorsements "one of the *least* effective methods of ensuring special preparation for middle grades teachers" (p. 104). They explain:

If the endorsement route has been so unsuccessful, why does it continue to reappear year after year, decade after decade? The answer is that it is a politically expedient solution (or "nonsolution") to the kinds of highly charged issues of teacher employment and assignment noted earlier.... All too often, policymakers and other influential individuals and groups agree to leave existing licenses as they are (i.e., K-8, 7-12) while adding a voluntary endorsement that includes the middle grades (e.g., 5-8, 6-9). Unfortunately, since the endorsement is not required, few teacher preparation institutions create such programs and few teachers bother to apply for the endorsement. After a few years, most or all of the few teacher preparation institutions that developed middle grades endorsement programs drop them because of low enrollments. State licensing agencies eventually drop the license endorsement because "it is not being used." The result is that young adolescents continue to be taught by teachers with a wide range of professional preparation, some of which is far removed from their middle grades teaching assignments. (Jackson & Davis, 2000, p. 105)

Teacher shortages have also played a role in heightening the demand for broader certification, especially among hard-pressed state and local administrators who want the best qualified teachers in their classrooms but just need teachers, period. Education reporter Lynn Olson described the pattern:

As the ultimate arbiters of who is permitted to teach, states ... raise standards for who can enter the profes-

sion on the front end, while keeping the door cracked open on the back end to ensure that every classroom will be staffed come September. (2000, p. 12)

Finally, the No Child Left Behind Act of 2001 (NCLB, 2002) has played an incredibly significant role in the current debate over middle grades certification and licensure. In an overview of NCLB, George Wood described its historical antecedents, its promise, and the pessimism of many educators:

Who could object to a law that promises no child left behind when it comes to our schools? After all, isn't this the great promise of our public school system—that all children, regardless of race, socioeconomic status, gender, creed, color or disability will have equal access to an education that allows them to enjoy the freedoms and exercise the responsibilities of citizenship in our democracy?

As proposed, the federal No Child Left Behind legislation stood as a continuation of this historic promise. It is a promise that began with Thomas Jefferson's proposal for the first free system of public education in Virginia; a promise offered as the balance wheel of society by the first state superintendent of education, Horace Mann; a promise put forward as the most basic of human rights by W. E. B. DuBois.... [However,] [t]he premise of this book is that ... *NCLB cannot, will not, and perhaps was even not intended to deliver on its promises* (Wood, 2004, pp. vii, xi).

In defining highly qualified teachers, NCLB focuses almost exclusively on subject matter knowledge, using degree of content expertise as the marker of quality. That focus on content harkens back to Charles Eliot and the Committee of Ten, skirting any hint of progressivism along the way. Teaching at any level requires more than content knowledge, but the focus on discipline expertise—often to the virtual exclusion of pedagogical skill, knowledge of youth development, and experience in schools—has been particularly hard on the effort to provide specialized preparation and licensure for middle grades teachers (see McEwin, Dickinson, & Anfara in this volume). The "back door" to teaching that Olson described has been opening ever wider for alternatively certified educators, many of whom have had little or no introduction to pedagogy, much less young adolescents or middle schools. To make matters worse, those teachers who had been certified in middle grades education as generalists, a status that allowed them to easily integrate curriculum across subject areas and in line with Dewey's conception of "real life" (1900/1915), have had their qualifications challenged and their college transcripts scrutinized, not for methods courses but for "pure" content courses untainted by any hint of pedagogy. Many states, including my own adopted state of Georgia, are defining content knowledge in terms of the number of courses taken in arts and sciences; courses taken through colleges of education either do not count at all or do not count for as much. Much more could be said, and has been said elsewhere, about No Child Left Behind and its implications for middle grades schools and educators (see, for example, Andrews & Anfara, 2003; Meier & Wood, 2004; Thompson, 2004). For now, let's turn back to the future.

BACK TO THE FUTURE

In *Turning Points 2000: Educating Adolescents in the 21st Century* (2000), Anthony Jackson and I described our vision of a 15-year-old who had experienced the best we could hope for during the middle grades.

Demonstrating five characteristics of effective human beings, that 15-year-old would be

- An intellectually reflective person
- A person en route to a lifetime of meaningful work
- A good citizen
- A caring and ethical individual
- A healthy person (p. 22)

Our vision came directly from the vision articulated in Carnegie's landmark 1989 report from the Task Force on Education of Young Adolescents, *Turning Points: Preparing American Youth for the 21st Century* (Carnegie Council on Adolescent Development), but it goes deeper than that. Our vision can be traced directly to those who advocated improving schooling for young adolescents in the first half of the twentieth century (e.g., Briggs, 1920; Gruhn & Douglass, 1947; Koos, 1920, 1927), the second half of the twentieth century (e.g., Beane, 1993; Lipsitz, 1977; Van Til, Vars, & Lounsbury, 1961), and the first few years of the twenty-first (e.g., Andrews & Anfara, 2003; Oakes, Quartz, Ryan, & Lipton, 2000; Thompson, 2004).

Will 15-year-olds like the one we have envisioned ever emerge from a middle grades school? Our 15-year-old could have, and probably has, already emerged from one of the 55 Schools to Watch identified by the National Forum to Accelerate Middle-Grades Reform (2004a, 2004b). The criteria for the Schools to Watch reflect the National Forum's vision of a high-performing middle grades school that is academically excellent (see Pate's anchor essay), developmentally responsive (see Nesin & Brazee's anchor essay), and socially equitable (see Doda's anchor essay). Our 15-year-old could have already emerged from one of the many schools implementing the *Turn-*

ing Points 2000 recommendations. *Turning Points 2000* called for middle grades schools that

- Teach a curriculum grounded in rigorous, public academic standards for what students should know and be able to do, relevant to the concerns of adolescents, and based on how students learn best.
- Use instructional methods designed to prepare all students to achieve higher standards and become lifelong learners.
- Staff middle grades schools with teachers who are expert at teaching young adolescents, and engage teachers in ongoing, targeted professional development opportunities. (See McEwin, Dickinson, & Anfara's anchor essay.)
- Organize relationships for learning to create a climate of intellectual development and a caring community of shared educational purpose.
- Govern democratically, through direct or representative participation by all school staff members, the adults who know students best. (See Williamson & Johnston's anchor essay on leadership.)
- Provide a safe and healthy school environment as part of improving academic performance and developing caring and ethical citizens.
- Involve parents and communities in supporting student learning and healthy development (Jackson & Davis, 2000, pp. 23-24).

Fifteen-year-olds who reflect our vision have been emerging from the doors of some middle grades schools for decades, just not nearly enough: Only all of them will be enough. Those of us who care about middle grades schools and the young adolescents they serve face many challenges along the way to our vision; I have described many of those challenges in this essay. We can build on a few current realities, though, to strengthen our capacity to face those challenges. No Child Left Behind, whether we love or hate it, has focused attention on students whose poor performance often went unremarked and unnoticed. We can build on that attention by heightening our efforts to ensure the success of every student (Jackson & Davis, 2000), and highlighting the success of those efforts publicly and frequently. We need positive press, publicity for what is working and what is going well. Many national associations seek to bring attention to what works, most notable among them National Middle School Association and the National Forum. But, they cannot do the job of "talking up" our successes alone. As Lew Armistead pointed out in remarks to National Forum members in 2002, each one of us has the responsibility to share what's working with the people around us wherever we are, whether it's on the soccer field sideline, in the grocery store line, or in conversations, casual and formal, with decision makers who can make a difference (L. Armistead, personal communication, January 2002).

We can also build on the current attention to high school reform, which represents yet another improvement effort with echoes from the past. Except, in the case of the current calls for improving high schools, it's the middle school's past we're hearing, not the high school's. In their move to block scheduling, building and strengthening relationships, and engaging students in hands-on and minds-on learning, high school educators could learn from us. And, we could remind folks that the high school is now moving back to our future, a future we do not want to abandon in the face of the calls we in middle grades education now hear to go back to the past, back to junior high schools that turned into mini-high schools, thus emulating the very high school structure that high school reformers are trying to change.

In point of fact, I believe that many young adolescents are being well served during the middle grades, and will continue to be well served if we, middle grades educators, researchers, and advocates, can learn from the past, stick to our vision, and rely on young adolescents and one another to keep us on the path back to the future.

REFERENCES

Alexander, W. M., & McEwin, C. K. (1988). *Preparing to teach at the middle level.* Columbus, OH: National Middle School Association.

Andrews, P. G., & Anfara, V. A., Jr. (Eds.). (2003). *Leaders for a movement: Professional preparation and development of middle level teachers and administrators.* Greenwich, CT: Information Age.

Arhar, J. (1990). Interdisciplinary teaming as a school intervention to increase the social bonding of middle level students. *Research in middle level education: Selected studies 1990.* Columbus, OH: National Middle School Association.

Arhar, J. (1997). The benefits of interdisciplinary teaming on teachers and students. In J. Irvin (Ed.), *What research says to the middle level practitioner* (pp. 49-56). Columbus, OH: National Middle School Association.

Beane, J. A. (1993). *A middle school curriculum: From rhetoric to reality* (2nd ed.). Columbus, OH: National Middle School Association.

Beane, J. A. (1997). *Curriculum integration: Designing the core of democratic education.* New York: Teachers College Press.

Beane, J. A., & Brodhagen, B. L. (2001). Teaching in middle schools. In V. Richardson (Ed.), *Handbook of research on teaching* (4th ed.) (pp. 1157-1174). Washington, DC: American Educational Research Association.

Briggs, T. H. (1920). *The junior high school.* Boston: Houghton Mifflin.

Carnegie Council on Adolescent Development. (1989, June). *Turning points: Preparing American youth for the 21st century* (Report of the Task Force on Education of Young Adolescents). New York: Carnegie Corporation of New York.

Carnegie Foundation for the Advancement of Teaching. (1906). *First annual report of the president and treasurer.* New York: Author.

Carnegie Foundation for the Advancement of Teaching. (1907). *Second annual report of the president and treasurer.* New York: Author.

Curtis, T. E. (1972). Preparing teachers for middle and junior high schools. *NASSP Bulletin, 56*(364), 61-70.

Davis, G. A. (1996). *Is everything old new again? Influences on the evolution of the junior high school and the middle school.* Unpublished doctoral dissertation, University of North Carolina at Chapel Hill.

Dewey, J. (1915). *The school and society* (Rev. ed.). Chicago: University of Chicago Press. (Original work published 1900)

Dickinson, T. S. (2001). Reinventing the middle school: A proposal to counter arrested development. In T. S. Dickinson (Ed.), *Reinventing the middle school* (pp. 3-20). Columbus, OH: National Middle School Association.

Dicksinson, T. S., & Erb, T. E. (1997). *We gain more than we give: Teaming in middle schools.* New York: Routledge Falmer.

Dorman, G. (1984). *Middle grades assessment program: User's manual* (2nd ed.). Carrboro, NC: Center for Early Adolescence.

Dutton, S. T., & Snedden, D. (1912). *The administration of public education.* New York: Macmillan.

Eichhorn, D. H. (1966). *The middle school.* New York: The Center for Applied Research in Education.

Eliot, C. (1888). *Shortening and enriching the grammar school course.* Address to the annual convention of the National Education Association.

Flowers, N., Mertens, S., & Mulhall, P. (1999). The impact of teaming: Five research-based outcomes of teaming. *Middle School Journal, 31*(2), 57-60.

Flowers, N., Mertens, S., & Mulhall, P. (2000). What makes interdisciplinary teams effective? *Middle School Journal, 31*(4), 53-56.

Floyd, O. R. (1932). *The preparation of junior high school teachers.* U.S. Office of Education Bulletin 20, Washington, DC: U.S. Government Printing Office.

Gaskill, P. E. (2002). Progress in the certification of middle level personnel. *Middle School Journal, 33*(5), 33-40.

Goodenow, C. (1993). Classroom belonging among early adolescent students: Relationships to motivation and achievement. *Journal of Early Adolescence, 13*(1), 21-43

Gruhn, W. T., & Douglass, H. R. (1947). *The modern junior high school.* New York: Ronald Press.

Hall, G. S. (1905). *Adolescence: Volume I.* New York: Appleton-Century.

Jackson, A. W., & Andrews, P. G. (2004). *Making the most of middle school: A field guide for parents and others.* New York: Teachers College Press.

Jackson, A. W., & Davis, G. A. (2000). *Turning points 2000: Educating adolescents in the 21st century.* New York: Teachers College Press.

Koos, L. (1920). *The junior high school.* New York: Harcourt, Brace, and Howe.

Koos, L. V. (1927). *The junior high school.* Boston: Ginn and Company.

Kuntz, S. (2004). *The story of Alpha: A multi-age, student-centered team—33 years and counting.* Columbus, OH: National Middle School Association.

Lounsbury, J. H. (1991). *As I see it.* Columbus, OH: National Middle School Association.

Lipsitz, J. (1977). *Growing up forgotten: A review of research and programs concerning early adolescence: A report to the Ford Foundation.* Lexington, MA: Lexington Books.

McEwin, C. K., Dickinson, T. S., Erb, T. O., & Scales, P. C. (1995). *A vision of excellence: Organizing principles for middle grades teacher preparation.* Westerville, OH: National Middle School Association.

McEwin, C. K., Dickinson, T. S., & Smith, T. W. (2003). Middle level teacher preparation: Status, progress, and challenges. In P. G. Andrews & V. A. Anfara (Eds.), *Leaders for a movement: Professional preparation and development of middle level teachers and administrators* (pp. 3-26). Greenwich, CT: Information Age.

Montgomery, T. S. (1940). *A study of philosophy and changing practices in the junior high school.* Unpublished doctoral dissertation, University of Texas.

National Education Association. (1894). *Report of the committee of ten on secondary school studies.* New York: American Book.

National Education Association. (1895). *Report of the committee of fifteen on elementary education, with reports of the sub-committees: On the training of teachers; On the correlation of studies in elementary education; On the organization of city school systems.* New York: American Book.

National Forum to Accelerate Middle-Grades Reform. (1998). *Vision statement of the National Forum to Accelerate Middle-Grades Reform.* Newton, MA: Education Development Center.

National Forum to Accelerate Middle-Grades Reform. (2002). *Policy statement: Teacher preparation, licensure, and recruitment.* Newton, MA: Education Development Center. Retrieved August 11, 2004, from http://www.mgforum. org

National Forum to Accelerate Middle-Grades Reform. (2004a). *What are schools to watch.* Retrieved November 1, 2004, from http://www.schoolstowatch.org/what/htm

National Forum to Accelerate Middle-Grades Reform. (2004b). *Our schools.* Retrieved November 1, 2004, from http://www.schoolstowatch/visit.htm

National Middle School Association. (2003). *This we believe: Successful schools for young adolescents.* Columbus, OH: Author.

No Child Left Behind Act of 2001, Pub. L. No. 107-110, 115 Stat. 1425 (2002). Retrieved August 9, 2004, from http://www.ed.gov/offices/OESE/asst.html

Oakes, J. (1985). *Keeping rack: How schools structure inequality.* New Haven, CT: Yale University Press.

Oakes, J., Quartz, K. H., Ryan, S., & Lipton, M. (2000). *Becoming good American schools: The struggle for civic virtue in education reform.* San Francisco: Jossey-Bass.

Olson, L. (2000, January 13). Finding and keeping competent teachers. *Education Week, XIX*(18), 12-18.

Pate, P. E., Homestead, E. R., & McGinnis, K. L. (1997). *Making integrated curriculum work: Teachers, students, and the quest for coherent curriculum.* New York: Teachers College Press.

Perlstein, D., & Tobin, W. (1988). *The history of the junior high school: A study of conflicting aims and institutional patterns.* A paper commissioned by Carnegie Corporation of New York.

Springer, M. (1994). *Watershed: A successful voyage into integrative learning.* Columbus, OH: National Middle School Association.

Stevenson, C. (1992). *Teaching ten to fourteen year olds.* New York: Longman.

Stevenson, C., & Carr, J. F. (Eds.). (1993). *Integrative studies in the middle grades: Dancing through walls.* New York: Teachers College Press.

Task Force of the National Council for the Social Studies. (1994). *Expectations of excellence: Curriculum standards for social studies.* Waldorf, MD: National Council for the Social Studies.

Thompson, S. (Ed.). (2004). *Reforming middle level education: Considerations for policymakers.* Greenwich, CT: Information Age.

Tomlinson, C. A. (1999). *The differentiated classroom: Responding to the needs of all learners.* Alexandria, VA: Association for Supervision and Curriculum Development.

Tucker, M. S., & Codding, J. B. (1998). *Standards for our schools: How to set them, measure them, and reach them.* San Francisco: Jossey-Bass.

Tyack, D., & Cuban, L. (1995). *Tinkering toward utopia: A century of public school reform.* Cambridge, MA: Harvard University Press.

United States Department of Education. (2005). *Gaining Early Awareness and Readiness for Undergraduate Programs (GEAR-UP).* Retrieved July 2, 2005, from http://www.ed.gov/programs/gearup/index.html

Valentine, J. W., Clark, D. C., Hackmann, D. G., & Petzko, V. N. (2002). *A national study of leadership in middle level schools: Vol. I. A national study of middle level leaders and school programs.* Reston, VA: National Association of Secondary School Principals.

Valentine, J., Clark, D., Irvin, J., Keefe, J., & Melton, G. (1993). *Leadership in middle level education: Vol. I. A national survey of middle level leaders and schools.* Reston, VA: National Association of Secondary School Principals.

Van Til, W., Vars, G. F., & Lounsbury, J. H. (1961). *Modern education for the junior high school years.* Indianapolis, IN: Bobbs-Merrill.

Warren, L. L., & Muth, K. D. (1995). The impact of common planning time on middle grade students and teachers. *Research in Middle Level Education, 18*(3), 41-58.

Watson, M. Battistich, V., & Solomon, D. (1997). Enhancing students' social program and its effects. *International Journal of Education Research, 27,* 571-586.

Wood, G. (2004). Introduction. In D. Meier & G. Wood (Eds.), *Many children left behind: How the No Child Left Behind Act is damaging our children and our schools* (pp. vii-xv). Boston: Beacon Press.

Yecke, C. (2003). *The war against excellence: The rising tide of mediocrity in America's middle schools.* Westport, CT: Praeger.

ABILITY GROUPING

The educational terms "tracking" and "ability group-ing" are often seen as synonymous, and since tracking is widely viewed to have negative effects, so is ability grouping. While the two can share very similar characteristics depending on how they are used within a school framework, it is also important to note that ability grouping can, and often is, radically different from tracking in the ways in which it is used structurally and philosophically. Moreover, ability grouping can and does have tremendously positive effects on students' performance. In order to clear up any misconceptions, though, it is essential to differentiate between the two terms.

TRACKING: DEFINITIONS AND DOWNFALLS

Tracking has been called a result of "20th century efforts to prepare youngsters for the quite different careers and lifestyles awaiting them," according to Marsh and Raywid (1994, p. 268) in their article "How to Make Detracking Work." In reality, though, track-ing is the process of judging students' abilities, often earlier than middle school, and defining the course of their academic careers as a result of those (often too early) findings. Based on such characteristics as early reading skills or middle school math levels, students can be placed in higher or lower groups or classes, a process that can be carried out throughout the entire schooling experience. Indeed, Herb Frazier (1997, 1999) upholds Breard's statement that "tracking is when you label a student and it never changes (p. 15)," meaning that once a student has been placed in a

certain track, it is often impossible to move from that position.

Since the Civil Rights Movement, many have argued against the practice of tracking saying that it not only fosters inequality for students of differing levels, but that it also perpetuates segregation within schools. Furthermore, Herb Frazier has found that "tracking has led to a disproportionately lower num-ber of black children in programs for gifted students" (1999, p. 16). In South Carolina, White students make up 57% of the state's students and fill 87% of the avail-able slots in programs for gifted students. Black stu-dents represent 43% of the state's public school students, but only 13% of the enrollment in gifted programs, according to statistics from the U.S. Depart-ment of Education. There are similar statistics throughout the United States. The same is true of poor White and other minority students as it is for Blacks. Given the numbers, it is easy to see how many find the practice of tracking in schools offensive.

RESISTANCE TO DETRACKING

Despite the pitfalls of the tracking process, there is also considerable resistance to eliminate the process entirely. According to Marsh and Raywid (1994), "teachers have come to endorse tracking, believing that they can deal effectively only with groups of youngsters whose abilities all fall into the same nar-rowly defined range" (p. 269). In fact, teachers fear that detracking will only "remove ability grouping without making any other changes" to the system. Therefore, they would be on their own in the difficult process of adapting to a new method of education. It is true that having all students on a similar level makes it easier to ensure that students are getting instruction that fits their needs. It certainly makes the planning process easier.

Teachers are not alone in their resistance to change. Parents, obviously, are very concerned with the effects of shaking up the whole system. There are concerns, as cited in *The Roeper Review* ("Ability grouping," 2003) that the results of detracking have "been the degradation of educational opportunities for students identified as gifted and talented and the lack of concern for students identified as needing extra assistance." These pitfalls are the result of trying to maintain equality, and thus teaching only to the mid-range kids.

Reis, Kaplan, Tomlinson, Westberg, Callahan, and Cooper (1998) cite parents' complaints that when detracking occurs, there is often "no appropriate differentiation in the classroom," and parents perceive that their children are "not being academically challenged." Now, these objections are not only on the part of the more academically talented students. The parents of students who are more likely to fall behind also are concerned that detracking could make it more difficult for their students to keep up.

THE ANSWER? WITHIN-CLASS ABILITY GROUPING

While tracking is often a permanent solution that causes more problems than it solves, within-class ability grouping is a concept that allows detracked students in the same class to break into smaller groups in order to accomplish specific instructional goals. The Fall 2003 *Roeper Review* cites Kulik (1992) as saying "ability grouping has been defined as a practice that places students into ... small groups based on an initial assessment of their levels of readiness or ability." The groups can be made to include students of varying or similar abilities in a given area, or students sharing similar interests.

The beauty of this arrangement is that it is easily manipulated to be beneficial to the students, as proven by Frazier's support of Breard's claim that "ability grouping is more flexible, and it has to do with performance," rather than with test scores, and other perceived indicators. In fact, "it can be done in classrooms" where "teachers continue to look at students" and place them where they should be. Changes in placement can always be made. In fact, placement need not only be made based on academic ability. Groups can be arranged based on interests, learning styles, and any other combination of characteristics that can be imagined, and as student needs change, groups can easily be rearranged.

SUCCESSES OF ABILITY GROUPING

Given parents' and teachers' concerns over the hardships encountered with changing an academic program, it is essential to note the positive effects of detracking and the subsequent change to within-class ability grouping. In order to ensure that all students' needs are met, it is necessary to see the proof of success. Holloway (2001) cites Sheppard and Kanevsky's 1999 study in which they found that, while "students in [a] ... homogeneous gifted class" were able to work together to formulate more ideas for a project, while "the gifted students in the heterogeneous class were more hesitant and conforming" to the lower-ability students, these findings are not supported by the rest of the research. He goes on to report that Lloyd's 1999 findings indicate that "the overall achievement effect of homogeneous grouping was essentially zero at all grade levels from elementary through high school" (p. 189), therefore proving that tracking students by ability provides no discernible positive effects. Another study (Nyberg, McMillin, O'Neill-Rood, & Florence, 1997), again discussed by Holloway, found that "average to below-average students, of all races, can achieve academic success and prosper in a more rigorous academic environment and that midrange minority students perform as well as, or better than, white students in a curriculum that retracks general students into a college-preparatory curriculum" (p. 35). It is clear through these findings that tracking, when replaced by ability grouping within classrooms that contain students of vastly varied ability levels, can be successfully eradicated in order to improve student success at all levels.

METHODS FOR SUCCESSFULLY IMPLEMENTING AN ABILITY GROUPING PROGRAM

Teaching under such a new system can prove extremely difficult, as "instructional strategies most familiar to them (teachers) will not work in heterogeneous classrooms." In fact, new ways of gauging students' strengths, weaknesses, and successes will have to be continually monitored and implemented to ensure that all students are presented with opportunities that still meet their individual needs (Marsh & Raywid, 1994). Certainly, as stated in Frazier's article "Derailing Student Tracking, "It takes a very special teacher to teach ... kids of all levels at the same time" (1997, p. 12).

However, it is possible to tackle the difficult aspects of such a program in order to implement a policy of successful and equitable ability grouping within classrooms of all sizes and varied abilities. For instance, keeping class sizes small, and providing much needed support for kids and teachers can certainly aid in this regard. Some schools have taken teachers from certain disciplines and turned them into all-day tutors who are available at all times to make certain that extra help and challenges are available for all students (Marsh & Raywid, 1994).

There are several different methods for ensuring the success of replacing tracking with within-class ability grouping. These approaches focus on both whole-school and single-class advice. For entire schools to successfully embark on such a task, Marsh and Raywid (1994) discuss several effective methods of detracking. First, it must not be considered a separate undertaking. Instead, it must be part of a broader change in both structure and mindset. Many systems have detracked with a switch from junior high schools to middle schools, where more emphasis is placed on success and personal awareness than on academic rigor. Sometimes it is best, though, to start small, such as with a single grade or discipline (such as sixth graders or English classes). This slow process allows small groups to work together to implement a new design without the whole school having to make drastic changes, which can prove to be too big all at once. In making any change, administrative leadership and support are crucial. The authors, as well as Oakes and Wells (1998), also point out that, when moving away from a tracking system, it is essential that extra services be provided for both the lower and upper echelon students. Extra tutoring and summer programs are effective for both groups as they are both challenged and allowed to exhibit some successes.

In order to meet the needs of all students who are within the detracked classroom (mid-range as well as upper and lower level students), it is essential that some differentiated instruction be provided. It is for this reason that ability grouping can come in handy for all involved. For instance, you can group children based, according to Marsh and Raywid, "on the basis of interest," not just on academic success levels. Successful detracking and within-class ability grouping can only come to be if "it is combined with curricula that have been created based on students' learning styles, interests, and abilities. When ability grouping is utilized in a flexible and temporary manner, with appropriate curricular adjustment, significant achievement gains can be realized" ("Ability grouping," 2003, p. 30).

Ability grouping, clearly, is not just tracking or segregation on a smaller scale. It provides students of all levels with much greater avenues for success and socialization. Despite the extra planning on the part of teachers and administrators, this method promotes equality and academic excellence for all students, which, when you think about it, is that not what we are all seeking?

REFERENCES

Ability grouping is not just tracking anymore. (2003). *The Roeper Review, 26*, 29-36.

Frazier, H. (1997). Derailing student tracking. *Black Issues in Higher Education, 13*(25), 12-13.

Frazier, H. (1999). Rising up against tracking. *Black Issues in Higher Education, 15*(24), 16-17.

Holloway, J. H. (2001). Grouping students for increased achievement. *Educational Leadership, 59*(3), 84-85.

Kulik, J. A. (1992). *An analysis of the research on ability grouping: Historical and contempoary perspectives.* Storrs, CT: National Research Center on the Gifted and Talented.

Lloyd, L. (1999). Multiage classes and high-ability students. *Review of Educational Research, 69*(2), 187-212.

Marsh, R. S., & Raywid, M. (1994). How to make detracking work. *Phi Delta Kappan, 76*, 268-269.

Nyberg, K., McMillin, J., O'Neill-Rood, N., Florence, J. (1997). Ethnic difference in academic retracking: A four-year longitudinal study. *The Journal of Educational Research, 91*(1), 33-41.

Oakes, J., & Well, A. S. (1998). Detracking for high student achievement. *Educational Leadership, 55*(1), 38-41.

Reis, S. M., Kaplan, S. N., Tomlinson, C. A., Westburg, K. L., Callahan, C. M., & Cooper, C. R. (1998). Equal does not mean identical. *Educational Leadership, 56*(3), 74-77.

—Elizabeth Albright
The University of Tennessee

ACADEMIC ACHIEVEMENT

Academic achievement is at the forefront of all educational reform in our country. For this reason, many well-respected in education have debated both the meaning and the measurement of academic achievement, as concurrently, our nation's leaders have initiated educational programs aimed at improving education for all children as part of their legacy (see Achievement Gap for more information). Though it would seem, however, that before a statistically sound measurement of academic achievement can be realized definitively, and even before the prototypical student could be said to have made an academic achievement, academic achievement, itself, will have been deduced as the product of the student's academic ability set against the status quo of the localized curriculum and a multitude of environmental, social, and psychological factors. Academic ability, therefore, is a fundamentally important aspect of academic achievement. It is defined as "an estimate of an individual's actual or potential power to perform well in school tasks" (Harris & Hodges, 1995), and is publicly determined by standardized test scores and information assessed by teachers as they work with students in classrooms.

FACTORS AFFECTING ACADEMIC ACHIEVEMENT

The best education for all children at the middle school level incorporates teaming, advisory groups, block schedules, and flexible grouping (George, Lawrence, & Bushnell, 1998), utilizing an engaging, rigorous curriculum that both emphasizes the social and intellectual development of young adolescents (Arambula-Greenfield & Gohn, 2004; Jackson & Davis, 2000), and offering a comprehensive model for increasing middle school effectiveness and academic achievement. After 10 years of collaborative research, the authors recommend a developmentally responsive curriculum that is grounded in public academic standards; expert middle school teachers who know their content and their students' needs, and very importantly, who see themselves as learners, adapting amidst a caring climate of intellectual development in schools governed democratically with concern for all students, and surrounded by a safe and healthy school environment fostered predominantly by parent and community involvement in their continuous support of healthy student learning and development.

Clearly, there are many factors involved in increasing and maintaining successful academic achievement for all students. Statistics show, that children spend only 9% of their time at school compared to the 91% of their time they spent out of school from birth to 18 years (Will, 1997). Given this limited, miniscule amount of time, it is essential that schools include parents and community members in the education process. Of the myriad factors, parental involvement is undoubtedly critical, especially during the middle level years, as students are undergoing physical, social, cognitive, and emotional changes (Epstein, 1995). In helping to assuage the children's anxieties accompanying aspects of these aforementioned adolescent developmental processes through their attentiveness, parents first must feel welcomed by schools to work together so that their children will be academically successful and treated as socially equitable individuals (National Forum to Accelerate Middle-Grades Reform, 2002). Mulhall, Mertens, and Flowers (2001) report that four of the six practices identified as essential to high performing middle level schools are not familiar to 60% of the parents. This is cause for concern because parents are important partners for students' success and must join with schools to serve as advocates for middle level reform practices.

In a study of over 32,000 sixth, seventh, and eighth graders, Mulhall, Flowers, and Mertens (2002) concluded that several possible indicators of student academic success are: (a) students who had future expectations of their own educational success, (b) the number of books read and the presence of literacy material in the home and school, (c) students who are confident and competent as they meet demands in their school and classroom experiences, (d) students indicating a possible elevated report of past grades during middle school, and (e) parental involvement in their education. "If we have learned anything over the last ten years, it is that gains in student achievement and other positive outcomes for students require comprehensive implementation of reforms over an extended period of time" (Jackson & Davis, 2000, p. 16). The following factors involved in helping students achieve academic success make up a short, but important list among the many factors reported by many researchers.

Teacher Competence and Practice. In order to improve academic achievement in middle schools, we must ensure that there are competent teachers in every classroom. In addition to a competent teacher, schools need to include teacher collaboration through common planning time (Cooney & Bottoms, 2003; Miles & Darling-Hammond, 1998), an integrated curriculum, flexible scheduling, teaming, continuous professional development (Flowers, Mertens, & Mulhall, 2002; Wenglnsky, 2000), implementation of small group collaborative learning (Flowers et al., 2002; Johnson & Johnson, 1999), and provisions for extra help and instructional resources to students in need (Balfanz & MacIver, 2000; McLaughlin & Talbert, 1993; Middle Start, 2002; Trimble, 2003). An in depth understanding of the content area allows teachers to incorporate higher level questioning and reasoning skills (Southern Regional Education Board, 2001). Teachers then utilize their knowledge of content and their knowledge of students to create instruction for better understanding of content for students (Darling-Hammond, 1996). An emphasis on multisensory instructional methods as opposed to traditional teaching has shown greater student achievement results (Farkas, 2003).

Social Competence. Competence in interpersonal skills and social behaviors influences achievement more often than intellectual ability at the middle level. Students who are responsible and socially accepted by school peers tend to do better academically (Wentzel, 1991). Schools must attend to the "social side of learning" (Rutter et al., 1979), where everyone in the school focuses on higher student academic achievement. Counselors can increase achievement by teaching coping skills and educational planning (Dahir & Stone, 2003).

Transition to Middle School. The transition to middle school causes a significant loss of academic achievement for many students as they are put into a different, more impersonal and competitive environment (Alspaugh, 1998; Seidman, Allen, Aber, Mitchell, & Feinman, 1994). The loss of achievement is greater when self-contained elementary classrooms or multiple elementary schools combine into one middle school (Alspaugh, 1998). Provisions of a variety of school activities, such as counseling and summer orientation, are needed to address the transition to middle school (Hertzog & Morgan, 1999; McAdoo, 1999).

Parental Involvement. Parental involvement and academic achievement research have had conflicting results (Epstein, 1995; McNeal, 2001); however, as Desimone (1999) reports, practices and behaviors that can make a positive difference in academic achievement are authoritative parenting, high expectations, parent-teacher communications, parental assistance at home, and parent-school interactions. However, these indicators may differ in importance across social, economic, and ethnic groups (McNeal, 2001).

Classroom Climate. Since teaching is the most important element of successful learning, academic achievement depends on creating a place where teachers can practice their best teaching (Darling-Hammond, 1996). School climate is thus defined as the quality of interactions between students and teachers in the classroom. A positive school climate affects school achievement, as well as encouraging problem solving, risk taking, and increased production. Successful achievement has been shown to be present when teachers are supportive and involved, but also feel empowered to assert firm discipline while maintaining high expectations for achievement. All adults in a successful middle school collaborate as partners in a positive atmosphere of caring and support for young adolescents (Erb, 2001). Specifically, Erb (2001) suggests that possible indicators for this type of environment are: (a) the environment promotes creativity, responsible risk taking, cooperation, and mutual trust and respect; (b) staff and students feel safe at school and in work-related activities; and (c) staff, students, and parents all report that the learning environment is academically stimulating (p. 56).

High Expectations. Teacher expectations greatly influence students' academic performance (Turnbull, Fiester, & Wodatch, 1997) and studies show that students' perceptions of teacher expectations are lower than the expectations that teachers profess (Carpenter, Flowers, Mertens, & Mulhall, 2004). Student success is often dependent on teacher standards for the quality of students' work and the instructional methods that teachers use in class (Erb, 2001; Haynes, Emmons, & Ben-Avie, 1997).

Class size. Class size and its effect on student achievement continue to be topics of debate among researchers (Hanushek, 1998), who contend that reduction in class size does not aid achievement, but compels school districts to hire additional faculty and thus drive school costs up. Others claim that lower class size helps to enrich the quality of instruction because of added time for individual attention to students, especially those in need of extra help (Wenglinsky, 1997). Ehrenberg, Brewer, Gamoran, and Willms (2001) suggest that implementation of methods of instruction and assessment should be the focus, not only class size.

Technology. The use of technology to enhance student achievement comprises a positivepartnership at the middle school level because it encourages hands-on student engagement, which is critical to learning to adolescent development (Middleton & Murray, 1999; Wenglinsky, 1998). Again, regarding the implementation of technology, teacher competence is of the utmost importance. In teaching utilizing technology, it is most effective when the instructor is knowledgeable and has experience with the relevant software, where the technology is interactive, and a clear focus in instructional design is incorporated (Cradler & Bridgforth, 1996).

Literacy. Along with the transitional adjustments, while moving from elementary school to middle school, students are introduced to a complex and challenging perspective of reading to learn, rather than learning to read. Literacy competency is a prerequisite for academic success across the middle school curriculum (Hosking & Teberg, 2004; Hynds, 1997; Irvin & Strauss, 2000). Effective literacy instruction, which leads to improved academic achievement, should be student-centered, flexible, and responsive to the developmental needs of the young adolescent (Irvin & Strauss, 2000).

Self-Efficacy. Self-efficacy, defined as the level of confidence a student has in his or her ability to succeed in school, is a large-scale determiner of academic achievement (Jinks & Morgan, 1999; Roesar, Van der, Wolf, & Strobel, 2001). Also, studies have shown that confidence in performing a task successfully perpetuates feelings of competence (Bandura, 1986). Obviously, maintaining self-efficacy and achieving success in school also depends partly on teachers, as they critique academic work, offer affirming expectations, and provide support (Colvin & Schlosser, 1998; Kramer Schlosser, 1992). Equally as important, though, is engagement, the quality of being psychologically involved in one's own learning; engagement is a necessary step in the process to acquiring self-efficacy (Bandura, 1993; Walker, 2003).

CONCLUSION

Anne Lewis (2003), a national education policy writer, claims that, because children are not born with predetermined achievement they will achieve when they are effectively taught how to learn. She goes on to say that, "Schools should be considered excellent only when students of all racial and ethnic groups are achieving at high levels" (p. 260). Joftus (2002) states that, "Less than 75 percent of all eighth graders graduate from high school in five years, and in urban schools these rates dip below 50 percent" (p. 1).

The National Middle School Association Research Committee in their report, *Research and Resources in Support of This We Believe* (Anfara et al., 2003), concludes that all in a middle school, teachers, principals, counselors, and staff members must understand adolescent development and how curriculum, instruction, and assessment should all contribute to this development to ensure that learning takes place. Finally, academic achievement for all students takes work, time, and effort to reach this plateau of understanding.

REFERENCES

Alspaugh, J. (1998). Achievement loss associated with the transition to middle school and high school. *The Journal of Educational Research, 92*(1), 20-25.

Anfara, V. A., Jr., Andrews, P. G., Hough, D. L., Mertens, S. B., Mizelle, N. B., & White, G. P. (2003). *Research and resources in support of This We Believe*. Westerville, OH: National Middle School Association

Arambula-Greenfield, T., & Gohn, A. J. (2004). The best education for the best is the best education for all. *Middle School Journal, 35*(5), 12-21.

Bandura, A. (1986). *Social foundations of thought and action: A social cognitive theory*. Englewood Cliffs, NJ: Prentice-Hall.

Bandura, A. (1993). Perceived self-efficacy in cognitive development and functioning. *Educational Psychologist, 28*(2), 117-148.

Balfanz, R., & MacIver, D. J. (2000). Transforming high poverty urban middle schools into string learning institutions: Lessons from the first five years of the talent development middle school. *Journal of Education for Students Placed At Risk, 5*(1-2), 23-45.

Carpenter, D. M. H., Flowers, N., Mertens, S. B., & Mulhall, P. F. (2004). High expectations for every student. *Middle School Journal, 35*(5), 64-69.

Colvin, C., & Schlosser, L. K. (1998). Developing academic confidence to build literacy: What teachers can do. *Journal of Adolescent and Adult Literacy, 41*(4), 272-282.

Cooney, S., & Bottoms, G. (2003). *What works to improve student achievement in the middle grades*. Atlanta, GA: Southern Regional Education Board.

Cradler, J., & Bridgforth, E. (1996). *Recent research on the effects of technology on teaching and learning* (Policy Brief). San Francisco: WestEd Regional Educational Laboratory.

Darling-Hammond, L. (1996). The right to learn and the advancement of teaching: Research, policy, and practice for democratic education. *Educational Researcher, 25*(6), 5-17.

Dahir, C. A., & Stone, C. (2003). Accountability: A m.e.a.s.u.r.e. of the impact school counselors have on student achievement. *Professional School Counseling, 6*, 214-221.

Desimone, L. (1999). Linking parent involvement with student achievement: Do race and income matter? *The Journal of Educational Research, 93*(1), 11-30.

Ehrenberg, R. G., Brewer, D. J., Gamoran, A., & Willms, J. D. (2001). Class size and student achievement. *Psychological Science in the Public Interest, 2*(1), 1-30.

Epstein, J. L. (1995). School, family, and community partnerships: Caring for the children we share. *Phi Delta Kappan, 79*(9), 701-712.

Erb, T. O. (Ed.). (2001). *This we believe, and now we must act*. Westerville, OH: National Middle School Association.

Farkas, R. D. (2003). Effects of traditional versus learning-styles instructional methods on middle school students. *The Journal of Educational Research, 97*(1), 42-51.

Flowers, N., Mertens, S., & Mulhall, P. (2002). Four important lessons about teacher professional development. *Middle School Journal, 33*(5), 57-61.

George, P., Lawrence, G., & Bushnell, D. (1998). *Handbook of middle school teaching* (2nd ed.). New York: Longman.

Hanushek, E. (1998). The evidence on class size. Retrieved January 20, 2005, from http://www.edexcellence.net/library/sunhanu.html.

Harris, T. L., & Hodges, R. E. (1995). *The literacy dictionary: The vocabulary of reading and writing*. Newark, DE: International Reading Association.

Haynes, N. M., Emmons, C., & Ben-Avie, M. (1997). School climate as a factor in student adjustment and achievement. *Journal of Educational and Psychological Consultation, 8*(3), 321-329.

Hertzog, J., & Morgan, P. L. (1999). *Transition: A process not an event*. Reston, VA: National Association of Secondary School Principals.

Hosking, N., & Teberg, A. (1998). Bridging the gap: Aligning current practice and evolving expectations for middle years literacy programs. *Journal of Adolescent and Adult Literacy, 41*(5), 332-340.

Hynds, S. (1997). *On the brink: Negotiating of literature and life with adolescents*. New York: Teachers College Press.

Irvin, J. L., & Strauss, S. E. (2000). Developmental tasks of early adolescence: Foundation of an effective literacy program. In K. Wood & T. Dickinson (Eds.), *Promoting literacy in grades 4-9: A handbook for teachers and administrators* (pp. 115-127). Boston: Allyn & Bacon.

Jackson, A. W., & Davis, G. A. (2000). *Turning Points 2000: Educating adolescents in the 21st century*. New York: Teachers College Press.

Jinks, J., & Morgan, V. (1999). Children's perceived academic self-efficacy: An inventory scale. *The Clearing House*, 72(4), 224-231.

Joftus, S. (2002). *Every child a graduate: A framework for an excellent education for all middle and high school students.* Washington, DC: Alliance for Excellent Education.

Johnson, D. W., & Johnson, R. T. (1999). *Learning together and alone: Cooperative, competitive, and individualistic learning.* Boston: Allyn & Bacon.

Lewis, A. (2003) Washington commentary: A continuing American dilemma. *Phi Delta Kappan*, 85(4), 259-260.

Kramer Schlosser, L. (1992). Teacher distance and student disengagement: School lives on the margin. *Journal of Teacher Education*, 43, 128-140.

McAdoo, M. (1999). Studies in transition: How to help adolescents navigate the path to and from middle school. *Middle Ground*, 2(3), 21-23.

McLaughlin, M. W., & Talbert, J. E. (1993). *Contexts that matter for teaching and learning.* Retrieved January 20, 2005, from the Center for Research on the Context of Secondary School Teaching, Stanford University Web site: http://www.stanford.edu/group/CRC/Context_That_Matter.pdf

McNeal, R. B. (2001). Differential effects of parental involvement on cognitive and behavioral outcomes by socioeconomic status. *Journal of Socio-Economics*, 30(2) 171-179.

Middle Start. (2002). Effectiveness of Middle Start. Retrieved January 20, 2005, from http://www.middlestart.org

Middleton, B., & Murray, R. (1999). The impact of instructional technology on student achievement in reading and mathematics. *International Journal of Instructional Media*, 26(1), 109-117.

Miles, K. H., & Darling-Hammond, L. (1998). Rethinking the allocation of teaching resources: Some lessons from high-performing schools. *Educational Evaluation and Policy Analysis*, 20(1), 9-29.

Mulhall, P. F., Mertens, S. B., & Flowers, N. (2001). How familiar are parents with middle level practices? *Middle School Journal*, 33(2), 33-43.

Mulhall, P. F., Flowers, N., & Mertens, S. B. (2002). Understanding indicators related to academic performance. *Middle School Journal*, 34(2), 56-61.

National Forum to Accelerate Middle-Grades Reform. (2002). Retrieved May 2, 2004, from http://www.mgforum.org

Roesar, R. W., Van der Wolf, K., & Strobel, K. R. (2001). On the relations between social-emotional and school functioning during early adolescence: Preliminary finding from Dutch and American samples. *Journal of School Psychology*, 39(2), 111-144.

Seidman, E., Allen, L., Aber, J. L., Mitchell, C., & Feinman, J. (1994). The impact of school transitions in early adolescence on the self-system and perceived social context of poor urban youth. *Child Development*, 65, 507-522.

Southern Regional Education Board. (2001). Making middle grades work. Retrieved January 20, 2005, from http://www.sreb.org

Trimble, S. (2003). Common elements of high performing, high poverty middle schools. *Middle School Journal*, 33(4), 7-16.

Turnbull, B. J., Fiester, L., & Wodatch, J. (1997). *"A process, not a program:" An early look at the Comer Process in Community School District 13.* Washington, DC: Policy Studies Associates.

Walker, B. J. (2003). The cultivation of student self-efficacy in reading and writing. *Reading & Writing Quarterly*, 19, 173-187.

Wenglinksy, H. (1997). *When money matters: How educational expenditures improve student performance and how they don't.* Princeton, NJ: Policy Information Center, Educational Testing Service.

Wenglinsky, H. (1998). *Does it compute? The relationship between educational technology and student achievement in mathematics.* Princeton, NJ: ETS Policy Information Center-Research Division.

Wenglinsky, H. (2000). *How teaching matters: Bringing the classroom back into the discussions of teacher quality.* Princeton, NJ: Educational Testing Service.

Wentzel, K. R. (1991). Social competence at school: Relation between social responsibility and academic achievement. *Review of Educational Research*, 61(1), 1-24.

Will, G. (1997, August 10). 187: Young men on the edge. *Washington Post*, p. C7.

—Shirley Theriot
The University of Texas, Arlington

ACADEMIC EXCELLENCE

The term "academic excellence" refers to one of the four essential components of high-performing middle grades schools. In order to achieve its goal of improved academic and developmental outcomes for all young adolescents, the National Forum to Accelerate Middle-Grades Reform articulates best middle grades practices through this evaluation criteria. According to the National Forum, "high performing schools with middle grades are academically excellent. They challenge all students to use their minds well" (National Forum to Accelerate Middle-Grades Reform, n.d.a). As its vision emerged, the National Forum sought to impact classrooms with schools to model exceptional middle grades instruction and structures. In 1999, a new initiative, Schools to Watch, emerged leading to what is now a nationally-endorsed recognition system for middle schools (National Forum, n.d.b).

To transport the vision into fruition, members of the National Forum further developed these four essential concepts: academic excellence, developmental responsiveness, social equity, and effective organizational structures and processes. Through its Schools to Watch program, the National Forum has determined the criteria for identifying high-performing middle-grades schools, forged tools so that schools could utilize the criteria, selected and honored four high-performing schools across the country, made on-line tours to showcase those schools' successful practices, and then expanded the selection program to individual states (National Forum, n.d.b). Therefore, numerous schools and educators have been able to seek recognition, to self-assess school practices, and to pursue effective educational structures to support young adolescents through the use of the criteria. Ultimately, academically excellent schools aspire to lead all young adolescents to educational success.

ACADEMIC EXCELLENCE AND SCHOOL CURRICULUM

A significant component of academic excellence is the notion that all students are expected to meet high academic standards. Middle level education in the twenty-first century warrants a careful understanding of local, state, and federal standards, yet high achievement for all students supersedes mere standardized test scores. According to *This We Believe, Successful Schools for Young Adolescents* (2003), the National Middle School Association (NMSA) advocates that if all members of a school are expected to meet high standards—adults and young people alike—high achievement results. Schools that meet the needs of young adolescents conscientiously dedicate themselves to analyzing such standards and, consequently, augmenting a meaningful curriculum. For example, by providing students with exemplars of high quality work that meet the academic standard, teachers can guide students to achieving academic excellence and provide them with clear expectations. In such a way, educators translate expectations into tangible products (NMSA, 2003). Teachers can also utilize scoring guides like rubrics and checklists for projects and activities. Likewise, high-performing schools encourage students to consistently revise their work based on teacher and peer feedback until they meet or exceed the established performance standards. In such ways, educators inspire their students to perform well and lead them to greater academic achievement.

Academic excellence is highly reliant on a school's curriculum, instruction, and assessment simultaneously aligning with high standards. According to *Turning Points 2000: Education Adolescents in the 21st Century,* "curriculum defines the specifics of *what* students should learn: the concepts and generalizations, the related topics and facts, and the skills and habits

of mind that will enable learning" (Jackson & Davis, 2000, p. 40). As educators work to develop an academically excellent curriculum, assessments should determine what students really know. With a developmentally appropriate rigor and an avoidance of repetition, a curriculum should propel young adolescents through their middle school years. Ideally, the level of student work should increase from the school year's beginning to end and from one grade to the next. Therefore, schools seeking academic excellence carefully align their curriculum, instruction, and assessment tools to ensure that their students' learning is intentionally and meaningfully developed.

An academically excellent curriculum emphasizes the deep understanding of important concepts, development of essential skills, and the ability to apply new knowledge to real-world problems. Concepts are those "big picture ideas" that are the foundation for a unit of study and draw connections across the disciplines (Jackson & Davis, 2000). Furthermore, by linking curriculum across the disciplines, such important concepts are reinforced; a relevant curriculum depends on an integrative approach. Likewise, students learn problem-solving skills in order to critically examine skills; they learn how to perform research and analyze. For instance, students may use writing skills in math and science class to explain their approaches to problem solving. In high performing schools, both strategies and content evolve while classrooms purposefully adapt to the ever-changing needs of students. A relevant curriculum is a vehicle that moves students beyond mere memorization and isolated facts into an analysis of overarching ideas (Anfara et al., 2003).

ACADEMIC EXCELLENCE IN THE CLASSROOM

By employing both challenging and engaging instructional strategies, important concepts and skills can be taught more effectively. Although each young adolescent is developmentally unique, vast cognitive growth occurs between the ages of 10 and 15 (NMSA, 2003). Therefore, students are capable of being active participants in the learning process. An academically excellent classroom should encourage students' abilities to hypothesize, organize information, and analyze cause-and-effect relationships. Teachers dedicated to academic excellence invite students to critically process their own learning, so that they are able to explain learning goals for all classroom projects and activities. Such authentic learning occurs when students are genuinely excited about learning and want to talk about it. Many times students may participate in activities that personally interest them, and their teachers allow them to design their own projects. Using a variety of instructional approaches, teachers can incorporate the use of technology, the arts, the media, and group work. In fact, many schools have embellished the notions of hands-on learning activities and embraced what is known as "hands-joined" activities that promote the collaboration of teachers and students (NMSA, 2003). Ownership and choice motivate young adolescents, and they master standards when teachers utilize a variety of methods to capitalize on those classroom attributes.

Academic excellence is also apparent in exemplary classrooms which utilize a variety of quality methods to assess student performance. According to *This We Believe: Successful Schools for Young Adolescents*, assessment is "the process of estimating a students' progress toward an objective and using that information to help students continue their learning" (NMSA, 2003, p. 27). Although traditional quizzes or tests may be used frequently, they are not the sole means for assessing students' critical thinking, independence, responsibility, or other life-long skills (Anfara et al., 2003). Teachers can assess student learning in the classroom on a daily basis with informal checks for understanding like oral questions, classroom discussions, and general observations. Additionally, projects and performance tasks provide students with meaningful opportunities to demonstrate learning and offer their teachers greater insight into both their own practice as well as students' intellectual growth. Portfolios, or accumulated collections of student products and reflections, provide evidence of a student's academic accomplishments. In high-performing schools, students can explain their products and compare them to performance standards. They can use scoring to critique their own work as well as that of their classmates (Jackson & Davis, 2000). Many times, students are invigorated by the opportunity to present their learning to parents and community members, too. As middle grades educators seek to balance between the demands of standardized tests and young adolescent needs, varied assessment methods must be designed to complement both curriculum and instruction in order to promote academic achievement.

ACADEMIC EXCELLENCE SUPPORTED BY SCHOOL STRUCTURES

A school seeking academic excellence realizes the importance of best utilizing its instructional minutes and allows students time to meet those rigorous learning standards. A flexible time arrangement, a characteristic of middle grades schools, allows teams of teachers to schedule instructional time in flexible time periods to better meet the academic as well as social needs of students. Team teachers can autonomously vary both the frequency and order of classes as well as lengthen or shorten class periods. Extending the regular schedule can offer students more time for projects, hands-on activities, and inquiry-based learning. Because time is such a precious commodity in American middle schools, classroom minutes should be devoted to teaching and learning instead of classroom management issues or discipline problems. As a result, students can feel empowered to learn, not just do as their teachers tell them to do.

High-performing schools recognize that young adolescents may need significant academic support systems in order to help students reach high academic standards. With a keen awareness that middle grades learners bring with them numerous learning styles and—in many cases—a variety of learning challenges, teachers should understand their modalities and offer students different ways to learn. In order to advance academic success for all learners, teachers should know students have or have not learned; they work to eliminate students falling behind in class. In the event of academic difficulty, students can get the extra help they need in order to be successful. Many schools form support teams comprised of school personnel like the teachers, administrators, school nurse, social worker, guidance counselor, and sometime community health representatives. The team regularly discusses concerns and offers recommendations to bolster student achievement and solutions that involve the student, parents, and his/her teachers (Jackson & Davis, 2000). If students have difficulties learning, academically excellent schools dedicate themselves to offering students extra time for work and the opportunity to revise the work. Furthermore, many schools use advisory time to promote academic skills and support academic difficulties. Academically excellent schools offer students multiple opportunities to succeed and promote various structures like before or after school tutoring programs when students need extra help.

In order to embed academic excellence, professional development is a vital link to school-wide success. High-performing schools esteem teacher collaboration so that they may reflect on instruction, expand on their knowledge, and form supporting school structures. By working with colleagues, educators make decisions about their curriculum and refine their instructional practices. Academically excellent schools value observing one another's classrooms and invest time reviewing various forms of pertinent student data like student work samples or state test scores. In order to yield higher school performance, schools review their progress by closely examining these data forms and then create targeted staff learning programs accordingly. Meanwhile, the building administrator serves as an informed instructional leader and a resource for his/her staff's professional growth. In a high-performing school, school improvement and staff development are unending endeavors.

CONCLUSION

Academic excellence is a multifaceted criterion of the National Forum's vision statement and an essential component of its Schools to Watch program. For schools on a trajectory toward exemplary performance, high academic standards lead curriculum, instruction, and assessment efforts. Students should learn essential skills and concepts as their teachers utilize a variety of instructional and assessment methods to ensure quality learning in the classroom. Furthermore, students should have adequate time and multiple chances to be successful, and they can receive academic assistance if they need it. High-performing schools should also seek to advance the knowledge and skills of staff members through focused and meaningful professional development. In tandem with the other Schools to Watch criteria—developmental responsiveness, social equity, and effective organizational structures and processes—schools have the opportunity to measure their progress and guide school improvement efforts. But ideally, these criteria exist to make middle grades learning relevant and engaging for all students. Educational authorities like the National Middle School Association and the National Forum to Accelerate Middle-Grades Reform contend that academic excellence should be the "norm, not the exception" for the young adolescents in America's schools.

REFERENCES

Anfara, V. A., Andrews, P. G., Hough, D. L., Mertens, S. B., Mizelle, N. B., & White, G. P. (2003). *Research and resources in support of This We Believe*. Westerville, OH: National Middle School Association.

Jackson, A. W. & Davis, G. A. (2000). *Turning points 2000: Educating adolescents in the 21st century*. New York: Teachers College Press.

National Forum to Accelerate Middle-Grades Reform. (n.d.a). *Schools to Watch selection criteria: Academic excellence*. Retrieved May 23, 2005, from http://www.mgforum.org/ Improvingschools/STW/STWcriteria. asp#academic

National Forum to Accelerate Middle-Grades Reform. (n.d.b). *Schools to Watch background and information.*
Retrieved May 23, 2005, from http://www.mgforum.org/ Improvingschools/STW/STWbackground.htm

National Forum to Accelerate Middle-Grades Reform. (n.d.c). *Schools to Watch state program*. Retrieved May 23, 2005, from http://www.schoolstowatch.org/state/state. htm

National Middle School Association. (2003). *This we believe: Successful schools for young adolescents*. Westerville, OH. Author.

—Gena M. Bramlett
Association of Illinois Middle-Level Schools (AIMS)

ACCELERATED SCHOOLS

Accelerated Schools PLUS originated in 1986 as the Accelerated Schools Project when Dr. Henry Levin of Stanford University acted on his belief that all students, especially those designated as at-risk, can thrive academically when challenged and provided with engaging curriculum in an atmosphere of high expectations. As founder of the Accelerated Schools Project, Dr. Levin based his belief on the questions and challenges presented in the 1983 report, *A Nation at Risk*. What started with two schools in Northern California has grown into a vibrant, systemic vehicle for school reform which has, as of 2005, served over 1,500 elementary, middle, and high schools in almost every state in America (The National Center for Accelerated Schools, 2005). In 2000 the national headquarters for ASPLUS moved to the University of Connecticut to work more closely with the National Research Center on Gifted and Talented. The Accelerated Schools Project became known as Accelerated Schools PLUS (ASPLUS) in 2003, an acronym for Accelerated Schools: Powerful Learning Unlimited Success. In 2005, 90 schools were actively involved in Accelerated Schools PLUS, including 11 middle schools (S. Choi, personal communication, May 23, 2005).

The vision of ASPLUS is to be "recognized as an exemplary process for accelerating learning of all students through data driven inquiry, reflective teaching, and powerful learning" (The National Center for Accelerated Schools, 2005). According to two of the original leaders, Finnan and Hopfenberg (1997), the Accelerated Schools model is "a comprehensive approach to school change that offers both a philosophy about academic acceleration and a concrete process for achieving it" (p. 482). Each school's unique goals are determined by an analysis of its existing culture and are set by internal, rather than external, decision makers. The entire school staff participates in the change process with each individual contributing to a specific cadre addressing issues impacting student learning. The instructional focus of Accelerated Schools PLUS is based on pedagogy most often implemented in gifted and talented programs, thus providing opportunities for all young adolescents to experience powerful learning.

This process-oriented reform model adapts to each school's culture and goals requiring that they examine data to determine a baseline on demographics, perceptions, student achievement, and existing programs/processes. Based on this foundation, and consistent with Accelerated Schools' philosophy and commitment to powerful learning, they form individual, classroom, and school visions. The visions and baseline data are compared and priorities set to address gaps between the vision and the data collected. Cadres conduct additional inquiry into why challenge areas exist and propose solutions based on data. All of this is supported through a collaborative decision-making process that involves all members of the school community.

Accelerated Schools has always supported and encouraged research and evaluation. One of the earliest studies, conducted in 1990-1991, was an ethnographic study of one of the first middle schools to embrace ASPLUS. The study found that school reform is best seen as a process of school culture change and that reform is more likely to be successful when compatibility exists between the existing school culture and the culture of the reform (Finnan & Hopfenberg, 1997). Additional information is available at http://web.uconn.edu/asp

REFERENCES

Finnan, C., & Hopfenberg, W. (1997). Accomplishing school: The journey of an accelerated middle school. *Journal for a Just and Caring Education, 3*(4), 480-493.

The National Center for Accelerated Schools. (2005). *ASPLUS: Powerful learning unlimited success.* Retrieved May 22, 2005, from http://web.uconn.edu/asp

National Commission on Excellence in Education. (1983). *A nation at risk: The imperative for educational reform.* Washington, DC: U.S. Government Printing Office.

—Sara Davis Powell
—Christine Finnan
College of Charleston

ACCOUNTABILITY

OVERVIEW

It is helpful to think about accountability in public schools, and in particular, the middle grades, by revisiting the definition of the word accountability. According to the Merriam-Webster Online Dictionary (2003), accountability means, "the quality or state of being accountable; *especially:* an obligation or willingness to accept responsibility or to account for one's actions." Accountable means, "subject to giving an account: answerable, and capable of being accounted for: explainable. And finally, account means, "a statement explaining one's conduct," or "a statement or exposition of reasons, causes, or motives."

Essentially, accountability means an obligation and willingness to accept responsibility to explain and be answerable to one's actions, including the reasons, causes, and motives. Applied to the education arena, this definition implies distributing responsibility for student outcomes more equitably. Not only should we be measuring the outcomes of student learning in multiple ways, we should also be closely examining and assessing teacher, school, and district practices—practices which we know make a profound difference in how much students are engaged in learning, in the quality of what students learn, and, ultimately, on student performance. True accountability calls for a strong emphasis on how we educate students, knowing that it is the quality of this process that will be the strongest determinant of what students learn and how they demonstrate their learning. As stated by Linda Darling-Hammond, "An accountability system is a set of commitments, policies, and practices that are designed to: (1) heighten the probability that schools will use good practices on behalf of students; (2) reduce the likelihood that schools will engage in harmful practices; and (3) encourage self-assessment on the parts of schools and educators to identify, diagnose, and change courses of action that are harmful or ineffective" (Darling-Hammond, 1993, p. 40).

This definition of accountability means creating assessment opportunities in which students must demonstrate their knowledge, skills, and understanding, and be able to explain the underlying concepts of what they have learned, the process of their learning, and its application to the real world. Such assessment must be based on students' curriculum experiences and provide opportunities for students to demonstrate, in multiple ways, what they have learned and its application.

This more comprehensive notion of accountability also calls for teachers, schools, and districts to be intensely reflective of their practices, and their impact on student learning. The most successful schools—those able to improve student learning over time—are those in which teachers are most reflective about their craft and the art of teaching. In fact, one of Carl Glickman's (1993) key findings is that teachers in the most successful schools are less satisfied with their instructional practice than teachers in less successful schools. This finding indicates a continuous process of seeking to refine and improve one's teaching. Such a professional culture requires teachers to be able to justify and validate why they choose certain practices and how these choices shape each and every student's engagement in learning, leading to higher student performance in its multiplicity of forms.

We will only reach the universal goal of successfully educating all students by creating adult cultures of reflection and inquiry at the state, district, and school levels, and holding those cultures responsible for explaining their educational practices and justifying how they enable all students to learn in meaningful ways. According to Richard Elmore, this definition of accountability is "internal accountability" where one is able to articulate and put into practice "a coherent, explicit set of norms and expectations about what a good school looks like (2002, p. 37).

School Accountability

School accountability means holding students accountable for their learning and measuring what they have learned, as well as assessing and reflecting on a school's practices and the impact of these practices in leading to quality instruction and high student engagement and achievement. How do schools create professional learning communities of adults who are engaged in the discourse of their craft and practice of teaching? How can a school be structured to ensure that every student is engaged in demanding and challenging academic work? How do middle schools engage families in meaningful ways that enhance a student's performance? These are the questions that should drive school accountability practices and measures.

Middle schools in which teachers are actively engaged in collaboratively looking at student and teacher work, in peer observation, action research, and other collaborative work focused on teaching and learning, are holding themselves accountable to hone their instructional practices. Middle schools in which teaching teams share the same students, and in which every teacher has a student load of no more than 80

students, are accountable adult cultures. Schools in which students are grouped into heterogeneous and flexibly grouped classes are holding themselves accountable for providing every student with access to a quality curriculum. Schools in which families are asked in meaningful ways to engage in their child's education and in the life of the school, rather than contacting families only when their child has done something wrong, are holding themselves accountable for building the types of family involvement that have been proven to raise student performance. These are a few of many factors that we know contribute to high student engagement and quality instruction, and subsequently, high student achievement.

The critical question is what would a high quality, school accountability component look like? Periodic school quality reviews are a promising model that have demonstrated the potential of thoughtful school examinations leading to improved practice and hence, higher student engagement and achievement. This process has been successfully used as an accountability tool in Rhode Island, as part of their state accountability system; in Massachusetts state charter schools; and in *Turning Points*, a national model of middle school reform, to identify demonstration schools. School quality reviews generally include the following components:

- They are based on a set of public benchmarks of what constitutes the practices and policies of an effective school.
- They require a process of self-examination, reflection, and assessment by the school, based on the benchmarks, and the synthesis of this self-assessment into a document for public review, which is often a school portfolio.
- They involve a team of external practitioners, usually teachers and administrators from other schools and districts; higher education, community, and business representatives; and parents, who spend several days to review data and collect other multiple forms of documentation (e.g., school portfolios, classroom and team observations, shadowing students, interviews) that provide evidence of a school's progress in meeting the benchmarks.
- The team reports findings and recommendations from the external review that are made public to the school administration and faculty, the larger public, and an accrediting body. The report articulates a set of strengths, concerns, and recommendations. These recommendations effectively become a roadmap for future school improvement efforts.
- A school's status with the district is directly tied to its performance on the school quality review. Based

on the review the accrediting body may approve the school for continuation, continuation on probation or with explicit target goals, or closure.

- They are cyclical, occurring every 4 to 5 years, significantly reducing the chances of a school's performance markedly deteriorating and having a harmful effect on students (Center for Collaborative Education, 1998; Massachusetts Department of Education, 1999; Rhode Island Department of Education, 1998).

The school quality review process is a proactive accountability strategy ensuring that schools are engaged in quality educational practices that lead to high student engagement and achievement. Many schools that have undertaken school quality reviews have found that this process, while requiring an intense level of self-assessment and examination by the entire school community, has resulted in substantial improvements in teaching and learning—often prior to the external review team's visit.

STUDENT ACCOUNTABILITY AND DIAGNOSTIC TESTING

Assessment has its greatest impact on improving student learning and in accurately gauging a student's performance when it is embedded in curriculum and instruction in meaningful ways and when it is the result and product of authentic intellectual work. It is virtually impossible for authentic intellectual work to be adequately captured by state-administered standardized tests. Rather, the goal should be to create a system of locally developed and administered assessments that measure whether students have mastered state competencies.

A locally administered assessment system, governed by state guidelines that provide consistency while also allowing flexibility and innovation, does not preclude the need for state-wide assessment data that allows for diagnosis in literacy and math, as well as data that can be used for comparison purposes among districts enrolling similar demographics of students. Standardized tests provide one legitimate method of publicly tracking the progress of schools and students from year to year, both their overall progress and their progress in closing the achievement gap between low-income students and their more affluent peers, and between White students and African-American and Latino students.

What would a locally-based student assessment and diagnostic testing system look like? Under such a system, each school in the state would develop its own accountability and assessment plan, using state and district guidelines. The plan, developed by teachers, administrators, and parents and approved by the school governing body and the district, would outline how the school will ensure that students will demonstrate that they meet the state competencies. Plans would be encouraged to include authentic assessments, including portfolios, exhibitions, performance tasks, student products, and external reviews, as well as a description of how the school will use this information to improve itself. Such a plan would assist teachers to focus on high quality instruction and curriculum, rather than teaching to the test. These plans would be subject to review by the state department of education (Coalition for Authentic Reform in Education, 1997).

The Maine Department of Education has endorsed just such a local assessment model. While using a state standardized test, the Maine Educational Assessment (MEA), as a diagnostic assessment tool that allows district comparison of student performance, the beacon of its assessment program is a requirement for every district to develop a local assessment system to measure student performance. "It is important to recognize that districts and schools have a great deal of latitude in determining what to include in their assessment system.... Local assessments may include portfolios, performances, and demonstrations, in addition to other measures of achievement. Commercially produced assessment tools may be part of the local assessment system but may not carry a majority of the weight in determining student performance" (Maine Department of Education, 2003).

ACCOUNTING TO THE PUBLIC

A true accountability system must track student engagement and performance in multiple ways across time; there must be meaningful ways in which we assess how our students are doing. Certainly, the results of school and district quality reviews and the engagement of parents and community members in the review of authentic student assessments provide considerable information to the public on how their schools are faring. In addition, we need to be able to report a range of data on student engagement and performance in understandable and accessible ways to the public.

What would a system of accounting to the public look like? Within a public reporting system, multiple indicators of student engagement and performance would be included, all disaggregated by race, income, gender, school, and language. Student engagement, which indicates a school's power of attracting and holding students' interests, includes such indicators as waiting lists and rates of attendance, suspension, expulsions, dropouts, and transfers. Student achievement includes such indicators as course failures, grade retentions, enrollment in high-level classes and special education, achievement on standardized tests and authentic assessments, and graduation and college-going rates (tracked graduation back to the sending middle school).

These aggregated data should be provided annually in easy-to-read form for the general public, encouraging widespread discussion of the data. Presentations, focus groups, poster analysis, and newsletter syntheses are all good ways to get the data distributed and discussed. A school open to conversing about its data is usually a school that is likely to search for and adopt effective practices for meeting the needs of all its students.

REFERENCES

Coalition for Authentic Reform in Education. (1997, December). *A call for an authentic state-wide assessment system.* Cambridge, MA: Author.

Center for Collaborative Education. (1998). *The Boston public schools' school self-study guide: As prepared for the Boston Pilot Schools' accountability process for use with the school quality review process.* Boston, MA: Author.

Darling-Hammond, L. (1993). Creating standards of practice and delivery for learner-centered schools. *Stanford Policy and Law Review,* 37-52.

Elmore, R. (2002). Testing trap. *Harvard Magazine, 105*(1), 35-40.

Glickman, C. (1993). *Renewing America's schools.* New York: Jossey-Bass.

Massachusetts Deparment of Education. (1999). Massachusetts charter school inspection handbook. Malden, MA: Author.

Maine Department of Education. (2003). *Local assessments.* Retrieved August 13, 2003, from http://www.state.me.us/education/lsalt/localassess.html

Merriam-Webster On-Line Dictionary. Retrieved August 8, 2003, from http://www.com/home.html

Rhode Island Department of Education. (1998). *SALT pilot visit documents.* Providence, RI: Author.

—Dan French
Center for Collaborative Education

ACCREDITATION AND MIDDLE LEVEL TEACHER PREPARATION PROGRAMS

The decision by escalating numbers of states to use National Middle School Association/National Council for Accreditation of Teacher Education-Approved Middle Level Teacher Preparation Standards (National Middle School Association, 2001) as requirements for program approval and teacher licensure has significantly strengthened efforts by National Middle School Association (NMSA) to promote the specialized professional preparation of middle level teachers. The NMSA/National Council for Accreditation of Teacher Education-Approved Middle Level Teacher Preparation Standards exert a powerful influence on the nature of undergraduate and graduate middle level teacher preparation programs across the nation. These standards, created by the NMSA Professional Preparation Advisory Board and approved by the National Council for Accreditation of Teacher Education (NCATE), are used in the review of middle level teacher preparation programs as part of the accreditation process for institutions seeking NCATE accreditation for their education unit (e.g., college or school of education). By creating standards for middle level teacher preparation and utilizing them as part of the NCATE national accreditation system, NMSA has helped assure that increasing numbers of middle level teachers enter their classrooms with the specialized knowledge, skills, and dispositions to be highly successful teaching young adolescents.

States have two options regarding program approval in their partnership agreements with NCATE. Twenty-four states have selected the option which provides for the review of specialty programs by professional associations such as NMSA to determine the viability and sustainability of those programs. In these states, approval of middle level teacher preparation programs by NMSA through the NCATE review process is required for middle level teacher preparation programs to be established and to continue to recommend teacher candidates for middle level certification/licensure. Individual middle level teacher preparation programs that meet NMSA standards and have their overall teacher preparation programs accredited by NCATE are nationally recognized by NMSA.

Twenty-six states have selected the option of having program reviews conducted at the state level. However, many of these states use the NMSA/ NCATE-Approved Middle Level Education Standards for program approval and licensure purposes (e.g.,

Georgia, Ohio, South Carolina). Approximately seventeen states selecting one of these two options have adopted the NMSA/NCATE-Approved Middle Level Teacher Preparation Standards as state standards and require middle level teacher preparation programs to meet these standards to recommend teacher candidates for licensure. One result of the decision of states to take this route is that all teacher preparation programs in these respective states, whether or not they seek national accreditation through NCATE, have to meet the NMSA standards.

NATIONAL COUNCIL FOR ACCREDITATION OF TEACHER EDUCATION

NMSA is a constituent member of NCATE. NCATE is a national accreditation organization that provides a process for the professional accreditation of schools, colleges and departments of education. NCATE accreditation demonstrates that the college or university operates at a high level of educational quality and integrity. NCATE accreditation is the process by which a professional education unit is recognized by the profession as meeting national standards for the content and operation of the unit (NCATE, 2002).

Accreditation of colleges or schools of education indicates that teacher preparation programs have undergone rigorous external review by professionals and that the performances of teacher candidates have been thoroughly assessed before being recommended for initial or advanced licensure, and that preparation programs meet standards set by the teaching profession at large. The NCATE accreditation process "establishes rigorous standards for teacher education programs, holds accredited institutions accountable for meeting these standards, and encourages unaccredited schools to demonstrate the quality of their programs by working for and achieving professional accreditation" (NCATE, 2005, p. 1). NMSA is one of more than 30 professional associations representing millions of Americans that support and sustain NCATE. NCATE is the largest coalition of education and public organizations in the nation devoted to quality teaching.

MIDDLE LEVEL TEACHER PREPARATION STANDARDS

The NMSA/NCATE-Approved Middle Level Teacher Preparation Standards reflect a strong consensus that exists among middle level educators regarding the essential components of middle level teacher preparation programs (McEwin, Dickinson, & Smith, 2003, 2004). These standards that are provided below represent only those program components that are unique to middle level teacher preparation programs. Other key program components that are common to all teacher preparation programs are not discussed here (e.g., diversity, technology) because they are required of all teacher preparation programs seeking national accreditation from NCATE through unit level standards (e.g., core professional courses, field experiences, and performances). Middle level teacher preparation programs cannot be approved nor receive national recognition without having also met these unit standards (NCATE, 2002).

NMSA/NCATE-Approved Middle Level Teacher Preparation Standards for the initial, masters, and doctoral levels consist of two programmatic standards and seven performance-based standards. The programmatic standards incorporate indicators describing the nature of the standards while the performance-based standards include examples of knowledge, dispositions, and performances that help describe the meaning of the respective standards (NMSA, 2001). The programmatic standards are as follows:

- **Programmatic Standard 1.** Middle Level Courses and Experiences: Institutions preparing middle level teachers have courses and field experiences that specifically and directly address middle level education.
- **Programmatic Standard 2.** Qualified Middle Level Faculty: Institutions preparing middle level teachers employ faculty members who have middle level experience and expertise.

One overall purpose of the programmatic standards is to assure that teacher candidates enrolled in middle level teacher preparation programs have middle level courses that address topics such as middle level philosophy and organization, young adolescent development, and middle level curriculum and instruction. The standards also require that clinical experiences be conducted in middle level classrooms. Additionally, these programmatic standards address the qualifications of instructors teaching in middle level teacher preparation programs.

- **Performance-Based Standard 1.** Young Adolescent Development: Middle level teacher candidates understand the major concepts, principles, theories, and research related to young adolescent development, and they provide opportunities that support student development and learning.

Standard one focuses on the importance of middle level teacher preparation programs including a strong emphasis on providing teachers opportunities to obtain a comprehensive understanding of the development of young adolescents, and the implications of that knowledge.

- **Performance-Based Standard 2.** Middle Level Philosophy and School Organization: Middle level teacher candidates understand the major concepts, principles, theories, and research underlying the philosophical foundations of developmentally responsive middle level programs and schools, and they work successfully within these organizational components.

Standard two was developed to assure that middle level teacher candidates develop a comprehensive understanding of middle level philosophy and organization. Course topics addressing this standard typically include, but are not limited to (a) the origins and development of middle level schools, (b) effective middle level school organizational features and practices, (c) middle level philosophy, (d) middle level trends and issues, and (e) other information that helps middle level teacher candidates understand the rationale for and context of middle level schooling.

- **Performance-Based Standard 3.** Middle Level Curriculum and Assessment: Middle level teacher candidates understand the major concepts, principles, theories, standards, and research related to middle level curriculum and assessment, and they use this knowledge in their practice.

Standard three recognizes the importance of teacher candidates developing a thorough understanding of middle level curriculum. Study in this area typically includes an emphasis on curriculum that is discipline specific, integrative and interdisciplinary. Emphasis is also placed on the key role of assessment of middle level curriculum.

- **Performance-Based Standard 4.** Middle Level Teaching Fields. Middle level teacher candidates understand and use the central concepts, tools of inquiry, standards, and structures of content in their chosen teaching fields, and they create meaningful learning experiences that develop all young adolescents' competence in subject matter and skills.

Standard four notes the importance of middle level teacher candidates demonstrating two areas of content knowledge. Knowledge in two content areas, rather than a single area, provides a solid academic foundation for effective middle level teaching and promotes an understanding of the connections and interrelationships among the various subject areas.

- **Performance-Based Standard 5.** Middle Level Instruction and Assessment: Middle level teacher candidates understand and use the major concepts, principles, theories, and research related to effective instruction and assessment, and they employ a variety of strategies for a developmentally appropriate climate to meet the varying abilities and learning styles of all young adolescents.

Standard five emphasizes the key role middle level planning, teaching, and assessment in middle level teacher preparation programs. Middle level teacher preparation programs meeting this standard must demonstrate that their teacher candidates can effectively plan, teach, and assess student work based on content knowledge as well as demonstrate a comprehensive understanding of young adolescent development. They must also be competent in constructing and employing appropriate and effective assessment techniques.

- **Performance-Based Standard 6.** Family and Community Involvement: Middle level teacher candidates understand the major concepts, principles, theories, and research related to working collaboratively with family and community members, and they use that knowledge to maximize the learning of all young adolescents.

Standard six recognizes the importance of teacher candidates demonstrating their abilities to work effectively with family and community members. It includes a focus on establishing and maintaining respectful and productive relationships with family and community members that maximize student learning and well-being. Designing instruction that utilizes the diverse community experiences of all young adolescents is also an emphasis of this standard.

- **Performance-Based Standard 7.** Middle Level Professional Roles: Middle level teacher candidates understand the complexity of teaching young adolescents, and they engage in practices and behaviors that develop their competence as professionals.

Standard seven addresses the many important professional roles and responsibilities of middle level teachers. These roles include, but are not limited to, specialized responsibilities such as serving as team members, serving as advocates for young adolescents and middle level schooling, and engaging in ongoing professional practices that will improve their practice.

Readers should visit the Web sites of NMSA (http://www.nmsa.org) and NCATE (http://www.nmsa.org) for the most current information and a more detailed explanation of the national accreditation review.

REFERENCES

McEwin, C. K., Dickinson, T. S., & Smith, T. W. (2003). Middle level teacher preparation: Status, progress, and challenges. In P. G. Andrews & V. A. Anfara, Jr. (Eds.), *Leaders for a movement: Professional preparation and development of middle level teachers and administrators* (pp. 3-26). Greenwich, CT: Information Age.

McEwin, C. K., Dickinson, T. S., & Smith, T. W. (2004). The role of teacher preparation, licensure, and retention in creating high performing middle schools. In S. Thompson (Ed.), *Creating high performing middle schools: A focus on policy issues* (pp. 109-129). Greenwich, CT: Information Age.

National Council for the Accreditation of Teacher Education. (2002). *Professional standards for the accreditation of schools, colleges, and departments of education.* Washington, DC: Author.

National Council for Accreditation of Teacher Education. (2005). *About NCATE.* Retrieved May 26, 2005, from http://www.ncate

National Middle School Association/National Council for Accreditation of Teacher Education-approved middle level teacher preparation standards. (2001). Westerville, OH: Author. Retrieved May 26, 2005, from http://www.nmsa.org

—C. Kenneth McEwin
Tracy W. Smith
Appalachian State University

ACHIEVEMENT GAP

The term "achievement gap" refers to a difference in educational performance between groups of students. The gap typically refers to differences in standardized test scores that are tied to socioeconomic, racial, and ethnic differences among students. Standardized tests include the National Assessment of Educational Progress (NAEP) and college admission tests like the Scholastic Aptitude Test (SAT) among others (Stevens, 1995). The achievement gap first received national attention in the 1960s (Viadero, 2000a) when studies highlighted the differences in performance between poor and minority students and their middle- and upper-class White peers. The achievement gap remains a reality today despite massive efforts by both the federal and state governments to eliminate it.

Poor and minority students enter school slightly behind their wealthier White peers; these slight differences accumulate and become obvious differences by middle school (Bracey, 1996; Gutman, Sameroff, & Eccles, 2002; Newman, Myers, Newman, Lohman, & Smith, 2000). Midgley and Edelin (1998) report poor children experience a loss in achievement during the middle school years. Gutman et al. (2002) contend that African American students fall behind their White peers as much as two grade levels by the end of middle school. Inner-city and rural young adolescents are particularly at risk due to environmental and family factors that work against academic achievement (Norton & Lewis, 2000). Research indicates a myriad of factors contribute to the existence of this gap as well as educational responses that can reverse it.

REALITY

After the achievement gap first received national attention, the United States Congress enacted legislation in 1965 as part of the *Elementary and Secondary Education Act*, creating the Chapter I program to provide extra funding to schools with high concentrations of poor students (D'Agostino, Borman, Hedges, & Wong, 1998; Jennings, 2000; Tirozzi & Uro, 1997). The additional funding provided instructional opportunities in basic skills for poor children, defined as students who qualified for free and reduced-price lunch programs (D'Agostino et al., 1998; Jennings, 2000; Mertens & Flowers, 2003). This focus on improving the basic skills of economically disadvantaged students resulted in a narrowing of the achievement gap during the 1970s and 1980s (Haycock, 2001; Jennings, 2000; Tirozzi & Uro, 1997). African American students cut the performance gap between themselves and White students in half; the gap between Hispanic and White students closed by one third (Haycock, 2001; Jennings, 2000; Viadero, 2000a). This improvement trend halted in the 1990s, however, when the gap began to increase again in reading and math achievement (Haycock, 2001; Jennings, 2000; Johnston & Viadero, 2000). By 1999, NAEP results revealed that the reading and math skills of African American and Hispanic high school *seniors* were on par with those of White eighth graders (Haycock, 2001; Johnston & Viadero, 2000; Maruyama, 2003).

The achievement gap also appears in course grades, high school course selections, and high school and college graduation rates (Haycock, 2001; Singham, 2003). Students in high-poverty schools who score A's do as well on standardized tests as students from wealthier schools who score C's and D's (Anyon, 1997; Noguera, 2003; Viadero, 2000a). Researchers also note the tendency of African American students to settle for C's and D's because they perceive making better grades as "acting white" (Noguera, 2003; Viadero & Johnston, 2000). Generally, African American and Hispanic students comprise a small percentage of the students enrolled in gifted, honors, and Advanced Placement classes (less than 10%) compared to their White and Asian peers (Ford, Harris, Tyson, & Trotman, 2002; Noguera, 2003; Wheelock, 1992). Conversely, these African American and Hispanic students are disproportionately represented in vocational and remedial courses that do not provide a rigorous academic challenge (Midgley & Edelin, 1998; Tirozzi & Uro, 1997; Wheelock, 1992). More African American (19%) and Hispanic (37%) students fail to obtain a high school diploma or its equivalency by the age of 24 compared to White (10%) and Asian (6%) students (Haycock, 2001; Maruyama, 2003). Thus, African American and Hispanic students are less likely than their more advantaged peers to enroll in postsecondary education and even less likely to graduate from it (Anyon, 1997; Maruyama, 2003; Newman et al., 2000; Singham, 2003).

The achievement gap predicts a bleak future for many poor and minority students in the United States. The lack of a high school diploma or its equivalent limits the opportunities available to students, consigning many of them to poverty as adults. The majority of jobs in urban areas are either low-paying service jobs or high-paying technical or professional jobs (Anyon, 1997). For rural students, since occupational choices are limited in areas with smaller populations, educational achievement is linked to the ability to move to locales with higher-paying opportunities (Perry & Quaglia, 1995). Demographic statistics indicate that minority students comprise one third of the nation's students (Johnston & Viadero, 2000); in some states, minority students comprise well over half the student population (Anyon, 1997; Datnow, Borman, Stringfield, Overman, & Castellano, 2003). Within the next 15 years, they may comprise as much as two thirds of the nation's student population (Anyon, 1997; Maruyama, 2003). Failure to improve the educational performance of minority students when they represent such a large percentage of the nation's population poses serious implications for the economic future of the United States.

REASONS

Family socioeconomic status (SES) is the single greatest predictor of academic achievement for students (Brown, Roney, & Anfara, 2003; Gutman et al., 2002; Mertens & Flowers, 2003; Roscigno, 1998). In schools, qualifying for the free or reduced-priced lunch program serves as an indicator of low SES, or put more simply, poverty (Mertens & Flowers, 2003; Urban Schools, 1996). Schools with poverty levels as low as 25% experience lower achievement for both poor and wealthier students (Viadero, 2000b). As the percentage of poor students in a school increases, school-wide achievement levels decrease (Mertens & Flowers, 2003; Urban Schools, 1996). Payne and Biddle (1999) make a startling comparison that highlights the link between poverty and achievement. On the Second International Mathematics and Science Study (McKight et al., 1987), U.S. schools with low levels of poverty posted achievement scores second only to the leading nation in the study. High-poverty schools, however, posted achievement results lower than any other industrialized nations participating in the study—and on par with students from Nigeria and Swaziland!

Why is poverty such an important indicator? Guo (1998) reports that poverty during childhood affects cognitive ability, while poverty during adolescence impacts achievement. Poor children have access to fewer resources that stimulate learning, such as books in the home, preschool experiences, summer learning opportunities, and tutors (Maruyamo, 2003; Viadero, 2000a). They are also more likely to live in a single-parent home or a two-parent home where the parents are either on welfare or work low-paying jobs (Biddle, 1997).

Poverty is linked to lower levels of parental education (Perry & Quaglia, 1995; Roscigno, 1998), which often translates into less influence for poor families as an advocate for their students' education (Anyon, 1997; Dornbusch, Glasgow, & Lin, 1996; Noguera, 2003). Parents with lower educational levels also have lower grade expectations for their children (Dornbusch et al., 1996; Noguera, 2003).

The location of children living in poverty varies along racial/ethnic lines. Poor children in rural areas tend to be White (Urban Schools, 1996). Their parents have lower expectations for their children's futures and thus do not push for high levels of academic achievement (Perry & Quaglia, 1995). Urban children living in poverty are more likely to be minorities (Anyon, 1997; Noguera, 2003). They experience problems that increase the risks of educational failure such as inadequate health care, increased violence, and the physical and psychological stresses that accompany violence (Gutman et al., 2002; Kozol, 1991; Wang & Kovach, 1995). Viadero (2003) reports indicators linked to the achievement gap that place African American and Hispanic students at a disadvantage compared to White students. These indicators include low birth weight, poor nutrition, higher risks of exposure to lead paint, and lower levels of parental interactions such as reading to or talking with their children.

Maruyama (2003), reviewing the results of the 1998 NAEP, reports drastic achievement differences along racial/ethnic lines at all three grade levels (4th, 8th, and 12th) tested. Among White students, 27% of 4th graders, 18% of 8th graders, and 17% of 12th graders scored below the proficiency level. For African American students, 60%, 46%, and 36% at the respective grade levels scored below the proficiency level. Results for Hispanic students mirrored those of African American students with 64% of 4th graders, 47% of 8th graders, and 43% of 12th graders scoring below the proficiency level. In this same study, Maruyama reports that achievement differences along racial/ethnic lines narrow as family income increases, although the differences do not disappear entirely. The greatest achievement differences between White and African American students appear when family income is less than $25,000; as family income increases, the differences become more modest. Hispanic students with family income below $25,000 mirror the results of African American students in the same income level. At family income levels above $25,000, however, Hispanic students trail all other racial/ethnic groups in academic achievement. Asian-American students, on the other hand, outpace all other racial/ethnic groups in educational achievement, regardless of family income.

School-related factors also influence achievement. Viadero (2003) suggests school-related factors include class size and teacher preparation, with minority students more likely to be in overcrowded classrooms and to have teachers who are less experienced and less prepared to teach. Anyon (1997) and Noguera (2003) concur that urban children tend to be taught by teachers who are either not certified or lack confidence in their abilities/ knowledge, especially in the fields of math and science. Minority and poor students also experience a less rigorous academic curriculum than their White and Asian peers, either through the classes they choose or the classes they are enrolled in based on ability tracking (Anyon, 1997; Kozol, 1991; Noguera, 2003; Roscigno, 1998; Wheelock, 1992). Other educational factors contributing to the low achievement levels of poor and minority students include lower levels of funding for rural and urban schools in comparison to suburban schools, and

severely restricted access to resources such as textbooks, supplies, and laboratories (Anyon, 1997; Biddle, 1997; Noguera, 2003).

REMEDIES

Poor and minority students enter school lagging behind their White classmates in reading and math achievement (Viadero & Johnston, 2000). This difference stems, in part, from the resources available to middle- and upper-class families to provide their children with rich learning environments (Anyon, 1997; Viadero, 2000a). Poor and minority students, on the other hand, rely on their teachers and schools to provide supportive, literate learning environments (Stevens, 1995). That said, research indicates schools are not hostage to the socioeconomic context of their locations. Some common themes emerge from research on successful schools.

HIGH STANDARDS AND EXPECTATIONS

Negative attitudes toward diverse racial, ethnic, or language groups often lead to low teacher expectations and a watered-down curriculum (Zeichner, 1995). Teachers need to establish high expectations for their students and communicate those expectations to their students (Noguera, 2003; Wheelock, 1992; Zeichner, 1995). Performance benchmarks for each grade level, establishing what all students should know and be able to do, provide measurable goals for teachers. Systems adopting standards-based reforms like these have experienced achievement gains for all students, but especially for minorities (Datnow et al., 2003; Johnston, 2000; Mulhall, Flowers, & Mertens, 2002; Singham, 2003).

CHALLENGING CURRICULUM

All students need a challenging curriculum that reflects rigorous academic standards, relates to student interests, and relies on strong instructional practices (Jackson & Davis, 2000; Midgley & Edelin, 1998). Instructional strategies traditionally used with poor and minority students rely on isolated drill and practice of basic skills (Anyon, 1997; Noguera, 2003). Wheelock (1992) points to the harmful effects of "tracking," or ability grouping, for disadvantaged students. This practice never exposes them to the rich learning environments needed to develop higher order skills. Bracey (2001) found students more engaged during instructional activities like discussions, lab work, group work, and individualized instruction as well as instruction that was both relevant and academically challenging. McMillen (2001) reports that time engaged in active learning is more important to achievement than merely increasing instructional time.

Stevens (1995) refers to the teaching and learning conditions in a classroom or school as "opportunity-to-learn" variables (p. 54). These variables include the following: (1) content coverage that matches assessments, (2) exposure to higher-order skills in content-area materials, (3) depth of curriculum coverage, (4) quality instructional experiences that link to students' prior knowledge and experiences and provide corrective feedback, (5) active learning focused on real-life problem solving, and (6) performance and behavior standards that motivate all students to learn and to take responsibility for their actions. These opportunity-to-learn variables reflect the suggestions long offered by middle school proponents to engage all students in meaningful learning (Carnegie Council on Adolescent Development, 1989; Jackson & Davis, 2000; National Middle School Association, 2003).

Instructional Assistance

All students can learn at high levels, but Haycock (2001) points out that some students require more time and assistance to do so. To provide this support, schools are offering instructional assistance through before- and after-school programs, evening or weekend classes, and summer programs (D'Agostino et al., 1998; Haycock, 2001; McMillen, 2001). Datnow et al. (2002), studying programs for English language learner students, found "dual language and bilingual immersion programs" (p. 155) the most successful methods of improving achievement for these students.

Multicultural Differences

To successfully educate minority students, teachers must first appreciate and understand the home cultures of these students (Zeichner, 1995). Greenfield, Raeff, and Quiroz (1995) assert that children enter school already competent in many areas of functioning; these competencies, however, may not lend themselves to competency at school. Teachers, both pre-service and in-service, need training to recognize these differences in order to build on the strengths students bring to the classroom. When a student's home culture is both validated and understood, students and parents feel less threatened, and teachers can better connect learning between the home and school cultures to develop new learning (Anyon, 1997; Greenfield et al., 1995; Noguera, 2003; Zeichner, 1995).

Minority students need help to develop an "academic identity" (Jackson, 2003, p. 580) since many come from backgrounds lacking in strong academic traditions and expectations. Requirements for developing such an identity include teaching the codes and customs of the school culture as well as "code switching" (Jackson, 2003, p. 584) behaviors that allow students to transition between the different expectations of their home, school, and peer cultures (Greenfield et al., 1995; Newman et al., 2000; Noguera, 2003).

Pre- and In-Service Teacher Development

Erasing the achievement gap demands much of preservice teacher preparation programs and in-service professional development programs. Many preservice teacher candidates are White and speak only one language (Anyon, 1997; Zeichner, 1995). They bring their own cultural biases to the classroom, often resulting in low expectations for students who are different from them; the same holds true for many practicing teachers (Anyon, 1997; Noguera, 2003; Zeichner, 1995). Teachers and teacher candidates need a better understanding of second language acquisition as well as a greater awareness of how language and culture impact school performance (Benard, 1995; Datnow et al., 2002; Zeichner, 1995).

Singham (2003) suggests new teachers need as many as 10 years of professional development in content knowledge, teaching skills, and pedagogical content knowledge to become effective teachers. Other researchers (Dornbusch et al., 1996; Haycock, 2001; Jackson & Davis, 2000; Norton & Lewis, 2000) echo the call for teachers to possess strong content knowledge and an understanding of the ways students learn. Research consistently reveals the impact good teaching has on improving the achievement of the weakest students (Dornbusch et al., 1996; Haycock, 2001).

Dornbusch et al. (1996) report interesting changes in teacher-student interactions and teacher-parent collaborations during the transition to middle school. Middle school students participate in multiple classrooms, a very different situation from the self-contained classrooms they occupied at the elementary level. This change in classroom organization results in a more impersonal environment. The earlier this impersonal environment occurs, the greater the declines in self-esteem and academic performance that students may experience as a result of the changes of adolescence. The increasingly impersonal environment also weakens the collaborative relationship between schools and parents as students move into young adolescence. Other researchers note the need that students, especially poor and minority students, have for caring relationships with teachers (Jackson & Davis, 2000; Midgley & Edelin, 1998). Many teachers, however, perhaps in their empathy for the plight of poor and minority students, lower their academic expectations for mastery learning beginning in the middle school years (Norguera, 2003; Norton & Lewis, 2000). The challenge is to maintain both positive relationships and high expectations that all students can succeed.

Finally, preservice and practicing teachers need training in using achievement data to design curriculum and assessments that measure learning (Viadero & Johnston, 2000). Stevens (1995) asserts that most teachers know little about alternative assessment techniques such as portfolios or how to integrate them in curriculum design.

REFLECTIONS

Many of the remedies suggested for erasing the achievement gap among American students reflect the middle school reforms suggested by both *Turning Points* (Carnegie Council on Adolescent Development, 1989) and *Turning Points 2000* (Jackson & Davis, 2000). Researchers (Midgley & Uro, 1998; Norton & Lewis, 2000; Trimble, 2002) report that many middle schools adopting the *Turning Point* recommendations stop with creating more caring environments. Schools must also implement the *Turning Points* recommendations for a strong academic curriculum in order to prepare students for the rigorous academic curriculum needed at the secondary level. The teachers and/or counselors who make placement recommendations place students not academically prepared for high school in lower academic tracks at the beginning of their high school careers. Less learning occurs in these lower academic tracks, making it difficult for students to later switch to a more challenging college-preparatory curriculum (Anyon, 1997; Dornbusch et al., 1996; Midgley & Edelin, 1998; Noguera, 2003). Research indicates that a challenging academic curriculum in high school is the best predictor of college completion for all students (Singham, 2003). Since educational credentials rather than cognitive abilities predict future earnings and occupational status (Dornbusch et al., 1996), students need to obtain a high school diploma and some form of postsecondary education. Otherwise, poor and minority students will fall further behind their more advantaged peers and will find themselves more likely to experience poverty and unemployment as adults, thus perpetuating the achievement gap for future generations.

REFERENCES

Anyon, J. (1997). *Ghetto schooling: A political economy of urban educational reform*. New York: Teachers College Press.

Benard, B. (1995). Fostering resiliency in urban schools. In B. Williams (Ed.), *Closing the achievement gap: A vision to guide change in beliefs and practice* (pp. 65–80). Philadelphia: Research for Better Schools.

Biddle, B. J. (1997). Foolishness, dangerous nonsense, and real correlates of state differences in achievement. *Phi Delta Kappan, 78*(1), 8.

Bracey, G. W. (1996). The impact of early intervention. *Phi Delta Kappan, 77*(7), 510-511.

Bracey, G. W. (2001). Research—At the beep, pay attention. *Phi Delta Kappan, 82*(7), 555.

Brown, K. M, Roney, K., & Anfara, V. A., Jr. (2003). Organizational health directly influences student performance at the middle level. *Middle School Journal, 34*(5), 5-15.

Carnegie Council on Adolescent Development. (1989). *Turning points: Preparing American youth for the 21st century* (The Report of the Task Force on Education of Young Adolescents). New York: Carnegie Corporation of New York.

D'Agostino, J. V., Borman, G. D., Hedges, L. V., & Wong, K. K. (1998). Longitudinal achievement and chapter I coordination in high-poverty schools: A multilevel analysis of the prospects data. *Journal of Education for Students Placed at Risk, 3*(4), 401-420.

Datnow, A., Borman, G. D., Stringfield, S., Overman, L. T., & Castellano, M. (2003). Comprehensive school reform in culturally and linguistically diverse contexts: Implementation and outcomes from a four-year study. *Educational Evaluation and Policy Analysis, 25*, 143-170.

Dornbusch, S. M., Glasgow, K. L., & Lin, I. C. (1996). The social structure of schooling. *Annual Review of Psychology, 47*, 401-402.

Ford, D. Y., Harris, J. H., III, Tyson, C. A., & Trotman, M. F. (2002). Beyond deficit thinking: Providing access for gifted African American students. *Roeper Review, 24*(2), 52-53.

Greenfield, P. M., Raeff, C., & Quiroz, B. (1995). Cultural values in learning and education. In B. Williams (Ed.), *Closing the achievement gap: A vision to guide change in beliefs and practice* (pp. 25-38). Philadelphia: Research for Better Schools.

Guo, G. (1998). The timing of the influences of cumulative poverty on children's cognitive ability and achievement. *Social Forces, 77*(1), 257–288.

Gutman, L. M., Sameroff, A. J., & Eccles, J. S. (2002). The academic achievement of African American students during early adolescence: An examination of multiple risk, promotive, and protective factors. *American Journal of Community Psychology, 30*(3), 367–369.

Haycock, K. (2001). Closing the achievement gap. *Educational Leadership, 58*(6), 6–11.

Jackson, D. B. (2003). Education reform as if student agency mattered: Academic microcultures and student identity. *Phi Delta Kappan, 84*(8), 579–585.

Jackson, A. W., & Davis, G. A. (2000). *Turning points 2000: Educating adolescents in the 21st century.* New York: Teachers College Press.

Jennings, J. F. (2000). Title I: Its legislative history and its promise. *Phi Delta Kappan, 81*(7), 516.

Johnston, R. C. (2000). In a Texas district, test scores for minority students have soared. *Education Week, 19*(30), 14–15.

Johnston, R. C., & Viadero, D. (2000). Unmet promise: Raising minority achievement. *Education Week, 19*(27), 18–19.

Kozol, J. (1991). *Savage inequalities: Children in America's schools.* New York: Harper Perennial.

Maruyama, G. (2003). Disparities in educational opportunities and outcomes: What do we know and what can we do? *Journal of Social Forces, 59*(3),653–654.

McMillan, B. J. (2001). A statewide evaluation of academic achievement in year-round schools. *Journal of Educational Research, 95*(2), 67–69.

McKight, C., Crosswhite, F. J., Dossey, J., Kifer, A., Swafford, J., Travers, K., & Cooney, T. (1987). *The underachieving curriculum: Assessing U.S. school mathematics from an international perspective.* Champaign, IL: Stipes.

Mertens, S. B., & Flowers, N. (2003). Middle school practices improve student achievement in high poverty schools. *Middle School Journal, 34*(1), 33–43.

Midgley, C., & Edelin, K. C. (1998). Middle school reform and early adolescent well-being: The good news and the bad. *Educational Psychologists, 33*(4), 195–217.

Mulhall, P. F., Flowers, N., & Mertens, S. B. (2002). Understanding indicators related to academic performance. Retrieved on November 3, 2003, from http://www.nmsa.org/research/articles/res_articles_nov2002htm

National Middle School Association. (2003). *This we believe: Successful schools for young adolescents.* Westerville, OH: Author.

Newman, B. M., Myers, M. C., Newman, P. R., Lohman, B. J., & Smith, V. L. (2000). The transition to high school for academically promising, urban low-income African American youth. *Adolescence, 35*(137), 45–46.

Noguera, P. (2003). *City schools and the American dream: Reclaiming the promise of public education.* New York: Teachers College Press.

Norton, J., & Lewis, A. C. (2000). Special report—Middle grades reform. *Phi Delta Kappan, 81*(10), 1.

Payne, K. J., & Biddle, B. J. (1999). Poor school funding, child poverty, and mathematics achievement. *Educational Researcher, 28*(6), 4–18.

Perry, C. M., & Quaglia, R. J. (1995). A study of underlying variables affecting aspirations of rural adolescents. *Adolescence, 30*(117), 233–234.

Roscigno, V. J. (1998). Race and reproduction of educational disadvantage. *Social Forces, 76* (3), 1033–1062.

Singham, M. (2003). The achievement gap: Myths and realities. *Phi Delta Kappan, 84*(8), 586-591.

Stevens, F. I. (1995). Closing the achievement gap: Opportunity to learn, standards, and assessments. In B. Williams (Ed.), *Closing the achievement gap: A vision to guide change in beliefs and practice* (pp. 53-64). Philadelphia: Research for Better Schools.

Tirozzi, G. N., & Uro, G. (1997). Education reform in the United States: National policy in support of local efforts for school improvement. *American Psychologist, 52*(3), 243-252.

Trimble, S. (2002). Common elements of high performing, high poverty middle schools. *Middle School Journal, 33*(4), 7-16.

Urban Schools: The Challenge of Location and Poverty. (1996). (NCES Report 96-184). Washington, DC: National Center for Education Statistics. Retrieved December 6, 2003, from http://nces.ed.gov/pubs/96184.html

Viadero, D. (2000a). Lags in minority achievement defy traditional explanations. *Education Week, 19*(28), 1, 18–22.

Viadero, D. (2000b). Minority gaps smaller in some Pentagon schools. *Education Week, 19*(29), pp. 1, 20–21.

Viadero, D. (2003). Study probes factors fueling achievement gap. *Education Week, 23*(13), pp. 1, 12.

Viadero, D., & Johnston, R. C. (2000). Lifting minority achievement: Complex answers. *Education Week, 19*(30), 1, 14–16.

Wang, M. C., & Kovach, J. A. (1995). Bridging the achievement gap in urban schools: Reducing educational segregation and advancing resilience-promoting strategies. In B. Williams (Ed.), *Closing the achievement gap: A vision to guide change in beliefs and practice* (pp. 9–24). Philadelphia: Research for Better Schools.

Wheelock, A. (1992). *Crossing the tracks: How "untracking" can save American schools.* New York: The New Press.

Zeichner, K. M. (1995). Educating teachers to close the achievement gap: Issues of pedagogy, knowledge, and teacher preparation. In B. Williams (Ed.), *Closing the achievement gap: A vision to guide change in beliefs and practice* (pp. 39–52). Philadelphia: Research for Better Schools.

—Cathy Carter
The University of Georgia

ACHIEVEMENT TESTS

Horace Mann, secretary of the State Board of Education in Massachusetts, used standardized achievement tests as early as the 1840s to monitor the state's school systems. In the 1920s interests in the scientific movement brought standardized assessments to the nation's attention and by the end of the 1960s state and federal testing became a very important accountability measure (Pearson, Vyas, Sensale, & Kim, 2001). The No Child Left Behind Act of 2001 (NCLB) requires that all states in the nation administer annual tests to students in the third through eighth grades. These achievement tests are accountability measures, which aim at raising standards and student performance. Test results are then distributed to state, district, and local schools and oftentimes have overwhelming influence on students' placement and promotion. The accountability influences attached to these tests have raised concerns about this type of measurement and its impact on teaching and learning (Amrein & Berliner, 2003; Braun, 2004).

NCLB requires that all schools administer standardized achievement tests to students in grades three through eight in reading, language arts, and math by the year 2005-2006 and to students in grades three through five in science at least once and then once again in one of the grades six through nine by the year 2007-2008. This includes all students, even limited-English-proficient students (LEP), who for the first 3 years will be allowed to have a test in their first language. Also, of important note is that learning disabled students will be included in this testing with possible adaptations and accommodations, such as extra time for testing. High-stakes tests, which determine whether a student will go on to the next grade or even graduate, focus on every child in the school system including students with disabilities. Protected by the Individuals with Disabilities Education Act (IDEA) of 1975, students with disabilities by law have access to appropriate accommodations in instruction and assessments. Concurrently, the federal mandates for testing all students provide for access to opportunities without discrimination based on disability (Albrecht & Joles, 2003).

TYPES OF ACHIEVEMENT TESTS

Norm referenced tests and criterion referenced tests are two types of achievement tests. Norm referenced tests (NRTs) compare a person's score against the scores of a group of people who have already taken the same exam. Criterion reference tests (CRTs) measure a student's performance as compared to specifically identified grade-level criteria. This measure allows students, parents, and schools to compare the effectiveness of instruction and learning of the body of intended knowledge and skills. NRT content is based on national standards and curriculum and is usually presented in multiple-choice form, possibly including open-ended, short-answer questions. Some examples of NRTs are the California Achievement Test (CAT), Comprehensive Test of Basic Skills (CTBS), Iowa Test of Basic Skills (ITBS), and the Metropolitan Achievement Test (MAT).

The National Assessment of Educational Practice (NAEP) is a criterion-referenced test. Scores on the NAEP are arranged in three categories: basic, proficient, and advanced. The NAEP was first administered in 1969 and is commonly known as the "The Nation's Report Card." NAEP is a federally mandated assessment, which was created by the U.S. Department of Education. It is the only nationally represen-

tative achievement test and has continued since 1969. The examination measures academic achievement of 4th, 8th, and 12th grade students in reading, writing, mathematics, science, geography, civics, the arts, and other fields. Tests in math and reading are given more often than those for other subjects. It provides a state or national assessment of skills and knowledge among students of a small random sampling of each state. It also provides a rich database of educational performance and student demographics, as well as state ranking comparisons, but does not allow for comparison across schools. Calkins, Montgomery, and Santman (1998) explain that concern for low NAEP and state testing reading scores often results in a spontaneous reaction by school districts to attempt to provide what are thought to be immediate solutions.

SUPPORT FOR TESTS

Quality achievement testing can bring about academic success if the following are present: response to instruction and further assessment, distribution and explanation of test results in a timely manner, test data that are in a form that educators can understand and utilize to improve instruction, clear indicators to identify students' strengths and weaknesses, and the same achievement standards for everyone regardless of ethnic or cultural differences (Gandal & McGiffert, 2003). Achievement tests contain specific tasks and procedures, which measure specific skills and formal learning (Sattler, 2001) and are constructed so that school districts in all locations can discover how their students compare academically with students in other school districts. Standardized achievement tests are relatively inexpensive, can be easily mandated by policy makers, can be rapidly implemented, and the results are usually clearly understood (Barton, 1999).

Federal mandates have established yearly measurements of academic achievement in the core subjects with many parents pleased to have academic reports about their childrens' progress each year (Education Trust, 2003). These annual assessments allow parents and school personnel to tract students' progress, to give support to students quickly, and to suggest extra instruction in order to strengthen specific weaknesses and to prevent future academic problems. Testing requirements of NCLB do not include conditions for promotion or graduation (Education Trust, 2003).

CHALLENGES TO TESTING

It is extremely important that educators follow the curriculum, and ultimately plan, present, and assess educational content based on the standards, where success or failure is determined by multiple assessments and not solely on one measure (Barton, 1999; National Forum to Accelerate Middle-Grades Reform, 2002; Wiggins, 1993). Alternate assessments other than standardized tests may include portfolios, exhibitions, performances, demonstrations, and formative or classroom tests that measure how well students achieve state standards.

Some researchers (Amrein & Berliner, 2003; Bracey, 2003; National Forum, 2002; Neill, 2003) suggest that educators should focus on formative assessment practices that encourage quality teaching and higher-level learning, not only measurements that are easy and quick, such as multiple choice. When test scores are used to determine success or failure of schooling, often called high-stakes tests, many understand this to mean that they must teach to the tests (Stake, 2002). High-stakes testing (Amrein & Berliner, 2003; Jacob, 2001; Neill, 2003) has not improved academic achievement; is associated with higher dropout rates, because of fear of not graduating or not being promoted; is causing good teachers to leave the profession (Droege, 2004), and is not a reliable measure of individual student achievement (Heubert & Hauser, 1999; Linn, 2000). Some believe that the ones being assessed are the teachers, which sometimes leads to job loss or cuts in salary (Wiggins, 1993). These tests (Barton, 1999) have produced numbers and quantitative data, but do not add to teachers' and schools' improvement of student performance. Barton (1999) suggests that a random sampling, such as the NAEP tests, administered every four years, would be just as effective as annual testing of all students.

Debate about the influence of these tests on student achievement is ongoing due to the observational nature of student achievement and translating the data from tests into actual measurements of student learning and school ratings (Braun, 2004; Raymond & Hanushek, 2003). Some report that there has been no improvement on NAEP scores and no measurable improvement in student learning as a result of high-stakes testing policies, even with states, which have shown improvement on their own state tests (Amrein & Berliner, 2003; Linn, 2000) and others who disagree with this conclusion and who suggests that these assessments need refining and not exclusion from accountability measures (Braun, 2004; Raymond & Hanushek, 2003).

FACTORS INFLUENCING ACHIEVEMENT TESTS SCORES

There are multiple factors which influence academic success in achievement scores in middle school, such as, individual, family, school, and community factors (Mulhall, Flowers, & Mertens, 2002). In addition to understanding that these factors are indeed extremely important to student development and well-being, we know very little about how these factors play into the school environment; specifically, the students' culture, motivation, interests, and their instructional experiences (Alexander, 2000). Parental involvement has repeatedly demonstrated positive results in achievement test results (Desimone, 1999). Children from middle-class families tend to score higher than lower-socioeconomic class families and also attain higher levels of education (Hanson, 1994). Girls generally score higher than boys on standardized tests (Halpern, 2002). School systems have witnessed the effects of public support and community efforts on student achievement.

REFLECTIONS

Federal legislation and mandates for high stakes testing have placed added challenges before middle school faculties as they strive to improve student performance. As measures and guidelines are imposed, little direction and support in implementation of achievement strategies is given to those who are closest to the students (Meier, 2002).

REFERENCES

Albrecht, S. F., & Joles, C. (2003). Accountability and access to opportunity: Mutually exclusive tenets under a high-stakes testing mandate. *Preventing School Failure, 47*(2), 86-91.

Alexander, P. A. (2000). Toward a model of academic development: Schooling and the acquisition of knowledge. *Educational Researcher, 4,* 28-33.

Amrein, A. L., & Berliner, D. C. (2003). The effects of high-stakes testing on student motivation and learning. *Educational Leadership, 60*(5), 32-38.

Barton, P. E. (1999). Too much testing of the wrong kind; Too little of the right kind in K-12 education. Princeton, NJ: Educational Testing Service.

Bracey, G. W. (2003). The 13th Bracey Report on the condition of public education. *Phi Delta Kappan, 85*(2), 148-164.

Braun, H. (2004). Reconsidering the impact of high-stakes testing. *Education Policy Analysis Archives, 12*(1). Retrieved June 20, 2004, from http://www.epaa.asu.edu/epaa/v12n1/

Calkins, L., Montgomery, K., & Santman, D. (1998). *A teacher's guide to standardizedrReading tests: Knowledge is power.* Portsmouth, NH: Heinemann.

Desimone, L. (1999). Linking parent involvement with student achievement: Do race and income matter? *The Journal of Educational Research, 93*(1), 11-30.

Droege, K. L. (2004) Turning accountability on its head: Supporting inspired teaching in today's classroom. *Phi Delta Kappan, 85*(8), 610

Education Trust. (2003). *Fact sheet #2.* Retrieved July 1, from http://www2.edtrust.org/NR/rdonlyres/82FA87DD-62D2-415E-8426-32FD14CF2EF8/0/factsheetrev4.pdf

Gandal, M., & McGiffert, L. (2003). The power of testing. *Educational Leadership, 60*(5), 39-42.

Halpern, D. F. (2002). Sex differences in achievement scores: Can we design assessments that are fair, meaningful, and valid for girls and boys? *Issues in Education, 8*(1), 2-18.

Hanson, S. L. (1994). Lost talent: Unrealized educational aspirations and expectations of U.S. youths. *Sociology of Education, 67,* 159-183.

Heubert, J. P., & Hauser, R. M. (1999). *High stakes: Testing for tracking, promotion, and graduation.* Washington, DC: National Academy Press.

Jacob, B. (2001). Getting tough? The impact of high school graduation exams. *Educational Evaluation and Policy Analysis, 23*(2), 99-121.

Linn, R. (2000). Assessment and accountability. *Educational Researcher, 29*(2), 4-16.

Meier, D. (2002). Standardization versus standards. *Phi Delta Kappan, 84*(3), 190-198.

Mulhall, P. F., Flowers, N., & Mertens, S. (2002). Understanding indicators related to academic performance. *Middle School Journal, 34*(2), 56-61.

National Forum to Accelerate Middle-Grades Reform. (2002, July). *Position statement of the National Forum to Accelerate Middle Grades Reform. High-stakes testing.* Issue 3. Retrieved May 24, 2005, from http://www.nmsa.org/news/positionpapers/highstakestesting_nationalforum.htm

Neill, M. (2003). The dangers of testing. *Educational Leadership, 60*(5), 43-46.

No Child Left Behind Act of 2001. (2001). Public Law 107-110, 107th Cong, Cong. Rec. 1425. (enacted 2002). Washington, DC: U.S. Department of Education Web site: www.ed.gov./offices/OESE/esea

Pearson, P. D., Vyas, S. , Sensale, L .M., & Kim, Y. (2001). Making our way through the assessment and accountability maze: Where do we go now? *The Clearing House, 74*(4), 175-182.

Raymond, M. E., & Hanushek, E. A. (2003). High-stakes research. *Education Next, 3*(3), 48-55. Retreived June 4, 2004, from http://www.educationnext.org

Sattler, J. M. (2001). *Assessment of children: Cognitive applications* (4th ed.). La Mesa, CA: Author.

Stake, R. E. (2002). Teachers conceptualizing student achievement. *Teachers & Teaching: Theory and Practice, 8*(3/4), 303-372.

Wiggins, G. P. (1993). *Assessing student performance: Exploring the purposes and limits of testing.* San Francisco: Jossey-Bass.

—Shirley Theriot
University of Texas, Arlington

ADMINISTRATORS: MIDDLE LEVEL PRINCIPALS

Almost all educational reform reports have come to the conclusion that the nation cannot attain excellence in education without effective school leadership. We know that effective school leaders: (1) recognize teaching and learning as the main business of school, (2) communicate the school's mission and vision clearly and consistently to all constituents, (3) promote an atmosphere of trust and collaboration, and (4) emphasize professional development (see Bauck, 1987; George & Grebing, 1992; Weller, 1999). Despite the consensus that leadership counts, deep philosophical and political disagreements remain about what kind of educational leaders are needed, what knowledge and skills they should possess, and how they should be professionally prepared. Many policymakers criticize the preparation of school administrators in colleges and universities as outmoded and ineffective, unable to address adequately the complexities found in schools.

As middle level education enters the twenty-first century new questions need to be asked and old ones revisited. Middle level principals are essential to current school reform initiatives; yet rhetoric about their importance is often unaccompanied by sufficient attention to the new knowledge and skills they need or how they might acquire these through professional development.

There is a lack of research focused on the middle level principal. Between 1981 and 1983 the National Association of Secondary School principals (NASSP) conducted a national study of the middle level principalship which resulted in two publications. *The Middle Level Principalship, Volume I. A Survey of Middle Level Principals and Programs* (Valentine, Clark, Nickerson, & Keefe, 1981) and *The Middle Level Principalship, Volume II. The Effective Middle Level Principal* (Keefe, Clark, Nickerson, & Valentine, 1983). Analyzing the data from these two studies, Bauck (1987) attempted to determine the difference and similarities between typical and effective middle level principals. He concluded that while effective middle level teachers are teacher oriented and encourage parent and community involvement in the school, they do not feel that formal education or participation in professional organizations have contributed to their success.

Following these two publications Valentine and his associates have published three additional studies for the National Association of Secondary School Principals. In 1993 *Leadership in Middle Level Education: Volume I. A National Survey of Middle Level Leaders in*

Schools (Valentine, Clark, Irvin, Keefe, & Melton, 1993) was released. In 2002 *A National Study of Leadership in Middle Level Schools: Volume I. National Study of Middle Level Leaders and School Programs* (Valentine, Clark, Hackman, & Petzko, 2002) was published. More recently, in 2003 *A National Study of Leadership in Middle Level Schools: Volume 2. A National Study of Highly Successful Leaders and Schools* (Valentine, Clark, Hackman, Lucas, & Petzko, 2003) was published.

Kilcrease (1995), in her study of middle level principals, concluded that administrators performed three broad functions that enabled them to be successful: (1) providing a program especially adapted to diverse student needs, (2) promoting continuity of education, and (3) introducing needed innovations in curriculum and instruction. In addition, middle level administrators must have the skills to ensure that teaming and shared decision making processes work well in the school (George & Grebing, 1992). Not surprisingly, several theorists and researchers assert that middle level principals should be knowledgeable about young adolescents, their development, and their learning styles (Eichhorn, 1966; George, 1990; Schmidt, 1998). The reform literature (i.e., National Middle School's, 2003, *This We Believe: Successful Schools for Young Adolescents*) also strongly advocates that middle level principals possess a special set of skills, knowledge, and dispositions appropriate for middle grades students.

The literature about the personal nature of middle level principals is not usually research based; however, it sets forth such expectations as personal confidence (Rubenstein, 1990), trustworthiness (Tarter, 1995), and instructional leadership (Williamson, 1991). Neufeld (1997) asserted that middle level principals, especially those in urban schools, can reform schools if they transform themselves from managers to leaders. Montgomery (1995) concurs that principals working with teachers can make great changes. "If only the principal will grow, the school will grow. To change something, someone has to change first" (Barth, 1985, p. 92). Hipp (1997) extends the idea of principal and teacher collaboration and makes suggestions for principals to reinforce teacher efficacy. These suggestions include, among others (1) modeling behavior, (2) promoting teacher empowerment and decision making, (3) managing student behavior, (4) creating a positive climate for success, and (5) inspiring respectful and caring relationships.

PERFORMANCE STANDARDS FOR ADMINISTRATORS

Many professional organizations have developed performance standards that are meant to govern the work of school administrators. These organizations include the American Association of School Administrators (AASA), the National Policy Board for Educational Administration (NPBEA) and the Interstate School Leadership Licensure Consortium (ISLLC). ISLLC standards have been widely adopted by states across the nation and successful completion of an examination, the School Leaders Licensure Assessment (SLLA), has become part of the process of obtaining administrative licensure.

Of all of the national organizations that focus on school administrators only one has turned its attention on middle schools. In 1986 (revised 1991 and 1997) the National Association of Elementary School Principals (NAESP) published *Elementary and Middle School Proficiencies for Principals*. NAESP recognized that middle level schools are extremely complex organization that requires a wide range of leadership proficiencies. While NAESP notes that it is unrealistic to expect that all principals will possess all of the proficiencies cited in the report, an outstanding principal is characterized by 96 proficiencies. These include: (1) involves the school community in identifying and accomplishing the school's mission; (2) recognizes the individual needs and contributions of all staff and students; (3) applies effective interpersonal skills; (4) conducts needs assessments; (5) advances the profession through participation in professional organizations; (6) uses active listening skills; (7) works to build consensus; (8) understands group dynamics; (9) maintains a visible presence in the classrooms; (10) engages the staff in the study of effective teaching practices; and (11) uses effective strategies to deal with political forces that affect the school (NAESP, 1997, p. 3).

In addition to these proficiencies NAESP also identified four prerequisites for success as an elementary and middle level leader. These include: (1) an advanced understanding of the teaching and learning processes; (2) a thorough understanding of child growth and development; (3) a broad base of knowledge, including a solid background in the liberal arts; and (4) a sincere commitment to educational equity and excellence.

MIDDLE LEVEL PRINCIPAL PRESERVICE PREPARATION

Currently, few middle level principals are specifically prepared to work with young adolescents and most have not received any formal preparation in the instructional and organizational needs of a middle school. In 2002 Gaskill reported only seven states with special certification programs for middle level principals: Alaska, Kentucky, Massachusetts, Missouri,

Nebraska, Ohio, and Oklahoma. Only five of the seven states require the middle level credential. A closer examination of the programs offered in these states reveals a troublesome finding. Many of these states require only that the internship (field experience) is completed in a middle school. A well-designed program that one would expect and that truly addresses the needs of a middle school principal does not exist. Currently, the trend in administrative preparation at colleges and universities is to offer generic K-12 certification programs.

In 1997, Haller, Brent, and McNamara noted that "overall, our reading of the limited literature on this subject suggest that there is little evidence that graduate training increases the effectiveness of school managers" (p. 224). According to the candid remarks of the middle school principals in a study conducted by Anfara, Brown, Mills, Hartman, and Mahar (2000), formal college/university coursework was not perceived to be a major influence in middle level principals' acquisition of essential skills. Many middle level principals describe their pre-service preparation as inadequate, impractical, and unrealistic. Several principals commented about the disconnection between what they were taught and what they needed to know in the world of practice. Interestingly enough, the middle school principals who participated in the Anfara et al. study were not willing to go as far as calling for specific middle level certification/licensure.

Middle Level Principal Professional Development

The primary purpose of professional development for school administrators is to increase professional and personal effectiveness while simultaneously increasing organizational effectiveness. For middle school principals this purpose is even more urgent in light of the context in which they work and the knowledge and skills that are deemed essential for creating effective middle schools. Issues related to the professional development of middle school administrators are rooted in the preparation programs that have been criticized in recent years (Murphy, 1992). Unfortunately, the professional development of middle level administrators is reported to be in even worse shape than the initial preparation (Hallinger & Murphy, 1991).

Securing an administrative certification by completing a graduate degree has often been viewed as the end of formal training with subsequent professional development being hit or miss. If today's middle level principals want to be effective and escape the ever-present danger of professional obsolescence,

they must regularly participate in appropriate professional development. Daresh and Playko (1992) admit, "it takes hard work to learn the art, science, and craft of educational administration, and it takes a similar amount of hard work to keep the needed leadership skills well tuned over time" (p. xi).

A review of the literature on the professional development of middle level principals reveals descriptors such as "wasteland," "meager," "neglected," "poverty stricken," and "deplorable." Based on the interview data in the Brown, Anfara, Hartman, Mahar, and Mill study (2001), middle school principals do not believe that their school districts or professional organizations provide the necessary opportunities for them to learn what they need to know to effectively lead a middle school and implement reform initiative at both school and classroom levels. When asked what they wanted to learn from professional development, middle level principals in the Brown et al. study reported: (1) creating a respectful, collaborative, and collegial school culture; (2) understanding, implementing, and assessing newly proposed approaches to teaching and learning; (3) remaining up-to-date with the legal, financial, and technological issues related to their schools; and (4) understanding the nature of young adolescents and its implications for schooling, and the meaning of the term "developmentally appropriate."

Many of the participants in the Brown et al. (2001) study recognized the importance of conferences, presentations, and a wide variety of opportunities offered by professional associations. They look to professional organizations to help them develop a greater sense of efficacy, a sense that they are capable of learning, improving, and gaining insights. They would like to see national, regional, and state middle level associations consider collaborative efforts in establishing approved programs that would meet both administrative standards (i.e., Interstate School Leaders Licensure Consortium) while simultaneously addressing relevant and practical learning opportunities.

We must continue to explore and discuss issues surrounding the preservice preparation and professional development of middle level principals. The challenges that an administrator faces in a middle school are great.

References

Anfara. V. A., Jr., Brown, K. M., Mills, R., Hartman, K. J., & Mahar, R. J. (2000, April). *Middle level leadership for the 21st century: Principals' views on essential skills and knowledge, Implications for successful preparation*. Paper presented at the annual meeting of the American Educational Research Association. New Orleans, LA.

Barth, R. (1985). The leader as learner. *Educational Leadership, 42*(6), 92-93.

Bauck, J. (1987). Characteristics of the effective middle school principal. *NASSP Bulletin, 71*(500), 90-92.

Brown, K. M., Anfara, V. A., Jr., Hartman, K. J., Mahar, R. J., & Mills, R. (2001, April). *Professional development of middle level principals: Pushing the reform forward.* Paper presented at the annual meeting of the American Educational Research Association. Seattle, WA.

Daresh, J., & Playko, M. (1992). The professional development of school administrators: Preservice, induction, and inservice applications. Boston, MA: Allyn & Bacon.

Eichhorn, D. (1966). *The middle school.* New York: The Center for Applied Research in Education.

Gaskill, P. (2002). Progress in certification of middle level personnel. *Middle School Journal, 33*(5), 33-40.

George, P. (1990). From junior high to middle school—Principals' perspectives. *NASSP Bulletin, 74*, 86-94.

George, P., & Grebing, W. (1992). Seven essential skills of middle level leadership. *Schools in the Middle, 1*(4), 3-11.

Haller, E., Brent, B., & McNamara, J. (1997). Does graduate training in educational administration improve America's schools? *Phi Delta Kappan, 79*(3), 222-227.

Hallinger, P., & Murphy, J. (1991). Developing leaders for tomorrow's schools. *Phi Delta Kappan, 72*(7), 514-520.

Hipp, K. (1997). The impact of principals in sustaining middle school change. *Middle School Journal, 28*(2), 42-45.

Keefe, J., Clark, D., Nickerson, N., & Valentine, J. (1983). *The middle level principalship: Volume II. The effective middle level principal.* Reston, VA: National Association of Secondary School Principals.

Kilcrease, A. (1995, November). *Principals' perceptions of the functions and characteristics of middle schools in Mississippi.* Paper presented at the annual meeting of the Mid-South Educational Research Association. Biloxi, MS.

Montgomery, J. (1995). From K-3 to junior high: A principal's challenge. *Principal, 74*, 51-53.

Murphy. J. (1992). *The landscape of leadership preparation: Reframing the education of school administrators.* Newbury Park, CA: Corwin Press.

National Association of Elementary School Principals. (1997). *Elementary & middle school proficiencies for principals* (3rd ed.). Alexandria, VA: Author.

National Middle School Association. (2003). *This we believe: Successful schools for young adolescents.* Westerville, OH: Author.

Neufield, B. (1997). Responding to the expressed needs of urban middle school principals. *Urban Education, 31*(5), 490-510.

Rubenstein, R. (1990). A teacher's view of the quality principal. *Educational Horizons, 66*, 151-152.

Schmidt, D. (1998). Do squirrely kids need squirrely administrators? *Principal, 68*, 48-53.

Tarter, J. (1995). Middle school climate, faculty trust, and effectiveness: A path analysis. *Journal of Research and Development in Education, 29*, 41-49.

Valentine, J., Clark, D., Nickerson, N., Jr., & Keefe, J. (1981). *The middle level principalship: Vol. 1. A survey of middle level principals and programs.* Reston, VA: National Association of Secondary School Principals.

Valentine, Clark, D., Irvin, J., Keefe, J., & Melton, G. (1993). *Leadership in middle level education: Vol. 1. A national survey of middle level leaders in schools.* Reston, VA: National Association of Secondary School Principals.

Valentine, J. W., Clark, D. C., Hackman, D. G., & Petzko, V. N. (2002). *A national study of leadership in middle level schools: Vol 1. A national study of middle level leaders and school programs.* Reston, VA: National Association of Secondary School Principals.

Valentine, J. W., Clark, D. C., Hackman, D.G., Lucas, S. L., & Petzko, V. N. (2003). *A national study of leadership in middle level schools: Vol. 2. A national study of highly successful leaders and schools.* Reston, VA: National Association of Secondary School Principals.

Weller, L. (1999). *Quality middle school leadership: Eleven central skill areas.* Lancaster, PA: Technomic.

Williamson, R. (1991). Leadership at the middle level. In J. Capelluti & D. Stokes (Eds.), *Middle level education: Program, policies, and practices* (pp. 36-41). Alexandria, VA: National Association of Secondary School Principals.

—Vincent A. Anfara, Jr.
The University of Tennessee

ADVISORY PROGRAMS

According to *This We Believe: Successful Schools for Young Adolescents* (National Middle School Association, 2003), middle schools should provide an adult advocate to address the academic and affective needs of every student. The official position statement of the National Middle School Association (NMSA) notes, "Therefore, all adults in developmentally responsive middle level schools are advocates, advisors, and mentors" (p. 16). This entry focuses on one aspect of the advocacy that is needed—the advisor-advisee program.

Beane and Lipka (1987) offered the following description of advisory programs:

> Advisory programs are designed to deal directly with the affective needs of transescents. Activities may range from non-formal interactions to use of systematically developed units whose organizing center are drawn from the common problems, needs, interests, or concerns of transescents, such as "getting along with peers," "living in the school," or "developing self-concept." In the best of these programs, transescents have an opportunity to get to know one adult really well, to find a point of security in the institu-

tion, and to learn about what it means to be a healthy human being. (p. 40)

The NMSA (2003) recognizes that in the context of a caring environment "the advisor is the primary liaison between the school and family and often initiates contact with parents, providing pertinent information about the student's program and progress" (p. 17).

While recent research points to positive results of advisory programs (Connors, 1991; Mac Iver, 1990; Putbrese, 1989; Vars, 1989), it remains one of the most difficult of the middle level concepts to implement (Fenwick, 1992; Lounsbury & Clark, 1990). Many advisory programs are not functioning as they were initially intended and have simply taken the place of homeroom. Because of the tremendous potential of the middle school concept to contribute to the improvement of schools and their students' intellectual growth, it is most important to investigate the current status, strengths, and shortcomings of advisory programs.

While there is still a need for considerably more research about the effectiveness of advisory programs (Clark & Clark, 1994), some of the most frequently mentioned purposes of advisories include:

1. promoting opportunities for social development,
2. assisting students with academic problems,
3. facilitating positive involvement between teachers and administrators and students,
4. providing an adult advocate for each student in the school, and
5. promoting positive school climate (Clark & Clark, 1994, pp. 135-136).

Regarding the effectiveness of such programs, Mac Iver (1990) found that when teacher advisories focused on social and academic support activities that a strong relationship existed to the reduction of dropouts. Connors (1986) found evidence that advisory programs helped students grow emotionally and socially, contributed to a positive school climate, helped students learn about school and get along with their classmates, and enhanced teacher-student relationships. George and Oldaker (1985) suggested that when advisory programs are combined with other components of the middle school concept that student self-concept improves, dropout rates decrease, and school climate becomes more positive.

While these studies focus on the possible positive effects of advisory programs, we are warned that schools have a very difficult time both implementing and sustaining this component of middle school

reform (Fenwick, 1992; Lounsbury & Clark, 1990). A number of studies (Batsell, 1995; Bunte, 1995; Dale, 1993; Lee, 1995; Mosidi, 1994) addressed the issue of implementation of advisory programs. Findings from these research projects note that successful implementation must address issues related to staff capacity, professional development, technical/administrative support, limiting the number of students (15-20) in each advisory, differing expectations on the part of teachers and administrators, the allotment of time to advisory periods as well as to teacher planning, a well defined advisory curriculum, a feedback/maintenance loop for program review and revision, the transformation of the school's cultural norms, and the management of organizational politics.

Some researchers provide their readers with sample program development time lines (Ayres, 1994) or a listing of the "Ten Steps to a Successful Advisory Program" (Hertzog, 1992). Others suggest what the critical program features are (see Table 1) and how best to prepare teachers for their role in the program (Gill & Read, 1990; James, 1986).

Few researchers have systematically probed the subjective experiences of participants in advisory programs as disclosed by both students and teachers. Exploring the everyday experiences of middle school teachers, Anfara and Brown (2001), utilizing qualitative methods, found that:

- caring was perceived to be women's work,
- some teachers feared relating to students in the affective domain,
- battle lines were drawn between teachers and administrators over the implementation of advisory programs,
- there was a fine line between student mingling and teacher meddling, and
- teachers unwilling to effectively implement advisory programs moved from being "attention providers" to "detention givers" (see pp. 12-22).

The rationale for middle school advisory programs is multifaceted. Alexander and George (1981) noted that "Teachers need this type of involvement no less than students. Since most teachers really do seem to have a deep felt need to make a significant positive difference in the lives of their student, and the daily demands of the classroom often seem to make this difficult or impossible, the advisor-advisee program provides teachers with an opportunity to get to know some manageable number of students in a meaningful way" (p. 90).

Table 1
Components of Successful Advisor-Advisee Programs:
Rationale, Design, and Emphasis

Rationale for Advisor-Advisee Programs
　　Promote small, caring communities of learners
　　Promote mutually respectful and meaningful relationships
　　Provide individual attention to students
　　Provide each student with an opportunity to "belong"
　　Allow teachers to be actively involved in the affective development of students
　　Emphasize the social and emotional development of every young adolescent
　　Assist students with interpersonal communication skills development

Design of Advisor-Advisee Programs
　　Need careful organizing, planning, preparing, implementing and monitoring
　　Need guidance department, administration, and district-level support
　　Need teacher, parent, student input and active involvement
　　Need teachers/advisors trained and committed to teaching young adolescents
　　Need relevant, ongoing professional development opportunities
　　Number of meetings per week—scheduled daily and/or regularly
　　Length of advisory meetings—20 to 40 minutes, uninterrupted
　　Time of day advisories scheduled—morning, flexible
　　Number of students assigned to advisory groups—10 to 20 students
　　Assigning students—see advisor during the course of the day

Emphasis of Advisor-Advisee Programs
　　Based on teacher and student input
　　Based on the affective domain
　　Address needs of specific school and community
　　Social/Communication/Positive interpersonal relationships
　　Respect for self and others/Good citizen
　　Accepting responsibility for education and actions
　　Develop group, team, and school spirit
　　Academic monitoring/Assistance/Motivation
　　Study, test-taking, and note-taking, and skills instruction
　　Self-esteem activities/Self-awareness growth
　　Appreciating talents, health, and potential
　　Understanding and making commitments
　　Decision making/Coping skills/Problem solving
　　Career education/Guidance/Future planning
　　Setting and obtaining goals/Organizing time
　　Intramural activities/Community service projects
　　School issues and concerns/Adjustments
　　Substance abuse/Current adolescent issues

SOME PRACTICAL SUGGESTIONS

Lessons from the "the field" point to the following suggestions to assist in the development and implementation of a successful advisory program:

1. develop both short and long range goals;
2. be cognizant of students', teachers', and parents' needs;
3. provide for initial and ongoing staff training and development;
4. provide an orientation for students, teachers, and parents;
5. honor small teacher-student ratios;
6. structure advisory time in the daily schedule of the school;
7. be aware of school climate/culture;
8. involve students, teachers, and parents in the planning phase; and
9. respect teachers' and students' right to privacy.

Despite an expanding amount of literature on advisory programs, additional research is needed on the development, implementation, and sustainability of this programmatic component. It remains one of the hardest elements of the middle school concept to effectively implement.

REFERENCES

Alexander, W., & George, P. (1981). *The exemplary middle school*. New York: Holt, Reinhart, and Winston.

Anfara, V., & Brown, K. (2001). Advisor-advisee programs: Community building in a state of affective disorder? In V. A. Anfara, Jr. (Ed.), *The handbook of research in middle level education* (pp.3-34). Greenwich, CT: Information Age.

Ayres, L. (1994). Middle school advisory programs: Findings from the field. *Middle School Journal, 25*(3), 8-14.

Batsell, G. (1995). *Progress toward implementation of developmentally responsive practice in Arizona middle level schools, 1989-1994*. Unpublished doctoral dissertation, University of Arizona.

Beane, J., & Lipka, R. (1987). *When kids come first: Enhancing self-esteem*. Columbus, OH: National Middle School Association.

Bunte, A. (1995). *Success factors in the implementation of advisory programs in selected Illinois middle schools*. Unpublished doctoral dissertation, Southern Illinois University at Carbondale.

Clark, S., & Clark, D. (1994). *Restructuring the middle level school: Implications for school leaders*. Albany: State University of New York Press.

Connors, N. (1986). *A case study to determine the essential components and effects of an advisor/advisee program in an exemplary middle school*. Unpublished doctoral dissertation. Florida State University, Tallahassee, FL.

Connors, N. (1991). Teacher advisory: The fourth r. In J. L. Irvin (Ed.), *Transforming middle level education: Perspectives and possibilities* (pp. 162-178). Needham Heights, MA: Allyn & Bacon.

Dale, P. (1993). *Leadership, development, and organization of an advisor/advisee program: A comparative case study of two middle schools*. Unpublished doctoral dissertation, Fordham University, New York.

Fenwick, J. (1992). *Managing middle grade reform—An "American 2000" agenda*. San Diego, CA: Fenwick and Associates.

George, P., & Oldaker, L. (1985). *Evidence for the middle school*. Columbus, OH: National Middle School Association.

Gill, J., & Read, E. (1990). The experts comment on advisor-advisee programs. *Middle School Journal, 21*(5), 31-33.

Hertzog, C. (1992). Middle level advisory programs: From the ground up. *Schools in the Middle, 2*(1), 23-27.

James, M. (1986). *Adviser-advisee programs: Why, what, and how*. Columbus, OH: National Middle School Association.

Lee, S. (1995). *Implementing the teacher advisory program at the middle school: A case study of technical, normative and political perspectives of change*. Unpublished doctoral dissertation, University of California, Los Angeles.

Lounsbury, J., & Clark, D. (1990). *Inside grade eight: From apathy to excitement*. Reston, VA: National Association of Secondary School Principals.

Mac Iver, D. (1990). Meeting the needs of young adolescents: Advisory groups, interdisciplinary teaching teams, and school transition programs. *Phi Delta Kappan, 71*(6), 458-464.

Mosidi, M. (1994). *A qualitative study of the process of implementing the advisor-advisee program in a school setting.* Unpublished doctoral dissertation. The University of Toledo.

National Middle School Association. (2003). *This we believe: Successful schools for young adolescents*. Westerville, OH: Author.

Putbrese, L. (1989). Advisory programs at the middle level— The students' response. *NASSP Bulletin, 73*(514), 111-115.

Vars, G. (1989). A new/old look at the needs of transescents. *Transescence, 9*(2), 15.

—Vincent A. Anfara, Jr.
The University of Tennessee

AFFECTIVE DEVELOPMENT

INTRODUCTION

Children between the ages of 11 and 14 are known to educators, researchers, and administrators as young adolescents (Stevenson, 2002), and they undergo more physical, cognitive, emotional, and social changes during that time period than at any other time in their lives with the exception of infancy (Eccles & Wigfield, 1997). Although middle school educators have primarily been interested in the cognitive growth of young adolescents, the 1990s saw increased attention to other aspects of their development (National Middle School Association, 2003). These aspects include social and emotional needs and issues, otherwise known as affective development.

Because the most intense physical, cognitive, emotional, and social changes occur when young adolescents are typically in Grades 6-8, middle schools focus on creating environments that address all of these developmental issues. In *This We Believe*, the National Middle School Association (NMSA) encourages middle school educators to create environments that not only challenge students academically but also respond to the unique developmental needs of young adolescents (NMSA, 2003). Teachers who are familiar with the changes young adolescents undergo between the ages of 11 and 14 (approximately) are able to address their social and emotional issues as well as fostering cognitive growth.

WHAT IS AFFECT?

A student's social and emotional well-being can also be called the affective state. When used as a noun, the term affect refers to a feeling or emotion. A person's affective status is generally measured or observed through facial expressions or body language

(Merriam Webster, 2004). Affect is influenced by contextual factors such as success or failure in school or on the job, feedback one receives from any given experience, and personal relationships, in other words, an individual's environment (Lipka, 1997). One's sense of competence and the ability to control what happens to him/her (Deci, 1995), which is known as self-efficacy, also acts on the affective state. When an individual feels competent, loved, and has a good sense of self-efficacy (Daniels & Arapostathis, 2005), he/she has a positive affect. Self-efficacy in students is evident when they willingly attempt challenging assignments or take risks with their learning. They exert effort because they feel in control of the outcome, which is evidence of a positive affect. In middle school students, their affective state is at least as important, if not more so, than their cognitive abilities in terms of academic success (Daniels, 2004; Perlstein, 2003).

Self-concept and self-esteem also determine an individual's affective state. Self-concept is how people perceive their abilities and intelligence while self-esteem describes how they feel about those abilities and that intelligence (Lipka, 1997). While self-esteem places a value judgment on ability, self-concept is a neutral assessment of strengths and weaknesses (Lipka, 1997). Students with high self-esteem capitalize on their strengths and do not view their weaknesses as detrimental to their overall well-being and success.

Social and Emotional Needs

As they enter adolescence, children's reasoning ability and cognitive capacity rapidly develop in complexity, and they need coaching and guidance as they learn to deal with the changes. At the same time, they experience significant social and emotional changes and need support in adjusting to and managing these new feelings and experiences. Understanding affective development matters because success is highly dependent upon middle school students' social and emotional needs being met (NMSA, 2003).

Young adolescents want to understand why they have to complete certain tasks, and they want to know that their work matters to a larger context (Perlstein, 2003). Meaningful tasks are important. Because of their increasing intellectual skills, young adolescents are not as likely to acquiesce to teachers' demands or to believe that work matters simply because the teacher says so. They need to see the meaning for themselves (Daniels & Arapostathis, 2005). As children's free time diminishes because of increased homework, after school activities, and fam-

ily responsibilities, many students want their own opportunities to determine "how to allocate their own limited resources of attention" (Csikszentmihalyi, Rathunde, & Whalen, 1993, p. 42).

Because adolescence is a time when people struggle to determine what their identities are and what they stand for, middle school students are extremely aware of how others perceive them (Lipka, 1997). They are struggling to preserve their sense of self and to maintain positive self-esteem which is challenging if they feel that they are different from the mainstream or popular kids in terms of their wants, needs, or abilities (Lipka, 1997). Although they tend to push adults away in their quest to develop independence, young adolescents also want and need to engage with positive adult role models (Perlstein, 2003). As they struggle to find their emotional and social places in the world, the students learn from the relationships that they build with the adults around them. They learn from the behavior of their teachers and from the implicit lessons—"the way adults treat each other, set priorities, and make decisions" (NMSA, 2003, p. 11)—what behaviors are desired and/or rewarded in society. As young adolescents undergo substantive emotional changes, they increasingly want and need guidance in making their own moral and social choices. The guidance they do or do not receive during this time largely determines their affective states. If supportive adult role models are missing, they often feel isolated which leads to a negative affect.

The social and emotional hallmarks of young adolescence include increased dependence on peer approval, a need for social acceptance, and a struggle to find individual identity. Because the latter two can be contradictory, young adolescents' affective health is tenuous and ever changing. Their affect is positive when their friendships are strong, when they feel important at school, and when they are clear on their personal values. If any of these components are missing, young adolescents tend to feel angry, upset, or sad (Perlstein, 2003).

Influences on Affective Development

Many factors influence affective development in young adolescents. Examples include their feelings of competence (Csikszentmihalyi et al., 1993), how interested they are in what they are learning and whether or not they see its relevance to their own lives (McPhail, Pierson, Freeman, Goodman, & Ayaapa, 2000), and the relationships they build with peers and trusted adults (Daniels, 2004).

Students need to feel they have the skills necessary to meet challenges they confront (Csikszentmihalyi,

1990). If they feel a task is too easy, they will become bored quickly. If they feel a task is too difficult, they will shut down. Educators must provide enough support and adequate challenge to develop students' confidence. When teachers achieve this balance, students are neither frustrated nor bored—they are engaged in the learning which leads to academic success (Csikszentmihalyi, 1990; McPhail et al., 2000). One way to encourage students to exert effort, which builds competence, is to create lessons that incorporate students' outside interests. When young adolescents feel interested in school concepts and can immediately apply that learning to their own lives, they are more likely to be engaged in school (Smith & Wilhelm, 2003). They want to feel compelled by what they are learning; their rapidly maturing intellect and affect increase their need for relevance and self-management (Eccles & Wigfield, 1997). When educators actively work on meeting social and emotional needs, they positively influence young adolescents' affect.

SCHOOL CONTEXTS

In middle school, student populations increase and departmentalization and ability grouping are more commonplace. Young adolescents' affective development depends on adults in the middle school setting knowing who they are and what matters to them. In this way, young adolescents to explore different experiences and adopt different attitudes within the safety of supportive adult supervision. They need individualized attention from teachers who understand them as they search for what matters to them and identify what they stand for (Mizelle & Mullins, 1997).

Departmentalization and ability grouping also undermine young adolescents' affective development by separating them from close friends when they most need that support and highlighting the differences among students. In middle school, students want to develop and articulate their own, unique identities, but they do not want to do so at the risk of appearing too different (Perlstein, 2003). A middle school best supports affective development when it allows young adolescents to explore without standing out negatively from their peers.

The physical environment of middle school creates more stress than elementary school because homework increases, friend groups shift and weaken before they crystallize, and teachers often become less approachable due to the increased number of students they teach every day (Daniels, 2004). All of these factors affect students' social and emotional well-being. Young adolescents need to be taught how to deal with the changes middle school brings in addition to learning about math, science, and social studies (Daniels, 2004). While middle school educators cannot completely control how their students feel, they are able to create environments that promote positive affect (Anderman & Midgley, 1997).

CONCLUSION

Affective development for middle school students depends upon their social and emotional needs being addressed by the adults in their lives. Feelings and emotions, while less concrete than academic goals, influence the way in which young adolescents learn, the effort they choose to exert, and the success they experience in school. Thus, it is imperative that all adults who work with young adolescents understand what affect is, how it is influenced by contextual factors, and why it is as important as measurable academic goals.

REFERENCES

Anderman, L., & Midgley, C. (1997). Motivation and middle school students. In J. Irvin Ed.), *What current research says to the middle level practitioner* (pp. 41-48). Columbus, OH: National Middle School Association.

Csikszentmihalyi, M. (1990). *Flow: The psychology of optimal experience.* New York: HarperPerennial.

Csikszentmihalyi, M., Rathunde, K., & Whalen, S. (1993). *Talented teenagers: The roots of success and failure.* New York: Cambridge University Press.

Daniels, E. (2004). *Nobody's ever asked me that before.* Unpublished doctoral dissertation, California State University, San Marcos.

Daniels, E., & Arapostathis, M. (2005). What do they really want: Student voices and motivation research. *Urban Education, 40*(1), 34-59.

Deci, E. (1995). *Why we do what we do.* New York: Penguin Books.

Eccles, J., & Wigfield, A. (1997). Young adolescent development. In J. Irvin (Ed.), *What current research says to the middle level practitioner* (pp. 15-30). Columbus, OH: National Middle School Association.

Lipka, R. (1997). Enhancing self-concept/self-esteem in young adolescents. In J. Irvin (Ed.), *What current research says to the middle level practitioner* (pp. 31-40). Columbus, OH: National Middle School Association.

Merriam Webster. (2004). *The Merriam Webster Dictionary.* New York: Author.

McPhail, J., Pierson, J., Freeman, J., Goodman, J., & Ayaapa, A. (2000). The role of interest in fostering sixth grade students' identities as competent learners. *Curriculum Inquiry, 30*(1), 43-70.

Mizelle, N., & Mullins, E. (1997). Transition into and out of middle school. In J. Irvin (Ed.), *What current research says to the middle level practitioner* (pp. 303-316). Columbus, OH: National Middle School Association.

National Middle School Association. (2003). *This we believe: Successful schools for young adolescents.* Columbus, OH: Author.

Perlstein, L. (2003). *Not much just chillin: The hidden lives of middle schoolers.* New York: Farrar, Straus, and Giroux.

Smith, M., & Wilhelm, J. (2002). *Reading don't fix no chevys: Literacy in the lives of young men.* Portsmouth, NH: Heinemann.

Stevenson, C. (2002). *Teaching 10 to 14 year olds, third edition.* Boston: Allyn & Bacon.

—Erika Dale Daniels
California State University, San Marcos

AFTER-SCHOOL PROGRAMS

After-school programming is a broad term encompassing a range of activities designed to serve school-aged youth during their out of school time. Traditionally after-school programming referred to activities for school-aged children or adolescents that occurred after the school day anytime between 2 p.m. and 6 p.m. but this definition has been expanded to include any activities that occur during out-of-school time (OST) including before school time, during school lunch hours or breaks, summers, weekends, and holidays. The terms, after-school programming and out-of school time programming, are used interchangeably in the literature.

After-school programs range in scope, focus, and structure. Some programs are comprehensive and address a broad range of topics and activities whereas others are focused on just one topic or area. Programming focus ranges from remediation to enrichment opportunities and in many cases programs offer both types of opportunities. Some programs have formal enrollment periods while others are more unstructured and operate on a "drop-in" basis. Additionally, some programs are only offered during the after-school hours (2 p.m. to 6 p.m.) whereas other programs are offered during weekends or over the holidays (Gootman, 2000).

Programs are designed to address deficits or enhance assets, prevent problems or promote positive developmental outcomes. After-school programs often focus on offering safe, engaging environments that motivate and inspire learning outside the regular school day. Some out-of-school time programs are designed to be safe havens, some focus on recreation, and others have a strong academic focus. Even though after-school programs range in domain and quality, all programs strive to achieve some sort of positive outcome for youth. Program objectives are often overlapping and range from academic, social and emotional, health and safety, and community engagement (C.S. Mott Foundation, 2005).

Despite the many types and purposes of after-school programs, they typically fall into one of three wide-ranging and overlapping categories:

1. *School-aged child care.* This type of programming is typically for younger, elementary school aged children whose primary caregivers work during nonschool hours.
2. *Youth development.* This type of programming aims to increase social competencies, bolster emotional and physical health, and/or hone social and athletic skills. Oftentimes, these types of programs simply offer safe places for addressing developmental needs and fostering a sense of belonging, steering youth away from negative behavior and outcomes (drug and alcohol abuse, teen pregnancy, crime and violence) toward healthy lifestyles and relationships.
3. *Educational enhancement.* Programs that focus on academic performance and proficiencies are typically school based and consist of tutoring, homework assistance, academic enrichment, and/or recreational, social and cultural activities.

After-school programs locales are either community based or school based. National organizations like the YMCA, the Boys and Girls Club and the 4-H club are the largest category of community-based programs. Publicly sponsored programs directed by libraries, parks, recreation departments, and youth sports organizations also offer community-based programming for youth. Multiservice agencies often have after-school opportunities as one facet of diverse program offerings. Finally, independent youth organizations, grassroots, and community sponsored organizations, provide local after-school programming (Gootman, 2000; Rinehart, 2003).

There are several types of after-school programming located in school buildings. School-based after-school programming is usually academic and tutoring focused and is staffed by teachers and ideally aligned with academic standards to enhance classroom learning. Community-based organizations also use school facilities as a locale for their programming. Schools and community-based agencies also partner to transform schools into full-time community centers, "Community Schools," that offer activities to community residents of all ages (Gootman, 2000; Walker, Grossman, & Raley, 2000).

HISTORICAL CONTEXT

When after-school programs first appeared, only YMCAs, YWCAs, Boys and Girls Clubs, and a handful of other national and state organizations offered after-school programming. These after-school opportunities were almost exclusively fee-based services and prohibitive to many either because of cost or transportation limitations to youth who were the most likely beneficiaries?—children from low income, socially disorganized communities with few of any OST opportunities. There were a few instances of no cost after-school programming available to youth. One of the most cited instances is the New York Beacon Institute which started in 1991 as a city-funded, school-based youth program (Walker, Grossman, & Raley, 2000).

After-school programming became more prolific in the mid-1990s. Widely cited research showed elevated rates of youth crime, victimization, and other high risk behavior during after-school hours (Fox & Newman, 1997). The number of parents and guardians working during their children's OST has increased and many youth have no adult supervision during their out-of-school time. Youth who go home to an empty house during OST are called "latch-key" children and research shows that these youth have greater risk of academic failure and high risk behavior than youth who have OST supervision. School administrators and educators are increasingly being pressured to bolster students' academic performance and competence via the standards movement. All these factors influence the expansion of extended learning and enrichment programs (Brown, 2001; Gootman, 2000). Parents, educators, and the public were primed to favor and demand more after-school alternatives and programming for youth and these pressure jumpstarted policy makers.

In the mid-1990s, after-school programming gained widespread popularity and the federal and state governments attempted to make it more democratized and institutionalized through legislation like Title X which authorized the federal government to support expanded learning opportunities and initiatives like the 21st Century Community Learning Centers (21st CCLC). In 1997, the federal government funded 21st CCLC for one million dollars and in 2000 the 21st CCLC funds were increased to 450 million dollars (Gootman, 2000). The 2002 passage of the No Child Left Behind Act changed the 21st CCLC from a federally administered program to state administered. Due to variety of social factors, favorable public opinion, and increased funding after-school programming gained enormous support in the last 2 decades.

RESEARCH ON AFTER-SCHOOL PROGRAMS

Out-of-school time research is in its infancy in terms of looking at the connection between specific program elements and outcomes. Some organizations promote "standards" that are thought to be characteristic of successful out-of-school time programs. These standards have been advanced by national organizations such as the National School-Age Care Alliance, National Institute on Out-of-School Time (2000), the National Research Council and Institute of Medicine (2002); local organizations including YouthNet of Greater Kansas City and New York State Afterschool Network; state agencies such as the Illinois Department of Human Services; and at the federal level by the U.S. Department of Education.

Although research and theory suggest that after-school programming "might provide an effective mechanism to reduce juvenile delinquency, drug use, victimization, school dropout, pregnancy, and other negative outcomes associated with lack of supervision in after-school hours" (Weisman & Gottfredson, 2001, p. 202), the research on the effectiveness of after-school programming is scant and the findings are often mixed. Additionally, some types of after-school programming have been more extensively evaluated than others. Even though after-school programs are not created (or implemented) equally, research has generally shown that after-school programming has positive impact on youth.

After-school program participation is associated with better grades, peer relations, emotional adjustment, leadership skills, and conflict resolution skills (Noam, 2003). Research also shows that students involved in extracurricular activities are less likely to use drugs, become teen parents, and drop out of school (Mahoney & Cairns, 1997). Despite many positive findings, there is still a great need for research-based evidence that shows that after-school programs work and that articulates the elements that comprise effective programming.

Research of after-school programming needs to pay particular attention to program attendance and attrition and participant characteristics. In some instances after-school programming may not be serving the population that many intended to serve, at risk and high risk youth. Weisman and Gottfredson (2001) found that "withdrawal and poor attendance in after-school programs results in programs serving a lower-risk population than they intended" (p. 203).

After-school programming research needs to focus on program replication, age of participants, recruiting, mandatory or voluntary, transportation, selection bias, program purpose, and outcomes. One of the largest research shortcomings is that random assignment is rarely used in evaluations of after-school programming making it difficult what outcomes would have resulted in absence of the program (Fashola, 1998).

QUALITY AFTER-SCHOOL PROGRAMS

Partnering with parents, participants, districts and schools, and members of the broader community is essential in identifying program goals grounded in the ideas, values, people and institutions in the community. (C.S. Mott Foundation, 2005, p. 1)

There is no single formula for quality after-school programming. However, many organizations have tried to summarize some of the essential elements needed for both the foundation and the implementation of after-school programming. The most recent list of necessary after-school programming fundamentals were developed following the After-school summit hosted by the U.S. Department of Education and Arnold Schwarzenegger, a committee of researchers and program experts developed the Framework for After-School Programs (C.S. Mott Foundation, 2005) and they summarized the operational conditions that needed to be constant in order to sustain high quality after-school programs:

1. Effective partnerships.
2. Strong program management.
3. *Qualified staff and volunteers.* Out-of-school time program staff is one of the most important ingredients of an effective program. Staff quality includes the aptitude, skills, experience, and beliefs that a staff member brings to the program, as well as the structures, processes, resources, and requirements that influence who becomes a staff member and what they do in the program. Overall, a quality program staff member is someone who has the necessary content knowledge, can effectively use multiple strategies or approaches depending upon youth needs, is sensitive to cultural and social conditions, values youth participants as individuals, and is committed to ongoing professional development. In order to achieve true youth enrichment, the staff-to-youth ratio should be low, especially when tutoring or mentoring. A low youth-to-staff ratio may

increase the likelihood that youth will have one-on-one time with adult as well as develop a personal relationship with an adult staff member.

4. *Enriching learning opportunities* that complement school-day learning, utilize project-based learning, and explore new skills and knowledge. Intentional linkages between school-day and after-school staff including coordinating and maximizing use of resources and facilities. Out-of-school time programs should strive to promote knowledge, skills, and understanding through the provision of enriching learning opportunities that both complement and expand the school day (Fashola, 1998; Halpern, 1992; U.S. Department of Education & U.S. Department of Justice, 2000).

The curriculum used in out-of-school time programs (particularly in academic-focused programs) should be challenging but not overwhelming. A challenging curriculum accommodates individual student needs, coordinates with in-school instruction, and focuses on more than remedial work. It also combines direct teaching with indirect instruction, such as computer use, scientific experiments, and other hands-on projects. The combination of these approaches helps students acquire a set of skills useful in school and in life (U.S. Department of Education & U.S. Department of Justice, 2000).

5. Appropriate attention to safety, health, and nutrition issues.
6. *Strong family involvement* in participants' learning and development.
7. Adequate and sustainable funding.
8. Evaluation for continuous improvement and assessing program effectiveness.

These elements that should be in place in order to effectively recruit and retain targeted populations and maximize after-school program efficacy.

LATEST TRENDS

The latest after-school programming trend is extended-service schools, opening the school building to youth, families and the community and offering programming such as GED (general equivalency diploma), ESL (English as a second language), and parenting classes as well as family literacy programs. Because school buildings have facilities for meeting educational, developmental, and recreational needs of youth and families, "community schools" are popular and practical. Schools and community-based agencies partner and collaborate to transform schools into full-time community centers that offer activities to community residents of all ages (Gootman, 2000; Walker et al., 2000).

Youth who participate in an out-of-school time program with a positive emotional climate are exposed to role models as well as skills for making decisions, resolving conflicts, solving problems, accepting their own and others' feelings, and developing a sense of control over their environment. Developing a program environment in which positive and supportive relationships are customary can provide a healthy alternative to negative peer influences and pressures. Positive relationships can have a powerful impact on youth development (Gootman, 2000; Halpern, Spielberger, & Robb, 2000; Illinois Teen REACH Advisory Group, 2003; National Research Council & Institute of Medicine, 2002).

Out-of-school time programs provide youth with opportunities to build consistent positive relationships with adults and peers which helps create the foundation on which youth can build additional strengths, assets, and competencies needed for future success (Illinois After-School Initiative, 2002; Illinois Teen REACH Advisory Group, 2003; U.S. Department of Education & U.S. Department of Justice, 2000).

After-school programming covers a wide range of recreational, social service, educational enrichment, and vocational activities that emphasize social competencies (e.g., interpersonal skills), life skills (e.g. time management, goal setting, etc), and academic achievement. These programs vary in quality, depth, and breadth but they all have the aims of positively influencing youth during out-of school time. This type of programming can be especially important for youth without support, guidance, or positive and stable relationships at home, after-school programming may serve as a positive environment that may be crucial to their healthy development. Out-of-school time programs may be one of the few, if not only, places where such youth can receive such benefits.

REFERENCES

Brown, C. G. (2001). Extended learning: What are the states doing? *Principal, 80*(3), 12-15.

C. S. Mott Foundation Committee on After-School Research and Practice. (2005). *Moving towards success: A framework for after-school programs.* Washington, DC: Collaborative Communications Group.

Fashola, O. S. (1998). *Review of extended-day and after-school programs and their effectiveness. Report No. 24.* Center for Research on the Education of Students Placed at Risk. (ERIC ED424343).

Fox, J. A., & Newman, S. A. (1997). *After-school crime or after-school programs?* Report to the U.S. Attorney General. Washington, DC: Fight Crime: Invest in Kids.

Gootman, J. A. E. (2000). *After-school programs to promote child and adolescent development: summary of a workshop.* Washington, DC: National Research Council and Institute of Medicine. (ERIC. ED446849)

Halpern, R. (1992). The role of after-school programs in the lives of inner-city children: A study of the "Urban Youth Network." *Child Welfare, 71*(3), 215-230.

Halpern, R., Spielberger, J., & Robb, S. (2000). *Evaluation of the MOST (making the most of out-of-school time) initiative: Final report and summary of findings.* Chicago: Chapin Hall Center for Children at the University of Chicago.

Illinois After-School Initiative. (2002). *The Illinois after-school initiative 2002 task force report.* Chicago, IL: Illinois Center for Violence Prevention.

Illinois Teen REACH Advisory Group. (2003). *Illinois teen REACH benchmarks.* Chicago, IL: Illinois Teen REACH Advisory Group in conjunction with the Center for Prevention Research and Development, University of Illinois.

Mahoney, J. L., & Cairns, R. B. (1997). Do extracurricular activities protect against early school dropout? *Developmental Psychology, 33,* 241-253.

National Research Council & Institute of Medicine. (2002). *Community programs to promote youth development.* Washington, DC: National Academy Press.

National Institute on Out-of-School Time. (2000). *Making an impact on out-of-school time: a guide for corporation for national service programs engaged in after school, summer, and weekend activities for young people.* (ERIC ED449236).

Noam, G. G. (2003). After-school education: what principals should know. *Principal, 82*(5), 18-21.

Rinehart, J. (2003). A new day begins after school. *Principal, 82*(5), 12-16.

U.S. Department of Education & U.S. Department of Justice. (2000). *Working for children and families: Safe and smart after-school programs.* Washington, DC: Author.

Walker, K. E., Grossman, J. B., & Raley, R. (2000). *Extended service schools: putting programming in place.* New York: Manpower Demonstration Research Corp.

Weisman, S. A., & Gottfredson, D. C. (2001). Attrition from after school programs: characteristics of students who drop out. *Prevention Science, 2*(3), 201-205.

—Cody Stephens
CPRD, University of Illinois

AIM AT MIDDLE-GRADES RESULTS

AIM's goal is that all middle-grades students meet challenging standards and are prepared to succeed at the next stage of learning and growing. AIM uses a set of structures, processes, tools and materials to guide school improvement. A basic tenet is that all schools have the capacity to accelerate student learning and development when they exercise strong and collaborative leadership, create a powerful professional learning community, and build bridges with parents and the community. What's more, schools need to be at the center of their own improvement efforts.

GUIDING PRINCIPLES

All of AIM's professional development and technical assistance activities are based on the following principles:

- *Technical assistance must be contextualized.* Every school is different, given its particular student population, faculty, local community, and organizational history. And, every school faces a different set of challenges, based on state and local standards, past performance, and resources. AIM staff helps schools analyze their strengths and needs, determine priorities, and develop a tailored approach to school improvement.
- *Relationships matter.* AIM works in collaboration with member schools, building long-term relationships characterized by trust and mutual respect. A local *Site Developer* visits frequently to provide ongoing support, not just two or three times a year to monitor progress.
- *Capacity building is the key to long-term sustainability.* Through leadership development, professional development, and ongoing technical assistance, AIM helps schools build the knowledge and skills to continue their improvement efforts. AIM schools also create an inclusive culture and supportive structures that facilitate professional learning.
- *Continuous Improvement.* School improvement is not a one-time event. AIM schools learn how to use data for decision-making, set performance goals and benchmarks, take concrete actions, and track changes in performance by all segments of the student population.

AIM SUPPORT SERVICES

AIM works with schools for three or more years to build the internal capacity for continuous improvement. Schools begin with *Creating Tomorrow,* a structured process for assessing current strengths and needs and developing a long-term improvement plan. Through participation in *Faculty Inquiry Teams* teachers engage in collaborative work that improves teaching and learning. *Teaching for Understanding* institutes enable teachers to design a rigorous and devel-

opmentally appropriate curriculum based on student needs and local and state requirements. *Collaborative Leadership Teams* assess the current status of teaching and learning in the school, build a shared vision, create conditions for school improvement, and monitor progress. *Ongoing and Intensive Technical Assistance* facilitates the improvement process.

BENEFITS/RESULTS OR EVIDENCE OF IMPACT

Among the benefits *AIM* schools can expect are:

- Clearer expectations about what learning should take place;
- More rigorous curriculum aligned with local and state standards;
- Greater reflection and discussion about effective practice;
- More meaningful assessment of student learning;
- Greater focus on each student and the supports necessary for success;
- Active engagement of parents and community members in the school improvement process;
- A respectful, trusting school culture that fosters improved learning and healthy development for all students; and
- Significant improvements in student engagement, achievement, and behavior

—Nancy Ames
Educational Development Center, Inc.

ALEXANDER, WILLIAM M.

William M. Alexander was one of the pioneers and founders of the American middle school movement. Dr. Alexander received his undergraduate degree from Bethel College in his hometown of McKenzie, Tennessee, his masters degree from George Peabody College for Teachers, and his doctorate from Columbia University. He began his career as a teacher in McKenzie and later served as a curriculum specialist in Cincinnati, Ohio and Battle Creek, Michigan, and was superintendent of schools in Winnetka, Illinois. He also held posts at the University of Tennessee, the University of Miami, George Peabody College for Teachers, and the University of Florida. Dr. Alexander retired as Professor Emeritus at the University of Florida in 1977. However, he continued to share his middle school expertise through teaching, writing, and research for many years after his retirement.

In 1963, Dr. Alexander presented his conceptualization of what middle schools should be at a junior high school conference held at Cornell University. This groundbreaking address, titled "The Junior High School: A Changing View," followed by numerous professional publications, national studies, and other scholarly work provided a construct for the middle school movement that remains relatively unchanged today. Although he steadfastly pointed out that others had conceived the need for developmentally responsive, restructured middle schools before his proposal, his many contributions toward conceptualizing and popularizing the middle school concept have led many to recognize him as the "father of the American middle school."

William Alexander authored and coauthored over 200 articles, books, and other professional publications, the majority of which directly addressed middle school education. His landmark publications include *The Emergent Middle School* which helped shape the middle schools movement and *The Exemplary Middle School*, an authoritative text authored with his good friend and colleague Paul S. George. Dr. Alexander also served as consultant to numerous school districts, state departments of education, higher education institutions, and agencies throughout his career.

Dr. Alexander held many leadership positions during his distinguished career. He served as president for the Association for Curriculum Development, and in leadership positions for National Middle School Association. Among his numerous honors, Dr. Alexander was recipient of the John H. Lounsbury Distinguished Service Award, the highest award given by National Middle School Association. In 1984, he also received an award for "Sustained Contribution to the Field of Curriculum" from the American Educational Research Association.

William Marvin Alexander left an immeasurable legacy in American education that includes not only pioneering accomplishments in middle school education, but also renowned curriculum work for all levels of education. His staunch advocacy of middle school education, however, was one of his favorite causes and one which received the major share of his attention.

REFERENCES

Alexander, W. M., & George, P. S. (1981). *The exemplary middle school*. New York: Holt, Reinhart, and Winston.

Alexander, W., Williams, E., Compton, M., Hines, V., & Prescott, D. (1968). *The emergent middle school*. New York: Holt, Reinhart, and Winston.

—C. Kenneth McEwin
Appalachian State University

ALTERNATIVE MIDDLE SCHOOLS

Alternative middle schools provide learning experiences that differ from those offered at more traditional schools and their philosophies, goals, and practices differ substantially from those of more traditional schools (Dunbar, 2001). Students who attend alternative middle schools have tended to be students either who have had little success in regular schools or who required, or desired, a type of learning approach that better met their educational needs (Mottaz, 2002). Several kinds of alternative middle schools, both public and private, have appeared over the past 40 years to meet the needs of diverse young adolescent learners.

The first alternative middle schools, which emerged in the 1960s, tended to be either dumping grounds for urban children who did not succeed academically or behaviorally in regular urban middle schools or schools that provided an alternative curriculum for suburban gifted and talented youth (Mottaz, 2002). Another type of alternative middle school that emerged at this time was the *freedom school*, a type of school for African American children in the south that emerged from the struggles over civil rights and concerns that Black children understand the realities of racism and social action (Fantini, 1976). In the 1970s, hundreds of *free*, or *open, schools*, based on Dewey's principles of progressive education, opened that emphasized flexible space and informal learning activities. In the 1990s, a number of alternative schools were opened to better educate underserved children in economically poor urban settings.

The institution of the middle school and the promotion of the middle school concept some 40 years ago itself represented an alternative to the junior high school that dominated the educational landscape through the 1960s. Much has been written about how replacing the 6-3-3 grade structure with the 5-3-4 framework, thereby establishing the Grades 6 through 8 middle school, provides a better structure for meeting the developmental needs of young adolescents. A plethora of books and other writings, beginning in the 1960s influenced the thinking of many educators about how best to provide learning and growth opportunities for young adolescents in the new middle schools. Unfortunately, however, many children in the middle schools continued to be disengaged and at risk for school failure and early school leaving.

Alternatives to the large middle schools came to the fore in an attempt to engage those young people who were not succeeding in middle schools or to provide educational experiences consistent with contemporary movements in education. In contrast to larger regular middle schools, alternative middle schools, along with alternative elementary and high schools, tend to be characterized by small school and class size, thereby providing more individual and small group instruction for students. In addition, these schools adopted discipline and instructional practices designed to engage the diverse learner and promote academic learning and positive social development.

Alternative middle school programs could be categorized in one of three ways. First are the preventative programs, those which identify young people at risk for school failure and dropping out and provide them with the skills needed to be successful in a supportive environment. Second are the schools that serve as interventions for those who have already experienced school failure or who may have been labeled as uneducable. Third are those schools that meet special learning needs, including those that provide enrichment or magnet programs, such as in the arts, and those that are specific to children with learning differences.

Intervention-type alternative middle schools appear to be the most common among the three basic types. Many, if not most, school districts provide education in separate buildings for young adolescents who have performed poorly academically (i.e., retained in one or more grades) or who have been particularly disruptive (including having frequent suspensions) in regular middle schools. These schools tend to be very small with low student-to-teacher ratios and focus on students' behavioral issues and self-perceptions. Individual and group counseling and one-on-one mentoring and support are often aspects of these schools. The Milwaukee, Wisconsin school district Web site lists 10 such alternative middle schools, Grades 6 through 8, with enrollments of between 30 and 60 students and several Grade 6 through 12 alternative schools with small enrollments (http://www2.milwaukee.k12.wi.us/scs/altpart. htm#mps).

Often these alternative schools are established on a regional basis (e.g., through the Board of Cooperative Educational Services, BOCES, in New York State) to serve students in neighboring school districts. In addition, residential alternative programs, such as Discovery Academy in Provo, Utah, have been established to educate middle and high school students who have had significant behavioral difficulties in regular schools (see http://www.discoveryacademy.com). Wilderness, therapeutic, and military schools also provide such an alternative (see http://www. teenprogram.info/schools/index?state=ut).

A magnet middle school program in Baltimore County, Maryland, provides the type of curriculum consistent with the third type of alternative middle school identified above. Loch Raven Academy, a public magnet school, offers programs in health, law, finance, environmental science, visual arts, and performing arts to students in Grades 6 through 8 (see http://www.bcps.org/schools/cms/lra/). Betsy Ross, an arts magnet school in New Haven, Connecticut, offers instruction in the creative arts and a comprehensive core academic curriculum to any interested student in the area (see http://www.rossarts.org/). Many other alternative middle schools throughout the United States provide interdisciplinary programs rich in the creative and scientific arts.

Alternative middle schools that fit the preventative model have been growing in the past 10 years, particular in urban areas. These schools select children who are at risk, for a variety of reasons, for school failure and early school leaving. Risk factors include elementary school academic or behavioral difficulties, poor English language proficiency, homes in economically poor and dangerous neighborhoods, and the lack of adequate educational opportunities.

One example of the prevention type of middle school is the Nativity model school (www.nativity network.org). Named for the first school of its kind that opened on the lower east side of Manhattan in 1971, this type of school is a privately funded enterprise that caters to children in the inner city who have shown some potential for a relatively high level of school achievement but test at one or more years behind grade level in elementary school in reading and math. A vast majority of the children who enroll in Nativity schools are children of color who qualify for federal lunch programs. Nativity schools, of which there are 39 in operation in the United States at the beginning of 2004, and the very similar San Miguel schools that number 14, emphasize small class size, an extended day for study and tutoring, individual attention and mentoring, and summer enrichment, as well as support for high school and college admissions and high school achievement. These 53 alternative schools enroll a total of nearly 2,900 middle school children. Using both professional teachers and volunteers, through Americorps and other programs, in the classrooms, these schools provide extensive academic preparation that enables most students to qualify for private or parochial high school educations and attend college. Nativity and San Miguel schools provide a safe and nurturing community-type environment that supports students' social, emotional, physical, and spiritual development. In most of these schools, parents or guardians are closely involved in the educational enterprise.

Another type of prevention-type alternative middle school for inner city children that incorporates many of the structural elements of the Nativity schools is the KIPP (Knowledge Is Power Program) school, a public school program that first appeared in the mid 1990s in New York and Houston (www. kippschools.com). At the beginning of 2004, KIPP schools numbered more than 30 in which over 4,000 middle school children have been served. The same type of academic rigor that characterizes the Nativity schools is also found in KIPP schools. In addition, like the Nativity school students, children in KIPP schools face a longer school day than is found in regular middle schools, as well as over two hours of homework each night, Saturday attendance, and summer enrichment. Parents' commitment to their children's education is also mandated.

Prevention-type middle schools that work well to help underserved young adolescents achieve academically and grow socially and emotionally are characterized by well-managed classrooms in which time-on-task is maximized, effective mentoring programs, extended instructional days or weeks or both, extensive tutoring, summer enrichment or remediation programs, a caring and dedicated staff, a culturally relevant curriculum, and high expectations of students, parents, and staff. Some of these schools are enhanced by partnerships with companies and other educational institutions.

REFERENCES

Betsy Ross: An arts magnet middle school. (n.d.). Retrieved January 23, 2004, from http://www.rossarts.org/

Discovery Academy. (n.d.). Retrieved January 16, 2004, from http://www.discoveryacademy.com

Dunbar, Jr., C. (2001). *Alternative schooling for African American youth: Does anyone know we're here?* New York: Peter Lang.

Fantini, M. D. (Ed.). (1976). *Alternative education: A sourcebook for parents, teachers, students, and administrators.* Garden City, NY: Anchor Books.

KIPP: Life.Lessons. (n.d.). Retrieved January 23, 2004, from http://www.kippschools.com.

Loch Raven Academy. (n.d.). Retrieved January 23, 2004, from http://www.bcps.org/schools/cms/lra/

Mottaz, C. (2002). *Breaking the cycle of failure: How to build and maintain quality alternative schools.* Lanham, MD: Scarecrow Press.

MPS alternative and partnership schools. (n.d.).Retrieved January 16, 2004, from http://www2.milwaukee.k12.wi.us/scs/altpart.htm#mps.

Nativity Network: Breaking the cycle of poverty through education. (n.d.). Retrieved January 23, 2004, from http://www.nativitynetwork.org

Teen Program.info: A parent's guide to teen programs & schools. List of schools in Utah. (n.d.).Retrieved January 25, 2004, from http://www.teenprogram.info/schools/index?state=ut

—L. Mickey Fenzel
Loyola College, Maryland

ARTS EDUCATION

The inclusion of the arts as a core subject area in the No Child Left Behind Act of 2001 increased attention on the role of music, visual art, dance and theater in America's public schools (Arts Education Partnership, 2004b; Meyer, 2004). This attention coincided with the 10-year anniversary of the *National Standards for Arts Education* (Music Educators National Conference, 1994a) that have been widely adopted by states and individual school districts nationwide. The *National Standards* document has profoundly influenced the quality and scope of education in the arts—and it is education *in the arts* that is central to the role of arts education. At the same time, however, the increased attention paid to arts education continues to produce a large body of research indicating the benefits of arts study for other core academic subjects, students with special needs, whole school reform efforts, and student attitudes toward learning, school and community (Manzo, 2002).

Political and educational leaders nationwide have demonstrated a renewed commitment to the improvement of school curricula. This is nowhere more evident than in the development, adoption, and revision of high-level standards for all students in the core subject areas (President's Committee on the Arts and the Humanities, 1999). Though it might seem logical to invest resources solely in such traditional academic subjects as mathematics, language arts and science, a large body of research substantiates the essential role of the arts as a *partner* in academic success for all students, particularly for young adolescents (Healy, 2004; Konrad, 1999; Paige & Huckabee, 2005; Smar, 2000).

Arts education is broadly defined as encompassing the disciplines of music, visual art, dance and drama. According to the 1997 National Assessment of Education Progress in the Arts, U.S. eighth graders usually receive formal instruction in music and visual art, they may receive formal instruction in drama, and they rarely receive formal instruction in dance (National Center for Education Statistics, 1998). At the time of this writing, the next NAEP eighth grade assessment in the arts is scheduled to occur in 2008. Schedules for arts instruction at the middle school level are as varied as middle schools themselves, with formal instruction frequently offered as part of an exploratory series of courses and supplemented with performing arts rehearsals and other arts activities outside the normal school day (Music Educators National Conference, 1994b).

SEQUENTIAL ARTS EDUCATION

Arts education must be available to all students if it is to produce the benefits identified by research. The arts encourage all students to "cultivate and refine their sensibilities," provide a "fundamental appreciation between the individual and the cultural heritage of others," and offer a "crucial aesthetic metaphor of what life at its best might be" (Fowler, 1996, p. 106). Programs and curricula that demonstrate the influence of the arts on other types of academic learning can only be successful when they are sustained, and this sustainability is significantly influenced by state-level standards and legislation (National Association of State Boards of Education, 2003; Rabkin & Redmond, 2005).

Public support for arts education, while historically strong, has recently trended higher. Poll results indicate that adults "strongly believe that arts and culture benefit education and business" (e.g., Sabulis, 2004).

THE ARTS AND ACADEMIC ACHIEVEMENT

Arts education has long been known to have extra-musical outcomes, including an association with above-average scores on the SAT (Rarus, 2000). Several recent efforts have been made to gather all published research indicating the effect of arts on other academic success—such as higher order thinking, verbal, and mathematical skills; some effects have been conclusively identified, while others require further research (e.g., Abeles, Hafeli, Horowitz, & Burton, 2002; Arts Education Partnership, 2002, 2004a; Winner & Hetland, 2000). These positive effects of arts-rich curricula occur across ethnic and socio-economic boundaries. Significantly, it has been repeatedly shown that students' overall academic achievement may actually *increase* when the arts are added to the curriculum (e.g., Andrews, 1997; Cat-

terall, Chapleau & Iwanaga, 1999; Catterall & Waldorf, 1999).

THE ARTS AND FUNDAMENTAL SKILLS, ATTITUDES AND BEHAVIORS

The influence of arts education extends to other critical factors of student learning not easily measured by test scores (Bresler, 2002; Marshall, 1998). These factors include the desire to learn, facilitation of problem-solving skills, the enhancement of creativity, a reduction in school dropout rates, and improved school attendance (Cutietta, Harmann & Walker, 1995). Music education, in particular, has been found to increase students' recall and memory skills, academic self-concept, risk-taking, and the willingness to sustain effort (Campabello, DeCarlo, O'Neil, & Vacek, 2002; Eisner, 1998). Research has also begun to identify the specific ways in which arts education is of particular benefit to students with physical disabilities, behavioral issues, and cognitive impairments.

THE ARTS AND POSITIVE LEARNING ENVIRONMENTS

In schools that offer both sequential arts instruction and arts-infused curricula, students demonstrate an increased enthusiasm for learning, readily pursue cross-cultural understandings, and are more likely to be recognized for academic achievement (Corbett, Wilson, Noblit, & McKinney, 2001). Students in these schools read for pleasure nearly twice as often as students who do not receive arts instruction (Heath, Soep, & Roach, 1998). Arts-rich schools are characterized by increased teacher collaboration, parental involvement, and community support (Tabereaux, 2002). High-quality sequential arts education, rather than mere arts exposure, motivates school improvement and fosters equity in excellence among students with diverse backgrounds and capabilities (Darby & Catterall, 1994). Teachers in these schools develop more positive classroom climates, create more student-centered classrooms, and use a greater variety of teaching materials (Wolf, 2003).

While adolescents with disabilities often lag behind their peers in many areas of cognitive and motor function, research suggests that these students often possess music aptitudes (musical potential) similar to non-disabled students, especially those matched with regard to mental age (Darrow & Armstrong, 1999). Research has shown that music aptitude is independent of intellectual and academic achievement, indicating that music is a unique way for adolescents with disabilities to learn, process information, interact with their environments, and express themselves (Goldberg & Scott-Kassner, 2002).

THE ARTS AND LEARNING FOR ALL

The opportunity to participate and learn in the arts is not only every young adolescent's right but is essential to every person's development (Jensen, 2001; Peter, 1998). Research indicates that early exposure to music has a profound impact on children's ability to learn and grow. The cognitive, social, and physical benefits of arts education for students of all ages are a pervasive theme in research and literature addressing educational reform, learning development, and aesthetic understanding (Harvard University, 2000).

The growing body of arts education research presents challenges to those with influence over educational policy. The arts must be cemented into the core structures of our educational processes; they must no longer be considered frills for the wealthy or diversions for the needy (Elliott, 2004). Particularly at the middle school level, arts educators must be included on interdisciplinary teams (Hickey, 1995; Stewart, 1997) and must be encouraged to contribute to the conversation about how adolescents learn and grow (Freer, 2003).

REFERENCES

Abeles, H., Hafeli, M, Horowitz, R., & Burton, J. (2002). The evaluation of arts partnerships and learning in and through the arts. In R. Colwell & C. Richardson (Eds.), *The new handbook of research on music teaching and learning* (pp. 931-940). New York: Oxford University Press.

Andrews, L. J. (1997). *Effects of an integrated reading and music instructional approach on fifth-grade students' reading achievement, reading attitude, music achievement, and music attitude.* Unpublished doctoral dissertation, The University of North Carolina at Greensboro.

Arts Education Partnership. (2002). *Critical links.* Washington, DC: Author.

Arts Education Partnership. (2004a). *The arts and education: New opportunities for research.* Washington, DC: Author.

Arts Education Partnership. (2004b). *No subject left behind: A guide to arts education opportunities in the 2001 NCLB Act.* Washington, DC: Author.

Bresler, L. (2002). Research: A foundation for arts education advocacy. In R. Colwell & C. Richardson (Eds.), *The new handbook of research on music teaching and learning* (pp. 1066-1086). New York: Oxford University Press.

Campabello, N., DeCarlo, M. J., O'Neil, J., & Vacek, M. J. (2002). *Music enhances learning.* MA research project. Saint Xavier University.

Catterall, J., Chapleau, R., & Iwanaga, J. (1999a). Involvement in the arts and human development: General involvement and intensive involvement in music and theater arts. In E. B. Fiske (Ed.), *Champions of change: The impact of the arts on learning* (pp. 1-18). Washington, DC: The Arts Education Partnership and The President's Committee on the Arts and the Humanities.

Catterall, J., & Waldorf, L. (1999b). Chicago arts partnerships in education: Summary evaluation. In E. B. Fiske (Ed.), *Champions of change: The impact of the arts on learning* (pp. 47-62). Washington, DC: The Arts Education Partnership and The President's Committee on the Arts and the Humanities.

Corbett, D., Wilson, B., Noblit, G., & McKinney, M. (2001). *The arts, identity, and comprehensive education reform: A final report from the evaluation of the A+ Schools program.* Winston Salem, NC: Thomas S. Kenan Institute for the Arts.

Cutietta, R., Harmann, D., & Walker, L. M. (1995). *Spin-offs: The extra-musical advantages of a music education.* Elkhart, IN: United Musical Instruments.

Darby, J. T. & Catterall, J. S. (1994). The fourth r: The arts and learning. *Teachers College Record, 96, 2,* 299-329.

Darrow, A., & Armstrong, T. (1999). Research on music and autism: Implications for music educators. *Applications of Research in Music Education, 18*(1), 15-20.

Eisner, E. (1998). Does experience in the arts boost academic achievement? *Art Education, 51*(1), 7-15.

Elliott, K. J. (2004). *Art expression and experience in a middle school classroom.* Unpublished MAE dissertation, Pacific Lutheran University.

Fowler, C. B. (1996). *Strong arts, strong schools: The promising potential and shortsighted disregard of the arts in American schooling.* New York: Oxford University Press.

Freer, P. K. (2003). Rehearsal discourse of choral conductors: Meeting the needs of young adolescents. *Dissertation Abstracts International, 64* (5), 1574A. (UMI No. 3031248)

Goldberg, M., & Scott-Kassner, C. (2002). Teaching other subjects through music. In R. Colwell & C. Richardson (Eds.), *The new handbook of research on music teaching and learning* (pp. 1053-1065). New York: Oxford University Press.

Harvard University. (2000). *Harvard Project Zero.* Retrieved May 30, 2005, from hppt://pzweb.Harvard.edu.

Healy, K. (2004). *The effects of integrating visual art on middle school students' attitude toward mathematics.* Unpublished doctoral dissertation, University of Alaska, Anchorage.

Heath, S.B., Soep, E., & Roach, A. (1998). Living the arts through language and learning: A report on community-based youth organizations. *Americans for the Arts Monographs, 2*(7), 1-20.

Hickey, D. (1995). *Reforming arts in the middle grades: A study of visual and performing arts teacher teams.* Unpublished doctoral dissertation, California: University of La Verne.

Jensen, E. (2001). *Arts with the brain in mind.* Alexandria, VA: Association for Supervision and Curriculum Development.

Konrad, R. R. (1999). *Empathy, art, and the social studies: The effect of an empathy based, arts enriched United States history curriculum on middle school students.* Unpublished doctoral dissertation, University of California, Los Angeles.

Manzo, K. (2002). Study identifies benefits of arts curriculum. *Education Week 22* (11), 10.

Marshall, J. N. (1998). *Making meaning: Transformative art education for middle school.* Unpublished doctoral dissertation. University of San Francisco.

Meyer, L. (2004). The complete curriculum: Ensuring a place for the arts in America's schools. *The State Education Standard, 4*(4), 11-15.

Music Educators National Conference. (1994a). *National standards for arts education.* Reston, VA: Author.

Music Educators National Conference. (1994b). *An agenda for excellence in music at the middle level.* Reston, VA: Author.

National Association of State Boards of Education. (2003). *The complete curriculum: Ensuring a place for the arts and foreign languages in America's schools.* Alexandria, VA: Author.

National Center for Education Statistics. (1998). *The NAEP 1997 arts report card (NCES 1999-486).* Washington, DC: U.S. Department of Education.

Paige, R., & Huckabee, M. (2005). Putting arts education front and center. *Education Week, 24*(20), pp. 40, 52.

Peter, M. (1998). 'Good for them, or what?': The arts and pupils with SEN. *British Journal of Special Education, 25*(4), 168-172.

President's Committee on the Arts and the Humanities. (1999). *Gaining the arts advantage: Lessons from school districts that value arts education.* Washington, DC: Author.

Rabkin, N., & Redmond, R. (2005). Arts education: Not all is created equal. *Education Week, 24*(31), pp. 46-47.

Rarus, S. (2000). SAT scores of students in the arts. InB. Leung (Ed.), *Music makes the difference: Music, brain development, and learning* (pp. 56-57). Reston, VA: MENC: National Coalition for Musci Education.

Sabulis, T. (2004, May 13). Arts score high in poll. *The Atlanta Journal-Constitution,* p. A1.

Smar, B. J. (2000). *Integrating art and science: A case study of middle school reform.* Unpublished doctoral dissertation, The University of Toledo.

Stewart, P. J. (1997). *A case study of the role of a middle school art teacher in interdisciplinary teaming.* Unpublished doctoral dissertation, University of Arkansas.

Tabereaux, C. B. (2002). *An investigation of arts-infused schools in Mississippi: The Whole Schools Initiative.* Unpublished doctoral dissertation, Mississippi State University.

Winner, E., & Hetland, L. (Eds.). (2000a). The arts and academic achievement: What the evidence shows [Special issue]. *The Journal of Aesthetic Education, 34*(3-4).

Wolf, D. P. (2003). *The arts and school reform: Lessons and possibilities from the Annenberg Challenge Arts Projects.* Providence RI: Annenberg Institute for School Reform at Brown University.

—Patrick K. Freer
Georgia State University

ASSESSMENT: FORMATIVE EVALUATION

When evaluating schools and their programs, there are two basic kinds of evaluations available to educators, summative and formative. Summative evaluation is designed to provide an overall picture of how a particular educational program or curriculum is working in relation to stated goals or expectations of the program, or against selected comparison groups. The purpose of summative evaluation is to assist in making a determination as to the efficacy of a program. These types of evaluations are important for program developers, funders of educational programs, and educators themselves to determine if students are being adequately served by a particular program (versus other programs that could be implemented in schools).

Formative evaluation on the other hand has a different purpose. Whenever an intervention or program is implemented in a school, the implementation and maintenance processes are fraught with difficulties (Ross et al., 1997). These difficulties could include inadequate teacher training, curriculum materials that are unavailable, or insufficient staffing levels. Even though good interventions or programs exist, if they are not appropriately implemented or adequately maintained at a school, they may not make a difference in the lives of students (Stigler & Hiebert, 1999; Trimble, 2003).

The purpose of formative evaluation is to determine how a particular program or curricular change is doing (Bloom, Hastings, & Madaus, 1971). It can help identify problems in the implementation process so that these problems can be remedied, document early success as positive feedback to school staffs, function as supportive evidence for continuing the program, and enable school staffs to base improvement planning on objective data. It can also formalize teachers' and principals' accountability for the success of their school improvement program.

Principals however, are busy with the daily demands of running a school and are often tempted to use an informal approach to addressing these issues. Unfortunately, informal approaches are open to potential biases such as basing decisions on the opinions of a few trusted teachers, observing classrooms informally via the "drive-by" method, and listening to the parents who complain the loudest. The shortcomings of these methods are obvious, but they are used more often than educators would care to admit. Systematic formative evaluation on the other hand, can yield valid data to address the aforementioned issues.

There are six basic steps in a formative evaluation. Remember those science fair projects displayed in the middle school hallway last year? The same steps of the scientific method are also used in formative evaluations. They have been tailored for school evaluations and include (1) identification of issues, (2) development of benchmarks, (3) identification/development of instruments, (4) gathering data, (5) analyzing data, and (6) reporting results.

IDENTIFICATION OF ISSUES

School communities (administrators, teachers, students, and parents) should engage in a dialog to identify the factors believed to most directly impact student learning and achievement at their schools (e.g., more active teaching methods, positive climate, etc.). These factors should be "controllable" as opposed to wishful thinking (as in, "If only a lot more high-ability students happen to enroll here..."). Once the factors have been identified, they should be prioritized according to importance and practicality for evaluating.

DEVELOPMENT OF BENCHMARKS

When most of us fly to a distant location, we simply tell the reservation agent where we are (point A) and where we are going (point B). We don't think about the amount of fuel in the plane, needed repairs to the airplane, or the flight path. We assume those details have been taken care of, then sit back and relax. Getting a school to proceed from point A to point B, however, requires educators to incrementally address many critical details.

Implementation of a middle school's program requires careful sequencing of events, beginning with a starting point and ending with a fully implemented

program (Felner et al., 1997; Trimble, 2002). An innovative approach to representing a school's overall implementation plan in sequential steps that can also be easily communicated and monitored is "Implementation Benchmarking" (Ross & Alberg, 2001). As a first step, selected school staff (usually a leadership team) meet several times during the school year to "document" the desired major structures and programs of the school with regard to *curriculum* (what needs to be taught), *instruction* (how teaching takes place), and *organization* (resources, scheduling, faculty and principal roles, professional development, evaluation, etc.). The "benchmark" statements are then divided into three phases (beginning, intermediate, and full). Each phase has "indicator" and "evidence" columns that specify how attainment of implementation level will be verified (see Table 1 for a sample "benchmark" item). The process is then repeated for all key programs and activities in the three broad categories.

IDENTIFICATION/DEVELOPMENT OF INSTRUMENTS

The type of data collection instruments you use at your school will be determined by the issues identified in the benchmarks and the types of evidence that will be accepted for each item. Typically, evaluations include such measures as school climate, teacher/student/parent perception surveys, classroom observations, and student achievement.

Your school can develop its own instruments to measure each of these elements, or can use an off-the-shelf instrument that is reliable and has been used in numerous school contexts.

SCHOOL CLIMATE

Much can be learned about the success or failure of school interventions by "examining the culture of a school and the extent to which school members have

Table 1
Sample Benchmark Item

Phase 1 (Beginning)		Phase 2 (Intermediate)		Phase 3 (Full)	
Indicators	Evidence	Indicators	Evidence	Indicators	Evidence
All teachers are introduced to evidence-based alternative strategies, and some are using them intermittently	Lesson plans. Classroom observations.	Most teachers are using alternative strategies intermittently or regularly.	Lesson plans. Classroom observations.	All teachers regularly use evidence-based alternative strategies with direct linkage to standards	Lesson plans. Classroom observations.

created an environment where strategic interventions are supported and sustained" (Desjean-Perrotta, 2003, p. 9). Numerous school climate surveys have been developed and can be found in the literature. One instrument that has been used in hundreds of schools is the School Climate Inventory (SCI©) developed by the Center for Research in Educational Policy at The University of Memphis (Butler & Alberg, 1991). The SCI assesses seven separate climate dimensions:

1. Order (discipline and classroom management)
2. Leadership (principal and teacher roles)
3. Environment (Appearance/comfort of school)
4. Involvement (Parents, community teacher activities)
5. Instruction (Effectiveness, variability, appropriateness)
6. Expectations (Goals for studies, belief in success)
7. Collaboration (Cooperation among leaders, teachers, students).

The percentage of teachers who strongly agree to strongly disagree with each item can provide critical information for the school improvement process. Where there is improvement in school climate, the school has documented evidence to show progress. Importantly, where a positive school climate is cultivated, improvements in test scores should not be far behind (Bryk & Schneider, 2002).

TEACHER, STUDENT, AND PARENT SURVEYS

Although a school climate survey provides useful information about the general health of the school, it will not deal with specific interests, such as the newly adopted block scheduling system, the after-school tutoring program, or the adequacy of technology for student and faculty use. Surveys to solicit valuable feedback and reactions from teachers, parents, and students about these specific interests can be developed by the school or prepackaged surveys (that can be tailored) can be used.

CLASSROOM OBSERVATIONS

One of the most valuable types of data for strengthening improvement planning is observation of classroom teaching (Mertens & Flowers, 2003; Ross, 2003). However, to be effective, an observation process needs to be implemented systematically using a reliable observation instrument (Sterbinsky & Ross, 2003). At many schools, the overriding purpose of classroom observations is to assess teachers' effectiveness (summative evaluation) rather than to help

teachers to reflect on their practices and how they can better meet the needs of their students. For a formative evaluation however, the observation process should simply include a description of classroom practices, not a judgment of teaching effectiveness. Teachers (in conjunction with their mentors) can then ask themselves the hard questions such as: "Do student achievement results support the continuance of current practices?" and "If not, where are changes in teaching methods most likely to have a positive impact?" and still, "If we were going to try to realize these changes, what types of professional development support and resources are needed?"

Observations can be conducted for specific teachers or subject areas, or can be conducted at the school level. One observation instrument that provides data at the whole-school level is the School Observation Measure (SOM©) developed by Ross, Smith, and Alberg (1998). The SOM reliably measures 24 classroom practices and reports the frequency of use for each classroom practice observed throughout the school. The choice of an observation instrument depends on the purpose of the observation.

STUDENT ACHIEVEMENT AND ARCHIVAL DATA

In today's current educational environment, scores on state-mandated student achievement tests are used to determine if a school is proficient in reading, mathematics, and other subjects. In fact, under the federal No Child Left Behind (NCLB, 2001) Act, schools are expected to ensure all students are proficient in reading, mathematics, and other subjects by 2014. While this use of student achievement scores is typical of summative evaluations, student achievement can also be used in formative evaluations. For example, student achievement scores can be used in school improvement planning to identify deficits in specific subject areas. A school's Benchmarks can then identify programs or interventions that will be implemented to meet specific needs in student achievement.

GATHERING DATA

Once the instruments and sources of data have been identified, decisions should be made regarding who will gather the data, when they will gather it, and under what conditions the data collection will take place. Surveys should be administered in a way that will maintain the confidentiality of respondents and ensure that the final report will contain accurate results. Typically, teacher surveys are distributed and collected during a faculty meeting, or are distributed with a return-addressed envelope. Allowing a school staff member to distribute and collect the completed surveys is inadvisable due to the perceived potential breech of confidentiality and data accuracy. Using an outside agency to administer the surveys is a relatively safe way of ensuring the confidentiality of responses.

Observers in classrooms should be credible to teachers (e.g., retired teachers, university education faculty). Observers with substantive classroom experience will be quick to accurately identify specific classroom practices, and teachers will have more confidence in their results. Until teachers are comfortable with observations, it would be inadvisable to use observers who have direct supervisory roles (e.g., the principal) or even peers who teach at the same school.

It is important that observers not be in direct supervisory role for the teacher or be a peer of the teacher.

ANALYZING DATA

There are a variety of ways the data can be analyzed. Although complex statistics statistical procedures are available, the most useful approach includes the simplest analyses (e.g., totals, averages, frequencies). Classroom observations and responses to open-ended survey questions can be analyzed qualitatively, which includes the identification of themes or patterns in the data. Questionnaire data are typically analyzed quantitatively, indicating the percentage of teachers who agreed with a specific survey item, or the means for those items. Student achievement data may be available from the school district.

REPORTING DATA

Results should be combined into a single report that can be used by school faculty and staff for school improvement purposes. The report should contain sections for each source of data, allowing faculty and staff to easily identify themes and patterns in the data.

Results of classroom observations should be reported for the school as a whole (e.g., "The data show that 'we' are extensively using direct instruction but rarely using cooperative learning.") rather than for identifiable subgroups (e.g., "The three math teachers rarely use technology."). Once the faculty is comfortable with using evaluation data, the shift to subgroup and individual teacher findings can be made.

Achievement data are are typically available at the student/classroom/grade level, but with the advent of NCLB reporting requirements, disaggregation of data is also available for specific groups such as children with special needs and minority students.

Disaggregation is essential for the formative evaluation process, allowing teachers to use these data as "needs analysis" results and plan any needed changes in their classroom practices. Results from the teacher/student/parent questionnaires can also be disaggregated presented in a variety of ways that are meaningful to faculty, staff, and teachers. It is essential that the results of these questionnaires do not violate the confidentiality of respondents. For example, if a teacher survey is disaggregated by grade level, teachers may be able to identify individual teachers due to an identifiable pattern of responses. This is especially true when only a few teachers in a group responded to the survey. In these cases, it is best to generate results for groups only where there are more than three participants.

When the data from all instruments have been reported, teachers should have free access to the reports and ample time to assess and discuss it them. These data can provide a rich source of reliable information that can identify implementation progress and the need for further intervention. The venue for this discussion may be a faculty meeting with opportunities for follow-up meetings to discuss specific topics. Each school will handle the discussion process in their own way, but the results should be fully discussed by all faculty and staff, and any decisions should be incorporated into the school improvement plan. Hopefully, the end product of this formative evaluation process will be a better learning environment for both students and teachers alike.

REFERENCES

Bloom, B., Hastings, T., & Madaus, G. (1971). *Handbook on formative and summative evaluation of student learning*. New York: McGraw-Hill.

Bryk, A., & Schneider, B. (2002). *Trust in school: A core resource for improvement*. New York: Russell Sage Foundation.

Butler, E. D., & Alberg, M. J. (1991). *The Tennessee School Climate Inventory: Resource manual*. Memphis, TN: The University of Memphis, Center for Research in Educational Policy.

Desjean-Perrotta, B. (2003). The middle school achievement project: A grassroots effort improves middle level education. *Middle School Journal, 34*(3), 5-11.

Felner, R, Jackson, A., Kasak, D., Mulhall, P., Brand, S., & Flowers, N. (1997). The impact of school reform for the middle years. *Phi Delta Kappan, 78*(7), 528-532.

Mertens, S., & Flowers, N. (2003). Middle school practices improve students achievement in high poverty schools. *Middle School Journal, 35*(1),33-43.

No Child Left Behind Act of 2001. (2001). Public Law 107-110, 107th Cong, Cong. Rec. 1425. (enacted 2002). Washington, DC: U.S. Department of Education Web site: www.ed.gov./offices/OESE/esea

Ross, S. M. (2003). How to get off the reform roller coaster. *Principal Leadership*, High School Edition, 2(4), 16-21.

Ross, S. M., & Alberg, M. J. (2001). Implementation benchmarking. Memphis, TN: The University of Memphis, Center for Research in Educational Policy.

Ross, S. M., Smith, L. J., & Alberg M. J. (1998). *School observation measure*. Memphis, TN: The University of Memphis, Center for Research in Educational Policy.

Ross, S. Troutman, A, Horgan, D., Maxwell, S., Laitinen, R., & Lowther, D. (1997). The success of schools in implementing eight restructuring designs: A synthesis of first-year evaluation outcomes. *School Effectiveness and School Improvement, 8*(1), 95-124.

Sterbinsky, A., & Ross, S. M. (2003). *School observation measure reliability study*. Memphis, TN: The University of Memphis, Center for Research in Educational Policy.

Stigler, J., & Hiebert, J. (1999). *The teaching gap: Best ideas from the world's teachers for improving education in the classroom*. New York: The Free Press.

Trimble, S. (2002). Common elements of high performing, high poverty middle schools. *Middle School Journal, 38*(4), 7-16.

Trimble, S. (2003). Research-based classroom practices and student achievement. *Middle School Journal, 35*(1), 52-58.

—Allan Sterbinsky
—Steven M. Ross
The University of Memphis

ASSESSMENT: SUMMATIVE EVALUATION

"'Whaja' get on the final?", a sixth grader asks his best friend. "How many of my seventh graders reached 'proficiency' in math?," a teacher wonders. "How effective is this new science program for raising student achievement?" a middle school principal asks a sales representative. Such inquiries occur every day in schools as part of efforts to gauge the effectiveness of different learning experiences. Educational researchers and policy makers view this process very seriously and refer to it by a formal name—*summative evaluation*.

Summative evaluation measures how well the major outcomes of a course or program are attained at the conclusion of instruction (posttest) or thereafter on the job (Morrison, Ross, & Kemp, 2004, p. 426). Student learning is usually the primary outcome of interest. Other outcomes that are frequently assessed include: (a) efficiency of learning, (b) cost of program development and implementation, (c) reactions toward the course or program, and (d) long-term benefits of the program. As will be illustrated below, it is beneficial for summative evaluations to include multiple outcome measures to increase information for

decision making. For example, it would be quite important to know that a new program, which produces only marginally better student learning than the currrent program, costs five times more to implement!

Summative evaluations essentially ask "how did we do?" In contrast, a complementary orientation called *formative* evaluation asks "how are we doing?" Thus, summative evaluations focus on final results or "products," whereas formative evaluations focus on intermediate results or "processes." To sharpen this distinction, consider a social studies teacher who presents a week-long unit on the Revolutionary War. From time to time, she gives informal quizzes and asks questions to gauge how well students understand the material. Unfortunately, the "formative" results prove discouraging—nearly half of the students fail the quizzes. On this basis, the teacher decides to use more concrete examples and teach at a slightly slower pace. At the end of the week, she administers the final unit test. The results on this "summative" test are outstanding—tthe vast majority of the students earn A's and no one scores lower than 80% correct. Formative and summative evaluations are thus being used in combination to (a) judge progress (formative), (b) make refinements in instruction, and (c) judge culminating products (summative).

Today, U.S. schools are being judged on a very familiar type of summative evaluation—the state-mandated standardized achievement tests in reading, mathematics, and other subjects. Under the federal No Child Left Behind (NLCB) Act, every public school in the United States is expected to bring all of its students to proficiency in reading and mathematics by the 2013-2014 school year. Schools that fail to make Adequate Yearly Progress (AYP) are subject to progressively more severe sanctions each year, culminating in restructuring and possible state takeover. Never in our history has summative evaluation been such a dominant a force for requiring educational accountability.

Aside from judging the success of schools and courses, summative evaluation is widely used for assessing the effectiveness of educational programs. Such evaluations are exemplified in questions such as, "Is Program A a better choice for improving first graders' reading skills than is Program B?" To address this question, the preferred summative evaluation approach uses an experimental-type design to compare outcomes for a group of students (or classrooms or schools) using "Program A" and a similar group using "Program B." If one group significantly outperforms the other on an appropriate assessment of reading skill, the evaluator can infer that the associated reading program has a positive effect.

To illustrate an actual design of this type, several colleagues and I recently evaluated, in Memphis, Tennessee, a middle school educational reform called the KIPP Academy (Alberg, 2003; Ross, McDonald, & Gallagher, 2004; Sterbinsky & Ross, 2003). The KIPP program was developed in 1994 with the explicit goal of increasing achievement of at-risk young adolescents. Major program components used to accomplish this goal include extending the school day, increasing academic rigor of instruction and student work, setting high goals for achievement, and requiring participation and commitment by students, their parents, and the faculty (see www.kipp.org). In this summative evaluation study, we examined the KIPP Academy's end-of-year results on multiple measures including student achievement, teacher perceptions, school climate, and teaching methods. Most critical was the analysis of student achievement, which would establish the primary basis on which the school district and the public would judge the success of the school. In this situation (as in nearly all educational settings), it was not feasible or desirable to randomly assign students or teachers to the KIPP Academy and a control school (experimental design). Nor was it possible to find an existing school in the district that was sufficiently similar to KIPP to serve as a control school (matched-control school design). What we could do, however, was establish a control group at the *student* level. Specifically, we first individually matched each KIPP student to a student of the same grade level, gender, ethnicity, SES status, and ability (prior reading and math achievement) who attended a similar neighborhood school. Then, we compared the end-of-year achievement of the KIPP and control students on the state-mandated achievement test. The results showed significant advantages for KIPP in nearly all of the subject area tests. Coupled with positive results from the teacher attitude and climate surveys, the final report presented a favorable evaluation that justified both continuation of the KIPP Academy and its possible expansion to other schools.

Studies such as the one just described are being increasingly advocated under NCLB's focus on using "scientifically-based research" to determine "what works" in education (Eisenhart & Towne, 2003). In fact, in association with the NCLB legislation, the What Works Clearinghouse (WWC) was awarded, in August 2002, $18.5 million to assess and report the strength of scientific evidence on the effectiveness of different educational programs used to improve important student outcomes (see http:www.ed.gov/offices/OERI/what works/). Emphasis will be placed on using rigorous experimental-type studies to determine program effects on student achievement. How the program can be better implemented or improved (formative evaluation) will not be of interest. The WWC orientation thus represents about as pure a form of summative evaluation as can be applied.

Given their different goals, how do summative and formative evaluation compare procedurally? Outlined below are the basic steps for applying each. As will be seen, the first three steps show slight differences for the two orientations. The last four steps, however, are virtually identical for both.

1. Specifying evaluation objectives

   Summative example: To determine the effects of Reading Program A on increasing student achievement

   Formative example: To determine whether each major component of Reading Program A is working as designed.

2. Determining the evaluation design for each objective

   Summative example: Experimental-control group design (compare Program A to Program B using two different classes)

   Formative example: Descriptive design (observe and interview teachers and students regarding Program A implementation)

3. Developing data collection instruments and procedures for each objective

   Summative example: Achievement test scores, questionnaires, interviews, observations, development costs, implementation costs

   Formative example: Interviews, questionnaires, course exams and quizzes, observations

4. Conducting the study

   Summative and formative example: The data collection is scheduled at the target school or schools. Evaluators visit the school to administer questionnaires, conduct interviews, observe program implementation, and collect test scores.

5. Analyzing the results from each instrument

   Summative and formative examples: The interview and observation data are analyzed *qualitatively* to determine trends, themes, and categories of outcomes. Questionnaire data are analyzed *quantitatively* to indicate response frequencies (e.g., what percent of the teachers "strongly agreed" that they liked the program?). Test data are analyzed *quantitatively* to determine gains from pre- to post-testing (formative and summative) or differences between treatment and control students (usually summative).

6. Interpreting the results

   Summative and formative example: A final report might read: "Interview and questionnaire results overall indicate positive reactions to the program by teachers. Observations, however, reveal some weaknesses in the implementation. Student achievement show 'statistically significant' improvements in test scores for students using the program."

7. Disseminating the results and conclusions

   Summative and formative example: An interim (formative) or final (summative) evaluation report is written. The evaluators may meet with the program developers and school representatives to discuss the results. Presentations at various forums or meetings may be given.

Although the last four steps show much overlap between summative and formative evaluations, it is generally the case that summative evaluations will place relatively more emphasis on:

- Objective as opposed to subjective measures of student learning
- Quantitative analyses that determine program outcomes, particularly student achievement, by comparing treatment (program) groups to control groups.
- Interpretations of program effects in terms of "statistical significance" (reliability) and "effect sizes" (educational meaningfulness)
- Publication of reports in refereed educational research journals; presentation of reports at professional meetings.

As discussed above, current national emphases on educational accountability are elevating the visibility and importance of summative evaluation. The obvious advantage is increased accessibility to scientifically valid evidence about the effectiveness of educational programs. A disadvantage, however, may occur if summative evaluation is made so distinct from formative evaluation that potentially good programs (with correctable weaknesses) are discarded prematurely. In other domains, such as the aviation or automobile industry, "completed" or "finished" prod-

ucts are quite easy to identify. (Imagine your pilot announcing that the new jet aircraft in which you are seated at 40,000 ft. is still "under development.") By comparison, the status of educational products at any given time is usually indeterminate. That is, can any educational program (e.g., in reading, math, or science) ever be considered *complete*? In educational contexts, there is almost always the opportunity to use evaluation (whether formative or summative) to make improvements in courses and programs. Suppose, for example, that a summative evaluation reveals that a new program is ineffective due to, say, being too difficult for students, too demanding for teachers to implement, or too time-consuming to integrate with the current curriculum. Surely, if motivated, the developers or teachers could make subsequent adaptations to address the particular problems and improve results. Such is exemplified by the ongoing efforts of the KIPP Academy (see above illustration) to use its "summative evaluation" results to make desired enhancements in its programs (e.g., increasing usage of student-centered teaching). Together, formative and summative orientations establish an evaluation continuum having generally similar methodologies and purposes. As presented in this chapter, summative evaluation approaches will become favored over formative approaches with increases in (a) the maturity of courses/programs to be examined and (b) the stakes for determining their effectiveness on measures considered educationally important.

REFERENCES

Alberg, M. (2003). *KIPP D.I.A.M.O.N.D Academy: The first year.* Memphis, TN: Center for Research in Educational Policy, The University of Memphis.

Eisenhart, M., & Towne, L. (2003). Contestation and chang in national policy on "scientifically based" education research. *Educational Researcher, 32*(7), 31-38.

Morrison, G. R., Ross, S. M., & Kemp, J. E. (2004). *Designing effective instruction* (4th ed.). Hoboken, NJ: Wiley.

Ross, S. M., McDonald, A. J., & Gallagher, B. M. (2004). *Year 1 evaluation of the KIPP DIAMOND Academy: Analysis of TCAP scores for matched program-control students.* Memphis, TN: Center for Research in Educational Policy, The University of Memphis.

Sterbinsky, A., & Ross, S. M. (2003). *KIPP D.I.A.M.O.N.D. Academy: Three comparison studies.* Memphis, TN: Center for Research in Educational Policy, The University of Memphis.

—Steven M. Ross
The University of Memphis

ASSOCIATION FOR SUPERVISION AND CURRICULUM DEVELOPMENT

Founded in 1943, the Association for Supervision and Curriculum Development (ASCD) is an international, nonprofit, nonpartisan organization that represents 160,000 educators from 135 countries and more than 60 affiliates. ASCD's members span the entire profession of educators—superintendents, supervisors, principals, teachers, professors of education, and school board members. Because ASCD's membership is so large, it represents as many members of individual professions as do the individual cohort groups, with the exception of teachers. Approximately 41 percent of ASCD's members work in middle level education.

As ASCD's name reflects, the association was initially envisioned to represent "curriculum" and "supervision" issues. Over the years, its focus has changed. ASCD now addresses *all aspects of effective teaching and learning*—such as, professional development, educational leadership, and capacity building.

ASCD AS AN EXPERT SOURCE AND CONTENT PROVIDER

ASCD is known throughout the profession for its ability to identify educational trends and to translate research into practice. Areas, for example, that show promising results in improved student achievement include: differentiated instruction; Understanding by Design, a framework for curriculum design and assessment for deep student understanding; the brain and learning; and What Works in Schools, a synthesis of 35 years of education research that identifies 11 factors that have the greatest effect on student achievement.

ASCD has been advocating for educational excellence and equity since the mid-1940s—shortly after the organization's inception. Through its involvement in key national and international issues, ASCD has provided resources and expert opinion ranging from broad-based issues (such as school reform, professional development, organizational leadership, technology, and brain-based research) to specific issues (such as high-stakes testing, commercialism in schools, character education, service learning, First Amendment rights in education, and school violence).

ASCD'S "IN THE FIELD" EDUCATOR PERSPECTIVES

ASCD as an organization is composed of multiple and overlapping communities–interconnected by physical location and common interests. For example:

- **ASCD's affiliates** serve as key educational links at local, state and international levels.
- The **ASCD Student Chapter Program** continues to be an important resource for pre-service, novice, and graduate level teachers.
- **The ASCD Networks** continue to provide forums for educators and noneducators alike on various themes that address traditional teaching and learning, progressive approaches, classroom and non-classroom delivery, and management-related topics. There are now more than 50 ASCD-sponsored networks, including the middle grades network.

ASCD'S MIDDLE GRADES NETWORK

The ASCD Middle Grades Network is an alliance of educators who discuss, develop, promote, disseminate, and evaluate new knowledge and practices designed to improve learning and success for all middle grades youth. The network provides high quality learning and professional growth opportunities and fosters innovations that are cooperative, interactive, rigorous, and responsive to the needs of diverse learners.

—Christy Guilfoyle
Association for Supervision and Curriculum Development

ASSOCIATION OF ILLINOIS MIDDLE-LEVEL SCHOOLS

The Association of Illinois Middle-Level Schools (AIMS) is a private nonprofit organization committed to exemplary programs, practices, and policies that support professionals, families, and communities educating students, typically ages 10-14, during their journey through Grades 5-8 and their transition into ninth grade.

AIMS takes a leadership role in building and promoting excellence and equity in professional preparation and practice for the middle-level. The organization has emerged as the leader and professional development provider for Illinois middle-grades teachers and principals. AIMS promotes and advocates for middle-grades best practices, and its contributions have impacted both state and national priorities.

AIMS has four primary goals:

- Serve as a forum for generating and gathering ideas regarding exemplary programs, practices, and policies in middle-level education.
- Promote and disseminate contemporary philosophy, programs, curricula, and instructional practices.
- Represent middle-level education in professional and public settings.
- Encourage colleges and universities to prepare educators and administrators to meet the needs of middle-level schools, students, staff, and parents.

To reach these goals, AIMS hosts conferences, institutes, seminars, and workshops. It also publishes a quarterly newsletter and annual journal, and maintains a Web site dedicated to middle-level education in Illinois. The organization has been a leader in pursuing multiple avenues for helping schools improve their practices. To assist in quality control of desirable practices, AIMS began its Summer Institutes in 1986. The goals of this institute, as well as other AIMS events, are to provide relevant content in Illinois, where no middle-level preparation standards are defined or required. Thus, AIMS continues to seek to create a cadre of "state-level" experts to assist other schools, and offer schools opportunities to learn from one another.

AIMS has been in operation since 1976, when it began with 20 Illinois educators attending the National Middle School Association (NMSA) Annual Conference. By 1984, AIMS had merged with the Early Adolescent Education Association of Illinois. AIMS reached national prominence in 1989, when it started a network of schools through an Innovation in Education award from the U.S. Department of Education. This network of 12 demonstration/partnership schools set the gold standard for school reform networks nationwide. Originally known as Project Initiative Middle Level, and now called the Illinois Middle Grades Network, it has grown to include over 150 schools in 2003-04. Network schools participate in school mentoring, network-wide data development and collection, professional development, and leadership development using NMSA's *This We Believe* and the Carnegie Corporation of New York's *Turning Points*.

To aid the data collection process, AIMS jointly developed the Middle Grades Self Study with the Center for Prevention Research and Development (CPRD), a unit of the University of Illinois' Institute of Government and Public Affairs. The self study was used in the network schools as part of the country's first large-scale, quantitative research project demonstrating the relationship between middle-grades practices and school achievement (Felner et al., 1997). This 7-year study, along with the self study instrument, significantly influenced the national middle-grades movement and agenda.

By 1995, AIMS and the Illinois State Board of Education (ISBE) were codirectors of Illinois' Middle Grades School State Policy Initiative (MGSSPI), a project of the Carnegie Corporation. This unique public/private relationship increased state-level awareness and consideration about the needs of early adolescents, and fostered policy development, including middle-grades teacher preparation.

In 1998, AIMS expanded its services to Illinois schools qualifying for Comprehensive School Reform funding. AIMS became the first regional center for the National Turning Points Design, a New American Schools model. In 2003, AIMS began coordinating the Illinois Horizon Schools: Schools to Watch program, a state version of the nationwide program run by the National Forum to Accelerate Middle-Grades Reform. (AIMS has been a member of the forum since its inception in 1997.) The Illinois Horizon Schools program allows AIMS to identify exemplary middle-level schools within the state, as well as connect to the larger national initiative.

As a result of the collaborations with ISBE and CPRD, AIMS has been awarded special grants for Education to Careers programming, networking support, adolescent literacy and reading, scientific literacy, drug prevention, and parental involvement. AIMS is located at the University of Illinois at Urbana-Champaign within the Institute of Government and Public Affairs, alongside the offices of Center for Prevention Research and Development.

REFERENCE

Felner, R. D., Jackson, A. W., Kasak, D., Mulhall, P., Brand, S., & Flowers, N. (1997). The impact of school reform for the middle years: Longitudinal study of a network engaged in Turning Points-based comprehensive school transformation. *Phi Delta Kappan, 78*(7), 528-532, 541-550.

—Deb Schrock
Association of Illinois Middle-Level Schools

—Deborah Kasak
National Forum to Accelerate Middle-Grades Reform

AUTHENTIC ASSESSMENT

In the postmodern world, educational assessments must measure or sample a wide range of cognitive processes and/or abilities. The term "authentic" represents a broad concept of assessment, one that is interrelated and interconnected to numerous innovative strategies. The major criteria for an authentic assessment are that it engages students in real-life situations, rather than in completing isolated tasks, and requires students to show what they have learned in a context that is congruent with real-life experience (Leon & Elias, 1998).

In the late 1970s, a reawakened interest in the theories and research of intelligence led to scrutinizing assessment practices with broader lenses. Children's achievement and performance received increasing public attention during the latter 1980s and early 1990s. The volume and variety of professional literature on various methods of assessment and the number of states seeking alternative means to evaluate students demonstrates this interest (Grace, 1992; Maurer, 1996). The rise of authentic assessment resulted from demands for higher standards, work force 2000 which recognized skills needed to be successful in later life, and cognitive and developmental psychological research (Maurer, 1996). Cognitive psychologist Howard Gardner's (1983) theory of multiple intelligences became part of this assessment reform movement as he focused on the many kinds of knowledges, talents, abilities, and skills that exist beyond the two that traditional schooling has emphasized and usually tested: verbal-linguistic and logical-mathematical.

Most tests measure only a small part of children's linguistic and mathematical abilities and fail to reflect students' ability to think critically and creatively. They do not reflect students' motivation to learn or their capacity to engage in self-assessment (Kulieke et al., 1990). In addition, traditional tests may restrict resources or limit the time available to complete the test. Unlike the need to memorize that is emphasized in many tests, authentic assessment focuses on increased understanding with students demonstrating their own thinking and meanings—"a process of gathering and synthesizing information to help us understand and describe" (Schurr, 1999, p. 2). Critical and higher-order thinking skills are stressed through these assessments and often multiple approaches or answers can be correct as students demonstrate their use of the knowledge.

Assessment labels under the authentic umbrella typically include process, product, and performance.

Usually tied closely to the instructional process and course standards, these assessments can take many forms such as projects, demonstrations, exhibitions, and portfolios. Assessment is considered an ongoing dynamic process, not a one time test-only event, in which "students orchestrate learning strategies in a dynamic flow as they move in and out of different tasks and phases of learning" (Isolated Versus Integrated Assessment, ¶ 1; Kulieke et al., 1990). Regardless of the label, each of these techniques has moved beyond the concept of measuring student learning using multiple choice and other simple tests as single measures of student learning at one point in time. Judgment about students' abilities is based on the integration of many different sources of information gathered over time (Maurer, 1996).

Schurr (1999) in her text *Authentic Assessment* summarizes the characteristics of authentic assessment as general, complex tasks involving interrelated subtasks and internalization and application of knowledge and thinking processes generalizable to all sorts of knowledge. Authentic Assessment adapts more to strengths, needs, and choices of unique students; encourages critical and creative thinking in which students have time to arrive at the best of many possible answers; and involves students very actively and cooperatively in productive processes. Kulieke et al. (1990) describe these multidimensional assessments in continuums: from decontextualized, atomistic tests (short answer, fill-in blank, multiple choice, true/false, etc.) to authentic, contextualized tasks such as performances and/or products; from a single measure of student learning to multiple measures; from simple to complex dimensions of learning; from assessment of few dimensions of intelligence to assessment of many dimensions.

These characteristics of authentic assessment complement the developmental characteristics and needs of middle school students. Critical thinking, inquiry, and discovery-oriented assessments such as multidimensional projects and exhibitions complement students' expanding cognitive abilities, especially for abstract thinking. With the focus on real world knowledge and contexts, students' growing interests in the larger community and their own self identity within it are nourished. This more qualitative approach to assessment encourages students to self express, create in many directions, and exhibit various abilities and multiple intelligences. As Alexander, Carr, and McAvoy state in their text *Student Oriented Curriculum*, "Young adolescents want desperately to do 'real' work, things that have meaning for them and significance in their community" (1995, p. 56). They have legitimate and significant concerns about themselves and the larger social, political world around them (Alexander et al., 1995; Beane, 1993).

CURRICULUM, INSTRUCTION, AND ASSESSMENT LINKED: EMPOWERING TEACHERS AND STUDENTS

The middle level movement stresses the interdependent priorities of curriculum, instruction, and assessment. When assessment is viewed as an equal component, educators, often with the help of students, can establish an agenda, communicate it, and learn the extent to which it has impacted students' learning (Gross, 2002). Authentic assessment should be aligned with curriculum and instruction, should promote student centered and individualized attention and thus empower teachers and students to maintain closer, more communicative relationships and to find and measure each student's potential.

With increased expectations such as accountability demands from the federal, state, and community levels, the issue of alignment can become difficult. Yet in an educational environment where instruction and assessment are integrated and where the concept of dynamic assessment is an active process in which students and teachers participate, new assessment techniques can be aligned with the newer constructivist vision for teaching and learning (Leon & Elias, 1998, Maurer, 1996). Using authentic curriculum ensures real-world learning, content connections and coherence as in interdisciplinary and integrated approaches and brings forward the student voice for a more democratic, student-centered focus (Beane, 1993; Caskey, 2002). Standards and skills promoted in all subject areas can be planned and integrated into an assessment that reflects the criteria from an interdisciplinary unit.

Instructional strategies that are varied, stress cooperative learning, performance and oral demonstrations, and strategies that incorporate numerous multiple intelligence opportunities, can bring out the strengths in students that probably would not be seen in typical or standardized test situations. Traditional tests can misjudge the abilities of some students and lead to damaging mistakes regarding the curricular and placement decisions. Leon and Elias' (1998) findings suggest that "authentic assessments may provide a method with which we can 'save' those students who have traditionally been regarded as failures and passed through the system until they drop out or graduate from high school without adequate skills or a sense of accomplishment" (p. 31). Those students evaluated more highly by authentic assessments will thus be allowed to reach their potential, be treated more fairly, not fall through the cracks, and not be

held back from challenging courses and opportunities by their low standardized test scores. Thus, the authentic assessments also hold strong potential for increasing students' motivation levels. Instruction that is relevant, academically challenging, and actively engaging will increase students' levels of motivation and ultimately is more important to achievement (Bracey, 2001). Actively engaging forms of assessment, as with instruction, are also more fun. Young adolescents often have their best learning experiences when they are also having fun in the process (Alexander et al., 1995; Vars, 1993).

Teachers are more empowered with authentic assessment practices as they, not a national test manufacturing company, make decisions about which knowledge tied to their own curriculum and instruction should be assessed and how. "A teacher interested in whether a student can transfer what is known to solve a problem in a different but real context is one who is interested in using an assessment tool that is authentic (Maurer, 1996). Students are also more empowered as these assessments meet their growing needs as individuals, responsible for their own learning. Alexander and colleagues' (1995) experience with sixth grade students in a student-oriented curriculum demonstrated that students responded positively to empowerment and that teachers should not fear students making their own choices and decisions. Students can become strategic in their own learning process and teachers can better adapt the instructional process to individuals and communicate to students, expectations and standards so that students can know what is valued, set personal goals, internalize the required knowledge and skills, and understand that they can help to control and improve their learning (Kulieke et al., 1990). This improved communication between teachers and students can lead to improved relationships, affective gains, and an overall warmer classroom environment and culture (Grace, 1992).

DESIGNING AND MEASURING AUTHENTIC ASSESSMENT

With the focus on more student-centered learning, measuring understanding with authentic assessment requires different criteria. Among these criteria, assessments should be credible, reliable, valid, generalizable, feasible, and user-friendly (Kulieke et al., 1990; Maurer, 1996; Wiggins 1989). Maurer also indicates that evaluation can include four sources: students, peers, parents/community, and teachers, both formal and informal. If performance assessments are to gain credibility with students, parents, and the community, they need to be reliable, valid, and generalizable. Reliability entails the consistency of the scores when different evaluators rate a student and when rated on the same task over time. Validity refers to the assessment accurately measuring the learning domain. "The closer the assessment is to the real context of the classroom instruction, the more valid it is" (Maurer, 1996, p. 114). Generalizability means that the tasks involve real life skills that can be transferred to solving real world challenges and problems.

A good school practice is for the teaching faculty to develop together some common sets of criteria so that individual, idiosyncratic criteria are not used. Such efforts are more likely to result in valid and reliable assessment. By participating in the process of setting criteria, teachers will be more likely to understand and adhere to these criteria. A purpose and use of each assessment must be clear. Generally, the overall purpose of student assessment is to provide valid information for decision making. These decisions can include diagnosis, placement, guidance and counseling, admissions, or certification.

The scoring requires complex and more subjective considerations and tests depth of knowledge better, yet the contextual aspects often make authentic assessment more difficult to compare (Schurr, 1999). Thus, rubrics are often used to aid evaluation, either holistic or analytic, which provides a more thorough analysis of specific strengths and areas for improvement. Students often view standards and rubrics for assessing the work beforehand; thus, teachers provide students guidelines for judging their own work and encouraging valid self-assessment (Maurer, 1996).

PORTFOLIOS

Portfolios represent many forms of authentic assessment that can include process, performance, and product. Although most of the characteristics of authentic assessment addressed in previous sections pertain to portfolios, the concept of multiple, varied tasks worked on, collected, and measured over time helps to define a portfolio. For Schurr (1999), a portfolio is a "systematic, integrated, and meaningful collection of a student's day-to-day work showing that student's efforts, progress, or achievement in one or more subjects. A portfolio includes evidence of the student's critical self-reflection and participation in setting the focus of the portfolio, selecting the contents of the portfolio, and judging the portfolio's merit" (p. 4).

Essays, reports, letters, creative writing pieces, poetry, problems and solutions, response logs, reviews, journal entries, interviews, illustrations, maps, photographs, comic strips, dioramas, collaborative works, workbook exercises, quizzes, self assessment checklists, teacher comments, peer reviews, parental observations and comments, and rough drafts and revisions might all be components of a portfolio. Other items could include a check list or inventory, work samples showing progress and success, anecdotal nonjudgmental records, rating scales, questions and requests, and screening tests that assess what a student already knows on a particular topic, as in differentiated learning approaches (Grace, 1992). Ways to organize the portfolio can include chronologically or categorically by skill development area or curriculum area, on-going versus finished work, medium in which it is created, or rank in quality. This multidimensional exhibition can demonstrate numerous skills related to defined standards such as reading, writing, questioning, expressing, and listening.

The portfolio must have a defined purpose that the components will help illuminate. A portfolio can represent a journey over time with drafts and showing progress on particular pieces as well as showing the breadth or scope of a student's efforts and achievements. Portfolios enable children to participate in evaluating their own work, track individual children's progress, and allow for evaluating the quality of individual children's overall performance. Parents and others beyond the teacher become the audience for the portfolio as various sources contribute to the authentic assessment work. Portfolios can be helpful demonstrations of student work in parent-teacher discussions.

Some educators value videotaped portfolios. These document the learner's interests and accomplishments and assist teachers in evaluating each student's progress from year to year. The portfolios usually include tapes of an initial interview and excerpts of the student's work throughout the year. As parents receive the videotape at the end of the year, they better understand their children's growth. This provides an important supplement to information from report cards and results of standardized tests. "Wide use of portfolios can stimulate a shift in classroom practices and education policies toward schooling that more fully meets the range of children's developmental needs" (Grace, 1992).

REFERENCES

Alexander, W. M., Carr, D., & McAvoy, K. (1995). *Student-oriented curriculum: Asking the right questions*. Westerville, OH: National Middle School Association.

Beane, J. A. (1993). A middle school curriculum: From rhetoric to reality (2nd ed.). Columbus, OH: National Middle School Association.

Bracey, G. W. (2001). Research—At the beep, pay attention. *Phi Delta Kappan, 82*(7), 555.

Caskey, M. (2002). Authentic curriculum: Strengthening middle level education. In V. A. Anfara, Jr. & S. L. Stacki (Eds.), *Middle school curriculum, instruction, and assessment* (pp. 103-117). Greenwich, CT: Information Age.

Gardner, H. (1983). *Frames of mind.* New York: Basic Books.

Grace, K. (1992). The portfolio and its use: Developmentally appropriate assessment of young children. Retrieved June 16, 2005, from http://ceep.crc.uiuc.edu/eecearchive/digests/1992/grace92.html

Gross, S. J. (2002). Introduction: Middle-level curriculum, instruction, and assessment. In V. A. Anfara, Jr. & S. L. Stacki (Eds.), *Middle school curriculum, instruction, and assessment* (pp. ix-xxxii). Greenwich, CT: Information Age.

Kulieke, M., Bakker, J., Collins, C., Fennimore, T., Fine, C., Herman, J., et al. (1990). *Why should assessment be based on a vision of learning?* North Central Regional Educational Laboratory. Retrieved on July 21, 2004, from http://www.ncrel.org/sdrs/areas/rpl_esys/assess.htm

Leon S., & Elias, M. (1998). A comparison of portfolio, performance, and traditional assessment in the middle school. *Research in Middle Level Education Quarterly, 21*(2), 21-37.

Maurer, R. E. (1996). *Designing alternative assessments for interdisciplinary curriculum in middle and secondary schools.* Boston: Allyn & Bacon.

Schurr, S. (1999). *Authentic assessment: Using product, performance, and portfolio measures.* Columbus, OH: National Middle School Association.

Vars, G. F. (1993). *Interdisciplinary teaching: Why & how.* Westerville, OH: National Middle School Association.

Wiggins, G. (1989). A true test: Toward more authentic and equitable assessment. *Phi Delta Kappan, 70,* 703-714.

—Sandra L. Stacki
Hofstra University

BEANE, JAMES A.

James Beane is a curriculum theorist, scholar, and teacher whose life-long focus has been on the nature of the democratic school, human dignity, and the commensurate mandate on curriculum to integrate all aspects of student experience and knowledge. This theme is evident in the very titles of his three most influential books: *Affect in the Curriculum: Toward Democracy, Dignity, and Diversity* (1990); *A Middle School Curriculum: From Rhetoric to Reality* (1990/1993); and *Curriculum Integration: Designing the Core of Democratic Education* (1997).

Following graduation from the State University of New York, Buffalo, with a major in English, Beane taught in the Amherst Public Schools (NY) for 3 years. He worked at the state education level from 1971–1973. During this time, Beane completed his graduate studies, with an EdD in curriculum development. His major professor was Conrad Toepfer, one of the founders of the middle school movement, and also a staunch defender of human rights, dignity, and equity. Beane approached his doctoral study in a manner fitting of his interests. Dr. Toepfer has commented of his student, "His scholarship in graduate study was surpassed only by his passion for human justice" (Lounsbury, 1997). Rather than study the accepted education texts of the day, Beane studied the works of early progressive educators, from which he synthesized his strongly held and well articulated philosophy of education.

In 1973 Beane joined the faculty at St. Bonaventure University (NY) and became chair of the Department of Administration, Supervision, and Curriculum in 1976. He continued his teaching and scholarship at St. Bonaventure for the next five years. He then returned to the middle school as a seventh grade team teacher before joining the faculty of the National College of Education at National-Louis University (IL) in 1989 as a member of the Interdisciplinary Studies Program. He was instrumental in planning the Middle Level Curriculum Center at National-Louis University.

Beane is the recipient of the Distinguished Alumni Award from the Graduate School of Education, SUNY, Buffalo; the James E. Stoltenberg Award from the Wisconsin Association for Middle Level Education; and the University-Wide Faculty Award for Professional Excellence from St. Bonaventure University.

REFERENCES

Beane, J. A. (1990). *Affect in the curriculum: Toward democracy, dignity, and diversity.* New York: Teachers College Press.

Beane, J. A. (1993). *A middle school curriculum: From rhetoric to reality* (Rev. ed.). Columbus, OH: National Middle School Association(Orignal work published 1990)

Beane, J. A. (1997). *Curriculum integration: Designing the core of democratic education.* New York: Teachers College Press.

Lounsbury, J. (1997, November). Introduction speech. Presented at the annual conference of the National Middle School Association, Indianapolis, IN.

—Mary Henton
National Middle School Association

BERGMANN, SHERREL

A member of the "second generation" of middle school advocates, according to Gordon Vars who was her major professor, Sherrel Bergmann has focused her work on young adolescent social and emotional development. Specifically, she has contributed to the literature on advisory, guidance, young adolescent decision-making skills, and family/parent relationships. Her research, practice, and writing on the guidance and advisory roles that teachers fulfill have helped to shape the conversations about student needs and teacher responsibilities. In addition, Bergmann has been a defender of arts and exploratory programs for middle school students.

The titles of her publications, speeches, and presentations reflect her keen interest in the social and emotional development of young adolescents: *Discipline and Guidance: A Thin Line in the Middle School,* "There Must be Time for Guidance in the Middle School," "Divorce and the Middle School Student," "Teaching Middle-Schoolers Decision Making Skills," "You've Got to Reach Them if You Want to Teach Them," What Research Says About At-Risk Students in the Middle School," and "Spending an Hour With Some Middle Level Writers."

Bergmann began her professional career as a middle school teacher, serving in various districts, including the Kent State University School, Akron Public Schools (OH), and Calumet Public Schools (MI). She became Chair of the Department of Education at Lake Forest College (IL) in 1976, and later held several teaching and administrative positions at National Louis University between 1978 and 1996. Among the accomplishments during her tenure at the university is developing the Middle Level Curriculum Center, which she later directed. She has held numerous summer faculty appointments, as well.

Bergmann's contributions to the field of middle grades education have extended beyond her teaching to active membership and leadership on numerous professional committees and organizations, including committees of National Middle School Association (Research Committee, Professional Preparation Committee, Critical Issues Committee, Curriculum Task Force) and advisor to education and health organizations (JFK Healthworld, National Resource Center for Middle Grades Education, Center for Education of the Young Adolescent). Bergmann was cofounder of the Association of Illinois Middle Level Schools, and continues to be active at the state level.

—Mary Henton
National Middle School Association

BRAIN PERIODIZATION

Brain periodization is a theory of human brain growth stages advanced in the 1970s by Herman T. Epstein, a professor of biophysics in the Department of Biology at Brandeis University. This theory purports that the brain undergoes alternating periods of growth spurts and growth plateaus from birth to adolescence (Epstein, 1978). Epstein's research led him to hypothesize that there are five major brain growth stages at the ages of 3-10 months, 2-4 years, 6-8 years, 10-12 years, and 14-16 years in about 85% of children. Similarly, he reported that there is virtually no growth during the intervals between these stages. As a consequence of these hypotheses, a flurry of interest in the theory of brain periodization and its implications for middle level education emerged (Epstein & Toepfer, 1978). Interest in brain periodization waned in the mid 1980s as Epstein's research methodology and conclusions were called into question (Hutson, 1984; McQueen, 1984; Pellegrini, 1983). The literature on brain periodization reveals the rise and decline of the theory.

At the 1977 National Middle School Association's annual conference, Epstein's presentation on the theory of brain periodization caught the interest and attention of middle level educators (Brazee, 1983). Afterward Epstein and Toepfer (1978) called on educators to adjust middle level programs in light of the predicted slow brain growth period of ages 12 to 14. They postulated that during this period the brain did not have the capacity for complex thinking and recommended curricula that avoided the introduction of novel cognitive skills (p. 658). Epstein (1981) hypothesized that the brain growth stages corresponded to Piaget's cognitive stages of development and suggested altering curricula to match students' cognitive levels. For a time, brain periodization was given consideration. The National Middle School Association's position paper, *This We Believe* (1982) mentioned the emergence of brain periodization and other theories for their members' consideration. Several middle level educators (Brazee, 1983; Hester & Hester, 1983; Strahan, 1985; Strahan & Toepfer, 1984) summarized brain periodization theory and suggested implications for middle grades programs. Conversely, researchers, science specialists, and others (Gould, 1981; Hutson, 1985; McQueen, 1984; Pellegrini, 1984) thoroughly critiqued Epstein's theory and raised questions about his research methodology. Examination of original data sources led Gould (1981) to find fault with Epstein's work as reported in *The Mismeasure of Man.* Later, Pellegrini (1984) and McQueen (1984) criticized Epstein's assertions citing the misleading use of data and advised against classroom application of the theory. Epstein (1984) responded to early criticisms of brain periodization, however support for his theory of brain periodization diminished due to flawed research methods and analyses.

Brain periodization theory had a unique and brief appearance in middle level education. The theory had minimal effect on the curricula or instruction of middle schools (Brazee, 1983). Reference to brain periodization disappeared from educational journals and middle school literature in the late 1980s. In about a decade, the theory of brain periodization had gained and lost the attention of the educational community.

REFERENCES

Brazee, E. N. (1983). Brain periodization—Challenge not justification. *Middle School Journal, 15*(1) 8-9, 30.

Epstein, H. T. (1978). Growth spurts during brain development: Implications for educational policy and practice. In J. S. Chall & A. F. Mirsky (Eds.), Education and the brain (pp. 343-370). Chicago: University of Chicago Press.

Epstein, H. T. (1981). Learning to learn: Matching instruction to cognitive levels. *Principal, 60*(5), 25-30.

Epstein, H. T. (1984). Brain growth and cognitive development: A response to Richard McQueen. *Educational Leadership, 41*(5), 72-75.

Epstein, H. T., & Toepfer, C. F., Jr. (1978). A neuroscience basis for reorganizing middle grades education. *Educational Leadership, 35*(8), 656-658, 660.

Gould, S. J. (1981). *The mismeasure of man.* New York: Norton.

Hester, J. P., & Hester, P. J. (1983). Brain research and the middle school curriculum. *Middle School Journal, 15*(1) 4-7, 30.

Hutson, B. A. (1985). Brain growth spurts—What's left by the middle school years? *Middle School Journal, 16*(2), 8-10.

McQueen, R. (1984). Spurts and plateaus in brain growth: A critique of the claims of Herman Epstein. *Educational Leadership, 41*(5), 66-69, 71.

National Middle School Association. (1982). *This we believe.* Columbus, OH: Author.

Pellegrini, A. D. (1984). Some questions about the basic tenets of brain periodization research. *Journal of Instructional Psychology, 11,* 165-169.

Strahan, D. B. (1985). Brain growth spurts and middle grades curriculum: Readiness remains the issue. *Middle School Journal, 16*(2), 11-13.

Strahan, D. B., & Toepfer, C. F., Jr. (1984). Transescent thinking: Renewed rationale for exploratory learning. *Middle School Journal, 15*(2), 8-11.

—Micki Caskey
Portland State University

BREAKING RANKS: CHANGING AN AMERICAN INSTITUTION

The National Association of Secondary School Principals (NASSP) in partnership with the Carnegie Foundation for the Advancement of Teaching assembled this ambitious collection of recommendations for high schools called *Breaking Ranks: Changing an American Institution* (NASSP, 1996). Two years of collaboration from the Commission on the Restructuring of the American High School, the people "most profoundly involved in the American high school," culminated in this blueprint for improving and reforming high schools in the 21st century. This report was written for and by high schools principals and other educators in order to appeal to those who are involved in high school education reform on a day-to-day basis and in order to apply to high school principals as they have the best overview and they are best suited to know practical from impractical reforms.

The title, *Breaking Ranks*, emphasizes the purpose of this report. There are appeals to quash the status quo and demands to overhaul practices that do not contribute to students' academic success and ultimately life successes. Because students spend formative years in high school, the authors ask educators to reevaluate the purposes and functions of their high schools. This report stresses the importance of individualizing education rather than the traditional assembly line approach—"each student needs something different from high school." The authors also emphasize that reform is not as simple as implementing policies and tweaking practices. In order for reform to stick they are calling for systemic reform.

Breaking Ranks is grounded by six themes that appear throughout the report and that the authors insist are pivotal to the reformation of the American high school: (1) Personalization—high school educators must individualize instruction in order to accommodate all students; (2) Coherency—graduation requirements and "real world" applications of teachings should be clearly laid out for students; (3) Time—the traditional school day and year needs to change; (4) Technology—must be an integral aspect of every student's high school experience; (5) Professional Development—educators need focused preparation and support in the way of training and an elevated emphasis needs to be placed on their ongoing and evolving professional development; and (6) Leadership—everyone involved in the educational process, especially principals, need to contribute to building better high schools.

The themes listed above are reflected throughout the three sections that comprise *Breaking Ranks* and in the nearly 80 recommendations presented in these sections. The first section, "Priorities for Renewal," focuses on fundamental recommendations for high schools that instigate change in curriculum, instructional strategies, school environment, technology, organization and time, assessment and accountability. The entities, people and institutions, which enable and support the elemental changes proposed in the first section are the focus of the second section, "Web of support." Section two discusses professional development, diversity, governance, resources, ties to higher education, and relationships as areas integral to enhancing and supporting reform efforts. The final section, "Leadership," receives the least amount of page space but is the crux of the whole reform effort. In order for all the recommendations to gain a foothold and start to show success, educators, students, and communities must be willing to lead reform efforts and not balk in the face of seemingly insurmountable barriers, resistance to change, complacency, and acceptance of "good enough." One of the last statements of the authors' sums up the challenge facing high schools when *Breaking Ranks*, "Leadership requires that some people have the will and ability to act" (p. 96).

REFERENCE

National Association of Secondary School Principals. (1996). *Breaking ranks: changing an American institution.* Reston, VA: Author.

—Cody Stephens
CPRD,
University of Illinois

BREAKING RANKS II: STRATEGIES FOR LEADING HIGH SCHOOL REFORM

Breaking Ranks II: Strategies for Leading High School Reform (National Association of Secondary School Principals, 2004) is a complimentary, follow up report to *Breaking Ranks: Changing an American Institution* (NASSP, 1996) which presented ambitious high school reform recommendations. The general recommendations proposed in the initial *Breaking Ranks* serve as the foundation for *Breaking Ranks II* which is more applied, interactive, and specific to high school reforms in which principals play the central role. Assembled by the National Association of Secondary Schools Principals, *Breaking Ranks II* offers a template for principals, including tools, strategies, and examples of the successes and challenges that actual schools experienced when implementing school improvement recommendations. The *Breaking Ranks* series insists on broad reform in order to improve student performance and the "Seven Cornerstones Strategies to Improve Student Performance" presented in this report succinctly outline the "entry points" for reform and these Cornerstones provide the basis for successfully implementing all 31 of the *Breaking Ranks II* recommendations.

Breaking Ranks II begins with a battery of questions designed to assess a school's ability to serve all their students well. Once this assessment is complete and the need for reform is clear, the second section outlines how principals can institute a collaborative process to ensure buy in and enhance coordinated and sustained reform efforts by all parties. The authors believe that reforms will not stick if the principals are the only ones advocating for them. In addition to focusing on strategies for and barriers to enhancing student performance, the final section details real schools' experiences with reform efforts. In addition to being divided into several stepwise sections including the assessment, action strategies, and examples of reform in action. The recommendations cluster under one of three core areas: (1) Collaborative Leadership and Professional Learning Communities; (2) Personalization; and (3) Curriculum, Instruction and Assessment.

The most innovative aspect of *Breaking Ranks* is the appendices. These practical and instructive worksheets are tangible tools that facilitate principals' steps toward assessing and improving the staff and student performance.

Breaking Ranks is designed to serve as reference tool with recommendations and strategies that can be read, assimilated, and implemented in stages; however, the authors warn against piecemeal reform or focusing on a single strategy. They insist that substantive reform consists of constant, dedicated, and relentless efforts to assess schools' needs and implement good practice toward the ultimate goal of improving students' learning environment and achievements.

REFERENCES

National Association of Secondary School Principals. (1996). *Breaking ranks: changing an American institution.* Reston, VA: Author.

National Association of Secondary School Principals. (2004). *Breaking ranks II: Strategies for leading high school reform.* Reston, VA: Author.

—Cody Stephens
CPRD,
University of Illinois

THE BRIDGES PROJECT

Educational changes needed to occur as a growing concern mounted at the finding that a "volatile mismatch exists between the organization and curriculum of middle grade schools, and the intellectual, emotional, and interpersonal needs of young adolescents" (Carnegie Council on Adolescent Development, 1989, p. 32). This pronouncement lead the National Middle School Association, the Carnegie Corporation of New York, the National Education Association, and state and local educators and administrators to explore the need for more effective middle level practices. In 1990, this concerted effort along with state grants awarded by the Carnegie Corporation titled the Middle Grade School State Policy Initiative (MGSSPI) resulted in the formation of the BRIDGES Project in the state of North Dakota.

The BRIDGES Project was a voluntary program for North Dakota school districts that wanted to transition from the traditional junior high school structure to that of a middle school. The Project was a Professional Development/Education improvement effort aimed at assisting schools to develop curriculum and improve learning for all middle level students in North Dakota. The implementation of the Project lead to changes in school organization and management, curriculum, classroom practices and teacher attitudes as well as teacher education programs and teacher certification. It was from these changes that middle schools attempted to create a developmentally appropriate bridge between elementary and high school.

On receiving the initial state grant in 1990, study groups were formed with 24 communities across the state to explore the recommendations and implications of the middle school concept through the guidance of *Turning Points: Preparing American Youth of the 21st Century* (Carnegie Council on Adolescent Development, 1989). As it became evident that significant levels of commitment and interest existed in the state,

the Project embarked on the continuation grant for additional funding that was sought and obtained in 1993, 1995, and 1997.

At the onset of the 1993-1995 grant, the newly established BRIDGES Task Force III developed program standards. The standards were fashioned from the eight essential principles founded by the Carnegie Council's Task Force on Education of Young Adolescents (Carnegie Council on Adolescent Development, 1989). These standards described educational goals for all middle grade students within the state.

NORTH DAKOTA MIDDLE SCHOOL PROGRAM STANDARDS

- Standard 1: Establish a climate of trust between adults and students which fosters students' intellectual and individual growth.
- Standard 2: Provide students with opportunities to master a balanced body of knowledge and to develop thinking and processing skills.
- Standard 3: Provide all young adolescents with opportunities to experience success in every aspect of the middle school program.
- Standard 4: Share all decision-making responsibilities concerning students' school experience by empowering teachers, parents, and administrators who know them best.
- Standard 5: Employ a staff of teachers who are skilled in the instruction of young adolescents.
- Standard 6: Improve academic performance through the fostering of health and fitness opportunities for young adolescents.
- Standard 7: Provide opportunities for increased family involvement in the education of their children.
- Standard 8: Share the responsibility for each middle school student's success with both school and community organizations.

In addition, in the 1993 grant cycle, six systemic change (lead) schools were funded by MGSSPI to begin the transition process. The selection of the systemic change schools was based on the following criteria: (1) involvement with the project at its inception, (2) economically disadvantaged schools (high percentage of students receiving free or reduced lunch), and (3) documented commitment to effective middle school practice. The primary responsibility of these BRIDGES schools was to implement established middle school practices and provide statewide leadership for the education of young adolescents.

The Project expanded to 14 schools by 1996 to include eight new network schools. These schools were held to the same requirements (implementing established middle school practices enabling them to meet the eight ND middle school program standards) as the systemic change schools with the exception of providing state-wide mentoring.

In 1997, 10 new partner schools were added. These schools agreed to: (1) engage in annual school improvement planning, (2) implement study groups to address key challenge areas within the school, and (3) participate in the annual Fall and Spring BRIDGES conference and the Fall AMLEND (Association of Middle Level Educators in North Dakota) State Conference.

INDICATORS OF SUCCESS

The data reported were taken from aggregated student and teacher responses from the Middle Grade (MGSSPI) Self-Study Survey (Felner, 1999b) developed at the University of Rhode Island and administered in BRIDGES Project schools in North Dakota. Since the culmination of the Project, 10 schools have continued to offer the survey (now known as HiP-LaCes Self-Study (Felner, 1999a) on a rotating year basis.

INCREASED STUDENT ACADEMIC ACHIEVEMENT

From 1992 through 1996, the BRIDGES Project collected data from the six systemic change schools regarding academic achievement. These data demonstrate that indicators of school success had been very positive. The cohort of students in these systemic change schools (economically disadvantaged and ethnically diverse) had made significant gains in eight of the ten academic areas. In fact, the BRIDGES Project students had higher grade equivalency score gains than non-BRIDGES Project student in 6 of 10 cognitive areas.

Composite grade level equivalency scores on the Comprehensive Test of Basic Skills (CTBS) at the eighth grade level increased in all academic areas for the six systemic change schools. Academic areas that showed a two grade level increase in mean grade equivalence scores from 6th to 8th grade (middle schools) were: reading vocabulary (2.4), reading comprehension (2.0), language mechanics (2.0), language expression (2.1), mathematic computation (2.8), mathematics concepts and application (2.4), study skills (2.0), and science (2.2). These improvements in the BRIDGES middle schools supported the project's beliefs that the middle school philosophy and practice could make a difference in academic achievement (Backes, Ralston, & Ingwalson, 1999).

INCREASED PARENTAL INVOLVEMENT

Teachers reported in the MGSSPI Self-Study that parental involvement had risen steadily as the middle school concepts were more fully implemented. A parent survey conducted in 1996 by the BRIDGES Project indicated an increase in parental involvement in several areas: advisory committees, teaching exploratory classes, and regular communication with team teachers, and attendance at grade level teacher teams meetings to discuss their children's progress in school.

INCREASED STUDENT ATTENDANCE

Daily attendance for students in BRIDGES schools increased from 94.1 percent in 1992 to 95.3 percent in 1998.

INCREASED TEACHER SATISFACTION

Teachers reported increased satisfaction with school and the environment in which they work. Overall, the data point to a more positive school climate as measured by various dimensions of the MGSSPI Self-Study.

DECREASED STUDENT DISCIPLINE PROBLEMS

Middle schools in the BRIDGES Project used varied programs in an effort to improve student behavior and academic performance. Because of this variance, longitudinal data on suspension and discipline are not available. However, 8th grade students self-reported an 8% decrease in behavior problems amongst peers. Students also reported a 15% reduction in feelings of anxiety about school, a 20% reduction in the feelings of depression, and a 3% increase in feelings of self-esteem.

INCORPORATED HEALTH EDUCATION

All schools involved with the BRIDGES Project provide access to health services, physical fitness screening, and conduct the Youth Risk Behavior Survey (YRBS). The results of the YRBS are accessible on the Web site www.dpi.state.ud.us/

PROFESSIONAL DEVELOPMENT

A key factor to sustaining middle schools in the state is the enhancement of preservice and inservice education. This is accomplished through coursework and workshops offered at various levels that include a middle school endorsement, middle school minor, middle school major, and a masters of science in education with a middle school cognate. By 2005, the largest district in the state will require the completion of the endorsement for all of their middle school staff. In addition, a 2004 survey conducted by the University of North Dakota Continuing Education Department reported that 243 middle school teachers are interested in taking the endorsement coursework.

ESTABLISHED THE ASSOCIATION OF MIDDLE LEVEL EDUCATORS IN NORTH DAKOTA (AMLEND)

The Association of Middle Level Educators in North Dakota was established in 1993 to provide expertise and leadership for middle level teachers, parents, administrators, and university professors to sustain middle school education. This organization has sustained middle school education in the state since the culmination of the BRIDGES Project in 1999. AMLEND hosts two conferences a year to support the middle school movement within the state. The fall conference is held to enhance teacher and administrator effectiveness in dealing with the developmental needs of young adolescents. The spring conference focuses on the involvement and contributions of students and parents in middle school education. In addition, AMLEND conducts conference calls (4/year) with the principals and/or lead teachers to discuss middle school education. AMLEND has also created a website, (www.amlend.org) to disseminate information and share experiences amongst the middle school educators in the state.

ESTABLISHED THE CENTER FOR MIDDLE LEVEL EDUCATION

At the conclusion of the MGSSPI grant in 1999, the University of North Dakota established the Center for Middle Level Education (CMLE) to organize efforts to sustain middle school education in the state. The Center published the final report of the BRIDGES Project entitled, Last Best Chance: Middle Schools in North Dakota (2000). This report highlighted Project accomplishments, recommendations and five critical elements of middle level reform: (1) professional development, (2) administration/policy, (3) health education, (4) parent/family involvement, and (5) middle level practices with students.

One critical recommendation is the continuance of workshops/seminars for teachers/schools interested in becoming better acquainted with the essential knowledge of middle school education (resulting in a middle school endorsement). Continuing the collaborative relationship with the various state education departments was another recommendation. The CMLE has continued to assist the state in reviewing and updating standards as well as examining new laws and regulations that influence middle school education (e.g., No Child Left Behind Act).

SUSTAINED MIDDLE SCHOOL PRACTICE

Of the 24 schools involved with the BRIDGES Project, 21 are currently listed as North Dakota schools that employ the middle school philosophy (North Dakota Department of Public Instruction, 2004). The magnitude of this number is evident considering that the 24 BRIDGES schools constituted 85% of the middle grades school students in the state (Backes & Becker, 1999). It is even more promising that six additional schools (non-BRIDGES schools) have committed to the middle school practices and beliefs since the culmination of the Project.

REFLECTIONS

For 9 years, the BRIDGES Project successfully promoted middle school education in North Dakota. Since then there have been numerous times that the future of middle school education was endangered. Shortly after the funding was discontinued and the Project requirements lifted, many districts questioned the additional cost of middle schools, teacher occasionally lost sight of the purpose of teaming, administrators pondered how to promote advisory time, and parent involvement often took a backseat to other school responsibilities.

However, probably the biggest obstacle middle school education has faced is the No Child Left Behind Act of 2001 (NCLB). NCLB poses a unique problem as it "raised the hackles of many educators who considered its short timeline and emphasis on standardized assessment to be unreasonable and unwise" (George, 2002, p. 5). This was particularly true at the state level as the Education Standards and Practice Board (ESPB) struggled with the final descriptors for a "highly qualified" middle level teacher for months. The Board finally came to the decision to recognize a middle school degree as highly qualified (see Procedures and Guideline Toolkit at www.state.nd.us/espb/). This recognition provides the additional support needed to move middle school education forward so to provide our young adolescence with the type of education vital for their development.

REFERENCES

Backes, J., & Becker, G. (1999). *1997-1999 BRIDGES Project final report.* Grand Forks: University of North Dakota.

Backes, J., Ralston, A., & Ingwalson, G. (1999). Middle level reform: The impact on student achievement. *Research in Middle Level Education Quarterly, 22*(3), 43-57.

Carnegie Council on Adolescent Development. (1989). *Turning Points: Preparing American youth for the 21st century.* New York: Carnegie Corporation of New York.

Felner, R. D. (1999a). *High performance learning community assessment.* Kingston, RI: National Center on Public Education and Social Policy, University of Rhode Island.

Felner, R. D. (1999b). *Middle grade (MGSSPI) self-study.* Kingston, RI: National Center on Public Education and Social Policy, University of Rhode Island.

George, P. (2002). *No child left behind: Implications for middle level leaders.* Westerville, OH: National Middle School Association.

North Dakota Department of Public Instruction. (2004, May). *Title I News* [Brochure]. Bismarck, ND: Author.

—Gail Ingwalson
University of North Dakota

BRIGGS, THOMAS

Thomas Briggs was a leading scholar of junior high school education. He earned an AB degree from Wake Forest College (1896) and a PhD (1914) from Columbia University. From 1912-1942 he was on the faculty of Teachers College, Columbia University (Cattell, 1932; Clark & Clark, 1994; Cook, 1930).

In 1920, Brigg's ideas about junior high school education were published in *The Junior High School*. In this book he identified conditions that led to the dissatisfaction with the structure of eight years of elementary school followed by four years of high school. These conditions included the increasing number of high schools, the changes in the social and industrial life, and the need to differentiate the curriculum because of the increasing number of children continuing past elementary school (Clark & Clark, 1994).

In *The Junior High School*, he also explained that he believed that differences between elementary school and high school, such as the change in subjects, school organization and environment led to students dropping out of school after elementary school (Clark & Clark, 1994). In addition, he held that schools focused too narrowly on college preparation and stressed the importance of exploration in the curriculum (Clark & Clark, 1994).

REFERENCES

Cattell, J. M. (Ed.). (1932). *Leaders in education: A biographical directory.* New York: The Science Press.

Clark, S. N., & Clark, D. C. (1994). *Restructuring the middle level school: Implications for school leaders.* Albany: State University of New York Press.

Cook, R. C. (Ed.). (1930). *Who's who in American education* (Vol. II). New York: The Robert C. Cool Company.

—Jennifer S. Goodwin
Teachers College, Columbia University

CARDINAL PRINCIPLES OF SECONDARY EDUCATION

A key document in the development of the junior high and middle school movements is the 1918 National Education Association's report of the Commission on the Reorganization of Secondary Education (1918), also known as the "Cardinal Principals" (Clark & Clark, 1993; Cuban, 1992). The commission was composed of 28 members including university administrators, professors, educational specialists from the YMCA, superintendents, principals, and a representative of the United States Bureau of Education. The commission examined secondary schooling in the United States and developed recommendations to reorganize secondary schools to better meet the needs of students and a changing society. The opening section of the report stated that secondary education should be determined by three factors, the needs of society, the characteristics of the students being served, and the knowledge of currently available educational theory and practices. The commission further stated institutions, such as secondary education, resist modification and need reorganization at times to address these three factors. The report continued with specific recommendations that influenced the structural and curricular development of secondary schooling, including junior highs schools, throughout the twentieth century.

The recommendations of the commission, termed the "The Seven Cardinal Principles of Secondary Schooling," are: (1) Health—physical activity, health needs, safeguarding and promoting health interests; (2) Command of fundamental processes—reading, writing, arithmetic, and oral and written expression;

(3) Worthy home membership—development of qualities that make the individual a worthy member of a family; (4) Vocational skill development—development of differing skills for girls and boys; (5) Civic education—loyalty to ideals of civic righteousness, developed through cooperative student projects; (6) Worthy leisure—development of skills and attitudes necessary to be involved in worthy leisure activities such as music, art, literature, drama, social intercourse, and special vocational activities; and (7) Ethical character—personal responsibility and initiative, a spirit of service, and understanding of the principles of democracy.

The report recommended the development of "Junior Highs" instead of the elementary/high school configuration of the time. The commission listed the goals of the junior high as (a) the gradual introduction of departmental instruction, (b) some choices of subjects under guidance, (c) prevocational courses, and (d) social organizations that called for initiative and developed the sense of personal responsibility for the welfare of the group. Junior highs were also to involve students in exploratory activities in preparation for adult life with increasing specialization in vocational activities. Moreover, junior highs were to be comprehensive and avoid duplicating the specialized nature of the senior high school.

Criticisms of the cardinal principals over the decades include a lack of academic rigor, an overemphasis on vocational education, introduction of the tracking systems in schools by separating college bound from vocational students, and contributing to inequities in education by limiting expectations of vocational bound students (Cuban, 1993; Mitchell, 1982). Regardless of these criticisms, the roots of the current middle school movement are found in the cardinal principals, with the emphasis on relevance, the exploratory nature of middle grade education, and the unique needs of early adolescents.

REFERENCES

Clark, S. N., & Clark, D. C. (1993). Middle level school reforms: The rhetoric and the reality. *Elementary School Journal, 93*(5), 447-460.

Commission on the Reorganization of Secondary Education (1918). *Cardinal principles of secondary education.* Bulletin 1918, No. 35. Washington, DC: U.S. Department of Interior, Bureau of Education.

Cuban, L. (1993). What happens to reforms that last? The case of the junior high school. *American Educational Research Journal, 29*(2), 227-251.

Mitchell, R. (1981). *The graves of academe.* Boston: Little Brown.

—Dana L. Bickmore
The University of Georgia

CARNEGIE COUNCIL ON ADOLESCENT DEVELOPMENT

The Carnegie Council on Adolescent Development (CCAD) was formed in 1986 by the Carnegie Corporation of New York to shed national attention on the important, yet often neglected, challenges of early adolescence. The CCAD established the Task Force on Education of Young Adolescents in 1987 so that experts in the fields of education, research, government, health, nonprofit, and philanthropic sectors could study the education and healthy development of young adolescents.

The result of the work of the CCAD and the Task Force on Education of Young Adolescents was the ground-breaking 1989 report, *Turning Points: Preparing American Youth for the 21st Century* (Carnegie Council on Adolescent Development, 1989). This report focused national attention on the needs of young adolescents. It also made a set of recommendations for the education of young adolescents that included a support system of schools, families, and health and community organizations. This comprehensive approach to educating young adolescents highlighted eight core recommendations for middle grades schools including: creating a community for learning, teaching a core of common knowledge, ensuring success for all students, empowering teachers and administrators, preparing teachers for the middle grades, improving academic performance through better health and fitness, reengaging families in the education of young adolescents, and connecting schools with communities.

In the decade that followed the release of *Turning Points,* hundreds of middle grades schools across the country read about and adopted the principles outlined in the report. In fact, nearly 100,000 copies of the full report and over 200,000 copies of the executive summary were disseminated (Jackson & Davis, 2000). The CCAD continued its work of examining practices and research related to the education of young adolescents and released many reports including its concluding report in 1995 titled *Great Transitions: Preparing Adolescents for a New Century* (Carnegie Council on Adolescent Development, 1995). The CCAD indicated that a key lesson from their work was that a long-term view is essential for changes that impact the lives and education of young adolescents.

The long-term impact of the CCAD's work was recognized by the Carnegie Corporation who continued the work by funding a grant program called the Middle Grade School State Policy Initiative (MGSSPI) from 1990 to 1999 to encourage and support the systemic implementation of the Turning Points recommendations. The Carnegie Corporation also lent their support to the research, writing, and publication of *Turning Points 2000: Educating Adolescents in the 21st Century* (Jackson & Davis, 2000), a follow-up to the 1989 *Turning Points* report. *Turning Points 2000* reflects on the recommendations in the 1989 report, the lessons learned from MGSSPI, and the latest research to further guide educators in their implementation of Turning Points principles.

REFERENCES

Carnegie Council on Adolescent Development. (1989). *Turning points: Preparing American youth for the 21st century.* The report of the Task Force on Education of Young Adolescents. New York: Carnegie Corporation of New York.

Carnegie Council on Adolescent Development. (1995). *Great transitions: Preparing adolescents for a new century.* Concluding report. New York: Carnegie Corporation of New York.

Jackson, A. W., & Davis, G. A. (2000). *Turning points 2000: Educating adolescents in the 21st century.* New York: Teachers College Press.

—Nancy Flowers
CPRD, University of Illinois

CAUGHT IN THE MIDDLE

Published in 1987, the historic reform document, *Caught in the Middle: Educational Reform for Young Adolescents in California's Public Schools*, culminated a year of intense, pioneering work by California's Middle Grade Task Force (California Department of Education, 1987). The report emphasized the uniqueness of middle grade students and argued for the need to create educational settings specifically organized to meet these unique needs. *Caught in the Middle* remained available until July 2000 when it was retired from print. It was the largest selling document ever produced by the California Department of Education, selling over 135,000 copies.

Organized around 22 "principles for middle grade education," *Caught in the Middle* (1987) detailed 102 recommendations for action. The report is divided into five parts:

1. Curriculum and Instruction: Achieving Excellence
2. Student Potential: Realizing the 'Highest and Best'-Intellectual, Social Emotional, and Physical Development
3. Organization and Structure: Creating New Learning Environments
4. Teaching and Administration: Preparing for Exemplary Performance
5. Leadership and Partnership: Defining the Catalysts for Middle Grade Educational Reform.

One of the most enduring features of *Caught in the Middle* was its appendix, which in five pages distilled the existing research on the developmental characteristics of young adolescents. This distillation became a frequent handout in many university-level courses across the country.

A recurring theme throughout the 1987 report was the contrast between what was termed "effective schooling based on the needs of middle grade students" and "junior high school practices." School practices that were endorsed by *Caught in the Middle* included:

- Creating unified "humanities" core courses for all students;
- Providing extended blocks of uninterrupted instruction time;
- Encouraging student involvement and choice in their own learning;
- Offering exploratory courses that allow students to extend their base of experience;
- Teaching through interdisciplinary teams;
- Developing opportunities for teacher collaboration; and
- Connecting students to adult mentors through active advisement programs.

Practices that were discouraged included:

- Fixed-length classes with school-wide "passing periods;"
- Tracking, permanent, or semipermanent "ability" grouping; and
- Drill and rote instruction using only the available textbook.

An important legacy of *Caught in the Middle* came from its call to create a "partnership of state-of-the-art middle schools" to be the "catalyst for renewal and reform of middle grade education throughout California." As a follow-up, the California Department of Education formed the California Middle Grades Partnership Networks. California's middle schools responded eagerly to this call for mutual assistance, networking together to implement the recommendations from *Caught in the Middle*. Network schools called themselves "schools of un-common commitment" because no support was provided by the Legislature. Networks have been self-funded. Nonetheless, by the end of 2004, California had 30 regional partnership networks, involving almost 400 middle schools.

In March 2001, the California Department of Education published *Taking Center Stage: A Commitment to Standards-Based Education for California's Middle Grade Students* (California Department of Education, 2001) as a sequel to *Caught in the Middle*.

REFERENCES

California Department of Education. (1987). *Caught in the middle: Educational reform for young adolescents in California's public schools.* Sacramento, CA: CDE Press.

California Department of Education. (2001). *Taking center stage: A commitment to standards-based education for California's middle grades students.* Sacramento, CA: CDE Press.

—Jim Miller
California Department of Education

CENTER FOR EARLY ADOLESCENCE

Created in 1978, the Center for Early Adolescence (CEA) at the University of North Carolina at Chapel Hill worked to "increase the effectiveness of agencies and individuals that have an impact upon the lives of 10- to 15-year-olds" (Dorman, 1985a, p. ii). The Center's founder, Joan Lipsitz, studied young adolescents as a researcher at The Learning Institute of North Carolina. The result of her research was the landmark book, *Growing Up Forgotten: A Review of Research and Programs Concerning Early Adolescence* (Lipsitz, 1977). In conducting the research for the book, Lipsitz and her fellow researchers confirmed their original assumption "that young adolescence is the most overlooked age group among minors in America" (Lipsitz, 1977, p. xv).

In response to gaping holes in research, services, and advocacy described in the book, Lipsitz founded the Center for Early Adolescence. The Center focused on supporting young adolescents in their homes, schools, and communities by providing training to professionals and volunteers who worked with the age group, offering technical assistance to educators in schools and districts, and responding annually to thousands of requests for information from parents, educators, policymakers, and community members. The Center housed perhaps the only refereed collection of the best resources and research related to young adolescents. The Center's own groundbreaking publications included *3:00 to 6:00 p.m.: Planning Programs for Young Adolescents* (Dorman, 1985a); *Middle Grades Assessment Program* (Dorman, 1985b); *Building Youth Literacy: A Training Curriculum for Community Leaders* (Davidson & Pulver, 1991); and *A Portrait of Young Adolescents in the 1990s* (Scales, 1991).

Though the Center closed its doors in 1994, its impact continues through its publications and the continuing work of CEA alumni. Several Center alumni have served or continue to serve as program officers for national and regional foundations that have funded programs related to young adolescents: Joan Lipsitz at the Lilly Endowment, Inc., Leah Meyer Austin (formerly Lefstein) at the W.K. Kellogg Foundation, Gayle Williams (formerly Dorman) at the Mary Reynolds Babcock Foundation, Tara McKenzie Sandercock at the Community Foundation of Greater Greensboro, NC, and M. Hayes Mizell, a former CEA advisory board member, at the Edna McConnell Clark Foundation. Other Center alumni have authored or co-authored significant publications related to young adolescents, for example Gayle Andrews (formerly Davis) co-authored, with Anthony Jackson, *Turning*

Points 2000: Educating Adolescents in the 21st Century (2000) and Peter Scales wrote *Boxed in and Bored: How Middle Schools Continue to Fail Young Adolescents—And What Good Middle Schools Do Right* (1996).

REFERENCES

Davidson, J., & Pulver, R. (1991). *Building youth literacy: A training curriculum for community leaders.* Carrboro, NC: Center for Early Adolescence.

Dorman, G. (1985a). *3:00 to 6:00 p.m.: Planning programs for young adolescents.* Carrboro, NC: Center for Early Adolescence.

Dorman, G. (1985b). *Middle grades assessment program.* Carrboro, NC: Center for Early Adolescence.

Jackson, A. W., & Davis, G. A. (2000). *Turning points 2000: Educating adolescents in the 21st century.* New York: Teachers College Press.

Lipsitz, J. (1977). *Growing up forgotten: A review of research and programs concerning early adolescence.* New Brunswick, NJ: Transaction Books.

Scales, P. C. (1991). *A portrait of young adolescents in the 1990s: Implications for promoting healthy growth and development.* Carrboro, NC: Center for Early Adolescence.

Scales, P. C. (1996). *Boxed in and bored: How middle schools continue to fail young adolescents—and what good middle schools do right.* Minneapolis, MN: Search Institute.

—Gayle Andrews
The University of Georgia

CENTER FOR PREVENTION RESEARCH AND DEVELOPMENT

The Center for Prevention Research and Development (CPRD) at the University of Illinois has been involved in the evaluation of middle-level school reform for over 15 years. In 1990, CPRD developed the School Improvement Self-Study, a comprehensive, cost-effective evaluation and assessment system that has been completed by hundreds of schools across the nation. CPRD's experience and expertise in the evaluation of middle-level reform is best depicted by the number and types of evaluations they have undertaken. Beginning in 1989, CPRD, in partnership with the Association of Illinois Middle-Level Schools (AIMS), began an intensive evaluation of Project Initiative Middle Level, a network of Illinois middle-level schools undergoing substantive reform. This seminal work led to the evaluation of the Carnegie Corporation's Middle Grades Schools State Policy Initiative (MGSSPI), the Lilly Endowment's Middle Grades Improvement Program, the W. K. Kellogg

Foundation's Middle Start Initiative, the Foundation for the Mid South's Mid South Middle Start Initiative, and the National Turning Points Network.

The cornerstone of CPRD's evaluation of middle-grade schools is the School Improvement Self-Study. The Self-Study is a data collection system consisting of a set of surveys completed by teachers, principals, students, and parents in a school. The Self-Study provides schools with highly reliable and validated survey measures that provide ongoing opportunities to assess the comprehensive, complex, and multiple levels of reform. The key elements asked about in the confidential and anonymous surveys include classroom practices, instructional, and curricular integration, decision making practices, parent, and community involvement, climate, and attitudes, professional development needs, educational expectations, school safety, student health behaviors, and student socioemotional functioning. After participating in the Self-Study surveys, schools receive a site specific report containing charts, tables, and graphs for use in planning and monitoring school improvement efforts.

Thus far, CPRD's research has focused primarily on middle grades education. As a research and evaluation partner for the initiatives mentioned above, CPRD collected individual teacher, student, principal, and parent survey data for hundreds of schools on an annual basis. CPRD's analyses of Self-Study data are disseminated in a variety of forums. For over 6 years, CPRD has published findings from the Self-Study as part of their twice-a-year research column in the *Middle School Journal*. CPRD has published over 30 reports and articles focusing on varying aspects of middle grades education and school reform. CPRD has also made over 25 presentations of their research results at regional, state, and national meetings and conferences. These reports, publications, and presentations target varying audiences ranging from peer-review to policy to practitioners and advocates (most of CPRD's publications are available at their web site: www.cprd.uiuc.edu). One of CPRD's primary focus areas has been in establishing the link between the implementation of middle grade programs, practices, and policies and directly measurable outcomes, specifically student learning and achievement.

—Nancy Flowers
—Steven B. Mertens
CPRD, University of Illinois

COLLABORATIVE DECISION MAKING

Numerous decisions are made in schools every day in areas such as curriculum and instruction, student welfare, school and team organization, scheduling, and parent and community relations. These decisions may be made by administrators, teachers, support staff, students, and parents. A seventh grade social studies teacher, for example, may decide to organize an International Day celebration on his team. The principal may elect to hire a former marine biologist, who has no prior teaching experience, to teach sixth grade science. Students may decide to organize a petition to have the music program reinstated. A group of parents may plan a dance-off to raise money for the school. As each of these decisions is made, will the decision makers take into account how others might be affected by the decision? Will they gather input from other stakeholders? If the answer to these questions is "No," problems may ensue, not because the decisions themselves were necessarily flawed ideas but because these decisions were made in isolation and without consideration for the programs, people, and structures these decisions impacted.

WHAT IS COLLABORATIVE DECISION MAKING?

To avoid the pitfalls the well-intentioned people in the scenarios above may have encountered, a formal process should be established that brings stakeholders together for the purpose of making decisions. This process of *collaborative decision making*, often called site-based management, counters the notion of authoritarian, top-down management as being the most effective means for operating a school. Collaborative means joint or shared; thus, issues and concerns are considered jointly by the school's stakeholders. Stakeholders share in the identification of a problem, investigation of a solution, and recommendation of a course of action. While decision making by one person or a select few in the school may be an efficient means for getting work accomplished, it is surely not the most effective way. Better decisions are made when vested stakeholders, who offer a variety of perspectives, are involved in the process (Glickman, 1990). In schools where collaborative decision-making thrives, students and school personnel work in partnership with parents and community members to make decisions regarding a variety of issues including the school's mission, curriculum, and instruction, and professional development (Glickman, 1993).

In collaborative decision-making schools, elected representatives from the stakeholder groups (e.g., faculty, staff, parents, students, administrators, and community members) often form a leadership team (Jackson & Davis, 2000). The leadership team's elected participants should reflect the make-up of the school. Most school leadership teams have teacher representatives from each grade level or department so as to gain differing perspectives, as well as representatives from student support services (e.g., counselor, media specialist, or other student support personnel). Parental involvement in collaborative decision making is also important to the success of the process (Jackson & Davis, 2000). The parent representative can offer parents' perspectives on critical issues, as well as serve as a liaison for the school's parent organizations. Students and community members, as important stakeholders in the school's mission, should also be elected to the leadership team.

So as to include all who wish to participate in collaborative decision making, most schools establish subcommittees that identify and investigate areas of concern (Glickman, 1993; Jackson & Davis, 2000). These committees report their findings to the leadership team and make recommendations for the leadership team's consideration. Schools may decide to organize these committees according to school goals (e.g., literacy, professional development, or community involvement) or school improvement accreditation areas such as curriculum, assessment, professional development, and planning.

Decisions made collaboratively usually focus on teaching and learning (e.g., alignment of curriculum, implementation of innovative teaching strategies, and establishment of new academic programs) but may also center on administrative issues such as the hiring of new teachers, evaluation of job performance, and structure of school day (Glickman, 1993). In some middle schools, for example, teams of teachers participate in the hiring of colleagues by screening, interviewing, and recommending candidates that best fit the vacant position on their team. While the focus of collaborative decision making is usually on issues that directly impact teaching and learning, noninstructional issues may have an indirect impact on teaching and learning, and therefore, may also be addressed through collaborative decision making (Glickman, 1993). For example, stakeholders concerned about student safety during afternoon dismissal from school may approach the school's collaborative decision-making team with a request that the problem be studied and solutions be identified so as to ensure the safety of their middle school students.

Another area in which decisions should be made collaboratively is teachers' professional development. Rather than be told what courses or workshops in which they should participate, teachers in collaborative decision-making schools determine their own professional development needs and take action to address these accordingly (Pate & Thompson, 2003). Professional development can be acquired through (1) whole-school events such as faculty meetings, workshops, and seminars; (2) small group learning such as grade-level meetings, content area meetings, or learning community groups; and (3) individual action such as membership in educational organizations, presentations made at local, state, and national conferences, and enrollment in staff development or graduate courses. In schools where collaborative decision making is practiced, professionals within the school are recognized for their areas of expertise (Pate & Thompson, 2003). Rather than relying solely on outside specialists, these schools often solicit experts within the school to conduct professional development activities with the assurance that school personnel often understand the needs and issues of the school better than outside professionals.

In addition to school-wide issues, collaborative decision making is also important at the grade and team level (Pate, 1997). Types of decisions made at the grade or team level include team make-up and organization, instructional methods, curriculum emphases, scheduling and duty assignments. In many middle schools, teams of teachers designate a leader to whom they look for guidance. Collaborative decision-making teams, however, while officially designating a leader for office contact reasons, share the workload. Teachers with scheduling expertise take on duties of scheduling new students and communicating any schedule changes with the rest of the team or grade level. Other experts (e.g., instructional innovation) teach their colleagues about a new program or strategy that addresses an identified grade level or team need. Teachers at the grade and team levels meet regularly to discuss challenges and successes and identify ways to improve teaching and learning in their content areas. Social studies teachers, for example, may work together to identify strengths and weaknesses of their curriculum and plan professional development activities that will address theses areas, thereby enhancing and enriching the instruction they provide to their middle school students.

Collaborative decision making is not restricted to school-wide or team-level decisions; successful collaborative decision making also occurs in middle school classrooms. Together, teachers and students collaborate on issues such as curriculum planning, assessment, and classroom procedures (Beane, 1993; Larivee, 1999). An essential element of effective collaborative decision-making process is communication. When formal collaborative decision-making processes are not followed or understood, stakeholders experience frustration and confusion (Thompson, 1999). Participants must know how, why, and by whom decisions are made. The collaborative decision-making process should be communicated in writing so that all participants have a clear understanding of the procedures and roles and responsibilities of participants. Some schools draft formal by-laws that are approved by stakeholders and revisited each year for modification, while other schools develop a simple memorandum of understanding outlining the collaborative decision-making process and participation.

WHAT DOES COLLABORATIVE DECISION MAKING LOOK LIKE IN SCHOOLS?

Collaborative decision-making processes help to ensure that interested stakeholders are involved in decision-making and that the best decisions possible are made. The following are examples of how collaborative decision-making has occurred in middle schools:

- In a small urban middle school, stakeholders were concerned about the number of children who were getting into trouble after school hours. School personnel, students, parents, and community members studied the issue, examined successful programs in place at other schools, created a plan of action and made a recommendation to the school's leadership team to establish an after-school program.
- The school leadership team in a rural middle school addressed students' lack of interest in reading by establishing a daily silent reading time during which students read literature of their choice including books, magazines, or comic books. Prior to the creation of the sustained silent reading period, a committee studied the problem, identified possible solutions and resources, considered the potential impact on other areas (i.e., master schedule), and surveyed school stakeholders. The committee presented its proposal to the leadership team where it was approved for implementation.
- Teachers in an urban middle school realized through participation in a needs assessment that they needed professional development in working with diverse students. As a result, the teachers created a program called "Diversity Dinner Dialogue." Each month, the teachers read a new book focused

on diversity and attended an evening session to discuss their thoughts and determine new courses of action.
- In a diverse, suburban middle school, students and teachers made collaborative decisions about the curriculum. The students were knowledgeable about state and local standards and used this knowledge to determine how they would learn required content, as well as how they would demonstrate mastery of these standards.
- Sixth grade students in a large, suburban middle school participated in daily class meetings as a process for making decisions about issues ranging from rubric assessment to misbehavior in the hallway. The students and their teacher reached consensus on classroom rules, procedures, and student leadership positions that guided student action throughout the year.

WHY IS COLLABORATIVE DECISION MAKING IMPORTANT?

Collaborative decision-making results in leadership shared by all. Historically in schools, decisions have been made by administrators or a select few designees (Glickman, 1993). More recently, however, school personnel have witnessed the benefits of including in the decision-making process those most affected by the decisions. In collaborative decision-making schools, teachers experience higher morale than their counterparts in schools where decisions are usually made in an authoritarian, or top-down, manner (Conley, Schmidle, & Shedd, 1988). When teachers participate purposefully and consistently in the decision making of their schools, they also experience greater feelings of confidence in their abilities to impact student learning (Browder, 1994). Students who participate in collaborative decision making are more engaged learners and take greater ownership of their learning (Vattercott, 1999). Parents who have opportunities to take part in decision-making processes also benefit, for they experience greater feelings of ownership and are therefore, more committed to supporting the school's mission (Jackson & Davis, 2000). Both schools and communities profit when community members participate in collaborative decision making in local schools. When schools solicit input and participation from community members and organizations, participants begin to view education as the responsibility of everyone in the community, not just of those with school-aged children. As a result, schools have access to and benefit from the expertise and resources of the whole community. Schools fortunate enough to exist near institutions of higher learning can benefit from a variety of programs sponsored by the college or university, including research and grants, when professors and instructors are viewed as collaborative partners in the school's decision-making processes (Clift, Veal, Holland, Johnson, & McCarthy, 1995).

Middle school educators interested in collaborative decision-making need not wait for formal invitations to participate in school issues. Instead, they should look for ways to be involved in the daily operations of the school (e.g., seek elected positions on leadership team, engage in professional learning community groups, and participate in team, grade-level, and content area meetings), grow professionally (e.g., enroll in graduate courses, keep abreast of current educational issues, subscribe to educational journals, conduct research in the classroom, and try innovative teaching strategies), and encourage school stakeholders (e.g., students, parents, and community members) to join them in making collaborative decisions. If the culture of the school is one in which all professionals initiate participation in activities such as those listed above, the culture eventually becomes one where collaborative decision making is not only encouraged but also valued.

REFERENCES

Beane, J. A. (1993). *A middle school curriculum: From rhetoric to reality* (2nd ed.). Columbus, OH: National Middle School Association.

Browder, L. H. (1994). Exploring the meanings of teacher empowerment. *International Journal of Educational Reform, 3,* 137-53.

Clift, R. T., Veal, M. L., Holland, P., Johnson, M., & McCarthy, J. (1995). *Collaborative leadership and shared decision-making: Teachers, principals, and university professors.* New York: Teachers College Press.

Conley, S., Schmidle, T., & Shedd, J. (1988). Teacher participation in the management of school systems. *Educational Policy, 90,* 259-80.

Glickman, C. D. (1990). *Supervision of instruction: A developmental approach* (2nd ed.). Boston: Allyn & Bacon.

Glickman, C. D. (1993). *Renewing America's schools: A guide for school-based action.* San Francisco: Jossey-Bass.

Jackson, A. W., & Davis, G. A. (2000). *Turning points 2000: Educating adolescents in the 21st century.* New York: Teachers College Press.

Larivee, B. (1999). *Authentic classroom management: Creating a community of learners.* Boston: Allyn & Bacon.

Pate, P. E. (1997). Teaming and decision-making. In T. S. Dickinson & T. O. Erb (Eds.), *We gain more than we give: Teaming in middle schools* (pp. 425-442). Columbus, OH: National Middle School Association.

Pate, P. E., & Thompson, K. F. (2003). Effective professional development: What is it? In V. A. Anfara & P. G. Andrews (Eds.), *Leaders for a movement: Professional preparation and development of middle level teachers and administrators* (pp. 123-143). Greenwich, CT: Information Age.

Thompson, K. F. (1999). *Middle level teachers' interpretations of their experiences regarding empowerment.* Unpublished doctoral dissertation, The University of Georgia.

Vattercott, C. (1999). *Academic success through empowering students.* Columbus, OH: National Middle School Association.

—Katherine F. Thompson
The University of Georgia

COMER SCHOOL DEVELOPMENT PROGRAM

James P. Comer serves multiple roles at Yale University: the Maurice Falk Professor of Child Psychiatry, the Associate Dean of the School of Medicine, and the Director of the Child Study Center School Development Program. He is a national leader in school change. In 1968, Comer established the comprehensive school improvement model through his initial work with the New Haven, Connecticut inner-city, public school system. He applied the principles of psychiatry and the behavioral sciences to education. Currently, the Comer Project for Change (http://info.med.yale.edu/comer/) in Education is operating in more than 600 schools and 26 states.

The Comer model focuses on child development as the one aspect that should guide everything else in education, and the Comer's Schools and Families Initiative seeks to raise school achievement and promote healthy growth and development. Comer has determined that three mechanisms under gird the program in any school, "a governance and management team, a mental health or school support team, and a parents' program" (Goldberg, 1997). Comer also developed three operations that are a part of the philosophy: a comprehensive school plan, staff development, and assessment and modification. Three guiding principles permeate his work, collaboration, consensus decision making, and no fault problem solving. This is a comprehensive, collaborative school-based improvement process and it requires involvement and support of all school and community stakeholders with an emphasis on parent involvement.

The Comer model is rooted in child development, human development, and relationship concepts and is a comprehensive approach to school management. Comer Schools usually decide to focus attention to one group in school, the students, teachers or parents. Constituent groups work in collaboration and coordinate resources and programs to establish and achieve school objectives and goals that lead to improved educational outcomes for all students. Using the Comer model, the school learns that the culture must be "a cooperative, learning, trying, experimenting attitude rather than an obstructive, adversarial relationship" (Goldberg, 1997). According to Comer, "When a school becomes a community, when goals and programs are established, where there is determination to make progress, motivation to improve is high" (Goldman, 1997). Comer also says that, "Economic integration allows groups to come together in meaningful ways, then that makes school integration possible." Therefore, the model attempts to create a school climate that permits parents and staff to support the development of all students in a way that makes academic achievement and desirable social behavior possible and expected.

The Comer model and the National Middle School's publication, *This we believe: Successful schools for young adolescents* have many similar and overlapping beliefs: collaborative leadership, a shared vision to guide decision making, a supportive and safe environment, high expectations for every member of the learning community, an adult advocate for every student, and strong family and community partnerships (National Middle School Association, 2003). While the Comer model is not a quick fix or add on program, it is a model that has had positive effects on school change and improvement and replaces more traditional school management.

REFERENCES

Goldberg, M. (1997). Maintaining a focus on child development. *Phi Delta Kappan, 78*, 557-559.

National Middle School Association. (2003). *This we believe: Successful schools for young adolescents*. Westerville, OH: Author.

—Kimberly J. Hartman
University of North Carolina, Charlotte

COMMUNITY

A community is a group having similar interests (e.g., sports, music, theater), locale (e.g., classroom, school, neighborhood), commonalities (e.g., religion, ethnicity, nationality), or identities (e.g., team of seventh grade students, school club member, band member). Community members are in close proximity to each other; have a social structure resembling intergenera-tional closure; and foster, model, or explicitly teach shared communal values and a sense of place (Sampson-Cordle, 2001). Intergenerational closure is a social structure in which an extended network of kinship, friendship, and work relations pervade the community (Coleman, 1987). Being a part of a community means that students feel a sense of belonging and purpose. Students are more committed to learning when they believe that teachers and peers understand and care about them. Feelings of community in the classroom and school facilitate students' understanding of one another. Students see purpose in their learning when the knowledge and skills they have acquired help make their community a better place.

Students should have opportunities to experience community in individual classrooms, in the larger school context, and in the community beyond the school. In the classroom, students need frequent opportunities to learn with one another in pairs, small groups, and whole-class settings. A sense of community is also established when students participate in school-wide activities. Even as students and school personnel create community within their building, they must understand the role that the school plays in the larger community and the role that the community can play in education.

Several strategies are useful in creating and facilitating communities. These strategies include class meetings, inventories, surveys, interviews, walkabouts, maps, newspapers, and telephone books.

CLASS MEETINGS

Class meetings, as a strategy, is a simple and yet effective way for students to experience community. Class meetings are designed as a safe forum for students and teachers to brainstorm and share ideas, engage in decision making and goal setting, vent frustrations and celebrate successes. Class meetings facilitate the processes of reflection (looking back) and envisioning (looking forward), both important to the health of a community. Class meeting times can be set in advance or, if necessary, can be held on-the-spot to take care of urgent issues. They may be called or facilitated by students or teachers. The *McHome Team*, an eighth grade team of 58 students and two teachers, frequently held class meetings. During their first class meeting, they collaborated on the establishment of group norms (what behaviors were and were not acceptable). During subsequent meetings, students took turns conducting lively, but controlled, discussions. At the first "end of the grading period" class meeting, the first order of business was to discuss the grading policy. As a team, they discussed what was good about the policy, what students wanted changed, and why (Pate, Homestead, & McGinnis, 1997).

INVENTORIES

Inventories, as a strategy to develop community, can be used as tools to provide more information to both teachers and students about the students themselves. They build community in the classroom by pointing out commonalities. Inventories may identify such things as students' interests, concerns, needs, preferred learning methods/modalities, and knowledge of and/or access to technology. This information can then be used by teachers and students as they collaboratively plan curriculum, instruction, and assessment. Inventories can be used to enhance students' own understanding of how they learn best. Inventories serve as starting points for classroom discussions to develop and/or refine projects, curriculum, assessments, and instructional methods. They highlight the need for varied instructional strategies so that, over time, each student has the opportunity to learn in ways that align with his/her strengths and push the student to tackle challenges. Inventories also encourage students to be more appreciative of their peers' learning strengths and supportive in helping their peers address their learning challenges. Additionally, inventories provide guidance to teachers as they set up the classroom, make learning relevant to students' interests and concerns, support students' learning as individuals, groups or classes, and encourage collaboration among students.

SURVEYS

Surveys are useful for gathering community information through a series of directed questions. Surveys are designed to elicit perspectives, ideas, concerns, solutions, and problems surrounding a topic or idea. Survey types include: face-to-face, written, telephone, e-mail, and mail. In the *Kids in Partial Control* project, students stepped outside their own community and helped the teacher community with curriculum planning. Students began the project by surveying the sixth grade teachers in their school about unit topics the teachers might teach in their content areas the next school year. They used the results of their survey to search the Internet for resources and materials the teachers could use in their planning. As a result of this project, two diverse communities learned how to work together to plan developmentally appropriate and motivational curriculum (Payne, 1999).

INTERVIEWING

Interviewing is a strategy designed to obtain information about particular problems, ideas, answer, and/or personal insights from a person in a community by asking questions. Interviewing gives students a chance to get involved in a community. Seventh grade students involved in the *Stopping Poverty from Ending Everyone's Dreams* project were concerned about the number of homeless people living in their community. The students decided to learn more about homelessness issues. They wanted to interview community members to gain a better understanding of the causes and effects of homelessness in their area. Prior to the interviews, students brainstormed scenarios, framed interview questions, and practiced interviewing skills with each other. Following the interviews, the students analyzed their data and created informational brochures about homelessness. Through interviewing, students gained a broader perspective of their community and fostered compassion for others.

WALK-ABOUT

A walk-about is a type of observation and may serve a variety of purposes. It may be used to collect initial data regarding the needs, issues, or problems related to a particular community, or it may be used to focus in on the various factors affecting a previously identified need or issue. It may also be used to identify the strengths and weaknesses of a particular area or community. A walk-about may be conducted individually or in pairs. It may be silent or collaborative. On occasion, a small group of students may find it necessary to conduct a walk-about to find answers to a particular problem on which only they are working. Some walk-abouts may include photographs to support written documentation. Using a camera, students may take pictures of areas during or after the walk-about. In *Kids with Powers*, students participated in a walk-about to identify issues of concern in an area already designated as a problem in a community. These students had, in earlier documentation (observation, interviews, surveys), determined that the bus circle at their school needed beautification and maintenance. Each group participating in the walk-about was focused on particular area of concern (e.g., walkway, vegetation, sitting area). The responses generated from the walk-about were placed in a "top ten" list for the purpose of narrowing the responses. This list of ten was agreed upon by the group. The top ten list was then used to help students identify the underlying problem of the area of concern on which they were focused.

MAPS

Using maps is another way to learn more about a community. Through map activities, students can gather a variety of information regarding their communities. They can learn about neighborhoods (their own and others), location of businesses, industries and schools, and the location and equity of resources. The type of map used may depend upon the age and developmental level of the students. For older students, a standard map of the community is appropriate. For special needs students, the facilitator may need to modify the map to make it more visually readable. It may even be appropriate for the facilitator to take a single portion of the map (that focuses on a particular area of the community) and enlarge it for lower elementary students. Depending upon students' developmental needs, facilitators may also conduct this activity in a whole-group setting with a single map or orally with student pairs. Map activities can be used in the classroom to learn about the distribution of community resources; learn about the culture of the community (location of government, religious, cultural, educational institutions); learn about community infrastructure; and, identify community needs. In *Community Memory Banking*, students used maps to identify community needs. Using maps donated by the Chamber of Commerce, pairs of students answered specific questions to help them learn more about their community. They identified the location of schools, neighborhoods, governmental agencies, community services, industries, and businesses. Then they engaged in a series of discussions regarding the rationale of the locations. These discussions led students to the realization that there were services that were lacking in particular areas of the community, particularly where many of these students lived. The students then used their findings to create a class map of the community. They attached services (e.g., wider roads, sidewalks, recycling locations, playgrounds) to their class map using Velcro. The map, which was 20′ x 10′, was then presented to the mayor of the community at an exhibition and reception during National Community Development Week for use in decision making.

NEWSPAPERS

Newspapers are another meaningful and quick way of learning more about their community. Students and teachers can use newspapers to identify a community of interest; investigate that community's participants, concerns, and needs; view a community from the perspectives of various participants; and highlight community issues relevant to the curriculum and students' lives (e.g., interests, concerns, needs, and/or questions). In an eighth grade classroom, the teacher brought in copies of the local newspaper to share with his students. The students were asked to review the newspapers from three perspectives to identify articles and issues of interest: their own perspective as eighth graders, their families' perspectives as community members, and small business owners' perspectives. The students wrote on three charts what they found from each perspective. Then, through a consensus building process, they agreed on an issue that seemed to be of interest to all three. That issue became the focus of a service-learning project aimed to meet a community need and give a real-life focus and audience for the students' work.

TELEPHONE BOOK

Through telephone book surveys or scavenger hunts, students can learn about businesses, industries, agencies, schools, neighborhoods, and much more using the supplemental pages that are often included in a standard telephone book. Depending upon the developmental needs of the students, this can be an oral or written strategy. It can be traditional (e.g., survey) or nontraditional (e.g., scavenger hunt). This strategy may be done individually but is usually more engaging for students if done collaboratively. If more than three students will be working together, at least two telephone books should be available for their use. Telephone book surveys can be used to learn about the resources in a community (e.g., governmental, religious, cultural, educational); enhance awareness of community cultures; compare business, industry, and agency services and products; and discuss role and significance of advertisement, including issues of truth and propaganda. In the *Community Context Curriculum Project*, students engaged in a democratic learning experience focused on workplace knowledge, skills and ethics as these issues related to the school curriculum (Pate, Thompson, & Keyes, 2001). The students participated in the scavenger hunt for the purpose of learning more about the resources in their community, particularly those pertaining to businesses, industries, and agencies, as well as how these resources impacted them as citizens in the community.

REFERENCES

Coleman, J. S. (1987). The relations between school and social structure. In M. Hallinan (Ed.), *The social organization of schools: New conceptualizations of the learning process* (pp. 177-204), New York: Plenum Press.

Pate, P. E., Homestead, E. R., & McGinnis, K. L. (1997). *Making integrated curriculum work: Teachers, students, and the quest for coherent curriculum.* New York: Teachers College Press.

Pate, P. E., Thompson, K. F., & Keyes, M. (2001). Students, standards, and exploration: A responsive, relevant, and engaging curriculum. *Middle School Journal, 33*(1), 20-35.

Payne, J. (1999). *Kids in P.C. (Partial Control): A service-learning project.* Unpublished manuscript, The University of Georgia, Athens.

Sampson-Cordle, A. V. (2001). *Exploring the relationship between a small rural school in Northeast Georgia and its community: An image-based study using participant-produced photographs.* Unpublished manuscript, The University of Georgia.

—Katherine F. Thompson
The University of Georgia

—P. Elizabeth Pate
The University of Texas, San Antonio

COMPREHENSIVE SCHOOL REFORM DEMONSTRATION PROGRAM

Comprehensive School Reform Demonstration (CSRD) Program was established by the 1998 Fiscal Year Appropriations Act for the U.S. Department of Education as Public Law 105-78, commonly known as Obey-Porter. CSRD was designed, in part, to build on and strengthen school wide programs under the Improving America's Schools Act (IASA). CSRD programs are designed to support comprehensive school improvement strategies in a coordinated fashion to help students reach challenging standards (van Heusden Hale, 2000.) CSRD was designed to improve the entire school while addressing all key operations of a school. That is, it must address all aspects of school, from teaching to school structure, and must place focus on improving the learning of all students in all subjects rather than focusing solely on particular populations of students within a school or performance in particular subjects.

Under Obey-Porter, schools that sought eligibility for funding were required to develop comprehensive and coherent school wide plans that addressed nine specific areas. These nine components stress that schools incorporate measurable goals; support from staff members; research-based methods; external assistance; parental and community involvement; staff development; coordination of resources; evaluation; and a comprehensive approach into a school wide reform plan.

In the 1980s, a number of researchers and practitioners developed whole school models or designs for school reform that included such elements as curriculum, instructional methods, professional development, and restructuring of school organization and governance. CSRD, unlike Title I, placed a special emphasis on working with these expert partners. It allowed for and encouraged schools to implement whole school reform models that have a strong research base and a successful replication record (DeSimone, 2000.) Many of these reform models were already being implemented throughout the United States due to the efforts of programs like Annenberg Challenge Grant and the New American Schools Break the Mold Schools.

The legislation, provided states and schools wide autonomy in selecting which, if any reform models they could implement using CSRD funding. Encouraging them to also develop their own school-wide reform programs based on rigorous research, the legislation did not restrict schools to using only those approaches identified by the U.S. Department of Education. Having acknowledged the autonomy in selection, the legislation pointed out the following 17 reform models as possible external assistance providers: Accelerated Schools, ATLAS Communities, Audrey Cohen College, the Coalition of Essential Schools, Community for Learning, Co-NECT, Director Instruction, Expeditionary Learning Outward Bound, High Schools that Work, the Modern Red Schoolhouse, the National Alliance for Restructure Education (America's Choice), Paideia, Roots, and Wings, The School Development Program, Success for All, the Talent Development High School, and the Urban Learning Center (United States. Congress. House of Representatives. Committee on Appropriations, 1999).

Through a competitive grant process, in 1998 the CSRD program gave state education agencies $145 million to award financial support to schools adopting school-wide reform; of this amount, $120 million was reserved for Title I schools. It was recognized that a CSRD grant would not fully fund a school-wide reform program even though it guaranteed $50,000 per year for up to 3 years. Regardless, over 1,800 schools throughout all 50 states, the District of Columbia, and Puerto Rico, including schools funded through the Bureau of Indian Affairs (BIA), received grants as part of the original 1998 cohort. An additional 3,500 schools received grants through funding increases in 2000 and 2001 (Southwest Educational Development Laboratory, 2003.) According to a study of the CSRD award selection process in 28 states, fewer than 8% of the eligible Title I schools applied for funding. Nationally, urban schools received almost 70% of the grants, and elementary schools 60.5% (Buttram, 2000).

REFERENCES

Buttram, J. L. (2000). *Analysis of national comprehensive school reform demonstration program*. Austin, TX: Southwest Educational Development Laboratory.

DeSimone, L. (2000). *Making comprehensive school reform work*. New York: ERIC Clearinghouse on Urban Education.

Southwest Educational Development Laboratory. (2003). Retrieved July 12, 2004, from: http://www.sedl.org/csr/csr.html

United States. Congress. House of Representatives. Committee on Appropriations. (1999). Making Appropriations for the Departments of Labor, Health and Human Services, and Education, and Related Agencies for the Fiscal Year Ending September 30, 1998, and for other purposes on H. R. 2264. Washington, DC: Government Printing Office. (House Report 105-390)(f:hr390.105)

Van Huesden Hale., S. (2000). *Comprehensive school reform: Research-based strategies to achieve high standards*. San Francisco: WestEd.

—Monica Martinez
KnowledgeWorks Foundation

COMPREHENSIVE SCHOOL REFORM PROGRAM, TITLE I, PART F

The 2001 Elementary and Secondary Education Act (ESEA), Public Law 1-7-110, known commonly as the No Child Left Behind Act (NCLB), signaled important changes for the CSRD program. Under NCLB, CSRD was no longer designated as a "demonstration" program nor governed by language in the appropriations legislation or accompanying conference reports. Rather, the federal program is now known as the Comprehensive School Reform (CSR) Program and is regulated by the new CSR authority established in ESEA's Title I, Part F and also the Fund for the Improvement of Education. Regardless of these fiduciary changes, the CSR program remains committed to a school's need to engage in coherent and comprehensive school-wide reform rather than the adoption and implementation of isolated programs within a school.

Although maintaining much of CSRD's basic formula, the NCLB legislation was pivotal because of its inclusion of an additional two components to the original nine determinates of comprehensive school reform. Incorporating measurable goals; utilizing external assistance; engaging parents, and community members meaningfully; providing staff development; coordinating resources; evaluating the program; and designing a comprehensive approach into a school-wide reform plan were augmented by the addition of an importance on support both *from* staff members as well as support *for* teachers, principals, and supplementary staff as well as a new emphasis on scientifically-based research rather than the reliable research and effective practices.

Although the 11 components of the Comprehensive School Reform Program were to be considered an organizing framework that would help schools create a comprehensive, integrated reform program that affects all of a school's students, teachers, and subjects, the legislation also encouraged schools to build upon and leverage state and local school initiatives when creating a comprehensive plan for school improvement. Regardless of these local initiatives, however, schools can only employ strategies and methods deemed to be proven through scientifically based research, defined in Section 9101 (37)(A) of the No Child Left Behind Act as "research that involves the application of rigorous, systematic, and objective procedures to obtain reliable and valid knowledge relevant to education activities and programs."

Section 1606 (11)(A) of NCLB goes so far as to limit programs schools choose to those that meet one of the following requirements—"the program has been found, through scientifically based research, to significantly improve the academic achievement of participating students; or the program has been found to have strong evidence that it will significantly improve the academic achievement of participating children." Supporters of the use of scientifically based research believe that education research in general has lacked rigor and that the type of research supported in the legislation can help the field determine what works in education. However, others contend that it is not feasible or appropriate to conduct such research in educational contexts.

States receive CSR funding based on their Title I formula and may award CSR grants to schools whose CSR reform program addresses and aligns with eleven components outlined in the Comprehensive School Reform program guidance. For the 2003 fiscal year, $308 million was allocated for schools interested in CSR, twice the amount originally funded in 1998. Of this allocation, $233.5 million was directed towards Title I schools and $74.5 million was available to all public schools. Through state grants, the federal CSR program awards a minimum of $50,000 per year for three years.

REFERENCE

No Child Left Behind Act of 2001, Pub. L. No. 107-110. Retrieved July 12, 2004, from: http://www.ed.gov/policy/elsec/leg/esea02/index.html

—Monica Martinez
KnowledgeWorks Foundation

COOPERATIVE LEARNING

THE NATURE OF COOPERATIVE LEARNING

Cooperative learning is based on social interdependence theory. Social interdependence exists when each individual's outcomes are affected by the actions of others (Deutsch, 1962; Johnson & Johnson, 1989). Social interdependence may be positive (cooperation), negative (competition), or absent (individualistic efforts). Positive interdependence (cooperation) exists when individuals work together to achieve mutual goals, which results in individuals promoting each other's success. Negative interdependence (competition) exists when individuals work against each other to achieve a goal that only one or a few may attain, which results in individuals opposing each other's success. Social independence exists when the outcomes of each person are unaffected by others' actions, which results in no interaction among individuals. Social interdependence theory is based on the premise that the type of interdependence structured among individuals determines how they interact with each other which, in turn, largely determines outcomes.

Cooperative learning is the instructional use of small groups of students working together to maximize their own and each other's learning (Johnson, Johnson, & Holubec, 1998a). Any assignment in any curriculum for any age student can be done cooperatively. There are three types of cooperative learning—formal, informal, and cooperative base groups (Johnson, Johnson, & Holubec, 1998a, 1998b; Johnson, Johnson, & Smith, 1998).

Formal cooperative learning consists of students working together, for one class period to several weeks, to achieve shared learning goals and complete jointly specific tasks and assignments (such as decision making or problem solving, writing, conducting an experiment, or reading a chapter, or learning vocabulary). In formal cooperative learning teachers:

1. *Make a number of pre-instructional decisions.* Teachers specify the objectives for the lesson (both academic and social skills) and decide on the size of groups, the method of assigning students to groups, the roles students will be assigned, the materials needed to conduct the lesson, and the way the room will be arranged.

2. *Explain the task and the positive interdependence.* Teachers define the assignment, teach the required concepts and strategies, specify the positive interdependence and individual accountability, give the criteria for success, and explain the expected social skills to be used.

3. *Monitor students' learning and intervene to provide task assistance or increase students' interpersonal and group skills.* Teachers systematically observe and collect data on each group as it works. When needed, teachers intervene to assist students in completing the task accurately and in working together effectively.

4. *Assess students' learning and help students process how well their groups functioned.* Students' learning is carefully assessed and their performances evaluated. Members of the learning groups then discuss how effectively they worked together and how they can improve in the future.

Informal cooperative learning consists of having students work together to achieve a joint learning goal in temporary, ad hoc groups that last from a few minutes to one class period. During a lecture, demonstration, or film, informal cooperative learning can be used to focus student attention on the material to be learned, set a mood conducive to learning, help set expectations as to what will be covered in a class session, ensure that students cognitively process and rehearse the material being taught, summarize what was learned and precue the next session, and provide closure to an instructional session. The procedure for using informal cooperative learning during a lecture entails having 3-to-5 minute focused discussions before and after the lecture (i.e., bookends) and 2-to-3 minute interspersing pair discussions throughout the lecture.

Cooperative base groups are long-term, heterogeneous cooperative learning groups with stable membership whose primary responsibilities are to provide support, encouragement, and assistance to make academic progress and develop cognitively and socially in healthy ways as well as holding each other accountable for striving to learn. Typically, cooperative base groups (a) are heterogeneous in membership, (b) meet regularly (for example, daily or biweekly), and (c) last for the duration of the semester, year, or until all members are graduated. When students know that the base group will stay together for some time, they become committed to find ways to motivate and encourage their groupmates and solve any problems in working together. The procedure for using base groups is to assign students to base groups of three to four members, have them meet at the beginning and end of each class session (or week) to complete academic tasks such as checking each members' homework, routine tasks such as taking attendance, and personal support tasks such as listening sympathetically to personal problems or providing guidance for writing a paper.

The effectiveness of cooperative learning tends to increase as five basic elements are structured into the situation (Johnson & Johnson, 1989, 1999). First, there must be a strong sense of positive interdependence, so individuals believe they are linked with others so they cannot succeed unless the others do. Positive interdependence may be structured through mutual goals, joint rewards, divided resources, complementary roles, and a shared identity. Second, each collaborator must be individually accountable to do his or her fair share of the work. Third, collaborators must have the opportunity to promote each other's success by helping, assisting, supporting, encouraging, and praising each other's efforts to achieve. Fourth, working together cooperatively requires interpersonal and small group skills, such as leadership, decision making, trust building, communication, and conflict-management skills. Finally, cooperative groups must engage in group processing, which exists when group members discuss how well they are achieving their goals and maintaining effective working relationships.

RESEARCH ON COOPERATIVE LEARNING

During the past 110 years, over 550 experimental and 100 correlational studies have been conducted by a wide variety of researchers in different decades with diverse participants, in different subject areas, and in different settings (Johnson & Johnson, 1989, 1999). The research on cooperation, therefore, has a validity and a generalizability rarely found in the educational literature. The research results may be subsumed in the following categories (see Table 1 and Figure 1).

EFFORT TO ACHIEVE

The more successful middle school students are in facing academic challenges, the more positive their school experience tends to be. From Table 1 it may be seen that cooperation promotes considerably greater effort to achieve than do competitive or individualistic efforts (effect sizes = 0.67 and 0.64 respectively). Effort exerted to achieve includes such variables as achievement, retention, on-task behavior, higher-level reasoning strategies, generation of new ideas, intrinsic motivation, achievement motivation, continuing motivation, and transfer of learning. Thus, more successful coping with academic challenges tends to occur within cooperative than within competitive or individualistic situations.

INTERPERSONAL RELATIONSHIPS

The degree of emotional bonding that exists among middle school students has a profound effect on students' school experience. There have been over 175 studies that have investigated the relative impact of cooperative, competitive, and individualistic efforts on quality of relationships (Johnson & Johnson, 1989). From Table 1 it may be seen that cooperation generally promotes greater interpersonal attraction among individuals than do competitive or individualistic efforts (effect sizes = 0.67 and 0.60 respectively). Thus, more friendly, caring, and committed relationships tend to develop among students within cooperative than within competitive or individualistic situations. In addition, the results of over 106 studies indicate

Table 1
Mean Effect Sizes for Impact of Social Interdependence on Dependent Variables

	Cooperative vs. Competitive	Cooperative vs. Individualistic	Competitive vs. Individualistic
Achievement	0.67	0.64	0.30
Interpersonal Attraction	0.67	0.60	0.08
Social Support	0.62	0.70	-0.13
Self-Esteem	0.58	0.44	-0.23

Source: Johnson and Johnson (1989).

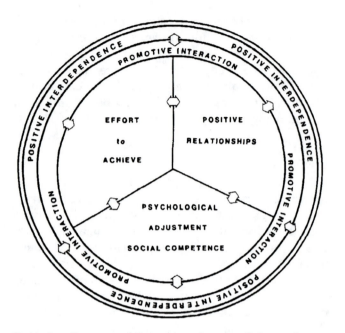

Figure 1.   Outcome of Cooperative Learning (Johnson & Johnson, 1989).

that cooperative experiences tend to promote greater perceived social support from peers and from teachers than do competitive (effect-size = 0.62) or individualistic (effect-size = 0.70) experiences.

It is difficult to overemphasize the importance of these research results. Supportive and caring friends give children, adolescents, and young adults a developmental advantage (Johnson & Johnson, 1989, 1999). Antisocial behavior and rejection by the normal peer group are positively correlated, inappropriately aggressive behavior tends to result in rejection by peers, and rejected children tend to be deficient in a number of social-cognitive skills (including peer group entry, perception of peer group norms, response to provocation, and interpretation of prosocial interactions). Children referred to child guidance clinics tend to experience peer difficulties twice as often as nonreferred children. Referred children also tend to have fewer friends, have less contact with friends, have less stable friendships over time, and have less mature understanding of the reciprocities and intimacies involved in friendships. Students who engage in violence and bullying in school, furthermore, are often reported as being alienated and isolated from their schoolmates.

PSYCHOLOGICAL HEALTH

The anthropologist Asley Montagu was fond of saying that with few exceptions, the solitary animal in any species is an abnormal creature. The psychoana-

lyst Karen Horney believed the neurotic individual is someone who is inappropriately competitive and, therefore, unable to cooperate with others. They recognized that psychological health is the ability to develop and maintain relationships in which cooperative action effectively takes place. Studies relating cooperative, competitive, and individualistic efforts and attitudes to various indices of psychological health have been conducted on middle-class middle-school students, middle-class high school seniors, high-school age juvenile prisoners, adult prisoners, Olympic ice-hockey players, and adult step-couples (see Johnson & Johnson, 1989). The results indicate that the more positive a person's attitudes toward cooperating with others, the less likely they are to engage in antisocial behaviors such as drug abuse and criminal activities, the less their tension and anxiety, the less their depression and dejection, the less their anger and hostility, the less forceful and demanding they are, and the less rebellious and egoistic they are. In addition, the more cooperative individuals are, the more they use socially appropriate and approved ways of meeting environmental demands, the more they see reality clearly without distorting it according to their own desires and needs, the greater their emotional maturity, the greater their ability to resolve conflicts between self-perceptions and adverse information about oneself, the higher their self-esteem and self-acceptance, the greater their basic trust in others and optimism, the more aware they are of their feelings, the more they can control their anger and frustration and express them appropriately, the more they take into account social customs and rules in resolving interpersonal and personal problems, the more willing they are to acknowledge unpleasant events or conditions encountered in daily living, the more their thinking is organized and focused on reality and free from confusion and hallucinations, the greater their leadership ability and social initiative, the more outgoing and sociable they are, the greater their sense of well-being (which includes minimizing their worries and being free from self-doubt and disillusionment), the greater their common sense and good judgment, and the more conscientious and responsible they are. All of these qualities are important for middle grade students.

INTERPERSONAL AND SMALL GROUP SKILLS

An essential aspect of middle school experience is the mastery of the interpersonal and small group skills needed to interact effectively with other people (Johnson, 2006; Johnson & Johnson, 2006). They include such skills as communication, trust building, self-disclosure, leadership, decision making, goal setting, social influence, and conflict resolution skills. Interpersonal and small group skills are mastered primarily in cooperative situations. The research indicates that socially isolated and withdrawn students learned more social skills and engaged in them more frequently within cooperative than within individualistic situations, especially when the group was rewarded for their doing so. Emotionally disturbed adolescents who experienced cooperative learning were more likely than traditionally taught students to interact appropriately with other students and even attended class more often. Cooperation tends to promote more frequent, open, effective, and accurate communication while communication among competitors tends to be infrequent, closed, ineffective, and inaccurate.

CONCLUSION

The pedagogy used may be the most important factor in helping students in the middle grades meet their development challenges. Middle grade students need to feel successful and academically capable, they need to have supportive and caring friendships with classmates, they need to resolve their developmental issues in psychologically healthy ways while building resilience and efficacy, and they need to master the social skills necessary to build and maintain constructive relationships with diverse peers. Cooperative learning has considerable impact on whether students successful achieve these developmental necessities.

REFERENCES

Deutsch, M. (1962). Cooperation and trust: Some theoretical notes. In M. R. Jones (Ed.), *Nebraska symposium on motivation* (pp. 275-319). Lincoln, NE: University of Nebraska Press.

Johnson, D. W. (2006). *Reaching out: Interpersonal effectiveness and self-actualization* (9th ed.). Boston: Allyn & Bacon.

Johnson, D. W., & Johnson, F. P. (2006). *Joining together: Group theory and group skills* (9th ed.). Boston: Allyn & Bacon.

Johnson, D. W., & Johnson, R. (1989). *Cooperation and competition: Theory and research.* Edina, MN: Interaction Book.

Johnson, D. W., & Johnson, R. (1999). *Learning Together And Alone: Cooperative, competitive, and individualistic learning* (5th ed.) Boston: Allyn & Bacon

Johnson, D. W., Johnson, R., & Holubec, E. (1998a). *Cooperation in the classroom* (7th ed.). Edina, MN: Interaction Book.

Johnson, D. W., Johnson, R., & Holubec, E. (1998b). *Advanced cooperative learning* (3rd ed.). Edina, MN: Interaction Book.

Johnson, D. W., Johnson, R., & Smith, K. (1998). *Active learning: Cooperation in the college classroom* (2nd ed.). Edina, MN: Interaction Book.

—David W. Johnson
—Roger T. Johnson
University of Minnesota

COUNSELING

Counseling has roots in both psychology and education, and today professional school counseling focuses on promoting the academic, career, and personal/social development of all students. Middle school counselors have the unique task of promoting normal and optimal development with students in the midst of puberty, school transition, and typical family redefinition. Middle school counselors also seek to ensure that the ecology or context of the school corresponds to the "developmentally appropriate context" endorsed by the middle school movement. Clearly, the distinctive development of early adolescents and the development focused context of middle school present challenges and opportunities for middle school counselors.

The practice of school counseling varies considerably based on training and particular school needs, although current national models have expanded upon traditional roles of remediation and individual counseling to include systemic functions such as leadership and advocacy to impact the school system. The American School Counselor Association (ASCA, 2003) indicates that professional school counselors, as members of the educational team, consult and collaborate with teachers, administrators, and families to assist students to be successful. They work on behalf of students and their families to ensure that all school programs facilitate the educational process and offer the opportunity for school success for each student.

School counselors provide direct services to students through individual and group interventions. Individual counseling consists of working with a student in a one-on-one relationship on normal developmental challenges where the school counselor facilitates the development of mutually determined goals. In group counseling, school counselors allow students to work together to resolve difficulties or develop skills. Groups typically focus on a specific topic (e.g., new student orientation, anger management, grief and loss, study skills). Large group guidance, often called classroom guidance, is planned developmental curriculum delivered in classrooms to teach skills and discuss important topics such as study skills or decision-making. Classroom guidance is often delivered in collaboration with teachers and in conjunction with their curriculum. Another collaborative process is consultation, where the school counselor serves as a consultant (e.g., behavioral management) to parents, teachers, or administrators in order to benefit a third party (student/child).

Several systemic functions have gained importance in recent years. Coordination and leadership of programs (e.g., peer mentoring, school improvement committees) and advocacy are used by school counselors to impact and promote student development by influencing and/or manipulating the environment. Advocacy refers to the important role that counselors play in ensuring a voice for the disenfranchised or in breaking down barriers to open access for all students.

In addition to direct services and systemic functions, school counselors often perform a wide range of additional duties. They may include: advising students, educational planning, and career development, referring students to community-based services, leading or contributing to 504 or IEP meetings, coordinating course scheduling, collecting, and evaluating data about counseling programming, and planning orientation programs or group meetings that promote student adjustment in school transitions. This list is not exhaustive, as school counselors tend to contribute to the school in a variety of ways depending on student and teacher needs, administrator philosophy, caseloads, and environmental circumstances.

School counselors are typically trained at the master's level and are licensed or certified by the state (only a few states still require previous teaching experience). Nationally accredited (Council for Accreditation of Counseling and Related Educational Programs) training programs include course work in professional identity, social, and cultural diversity, human growth, and development, career development, helping relationships, group work, assessment, and research and program evaluation. Additionally, many programs require supervised practicum and internship experiences that total 700 hours of service, 280 of which must be direct service to students, teachers, and/or parents.

HISTORY OF SCHOOL COUNSELING AND THE RISE OF THE MIDDLE SCHOOL COUNSELOR

School counseling historically has been responsive to meeting societal needs. There is evidence of guidance-related programs dating back to the early 1900s. In fact, as early as 1905 standardized intelligence and military tests were used to evaluate students' academic abilities and personal interests as a means of categorizing students and exploring career options. In the 1930s, directive guidance emerged as the new trend in school counseling. One of the most influential figures in this movement was E. G. Williamson, who promoted enhancing normal adjustment, goal setting, and overcoming obstacles, and assisting in the individual's quest for a satisfying lifestyle (Sweeney, 2001). With the work of Carl Rogers in the early 1940s (Sweeney, 2001) came the shift from problem-focus to person-focus, with an emphasis on the counseling relationship and climate. Rogers was a pioneer in the field of counseling in that he believed clients have the capacity to solve their own problems while in a therapeutic relationship with a counselor. His work led to the growth of individual counseling as a dominant function for school counselors. In the 1950s, The American School Counselor Association (ASCA) and the Association for Counselor Education and Supervision (ACES) developed and promoted standards regarding the training of school counselors with a strong emphasis in counseling theory and clinical training (Sweeney, 2001).

The National Middle School Association (NMSA), founded in 1973, brought a focus on early adolescents and middle level education. Two seminal documents that sharpened the middle school philosophy were *This We Believe* (NMSA, 1982) and *Turning Points: Preparing American Youth for the 21st Century* (Carnegie Council on Adolescent Development, 1989). Both articulated a road map for middle school education based on a plan for what developmentally responsive middle level schools could and should be (NMSA, 1992). While these reforms were broad and not necessarily focused on school counseling, a closer examination reveals significant overlap. School counselors play a significant role in operationalizing many of the middle school tenants. Middle school counselors achieve this goal by creating a community for learning, ensuring success for all students, reengaging families in the education of young adolescents, and connecting schools with communities. The *21st Century Research Agenda* created by the NMSA in 1997 outlined questions that target respect and appreciation for diversity, peer mentoring, psychologically, and physically safe environments, violence, and drug free schools, programs, and policies that foster health, wellness, and safety, and comprehensive guidance and support systems; all which middle school counselors are invested in.

In the late 1990s, ASCA introduced the National Standards of School Counseling (Campbell & Dahir, 1997). There are three main areas of development addressed: academic development, career development, and personal/social development. Under each of these main areas are three standards, each with specific competencies.

ACADEMIC DEVELOPMENT

1. Students will acquire the attitudes, knowledge, and skills contributing to effective learning in school and across the life span.
2. Students will complete school with the academic preparation essential to choose from a wide range of substantial post-secondary options, including college.
3. Students will understand the relationship of academics to the world of work and to life at home and in the community.

CAREER DEVELOPMENT

1. Students will acquire the skills to investigate the world of work in relation to knowledge of self and to make informed career decisions.
2. Students will employ strategies to achieve future career success and satisfaction.
3. Students will understand the relationship between personal qualities, education, and training, and the world of work.

PERSONAL/SOCIAL DEVELOPMENT

1. Students will acquire the attitudes, knowledge, and interpersonal skills to help them understand and respect self and others.
2. Students will make decisions, set goals, and take necessary action to achieve goals.
3. Students will understand safety and survival skills (Campbell & Dahir, 1997, p. 2).

Recently, the American School Counseling Association National Model for school counseling (ASCA, 2003), and reform efforts like the Transforming School Counseling Initiative (The Education Trust, 2003) continue to shape school counseling. While current reforms are helpful, it is essential for middle school counselors to institute helping services based on developmental theory and the specifics of early adolescent development in establishing these goals. The challenges of early adolescence influence how counselors help promote student development based on the ASCA National Standards. Personal/social devel-

opment, puberty, peer relations, cognitive development, moral dilemmas, family issues, and many other topics are salient to early adolescent life.

"Development" is the word most often times associated with middle school children. Aside from infancy, no other phase of life is characterized by greater, more rapid, and diverse development than early adolescence (Pruitt, 1999). Traditionalists have often viewed this period of development as being marred with "storm and stress," and a transition into a more complex interaction of self exploration, peer interaction, and intellectual expansion (Hall, 1904). There can be a great deal of interference for early adolescents as they journey towards adulthood. As theorized by the likes of Erikson, Freud, and Piaget, successful emergence to adulthood is determined by how well the early adolescent can adapt to, and persevere from, the new experiences of this time period. An examination of the cognitive and psychosocial development associated with early adolescence uncovers the many interactions, experiences, and challenges that occur in middle schools on a daily basis.

As transition from elementary to middle school occurs, changes in physical, mental, and social dynamics of these early adolescents are evident. As developmental advocates, middle school counselors can collaborate with school personnel to better recognize and understand the varying levels of development and the endless possibilities and struggles associated with this age group (Galassi & Akos, 2004). This developmental understanding is vital to the success of early adolescents. By working systematically and proactively these counselors can promote a healthy and prosperous journey towards adulthood for middle school students. The middle school counselor is charged to create programmatic services integrated with the school and community that promote awareness and understanding of the varying levels of development, the interaction between individual development and the environment, and how best to facilitate optimum development for all students.

REFERENCES

American School Counseling Association. (2003). *The ASCA national model: A framework for school counseling programs.* Alexandria, VA: Author.

Campbell, C., & Dahir, C. (1997). *Sharing the vision: The national standards for school counseling programs.* Alexandria, VA: American School Counselor Association.

Carnegie Council on Adolescent Development. (1989). *Turning points: Preparing American youth for the 21st century.* New York: The Carnegie Corporation of New York.

Galassi, J., & Akos, P. (2004). Developmental advocacy: 21st century school counseling. *Journal of Counseling and Development, 82,* 146-157.

Hall, G. S. (1904). *Adolescence: It's Psychology and its relations to Physiology, Anthropology, Sociology, Sex, Crime, Religion, and Education.* (Vols. 1-2). Norwalk, CT: Appleton-Century-Crofts.

National Middle School Association. (1982). *This we believe.* Columbus, OH: Author.

National Middle School Association. (1992). *This we believe: Developmentally responsive middle level schools.* Columbus, OH: Author.

National Middle School Association. (1997). *A 21st century research agenda: Issues, topics & questions guiding inquiry into middle level theory & practice.* Columbus, OH: Author.

Pruitt, D. B. (1999). *Your adolescent: Emotional, behavioral and cognitive development from early adolescence through the teen years.* New York: Harper Collins.

Sweeney, T. (2001). Counseling: Historical origins and philosophical roots. In D. Locke, J. Myers, and E. Herr (Eds.), *The Handbook of Counseling* (pp. 3-26). Thousand Oaks, CA: SAGE.

The Education Trust. (2003). *Transforming school counseling initiative.* Retrieved May 25, 2004, from: http://www2.edtrust.org/EdTrust/Transforming+School+Counseling/main

—Michael J. Brannigan
Queensbury Middle School,
Queensbury Union Free School District

—Patrick Akos
The University of North Carolina, Chapel Hill

CURRICULUM DEVELOPMENT

Curriculum development" is a comprehensive decision-making process that includes the phases of planning, implementation, and evaluation. The term is often used synonymously with curriculum improvement and ideally results in change and the enhancement of an existing program (Oliva, 2001). The foundation of curriculum development lies primarily in the fields of philosophy, sociology, and psychology. Philosophy outlines one's views of learners, educational purpose, and the value of what is to be learned. Sociology assists curriculum developers in understanding the relationship between people and their society and helps determine how schools relate to society. Psychology includes insight into the characteristics of the learners and provides the basis for how a curriculum can best be arranged to meet their needs (Beane, Toepfer, & Alessi, 1986). While curriculum specifies what students must learn including concepts, generalizations, relative facts, skills, and habits of mind (Jackson & Davis, 2000) and encompasses every planned component of a school's program (National Middle School Association, 2003), curriculum development serves as the vehicle for ensuring that these components are delivered to learners. This vehicle is driven by teachers, administrators, curriculum specialists, supervisors, students, parents, and other community members who are involved with the curriculum (Oliva, 2001).

HISTORY

Spirited debate over the definition and interpretations of middle school curriculum design models has continued for decades. Eichhorn's (1966) early model for curriculum development was based upon the physical, mental, social, and cultural characteristics of the young adolescent. Alexander's (1995) vision for the curriculum content initially involved three phases: (a) learning skills such as reading, writing, speaking, listening, computation and research skills; (b) common learnings such as literature, social studies, languages, mathematics, science, and fine arts; and, (c) personal development skills such as health and physical education, exploratory experiences, special interest courses, and advisor-advisee programs. Hamburg (1993) emphasized the need for curriculum to include knowledge and skills, a spirit of inquiry, respect, a sense of belonging, and a way to assist learners in becoming useful members of their own communities.

The position statement of the National Middle School Association (2003) asserts a developmentally responsive curriculum is characterized by learning experiences that are appealing to young adolescents and should provide rich opportunities for posing questions and seeking answers to them. No other aspect of a middle school is perceived to be as important as that of developing a quality curriculum resulting in young adolescents who acquire the knowledge, skills, and dispositions needed for leading productive lives. An essential programmatic feature in this position statement suggests that curriculum must be relevant, challenging, and exploratory thus providing a worthy challenge for curriculum developers. Similarly, Jackson and Davis (2000) recommend a curriculum grounded in standards, relevant to adolescents' concerns, and based on how students learn best using a mix of assessment methods.

Despite these recommendations, some authorities contend that curriculum development has been largely ignored as the middle school movement progressed (Beane, 1990; Knowles & Brown, 2000). Dickinson (2001) states that the absence of appropriate curriculum for young adolescents has had a debilitating effect on the reform efforts in the middle school movement. Lipsitz (1984) concurs and states the "translating philosophy into curriculum is the most difficult feat for schools to accomplish" (p. 188). Lounsbury (1993) challenged curriculum developers to "employ zero-based curriculum development" (p. 53) and create a new curriculum for young adolescents that transcends the core subjects, state curriculum guidelines, spiraling curricula, block scheduling and state mandates. Likewise, curriculum theorists in schools and universities have begun to seek best practices for asking and answering key questions related to curriculum development at the middle school level (Brazee & Capelluti, 1995). Inherent in this work is the concept that traditional curriculum had not been developed by or for the young adolescents that it serves. Resulting was a model that promoted agendas such as improving test scores or "inculcating American culture" (p. 187). Brazee and Capelluti challenge stakeholders to begin to view curriculum development as a "fluid process whereby we move along a scale" (p. 28) and provides a five-point continuum that outlines an approach to curriculum development will ultimately result in implementing a highly sophisticated curriculum for young adolescents.

A CONTINUUM FOR CURRICULUM DEVELOPMENT

In *Dissolving Boundaries: Toward an Integrative Curriculum*, Brazee and Capelluti (1995) introduce the idea that curriculum exists as points on a continuum ranging from a totally integrated curriculum that clearly is best suited to the needs of young adolescents to a plan that is best suited for the convenience of teachers. They surmise curriculum development is a fluid process that includes points on a scale ranging from most responsive to least responsive to student needs. This five point scale provides a framework for teachers as well as a reference for self-evaluation and goals for developing curriculum at more sophisticated levels (see Figure 1)

In Brazee and Capelluti's curriculum continuum, the first point refers to a conventional curriculum that is most widely recognized and utilized today. This conventional form of curriculum development is typically characterized by a teacher-centered classroom where subjects are taught in isolation and textbooks are key sources of information. The role of the teacher is active as information is delivered to students who passively answer worksheets, read textbooks, and complete tests that measure success. Underlying this type of curriculum development is the belief that the teacher knows what is best for learners and application to the lives of students is marginalized. Schools which operate under Point 1 may attempt interdisciplinary planning and give occasional opportunities for theme-based projects resulting in a lack of student engagement and boredom.

Point 2 in the continuum refers to a multidisciplinary approach that is characterized by the existence of curricular themes determined by teachers and delivered in separate classrooms where subjects are taught in isolation. For example, a novel may be assigned in a language arts classroom while the social studies teacher might study the geography related to the setting of the book. These connections often increase student interest as well as their intellectual and social skills. When students and teachers experience success with the multidisciplinary approach, it often provides encouragement to move to a further point on the continuum of curriculum development.

Integrated curriculum, the next step in the curriculum continuum builds upon the previous points and gets further impetus from increased student motivation and interest. Dissolved subject-area demarcation and flexible scheduling enables young adolescents to investigate broader themes and topics. Other curriculum experts recommend the need for an integrated curriculum that uses broad-based concepts, essential questions and themes drawn from the young adolescents' interests. They also suggest that teachers should rethink existing paradigms about the curriculum content and instructional techniques. This thinking requires professionals to rely on their expertise. Variations in the development and delivery of this model exist. Integrated curriculum can be used as a total program or can be implemented at various points in an academic day or at the conclusion of a multidisciplinary unit of study (Jackson & Davis, 2000).

Point 4 in the continuum refers to integrative curriculum and it minimizes the role of the teacher while maximizing the role of the learner. Students are the "prime curriculum developers" (McDonough, 1991) as they seek to resolve issues related to them and to their world. In the integrative process, the role of the teacher involves identifying key curricular areas and student expectations. Teacher responsibility is not diminished in truly integrative curriculum. While they continue to devote their time to teaching, their responsibility evolves as a facilitator of learning. Vars and Beane (2000) believe that integrative teaching has great potential for producing students who will be successful on mandated assessments as well.

Point 5 in the curriculum continuum, referred to as beyond integrative curriculum, places an enormous

Point 1	Point 2	Point 3	Point 4	Point 5
*_____*_____*_____*_____*				
Separate Subjects	Multidisciplinary Approach	Integrate Approach	Integrative Approach	Beyond Integrative

Figure 1.   Curriculum Continuum Scale.

responsibility on the student to plan, implement, and evaluate the content to be learned. Students would be allowed to pursue their own interests or those predetermined subjects designated by the school. Self directed learners in this model require individual pace and access to information and tools for learning. Learning would extend beyond the classroom and engage the students in service projects and real-world internships. Key aspects of this point have rarely been explored or implemented in schools.

Although not reflected in Brazee and Capelluti's continuum, Knowles and Brown (2000) suggest that an interdisciplinary approach to curriculum development fits between the multidisciplinary approach and the integrated model. This model differs from the multidisciplinary model as the content lines are blurred and themes are based on the interests of the students. Students initially have the opportunity to tell teachers about their interests, and curriculum is developed around these questions and concerns. This type of curriculum empowers young adolescents to make decisions and to experience a more democratic education.

CONCLUSION

It is essential that middle level curriculum development retain young adolescent needs and interests as its focal point. The successful implementation of any of these five points outlined by Brazee and Capelluti relies imminently upon the commitment of teachers and their implementation skills. However, proponents of the standards-based reform movement advocating high-stakes testing and accountability have threatened the work of middle level curriculum developers who maintain their commitment to developmentally responsive curriculum for the young adolescent. Their premise is that teachers must become more cognizant of national standards and teach them in a more deliberate manner to ensure student success in school (George & Alexander, 2003). Jackson and

Davis (2000) call for middle grades teachers to develop and present a curriculum rooted in standards that outline what students should know and be able to do while maintaining relevance and staying grounded in how young adolescents learn. Vars and Beane (2000) state teachers can engage students in inviting, student-centered, integrated curriculum while incorporating imposed standards.

As curriculum development occurs, the work may be better understood by the following axioms. Change is inevitable, desirable, and a product of its time. Curriculum change occurs over time and may overlap with old or new ideas. It is a cooperative activity that results when participants involved experience the change. Curriculum development is a decision making process that is cyclic and ongoing. The process is most successful when comprehensively done and when it follows a systematic process. Moreover, curriculum development must start at its existing point. Change may be a slow process, yet it is most successful when all stakeholders engage in collaborative efforts towards similar goals (Oliva, 2001).

REFERENCES

Alexander, W. A. (1995). The junior high school: A changing view. *Middle School Journal, 26*(3), 24.

Beane, J. A. (1990). *The middle school curriculum: From rhetoric to reality.* Columbus, OH: National Middle School Association.

Beane, J. A., Toepfer, C. F., & Alessi, S. J. (1986). *Curriculum planning and development.* Boston: Allyn & Bacon.

Brazee, E. M., & Capelluti, J. (1995). *Dissolving boundaries: Toward an integrative curriculum.* Columbus, OH: National Middle School Association.

Dickinson, T. S. (2001). Reinventing the middle school: A proposal to counter arrested development. In T. Dickinson (Ed.), *Reinventing the middle school* (pp. 3-20). New York: RoutledgeFalmer.

Eichhorn, D. (1966). The junior high school plan, Part III. *The fifteenth yearbook of the national society for the study of education.* Bloomington, IN: Public School.

George, P. S., & Alexander, W. M. (2003). *The exemplary middle school* (3rd ed). Belmont: CA: Wadsworth/Thomson Learning.

Hamburg, D. A. (1993). The opportunities of early adolescence. *Teachers College Record, 94*(3), 466-471.

Jackson, A. W., & Davis, G. A. (2000). *Turning points 2000: Educating adolescents in the 21st century.* New York: Teachers College Press.

Knowles, T., & Brown, D. F. (2000). *What every middle school teacher should know.* Portsmouth, NH: Heinemann.

Lipsitz, J. (1984). *Successful schools for young adolescents.* New Brunswick, NJ: Transaction.

Lounsbury, J. H. (1993). A fresh start for the middle school curriculum. In. T. Dickinson, (Ed.), *Readings in middle school curriculum: A continuing conversation* (pp. 53-62). Columbus, OH: National Middle School Association.

McDonough, L. (1991). Middle level curriculum: The search for self and social meaning. *Middle School Journal, 23*(2), 29-35.

National Middle School Association. (2003). *This we believe: Successful schools for young adolescents.* Westerville, OH: Author.

Oliva, P. F. (2001). *Developing the curriculum.* New York: Longman.

Vars, G., & Beane, J. A. (2000). *Integrative curriculum in a standards-based world.* Urbana-Champaign, IL: University of Illinois. (ERIC ED441618)

—Melanie W. Greene
Appalachian State University

CURRICULUM INTEGRATION

"Curriculum integration" refers to the collaborative process between teachers and young adolescents who organize curriculum around relevant themes of social and personal issues while transcending the limits of subject-area demarcations. In his important book, *Curriculum Integration: Designing the Core of Democratic Education*, James Beane (1997) describes curriculum integration as "a special kind of unity" (p. 2) that makes multiple connections among disciplinary knowledge and skills, young adolescents' experiences, and local and global social problems. The integrated nature of this curriculum calls for learning opportunities to be arranged around a broader conceptual theme (e.g., "Cooperation and Conflict") that is not only the focus of meaningful inquiry but also the context for how young adolescents acquire and apply knowledge and skills.

Beane (1997) asserts that there are four dimensions of curriculum integration: "the integration of experiences, social integration, the integration of knowledge, and integration as a curriculum design" (p. 4).

The first of these dimensions, the integration of experiences, is more than simply drawing upon young adolescents' interests and experiences into the curriculum; it involves actually using experience as a tool for learning. That is, as young adolescents experientially learn new concepts, both the process and product of learning become meaningful, relevant, and transformative. Furthermore, integrated experiences as part of the curriculum prepare young adolescents for what Dewey (1938) called "educative experiences;" Dewey (1938) put it this way: "only by extracting at each present time the full meaning of each present experience are we prepared for doing the same thing in the future. This is the only preparation which in the long run amounts to anything" (p. 49). The integration of experiences into a middle level curriculum can involve community-based activities, service learning, and nature studies, among others (Brazee & Capelluti, 1995; Fertman, White, & White, 1996; Meng, 2003; Stevenson & Carr, 1993; Warren & Flinchberg, 2003).

A second feature of an integrated curriculum is social integration (Beane, 1993a; Beane, 1997). Beane (1997) describes such social integration as a "problem-centered curriculum" that "involves collaborative work on common social issues" (p. 6). In this arrangement, adolescents' self-identified personal concerns are linked to social/global issues and are collaboratively studied in an integrated fashion (Apple & Beane, 1995; Beane, 1993a; Beane, 1997). A problem-centered approach can be used in an integrated curriculum to allow adolescents to identify, inquire into, and actively and democratically make decisions about their social worlds—while at the same time connecting this critical activity to broader global political issues. Such problem-based, democratic inquiry helps young adolescents to see the integrated and transformative nature of experience, social worlds, and knowledge (Beane, 1997; Drake, 1998; Glasgow, 1997; Jones, Rasmussen, & Moffitt, 1997; Kain, 2003; Stepian & Gallagher, 1993; Vossler & Moore, 1993).

A third aspect of an integrated curriculum is how knowledge becomes contextualized and as a source of empowerment (Beane, 1997). As contextualized, disciplinary knowledge is no longer acquired through a subject-centered, fragmented approach that tends to limit what students are able to know and how they learn it; rather, disciplines are integrated to *support* the exploration of a theme. Knowledge in curriculum integration, then, is neither predetermined nor pre-packaged by a teacher but emerges as a social construction that leads to a deeper, meaningful understanding of the relationship of the self to the world (Arnold, 1991; Beane, 1993a; Beane, 1997). Disciplinary knowledge is drawn upon to increase this understanding; subject-area content and skills are repositioned as resources rather than the focus of learning. This repositioning of knowledge from the dominant or high culture of academics to acknowledge and integrate the everyday or popular knowledge may empower adolescents to study social issues important to their lives as well as larger concerns of a democratic society (Apple & Beane, 1995; Beane, 1996; Beane, 1997). Such empowerment through the integration and valuing of all types of knowledges, experiences, and concerns is supported through a problem-based, experiential curriculum.

Finally, a feature of integration is the way in which curriculum development is democratic and participatory, and unique to curriculum integration is the shifting roles of teachers and students (Beane, 1993b; Beane, 1997; Brodhagen, 1995; Caskey, 2002; Erlandson & McVittie, 2001; Knowles & Brown, 2000; Manning & Bucher, 2005; Muir, 1998; Nesin & Lounsbury, 1999; Pate, 2001; Powell, 2001; Simmons & El-Hindi, 1998). Teachers come to be more facilitators, organizers, listeners, resources, and directors of learning, rather than the sole authority in the classroom. Young adolescents are no longer empty repositories for knowledge but take inclusive, active roles in decision-making, become support networks for each other in authentic learning opportunities, grow to understand themselves as learners, and accept responsibility for their learning.

The above essentials of an integrated curriculum are those identified and developed by James A. Beane whose work has impelled the theory and practice of integrated curriculum. Educators and scholars have taken up Beane's work to describe how these essentials might be implemented in middle level classrooms (Brazee & Capelluti, 1995; Brodhagen, 1994; Drake, 1998; Powell, Fussell, Troutman, Smith, & Skoog, 1998; Smith & Johnson, 1993; Springer, 2003; Stevenson & Carr, 1993). Furthermore, educators and scholars have articulated some of the challenges and obstacles to implementing an integrated curriculum such as the following: (1) the current political climate of standards and high-stakes testing (George & Alexander, 2003; Jackson & Davis, 2000; Pate, 2001; Paterson, 2003; Powell, 2001; Vars, 2001); (2) the intensive labor and unpredictable or incongruent outcomes inherent in planning and applying an integrated curriculum (George & Alexander, 2003; Powell & Van Zandt Allen, 2001; Thompson, 2002; Weilbacher, 2001); (3) a lack of both administrative and collegial support and faculty development in middle schools for curriculum integration (Gatewood, 1998; George & Alex-

ander, 2003; Thompson, 2002; O'Steen, Cuper, Spires, Beal, & Pope, 2002); (4) the existence of critiques of integrated curriculum as anti-intellectual and nonrigorous (Beane, 1999; Roth, 1994); and (5) misinterpretations and misapplications of curriculum integration (Bergstrom, 1998; Powell & Van Zandt Allen, 2001).

It is crucial to make the important distinction between integrated and interdisciplinary curriculum, and the differences are grounded in the approach to and process of curriculum design as well as how subject-area knowledge is included (Beane, 1997; Nesin & Lounsbury, 1999; Powell & Van Zandt Allen, 2001).

REFERENCES

Apple, M. W., & Beane, J. A. (Eds.). (1995). *Democratic schools*. Alexandria, VA: Association for Supervision and Curriculum Development.

Arnold, J. (1991). Towards a middle level curriculum rich in meaning. *Middle School Journal, 23*(2), 8-12.

Beane, J. A. (1993a). *A middle school curriculum: From rhetoric to reality* (2nd ed.). Columbus, OH: National Middle School Association.

Beane, J. A. (1993b). Problems and possibilities for an integrative curriculum. *Middle School Journal, 25*(1), 18-23.

Beane, J. A. (1996). On the shoulders of giants! The case for curriculum integration. *Middle School Journal, 28*(1), 6-11.

Beane, J. A. (1997). *Curriculum integration: Designing the core of democratic education.* New York: Teachers College Press.

Beane, J. A. (1999). Middle schools under siege: Points of attack. *Middle School Journal, 30*(4), 3-9.

Bergstrom, K. L. (1998). Are we missing the point about curriculum integration? *Middle School Journal, 29*(4), 28-37.

Brazee, E. N., & Capelluti, J. (1995). *Dissolving boundaries: Toward an integrative curriculum.* Columbus, OH: National Middle School Association.

Brodhagen, B. L. (1994). Assessing and reporting student progress in an integrative curriculum. *Teaching and Change, 1*(1) 238-254.

Brodhagen, B. L. (1995). The situation made us special. In M. Apple & J. Beane (Eds.), *Democratic schools* (pp. 83-100). Alexandria, VA: Association of Supervision and Curriculum.

Caskey, M. M. (2002). Authentic curriculum: Strengthening middle level education. In V. Anfara, Jr. & S. Stacki (Eds.), *Middle school curriculum, instruction, and assessment* (pp. 103-118). Greenwich, CT: Information Age.

Dewey, J. (1938). *Experience and education.* New York: Collier Books.

Drake, S. M. (1998). *Creating integrated curriculum: Proven ways to increase student learning.* Thousand Oaks, CA: Corwin Press.

Erlandson C., & McVittie, J. (2001). Student voices on integrative curriculum. *Middle School Journal, 33*(2), 28-36.

Fertman, C. I., White, G. P., & White, L. J. (1996). *Service learning in the middle school: Building a culture of service.* Columbus, OH: National Middle School Association.

Gatewood, T. (1998). How valid is integrated curriculum in today's middle schools? *Middle School Journal, 29*(4), 38-41.

George, P. S., & Alexander, W. M. (2003). *The exemplary middle school* (3rd ed.). Belmont, CA: Wadsworth/Thomson Learning.

Glasgow, N. A. (1997). *New curriculum for new times.* Thousand Oaks, CA: Corwin Press.

Jackson, A. W., & Davis, G. A. (2000). *Turning points 2000: Educating adolescents in the 21st century.* New York: Teachers College Press.

Jones, B. F., Rassmussen, C. M., & Moffitt, M. C. (1997). *Real-life problem solving: A collaborative approach to interdisciplinary learning.* Washington, DC: American Psychological Association.

Kain, D. L. (2003). *Problem-based learning for teachers, grades k-8.* Boston: Allyn & Bacon.

Knowles, T., & Brown, D. F. (2000). *What every middle school teacher should know.* Portsmouth, NH: Heinemann.

Manning, M. L., & Bucher, K. T. (2005). *Teaching in the middle school* (2nd ed.). Upper Saddle River, NJ: Pearson Education.

Meng, K. (2003). Spanning the curriculum: students build community ties. *Middle Ground, 7*(1), 19-21.

Muir, M. (1998). Planning integrative curriculum with skeptical students. *Middle School Journal, 30*(2), 9-17.

Nesin, G., & Lounsbury, J. (1999). *Curriculum integration: Twenty questions—with answers.* Atlanta: Georgia Middle School Association.

O'Steen, B., Cuper, P., Spires, H., Beal, C., & Pope. C. (2002). Curriculum integration: Theory, practice, and research for a sustainable future. In V. Anfara & S. Stacki (Eds.), *Middle school curriculum, instruction, and assessment* (pp. 1-21). Greenwich, CT: Information Age.

Pate, P. E. (2001). Standards, students, and exploration: Creating a curriculum intersection of excellence. In T. S. Dickinson (Ed.), *Reinventing the middle school* (pp. 79-95). New York: RoutledgeFalmer.

Paterson, J. (2003). Curriculum integration in a standards-based world. *Middle Ground, 7*(1), 10-12.

Powell, R., Fussell, L., Troutman, P., Smith, M., & Skoog, G. (1998). Toward an integrative multicultural learning environment. *Middle School Journal, 29*(4), 3-13.

Powell, R. (2001). On headpieces of straw: How middle level students view their schooling. In T. S. Dickinson (Ed.), *Reinventing the middle school* (pp. 117-152). New York: RoutledgeFalmer.

Powell, R., & Van Zandt Allen, L. (2001). Middle school curriculum. In V. A. Anfara, Jr., (Ed.), *The handbook of research in middle level education* (pp. 107-124). Greenwich, CT: Information Age.

Roth, K. (1994). Second thoughts about interdisciplinary studies. *American Educator, 18*, 44-48.

Simmons, S. L., & El-Hindi, A. E. (1998). Six transformations for thinking about integrative curriculum. *Middle School Journal, 30*(2), 32-36.

Smith, J. L., & Johnson, J. (1993). Bringing it together: Literature in an integrative curriculum. *Middle School Journal, 25*(1), 3-7.

Springer, M. (2003). A view from the top: Scaling the heights of curriculum integration. *Middle Ground, 7*(1), 14-18.

Stepian, W., & Gallagher, S. (1993). Problem-based learning: As authentic as it gets. *Educational Leadership, 50*(7), 25-28.

Stevenson, C., & Carr, J. F. (Eds.). (1993). *Integrated studies in the middle grades: Dancing through walls.* New York: Teachers College Press.

Thompson, S. (2002). Reculturing middle schools to use cross-curricular portfolios to support integrated learning. In V. Anfara, Jr. & S. Stacki (Eds.), *Middle school curriculum, instruction, and assessment* (pp. 157-179). Greenwich, CT: Information Age.

Vars, G. F. (2001). Can curriculum integration survive in an era of high-stakes testing? *Middle School Journal, 33*(2), 7-17.

Vossler, J., & Moore, T. (1993). Garbology. In C. Stevenson & J. F. Carr (Eds.), *Integrated studies in the middle grades: Dancing through walls* (pp. 165-175). New York: Teachers College Press.

Warren, L. L., & Flinchberg, M. E. (2003). Engaging students in meaningful, integrative environmental lessons. *Middle School Journal, 34*(3), 47-50.

Weilbacher, G. (2001). Is curriculum integration an endangered species? *Middle School Journal, 33*(2), 18-27.

—Alecia Youngblood Jackson
Appalachian State University

CURRICULUM: INTERDISCIPLINARY UNIT

As a plan for teaching an interconnected block of curriculum, interdisciplinary units are not unique to middle schools. Many elementary school teachers develop interdisciplinary units routinely to correlate the various disciplines or subject areas for enhanced understanding among their students. Such a unit plan for the self contained classroom necessitates planning by only one teacher.

In a typical middle school setting, interdisciplinary teaching presupposes the existence of interdisciplinary teams. Interdisciplinary teaching occurs when two or more disciplines or subject areas are linked to deepen student comprehension. Student interest is sparked as they grasp the interconnectedness of concepts and skills shared by the various subject matter areas. The blending of the disciplines more readily mirrors real life, which does not arbitrarily segregate language, math, social studies, and science skills into discreet elements. The interdisciplinary unit draws upon the rigorous knowledge of the disciplines, while helping students make connections for richer, more complete understanding.

Interdisciplinary units are often referred to as theme-based units (Keller, 1992; McArthur & McGuire, 1998; Meinbach, Rothlein, & Fredericks, 1995; Rothlein, Fredericks, & Meinbach, 1996; Strube, 1993). The theme for such a unit of study can come from one of the disciplines, an area of interest, the state standards, or almost any other venue. A helpful starting point for ideas to be developed into interdisciplinary units is the curriculum map. Middle level curriculum maps are drafted by interdisciplinary teams of teachers. Through mapping the curriculum for the year, teachers often discover common themes in their teaching. Using such themes as entry points for brainstorming ideas and activities in each of the disciplines is a crucial step in planning an interdisciplinary unit.

Curriculum Mapping

Curriculum maps are typically drawn up prior to the start of the school year. Curriculum maps can be thought of as longitudinal plans for a specific grade level that spans a school year or as multilayered blueprints which reveal areas taught across the grade level spectrum. The longitudinal, year-long plan is what influences the teaching of an interdisciplinary unit. A resource for learning more about curriculum mapping is *Mapping the Big Picture* by Heidi Hayes Jacobs (1997). According to Jacobs, the main components of a curriculum map are:

- the process and skills emphasized;
- the content in terms of essential concepts and topics; and
- the products and performances that are the assessments of learning. (Jacobs, 1997, p. 8)

These are all basic elements of a good unit plan. Jacobs suggests that each teacher independently map the upcoming year with what is expected to be taught. At an interdisciplinary team meeting, teachers can share their individual maps to look for "potential areas for integration." (Jacobs, p. 11) This is the beginning of an interdisciplinary unit.

Interdisciplinary Team

While it is certainly possible to plan and implement an interdisciplinary unit as an individual teacher, in a true middle school the more meaningful approach involves an interdisciplinary team. The interdisciplinary team was historically a major breakthrough for the middle school movement. This type of team arrangement typically consists of four teachers each with expertise in language arts, math, science, or social studies. Such a team of teachers is responsible for 80 to 125 students. Occasionally teams are formed with two or three teachers who are endorsed in more than one discipline. The interdisciplinary team arrangement makes the planning of interdisciplinary units more plausible, particularly with the inclusion of common planning time. "[T]eachers would find it very difficult to create an interdisciplinary curriculum in the departmental organizational structure, since that structure does not give them opportunities to coordinate" (Jackson & Davis, 2000, p. 136). Collaborative planning gives the interdisciplinary unit its depth and richness.

Themes

Themes for interdisciplinary units often stem from curricular subject areas. Social studies and science topics are frequently used as themes for units. A particular adolescent novel might serve as the underlying focus. When teams meet to look at their curriculum maps for the year, related topics emerge. A look at state and national standards for the grade level can produce ideas for themes. Students can come up with interest themes from which to plan. James Beane (1993) insists that themes chosen for study should be determined jointly by students and teachers, with teachers taking a facilitative role in the co-planning of the curriculum.

Themes can be thought of as broad or narrow topics. The more expansive the topic is, the richer your plans can be. Carol Ann Tomlinson (1998) makes a distinction between content themes and concept themes. Themes based on content can certainly be useful. An interdisciplinary team could come up with a good unit using the Civil War as its theme. Using this social studies content theme could spark interesting language arts, science and math lessons. A broader concept associated with the Civil War is conflict. Using the theme of conflict across the disciplines can include the Civil War, but opens up many more possibilities. Basing an interdisciplinary unit on a conceptual theme such as conflict, independence, change, patterns, justice, or similarly broad ideas, will facilitate the inclusion of discipline based standards in meaningful and genuine ways. A comprehensive conceptual theme is more likely to be relevant to young adolescents. Middle school students can sooner relate to the concept of independence than to the content of the U.S. Revolution. Within an interdisciplinary unit based on the concept of independence, the social studies content of the U.S. Revolution comes alive through the integration of all the disciplines.

BRAINSTORMING

Selecting a theme can occur through brainstorming. Once the theme is chosen, the process of brainstorming is essential to come up with possible activities and connections to the theme in all the subject areas. For a truly integrated unit, it is important for all faculty team members to have input during all stages of planning. It is equally important to involve students in the brainstorming of ideas. To facilitate creativity and productivity, it suggested that teachers brainstorm individually with the theme in mind, then interact with each other in a group brainstorming sessions (Jacobs, 1989). One way to approach the brainstorming process is to come up with associations to the disciplines based on the chosen theme. This process can be illustrated in the following discipline web (Figure 1).

Alternately teachers might brainstorm using a concept web, which often serves to further integrate the ideas produced. Rather than looking at the discreet disciplines for connections with the theme, teachers first brainstorm concepts associated with the theme. Then think of relevant activities to explicate these concepts for enhanced understanding with the students. Such a concept web might be illustrated as seen in Figure 2.

Many teachers prefer brainstorming with simple lists. Jacobs (1989, pp. 56-58) suggests spokes on a wheel with the theme as the hub and the disciplines as the spokes. Brainstormed ideas are then listed under each spoke. Whatever method is chosen, a record of the ideas should be kept to be incorporated into the interdisciplinary unit.

ELEMENTS OF AN INTERDISCIPLINARY UNIT PLAN

A wide body of literature depicts a range of basic characteristics which comprise an interdisciplinary unit and how to go about creating such a plan (Campbell & Harris, 2001; Erickson, 2002; Jacobs, 1989; Lacy,

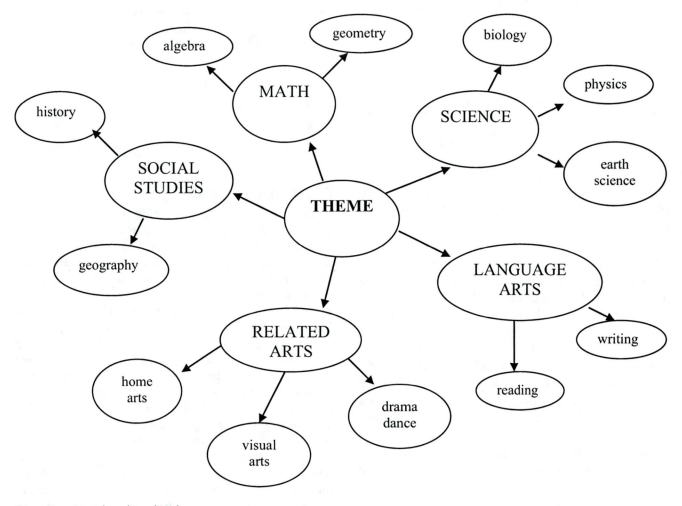

Figure 1.   Disciplinet-based Web.

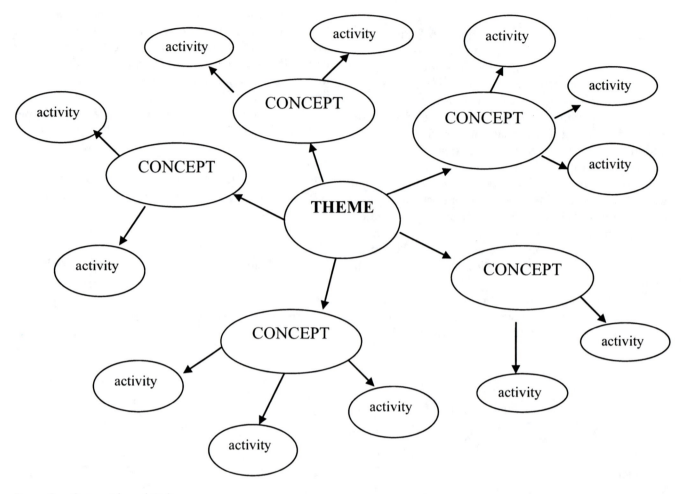

Figure 2.   Concept-based Web.

2002; Lounsbury, 1992; Martinello & Cook, 2000; Meinbach, Rothlein, & Fredericks, 1995; Roberts & Kellough, 2004; Strube, 1993; Vars, 1987, 1993; Wilson, Malmgren, & Ramage, 1993; Wineburg & Grossman, 2000). One can find previously developed interdisciplinary units ready to be adapted or adopted in books (Brazee, 2001; Forte & Shurr, 1994; Keller, 1992; Rothlein, Fredericks, & Meinbach, 1996; Schurr, Lewis, LaMorte, & Shewey, 1996) and internet sources posted by individual teachers, teams, schools, and school districts. Once developed, teachers often file these units to be used in subsequent years. Although no template should be thought of as mandatory, a few basic, accepted elements exist across many interdisciplinary unit plans. Some of these elements include essential questions, an overview of the unit, the launch and culminating experiences, daily lesson plans, schedule-altering whole team events, assessments, and evaluation.

ESSENTIAL QUESTIONS

Thoughtful questions to guide the unit are vital to ensure higher-level thinking. Although a variety of pertinent questions may be brainstormed and utilized throughout the unit, the essential questions should be those carefully selected few which frame the unit and serve to organize the planning of learning experiences (Erickson, 2002; Jacobs, 1989, 1997; Wiggins & McTighe, 1998). When meaningful essential questions are generated, they can "serve as the scope and sequence to the structure of the study." (Jacobs, 1997 p. 27). In order to function as the "table of contents" for the unit, the essential or guiding questions must be expansive, conceptual, and analogous to enduring understandings. Such questions are multifaceted with no simple answers. Essential questions naturally lead to further questions throughout the unit. By their nature, essential questions are interdisciplinary. Such questions are relevant across the curriculum. Answers to essential questions can lead students to conceptualize the big ideas or major understandings meant to be garnered through the course of the interdisciplinary unit. Essential questions should be pertinent to the students' experiences and understandings. They should foster creative and critical thinking.

Overview

Since a middle level interdisciplinary unit typically involves a few teachers, it is crucial to draw up some form of an outline to coordinate the planned experiences across and within the disciplines. The overview can take the form of a web, a calendar, or a more formal outline. A calendar-based overview can serve the team well as the unit progresses. Teams may find their brainstormed web useful as an initial overview. Those needing more structure might prefer to devise an ordered outline to follow.

Launch

The beginning activity, or launch, for the unit should be a thoughtfully planned, attention-getting experience which peaks the curiosity and interest of the students. The launch will set the stage for the rest of the unit. For a truly integrated unit, the launch should be interdisciplinary and be experienced by all the students involved across the subject areas. Teams often plan their unit's beginning and ending lessons first, but these experiences can evolve with the rest of the unit plans.

Daily Plans

Thoughtful, relevant daily plans will determine the cohesiveness of an interdisciplinary unit. Many of the ideas for activities and learning experiences come from earlier brainstorming with the team of teachers and students. These ideas are then developed into lesson plans. Typically each subject matter specialist will prepare individual daily lessons for the classes pertaining to that discipline. Coordination with other faculty team members is key to enhance the understanding of the connections related to the theme within and among the other subject areas. Each teacher should share tentative plans with the rest of the faculty team often during the planning stages to ensure relevant and worthwhile experiences for the students.

Whole Team Events

Some interdisciplinary unit activities will involve the entire team of 80 to 120 students participating together. Whole team events can include field trips, service learning projects, simulations, and guest speakers. Often the launch and culminating activities involve the entire team. Faculty team members can share the responsibilities involved in planning these larger scale events.

Assessments

Interdisciplinary units provide marvelous opportunities for authentic assessment, merging the various disciplinary standards in projects and activities. Formative assessment throughout the unit can help reshape initial plans for enhanced understanding. Informal teacher observation and questioning of students during the course of the unit can redesign aspects of the plans for more relevance and improved comprehension. Students can be given a selection of summative assessment strategies to demonstrate their grasp of enduring understandings. Summative assessments spanning the subject areas can include performances, research projects, presentations, portfolios, demonstrations, and artistic creations. The teaching team can collectively review student culminating projects with students for authentic assessment.

Culminating Experience

Often the beginning and culminating experiences are the first pieces of a unit to be designed. During the initial stages of brainstorming teams can come up with appropriate ways to end the unit with final projects, presentations, dramatic representations, gallery showings, celebrations, service days, field trips, simulations, fairs, and so forth.

Evaluation

All members of the team, faculty and students, should be involved in providing detailed feedback on all aspects of the unit. Some of the evaluation process can be ongoing in conjunction with formative assessments. Feedback forms can be designed for all involved including guest speakers, field trip providers, community participants, and parents. Of course the young adolescents who have just participated in the interdisciplinary unit can provide some of the most valuable feedback.

REFERENCES

Beane, J. A. (1993). *A middle school curriculum: From rhetoric to reality* (2nd ed.). Columbus, OH: National Middle School Association.

Brazee, E. (2001). *It's about time: A resource unit.* Columbus, OH: National Middle School Association.

Campbell, D. M., & Harris, L. S. (2001). *Collaborative theme building: How teachers write integrated curriculum.* Boston: Allyn & Bacon.

Erickson, H. L. (2002). *Concept-based curriculum and instruction: Teaching beyond the facts.* Thousand Oaks, CA: Corwin Press.

Forte, I., & Shurr, S. (1994). *Interdisciplinary units and projects for thematic instruction.* Nashville, TN: Incentive.

Jackson, A. W., & Davis, G. A. (2000). *Turning points 2000: Educating adolescents in the 21st century.* New York: Teachers College Press.

Jacobs, H. H. (Ed.). (1989). *Interdisciplinary curriculum: Design and implementation.* Alexandria, VA: Association for Supervision and Curriculum Development.

Jacobs, H. H. (1997). *Mapping the big picture: Integrating curriculum and assessment K-12.* Alexandria, VA: Association for Supervision and Curriculum Development.

Keller, E. (1992). *The big book of ready-to-use theme units.* New York: Scholastic.

Lacy, L. E. (2002). *Creative planning resource for interconnected teaching and learning.* New York: Peter Lang.

Lounsbury, J. H., (Ed.). (1992). *Connecting the curriculum through interdisciplinary instruction.* Columbus, OH: National Middle School Association.

Martinello, M. L., & Cook, G. E. (2000). *Interdisciplinary inquiry in teaching and learning* (2nd ed.). Upper Saddle River, NJ: Merrill.

McArthur, J., & McGuire, B. E. (1998). *Books on wheels: Cooperative learning through thematic units.* Englewood, CO: Libraries.

Meinbach, A. M., Rothlein, L., & Fredericks, A. D. (1995). *The complete guide to thematic units: Creating the integrated curriculum.* Norwood, MA: Christopher Gordon.

Roberts, P., & Kellough, R. D. (2004). *A guide for developing interdisciplinary thematic units* (3rd ed.). Upper Saddle River, NJ: Merrill

Rothlein, L., Fredericks, A. D., & Meinbach, A. M. (1996). *More thematic units for creating the integrated curriculum.* Norwood, MA: Christopher-Gordon.

Strube, P. (1993). *Theme studies, a practical guide: How to develop theme studies to fit your curriculum.* New York: Scholastic Professional Books.

Schurr, S., Lewis, S., LaMorte, K., & Shewey, K. (1996). *Signaling student success: Thematic learning stations and integrated units.* Columbus, OH: National Middle School Association.

Tomlinson, C. A. (1998). For integration and differentiation choose concepts over topics. *Middle School Journal, 30*(2), 3-8.

Vars, G. F. (1987). *Interdisciplinary teaching in the middle grades: Why and how.* Columbus, OH: National Middle School Association.

Vars, G. F. (1993). *Interdisciplinary teaching why & how.* Columbus, OH: National Middle School Association.

Wiggins, G., & McTighe, J. (1998). *Understanding by design.* Alexandria, VA: Association for Supervision and Curriculum Development.

Wilson, L., Malmgren, D., & Ramage, S. (1993). *An integrated approach to learning.* Portsmouth, NH: Heinemann.

Wineburg, S., & Grossman, P. (2000). *Interdisciplinary curriculum: Challenges to implementation.* New York: Teachers College Press.

—Virginia M. Jagla
National-Louis University

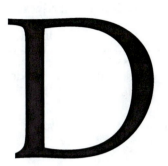

DEVELOPMENTAL RESPONSIVENESS

In education developmental responsiveness is grounded in the belief that schools should be organized around the developmental characteristics of the students they educate. Young adolescence is a particularly stressful and momentous developmental period with specific cognitive distinctions (Piaget, 1952) and social/emotional challenges (Erikson, 1964). Working with young adolescents requires a strong orientation toward the ethic of care (Beck, 1994; Noddings, 1992) as its underpinning coupled with challenging academic standards while middle grades students learn to interact with the demands of the adult world. Developmentally responsive educators will understand the conditions of their students and use this knowledge to understand middle grades learners' zone of proximal development or ZPD (Vygotsky, 1978). Effective scaffolds coming from this analysis are ones that are based upon understanding and responding to middle grades learners' needs.

DEVELOPMENTAL RESPONSIVENESS TO COGNITIVE DISTINCTIONS

The middle grades student is not merely in-between elementary and high school, but a special kind of learner with unique gifts that are short lived (since no one stays a middle grades student for very long) and, therefore, all the more precious. Developmentally appropriate practice requires that teachers and principals integrate what they know about young adolescent development and the implications of this knowledge for choosing curriculum content, how and when to teach the content of the curriculum, and how to assess what students have learned. Specific examples in the literature include a seven-element plan which includes: "focus on academic achievement in the core curriculum; daily teacher advisory; team organization at every grade; flexible block scheduling; an expanded menu of electives and student activities (cultural arts, athletics, and intramurals); differentiated instruction; heterogeneous grouping in science and social studies in all schools" (George, Weast, Jones, Priddy, & Allred, 2000, p. 5).

In the practice of teaching at the middle level, distinctions are made as to the teacher's educational objectives about knowledge and intellectual abilities and skills, categorized by Bloom and associates in a hierarchical order as outlined in Table 1. According Bloom's taxonomy, knowledge is defined in the following way:

> By knowledge, we mean that the student can give evidence that he remembers, either by recalling or by recognizing, some idea or phenomenon with which he has had experience in the educational process. For our taxonomy purposes, we are defining knowledge as little more than the remembering of the idea or phenomenon in a form very close to that in which it was originally encountered. (Bloom, Engelhart, Furst, Hill, & Krathwohl, 1956, pp. 28-29)

The distinction between knowledge and the higher levels of intellectual skills and abilities is helpful to our discussion of the cognitive domain. The hierarchical arrangement by Bloom, Engelhart, Furst, and Krathwohl (1956) leads to a dichotomy between lower-level and higher-level thinking. Middle grades learners are moving from the concrete—the level of knowledge, comprehension, and application—to the abstract level of analysis, synthesis, and evaluation.

Table 1
Bloom's Taxonomy of Educational Objectives in the Cognitive Domain

Level	Educational Objective
1. Knowledge	• Knowledge of specifics • Knowledge of ways and means of dealing with specifics • Knowledge of the universals and abstractions in a field.
2. Comprehension	• Translation • Interpretation • Extrapolation
3. Application	
4. Analysis	• Analysis of elements • Analysis of relationships • Analysis of organizational principles
5. Synthesis	• Production of a unique communication • Production of a plan, or proposed set of operations • Derivation of a set of abstract relations
6. Evaluation	• Judgments in terms of internal evidence • Judgments in terms of external criteria

Source: Adapted from Bloom et al. (1956, pp. 201-207) as cited in Dunkin & Biddle (1974, p. 234).

According to Ericksen (1984), "It is vital for students to know something about a field before engaging in the heuristic scramble for solutions to its problems" (p. 93). Using the taxonomy assembled by Bloom et al. (1956), the educational objectives of analysis, synthesis, and evaluation involve the teacher in higher-level thinking categories, whereby teachers lead students into learning by discovery. Supporters of developmentally responsive middle level schools recognize the importance of relationships. For example, the interdisciplinary curriculum advocated by middle level reformers provides powerful learning opportunities in the classroom. As stated by Clark and Clark (1994, p. 5), such opportunities help middle school students "find relevance in the content and become more actively engaged in learning. Students remember more and become more creative thinkers because they make these connections to their personal lives" (See also Berg, 1988; Jacobs, 1991).

DEVELOPMENTAL RESPONSIVENESS TO SOCIAL/EMOTIONAL ISSUES

Developmental trajectories diverge in early adolescence toward either healthy adjustment or psychopathology (Petersen & Hamburg, 1986). Declines in academic motivation, perceived competence, intrinsic interest in school (Harter, 1981) and self-esteem (Eccles, Midgley, & Adler, 1984) are common, not to mention anxiety, depression, substance abuse, and antisocial behaviors (see Hankin, Abramson, Silva, McGee, Moffitt, & Angell, 1998).

Relying on the work of Peter Scales at the Search Institute/Center for Early Adolescents, the National Middle School Association (1996) identified seven key developmental needs characteristic of young adolescence:

• positive social interaction with adults and peers;
• structure and clear limits;
• physical activity;
• creative expression;
• competence and achievement;
• meaningful participation in families, school communities; and
• opportunities for self-definition. (p. 1)

From their research into young adolescent development and school practices, Van Hoose, Strahan, and L'Esperance (2001) conclude that while portraying a buoyant and self-assured demeanor, young adolescents often mask deeper feelings of self-doubt and vulnerability. These researchers advise middle level educators to be proactive in addressing the social and personal needs of their young learners, which can be summed up in three words: security, support and success.

Stevenson (1992) offers a succinct summary of the psychosocial issues of adolescent development (Table 2).

Table 2
Psychosocial Issues in Adolescent Development

Issue	Adolescent Change
Attachment	Transforming childhood social bonds to parents to bonds acceptable between parents and their adult children.
Autonomy	Extending self-initiated activity and confidence in it to wider behavioral realms.
Sexuality	Transforming social roles and gender identity to incorporate sexual activity with others.
Intimacy	Transforming acquaintanceships into friendships; deepening and broadening capacities for self-disclosure, affective perspective-taking, and altruism.
Achievement	Focusing industry and ambition into channels that are future-oriented and realistic.
Identity	Transforming images of self to accommodate primary and secondary change; coordinating images to attain a self-theory that incorporates uniqueness and continuity through time.

Source: Hill (1980) as cited in Stevenson (1992, p. 11)

DEVELOPMENTAL RESPONSIVENESS AND THE MIDDLE SCHOOL PRINCIPAL

The literature regarding middle level education and middle school reform is replete with references to "developmental appropriateness" and "developmentally responsive" schools, curriculum, practices, structures, and strategies. Pivotal to this discussion, but conspicuously absent, is the role of middle level leadership in implementing such reform efforts.

Developmentally responsive leadership results from the process of making decisions about the well being and education of children, about faculty, and about the school itself based on the following kinds of information:

1. what is known about human development and learning—knowledge of age-related characteristics that permit general predictions within an age range about what activities, materials, interactions, or experiences will be safe, healthy, interesting, achievable, and challenging to young adolescents;
2. what is known about the strengths, interests, and needs of each individual student to be able to adapt for and be responsive to inevitable individual differences; and
3. knowledge of the social and cultural contexts in which children live to ensure that learning experiences are meaningful, relevant, and respectful for the participating children and their families (National Association for the Education of Young Children, 1997, p. 7).

Anfara, Roney, Smarkola, and DuCette (2004) proposed a three-dimensional model for understanding the developmentally responsive middle school princi-

pal, and developed an instrument for measuring it. The features of this model include: (a) responsiveness to the developmental needs of middle grades students, (b) responsiveness to the developmental needs of the faculty who support learning for middle grades students, and (c) responsiveness to the development of the middle school itself as a unique innovating entity. From extensive research (see Brown & Anfara, 2002) and feedback from middle level principals, Anfara et al. developed The Middle Level Leadership Questionnaire (MLLQ). The MLLQ focuses on the actions (behaviors) of middle level principals in areas related to students, teachers, parents, the curriculum, professional development, school-community relations, and the structuring of the school day. According to these researchers, the developmentally responsive middle level leader is defined as one who is:

(1) Responsive to the needs of students

- understands the intellectual, physical, psychological, social, and moral/ethical characteristics of young adolescents;
- establishes a learning environment that reflects the needs of young adolescents;
- purposely designs programs, policies, curriculum, and procedures that reflect the characteristics of young adolescents;
- believes that all students can succeed;
- views parents and the community as partners, not adversaries.

(2) Responsive to the needs of faculty:

- understands the necessity of reconnecting educational administration to the processes of teaching and learning;

- is emotionally invested in the job;
- shares a vision for continuous organizational improvement and growth;

(3) Responsive to needs of the school itself:

- is knowledgeable of and can implement the components of the middle school concept;
- acts as a responsible catalyst for change and understands that change requires time, training, trust, and tangible support;
- is flexible and able to deal with ambiguity and chaos. (p. 13)

If middle level reform is going to achieve its goals (a positive educational environment that ensures student cognitive and affective development), middle level principals must come to a more complete understanding of their role in this process. They must acknowledge that different skills and knowledge are necessary for leadership at this level. Being truly "responsive" entails a readiness and willingness to react to suggestions, influences, and appeals and to reply appropriately and sympathetically. It requires "responding to current challenges, engaging in thoughtful and reflective discussions, and actively and openly embracing the revision and refinement of programs" (Williamson & Johnston, 1999, p. 11). Developmentally responsive middle level leadership recognizes and embraces learners' developmental levels as providing the basis for all school curricular and instructional practices, as well as the overall teaching-learning environment (Manning, 1993).

CONCLUSION

Middle level education is rooted in relevant curriculum, instruction and assessment, and the related developmental issues of middle grades learners (see National Middle School Association, 2003, pp. 43-51). Middle schools require a particular kind of educator; one who is attracted to the energy and complexity of early adolescents and who combines empathy with skills in modeling effective strategies for students of this age. Knowledge of the developmental circumstances of middle grades learners matched with an affinity to curriculum content that is rich, demanding, and highly interactive is also important. In short, "middle schools provide 10- to 15-year olds with developmentally appropriate educational experiences that emphasize the education and overall well-being of the learners" (Manning & Bucher, 2005, p. 9).

Based upon years of practical experience in working with young adolescents—as teacher, principal, coach, professor, researcher, and author—Stevenson (2002) presents the following equation for understanding the concept of developmental responsiveness:

> *What to teach and how to teach* ÷ Developmental assessment = Responsive Education…. In other words, it is our purpose to provide education that is responsive to the developmental needs of young adolescents. Our decisions about what to teach and how to go about presenting it must be calculated on the basis of what we know about the multifaceted development of our students. (p. 76)

REFERENCES

Anfara, V. A., Jr., Roney, K., Smarkola, C., & DuCette, J. (2004). *Developmentally responsive leadership: A look at the middle school principal*. Paper presented at the American Educational Research Association Annual Meeting, San Diego, CA.

Beck, L. (1994). *Reclaiming educational administration as a caring profession*. New York: Teachers College Press.

Berg, M. (1988). The integrated curriculum. *Social Studies Review, 28*(1), 38-41.

Bloom, B., Engelhart, M., Furst, E., Hill, W., & Krathwohl, D. (Eds.). (1956). *Taxonomy of educational objectives: The classification of education goals, handbook I: Cognitive domain*. New York: David McKay.

Brown, K. M., & Anfara, V. A., Jr. (2002*). From the desk of the middle school principal: Leadership responsive to the needs of young adolescents*. Lanham, MD: The Scarecrow Press.

Clark, D., & Clark, S. (1994). Meeting the needs of young adolescents. *Schools in the Middle, 4*(1), 4-7.

Dunkin, M., & Biddle, B. (1974). *The study of teaching*. New York: Holt, Rinehart, and Winston.

Eccles, J., Midgley, C., & Adler, T. (1984). Grade-related changes in school environment: Effects on achievement motivation. In J. H. Nicholls (Ed.), *The development of achievement motivation* (Vol. 3, pp. 283-331). Greenwich, CT: JAI Press.

Erikson, E. (1964). *Childhood and society*. New York: Norton.

Ericksen, S. (1984). *The essence of good teaching: Helping students learn and remember what they learn*. San Francisco: Jossey-Bass.

George, P., Weast, J., Jones, L., Priddy, M., & Allred, L. (2000). Revitalizing middle schools: The Guilford County process. *Middle School Journal, 31*(3), 3-11.

Hankin, B., Abramson, L., Silva, P., McGee, R., Moffitt, T., & Angell, K. (1998). Development of depression from preadolescence to young adulthood: Emerging gender differences in a 10-year longitudinal study. *Journal of Abnormal Psychology, 107*, 128-140.

Harter, S. (1981). A new self-report scale of intrinsic versus extrinsic orientation in the classroom: Motivational and informational components. *Developmental Psychology, 17*, 300-312.

Jacobs, H. (1991). Planning for curriculum integration. *Educational Leadership, 49*(2), 27-28.

Manning, M. L. (1993). *Developmentally appropriate middle level schools*. Wheaton, MD: Association for Childhood Educational International.

Manning, M. L., & Bucher, K. T. (2005). *Teaching in the middle school* (2nd ed.). Upper Saddle River, NJ: Pearson Education.

National Association for the Education of Young Children. (1997). *Statement of the position*. Retrieved January 20, 2005, from: http://www.naeyc.org/resources/position_statements/ dap2.htm

National Middle School Association. (1996). *NMSA research summary #5: Young adolescents' developmental needs*. Retrieved May 17, 2004, from: http://www.nmsa.org

National Middle School Association. (2003). *This we believe: Successful schools for young adolescents*. Westerville, OH: Author.

Noddings, N. (1992). *The challenge to care in schools: An alternative approach to education*. New York: Teachers College Press.

Petersen, A., & Hamburg, B. (1986). Adolescence: A developmental approach to problems and psychopathology. *Behavior Therapy, 17*, 480-499.

Piaget, J. (1952). *The origins of intelligence in children*. New York: International Universities Press.

Stevenson, C. (1992). *Teaching ten to fourteen year olds*. New York: Longman.

Stevenson, C. (2002). *Teaching ten to fourteen year olds* (3rd ed.). Boston, MA: Allyn & Bacon.

Van Hoose, J., Strahan, D., & L'Esperance, M. (2001). *Promoting harmony: Young adolescent development and school practices*. Westerville, OH: National Middle School Association.

Vygotsky, L. (1978). *Mind and society: The development of higher psychological processes*. Cambridge, MA: Harvard University Press.

Williamson, R., & Johnston, J. H. (1999). Challenging orthodoxy: An emerging agenda for middle level reform. *Middle School Journal, 30*(4), 10-17.

—Kathleen Roney
The University of North Carolina, Wilmington

DEWEY, JOHN

John Dewey was considered to be the preeminent American philosopher of the twentieth century (Hickman, 1999). Dewey is identified with Instrumentalism, a branch of the Pragmatist school of philosophy. His philosophy incorporated psychology, evolutionary theory, and democracy into a framework of thinking based in the scientific method (Campbell, 1995). Dewey focused on learning and education as vital human functions. His work provided a foundation for the Progressive Education movement, which began in the late nineteenth century and continues into the present day. Dewey's most influential works include *The Child and the Curriculum* (1899), *Democracy and Education* (1916), and *Experience and Education* (1938).

Dewey was born in Burlington, Vermont on October 20, 1859 (biographical details taken from Dykhuizen, 1973, the standard biography of Dewey). He graduated from the University of Vermont in 1879, taught high school for a brief period, and then attended graduate school in philosophy at Johns Hopkins University. There Dewey was strongly influenced by the philosophy of Charles S. Pierce and George Sylvester Morris as well as the emerging study of experimental psychology led by G. Stanley Hall. He received his PhD in 1884. He joined the faculty of the University of Michigan in 1884, where he met his wife, Alice Chipman. Dewey moved to the University of Chicago in 1904, where he founded the influential Dewey School, an experimental school in which Dewey tested many of his educational ideas. Dewey later accepted a joint position at Columbia University in philosophy and in education at Teacher's College at Columbia. He taught there until his retirement in 1930. Dewey was a prolific writer throughout his adult life, and was involved in founding the American Civil Liberties Union and the American Association of University Professors, among other organizations. Dewey served frequently as a representative for the United States in international affairs. He died on June 1, 1952.

Although Dewey's life and work predated the middle school movement, his educational ideas form a foundation for many concepts associated with modern middle schools. Van Til, Vars, and Lounsbury (1967) identified Dewey's focus on the innate worth of the child (Dewey, 1902), and the value of organizing the school as a community (Dewey, 1899, 1916) as central values for educators of early adolescents. Dewey's concepts of the logical and psychological organization of subject matter (1902) provide a foundation for the idea of a developmentally appropriate curriculum (Anfara & Waks, 2000, 2001; George, Stevenson, Thomason, & Beane, 1992). The exploratory curriculum can be traced to Dewey's emphasis on the educational value of experience (1938) and human occupations (1899, 1902). Beane (1993, 1997) has advocated integrating the interests and concerns of the child and the needs and problems of society into a curriculum appropriate for early adolescent students, a position he traced in part to Dewey's ideas. Finally, Dewey's ideal of the school as a place for practicing democratic principles and developing the traits of democratic citizenship (1916) is advanced by many middle grades educators (Van Til et al., 1967; Beane, 1993; 1997; Pate, Homestead, & McGinnis, 1997; Kienholz, 2001). Dewey's ideas continue to influence middle schools and education in general today.

REFERENCES

Anfara, V. A., & Waks, L. (2000). Resolving the tension between academic rigor and developmental appropriateness, part I. *Middle School Journal, 32*(2), 46-50.

Anfara, V. A., & Waks, L. (2001). Resolving the tension between academic rigor and developmental appropriateness, part II. *Middle School Journal, 32*(3), 25-30.

Beane, J. A. (1993). *A middle school curriculum: From rhetoric to reality* (2nd ed.). Columbus, OH: National Middle School Association.

Beane, J. A. (1997). Social issues in the middle school curriculum. In S. Totten & J. E. Pedersen (Eds.), *Social issues and service at the middle level* (pp. 12-28). Boston: Allyn & Bacon.

Campbell, J. (1995). *Understanding John Dewey.* Chicago: Open Court.

Dewey, J. (1899). *The school and society.* Chicago: University of Chicago Press.

Dewey, J. (1902). *The child and the curriculum.* Chicago: University of Chicago Press.

Dewey, J. (1916). *Democracy and education.* New York: MacMillan.

Dewey, J. (1938). *Experience and education.* New York: MacMillan.

Dykhuizen, G. (1973). *The life and mind of John Dewey.* Carbondale, IL: Southern Illinois University Press.

George, P. S., Stevenson, C., Thomason, J., & Beane, J. (1992). *The middle school—and beyond.* Alexandria, VA: Association for Supervision and Curriculum Development.

Hickman, L. A. (1999). John Dewey. In J. A. Garraty & M. C. Carnes (Eds.), *American national biography* (pp. 514-518). New York: Oxford Press.

Kienholz, K. B. (2001). From Dewey to Beane, innovation, democracy, and unity characterize middle level education. *Middle School Journal, 32*(3), 20-24.

Pate, P. E., Homestead, E. R., & McGinnis, K. L. (1997). *Making integrated curriculum work: Teachers, students, and the quest for coherent curriculum.* New York: Teacher's College Press.

Van Til, W., Vars, G. F., & Lounsbury, J. H. (1967). *Modern education for the junior high school years* (2nd ed.). Indianapolis, IN: Bobbs-Merrill.

—Bryan Sorohan
Brenau University

DIFFERENT WAYS OF KNOWING

Different Ways of Knowing, a comprehensive school improvement design, is an initiative of The Galef Institute, an educational nonprofit that provides quality professional development services to strengthen teacher quality and instructional leadership and to accelerate school improvement plans. The Institute focuses its services for the middle grades on tools, products, and strategies that produce significant results for young adolescents (Ross & Muñoz, 2005).

Different Ways of Knowing services and tools are based on the belief that intelligence is the development of a wide range of expertise rather than fixed aptitude (Gardner, 1983; Sternberg, 1988) and on research on student and adult learning (Resnick, 1987; Knowles, Holton, & Swanson, 1998), organizational change (Senge, 1990), and the role of the arts and culture in education (Levine, 2002). By integrating the visual, performing, literary, and media arts, our classroom tools provide varied instructional pathways that promote academic excellence, developmental responsiveness, and equal access for all students; enhance and accelerate in-depth, creative thinking and content acquisition across all disciplines; and motivate students to think critically and gain deeper, long-lasting understandings.

Our comprehensive, professional development middle grades services and tools support schools and districts in providing experiences for young adolescents that are responsive to their unique academic, developmental, and social needs; that meet the requirements of federal and state accountability systems; that accelerate individual school improvement plans; that close achievement gaps for all student groups; and that operationalize the recommendations of *Turning Points 2000* (Jackson & Davis, 2000).

The organizing structure for Different Ways of Knowing implementation is a set of research-based practices for high-performing schools that serve as the basis for professional development, on-site coaching, leadership development, and school planning and organization. These best practices of teaching and learning are:

- Standards-based planning in curriculum, assessment, and instruction
- Student inquiry and self-directed learning
- School-wide literacy and mathematics achievement
- Integrating the arts for deeper content learning and differentiated instruction
- Shared leadership for results, including organizational structures that support teaching, learning, and a positive school climate

Our professional development services, adaptable to a variety of contexts—urban and rural, public and charter—focus on the core practices listed above and engage school and district stakeholders in: on-site, job-embedded coaching (one-to-one and grade-level or discipline-specific groups) that dramatically improve classroom and leadership practices; professional development workshops that provide hands-on experiences in classroom implementation of the Different Ways of Knowing design; print and Web-based resources that provide a solid infrastructure for developing and sustaining school improvement results; institutes for teachers, site administrators, specialists, and family and community members that deepen their understanding of instructional strategies that produce results; and leadership institutes for principals, administrators, teacher-leaders, and district liaisons that strengthen their capacity to sustain change over time.

REFERENCES

Gardner, H. (1983). *Frames of mind: The theory of multiple intelligences.* New York: BasicBooks.

Jackson, A., & G. A. Davis. (2000). *Turning points 2000: Educating adolescents in the 21st century.* New York: Teachers College Press.

Knowles, M. S., Holton III, E. F., & Swanson, R. A. (1998). *The adult learner: The definitive classic in adult education and human resource development.* Woborn, MA: Butterworth-Heinemann.

Levine, M. (2002). *A mind at a time.* New York: Simon & Schuster.

Resnick, L. B. (1987). *Education and learning to think.* Washington, DC: National Academy Press.

Ross, S. M., & Muñoz, M. (2005, February). *The effects of Different Ways of Knowing for the middle grades on student achievement in a large urban school district: Year 3 outcomes.* Memphis, TN: Center for Research in Education Policy.

Senge, P. M. (1990). *The fifth discipline: The art and practice of the learning organization.* London: Random House.

Sternberg, R. (1988). *The triarchic mind: A new theory of intelligence.* New York: Viking Press.

—Shelly Kale
The Galef Institute

DODA, NANCY

With a degree in English secondary education from Wake Forest University, Nancy Doda began her teaching career in 1974 as a middle school language arts teacher at the progressive Lincoln Middle School in Gainesville, FL. Between 1976 and 1980 she authored the column, "Teacher to Teacher, in National Middle School Association's *Middle School Journal.* During this time she completed masters work in curriculum and instruction at the University of Florida, where she ultimately completed her doctoral work under Paul George.

Her 6 years with young adolescents at Lincoln Middle School combined with graduate studies established a rich experience and knowledge base from which Doda developed expertise in several areas of middle level education, in particular: social equity and young adolescence, teaming, advisories, grouping, and language arts instruction.

Doda's contributions to the field of middle grades education extend through her extensive involvement as a professional development specialist. She has held numerous instructorships, and various faculty positions at George Mason University, Virginia Polytechnic Institute, and National-Louis University. Her work at National-Louis in DC included the development of a program for middle school teachers in the District that provided a middle level endorsement with graduate credit.

Involved in educational professional organizations, Doda has been active in Phi Delta Kappa, American Educational Research Association, the National Forum to Accelerate Middle Grades Reform, and the American Educational Research Association. She is the recipient of the Virginia Middle School Association Distinguished Service Award, The New England League of Middle Schools Distinguished Service Award, and the Connecticut Association of Secondary Schools Special Recognition Award.

Her publications include a compilation of her journal columns, *Teacher to Teacher* (Doda, 1981), *Team Organization: Promises, Practices, and Possibilities* co-authored with Tom Erb (1989); *Treasure Chest: A Teacher Advisory Source Book* coauthored with Cheryl Hoversten and John Lounsbury (1991); and *Transforming Ourselves, Transforming Schools: Middle School Change* co-edited with Sue Thompson (2002).

REFERENCES

Doda, N. (1981). *Teacher to teacher.* Columbus, OH: National Middle School Association.

Doda, N., & Thompson, S. C. (Eds). (2002). *Transforming ourselves, transforming schools: Middle school change.* Westerville, OH: National Middle School Association.

Erb, T. O., & Doda, N. M. (1989). *Team organization: Promise—practices, and possibilities.* Washington, DC: National Education Association.

Hoversten, C., Doda, N., & Lounsbury, J. (1991). *Treasure chest: A teacher advisory source book.* Columbus, OH: National Middle School Association.

—Mary Henton
National Middle School Association

DOUGLASS, HARL R.

Throughout his life and career Harl R. Douglass made numerous contributions to the field of education through his scholarship, consultation with school districts, and service in several administrative and leadership roles. According to Dr. Douglass his major interests were "teaching mathematics in secondary school, examining factors (of success) at the college and university level, secondary school methods, curriculum, administration and supervision especially at the junior high school level" (Douglass Personal Papers, Autobiography, n.d.).

Harl R. Douglass was the only child born to Joseph and Anna Douglass in Richmond, Missouri on June 22, 1892. After graduating from high school, his education included a Bachelor of Science (1915) and Master of Arts degrees (1921) from the University of Missouri and he later earned a Doctor of Philosophy from Stanford (1927) (Harte & Riley, 1969; Ohles, 1978).

During the early phase of his career, Dr. Douglass was as a high school mathematics teacher (1913) and as a superintendent in several school districts (1914-1919) followed by a directorship of the University of Oregon High School (1919-1928). As a beginning professor he taught at the University of Pennsylvania (1928-29) and University of Minnesota (1929-38) before moving to the University of North Carolina. There he became chairman of the division of teaching and was recognized as the Kenan Professor of Secondary Education (1938). During summer sessions, he would serve as a guest professor at other universities that included the University of Southern Illinois, Arizona University, Southern California University and Yale University. In 1940 he moved to the University of Colorado at Boulder where he served as dean of the college of education until 1958. He retired from the university in 1968 (Harte & Riley, 1969; Ohles, 1978).

Dr. Douglass served as vice president of American Educational Research Association and was a board member of the National Society for the Study of Education. From 1937-1938, he was president of the National Society of College Teachers of Education. He also was editor of the *Journal of Education Research* and the *Journal of Experimental Research* (Harte & Riley, 1969; Ohles, 1978).

Over 430 publications, including books, monographs and reports were authored or coauthored by Harl Douglass (Douglass Personal Papers, n.d.). Topics for his articles and books addressed a variety of topics from secondary school curriculum, instructional methods, classroom management, administration and supervision to testing and measurement. He was well known for his Douglass Series on Education (1947-1952) for which he was editor and authored three of the 31 volumes (Douglass Personal Papers, 1972; Ohles, 1978).

His special interest in junior high school education was demonstrated when coauthored *The Modern Junior High School* with William T. Gruhn in 1971. This book provided information about junior high school philosophy and curriculum for educators preparing to be junior high school teachers, administrators or supervisors in junior high schools. In honor of his work Douglass Junior High School in the Boulder Valley School District, Boulder, Colorado was named after him (Douglass Personal Papers, n.d., Douglass Personal Papers, 1972).

In addition to his many innovative ideas about teaching, curriculum, administration, and advocacy for junior high school, he stated "his major interest was bringing peace and fraternal feeling among the peoples of the world regardless of their race, religion, sex or level of cultures" (Douglass Personal Papers, Autobiography, n.d.).

REFERENCES

Douglass, H. R. (n.d.). *Personal papers folder, archives,* University of Colorado at Boulder Libraries.

Douglass, H. R. Personal Papers. (1972). *School & University Review, 2*(4), Boulder, CO: Archives, University of Colorado at Boulder Libraries.

Douglass, H. R. Personal Papers, Autobiography, (n.d.), *Box 1, folder 10.* Boulder, CO: Archives, University of Colorado at Boulder Libraries.

Harte, B., & Riley, C. (1969). *Contemporary authors: A bio-bibliographical guide to current authors and their works,* Vols. 5-8. Detroit, MI: Gale Research.

Ohles, J. F. (Ed.). (1978). *Biographical dictionary of American educators,* Vol. 1. Westport, CT: Greenwood Press.

—Barbara L. Whinery
University of Northern Colorado

E

EARLY AWARENESS

According to the U.S. Department of Education, early awareness programs and activities introduce middle-grades students to college and career goals and help them and their families understand the connection between education and career paths. Such programs also help middle-grades schools provide students with the academic and developmental opportunities they need to enter and complete high school as college-bound students (U.S. Department of Education, 2000).

Unlike college-prep programs, which tend to focus on high school students, early awareness programs usually focus on the middle grades, in line with the growing recognition that these are "pivotal years" that can establish the "habits and mind-set that will help students excel in high school and position them for college or the work force" (Kasak, 2004, p. 44). Most students think about attending college by early adolescence (Noeth & Wimberly, 2002) and those who get support during the middle grades are "far more successful at actually attending college despite other challenges" (Cabrera et al., 2001 cited in Camblin, 2003, p. 2).

Early awareness programs most often target low-income, minority, and first-generation students and usually provide an array of services, including academic preparation and enrichment, test-taking preparation, mentoring and tutoring, academic and career counseling, study and life skills development, college trips, and assistance with the financial aid process. While research on the success of early awareness programs is still limited, existing studies have found that participating students are more likely to attend college, have higher grades, and participate in more college prep activities (National Association of Student Financial Aid Administrators and The Education Resources Institute, 2005).

THE MIDDLE-GRADES AND COLLEGE READINESS

Much research has determined that it is the middle-grades experience that influences "whether students see themselves as smart and worthy of taking challenging courses in high school" (Camblin, 2003, p. 2). Conversely, research indicates that the middle grades is where an alarming number of students drop out: one in four eighth graders never goes to high school (Jonsson, 2004), and many who do are unprepared and fail to graduate, especially if they repeat ninth grade (Trejos, 2004). Of the 20% to 30% of students who drop out by, or during high school, a disproportionate number are Black and Latino, foreign-born Latinos being the highest (Greene & Forster, 2003). Further, of the approximately 75-80% of students who do complete high school, only 32% leave qualified to attend 4-year colleges. Of this 32%, only 9% are Black and another 9% are Latino. In short, Black and Latino graduates are disproportionately dropping out or exiting high school not "college ready" compared with their white and Asian peers (Greene & Forster, 2003). It is therefore essential that students, families, and educators realize that "preparing for college doesn't begin during a student's junior or senior year of high school—it begins even before a student first sets foot in school, and it continues through middle school and high school" (U.S. Department of Education, 2000).

ACADEMIC RIGOR FROM THE BEGINNING

Researchers and educators agree that a rigorous academic program is essential for preparing students for college and the world of work. According to the Pathways to College Network, such a curriculum "predicts college success better than high grades or test scores" (2004, p. 13). Most experts also concur that academic rigor must begin early to help alleviate the overwhelming number of students entering high school not prepared academically and already predisposed to dropping out, especially those students who have been retained in middle school (Woelfel, 2003) or grade nine as mentioned earlier.

Lack of college readiness usually means both low literacy skills and lack of preparation in math and science. While the connection between reading skills and student outcomes is a given, the extent of illiteracy is shocking, with "hundreds of thousands of high school students" barely able to read "on the eve of their high school graduation" (Joftus, 2002). Also disturbing is the extent to which these problems start early: Approximately 75% of students with reading problems in Grade 3 still have trouble reading in Grade 9 (Joftus, 2002). Once in college, students who enroll in remedial courses are less likely to obtain a degree or certificate, with a need for remedial reading acting as the most serious barrier to degree completion. Not surprisingly, these literacy problems are greater for minority students: 24.1 % of African Americans and 20.3 % of Latinos require remediation in reading, compared to only 7% of whites (National Center for Education Statistics, 2004).

CHALLENGING MATHEMATICS AND SCIENCE COURSES MATTER BIG TIME

While the importance of literacy has long been acknowledged in terms of student's academic and postacademic success, the vital importance of achievement in advanced mathematics and science course has emerged in the past decade. Simply put, algebra has come to be seen as a "gateway" course, an essential prerequisite for students to enroll in rigorous high school mathematics and science classes (U.S. Department of Education, 1997). Students who do not take courses covering algebraic concepts early in their schooling risk closing the door on many important opportunities, including opportunities to take courses outside of mathematics and science.

According to the National Education Longitudinal Study (NELS), a longitudinal survey of students who were in the Grade 8 in 1988, approximately 60% of students taking calculus in high school took algebra in Grade 8. NELS data also reveal that 93% of students

taking algebra I and geometry entered college while only 36% of students not taking these courses did so. The typical high school sequence of rigorous science courses (biology, chemistry, and physics) also necessitates a background in algebra and geometry (U.S. Department of Education, 1997).

However, despite recent increases in the proportion of students taking algebra I in Grade 8, in 1996, most students—especially minority and low-income students—were not enrolled in this course. The 1996 National Assessment of Educational Progress (NAEP) data reveal that minority and low-income students are less likely to report being enrolled in algebra in Grade 8 and therefore continue to be underrepresented in high-level math courses. While about two-thirds of Whites and Asians take algebra II, for example, only about half of Latinos, African Americans, and Native Americans take this course. Differences are even larger for precalculus (Haycock, 2002; U.S. Department of Education, 1997).

Further, research indicates that many students do not understand the importance of algebra and other math and science courses in terms of their educational futures. A nationally representative survey of public school students and parents commissioned by the National Action Council for Minorities in Engineering (NACME), Inc. found that large proportions of students wanted to stop taking mathematics and science. Distressingly, middle-grades minority students were more likely to indicate that they planned on dropping mathematics and science as soon as they could (61% planned to drop mathematics, and 58% planned on dropping science). Minority students of all ages were more likely than other students to say that they would like to stop taking mathematics and science as soon as they could (U.S. Department of Education, 1997).

However, the same students indicated that they would be interested in going to college, and taking college-level mathematics courses and other advanced placement courses. These contrasts signal that many students do not understand the importance of, and requirements for, taking rigorous mathematics and science courses in high school, including the need to take algebra by Grade 8. In fact, only 25% of minority and 42% of nonminority students in Grades 5-8 recognized that algebra was a requirement for future upper-level mathematics classes (U.S. Department of Education, 1997).

This is especially unfortunate, given the connection between taking rigorous mathematics and science courses and college enrollment. NELS data (1988) reveals that 83% of students who took algebra I and geometry enrolled in college within 2 years of their scheduled high school graduation, and "students who take algebra in eighth grade are very likely to apply to a four-year college, controlling for other high school course taking" (Atanda, 1999 cited in Noeth & Wimberly, 2002, p. 17).

In summary, students of all income levels who take rigorous mathematics and science courses, beginning with algebra in Grade 8 or 9 at the latest, are more likely to go to college, and among low-income students (students in the bottom third of the income distribution), the difference is particularly dramatic (U.S. Department of Education, 1997). Students from low-income families who took algebra I and geometry were almost three times as likely to attend college as those who did not. While 71% of low-income students who took algebra I and geometry went to college, only 27% of low-income students who did not take algebra I and geometry went on to college (U.S. Department of Education, 1997).

BEYOND ACADEMICS

Other important components of early awareness programs are discussed briefly below.

- *Advisory.* Some of the benefits of advisory are that it can be used to help students set personal goals, and make decisions and solve problems concerning academic and personal matters. Advisory can also bolster early awareness efforts by helping students develop a personal responsibility for learning (Arth et al., 2004).
- *Independent Reading and Study.* Independent reading and study help students develop interests, expand knowledge, and improve the vocabulary and reading comprehension skills needed for high school, college, and standardized exams such as 8th-grade exit exams as well as the PSAT, SAT I or ACT.
- *Extracurricular Activities.* Many activities such as school clubs, the student newspaper, athletics, musical activities, arts, and drama school enable middle-grades and high school students to explore their interests and talents; such activities also enhance a student's college application.
- *Work Experience and Community Service/Service Learning.* Work experience—paid or volunteer—can teach students discipline, responsibility, and teamwork, and help them identify their career interests and goals. Some schools offer academic credit for volunteer work through service-learning, a teaching method integrating hands-on learning based in the community into the school curriculum.

- *Career Awareness.* Helping students think early about the world of work will help them succeed in life (U.S. Department of Education, 2000). Growing in popularity are career academies based on themes such as international studies, biosciences, sports medicine, and media, with the overall goal of helping students see school as relevant to their lives (Jonsson, 2003). Other career awareness activities in many middle-grades schools include mentoring, trips to worksites, and presentations by individuals about their work.
- *Family Engagement.* Given the importance of family guidance in terms of student decisions about courses and school in general, early awareness must involve families in helping students prepare for college. For example, analysis of the course-taking patterns of the NELS students in grade 8 in 1988 reveals that higher levels of parental involvement were consistently associated with higher likelihoods of taking rigorous mathematics courses. (U.S. Department of Education, 1997). Families also need to be involved in discussions of financial aid. Above all, they need to understand that, while much financial aid is available, some sort of pre-college savings on the part of the family and the student will also probably be necessary. While it may be unrealistic for many families to set aside significant amounts of money on a monthly or yearly basis, just the expectation of college savings—from a summer job, for example—may be important in terms of preparing a young person for college.

In conclusion, a range of early awareness programs and activities can help prepare middle-grades students for college—in terms of their aspirations and their readiness to successfully take a rigorous college-prep curriculum in high school. Middle-grades educators and all who work with young adolescents clearly have important roles to play in supporting future high school students in setting and meeting high standards for themselves to prepare for the challenges of college and the world of work. Just as with effective college prep programs, school-based early awareness programs are most successful when early awareness is a central part of the school's mission, carefully aligned with the school's academic and extracurricular programs and strongly supported by the administration, staff, families, and community members.

REFERENCES

Arth, A., Ashford, A. Jenkins, J., Burns, J., Kane, T., Mitchell, K., et al. (2004). Present imperfect. *Principal Leadership, 4*(8), 37-42.

Camblin, S. (2003). *The middle grades: Putting all students on track for college*. Honolulu, HI: Pacific Resources for Education and Learning.

Greene, J. P., & Forster, G. (2003). *Public high school graduation and college readiness rates in the United States*. Retrieved June 24, 2005, from http://www.manhattan-institute.org/html/ewp_03.htm

Haycock, K. (2002). *Still at risk*. Washington, DC: The Education Trust.

Joftus, S. (2002). *Every child a graduate*. Washington, DC: Alliance for Excellent Education.

Jonsson, P. (2004, May 16). Ninth grade: a school year to be reckoned with. *The Christian Science Monitor*. Retrieved June 24, 2005, from http://www.csmonitor.com/2004/0316/p01s02-ussc.html

Kasak, D. (2004). What middle grades need: A five-point prescription for better middle-level education. *American School Board Journal, 191*(5), 44-45.

National Association of Student Financial Aid Administrators and The Education Resources Institute. (2005). *The abc's of early awareness: A resource guide and toolkit for helping students achieve a higher education*. Retrieved June 24, 2005, from http://www.nasfaa.org/subhomes/abcs/index.html

National Center for Education Statistics. (2004). *The condition of education 2004*. Retrieved June 24, 2005, from http://nces.ed.gov/pubs2004/2004077.pdf

Noeth, R. J., & Wimberly, G. L. (2002). *Creating seamless educational transitions for urban African American and Hispanic students*. Retrieved June 24, 2005, from http://www.act.org/path/policy/pdf/2181.pdf#search='Creating%20seamless%20educational%20transitions%20for%20urban%20African%20American%20and%20Hispanic%20students

Pathways to College Network. (2004). *A shared agenda: A leadership challenge to improve college access and success*. Retrieved June 24, 2005, from http://www.pathwaystocollege.net/pdf/sharedagenda.pdf

Trejos, N. (2004, May 12). The lost freshmen: Many students in area have to repeat 9th grade. *The Washington Post*. Retrieved June 24, 2005, from http://www.washingtonpost.com/wp-dyn/articles/A19034-2004May11.html

U.S. Department of Education. (1997). *Mathematics equals opportunity*. Retrieved June 24, 2005, from http://www.ed.gov/pubs/math/index.html

U.S. Department of Education. (2000). *Getting ready for college early, A handbook for parents of students in the middle and junior high school years*. Retrieved June 24, 2005, from http://www.ed.gov/pubs/GettingReadyCollegeEarly/index.html

Woelfel, K. (2003). Back on track. *Principal Leadership, 3*(9), 45-48.

—Maud Abeel
Academy for Educational Development

EDNA MCCONNELL CLARK FOUNDATION

From 1989 through 2003, the Edna McConnell Clark Foundation supported, first through its Program for Disadvantaged Youth and subsequently through its Program for Student Achievement, selected urban school districts to systemically reform schools serving Grades 6 through 8. The Foundation focused on the middle grades because it believed they are the years when schools need to provide students with both strong support and meaningful academic challenges.

In 1989, the Program for Disadvantaged Youth began to support initiatives in five urban school systems that wanted to learn more about middle school reform by focusing on school-wide change at two or three middle level schools. By 1992, the Program started to shift its efforts to school systems that sought district-wide improvements in student learning by advancing reform in all middle schools simultaneously. During these years, the Program worked with school systems in Baltimore, MD; Louisville, KY; Milwaukee, WI; Oakland, CA; San Diego, CA; Chattanooga, TN; Jackson, MS; and Long Beach, CA.

In March 1994, the Foundation's Trustees approved a new name and direction for the initiative—the "Program for Student Achievement." The new name did not represent a shift from the Foundation's long-standing commitment to inner city, low-achieving youth and those from low-income families. Rather, it signified the Foundation's conviction that urban middle schools must reform themselves in ways that enable large numbers of these young people to meet higher academic standards.

Through the Program, the Foundation initially assisted the Chattanooga Public Schools, Corpus Christi Independent School District, Jefferson County Public Schools (Louisville, KY), Long Beach Unified School District, Minneapolis Public Schools, and the San Diego Unified School District. With Foundation support, each of these districts established student performance goals and committed to reforming middle level schools and supporting students so they would perform at standard. By 2001, the Foundation was supporting only the Corpus Christi, Long Beach, and San Diego school systems.

Throughout both the Program for Disadvantaged Youth and the Program for Student Achievement, the Foundation published a wide variety of publicly-available reports, evaluations, and other materials describing the work of the Program's grantees and the results they achieved. Many of these publications are available either directly from the Foundation (250

Park Avenue, Suite 900, New York, NY 10177) or its web site, www.emcf.org. At the end of 2003 the Foundation concluded its support for middle schools and public education, and refocused its priorities on other areas of need.

—Hayes Mizell
National Staff Development Council

EFFECTIVE SCHOOLS

The goal of every school is to be an "effective" school. In the U.S., for example, federal state legislation has specifically mandated that every school report annual progress data on students' academic achievement and that schools specifically report on the performance of certain groups of historically underachieving students (e.g., ethnic minorities and students from low socioeconomic status). In many instances, a school that outperforms other schools with similar student demographics is recognized and receives both monetary and other tangible rewards. These types of schools are typically called "effective," although various synonyms like high performing, exemplary, and unusually successful are also used to describe these schools.

Research on effective schools has been both praised and criticized for its contributions to education. On the one hand, the research has provided educators with a knowledge base that has identified several salient characteristics, components, or processes of effective schools. Levine and Lezotte (1995), for example, describe several variables that have been found to correlate with schools that have unusually high achievement: "a safe and orderly environment, a shared faculty commitment to improve achievement, orientation focused on identifying and solving problems, high faculty cohesion, collaboration, and collegiality, high faculty input in decision making, and schoolwide emphasis on recognizing positive performance" (pp. 525-526). Other studies and reviews of the research have developed similar lists of effective factors or schooling practices that are related to students' academic achievement (Cotton, 2000).

On the other hand, school effectiveness research has been criticized for a number of methodological, technical, theoretical, and conceptual reasons (Levine, 1990; Scheerens, 1992; Scheerens & Creemers, 1990; Teddlie & Stringfield, 1993). Some of these concerns focus on the lack of theoretical models that explain the relations between school-level and classroom-level factors, while other criticisms have addressed how studies typically (a) focus on low-level basic skills

achievement, (b) do not examine classroom processes, and (c) ignore important school context variables. In addition, other educators have been critical of the generalized findings from effective schools research because they maintain that each school must "construct" the knowledge and processes to become successful schools on their own rather than apply these lessons learned from other schools (Darling-Hammond, 1997).

This chapter briefly highlights some of the common characteristics of effective middle level schools, and it also discusses some of the limitations and criticisms of this work. Finally, we address how this research could be applied in more productive ways.

EFFECTIVE MIDDLE LEVEL SCHOOLS

Research on effective schools has primarily focused on identifying factors or processes in elementary schools that have been found to have a positive impact on students' outcomes (Cotton, 2000; Reynolds, Teddlie, Creemers, Scheerens, & Townsend, 2000). Although most of the research on effective schools has been conducted at the elementary school level, there are a few studies that have been conducted at the secondary school level and specifically in middle level schools. There also are a number of theoretical/conceptual articles that have summarized the characteristics of effective middle level schools. The National Middle School Association, for example, has defined 14 characteristics crucial for effective middle level schools (NMSA, 1995). They include eight cultural qualities that should exist in the school setting: (a) educators who value working with this age group and are prepared to do so, (b) courageous, collaborative leadership, (c) a shared vision that guides decisions, (d) an inviting, supportive, and safe environment, (e) high expectations for every member of the learning community, (f) students and teachers engaged in active learning, (g) an adult advocate for every student, and (h) school-initiated family and community partnerships. They also include six critical program characteristics: (a) curriculum that is challenging, integrative, and exploratory, (b) varied teaching and learning approaches, (c) assessment and evaluation that promote learning, (d) flexible organizational structure, (e) programs and policies that foster health, wellness, and safety, and (f) comprehensive guidance and support services.

We categorized the findings from several effective middle level schools studies that have been published in recent years into the following seven areas: (a) school culture and expectations, (b) effective instructional strategies, (c) teacher/staff professional development, (d) parent and community involvement, (e) continuous student improvement, (f) strong school leadership, and (g) valuing student's needs and culture. These recent research-based characteristics or practices are very similar to the general lists of variables previously described.

One of the key components of effective schools in these studies is the prevailing culture of high expectations maintained by all stakeholders in the school community. In their study of effective middle level schools for English Language Learners, for example, Minicucci, Berman, McLaughlin, McLeod, and Wooodworth (2002) found that the effective schools in their sample maintained the expectation that all students will achieve literacy in English and then built their programs around that expectation. Other studies have also found that the level of expectation must be aligned to national, state, and district standards as well as the specific goals of the local school community. In other words, the work of the school is to reach the lofty goals and expectations established by the school community (Anderson & Pellicer, 1998; Cotton, 1995; Crispeels, 2002; Minicucci, et. al., 1995). These high expectations must be communicated directly as well as through the school's culture and climate. More than anything, the culture exudes a sense of determination, collaboration, and aspiration to doing whatever is required to make student learning and development the central focus of the entire school community.

In the area of effective instructional strategies, several practices were found to be effective. Teacher collaboration on interdisciplinary/thematic units, grade level planning, and vertical alignment, for example, were found to be effective (Anderson & Pellicer, 1998; Cotton 1995; Jackson & Davis, 2000; Miramontes, Nadeau, & Commins, 1997; Short, 1994). Further, middle school students' academic success was increased when they were allowed to collaborate with peers, work on open-ended projects, long term assignments, and focus on skill development with a transition into higher level, critical thinking requirements (Anderson & Pellicer, 1998; Cotton, 1995; Rosebery, Warren, & Conant, 1992). It is important to be responsive to students' status as adolescent learners by allowing them the opportunity to use their developing minds in a safe and stimulating learning environment. Movement from traditional modes of instructional delivery, such as whole group lecture and multiple selection tests at the end of a "unit"; and into collaborative classroom inquiry requires a lot of professional development.

Ongoing professional development; therefore, is another feature of effective middle level schools (Anderson & Pellicer, 1998; Chrispeels, 2002; Cotton, 1995; Jackson & Davis, 2000; Mora, 2000). Vertically aligning curriculum, designing, and implementing interdisciplinary units, and building a strong school culture with high expectations requires time and commitment, so it stands to reason that continuous professional development (PD) is a feature of effective schools. Chrispeels (2002) found that it is particularly effective for the PD to first build leadership capacity among key teachers and then move into developing literacy in the areas of curriculum, assessment, and instruction. Next, grade levels must be given the time to work on production and implementation of their units as well as reflect teaching practice. Building excellent teaching practices, instructional literacy, and leadership capacity is often the starting point of PD.

Just as teachers and administrators work to build effectiveness capacity in their schools, time and effort must also go into building community commitment through parental involvement. Parental involvement decreases as students grow older, this is evident on open house nights when kindergarten rooms are bursting at the seems with parents while fifth grade classes are glad to get more than a hand full; the same goes for middle school. Middle school stands out in this because kids are starting to push their parents away and gain more control in their own lives. Effective schools, however, have repeatedly been found to go to great lengths to involve parents in their child's learning, school programs, and shared governance structures (Anderson & Pellicer, 1998; Cotton, 1995; Minicucci et. al., 1995; Miramontes et. al., 1997; Reyes, Scribner, & Scribner, 1999).

School effectiveness research studies address the need for continuous assessment of student progress towards learning goals. According to Cotton (1995), effective schools use assessments to monitor student progress, modify curriculum, and adjust teaching practices. Just as teachers have ongoing development and reflection, the assessments, used for student growth and learning, are also continuous.

All of these effective practices can only take place with a strong instructional leader as principal. Principals in effective schools have been found to support innovative teaching, foster ongoing professional development, practice collaborative government structures, and provide the grand vision to which the entire school community aspires (Anderson & Pellicer, 1998; Chrispeels, 2002; Cotton, 1995; Jackson & Davis, 2000; Minicucci et. al., 1995; Reyes et. al., 1999).

The last common category of effective middle level schools' characteristics is valuing students' needs and culture. For many adolescent learners, valuing their unique instructional needs and culture has been repeatedly revealed in school effectiveness studies. This may mean instruction in their primary language, a structured immersion program, and/or diversity imbedded in the curriculum so that contributions of various ethnic groups are acknowledged and cultural differences are incorporated (Cotton, 1995; Minicucci et. al., 1995 ; Miramontes et. al. 1997; Mora, 2000; Reyes et. al., 1999; Short, 1994).

CRITICISMS OF EFFECTIVE SCHOOLS RESEARCH

For all its promise to educational practitioners, school effectiveness research has a number of critics among educational researchers. Nuthall (2004) challenges this type of research because the correlational relationship between teaching and learning is presumed to be causal, when in fact few studies actually make a direct link between teaching and learning. Nuthall explains that just because something is taught does not mean that learning occurs as a direct result of the act of teaching and that school effectiveness research is, "plagued by ambiguity" (2004, p. 282). Other critics of effective schools research are concerned because they feel that the research has produced no sustainable, significant improvement in students' learning. Schools and school-level variables have been found to have a very small effect on student outcomes and they may account for less than 10% of the variance in student achievement (Wang, Haertel, & Walberg, 1993; Wyatt, 1996). Another specific criticisms aimed at researchers in this field is that they have not investigated classroom processes as extensively (Good & Brophy, 1986), especially since there is some evidence that suggests that instructional and classroom processes account for differences between schools (Teddlie, Kirby, & Stringfield, 1989; Teddlie & Stringfield, 1993).

A final limitation of effective schools research is that the majority of the studies are merely descriptive or correlational studies. There have not been many experimental studies that have investigated the impact of effective school practices on teachers' and students' educational outcomes. Similarly, there have been very few naturalistic, longitudinal studies that have examined the success of effective schools on middle level students' long-term academic achievement and educational success. Mixed methods approaches that use systematic classroom observation, teacher self-report data, along with teacher, administrator, and student interview data supplement the survey data could also help us understand, from different perspectives, the complexity of issues surrounding the educational improvement of middle level students. Finally, ethnographic studies also are needed in order to help us uncover "grounded theoretical" explanations of factors that impact schools for middle level students.

SUMMARY

Effective schools research is helpful because this is a starting point for schools who are having difficulties serving their students. The research summarized in this synthesis are based on real schools who had similar problems to other schools serving middle level students, but they managed to overcome their difficulties and obtain real success. The critical question, however, is how do researchers reconcile the gap between empirical studies on effective schools for middle level students, while maintaining this practical significance?

The present chapter described some of the research-based components from effective middle level schools that have been found to be successful in improving the education of students. Several key elements or components that have been successful in middle level schools are discussed, but these are only suggestions, not "recipes" for improving schools. No program, however well implemented, will prove a panacea for all the educational problems of students. For the most part, each school must concern itself with the resolution of its own specific problems (Schubert, 1980). In that sense, every school should be considered unique, and educators should choose among research-based practices and programs according to the needs of the middle school students that they serve. Furthermore, critical out-of-school factors that affect the outcomes of schooling for students must also be addressed. If we only focus on school factors and ignore the importance of family, community, and societal influences on the education of students, we will clearly fail in our endeavors.

REFERENCES

Anderson, L. W., & Pellicer, L. O. (1988). Toward and understanding unusually successful programs for economically disadvantaged students. *Journal of Education for Students Placed at Risk, 3,* 237-263.

Cotton, K. (1995). *Effective schooling practices: A research synthesis 1995 update.* Northwest Regional Educational Laboratory. Retrieved May 19, 2005, from http://www.nwrel.org/scpd/esp/esp95.html

Cotton, K. (2000). *The schooling practices that matter most.* Alexandria, VA: Association for Supervision and Curriculum Development.

Crispeels, J. H. (2002). Effective schools—The California Center for Effective Schools: The Oxnard district partnership. *Phi Delta Kappan, 83,* 382.

Darling-Hammond, L. (1997). *The right to learn: A blueprint for creating schools that work*. San Francisco: Jossey-Bass.

Good, T. L., & Brophy, J. E. (1986). School effects. In M. Wittrock (Ed.), *Handbook of research on teaching* (3rd ed., pp. 570-602). New York: Macmillan.

Jackson, A. W., & Davis, G. A. (2000). *Turning points 2000: Educating adolescents in the 21st century*. New York: Teachers College.

Levine, D. U. (1990). Update on effective schools: Findings and implications from research and practice. *Journal of Negro Education, 59*, 577-584.

Levine, D. U., & Lezotte, L. W. (1995). Effective schools research. In J. A. Banks & C. A. M. Banks (Eds.), *Handbook of research on multicultural education* (pp. 525-547). New York: Macmillan.

Minicucci, C., Berman, P., McLaughlin, B., McLeod, B., Nelson, & Woodworth, K. (1995). School reform and student diversity. *Phi Delta Kappan, 77*(1), 77.

Miramontes, O. B., Nadeau, A., & Commins, N. L. (1997). *Restructuring schools for linguistic diversity: Linking decision making to effective programs*. New York: Teachers College.

Mora, J. K. (2000). Policy shifts in language-minority education: A mismatch between politics and pedagogy. *The Educational Forum, 64*(3), 204-214.

National Middle School Association. (1995). *This we believe: Developmentally responsive middle schools*. Columbus, OH: Author.

Nuthall, G. (2004). Relating classroom teaching to student learning: A critical analysis of why research has failed to bridge the theory-practice gap. *Harvard Educational Review, 74*, 273-306.

Reyes, P., Scribner, J., & Scribner, A. P. (1999). *Lessons from high-performing Hispanic schools: Creating learning communities*. New York: Teachers College.

Reynolds, D., Teddlie, C., Creemers, B., Scheerens, J., & Townsend, T. (2000). An introduction to school effectiveness research. In C. Teddlie & D. Reynolds (Eds), *The international handbook of school effectiveness research*. London: Falmer Press.

Rosebery, A. S., Warren, B., & Conant, F. R. (1992). Appropriating scientific discourse: Findings from language minority classrooms. *The Journal of the Learning Sciences, 2*(1), 61-94.

Scheerens, J. (1992). *Effective schooling: Research, theory, and practice*. London: Cassell.

Scheerens, J., & Creemers, B. (1990). Conceptualizing school effectiveness. *International Journal of Educational Research, 13*, 691-706

Schubert, W. H. (1980). Recalibrating educational research: Toward a focus on practice. *Educational Researcher, 9*(1), 17-24.

Short, D. J. (1994). Expanding middle school horizons: Integrating language, culture, and social studies. *TESOL Quarterly, 28*(3), 581-608.

Teddlie, C., Kirby, P. C., & Stringfield, S. (1989). Effective versus ineffective schools: Observable differences in the classroom. *American Journal of Education, 97*, 221-236.

Teddlie, C., & Stringfield, S. (1993). *Schools make a difference: Lessons learned from a 10-year study of school effects*. New York: Teachers College.

Wang, M. C., Haertel, G. D., & Walberg, H. J. (1993). Toward a knowledge base for school learning. *Review of Educational Research, 63*, 249-294.

Wyatt, T. (1996). School effectiveness research: Dead end, damp squib or smoldering fuse? *Issues in Educational Research, 6*(1), 79-112.

—Donna Davenport Price
—Hersh C. Waxman
University of Houston

EICHHORN, DONALD H.

Referred to as "the first major implementer of the middle school concept" (Lounsbury, 1984, p. 3), Donald H. Eichhorn was named the 1983 recipient of The John H. Lounsbury Award for Distinguished Service, the highest award given by the National Middle School Association (NMSA). As stated by NMSA, "This award is given only when an individual has demonstrated a level of service, integrity, and leadership in middle level education that warrants this special recognition" (2004, para. 1).

Eichhorn's doctoral dissertation resulted in a monograph entitled *The Middle School* (1966), now considered part of the middle level education research canon. From 1962-1979 Eichhorn served as assistant supervising principal/superintendent in the Upper St. Clair Township School District, Pittsburgh, Pennsylvania. Unsatisfied with junior high school education common during his tenure with the school district, Eichhorn conceived of a developmentally appropriate model of education rooted in the sociopsychological characteristics and needs of young adolescent learners. Eichhorn envisioned a nongraded transitional school between elementary school and high school. Attempting to clarify the type of student such a transitional school would serve, Eichhorn introduced the term "transescence" to refer to

> the stage of development which begins prior to the onset of puberty and extends through the early stages of adolescence. Since puberty does not occur for all precisely at the same chronological age in human development, the transescent designation is based on the many physical, social, emotional, and intellectual changes in body chemistry that appear prior to the puberty cycle to the time in which the body gains a practical degree of stabilization over these complex pubescent changes. (p. 3)

To test his theory of transcescent development., Eichhorn and the school district joined with Allan L. Drash of Pittsburgh Children's Hospital and initiated the Boyce Medical Study. Results of that 1969 study validated Eichhorn's initial work in identifying the middle level learner's unique characteristics and led Eichhorn to advocate "developmental age grouping rather than traditional grouping based on age and grade level" (Eichhorn, 1998, p. 87).

Eichhorn remained a steadfast supporter of the nongraded model of educating transcents, nevertheless, conceded to the notion of a middle school for such learners. While there was no agreement among educators at that time as to the program for the emerging middle school, Eichhorn confirmed three broad goals—value goal, learning goal, personal development goal—and an educational program for the emerging adolescent learner—curriculum, instruction, grouping—upon which the model stood (Eichhorn, 1972).

Reflecting upon the 32 years since his first publication, Eichhorn outlined six areas that "merit constant attention" by middle level educators:

1. To maintain the basic rationale of the middle school.
2. To develop programs that educate and prepare students for a rapidly changing technological world.
3. To expand the role of the home and community in the schools.
4. To seek creative ways to confront home, school, and community problems.
5. To use the great potential of the present program.
6. To encourage teacher preparation institutions to become involved with middle level learning. (Eichhorn, 1998, pp. 90-92)

REFERENCES

Eichhorn, D. H. (1966). *The middle school.* New York: The Center for Applied Research in Education, Inc.

Eichhorn, D. H. (1972). The emerging adolescent school of the future—Now. In J. G. Saylor (Ed.), *The school of the future—Now* (pp. 35-52). Washington, DC: Association for Supervision and Curriculum Development.

Eichhorn, D. H. (1998). Considering it all. In R. David (Ed.), *Moving forward from the past: Early writing and current reflections of middle school founders* (pp. 78-95). Columbus, OH: National Middle School Association & Pennsylvania Middle School Association.

Lounsbury, J. H. (1984). *Perspectives: Middle school education, 1964-1984.* Columbus, OH: National Middle School Association.

National Middle School Association. (2004). *John Lounsbury award.* Retrieved June 21, 2004, from: http://www.nmsa.org/about/awards/lounsbury_winners.htm

—Kathleen Roney
The University of North Carolina, Wilmington

ELEMENTARY AND SECONDARY EDUCATION ACT

In 1965, the Elementary and Secondary Education Act (ESEA) was first enacted by Congress. It has been regularly renewed ever since, usually every 5 years. It's most important title, Title I, now called Improving the Academic Achievement of the Disadvantaged, has focused federal government attention and money for 40 years on students in schools with large concentrations of low-income children. Title I was most recently renewed in the fall of 2001 as part of the law entitled the No Child Left Behind Act (NCLB). Title I is the largest federal education program for elementary and secondary schools.

—Cynthia G. Brown
Center for American Progress

ELIOT, CHARLES

Charles Eliot was a charismatic figure well known as a president of Harvard University and the chair of Committee of Ten for the Study of Secondary Education.

As president of Harvard University from 1869-1909, Eliot implemented an elective system broadening college curriculum and eventually influencing the curriculum of other colleges. His ideas about educational reform were influenced by his observation of European educational models, especially German universities (Popper, 1967; Rivlin, 1943).

As chair of the National Education Association's Committee of Ten on Secondary School Studies, Eliot found a forum to draw attention to his ideas for reform of elementary and secondary education. He believed that time was not used efficiently in American elementary and secondary education resulting in a late age of graduation from American colleges in comparison to their European counterparts. The committee's report, published in 1894, suggested broadening the curriculum of secondary school (Barton, 1976;

Clark & Clark, 1994; Pinar, Reynolds, Slattery, & Taubman, 1995; Rivlin, 1943). The report also recommended four courses of study in secondary schools Classical, Latin-Scientific, Modern Language, and English (Pinar et al., 1995). Calling for "the economy of time," the report recommended that secondary school begin in seventh grade and include subjects such as foreign languages and algebra. This change would lead to a 6 year elementary school. Many see this reform initiative as a precursor to the junior high school movement.

REFERENCES

Barton, R. R. (1976). *A historical study of the organization and development of the junior high and middle school movement 1920-1975*. Fayettville: The University of Arkansas.

Clark, S. N., & Clark, D. C. (1994). *Restructuring the middle level school: Implications for school leaders*. Albany, NY: State University of New York Press.

Pinar, W. F., Reynolds, W. M., Slattery, P., & Taubman, P. M. (1995). *Understanding curriculum: An introduction to the study of historical and comtemporary curriculum discourse*. New York: Peter Lang.

Popper, S. H. (1967). *The American middle school*. Waltham, MA: Blaisdell.

Rivlin, H. N. (Ed.). (1943). *Encyclopedia of modern education*. New York: The Philosophical Library of New York City.

—Jennifer S. Goodwin
Teachers College, Columbia University

ENGLISH LANGUAGE LEARNERS

By the year 2010, all middle grades teachers in the United States are likely to have English Language Learners (ELLs) in their classrooms. Between 1990 and 2000, the numbers of ELLs in the United States increased by 95%, and in several states (including Georgia, Minnesota, Nebraska, and Iowa), the ELL population has grown by over 200% (National Clearinghouse for English Language Acquisition, 2002). Today's middle grades teachers, no matter where they teach, will need new resources to understand and educate this increasingly linguistically diverse student body (Gebhard, Austin, & Nieto, 2002; Nieto, 2000). This entry addresses how educators, families, and communities can best support the learning of ELLs in the middle grades (Grades 4-8), discussing issues of diversity among the ELL population, methodology and program, family involvement in ELLs' education, and multilingualism as a resource for all middle grades children and their communities.

THE DIVERSITY OF ELLs

While it is undeniable that the numbers of ELLs is increasing, this broad label includes many different groups of people. ELLs come from myriad countries, language backgrounds, economic backgrounds, and levels of former schooling; some are from urban areas; some from remote rural villages; and some were born in the United States. All of these distinctions mean that ELLs have varied resources that they bring to the classroom, varied support systems at home, and varied concerns that might influence their school performance.

AN EXAMPLE

Julio Aceves came to Los Angeles in the summer of 2001, at age 12, and that fall was placed in Ms. Carter's seventh grade English for Speakers of Other Languages (ESOL) class. As an introductory diagnostic activity, Ms. Carter had her students write postcards to someone they knew who spoke English. Ms. Carter assured the students they would be able to write simple messages if they wanted to, but Julio did not feel capable of writing in English. He had just arrived from Mexico a month ago, after all. Ms. Carter suggested he write his postcard in Spanish. At the end of the activity, Ms. Carter collected the postcards to review and send. She was surprised when she looked at Julio's card. The words all flowed together like supercalifragilisticexpialidocious—in a roughly spelled Spanish. Now it was clear that Julio had minimal writing experience in any language. At the same time, others in the class had written entire letters to former English teachers. For Ms. Carter, supporting the language and academic development of all her ELLs this year was going to be a challenge.

COUNTRY AND LANGUAGE OF ORIGIN

Julio fits neatly into the statistics—he is one of the growing numbers of ELLs who have come to the United States from Mexico, appearing in school having just arrived, knowing little English, and speaking Spanish among their friends and family. In the Los Angeles Unified School District in 2001, over 40% of the student body was placed in classes for ELLs (National Center for Educational Statistics, 2005). And this Los Angeles number is echoed across the country. In 2001, over 10% of the entire U.S. population spoke Spanish at home, and another 7% spoke languages other than English or Spanish at home (Modern Language Association, 2004). These numbers represent continuing, exponential increases (Asia Society, 2005).

In many school districts, over 100 different home languages are represented.

RURAL VERSUS URBAN

While Julio represents the large numbers of ELLs who have arrived in the United States from Mexico for economic reasons, leaving rural farms or small towns in Mexico where minimal schooling is available (Valdez, 1996; Valenzuela, 1999), many ELLs come from urban areas, and their families have left their countries for political reasons, to pursue international careers or advanced degrees. Even a classroom that superficially seems to be full of recently arrived Mexicans from rural areas may also include an El Salvadoran son of a political refugee, or a Columbian whose parents are former University Professors (Bachtel, Bohon, & Atiles, 2005).

LEVEL OF EDUCATION

Rural and urban backgrounds also can provide very different educational opportunities. Children in rural Mexico, for example, often leave school by the time they reach the middle grades. Girls are often encouraged to stay home and help with household chores rather than attend school. Boys may miss school during harvest times or other periods of increased work requirements (Valdez, 1996). Also, refugees, from Somalia or Cambodia, for example, may have had their educations cut short due to political instability or civil war (Friedman, 2002; Quan, 2004). Even in the middle grades, these students may arrive in the United States still preliterate in their home languages. As such, middle grades curriculum, particularly if provided exclusively in English, is minimally accessible to these students. Other ELLs arrive in ESOL classrooms highly educated, and may even come to the United States having had many years of instruction in English in their home countries. Some refugees may have received English classes in camps before arrival in the U.S. (Friedman, 2002). So, while Ms. Carter's class was full of recently arrived immigrants, some composed full-length letters in English, while Julio struggled to write a short postcard in Spanish.

PEER GROUP AFFILIATION

In the middle grades, peer group affiliation strongly influences development and academic achievement; and, both for ELLs who have just arrived, and for those who have been in the states for many years (including those ELLs who were born in the U.S.), negotiating peer group affiliation and ethnic and linguistic identity is complicated and can have lasting ramifications for school performance (Harklau, 1994; Meador, 2005; Mehan, Hubbard, & Villanueva, 1994). Rural-origin, recently arrived ELLs, like Julio, may join together as a peer group with few collective resources to access school success (Valenzuela, 1999), while ELLs who have been in the U.S. long enough to be familiar with schools and their norms may actively resist school success or "acting white" (Noguera, 2003) to avoid sacrificing ethnic identity (Meador, 2005). Both these groups are at increased risk of dropping out of school (Valenzuela, 1999).

SOCIOECONOMIC STATUS

Just as ELLs differ in home language, country of origin, the rural or urban nature of their upbringing, and the peer group affiliations they form, ELLs range widely in terms of socioeconomic (SES) background. Still, the majority of ELLs are from low SES families and, SES remains the single most influential factor predicting dropout rate. Many ELLs live in households in which all the adults must work multiple low-wage jobs. This means ELLs may not have support for homework at home, have minimal ability to provide snacks and materials for school, and, in some cases, must stay home from school to, for example, take care of a sick sibling while the mother and father are working (Valdez, 1998; The Center for Education Research and Policy at MassINC, 2003).

FORMS OF SUPPORT

Neglect of ELLs' education became an official legal issue in 1974, when, in the Supreme Court case *Lau v. Nichols*, it was ruled that, "Students who do not understand English are effectively foreclosed from any meaningful education" (*Lau v. Nichols*, 1974). (For an extended chronology of court cases leading to *Lau v. Nichols*, see Santa Ana, 2004, pp. 87-106.) Partly as a result, the Equal Educational Opportunities Act (1974) was passed, ruling that, "No state shall deny equal educational opportunity to an individual on account of his or her race, color, sex, or national origin, by the failure of an educational agency to take appropriate action to overcome languages barriers that impede equal participation by its students in its instructional programs." This means, effectively, that schools are legally bound to serve ELLs' educational needs and that denying them their first language obstructs this responsibility. Any school with second language learners that does not have an educational program in place for them is considered out of compliance with federal law. This leaves open, however, what might count as effective programming for ELLs.

PROGRAMS FOR ELLS

Often the discussion of effective educational programs for ELLs is framed as a debate between bilingual education and total English immersion. This is especially true after California and Arizona passed legislation prohibiting bilingual education (Propositions 227 and 207, respectively). However, despite the tendency to polarize the debate as for or against bilingual education, in reality, there are as many programs for ELLs as there are school contexts. Still, research investigating program efficacy generally categorizes programs according to (1) where children go for instruction (do they stay in the mainstream classroom or go to a separate room?); and (2) what languages are used as the medium of instruction and in what proportion (Piper, 2001). Program types range along a continuum from dual language bilingual—in which the goal is for students to learn to function academically in two languages, (e.g., Spanish and English)—to an English to Speakers of other languages pull-out program—in which the ELLs are taken from the mainstream classroom to be taught English traditionally, and returned to the grade level classroom for content area instruction in English. Between these two extremes there are a range of combination approaches.

The question remains: Which program type is most effective? To date, the largest available long-term research study conducted indicates that ELLs' long-term achievement on standardized reading and other achievement tests is significantly augmented when ELLs participate in programs that lean toward the bilingual end of the spectrum (Thomas & Collier, 1997). This finding has been supported by smaller studies of individual programs (Krashen & Biber, 1988; Rosier & Holm, 1980) and school ethnographies (Olsen, 1997). While there are cases that provide evidence counter to the Thomas and Collier research (Gerston & Woodward, 1995; Porter, 1990), these do not refute the growing numbers of studies showing that bilingual programs that are carefully designed and competently implemented are successful (Adamson, 2005).

FORMS OF SUPPORT BEYOND PROGRAM AND METHOD

An Example, at Home

Two days after Ms. Carter had read Julio's Spanish postcard, she made a courtesy visit to Julio's home. Julio was setting the table. His mother, Maria Serrano, was preparing *comida*, the afternoon meal. Ms. Carter

was surprised to find another of her students, Juan Maldonado sitting in the living room. Juan, she soon learned, was Julio's cousin. Thirty minutes later, Ms. Serrano left the home having made connections that would help her to reach both Julio and Juan throughout the year.

Parents and Siblings as a Resource

This was the beginning of a peer network developing within the Aceves/Maldonado/Serrano household. Throughout the year, Ms. Carter knew she could answer questions about Julio by talking to Juan and vice versa. These are the kinds of networks that Luis Moll and his colleagues began to encourage teachers to develop in their studies investigating students' homes and communities as "Funds of Knowledge." (Moll & Vellez-Ibanez, 1992). As mentioned above, ELL's often come from low SES households—but if teachers, counselors, and administrators learn about the nonmonetary funds and personal connections that exist in those households, they can draw on those resources to help children be accountable to school, finish homework, bring their materials, and share books and other school necessities.

Home Language/Heritage Language as a Resource.

Making these connections with homes not only provides teachers with an understanding of the resources available to ELLs, it encourages students to draw more on their home language and culture in classroom interactions. Recognizing home language as a resource in the classroom can also highlight the multiple languages spoken in a middle grades classroom, building important relationships across peer and language groups (Rymes & Anderson, 2004). "Home languages," defined broadly, include not only official languages spoken within national borders like Spanish or Chinese, but also the multiple varieties of English spoken by all students in any middle grades classroom. Building on the variety all students have in their linguistic repertoire can build a recognition and appreciation for language as a tool that we draw on very differently in different contexts (Heath, 1983; Rymes & Anderson, 2004; Tatum, 1997).

Paraprofessionals as a Resource

Teachers can also draw on paraprofessional teaching assistants to make connections with ELL homes. Paraprofessionals (parapros) who work with ELLs often live within the same community, speak multiple languages, have been at the school for many years, and know the tensions and connections between and among students and other students, staff, and family (Haselkorn & Fideler, 1996; Rymes, 2004). Out of politeness or respect, students and families of ELLs may be resistant to approaching a teacher with their concerns (Stanton-Salazar, 1997). Parapros, however, may in some cases be more approachable. When parents, teachers, and paraprofessionals working with ELLs work closely and communicate well, school achievement improves (Rueda & DeNeve, 1998).

Multilingual Students as a Resource

Like paraprofessionals, students who are multilingual often function as mediators between households and teachers, and other novice English-speaking students and teachers (Orellana, 2001; Orellana, Reynolds, Dorner, & Meza, 2003). The range of levels of Spanish and English literacy and fluency present in ESOL classes like Ms. Carter's, for example, while daunting, also provides student assistants who can help novice ELLs access the curriculum and prevent them from drifting to the silent margins. This use of Spanish-speaking students as resources in the classroom potentially lessens the social distance between English-speaking teachers and Spanish-speaking students, while illustrating to ELLs in the classroom that learning English need not entail first language loss.

REFLECTIONS: FROM SILENCE TO SUCCESS

Throughout the literature on immigrant experience, there are narratives of children silenced by their lack of voice in their new home (Hart, 1999; Hoffman, 1990; Rodriguez, 1983). As these stories testify, when students grow up feeling that their home language silences them at school, they may come to view their home language as inferior or useless (Rodriguez, 1983). And, many children then grow up, in turn, neglecting their home language and the relationships cultivated through that language. These individual narratives are consistent with language statistics indicating that the majority of ELLs learn English—but also lose their first language (Tse, 2001).

Approaches to ELLs that treat home languages other than English as a deficit can lead to "subtractive schooling" in which schools, rather than adding English to the students' linguistic repertoire, subtract the first language foundation these students bring to school with them (Cummins, 1989; Piper, 2001; Valenzuela, 1999). This devaluing of the first language can be reinforced with forms of high-stakes tests that, while important for identifying and providing services for ELLs, potentially frame home languages not as a resource to build on but as a deficit. There are not yet standardized, high-stakes ways of counting multilingualism as an asset within a school or district test results profile (Coltrane, 2002).

Nevertheless, ELLs' growing numbers are necessarily changing what counts as knowledge in classrooms, and increasingly, multilingualism is seen as an asset for individuals joining the U.S. labor force (Humphreys, 2004). Students who grow up multilingual and attend schools that recognize multilingualism as a resource, not a deficit, can achieve high degrees of academic success and social mobility (August & Hakuta, 1997; Brisk, 1998). In a society and economy that are becoming more bilingual, leaving school speaking two languages rather than only one is valuable, and ELLs in the middle grades are potentially already more than halfway there.

REFERENCES

August, D., & Hakuta, K. (1997). *Educating language minority children.* Washington DC: National Academy Press.

Adamson, H. D. (2005). *Language minority students in American schools: An education in English.* Mahwah, NJ: Erlbaum.

Asia Society. (2005). World languages spoken at home in the U.S.: 1990 and 2000 compared. Retrieved June 27, 2005, from www.internationaled.org/BriefingBook/6.Building/6.j%20world%20lang.xls

Bachtel, D. C., Bohon, S. A., & Atiles, J. H. (2005). *Profiling America's growing Hispanic population.* [Informational poster]. Athens, GA: The University of Georgia Venture Fund.

Brisk, M. E. (1998). *Bilingual education: From compensatory to quality schooling.* Mahwah, NJ: Erlbaum.

The Center for Education Research and Policy at MassINC. (2003). *Head of the class: Characteristics of higher performing urban high schools in Massachusetts.* Boston: MassINC.

Coltrane, B. (2002). *English language learners and high-stakes tests: An overview of the issues.* Retrieved July 1, 2005, from Center for Applied Linguistics Web site: http://www.cal.org/resources/digest/0207coltrane.html

Cummins, J. (1989). *Empowering language minority students.* Sacramento, CA: California Association for Bilingual Education.

Equal Educational Opportunities Act. (1974). Title 20, Chapter 39, Subchapter I, Part 2, United States Court, Section 1703(f). Retrieved July 7, 2005, from, http://www.usdoj.gov/crt/cor/byagency/ed1703.htm

Friedman, A. A. (2002). Agents of literacy change: Working with Somali students in an urban middle school. In Z. F. Beykont (Ed.), *The power of culture: Teaching across language difference* (pp. 121-145). Cambridge, MA: Harvard Education Publishing Group.

Gebhard, M., Austin, T., & Nieto, S. (2002). "You can't step on someone else's words;" Preparing all teachers to teach language minority students. In Z. F. Beykont (Ed.), *The power of culture: Teaching across language difference* (pp. 167-

191). Cambridge, MA: Harvard Education Publishing Group.

Gerston, R., & Woodward, J. (1995). A longitudinal study of transitional and immersion bilingual education programs in one district. *Elementary School Journal, 95*(1), 223-239.

Harklau, L. (1994). Jumping track: How language-minority students negotiate evaluations of ability. *Anthropology & Education Quarterly, 25*(3), 347-363.

Hart, E. T. (1999). *Barefoot heart: Stories of a migrant child.* Tucson, AZ: Bilingual Press.

Haselkorn, D., & Fideler, E. (1996). *Breaking the class ceiling: Paraeducator pathways to teaching.* Belmont, MA: Recruiting New Teachers.

Hoffman, E. (1990). *Lost in translation: A life in a new language.* New York: Penguin.

Humphreys, J. (2004). The multicultural economy 2004: America's minority buying power. *Georgia Business and Economic Conditions, 64*, 3.

Krashen, S., & Biber, D. (1988). *On course: Bilingual education's successes in California.* Sacramento, CA: California Association for Bilingual Education.

Lau v. Nichols (1974). 94 Supreme Court, 786.

Mehan, H., Hubbard, L., & Villanueva, I. (1994). Forming academia identities: Accommodation without assimilation among involuntary minorities. *Anthropology & Education Quarterly, 25*(2), 91-117.

Meador, E. (2005). The making of marginality. *Anthropology & Education Quarterly, 36*(2), 149-164.

Modern Language Association. (2005). *Census data language map.* Retrieved June 29, 2005, from http://www.mla.org/census_main

Moll, L. C., & Vellez-Ibanez, C. (1992). Funds of knowledge for teaching: Using a qualitative approach to connect homes to classrooms. *Theory into Practice, 31*, 132-141.

National Center for Educational Statistics. (2005). *Characteristics of the 100 largest public elementary and secondary school districts in the United States: 2001-2002.* Retrieved June 28, 2005, from http://nces.ed.gov/pubs2003/100_largest/table_20_1.asp

National Clearinghouse for English Language Acquisition. (2002). *The growing number of limited English proficient students, 2000-2001.* Retrieved July 1, 2005, from http://www.ncela.gwu.edu/policy/states/stateposter.pdf

Nieto, S. (2000). Placing equity front and center: Some thoughts on transforming teacher education for a new century. *Journal of Teacher Education, 51*, 180-187.

Noguera, P. (2003). *City schools and the American dream: Reclaiming the promise of public education.* New York: Teachers College Press.

Olsen, L. (1997). *Made in America: Immigrant students in our public schools.* New York: The New Press.

Orellana M. F., Reynolds, J., Dorner, L., & Meza, M. (2003). In other words: Translating or "para-phrasing" as a family literacy practice in immigrant households. *The Reading Research Quarterly, 38*(1), 12-34.

Orellana, M. F. (2001). The work kids do: Mexican and Central American immigrant children's contributions to households and schools in California. *Harvard Educational Review, 71*(3), 366-389.

Piper, T. (2001). *And then there were two: Children and second-language learning.* Toronto, Ontario, Canada: Pippin.

Porter, R. P. (1990). *Forked tongue: The politics of bilingual education.* New York: Basic Books.

Quan, K. Y. (2004). The girl who couldn't sing. In O. Santa Ana (Ed.), *Tongue-tied: The lives of multilingual children in public education* (pp. 13-21). Lanham, MD: Rowman & Littlefield.

Rodriguez, R. (1983). *Hunger of memory: The education of Richard Rodriguez.* New York: Bantam.

Rosier, P., & Holm, W. (1980). *The Rock Point experience: A longitudinal study of a Navajo school program.* (Bilingual Education Series No. 8). Washington, DC: Center for Applied Linguistics.

Rueda, R., & DeNeve, C. (1998). How paraeducators build cultural bridges in diverse classrooms. *Community Circle of Caring Journal 3*(2), 53-55.

Rymes, B. (2004, Winter). Bilingualism as a resource: Finding and training teachers for Georgia's schools. *The Georgia Association for Supervision and Curriculum Development Reporter,* 36-37.

Rymes, B., & Anderson, K. (2004). Second language acquisition for all: Understanding the interactional dynamics of classrooms in which Spanish and AAE are spoken. *Research in the Teaching of English, 29*(2), 107-135.

Stanton-Salazar, R. (1997). A social capital framework for understanding the socialization of ethnic minority children and youths. *Harvard Educational Review, 67*(1), 1-39.

Santa Ana, O. (Ed.) (2004). *Tongue-tied: The lives of multilingual children in public education.* Lanham, MD: Rowman & Littlefield.

Tatum, B. (1997). *Why are all the black kids sitting together in the cafeteria? And other conversations about race.* New York: Basic Books.

Thomas, W., & Collier, V. (1997). *School effectiveness for language minority students.* Washington, DC: National Council for Bilingual Education.

Tse, L. (2001). *Why don't they learn English: Separating fact from fallacy in the U.S. language debate.* New York: Teachers College Press.

Valdez, G. (1996). *Con respeto: Bridging the distances between culturally diverse families and schools: An ethnographic portrait.* New York: Teachers College Press.

Valdez, G. (1998). The world outside and inside schools: Language and immigrant children. *Educational Researcher, 27*(6), 4-18.

Valenzuela, A. (1999). *Subtractive schooling: U.S.-Mexican youth and the politics of caring.* Albany, NY: SUNY.

—Betsy Rymes
The University of Georgia

THE EXEMPLARY MIDDLE SCHOOL

It is no surprise that Paul S. George and the late William M. Alexander's *The Exemplary Middle School* (George & Alexander, 2003) is a comprehensive, accessible text particularly useful for students in the field of middle school education, but also informative for middle school practitioners who may seek further edification about the middle school concept, as well as researchers interested in this unique age group. As was true in their first edition of *The Exemplary Middle School* in 1981, the characteristics of the middle school concept and its implementation are illustrated in the practice of 1,100 actual middle schools around the United States. George and Alexander, giants in the field of middle school education, have dedicated their careers searching for the enhancement of a developmentally appropriate education model for young adolescents. The authors have come to consensus on what is representative of exemplary practices in middle school education by utilizing their considerable expertise, including the recommendations of other middle school educators, and the literature on middle school education. This most recent text version critically examines the tenets of middle school philosophy and organization, attempting to bridge the gap between the theoretical underpinnings with the practices reported in schools. There are 10 chapters in this textbook along with references, a roster of exemplary middle schools, and an author and subject index. The chapter titles include: The Middle School Students (Chaper 1), the Middle School Movement and Concept (Chapter 2), the Middle School Curriculum (Chapter 3), Instruction (Chapter 4), Managing and Mentoring Middle Schoolers (Chapter 5), Interdisciplinary Team Organization (Chapter 6), Grouping Students in the Middle School (Chapter 7), Organizing Time and Space in the Middle School (Chapter 8), Planning and Evaluating the Exemplary Middle School (Chapter 9), and Middle School Leadership (Chapter 10). These topics remain fairly consistent with the organization of the first edition over 20 years ago, albeit the insertion of the middle school student as Chapter 1. This change is significant as it denotes the critical importance of understanding this unique developmental period of young adolescence and the student population often identified as "at-risk." Chapter 5 in the latest edition encompasses teacher guidance and infuses the preventive and supportive rationale of classroom management. The authors allude that the middle school organization itself can mitigate excessive discipline problems.

It is evident that this edition's reorganization incorporates research knowledge on content area reading and text organization and in addition provides extensive up-to-date illustrative materials. A text 'hook' introduces the chapter whereas the reader is usually introduced to an exemplary school, or in the case of Chapter 1, "The Middle School Student", information from the New York Times Magazine section illustrates the rise is early puberty in girls. Chapter 1 also provides a summary of the remaining chapters I the textbook. Next, a chapter preview alerts the reader as to the chapter's content and the remainder of the chapter content is organized by headings and subheadings. Beginning with Chapter 2, each chapter has a conclusion, a content summary, a connections to other chapters, questions for discussion, and action steps. The final chapter section suggestions for further study includes books, periodicals, ERIC sources, and dissertations and dissertation abstracts (Chapters 9 & 10), as did the first edition. In addition, this section lists, videotapes, and appropriate annotated Web sites along with the comprehensive reference section at the end of the text are especially useful for further study and exploration. The reference section includes supplemental middle school sources that are a part of the end of chapter references. This third edition is an excellent text resource for all those interested in middle school education.

REFERENCE

George, P. S., & Alexander, W. M. (2003). *The exemplary middle school* (3rd ed). Belmont: CA: Wadsworth/Thomson Learning.

—Michele Jean Sims
University of Alabama, Birmingham

EXPLORATORY CURRICULUM

The concept of exploratory curriculum is a cornerstone and integral component of middle level education. The concept brings together two critical elements of middle school organization: curriculum and exploration. Curriculum refers to the instructional program or plan to engage students in learning. Exploration is the act of exploring, which has multiple meanings such as investigating systematically, traveling over new territory for the purpose of discovery, and becoming familiar with by experimentation. In middle level education, exploration includes "those offerings in the middle level school that encourage and allow students to explore new arenas of interest, both as specific courses and as methodology within courses" (Bergman, 1992, p. 179). Broadly viewed, exploration applies to the entire middle level curriculum, though in practice it exists as a portion of the day in distinct "exploratory" courses (Brazee, 2000; George, 2000/2001). Exploratory curriculum is developmentally responsive to young adolescent in middle level schools.

The purposes of this unique curriculum component are: (1) to be responsive to the developmental needs and characteristics of young adolescent learners, 10 to 15 year olds (George & Lawrence, 1982); (2) to provide a balance or an extension of the curriculum (Curtis & Bidwell, 1977; George & Lawrence, 1982; Tanner & Tanner, 1980); and (3) to allow for opportunities to "look into" or "try out" a particular area of interest (Briggs, 1920). Participation in the exploratory curriculum allows young adolescents to develop areas of personal interest, a vocation or avocation, a leisure activity as well as to identify areas of disinterest or areas that they do not have the requisite aptitude, skills, or motivation needed to pursue a particular area. Further, students' lives can be greatly enriched when given opportunities in school to derive personal satisfaction and gratification from varied, exciting, and challenging activities that are not strictly academic (Romano & Georgiady, 1994). Overall, exploratory curricula enhance young adolescents' school experiences.

EMERGENCE OF EXPLORATORY CURRICULUM

The origins of exploratory curriculum for middle level education extend back to early education in America. The Academy founded by Benjamin Franklin in 1751 broadened educational opportunities for students. Franklin believed that secondary education needed to prepare students for occupations in the increasingly complex colonies (Curtis & Bidwell, 1977). Subsequently, a general education curriculum appeared in secondary schools. During the 1800s, the high school became the common secondary institution. High school curriculum expanded to include programs for students not bound for college (Gruhn & Douglass, 1947) and extracurricular activities (Bergman, 1992). Between the 1890s and 1920s, school reorganization studies and resulting reports provided the impetus for change in American education. In 1893, the Committee of Ten on Secondary Education made recommendations about preparation for higher education that led to the restructuring of the elementary and secondary education. The Commission on the Reorganization of Secondary Education (1918) released the *Cardinal Principals of Secondary Education* that included a clear recommendation for the division secondary education into "junior and senior periods" (p. 13). The report articulated, "In the junior period

emphasis should be placed upon the attempt to help the pupil to explore his own aptitudes and to make at least provisional choice of the kinds of work to which he will devote himself" (p. 13). The underlying aims of the *Cardinal Principals* included preparing young people for a democratic society, recognizing individual differences and the nature of adolescents, and providing for exploration and guidance (Koos, 1920).

In the early 1900s, the junior high school developed to "bridge the gap between the elementary grades and secondary education, to provide for the needs of early adolescence, and to direct them intelligently toward work or advanced study" (Briggs, 1933, p. 97). Exploratory curriculum was central to the junior high model. Exploration was inherent to the junior high school's five functions: (1) to continue common integrating curriculum, (2) to ascertain and satisfy students' immediate and future needs, (3) to explore students' interests, aptitudes, and capacity, (4) to reveal possibilities in the fields of learning, and (5) to start students on a career path (Briggs, 1920, pp. 162-174). Exploration connected initially with the advisory function of the secondary curriculum and addressed the "differentiation" of the curriculum for adolescents. Exploratory experiences helped students to make vocational decisions and extend the curriculum for students to pursue interests in the subject matter courses (Koos, 1920).

In an effort to realize the aims of education in the junior high school program, Gruhn and Douglas (1947) identified seven functions of the junior high school. *Function II: Exploration* listed explicitly the responsibilities of an exploratory curriculum: (1) to lead students to discover and explore their specialized interests, aptitudes, and abilities as a basis for education decisions; (2) to lead students to discover and explore their specialized interests, aptitudes, and abilities as a basis for vocational decisions; (3) to provide opportunities for students to develop cultural, social, civic, avocational, and recreational interests; and (4) to help students identify what motivate them to continue their formal education and participate in educational activities for individual growth and development (p. 75). Gruhn and Douglas also referenced exploration in the *Guidance* and *Differentiation* functions. The *Guidance* function supported students in making "intelligent decisions regarding present educational activities and opportunities and to prepare them to make future educational decisions" (p. 75). The function of *Differentiation* provided for "learning activities in all areas of the educational program which will be challenging, satisfying, and at a level of achievement appropriate for pupils of different backgrounds, interest, abilities, and needs" (p. 76). Exploration, as described for the junior high school, remains the foundation for exploratory curriculum in middle level education.

As the middle school emerged in the 1960s, leaders of the movement shared their vision of exploratory curriculum and articulated how to incorporate this component into the middle school. In many cases, middle school educators adopted the same philosophy and terminology of exploration outlined for high schools and junior high schools. To ensure that exploratory curriculum was developmentally appropriate for young adolescents, educators modified the design, purposes, and guidelines for student participation. Middle level educators came to view exploratory curriculum as program offerings that: (1) is short term in duration; (2) has high interest to young adolescents; (3) incorporates decision making; (4) typically involves hands-on experiences; (5) includes assessment appropriate for the nature of the course; and (6) allows students to select an area of interest (Alexander, Williams, Compton, Hines, & Prescott, 1968, Bergman, 1992; Eichhorn, 1966; Lounsbury & Vars, 1978; National Middle School Association NMSA, 1995).

Professional organizations acknowledged exploration as a critical component of middle level education throughout the 1980s, 1990s, and into the twenty-first century. The National Middle School Association (NMSA) advanced exploration in *This We Believe*, a position statement regarding the rationale and essential elements of the middle school concept (NMSA, 1982). The rationale for the middle school was to bridge young adolescent students' intellectual, social, physical, and emotional characteristics and needs to the school's programs and practices. One of the essential elements of the middle school was a "full exploratory" program to meet the developmental needs of young adolescents. The program included "minicourses, exploratory courses, service clubs, special interest activities, and independent study projects" (NMSA, 1982, p. 18). Next, the National Association of Secondary School Principal's (NASSP) Council on Middle Level Education reported that curriculum should include exploratory programs that introduce students to a variety of topics (NASSP, 1985). Then, the Carnegie Council on Adolescent Development (1989) called attention to the rapid developmental stage of young adolescence and recommended that curriculum transmit a core of common knowledge to foster curiosity, problem-solving, and critical thinking. Beane (1993) asserted that a middle school curriculum needed to emerge from the intersection of students' personal concerns and social issues. Less than a decade later, the focus shifted to include curriculum

grounded in public standards and relevant to students (Jackson & Davis, 2000). The notion of exploration broadened to encompass the entire middle school curriculum which needed to be challenging, integrative, and exploratory as well as relevant (NMSA, 1995, 2003).

CONCEPTUALIZING EXPLORATORY CURRICULUM

The idea of exploration is broad-based and many terms describe how exploratory curriculum occurs in middle level schools. Educators refer to exploratory curriculum as required exploratory, unified arts, electives, cocurricular activities, extracurricular activities, student activities, minicourses, and independent study (Alexander & George, 1981, Lounsbury & Vars, 1978). Terminology for these exploratory options changes depending on the era and the author's categorization or description. Other variables that influence exploratory terminology include the purpose, educational objectives, the design of the exploratory activity, the teachers involved, and the schedule of the offerings.

Exploratory programs afford young adolescents with opportunities to investigate areas of study not introduced as part of the core curriculum. Typically, core curriculum refers to English/Language arts, mathematics, social studies, and science, while exploratory curriculum extends beyond academic designations. Components of a broad exploratory program for the middle school include: (1) a required cycle of general exploratory experiences for 6, 9, or 12 weeks; (2) electives that follow the required exploratory experiences for a full-semester or year; (3) interest-centered minicourses for short-term enrichment; (4) independent study as an outgrowth of academic work or personal interest; (5) clubs, organizations, and assemblies that offer opportunities for governance and meaningful service; and (6) an exploratory approach to teaching all subject areas (Lounsbury, 1991, pp. 65-66). Central to the concept of exploration and the exploratory curriculum is "a conscientious effort of a school to provide opportunities for students to discover, in a fairly threat free setting, their strengths, weaknesses, likes, dislikes, and potential future curriculum choices" (Compton & Hawn, 1993, p. 16).

Middle level educators promote the concept and provide examples from middle schools as to the arrangement and activities included in exploratory program (Bergman, 1992; Brazee, 2000; George, Lawrence, & Bushnell, 1998; Waks, 2002). Some schools use a separate course approach, while others infuse exploration throughout the curriculum. Common to the design of exploratory curriculum is the participation of every student in exploration of the middle school curriculum (George & Lawrence, 1982; Lounsbury & Vars, 1978). Guidelines for exploration suggest that the activities provide for student choice, have high interest, be short term, and engage actively students. These activities may also be noncompetitive, nongraded, allow for noncompletion, and foster successful initial experiences for students.

PRACTICES AND RESEARCH

Researchers uncovered information about exploratory curriculum when examining middle school programs and practices in national studies. In 1968, Alexander examined the organizational patterns of more than 100 middle schools. He found that music, art, home economics, and industrial arts were required in about half of the middle schools; however, electives and other exploratory opportunities were thin in many schools (Alexander et al., 1968). In 1988, Alexander and McEwin replicated the study of middle schools and noted shifting organizational patterns from Grades 7-9 to Grades 6-8. After identifying popular electives and frequently offered electives, they concluded that middle schools should provide a full-scale exploratory program (Alexander & McEwin, 1989). In a study of successful middle schools, Lipsitz (1984) noted that exploratory courses provided the most interesting and innovative learning experiences for young adolescents. Epstein and Mac Iver (1990) found that middle grades schools provided academic subjects, physical education, but very few course choices. Only 30-40% of the survey students had opportunities to take elective/exploratory courses. In 1993 and 2001, McEwin, Dickinson, and Jenkins (2003) conducted additional studies that revealed little change in exploratory course offerings, yet increasing percentages of middle schools offering special interest classes or mini courses.

ISSUES WITH EXPLORATORY

Although many educators support exploratory curriculum (e.g., Lounsbury, 1991), others criticize this component. Criticisms include the perception that exploratory programs lack academic rigor and limit time and budgets of the academic core; create a regrettable tension between core and exploratory teachers; and place additional demands on teachers and administrators to design, implement, and evaluate this curriculum component. To ameliorate these concerns, Brazee (2000) recommends aligning exploratory courses and experiences with the core curriculum.

Standards-based educational reform also influences exploratory curriculum. Accountability pressures including the increase of high stakes tests compete for time within the regular academic schedule. Exploratory classes are limited to provide remedial or additional instruction for low performing students. George (2001) remains optimistic that exploratory curriculum will survive the standards-based reform movement and continue to be an important part of the middle school curriculum.

REFERENCES

Alexander, W. M., & George, P. S. (1981). *The exemplary middle school.* New York: Holt, Rinehart, & Winston.

Alexander, W. M., & McEwin, C. K. (1989). *Schools in the middle: Progress 1968-1988. Schools in the middle: A report on trends and practices.* Reston, VA: National Association of Secondary School Principals.

Alexander, W. M., Williams, E. I., Compton, M., Hines, V. A., & Prescott, D. (1968). *The emergent middle school.* New York: Holt, Rinehart, & Winston.

Beane, J. A. (1993). *The middle school curriculum: From rhetoric to reality* (2nd ed.). Columbus, OH: National Middle School Association.

Bergman, S. (1992). Exploratory programs in the middle level school: A responsive idea. In J. L. Irvin (Ed.), *Transforming middle level education: Perspectives and possibilities* (pp. 179-192). Boston: Allyn & Bacon.

Brazee, E. (2000). *Exploratory curriculum in the middle school.* (ERIC ED447970).

Briggs, T. H. (1920). *The junior high school.* Boston: Houghton Mifflin.

Briggs, T. H. (1933). *Secondary education.* New York: MacMillan.

Carnegie Council on Adolescent Development. (1989). *Turning points: Preparing American youth for the 21st century.* New York: Carnegie.

Commission on Reorganization of the Secondary School. (1918). Cardinal principles of secondary (Bulletin 1918 #35). Washington, DC: U.S. Department of the Interior, Bureau of Education. [Electronic version.] Retrieved May 5, 2005, from http://www.stanford.edu/~dlabaree/Cardinal%20Principles%20Report.doc

Compton, M. F., & Hawn, H. C. (1993). *Exploration: The total curriculum.* Columbus, OH: National Middle School Curriculum.

Curtis, T. E., & Bidwell, W. W. (1977). *Curriculum and instruction for emerging adolescents.* Reading, MA: Addision-Wesley.

Eichhorn, D. E. (1966). *The middle school.* New York: The Center for Applied Research in Education.

Epstein, J. L., & Mac Iver, D. J. (1990). *Education in the middle grades: National practices and research.* Columbus, OH: National Middle School Association.

George, P. S. (2000/2001). The evolution of middle schools. *Educational Leadership, 58*(4), 40-51.

George, P., & Lawrence, G. (1982). *Handbook for middle school teaching*. Glenview, IL: Scott, Foresman.

George, P., Lawrence, G., & Bushnell, D. (1998). *Handbook for middle school teaching* (2nd ed.) New York: Longman.

Gruhn, W. T., & Douglass, H. R. (1947). *The modern junior high school*. New York: The Ronald Press.

Jackson, A. W., & Davis, G. A. (2000). *Turning points 2000: Educating adolescents in the 21st century*. New York: Teachers College Press.

Koos, L. V. (1920). *The junior high school*. New York: Harcourt, Brace, & Howe.

Lipsitz, J. (1984). *Successful schools for young adolescents*. New Brunswick, NJ: Transaction.

Lounsbury, J. H. (1991). *As I see it*. Columbus, OH: National Middle School Association.

Lounsbury, J. H., & Vars, G. F. (1978). *A curriculum for the middle school years*. New York: Harper & Row.

McEwin, C. K., Dickinson, T. S., & Jenkins, D. M. (2003). *America's middle schools in the new century: Status and progress*. Westerville, OH: National Middle School Association.

National Association of Secondary School Principals. (1985). *An agenda for excellence at the middle level*. Reston, VA: Author.

National Middle School Association. (1982). *This we believe*. Columbus, OH: Author.

National Middle School Association. (1995). *This we believe: Developmentally responsive middle level schools*. Columbus, OH: Author.

National Middle School Association. (2003). *This we believe: Successful schools for young adolescents*. Westerville, OH: Author.

Romano, L. G., & Georgiady, N. P. (1994). *Building an effective middle school*. Madison, WI: WCB Brown & Benchmark.

Tanner, D. & Tanner, L. N. (1980). *Curriculum development: Theory into practice*. New York: Macmillan.

Waks, L. J. (2002). Exploratory education in a society of knowledge and risk. In V. A. Anfara, Jr. & S. L. Stacki (Eds.), *Curriculum, instruction, and assessment* (pp. 23-40). Greenwich, CT: Information Age.

—Barbara Whinery
University of Northern Colorado

—Micki M. Caskey
Portland State University

F

FAMILY INVOLVEMENT AND PARTNERSHIPS

The term "family involvement" refers to family member support of their child's academic and social development. Family involvement generally includes voluntary engagement in the school and at home and/or participation in planned programs that involve partnerships between families, schools, and community groups. In this entry, "family involvement" will refer to voluntary family involvement at school or home. The term "partnerships" will be used to describe planned, organized, goal driven, and purposeful programs that encourage family participation in school, family and community partnerships.

Many policy statements and reports call for increased family and community involvement at the middle level. Significant reports including *Turning Points 2000* (Jackson & Davis, 2000), three reports by the Carnegie Council on Adolescent Development (1989, 1992, 1995) and *This We Believe ... and Now We Must Act* (Erb, 2001) identify family and community support of children as paramount to increasing academic achievement and sustaining their healthy development. The No Child Left Behind Act of 2001 (2002) continues an emphasis on family involvement that has been federal policy and law since the 1988 Hawkins-Stafford Elementary and Secondary School Improvement Amendments to P.L. 100-297. NCLB requires that schools develop a written policy for parent involvement in consultation with parents.

Numerous researchers have identified ways that family involvement benefits children. Yap and Enoki (1995) found a significant relationship between home-based parental involvement activities and student achievement. Henderson and Mapp's (2002) examination of 51 studies found that the more families are involved with their children's education, the more successful their children are in school (see Bickel, 1995; Connors & Epstein, 1995; Flaxman & Inger, 1992; Hidalso, Siu, Bright, Swap, & Epstein, 1995; Hoover-Dempsey & Sandler, 1995; Moore, 1991; Riley, 1994; Rutherford, Billig, & Kettering, 1993). Much of the research regarding family involvement and partnerships is done at the elementary level. A smaller body of research examines family involvement at the middle level.

Programs involving educators and parents which modify what Walberg (1984) identified as the alterable curriculum of the home (including such factors as informed conversations, leisure reading, regulating television viewing, and peer activities) have an effect of twice that of socioeconomic status in children's achievement. Clark (1983) found that "linguistic capital" (the family members as teachers providing instruction in language skills) and what Coleman (1989) identified as "social capital" (family interest, intimacy and involvement with children over time) influence the school achievement of children.

Epstein (1995) developed a typology to provide a framework to identify ways that families are involved in their child's education. The typology includes six types of involvement—parenting, communicating, learning at home, decision making, and collaborating with the community. All six types of involvement are multidirectional. Each group (families, schools, and community resources and services) interacts with the others in a mutually supportive way. For example, involvement in parenting includes the school assisting families with parenting skills, the families assisting schools in understanding their backgrounds and cultures, and the community providing social services to support parenting (Epstein & Jansom, 2004).

The findings on the effectiveness of family involvement on achievement are mixed. The National Middle School Association (NMSA) research summary, *Parent Involvement and Student Achievement at the Middle Level*, indicates that although some studies find a relationship between family involvement and student achievement other studies do not support such findings (NMSA, 2000). The large number of variables that influence student achievement challenge researchers' ability to isolate single factors that influence student success in school and in life. The educational level of the parents, socioeconomic status, the culture or racial/ethnic groups involved, and the efforts of the school to invite family participation all contribute to family involvement. One finding is clear, family involvement decreases when children reach the middle level (Epstein, 1996).

FACTORS THAT INFLUENCE FAMILY INVOLVEMENT AT THE MIDDLE LEVEL

Families' ability to respond to opportunities to interact with the school and with their children at home is influenced by social class, family structure, employment obligations, the need for child care, transportation difficulties, inconvenient meeting time, and limited financial resources to provide materials for their children (Moles, 1993). One factor that shapes the way families are involved in their children's education is the family's perception of what their role should be (Hoover-Dempsey & Sandler, 1995). Many families, especially recent immigrant and minority families, may view their role in their children's education differently than the school views their role. Hispanic and Southeast Asian immigrants often come from countries where family involvement is viewed as interference. From this perspective, questioning the actions of the school or teachers would be inappropriate (Moles, 1993; Yap & Enoki, 1995). A family's belief in their ability to help their children is also influenced by their social class, how a family member's parents were involved with their education, and how a family's friends are involved in schools.

Family involvement in the school decreases when students reach the middle school for several reasons. The transition from elementary school to the middle school can be unsettling for families and children and present challenges to family involvement. If the school is departmentalized by content areas students often have several teachers and it is difficult for both families and teachers to build relationships (Epstein &

Connors, 1993; Musser, 1998). Early adolescent development in itself can be an obstacle to family involvement. The physical, mental, and social changes in early adolescent development result in children wanting more independence from their families but also needing support and reassurance. The middle school curriculum also may intimidate some families. Family members may lack the skills to assist children with homework. Families and children may also be confused regarding the role families should play in assisting with homework at the middle level. The challenges faced by families in the transition from elementary school to middle school are often compounded by a lack of outreach by the school to welcome family involvement and provide assistance to families (Juvonen, Le, Kaganoff, Augustine, & Constant, 2004).

PARTNERSHIPS

The term "partnerships" refers to planned, organized, goal driven, and purposeful programs developed over time that encourage family, school, and community members to work together to support children. The partners work toward shared goals, contributing strengths and assists, sharing information, and supporting each other (Swap, 1993). The concepts of partnerships are based on a child-centered model of human development formulated by Bronfenbrenner (1979) and applied by Connors and Epstein (1995) in the overlapping spheres of influence model. The overlapping spheres of influence model recognizes that schools, family, community, and peers all contribute to a child's academic achievement and social development in different ways at different times. There are some times when the spheres of influence (family, school, community, and peers) operate separately and other times when they overlap and interact with each other. The times when the spheres overlap and families, schools, and community forces work together to support children are theoretically the most effective in influencing children.

Administrators, policy makers, and teachers are key players in the implementation of partnerships. Rutherford et al. (1993) and Chavkin (1993) have identified elements that are critical factors to the implementation of partnerships. These are: (a) communication; (b) the involvement of key players; (c) the allocation of resources sufficient to provide training, implementation, and coordination of programs; and (d) formal written policies and goals. Epstein (2004) emphasized that an action plan for partnerships developed with input from all families can help focus partnerships to provide a welcoming environment where educators, students, families, and community partners work together to meet school goals for student achievement and success. The one-year action plan used by the National Network of Partnership Schools (NNPS) meets the NCLB requirements for a comprehensive partnership program.

Well-developed partnership programs that include outreach to families by teachers can overcome many of the challenges faced by families in meeting the expectations of family involvement mentioned above. When teachers encourage family members and provide opportunities to be involved their participation increases.

An inclusive partnership program includes community interactions that involve children participating in community-based programs, extracurricular activities, and services provided by community agencies. The Carnegie Council on Adolescent Development (1992) reported that there are more than 17,000 youth-serving organizations operating in the United States. They include national organizations such as the Boy Scouts and 4-H Clubs and many small local organizations such as religious youth groups and parks and recreation programs. Joekel (1985) reported that when examining influences on future achievement, participation in extracurricular activities was more indicative of success than high grades in high school, high grades in college, or high scores on the ACT. Clear communication and interactions between family, school, and community organizations can help all three groups coordinate efforts to give all children opportunities to participate in valuable community activities (Musser, 1998).

CHALLENGES TO THE FORMATION OF PARTNERSHIPS

Despite the indications from research of the benefits of school, family, and community partnerships, there are numerous obstacles to the formation of these partnerships. Perceptions, attitudes, and beliefs regarding partnerships may differ dramatically between and among the family, school, and community members. This is true regardless of the participants' class, ethnicity, or cultural background. However, the obstacles presented by differing perceptions, attitudes, values, and beliefs are exacerbated when teachers and parents come from different cultures, races, or class backgrounds, or when they view themselves as different from other groups because of memberships in a different culture, race, or class

(Chavkin, 1993; Epstein & Dauber, 1989; Musser, 2004).

Much of the research regarding partnerships has been from the school's perspective. As Ginn (1994) pointed out, research on family involvement focuses on the perspective of educators, and that families are "Somewhat depersonalized; they are 'objectified'; it is difficult to think of parents as living, breathing humans or know what involvement means for them" (p. 39). Frequently family members are viewed as deficient. Partnerships depend on cooperation and mutual respect. Overcoming an assumption of deficiency and the negotiation of value differences are necessary for partnerships to build a culture of support and care that benefits children.

Teachers face some of the same obstacles to participating in partnerships as families. Teachers are human beings who also have roles as family members and community members. Frequently teachers do not have training regarding how to communicate and interact with parents and community members (Kirschenbaum, 2001). Teachers may have difficulty communicating with all families but especially with families from cultures and socioeconomic groups that are different from the teachers'. This results in frustration and misconceptions on the parts of all involved.

Teachers also may feel threatened by family and community involvement in the school. Ryan and Freidlaender (1996) found that tensions develop if teachers perceive that families are overstepping their bounds and that parent scrutiny is viewed as a threat or as questioning their expert status as educators. There is also some evidence to suggest that teacher beliefs and misconception of family attitudes contribute to barriers developing between teachers and families. Some teachers blame families for their children's problems and see family attitudes as obstacles to developing partnerships (Leitch & Tangri, 1988). The formation of partnerships that provide training for teachers and provide the opportunity for teachers and families to build relationships can overcome these obstacles (Musser, 2004).

The obstacles to the development of partnerships can be overcome by establishing culture where the education of children is viewed as a joint effort between family, school and community members. To establish a context where this goal can be met, participants in a partnership need to recognize the importance of the contributions of all of the people who support the child's healthy development and academic achievement.

LINKS TO INFORMATION ABOUT PARTNERSHIP PROGRAMS

The value of partnerships in supporting children's' academic achievement and social development is demonstrated by the number of partnership models in place to help families, schools, and community members develop partnerships. The following are a few:

- The National Network of Partnership Schools (NNPS) at Johns Hopkins University (http://www.csos.jhu.edu/p2000/)
- The Family Involvement Network of Educators, Harvard Graduate School of Education (http://www.finenetwork.org)
- The Partnership for Family Involvement in Education (http://www.ed.gov/pubs/whoweare/intro.html#partership)
- In the August 2004 issue of *Middle Ground*, Brenda Dyck (2004) provides internet links to 13 organizations that provide information regarding school, family, and community partnerships.

REFERENCES

Bickel, A. S. (1995). *Family involvement: Strategies for comprehensive alcohol, tobacco, and other drug use prevention programs.* Portland, OR: Northwest Regional Educational Laboratory, Western Regional Center for Drug-Free Schools and Communities.

Bronfenbrenner, U. (1979). *The ecology of human development: Experiments by nature and design.* Cambridge, MA: Harvard University Press.

Carnegie Council on Adolescent Development. (1989). *Turning points: Preparing youth for the 21st century.* New York: Carnegie Corporation, Task Force on Education of Young Adolescents.

Carnegie Council on Adolescent Development. (1992). *A matter of time: Risk and opportunity in the nonschool hours.* New York: Carnegie Corporation, Task Force on Youth Development and Community Programs.

Carnegie Council on Adolescent Development. (1995). *Great transitions: Preparing adolescents for a new century.* New York: Carnegie.

Chavkin, N. F. (Ed.). (1993). *Families and schools in a pluralistic society.* Albany: State University of New York Press.

Clark, R. M. (1983). *Family life and school achievement: Why poor black children succeed or fail.* Chicago: University of Chicago Press.

Coleman, J. S. (1989). The family, the community, and the future of education. In W. J. Weston (Ed.), *Education and the American family: A research synthesis* (pp. 169-185). New York: New York University Press

Weston (Ed.), *Education and the American family: A research synthesis* (pp. 169-185). New York: New York University Press.

Connors, L. J., & Epstein, J. L. (1995). Parent and school partnerships. In M. H. Bornstein (Ed.), *Handbook of parenting, volume 4: Applied and practical parenting* (pp 437-458). Mahwah, NJ: Erlbaum.

Dyck, B. A. (2004). Hot Links. *Middle Ground, 8*(1), 13.

Epstein, J. L. (1995). School/family/community partnerships: caring for the children we share. *Phi Delta Kappan, 76*(9), 701-712.

Epstein, J. L. (1996). Improving school-family-community partnerships in the middle grades. *Middle School Journal, 28*(2), 43-48.

Epstein, J. L. (2004). Meeting NCLB requirements for family involvement. *Middle Ground, 8*(1) 14-16.

Epstein, J. L., & Connors, L. J. (1993). School and family partnerships in the middle grades. In RMC Research Corporation (Ed.), *Parent and community involvement in the middle grades: Evaluating education reform* (pp. 81-122). Denver, CO: RMC Research.

Epstein, J. L., & Dauber, S. L. (1989). *Teacher attitudes and practices of parent involvement in inner-city elementary and middle schools* (Report No. 32). Baltimore, MD: Center for Research on Elementary and Middle Schools, The Johns Hopkins University. (ERIC ED314 151)

Epstein, J. L., & Jansom, N. R. (2004). School, family, and community partnerships link the plan. *Education Digest, 69*(6) 19-23. Retrieved June 5, 2004, from: http://search.epnet. com/direct.asp?an=12233064&db=aph

Erb, T. (Ed.). (2001). *This we believe . . . and now we must act.* Columbus, OH: National Middle School Association.

Flaxman, E., & Inger, M. (1992). Parents and schooling in the 1990s. *Principal, 72*(7), 16-18.

Ginn, L. W. (1994). Understanding people one at a time: A portrait of parental involvement. *The School Community Journal, 4*(2), 39-51.

Henderson, A. T., & Mapp, K. L. (2002). *A new wave of evidence: The impact of school family ad community connections on student achievement.* Austin, TX: Southwest Educational Development Laboratory, National Center for Family and Community Connections with Schools.

Hidalso, N. M., Siu, S., Bright, J. A., Swap, S. M., & Epstein, J. L. (1995). Research on families, schools, and communities: A multicultural perspective. In J. A. Banks (Ed.), *Handbook of research on multicultural education* (pp. 498-524). New York: Macmillan.

Hoover-Dempsey, K. V., & Sandler, H. M. (1995). Parental involvement in children's education: Why does it make a difference? *Teachers College Record, 97*(2), 310-331.

Jackson, A. W., & Davis, G. A. (2000). *Turning points 2000: Educating adolescents in the 21st century.* New York: Teachers College Press.

Joekel, R. G. (1985). Student activities and academic eligibility requirements. *NASSP Bulletin, 69*(483), 3-9.

Juvonen, J., Le, V., Kaganoff, T., Augustine, C., & Constant, L. (2004). *Focus on the wonder years: Challenges facing the American middle school.* Santa Monica, CA: RAND.

Kirschenbaum, H. (2001). Educating professionals for school, family and community partnerships. In D. B. Hiatt-Michael (Ed.), *Promising practices for family involve-*

ment in schools (pp. 185-208). Greenwich, CT: Information Age.

Leitch, M. L., & Tangri, S. S. (1988). Barriers to home-school collaboration. *Educational Horizons, 66*(2), 70-74.

Moles, O. C. (1993). Collaboration between schools and disadvantaged parents: Obstacles and openings. In N. R. Chavkin (Ed.), *Families and schools in a pluralistic society* (pp. 21-49). Albany: State University of New York Press.

Moore, E. K. (1991). Improving schools through parental involvement. *Principal, 71*(1), 17-20.

Musser, P. M. (1998). *Partnerships at the middle level: Perception of family members, community members, and teachers.* Ann Arbor, MI: UMI Dissertation Services.

Musser, P. M. (2004). Listening to the voices of family members, teachers, and community members. *Research in Middle Level Education Online 27*(2). Retrieved August 20, 2004, from http://www.nmsa.org/research/rmle/spring04/article_2.htm

National Middle School Association. (2000). *Research summary # 18: Parent involvement and student achievement at the middle level.* Retrieved June 5, 2004, from http://www.nmsa.org/research/ressum18.htm

No Child Left Behind Act of 2001, Pub. L. No. 107-110, 115 Stat. 1425 (2002).

Riley, R. W. (1994). *Strong families, strong schools: Building community partnerships for learning.* Washington DC: U.S. Department of Education. (ERIC ED371909)

Rutherford, B., Billig, S. H., & Kettering, J. F. (1993). *Parent and community involvement in the middle grades: Evaluating educational reform.* Denver, CO: RMC Research.

Ryan, S., & Freidlaender, D. (1996). Strengthening relationships to create caring school communities. *Research in Middle Level Education Quarterly, 20*(1), 41-68.

Swap, S. M. (1993). *Developing home-school partnerships: From concepts to practice.* New York: Teachers College Press, Columbia University.

Walberg, J. J. (1984). Improving the productivity of America's schools. *Educational Leadership, 41*(8), 19-27.

Yap, K. O., & Enoki, D. Y. (1995). In search of the elusive magic bullet: Parental involvement and student outcomes. *The School Community Journal, 5*(2), 97-106.

—P. Maureen Musser
Willamette University

GARVIN, JAMES P.

James Garvin is responsible for leading the development of the nation's first middle school teacher preparation program for undergraduate students and founding and expanding the New England League of Middle Schools. Having received a BA in guidance from Gordon College, Garvin began his teaching career at Shore Country Day School, Beverly, MA, as a history teacher for grades seven to nine. Garvin joined the faculty of Gordon College in 1969 as Associate Dean of Students, after completing his masters degree in educational psychology. Middle school teacher preparation was only a small portion of Gordon's teacher preparation program at that time. Fifteen miles north in Newburyport, MA, the Rupert Nock Middle School was in development as a fully-functioning, model middle school. The school opened in 1972, and discussions between Garvin and Nock Middle School principal, Henry Criss revealed the twin needs of practicum placement for middle school pre-service teachers and middle school teacher preparation curriculum. Soon Gordon College had the nation's first middle school teacher preparation program, developed in collaboration with an existing middle school and with the guidance and input from practicing middle school educators.

Among its significant features, the program provided potential education majors early exposure to the middle school classroom. Garvin was convinced of the need for these students to experience the classroom early in their own academic career to observe, reflect, and analyze classroom dynamics, curriculum, and pedagogy. He felt this early introduction was necessary for education majors to begin examination of their own experiences, views, and expectations about

teaching and learning. Soon the teacher preparation curriculum across the K-12 continuum at Gordon College included early and frequent interactions between education majors and their intended teaching grade level. Garvin expanded his professional expertise as well as additional opportunities for middle school education majors to work directly with and learn from young adolescents by developing and directing the Gordon Summer Day Camp.

The quality and innovation of Gordon's middle school education program brought national recognition, and Garvin was invited to chair the Massachusetts Professional Advisory Committee to develop middle grades standards and competencies. Schools throughout the Commonwealth and across the nation sought his guidance as they examined their practices and professional development. As Executive Director of the New England League of Middle Schools, Garvin led the fight for the new middle level certification program. Garvin was a site visitor for the U.S. Department of Education's Schools of Excellence program, and was later invited to the White House by President Reagan in connection with this service.

Garvin is the recipient of the NELMS Distinguished Service Award (1987), which was subsequently renamed in his honor; the NMSA President's Award (1987); the Massachusetts Junior High/Middle School Principals Association Outstanding Service Award (1987); and the Gordon College Faculty Member of the Year (1976). After more than 20 years at Gordon College, Garvin moved to Florida where he has assisted Fortune 500 companies, including Champion International, MBNA, International Paper and Union Pacific Railroad, to develop business partnership programs.

—Mary Henton
National Middle School Association

GEORGE, PAUL S.

Identified in 1994 as the "number one ranking scholar" in the field of middle school education (Scales, 1994), Paul S. George has concentrated his research and teaching in the areas of school organization and management, including the application of corporate organizational strategies to the improvement of public education, and instructional grouping. He is responsible for six national institutes on alternatives to ability grouping, and has conducted and published funded research, reviews of research, and staff development materials on student grouping.

George began his teaching career in 1964 as a high school and middle grades social studies teacher in Ohio and Tennessee. He has taught at the college level since 1969, when he was instructor in education at Belmont College (TN), then Assistant Professor of Education, Monmouth College (IL). In 1971 Dr. George moved to University of Florida in 1971 as an Assistant Professor of Education. In 1976 he was granted status of Doctoral Research Faculty, and in 1981, became Professor of Education.

George's work extends far beyond the college classroom to extensive consultation work with schools, school districts, and other educational organizations. In addition, since 1982, he has developed additional expertise in Japanese schools.

George is responsible for expanding the knowledge capital of middle grades education by translating his research into over a hundred articles, monographs, videos, and other publications. He is author or coauthor of 10 books, including *The Theory of School: Beyond Effectiveness* (George, 1983) and *The Exemplary Middle School*, coauthored with William Alexander (1981). Considered a classic in the field, *The Exemplary Middle School* has been revised and expanded in second and third editions, and outlines the six elements which characterize a middle school:

1. School guidance systems in which each student has a counselor who knows him/her well and with whom the student can consult on academic, social, and personal matters.
2. A transitional curriculum which provides for careful articulation and coordination of learning experiences.
3. Daily schedules organized into blocks of instructional time to allow for interdisciplinary instruction and appropriate learning experiences.
4. Use of a variety of instructional strategies that have been demonstrated to be effective with early adolescents (such as cooperative learning, interdisciplinary instruction, team teaching).
5. A wide range of exploratory courses designed to develop student interests, and an emphasis on intramural athletics which encourages participation by all students.
6. A core of learning experiences appropriate to early adolescents focused on learning skills that students will need for future study (George & Alexander, 2003).

George is founder of the Florida League of Middle Schools and honored as its first Executive Director at the 25th Annual Florida League of Middle Schools Conference, 1995. He is also recipient of the Middle School Educator of the Year Award from the Florida League. George was a vanguard of the first European Conference on Middle Level Education, held in Brussels, January 1986. A direct result of his leadership role in the second European Conference, 1987, was the formation of the European League for Middle Level Education, the first overseas affiliate of National Middle School Association.

REFERENCES

Alexander, W., & George, P. (1981). *The exemplary middle school*, New York: Holt, Rinehart, and Winston.

George, P. (1983). *The theory of school: Beyond effectiveness.* Columbus, OH: National Middle School Association.

George, P., & Alexander, W. (2003). *The exemplary middle school* (3rd ed.). New York: Holt, Rinehart, and Winston.

Scales, P. C. (1994). Strengthening middle grade teacher preparation programs. *Middle School Journal, 26*(1), 59-65.

—Mary Henton
National Middle School Association

GIFTED STUDENTS/PROGRAMS

WHAT IS GIFTEDNESS?

Definitions of giftedness vary, but in general, gifted learners are those who, by virtue of their abilities, exhibit advanced performance or advanced potential in one or more areas (U.S. Department of Education, 1994). Advanced performance is evident through indicators such as standardized achievement scores at very high levels in one or more areas; consistently high grades in one or more areas; or precocity in application of skills in areas such as music, art, technology, and so forth. Advanced potential in the absence of high consistently outstanding performance is more difficult to recognize, but equally as important an indicator of potential giftedness. Students with high potential but not high performance may show remarkable insight or skill in some areas or at some times with weakness in other areas or contexts, inconsistent performance, high standardized test scores in the absence of high grades, and so on.

In the last century, conceptions of intelligence have broadened as our knowledge of psychology, human development, and the brain have increased. As a result, our conceptions of giftedness have steadily become more generous as well. Prior to the early twentieth century, giftedness was assumed to be "global"—or evident in most or all areas of functioning and was generally thought of as manifesting through a very high score on an intelligence test. At that point, fewer than 5% of individuals were thought of as gifted. In the first third of the twentieth century, psychologists concluded that giftedness could manifest itself in specific academic areas (such as math, science, language, etc.) as well as generally or globally (Tannenbaum, 1983, 2000). Still largely conceived in terms of test scores, the percentage of potentially gifted learners expanded somewhat because of the expanded conception of giftedness as domain specific. In the last quarter century, our understanding of intelligence has continued to broaden because of the work of psychologists like Howard Gardner (1993) and Robert Sternberg (1988) have extended areas of intelligence (and therefore giftedness) to include domains such as logical, spatial, interpersonal, intrapersonal, practical, analytic, and creative.

WHO ARE GIFTED LEARNERS?

Gifted learners exist in all subpopulations—including students from low economic backgrounds, English language learners, and students with handicaps. We often fail to see students from such groups as having high potential because they exhibit weakness in one or more facets of school performance, lack experiences that spur development of ability in more privileged students, or manifest cultural differences from the dominant group which those in the dominant group may interpret as deficiencies. In addition to school performances that may appear less than extraordinary, students from such groups may make artificially low scores on achievement and/or aptitude measures because of limited experiences, test bias, or handicaps that make it difficult to perform well on standardized measures (Ford & Harris, 1999; Tomlinson, Ford, Reis, Briggs, & Strickland, 2004).

In general, however, there are traits of giftedness often manifest across groups of students with high performance and/or potential. Among those are: verbal strength, retentiveness for information and ideas, high levels of curiosity, keen sense of humor, ability to make connections among ideas, generating pertinent and probing questions, and so on (Callahan & Tomlinson, 1997). When teachers see evidence of these traits in a student, it is wise to work with that student in ways that develop and extend advanced abilities. Effective curriculum and instruction for high ability learners will inevitably be a response to their traits. In addition, it is prudent to look for evidence of what students with these traits *can* or *might* do rather than to focus solely or predominately on what they *cannot* do or are not *currently* doing.

WHAT ISSUES ARISE FOR GIFTED STUDENTS DURING EARLY ADOLESCENCE?

Because gifted early adolescents are a diverse group, and because they are early adolescents, they are likely to experience the developmental challenges and milestones typical of most early adolescents. Nonetheless, the intersection of high ability and early adolescent development can "put a different spin" on the school experiences of high ability middle schoolers. Following are some potential challenges for high ability early adolescents and their teachers.

THE NEED TO BALANCE BELONGING AND ACHIEVING

A major developmental need of early adolescence is affiliating with peers and moving away from childlike dependence on adults. A vehicle for separating from adults during this developmental stage can be group disidentification with or rejection of things sanctioned by adults—such as buying into school and making good grades. While rejection of school as important is problematic for many early adolescents, it can be particularly so for early adolescents whose great strength is academics. For these young people, early adolescence can present an uncomfortable and unfortunate sense that they must choose a peer group over achievement or achievement over a peer group. For their continuing intellectual growth as well as their emotional and social development, it is important that highly able early adolescents have access to other students who value achievement and with whom they can also find a peer group. This need may be particularly potent for high ability young adolescents from low economic and/or minority groups who sometimes feel it necessary during this period to reject achievement in order to maintain status with cultural peers (Tatum, 1997).

THE NEED TO EMBRACE CHALLENGE

It is a paradox for many bright learners that they both hunger for genuine challenge and resist it. Many very bright students feel consistently under-challenged by school curriculum that does not extend their ability to think and to learn. Nonetheless, when presented with challenge appropriate to their ability, such learners will often balk at accepting the challenge. There are at least two reasons this is the case.

First, after years of high grades with little or modest effort, students learn to like "easy success." In fact, they can begin to see high grades as an entitlement which ought not to have to be earned.

Second, bright students often fail to develop the coping skills necessary to succeed with personally appropriate challenge. When they encounter such challenges, they feel inadequate, and sometime question their ability. In these instances, it becomes safer to reject the challenge than to take the chance of failure (Tomlinson, 1998).

During the middle school years, highly able learners—like other learners—will solidify habits of mind and work that will serve them well, or poorly, in shaping their futures. Research suggests (e.g., Bloom, 1985) that early adolescents may be a particularly important period for highly able learners to experience challenge, learn to tolerate challenge, and come to embrace challenge. Further, research suggests (e.g., Csikszentmihalyi, Rathunde, & Whalen, 1993) that highly able students who find satisfaction in and commitment to challenge during this time span are likely to emerge from adolescence in better academic and emotional condition than will early adolescents who do not find satisfaction in and commitment to challenge.

THE NEED TO BALANCE JOY AND RIGOR

Early adolescents generally learn more effectively when learning experiences are engaging or pleasurable. In other words, they respond well to learning opportunities that see fresh, pique curiosity, allow interaction with peers, have real audiences, provide choice, are personally relevant, enable them to make a difference in the world, and so on. As is the case with other young adolescents, highly able middle schoolers also generally learn better in such settings. At the same time, they need assistance in consistently developing knowledge, understanding, skill, attitudes, and habits of mind that push forward their capacity to "grow into" their possibilities. It is important for stu-

dents at this age to find pursuit of their talent areas to be joyful, or at least satisfying, without sacrificing the stretching necessary to grow—and vice versa. Middle grades curriculum that is flat in either engagement or level of demand often causes students of this age to become disillusioned with the process of learning at a time when identification of self as a learner is particularly critical (Tomlinson, 1998).

WHAT IS APPROPRIATE CURRICULUM AND INSTRUCTION FOR GIFTED MIDDLE SCHOOLERS?

Curriculum and instruction that are drill-based, right-answer oriented, teacher-centered, lock-step, concrete, test-driven, and low level will serve gifted middle schoolers poorly (Callahan & Tomlinson, 1997). It is likely that such curriculum will serve most middle schoolers poorly.

Good curriculum and instruction for gifted middle school students begins with good curriculum and instruction (Tomlinson, in press). In other words, to ensure that highly able learners develop the potential, it is important for them consistently to work with curriculum that is concept-based and principle driven so that they make sense of subjects in ways that experts make sense of them. They need consistently to work at high levels of thought, to apply what they learn to solving authentic problems, to develop meaningful products for meaningful audiences. They need guidance in becoming increasingly independent and self-aware as learners, and they need to work in learning environments that are safe, affirming, support affiliation, and provide a balance of challenge and support. These are descriptors of high quality curriculum for the vast majority of learners.

That is not, to say, however, that "good" curriculum and instruction addresses the spectrum of learning needs of high performance and/or high potential learners. In order to make "good curriculum and instruction" become "good curriculum and instruction for gifted learners," teachers need to modify or differentiated how students experience the curriculum and instruction to ensure that it is appropriately challenging to stretch advanced learners, that it addresses the particular strengths, talents, and interests of the student (or that it is designed in ways that support students in pursuing their own strengths, talents, and interests), and so that it attends to students' learning preferences. This is likely to imply varied and advanced materials and flexible use of time (so that students can move ahead more rapidly at times, and work more slowly to achieve depth of understanding at times). It is likely to imply some degree of supported independent inquiry, and it is likely to imply work at higher levels of abstraction, complexity, ambiguity, and open-endedness than may be appropriate for many agemates. Further, learners with advanced performance benefit from teachers who continually extend the challenges they encounter as well as support systems necessary to succeed at progressively greater levels of challenge (Tomlinson, in press). Learners with advanced potential but not advanced performance benefit from teachers who hold performance standards high for them and provide ways to fill knowledge and skills gaps even as students move forward at advanced levels—and teachers who enact consistent messages of belief in the students' potential to work at advanced levels.

WHAT ARE APPROPRIATE PROGRAMMING OPTIONS FOR GIFTED MIDDLE SCHOOLERS?

It can be argued that *how* and *what* we teach advanced middle level learners matters more than *where* we teach them. Given the middle school emphasis on heterogeneity, it would seem desirable to ensure carefully planned and appropriately challenging learning experiences in the context of heterogeneous classrooms. When teachers lack the skill and/or will to provide such learning opportunities, arguments for separate learning opportunities for high ability learners become more compelling.

In addition to providing classroom experiences designed to ensure consistent growth for high achievement and/or high potential early adolescents, it is important for middle schools to provide for the affective development of advanced learners as well. This may include special counseling opportunities designed with these students in mind—recalling always that students from many different backgrounds, with many different learning profiles, and with varied talents and dreams fall under the heading of "gifted middle school students." Just as they will need flexible curriculum and instruction based on a teacher's growing knowledge about the students, so will they need affective support that is responsive to their particular talent and developmental profiles. For some students, such services will focus on general issues of early adolescent development, for some it will focus on planning for on-going advanced learning options within and beyond the school day and beyond the middle school years. For some it will focus on special issues related to being "different" at a time when differences may be perceived to be distinctly negative. The goal of identifying, teaching, and providing affective support for highly able middle school students is meeting the obligation of schools to maximize the capacities of the students they serve.

REFERENCES

Bloom, B. (1985). *Developing talent in young people*. New York: Ballentine.

Callahan, C., & Tomlinson, C. (1997). The gifted and talented learner: Myths and realities. In *ASCD Yearbook* (pp. 309-332). Alexandria, VA: Association for Supervision and Curriculum Development.

Csikszentmihalyi, M., Rathunde, K., & Whalen, S. (1993). *Talented teenagers: The roots of success and failure*. New York: Cambridge University Press.

Ford, D., & Harris, J. (1999). *Multicultural gifted education*. New York: Teachers College Press.

Gardner, H. (1993). *Multiple intelligences: The theory in practice*. New York: Basic Books.

Sternberg, R. (1988). *The triarchic mind: A new theory of human intelligence*. New York: Penguin.

Tannenbaum, A. (1983). *Gifted children: Psychological and educational perspectives*. New York: Macmillan.

Tannenbaum, A. (2000). A history of giftedness in school and society. In K. Heller, F., Monks, R. Sternberg, & R. Subotnik (Eds.), *International handbook of giftedness and talent* (2nd ed.) (pp. 23-53). Oxford, England: Elsevier.

Tatum, B. (1997). *"Why are all the Black kids sitting together in the cafeteria?" And other conversations about race*. New York: Basic Books.

Tomlinson, C. (in press). Teaching gifted learners well: A general guide to quality curriculum and instruction for highly able students. *Theory Into Practice*.

Tomlinson, C. (1998). Curriculum and instruction for gifted learners in the middle grades: What would it take? (pp. 21-34). In R. Williamson & J. Johnston (Eds.), *Able learners in the middle level school*. Reston, VA: National Association of Secondary School Principals.

Tomlinson, C., Ford, D., Reis, S., Briggs, C., & Strickland, C. (2004). *In search of the dream: Designing schools and classrooms that work for high potential students from diverse cultural backgrounds*. Washington, DC: National Association for Gifted Children.

U.S. Department of Education Office of Educational Research and Improvement. (1994). *National excellence: A case for developing America's talent*. Washington, DC: Author.

—Carol Ann Tomlinson
University of Virginia

GRADE CONFIGURATION: K-8 VERSUS MIDDLE GRADES

INTRODUCTION

How do we configure schools to maximize student achievement, high attendance rates, and the development of a positive self-concept while minimizing discipline infractions, violence, and feelings of anonymity? What is the best configuration for K-12 schooling? Is it an elementary school, followed by a middle school, followed by a 4-year high school? Are there advantages to K-8 schools, followed by a 4-year high school? Seller (2004) reminds us "configuring schools by grade is a practice influenced by history, psychology, sociology, and pedagogy" (p. 2). Beyond what is best for students, administrative issues related to transportation, finances, and facilities usage all affect the final decision.

Answers to these questions are not easily obtained when we consider that Mac Iver and Epstein (1993) found that seventh and eighth-graders in the United States attend schools with about 30 different grade configurations. Over a decade ago, Jenkins and McEwin (1992) wrote "Grade organization remains a controversial topic in American education as it has for at least 80 years" (p. 8). Indeed, this issue of grade configurations has again surfaced in the current debate that has resulted in many major school systems abandoning middle schools in favor of K-8 schools. After reviewing the history of the junior high and middle school, one could easily conclude that there seems to be perennial dissatisfaction with how public schools educate young adolescents.

The junior high appeared at the turn of the twentieth century and with Grades 7, 8, and 9 brought the 6-3-3 grade configuration to the educational scene. In 1918, the Commission on the Reorganization of Secondary Education recommended the new organization in its annual report. It noted:

> We, therefore, recommend a reorganization of the school system whereby the first six years shall be devoted to elementary education…. The six years devoted to secondary education may well be divided into two periods that may be designated as the junior and senior high periods. (pp. 12-13)

In the 1960s, a plethora of questions surfaced about the effectiveness of the junior high and the nation embraced the idea of creating middle schools, traditionally configured with Grades 6 through 8. Many educators and policymakers believed that the three-tiered grade structure was physiologically, psychologically, sociologically, and logically correct (Frances cited in Popper, 1967).

Since the 1960s, the number of junior high schools has declined, signaling a conceptual change away from the junior high as a "preparation for high school" and toward the middle school as a "child-centered institution" that affords opportunities for team teaching, integrated curricula, advisory programs, and flexible scheduling.

According to data from the National Center for Educational Statistics (2001), 56% of the primary/elementary schools are configured to transition students into either middle schools or junior high at the end of fifth grade. Another 34% make the transition after the sixth grade. Only about 4,500 schools (about 10%) educate students from kindergarten to eighth grade. But there is more to this than meets the eye. Many schools changed the name above the school house door and never implemented the middle school concept that is explicated most fully in *Turning Points* (Carnegie Council on Adolescent Development, 1989), *Turning Points 2000* (Jackson & Davis, 2000), and *This We Believe* (National Middle School Association, 2003).

WHAT ARE THE ISSUES?

Issues that surface in grade configuration debates center on academic performance, school environment, social adjustment, transitioning, increased parent involvement, building usage, fiscal matters, personnel deployment, transportation efficiency, the creation of neighborhood schools, desegregation, and school survival (specifically in relation to rural schools). Let's take a look at a few of these.

As can be predicted, the academic performance of students is the major concern behind the return to K-8 schools. In New Orleans, eighth-graders in the school system's five K-8 schools were twice as likely to pass the state test as compared to students in middle schools. The K-8 students also performed better on the Iowa Test of Basic Skills (Rasheed, 2004). Researchers who conducted studies in the Philadelphia (Offenberg, 2001) and Baltimore (Pardini, 2002) school systems reached similar conclusions.

Each school system considers different factors when making grade span decisions. Not all movements in favor of K-8 schools emerge from discussions of student achievement or adolescent development. Some want K-8 schools to create true neighborhood schools. Others seek K-8 schools as a way to preserve racial and/or economic segregation (Look, 2001). This multiplicity of purposes seems to make the K-8 grade configuration more attractive because it appears to accomplish several desirable ends all at the same time.

Another major factor in the decision to adopt K-8 schools involves the issues of student control, discipline, and safety. Truancy, high dropout rates, violence, and substance abuse are all associated with middle schools, while K-8 schools are deemed to be "safe places." Because K-8 schools are smaller than many middle schools, they may provide young adolescents with the personalization they could not get in larger middle schools. The tendency to create narrow grade-span configurations (e.g., 6-8) reinforces the bad habit of building larger and larger schools (Howley, 2002). This can lead to students who become alienated and seek recognition through power and other aggressive behavior. Mizell (2004) concludes from this that one results can be "middle schools where children are more vulnerable rather than less so, and where administrators choose to devote more time to student control than to creating the conditions necessary for students' academic and personal development" (p. 8). Overall, the environment created by a school's grade structure may affect student attitudes (Blyth, Hill, & Smyth, 1981) and social adjustment (Wihry, Coladarci, & Meadow, 1992).

Converting to a K-8 configuration eliminates the transition from fifth to sixth grade that occurs in 6-8 middle schools. These transitions require developing new relationships with adults and peers in a typically larger, more bureaucratic school and negotiating unfamiliar school regulations and social norms (Siedman, Allen, Aber, Mitchell, & Feinman, 1994).

The K-8 configuration may also lead to sustained parent involvement in their children's schooling. We know that while many families are quite involved in their children's elementary schools, their participation declines dramatically when their children enter middle school.

THE RESEARCH EVIDENCE—SHOW ME THE DATA

Empirical research on the topic is sparse. Many reports are anecdotal in nature and describe the perceived benefits and drawbacks of various grade configurations. Very little research attempts the more difficult task of determining if a cause-effect relationship exists between grade configurations and academic achievement, while controlling for variables like school size, student socioeconomic status, teacher experience, and the like. (Wihry et al., 1992). None of the studies we found considered whether or not the middle school concept was implemented—K-8 schools were simply compared to middle schools. The results could be vastly different if exemplary middle schools were used in this research.

Research has not provided definitive answers to the myriad of possible questions about grade span, but the questions have never gone away. They are questions that linger whenever school reform or financial considerations bring about a reorganization of existing schools. One of the earliest studies on grade configuration focused on financial issues. Stetson (1917) examined the cost effectiveness of the Grand Rapids, Michigan, junior high school and concluded that the increased administrative cost produced no improvement in student achievement over the elementary school.

While the current research on K-8 schools may be a shallow body of literature, consistent findings surface while wading through it. Alspaugh (1999) found a significant achievement loss during each transition year. He explored achievement losses associated with school-to-school transitions from elementary to middle schools and to high school. A statistically significant achievement loss associated with the transition from elementary to middle schools at the sixth grade was found, as compared with K-8 schools that did not have a school transition at the sixth grade. The transition loss in achievement was larger when students from multiple elementary schools were merged into a single middle school. Students from middle schools and K-8 elementary schools both experienced an achievement loss when they made the transition to high school in the ninth grade. However, the achievement loss was greater for middle school students than for K-8 elementary students. High school dropout rates were higher for districts with Grades 6-8 middle schools than for districts with K-8 elementary schools. Wren (2004) analyzed data from 232 schools in a large Midwestern inner-city school system and concluded:

> As grade span configuration increases so does achievement. The more grade levels that a school services, the better the student perform. The more transitions a student makes, the worse the student performs. (p. 9)

Paglin and Fager (1997) concluded that each time students switched schools, feelings of anonymity increased. Simmons and Blyth (1987) studied over 600 students in Milwaukee whom they followed from sixth to eighth grade. During this 3-year period some students transitioned to junior high or middle schools while others remained in a K-8 setting. They found that young adolescent girls suffered from a drop in self-esteem, extracurricular participation, and leadership behaviors when they made the transition into middle school or junior high, but not if they remained in an elementary setting. For young adolescent boys, Simmons and Blyth found negative effects in extracurricular participation and grades, but not in self-esteem, when they made the transition into middle or junior high schools.

In a Philadelphia study conducted in 2001, Offenberg studied a large sample of K-8 and middle schools. Multivariate regression allowed Offenberg to control for the effects of poverty and race while analyzing school performance and student achievement. Positive results were revealed for Philadelphia's K-8 schools. SAT-9 scores in reading, math, and science were significantly higher in K-8 schools than in middle schools. Offenberg also found that the percentage of students in K-8 schools who enrolled in the special admit high schools was more than 11% higher than the percentage of students from middle schools and had a higher grade point average in ninth grade.

Franklin and Glascock (1998) found that sixth-grade boys experienced more suspensions in middle schools or junior highs than in elementary schools. Reasons for this are tied to transitions, the school organization, and school size.

Conclusion

There is little doubt that more research is needed on the topic. We have heard this disappointing refrain again and again when it comes to the research that is needed to answer some of the lingering questions about the middle school. We have evidence that academic achievement, social development, and dropout rates are all influenced by grade span configuration. We must remember that a myopic focus on one of these at the expense of the other two is a dangerous stance to take. Making changes to address one of these areas could adversely affect the other two. Additionally, it would be important to see how "true" middle schools compare to the K-8 schools.

No sequence of grades is perfect or in itself guarantees student academic achievement and healthy social and emotional development. As Paglin and Fager (1997) remind us, "sound educational practices are more important than grade span" (p. 9). The educational reform pendulum is swinging again. Where it stops is not yet known. The inability of the educational system to recognize the absolute necessity of specialized preparation for all middle grades teachers and administrators and its unwillingness to devote the needed resources, both personnel and financial, may have seriously contributed to the failure of middle grades reform. The traditional middle school that contains Grades 6-8 may become a less dominant feature on the educational landscape, as has the junior high. Promising, though, is the fact that many of the practices that we hold near and dear, like advisory, teaming, and integrated curricula, are currently being recommended for adoption in high schools (see The Comprehensive School Reform Quality Center, 2005) and are already being implemented in many elementary schools.

References

Alspaugh, J. W. (1999). *The interaction effect of transition grade to high school with gender and grade level upon dropout rates.* Paper presented to the annual meeting of the American Educational Research Association. Montréal, Quebec, Canada. (ERIC ED431066)

Blyth, D. A., Hill, J. P., & Smyth, C. K. (1981). The influence of older adolescents on younger adolescents: Do grade-level arrangements make a difference in behaviors, attitudes, and experiences? *Journal of Early Adolescence, 1*(1), 85-100.

Carnegie Council on Adolescent Development. (1989). *Turning points: Preparing youth for the 21st century.* Washington, DC: Carnegie.

Commission on the Reorganization of Secondary Education. (1918). *Cardinal principles of secondary education.* Washington, DC: Department of the Interior, Bureau of Education.

The Comprehensive School Reform Quality Center. (2005, January). *Works in progress: A report on middle and high school improvement programs.* Washington, DC: American Institutes for Research.

Franklin, B. J., & Glascock, C. H. (1998). The relationship between grade configuration and student performance in rural schools. *Journal of Research in Rural Education, 14*(3), 149-153.

Howley, C. B. (2002). Grade-span configurations: Where 6th and 7th grades are assigned may influence student achievement, research suggests. *School Administrator.* Retrieved on April 18, 2005, from http://www.aasa.org/publications/sa/2002_03/howley.htm

Jackson, A. W., & Davis, G. A. (2000). *Turning points 2000: Educating adolescents in the 21st century.* New York: Teachers College Press.

Jenkins, D., & McEwin, C. (1992). Which school for the fifth grader? Programs and practices in three grade organizations. *Middle School Journal, 23*(4), 8-13.

Look, K. (2001). The great K-8 debate. Retrieved April 18, 2005, from http://www.Philaedfund.org/notebook/TheGreatK8Debate.htm

Mac Iver, D., & Epstein, J. (1993). Middle grades research: Not yet mature, but no longer a child. *Elementary School Journal, 93,* 519-533.

Mizell, H. (2004, October). *Still crazy after all these years: Grade configuration and the education of young adolescents.* Keynote address presented to the annual conference of the National School Board Association's Council of Urban Boards of Education, San Antonio, TX.

National Center for Educational Statistics. (2001). *Digest of education statistics tables and figures.* Retrieved April 18, 2005, from http://www.nces.ed.gov/programs/ digest/d01/dt095.asp

National Middle School Association. (2003). *This we believe: Successful schools for young adolescents.* Westerville, OH: Author.

Offenberg, R. M. (2001). The efficacy of Philadelphia's k-to-8 schools compared to middle grades schools. *Middle School Journal, 32*(4), 23-29.

Paglin, C., & Fager, J. (1997). Grade configuration: Who goes where? Portland, OR: Northwest Regional Educational Laboratory. Retrieved April 18, 2005, from http://www.nwrel. org/request/july97/index.html

Pardini, P. (2002). Revival of the k-8 school. *The School Administrator*. Retrieved April 18, 2005, from http://www.aasa.org/publications/sa/2002_03/pardini.htm

Popper, S. H. (1967). *The American middle school: An organizational analysis*. Waltham, MA: Blaisdell.

Rasheed, A. (2004). N. O. closing book on middle schools. *The Times-Picayune*, New Orleans, LA. Retrieved April 18, 2005, from http://www.nola.com/news/tp/frontpage/index.ssf?/base/news-2/109349996872230.xml

Siedman, E., Allen, L., Aber, J. L., Mitchell, C., & Feinman, J. (1994). The impact of school transitions in early adolescence on the self-system and perceived social context of poor urban youth. *Child Development, 65*(2), 507-522.

Seller, W. (2004). *Configuring schools: A review of the literature*. Toronto, Ontario, Canada: OISE/UT Northwestern Centre.

Simmons, R. G., & Blyth, D. A. (1987). *Moving into adolescence: The impact of pubertal change and school context*. Hawthorne, NY: de Gruyter.

Stetson, P. C. (1917). A statistical study of the scholastic records of 404 junior and non-junior high school students. *School Review, 25*(9), 617-636.

Wihry, D., Coladarci, T., & Meadow, C. (1992). Grade span and eighth-grade academic achievement: Evidence from a predominantly rural state. *Journal of Research in Rural Education, 8*(2), 58-70.

Wren, S. D. (2004). The effects of grade span configuration and school-to-school transition on student achievement. *The Journal of At-Risk Issues, 10*(1), 5-11.

—Vincent A. Anfara, Jr.
The University of Tennessee

GRADE CONFIGURATIONS AT THE MIDDLE LEVEL

HISTORICAL PERSPECTIVE

The initial iteration of middle level education, the junior high school, had its origins in a series of national committees commissioned in the final years of the nineteenth century and the early years of the twentieth century charged. The national commissions were asked to analyze secondary education of the era and recommend changes that would lead to the enhanced preparation of students for postsecondary education. In 1894 the Committee of Ten (National Education Association, 1894) recommended a shift from an 8-year elementary program and a 4-year secondary program to two 6-year programs. Subsequent reports at the turn of the century supported the idea of a 6-6 grade organization but it was not until the Report of the Committee on the Economy of Time in Education (1913) discussed a 3-3 structure at the secondary level

that the junior high grade configuration concept was articulated. The report of the Commission on the Reorganization of Secondary Education (1918) then encouraged districts to establish a 3-3 structure at the secondary level with distinct "junior" and "senior" high schools. In 1920, 80% of high school graduates in the United States were educated in district organizational grade structures of eight elementary years and four high school years (Alexander & George, 1981). The junior high, however, grew steadily in popularity as an alternative, purposeful structure for addressing the needs of young adolescents. By 1965, 67% of the middle level schools in the United States were 7-8-9 junior high grade structures (Rock & Hemphill, 1966).

Throughout the middle decades of the twentieth century, junior high schools were criticized for failing to accomplish their mission of effectively addressing the developmental needs of young adolescents. By the late 1960s manuscripts endorsing a "middle school" philosophy and associated grade structures of 6-7-8 and 5-6-7-8 appeared with increasing regularity (Lawton, 1989). The emergence of the middle school grade organizational patterns were well chronicled by Cuff (1967) and Alexander, Williams, Compton, Hines, and Prescott (1968). Using a definition that a middle school included at least Grades 6 and 7 and with no grade below fourth or above eighth, Cuff (1967) found fewer than 500 schools nationwide in 1965. Alexander et al. (1968) reported the existence of 1,101 middle schools in 1967 using the grade structure definition that a middle school included at least three grades and not more than five and included Grades 6 and 7. Using Alexander's early definition as a basis for identifying middle level schools, in 2004 the number had exceeded 10,600 (Middle Level Leadership Center, 2004a).

As the middle school grew in popularity in the 1960s and 1970s, debates between proponents of the "middle school" and the "junior high school" escalated. In 1980 a research team sponsored by the Geraldine R. Dodge Foundation and the National Association of Secondary School Principals selected the descriptive phrase "middle level" as the term to describe what was to become a comprehensive study of middle schools, intermediate schools, junior high schools, and all other schools of single or multiple grades designed specifically to serve the needs of young adolescents (Clark & Clark, 1994; Valentine, Clark, Nickerson, & Keefe, 1981). The purposeful use of the term was an effort to capture under one educational roof the outspoken supporters of both the "junior high school" and the "middle school." The hope was to shift the debate of the era away from "which grade configurations were best" to a collaborative analysis of the most appropriate programs for the students the school served, regardless of the grade configuration or the name of the school. A second, and perhaps over the long-term just as important, purpose was to emphasize the fact that serving the unique educational needs of young adolescents was worthy of reference as a "level" of educational thought, not just a transitional period of education between the elementary level and the high school level. The term middle level was defined in 1980 by Valentine and his Dodge/NASSP research team colleagues as a school with an organizational structure "encompassing any grade or grade combinations from grades five through nine (Valentine et al., 1981, p. xv). The grade configuration data presented in the remaining sections of this manuscript reflect that comprehensive "middle level" definition.

As is evident from this introductory discussion, grade configurations of middle level schools across the United States have been changing since the inception of the junior high school in the early years of the twentieth century. In the early decades of the century the shift was away from the 8-year elementary and 4-year secondary configuration to the 3-year junior high configuration. In the latter half of the century the change was away from the junior high configuration to the middle school configuration. By 1990 the 6-7-8 grade configuration had become the predominant pattern (Valentine, Clark, Hackmann, & Petzko, 2002). Even junior high principals of the 1980s and 1990s believed the 6-7-8 grade configuration was the most appropriate for young adolescents (Valentine, Clark, Irvin, Keefe, & Melton, 1993; Valentine et al., 2002).

WHY HAVE MIDDLE LEVEL GRADE CONFIGURATIONS CHANGED?

Though the junior high schools of the nineteenth century were publicly criticized for failing to effectively respond to the developmental needs of young adolescents, the actual reasons for the dramatic shifts from 7-8-9 to the 6-7-8 and 5-6-7-8 grade configurations could be characterized as pedagogical as well as nonpedagogical. Pedagogical reasons reflected a significant shift in the overall philosophy and specific programs designed to meet the needs of young adolescents. Writers characterized the middle school concept as promoting a more student-centered approach when contrasted to the realities of the junior high approach that tended to focus more on the content to be covered (Clark & Clark, 1994). Hough (1997, p. 290) noted: "As higher grades are included … programs, policies, and practices tend to be more subject-cen-

tered. As lower grades are included … programs, policies, and practices tend to be more student-centered." Several researchers believed that after the 1960s a change occurred in the realization about the relative importance that programmatic characteristics and developmentally appropriate programs can have on students in middle-level schools (Clark & Clark, 1994; DeJong & Craig, 2002; Ecker, 2002; Hough, 1997; Lucas & Valentine, 2001; Valentine et al., 2002).

Valentine and his colleagues (2002) examined reasons given by school leaders for the adoption of the grade configurations 5-6-7-8 or 6-7-8. "Reasons identified in 1980 and 1992 to implement 5-6-7-8 or 6-7-8 were identified again in 2000: to provide programs best suited to the needs of young adolescents (89%) and to offer better transitions from elementary school to high school (84%)" (p. 4). The report confirmed earlier research (Valentine et al., 1993) that principals favored the 6-7-8 pattern and that many schools made configuration changes for pedagogical reasons.

George and Alexander (1993) provided convincing arguments that numerous nonpedagogical reasons or conditions significantly influenced the shift of grade organizations from the junior high pattern (7-8-9) to the middle school patterns (5-6-7-8 and 6-7-8). They noted the flexibility provided by rearranging grade patterns to create middle schools that would meet court-ordered desegregation plans and the efficiency of adapting facilities to increasing and decreasing enrollment demographics.

The findings presented in Table 1 from NASSP's *National Study of Leadership in Middle Level Schools* (Valentine et al., 2002) bring specificity to both the pedagogical and nonpedagogical reasons for grade configuration changes during the decades of the 1970s–1990s. The rank-order of the reasons and the percentage of respondents selecting that option are provided. As evident from the top four responses, school leaders have consistently indicated that grade configuration changes were made to support the implementation of better pedagogical practices for early adolescents. However, school systems across the nation have also changed grade configurations as to adapt to shifting enrollment demographics often coupled with construction of new buildings or rearrangement of grades within existing buildings to meet the enrollment changes. The findings continue to support the contention that schools make changes for both pedagogical and nonpedagogical reasons and the combinations of those reasons accelerated the demise of the junior high and the rise of the middle school grade configurations.

Table 1
Reasons for Changing to 5-6-7-8 or 6-7-8 Grade Configuration in Prior Decades

Reason	2000	1992	1980
Provide a program best suited to the needs of early adolescents	1 (89)	1 (86)	1 (61)
Provide better transition from elementary to high school	2 (84)	2 (82)	2 (57)
Employ a new curriculum or instructional innovation	3 (64)	3 (60)	4 (31)
Solve concerns about junior high program	4 (58)	5 (47)	7 (24)
Adjust to enrollment trends	5 (49)	6 (33)	3 (46)
Employ programs successfully implemented in other schools	6 (48)	4 (48)	9 (17)
Utilize a new facility	7 (32)	9 (20)	5 (28)
Provide fifth and sixth graders with a more specialized curriculum	8 (31)	7 (31)	6 (26)
Move ninth grade to the high school	9 (23)	8 (29)	8 (19)

Source: Valentine et al. (2002, p. 4).

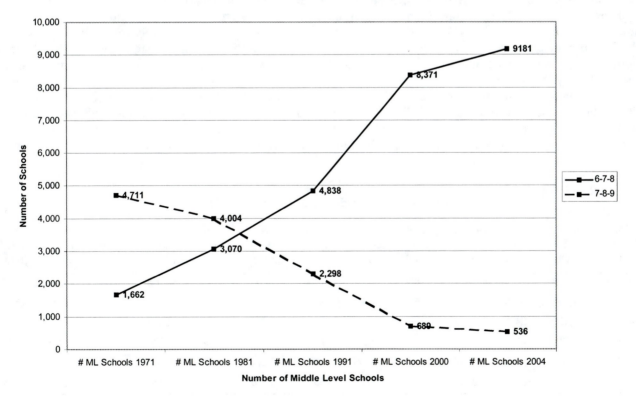

Figure 1.   Trends in grade configuration patterns.

HOW HAVE MIDDLE LEVEL GRADE CONFIGURATIONS CHANGED?

In examining the trends of grade level organization Lucas and Valentine (2001) wrote that, "Trends over the past two decades indicate a shift from junior high schools to middle schools" (p. 1). Reporting detailed data from a 2000 national study, Valentine and his colleagues (Valentine et al., 2002) noted:

> The 2000 data represent a very significant decline of the 7-8-9 middle level pattern with the percentage of responding schools in grades 7-8-9 dropping from 67% in 1965 to 6% in 2000. In the same time frame, the 6-7-8 pattern had grown from 5% to 59%. With evidence documented in each of the decade studies that developmentally appropriate practices were more likely to be present in 6-7-8 schools than in 7-8-9 schools, the shifting grade organizational patterns are favorable trends for middle level education. (Valentine et al., 2002, p. 137)

The authors concluded, "The 7-8-9 pattern has nearly disappeared, while the 6-7-8 grade pattern has emerged as the predominant pattern at the turn of the century" (Valentine et al., 2002, p. 142). The data presented in Table 2 provide insight into those major shifts and other less dramatic changes in middle level grade configurations.

In 1971 there were 10,445 middle level schools in the United States. By 2004 there were 14,956, an overall increase of 43%. The greatest increases in total number of middle level schools occurred in the seventies and nineties. There was a small decline in the eighties and a relatively small increase for the early years of the twenty-first century.

In 1971 the 5-6-7-8 middle schools comprised 7% of all middle level schools and increased slightly to 10% at the turn of the century. The greatest increase in numbers and percentages were for the 6-7-8 grade

configuration schools. In 1971 16% of all middle level schools had grade 6-7-8 patterns. That percentage rose significantly for 3 decades, reaching 61% in 2004. Over the 33-year period that represented a 452% growth. The 7-8 grade configuration was in moderate decline from 1971 at 24% to 16% in 2004 of the middle level schools in those respective timeframes. The 2% decline in total number of 7-8 schools from 1971 to 2004 paled in comparison to the decrease in the total number of 7-8-9 schools in that timeframe. In 1971 there were 4,711 schools with 7-8-9 configurations; by 2004 there were only 536, an 89% decrease. When compared to the total of middle level schools in each respective era, the 7-8-9 schools were 45% of the population in 1971, then 33% in 1981, 19% in 1991, and 5% in 2000. The 7-8-9 schools were declining at a rate of greater than 13% a decade.

In Table 2, the schools in the "other" category included all of the other sequential grade configurations such as 5-6, 5-6-7, 6-7, 7-8, and so forth and the single-grade schools of 5, 6, 7, 8, and 9. During the 33-year period, the number of "other" grade configurations rose from 850 to 1,334, an increase of 484 schools and 57%. The data presented in Table 3 provide specific insight into those grade patterns in 2000 and 2004.

From 2000 to 2004 the 5-6 grade configuration had an 86% increase. Except for the slight increase in the 6-7-8-9 configuration, the "other" nontypical multigrade configurations declined during that era. Most of the single grade schools (Figure 2) also experienced a slight decline during that same era. Fifth grade schools decreased from 47 in 2000 to 34 in 2004; sixth grade from 116 to 107; seventh grade from 28 to 21; and, eighth grade from 29 to 25. The notable exception was the ninth grade school, with an increase of 53% from 117 schools in 2000 to 170 in 2004. Data from Andrews (1993) documented 57 ninth grade schools,

Table 2
Middle Level Grade Configurations 1971-2004

Grade Config- urations	# ML Schools 1971	% of 1971 Total	# ML Schools 1981	% of 1981 Total	# ML Schools 1991	% of 1991 Total	# ML Schools 2000	% of 2000 Total	# ML Schools 2004	% of 2004 Total	1971- 2004 Change	1971- 2004 % Change
5-6-7-8	772	7%	1,024	8%	1,330	11%	1,379	10%	1506	10%	734	95%
6-7-8	1,662	16%	3,070	25%	4,838	40%	8,371	59%	9181	61%	7519	452%
7-8	2,450	24%	2,628	22%	2,902	24%	2,390	17%	2399	16%	−51	−2%
7-8-9	4,711	45%	4,004	33%	2,298	19%	689	5%	536	4%	−4,175	−89%
Other	850	8%	1,500	12%	727	6%	1,278	9%	1334	9%	484	57%
Total	10,445	100%	12,226	100%	12,095	100%	14,107	100%	14,956	100%	4,511	43%

Source: Middle Level Leadership Center (2004a).

Table 3
All Middle Level Grade Pattern Combinations 2000-2004

Grade Configurations	# ML Schools in 2000	% of 2000 Total	# ML Schools in 2004	% of 2004 Total	# of ML Change 2000 2004	% of Change 2000 to 2004
5	47	0.33%	34	0.23%	−13	−27.66%
5-6	475	3.37%	561	3.75%	86	18.11%
5-6-7	81	0.57%	73	0.49%	−8	−9.88%
5-6-7-8	1,379	9.78%	1,506	10.07%	127	9.21%
5-6-7-8-9	12	0.09%	13	0.09%	1	8.33%
6	116	0.82%	107	0.72%	−9	−7.76%
6-7	166	1.18%	134	0.90%	−32	−19.28%
6-7-8	8,371	59.34%	9,181	61.39%	810	9.68%
6-7-8-9	79	0.56%	84	0.56%	5	6.33%
7	28	0.20%	21	0.14%	−7	−25.00%
7-8	2,390	16.94%	2,399	16.04%	9	0.38%
7-8-9	689	4.88%	536	3.58%	−153	−22.21%
8	29	0.21%	25	0.17%	-4	−13.79%
8-9	128	0.91%	112	0.75%	−16	−12.50%
9	117	0.83%	170	1.14%	53	45.30%
Total	14,107	100.00%	14,956	100.00%	849	6.02%

Source: Middle Level Leadership Center (2004b).

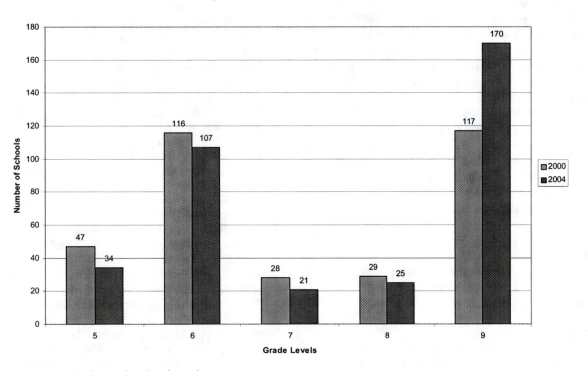

Figure 2.   Single-grade school trends.

establishing a growth percentage of 198% during the 1993-2004 period.

The most appropriate location of the ninth grade has been a issue of discussion since the noticeable growth spurt of the middle school in the 1970s. With the significant decline of the 7-8-9 schools, most ninth grades have shifted to the 9-10-11-12 high school configuration. Most researchers tend to agree with Andrews (1993) about the value of single-grade ninth grade centers: "ninth grade schools appear to be less desirable than junior high schools or senior high schools for the placement of ninth grade students" (p. 127). But the more significant issue may be the concerns about the single-grade school, regardless of the grade. Researchers (Alspaugh, 2001; Alspaugh & Harting, 1995) have documented that achievement declines each time a student transitions from one school building (grade configuration) to another. In most school districts the use of single grade schools increases the number of transitions. Alspaugh (2001) concludes that "students placed in relatively small cohort groups for long spans of time tend to experience more desirable educational outcomes" (p. 25). Such conclusions clearly imply that single-grade schools are not as appropriate as multigrade configurations.

CONCLUSIONS

Middle level grade configurations changed significantly throughout the twentieth century. Early data from the twenty-first century support continuing patterns of change toward middle school configurations. The grade configuration changes have been driven by pedagogical and nonpedagogical reasons and paralleled the evolving beliefs of school principals about the best grade configurations for young adolescents. With continuing evidence since 1980 confirming that "developmentally appropriate practices are more likely to be present in 6-7-8 schools than in 7-8-9 schools" (Valentine et al., 2002, p. 137), the direction of this shifting pattern holds promise for the continued evolution of more effective programs and practices throughout middle level education.

REFERENCES

Alexander, W. M., & George, P. S. (1981). *The exemplary middle school*. New York: Holt, Rinehart, and Winston.

Alexander, W., Williams, E., Compton, M., Hines, V., & Prescott, D. (1968). *The emergent middle school*. New York: Holt, Rinehart and Winston.

Alspaugh, J. W. (2001). Achievement loss associated with the transition to middle school and high school. *The Journal of Educational Research, 92*(1), 20-25.

Alspaugh, J. W., & Harting, R. D. (1995). Transition effects of school grade-level organization on student achievement. *Journal of Research and Development in Education, 28*(3), 145-149,

Andrews, D. R. (1993). *Grade organization patterns and ninth grade students*. Unpublished doctoral dissertation, University of Missouri, Columbia.

Clark, S. N., & Clark, D. C. (1994). *Restructuring the middle level school: Implications for school leaders*. Albany: State University of New York Press.

Commission on the Reorganization of Secondary Education. (1918). *Cardinal principles of secondary education* (Bulletin 1918, No. 35). Washington, DC: U.S. Department of Interior, Bureau of Education.

Cuff, W. (1967). Middle schools on the march. *NASSP Bulletin, 51*, 83-86.

DeJong, W. S., & Craig, J. (2002). How should schools be organized. *School Planning and Management, 41*(6), 26-32.

Ecker, M. (2002). Middle schools still matter: As new configurations grow, unique needs of young adolescents deserve attention. *School Administrator, 59*(3), 30-33.

George, P. S., & Alexander, W. M. (1993). *The exemplary middle school* (2nd ed.). New York: Harcourt Brace.

Hough, D. (1997). A bona fide middle school: Programs, policy, practice, and grade span configurations. In J. L. Irvin (Ed.) *What current research says to the middle level practitioner* (pp. 285-294). Westerville, OH: National Middle School Association.

Lawton, E. J. (1989). *A journey through time: A chronology of middle level education resources*. Columbus, OH: National Middle School Association and Reston, VA: National Association of Secondary School Principals.

Lucas, S. E., & Valentine, J. W. (2001). *NMSA research summary #1: Grade configuration*. Retrieved July 13, 2004, from http://www.nmsa.org/research/ressum1.htm

Middle Level Leadership Center. (2004a). *Middle level grade configurations (1971-2004)*. Retrieved June 22, 2005, from http://www.mllc.org/uploads/docs/mlgc71_04.pdf

Middle Level Leadership Center. (2004b). *Middle level grade configurations (2000-2004)*. Retrieved June 22, 2005, from http://www.mllc.org/uploads/docs/mlgc00_04.pdf

National Education Association. (1894). *Report of the committee of ten on secondary school studies*. New York: American Book.

Report of the Committee of the National Council of Education on Economy of Time in Education. (1913). Bulletin 1913, No. 38. Washington, DC: U.S. Department of Interior, Bureau of Education.

Rock, D. A., & Hemphill, J. K. (1966), *The junior high school principalship*. Reston, VA: National Association of Secondary School Principals.

Valentine, J. W., Clark, D. S., Nickerson, N. C., & Keefe, J. W. (1981). *The middle level principalship: Vol. 1. A survey of middle level principals and programs*. Reston, VA: National Association of Secondary School Principals.

Valentine, J. W., Clark, D. C., Irvin, J. L., Keefe, J. W., & Melton G. (1993). *Leadership in middle level education: Vol. I. A national study of middle level leaders and schools*. Reston, VA: National Association of Secondary School Principals.

Valentine, J. W., Clark, D. C., Hackmann, D. G., & Petzko, V. N. (2002). *A national study of leadership in middle level schools: Vol. I: A national study of middle level leaders and school programs.* Reston, VA: National Association of Secondary School Principals.

—Jerry Valentine
—Matthew D. Goodman
University of Missouri, Columbia

GROWING UP FORGOTTEN: A REVIEW OF RESEARCH AND PROGRAMS CONCERNING EARLY ADOLESCENCE

When Lispitz published *Growing Up Forgotten: A Review of Research and Programs Concerning Early Adolescence* in 1977 (first edition), she answered the question, "Who is doing what and where for people between the ages of twelve and fifteen?" In this landmark study, Lipsitz found that people in the stage of their life known as early adolescence are often overlooked by educational researchers, policymakers, and public service providers. The concept of early adolescence was virtually unknown and totally misunderstood. Lipsitz even contended, "as a society we have no coherent concept of adolescence" (p. 3) which has greatly impacted the support given to the biological, socioemotional, and cognitive development of adolescents.

Lipsitz's publication, funded by the Ford Foundation, was instrumental in bringing attention to this distinctive stage in human development. In addition to spotlighting issues related to early adolescence, Lipsitz confronted some of society's myths surrounding early adolescence. For example, society believes that adolescence is a time of turmoil for young people and the best approach to take when interacting with young people is to simply not interact, but to segregate. On the contrary, Lipsitz's research showed that for most adolescents, this stage of their life is quite stable and serene—not the tumultuous picture presented by mass media. Lipsitz acknowledged other myths as well, but did not focus her attention on society's misconceptions related to early adolescence. Nonetheless, these misconceptions have negatively influenced society's perceptions of adolescents.

Divided into two primary sections, the book explored general research on early adolescence and research about the young adolescent and social institutions. The social institutions examined were (1) the school; (2) service institutions and the handicapped young adolescents; (3) the family; (4) voluntary youth-serving agencies; and (5) the juvenile justice system. Lipsitz's research negated the popular opinion that the years between childhood and adulthood were not important. In fact, Lipsitz noted, "early adolescence is a time of growth and change second only to infancy in velocity" (p. xvi).

In conclusion, Lipsitz stated, "Society's present grasp of early adolescence is inadequate" (p. 207). Her study documented the limited amount research conducted focusing on early adolescence, the random attention paid to early adolescents with regard to social institutions, and the few advocates young adolescents have. Essentially, what Lipsitz found was that research then revealed precious little about the lives of young adolescents and which researchers failed to recognize the importance of the stage of life.

REFERENCE

Lipsitz, J. (1977). *Growing up forgotten: A review of research and programs concerning early adolescence.* Lexington, MA: Heath.

—Nicole L. Thompson
Mississippi State University

GRUHN, WILLIAM T.

William T. Gruhn is recognized for his contributions to educational administration and in particular to junior high school education. Because of his advocacy for the junior high school, the National Secondary School Principals gave him the title of "Mr. Junior High School." In addition to his many scholarly contributions, he provided leadership at various levels of education to administrators, teachers, graduate students, and colleagues.

William Theodore Gruhn was born in Bridgeport, Connecticut on November 11, 1904. His education included a bachelor of arts from Northern State College in Aberdeen, South Dakota in 1926, a master of arts degree from the University of Minnesota in 1933 and a doctor of philosophy from the University of North Carolina in 1940.

His career in education spanned 46 years from the time he began as a teacher in 1926 until he retired as a professor from the University of Connecticut at Storrs in 1973.

He taught social studies in Aberdeen, South Dakota and later became a principal. As a graduate student he studied at the University of Minnesota and the University of North Carolina. In 1940, he became an assistant professor of secondary education at the University of Connecticut at Storrs. Dr. Gruhn served as dean of the school of education from 1948-1949 and director of teacher education from 1949-1958. During the summers he would teach at other universities, one of which included the University of Colorado, where he met one of his mentors, Harl Douglass. While working with Dr. Douglass, he was known as one of the "Douglass Boys" (Douglass, H. R. Personal Papers, n.d.).

The list of his publications and scholarly works are lengthy. He authored and coauthored seven books on administration and education in addition to 50 articles in professional educational journals. His books and articles dealt with both theory and practice in the field primarily in secondary education. With his focus on junior high school administration, he coauthored the book *The Modern Junior High School* (1971) with Harl R. Douglass. This book was widely used in universities and by administrators across the country. Furthermore, he was a sought after consultant and successfully mentored many graduate students (Gruhn, 2000).

For his many outstanding contributions to the field he was honored with several citations and awards by the following organizations: the National Association of Secondary School Principals, the National Council for Junior High School Administration, and Northeast Council on Junior High School Administration, the Massachusetts Junior High School Principal Association, and the Connecticut Association of Secondary Schools. In 1983, The National Association of Secondary School Principals named an award in his honor. The Gruhn-Long-Melton Award was established to recognize distinguished service and leadership in improving middle level education (National Association of Secondary School Principals, 2004).

Dr. Gruhn died August 13, 2000 at the age of 96. His contributions to junior high school education were substantial. As a recognized authority in his field, he provided "distinguished service and leadership" to those who wanted to improve education for young adolescents.

REFERENCES

Douglass, H. R. Personal Papers. (n.d.). Autobiography, Box 1, Folder 10. Boulder, CO: Archives, University of Colorado at Boulder Libraries.

Gruhn, W. T. (2000, August 10). *The Hartford Courant*, p. B 4.

Gruhn, W. T., & Douglass, H. R. (1971). *The modern junior high school* (3rd ed.). New York: Ronald Pres.

National Association of Secondary School Principals. (2004). *The Gruhn-Long-Melton Award*. Reston, VA: Author.

—Barbara L. Whinery
University of Northern Colorado

HALL, G. STANLEY

G. Stanley Hall, an American developmental psychologist, is commonly considered psychology's greatest advocate in the United States (Bringmann, Bringmann, & Early, 1992; Ross, 1972). Remembered best, perhaps, for founding the American Psychological Association (APA) in 1892 and for bringing Freud to America in 1909, Hall was indeed a forward thinker ("G. Stanley Hall," 1991; Ross, 1972). Hall's contribution to psychology, however, tends to be forgotten—"he conducted few experiments, produced no lasting theory, and the bulk of his writing is long forgotten" ("G. Stanley Hall," 1991, p. 1). Nonetheless, in 1904, Hall authored his first major book, *Adolescence*, wherein he described the then modern concept of adolescence as a period of storm and stress. Before this publication, Hall was a leader in the child study movement. He brought the movement to the forefront of educational reform and helped create the platform for progressive education (Ross, 1972). Due to Hall's efforts, child development, educational psychology, and mental testing emerged as academic disciplines (Ross, 1972).

Granville Stanley Hall was born on February 1, 1844, in Ashfield, Massachusetts. Hall's mother, Abigail Beals, was a schoolteacher before marrying Hall's father, Granville Bascom Hall, a farmer (Hall, 1923). Being an educated woman, Hall's mother cultivated his intellectual talents. Hall's family, steeped in the Protestant faith, had hoped Hall would become a member of the clergy (Ross, 1972).

In 1863, Hall enrolled in Williams College and began studying religion, romantic literature, and philosophy. Upon graduation from Williams in 1867, Hall entered Union Theological Seminary in New York City. Although his schedule was demanding, Hall found time to explore. His interest in philosophy deepened. He dreamt of studying in Germany. In 1869, Hall secured funding that enabled him to study in Germany for 1 year ("G. Stanley Hall," 1991).

New opportunities caused Hall to rethink his choice of career. After working random jobs, Hall enrolled in the philosophy department at Harvard to earn his PhD (Bringmann et al., 1992). Hall studied under William James and in 1878, Hall was awarded his PhD in psychology. Hall's approach to psychology would later become a foundational element of the functionalist movement in the United States ("G. Stanley Hall," 1991).

Unable to find employment, Hall returned to Germany—where scientific psychology flourished. Hall was influenced by the work of du Bois-Reymond and Helmholtz (psychopathology), Wundt (physiology), and Haecket (recapitulation). Hall renewed his friendship with Cornelia Fisher and they were married in 1879. The couple returned to the United States in 1880 and Hall began lecturing at Harvard about philosophy and pedagogy ("G. Stanley Hall," 1991). During this time, Hall focused his studies on the child as an issue central to pedagogy. Due to the fame he achieved at Harvard, Hall was invited to lecture at Johns Hopkins University. After his lectures in 1884, Hall began teaching psychology and pedagogy in the philosophy department. Hall established a small laboratory used in conjunction with his teaching (Ross, 1972).

Although successful at Johns Hopkins, Hall accepted the presidency of Clark University in 1888 where he remained until he retired in 1920. During his tenure at Clark, Hall birthed the American Psychological Association and several journals related to psychology, hosted Freud, and became the leader of the child study movement in the United States. Hall died on April 24, 1924 (Ross, 1972).

REFERENCES

Bringmann, W., Bringmann, M., & Early, C. (1992). G. Stanley Hall and the history of psychology. *American Psychological Association, 47*(2), 281-289.

G. Stanley Hall: Founder of the *Journal of Genetic Psychology*. (1991). *Journal of Genetic Psychology, 152*(4), 397-403.

Hall, G. S. (1904). *Adolescence: Its psychology and its relations to physiology, anthropology, sociology, sex, crime, religion, and education* (Vols. 1-2). New York: Appleton.

Hall, G. S. (1923). *Life and confessions of a psychologist*. New York: Appleton.

Ross, D. (1972). *G. Stanley Hall: The psychologist as prophet*. Chicago: The University of Chicago Press.

—Nicole L. Thompson
Mississippi State University

THE HANDBOOK OF RESEARCH IN MIDDLE LEVEL EDUCATION

The *Handbook of Research in Middle Level Education* is a series of volumes containing articles on important research in the field of middle level education. Each volume of the handbook is focused on a specific topic related to the middle grades including curriculum, professional development, and policy issues. These are an invaluable source of the essential best practices and lessons learned based on research that provide both inspiration and support for middle level practitioners, scholars, and policymakers.

Volume 1 of the *Handbook of Research in Middle Level Education* (Anfara, 2001) begins with a history of the middle level concept. Volume 1 is then organized into two parts. Part 1 contains five chapters that focus on current research (1980s to present) regarding the middle school concept, including topics such as advisory programs, teaming, effective middle school teaching, and flexible scheduling. Part 2 provides a framework for moving middle level reform into the twenty-first century with four chapters on school staffing, teacher preparation, leadership, and an excellent discussion of the future of middle grades education from a *Turning Points 2000* (Jackson & Davis, 2000) author.

Middle School Curriculum, Instruction, and Assessment (Anfara & Stacki, 2002) is the title of volume 2 of the handbook. This volume is dedicated to linking the middle school concept to student achievement by focusing on what is taught and how it is taught. Volume 2 contains 11 chapters on middle school curriculum, instruction, and assessment. Chapter topics include curriculum integration, exploratory education, developmental appropriateness, authentic curriculum, and portfolios.

Volume 3 in the handbook series is titled *Leaders for a Movement: Professional Preparation and Development of Middle Level Teachers and Administrators* (Andrews & Anfara, 2003). This volume highlights issues around the education, training, and professional development of middle level teachers and administrators. Part 1 focuses on middle level teachers with eight articles on the history of teacher preparation, current challenges, and future potential. Part 2 addresses the preparation of middle level administrators with eight articles on topics that range from preservice preparation to models that support new and experienced principals. The final section of this volume contains resources including teacher interview protocols, policy statements, and course syllabi.

Reforming Middle Level Education: Considerations for Policymakers (Thompson, 2004) is the fourth volume in the handbook series. In this volume, middle level scholars highlight the most important issues about middle level education and their impact on state and national policy. The 12 chapters in this volume address issues including professional development, teacher preparation, recommendations for high-performing middle schools, and lessons from comprehensive school reform models.

Volume 5 in the handbook series is titled *Making a Difference: Action Research in Middle Level Education* (Caskey, 2005). This volume highlights action research in the middle grades and presents the many ways that educators and researchers use action research. The chapters in this volume focus on action research that is used to examine middle grades issues like classroom practices, peer evaluation, professional development, and teaming.

REFERENCES

Andrews, P. G., & Anfara, V. A., Jr. (Eds.). (2003). *Leaders for a movement: Professional preparation and development of middle level teachers and administrators*. Greenwich, CT: Information Age.

Anfara, V. A., Jr. (Ed.). (2001). *The handbook of research in middle level education*. Greenwich, CT: Information Age.

Anfara, V. A., Jr., & Stacki, S. L. (Eds.). (2002). *Middle school curriculum, instruction, and assessment*. Greenwich, CT: Information Age.

Caskey, M. M. (Ed.). (2005). *Making a difference: Action research in middle level education*. Greenwich, CT: Information Age.

Jackson, A. W., & Davis, G. A. (2000). *Turning points 2000: Educating adolescents in the 21st century.* New York: Teachers College Press.

Thompson, S. C. (Ed.). (2004). *Reforming middle level education: Considerations for policymakers.* Greenwich, CT: Information Age.

—Nancy Flowers
CPRD, University of Illinois

HEALTH: COMPREHENSIVE HEALTH PROGRAMS

BACKGROUND

With a few exceptions, middle grade students are generally very healthy in terms of their overall physical well-being. Early adolescents, normally characterized by student ages 10-15, are typically vibrant, active, and developing as they move from the quiet and stability of their home environment to the rough and tumble world of adolescents. This journey occurs in the face of numerous changes in physical, social, emotional, and intellectual development. Although increasing numbers of adolescents are contracting chronic diseases such as asthma, obesity, and diabetes, this age group remains one of the healthiest periods in the lifespan. In fact, the most serious adolescent health condition is their need for dental care (7.6%), while nearly 10% have not seen a dentist in 2-years (U.S. Department of Health and Human Services, 2003).

By contrast, the greatest risks associated with the early adolescent years are related to the developmental, socioemotional, and behavioral problems. That is, early adolescence is a time when many begin experimenting in high risk behaviors such as alcohol, tobacco, and drug use, sexual behavior, violence, delinquency, and suicidal ideation (Carnegie Council on Adolescent Development, 1989; Resnick et al., 1997). The causes and contributing factors to these social and behavioral problems are complex and relate to personal, community, developmental, family, and peer related factors (Hawkins, Catalano, & Miller, 1992). To understand the magnitude of high risk and problem behaviors among early adolescents, an examination of the onset, number, frequency, and severity of high-risk behaviors can be helpful. For example, 6% of eighth grade students are regular smokers (Substance Abuse and Mental Health Services Administration, 2003), and a 2002 national survey reports sizeable numbers of adolescent drug users who report first use of alcohol (39%), marijuana (18%), inhalants (10%), and hallucinogens (4.5%), before the age of 15 (Substance Abuse and Mental Health Services Administration, 2002a). These patterns are quite disconcerting since research shows that early onset of drug use increases associated personal and social problems, and in particular, the chance of becoming addicted to substances (Substance Abuse and Mental Health Services Administration, 2003). Similarly, research has also found strong interrelationships among problem behaviors. That is, a number of studies report that adolescents that engage in a problem behavior (e.g., alcohol and drug use, delinquency, early sexual debut) are much more likely to engage in multiple problem behaviors, which places them at even higher risk for serious behavioral problems and consequences (Hawkins et al., 1992; Resnick et al., 1997; Tubman & Wagner, 2004). It should also be noted that these are not only the "problem" students or "classical" troublemakers. A recent study of adolescents from affluent families report they are equally at risk for substance abuse and mental health problems (Luther, 2003). To that end, increasing evidence supports school-based health programs that promote healthier and engaged students appear to positively affect academic outcomes (Collaborative for Academic, Social, and Emotional Learning, 2003; Flay, Allred, & Ordway, 2001). These findings should further compel schools and communities to support school health programs.

SCHOOL HEALTH PROGRAMS

Schools, with American children as their captive audience, are viewed at the second most important socializing institution after the family, and have an enormous influence, both in a developmental and compensatory way that can impact on personal, social, and economic success. In other words, healthy schools promote healthy attitudes, norms, and behaviors that can have positive physical, social, and psychological benefits to early adolescents. Middle grade schools are particularly vital in this equation because of the emerging risks described above. In fact, both Turning Points documents vigorously document early adolescent needs, make important recommendations for action, and provide clear examples for comprehensive school health programming (Carnegie Council on Adolescent Development, 1989; Jackson & Davis, 2000).

The Centers for Disease Control and Prevention (CDC) propose the Comprehensive School Heath Programs (CSHP) framework as the cornerstone for healthy schools for school age children (Allensworth, Lawson, Nicholson, & Wyche, 1997; Centers for Disease Control and Prevention, 2005a). The CSHP is comprised of eight components that should guide middle grade schools in providing and promoting health behaviors and a health promoting environment. Each component is described below:

Health Education. The heart of a CSHP is an evidence-based health curriculum that targets developmentally appropriate contents and skills. CDC recommends a health curriculum containing the most salient and preventable health conditions—tobacco, diet, physical activity, alcohol and drugs use, unintentional injuries, and sexual behaviors. Recent federal funding guidelines require evidence-based health education/prevention programs to maximize the likelihood for reducing targeted health and problem behaviors (Centers for Disease Control and Prevention, 2005b; Substance Abuse and Mental Health Services Administration, 2002b). It is also becoming clear what does not work. For example, teaching the "facts" about the dangers of drugs alone or school assemblies are not effective in reducing alcohol, tobacco and drug use (National Institute on Drug Abuse, 2003).

Physical Education. Students must be physically active in their daily lives if they are to reduce the risks associated with sedentary lifestyles. Schools provide a unique opportunity for students to learn and practice knowledge and skills associated with active lifestyles in order to meet the recommended physical activity requirements of moderate to vigorous physical activity 3-5 days per week (Morbidity and Mortality Weekly, 1997). The "new" physical education uses more of a "personalized health and fitness" approach than the traditional "competitive sports" where individualized health and fitness assessments are conducted and a variety of fitness activities (power walking, resistance training, swim conditioning, ultimate Frisbee, aerobics, etc.) are taught to maximize participation, encourage success, and promote health-related fitness that can be maintained across the lifespan.

Health Services. Since middle grade schools are places where students, teachers, and staff spend a major portion of most days, it creates a common location for providing prevention, early intervention, referral, and treatment of acute and chronic physical and mental health problems. Numerous health service delivery models exist ranging from the traditional school nurse who visits a building once a week to a fully developed school-based clinic staffed with physicians, nurses, and related health personnel. Schools with well-developed health services depend on district resources and/or involvement of the com-

munity. Since school-based clinics are viewed as beyond the school mission, they are often operated by partner organizations such as health departments, hospitals, community health centers or clinics. These external partners must have expertise to provide high quality services for adolescents and their families. Adequate health services are particularly essential in middle grade schools with a high percentage of families lacking health insurance. With the advent of the Children Health Insurance Programs funded by the federal government in the late 1990s, school-based/ linked services have been more widely adopted across the U.S. school health services also provide opportunities for students and staff to gain knowledge and skills regarding the use of health care services, health literacy, and self-care.

Nutrition Services and Policies. Recent attention paid to the obesity epidemic has resulted in renewed efforts to ensure healthy foods and eating behaviors are promoted in schools. Federal programs provide disadvantaged students free and reduced breakfast and lunch to ensure appropriate quality and quantity of foods, which is particularly important for developing early adolescents. Many states and districts are changing school food polices by removing high fat and caloric foods from meals and banning vending machines with snacks and soda. Integrating effective nutrition education programs and policies with appropriate health and physical education curriculum provides the greatest opportunity to reduce the increasing rates of childhood obesity and prevent chronic diseases (Morbidity and Mortality Weekly Report, 1996).

Mental Health—Counseling, Psychological and Social Services. Similar to health services, many of today's youth, more than ever, require mental health and social services to help them navigate developmental challenges and the highs and lows of the adolescent years. The Surgeon General reports that 21% of school-age children (9-17) have mental health problems that require appropriate mental health services (U.S. Department of Health and Human Services, 1999). Moreover, many early adolescents struggle with one or more developmental challenges such as family conflict, academic/career expectations, finances, peer relationships, and autonomy. These problems are compounded in disadvantaged communities, where systems of support and positive role models are often lacking (Walrath, Bruns, Anderson, Glass-Siegel, & Weist 2004). Although most middle grade schools have counselors, student to counselor ratios make it impossible to meet the developmental and mental health needs of early adolescents. Some schools provide mental health services as part of a school based/linked clinic that counsels' students and families on or off the school grounds.

Recognizing developmental challenges, many middle grade schools implement advisor-advisee programs to provide a venue for teachers and staff to know, interact, and support students. Lastly, some middle grade schools are implementing Student Assistance Programs (SAP), where staff identifies students showing early signs of personal, social or educational problems, and provide appropriate assistance based on individual and family support plans.

Healthy School Environment. Research demonstrates that a positive school climate and student feelings of school attachment are major factors in promoting academic success and healthy behaviors (Resnick et al., 1997). Regardless of the type or location of a middle grade school, it must be safe, engaging, and empowering for teachers and students. Hazards such as traffic, noxious chemicals, and biological agents are obvious, but the threat to psychological safety is often more insidious. Bullying, fighting, harassment, and abuse frequently cause serious emotional harm, particularly to vulnerable early adolescents. School staff also can contribute to either feelings of psychological safety or intimidation depending on the level of caring, positive interactions, or support for students (Reddy, Rhodes, & Mulhall, 2003).

A recent approach to improving the school environment is the recognition and importance of socioemotional learning (Collaborative for Academic, Social, and Emotional Learning, 2003). Numerous schools are beginning to adopt a social emotional learning framework based on research that shows that emotional intelligence is a better predictor of academic and career success than one's intelligence quotient (Goleman, 1994). Emotional intelligence encapsulates skills of self-awareness and management, social awareness, relationship building, and responsible decision making, which appear to be essential for personal health and well-being and for promoting a positive school climate (Goleman, 1994; Collaborative for Academic, Social, and Emotional Learning, 2003).

Parent and Community Engagement. Families and communities must engage schools in ways that reinforce their positive values and expectations. Although parental influence remains important for early adolescents, peer influence significantly increases as youth reach out to cliques, teams, and subgroups. How families and communities provide constructive opportunities and outlets for early adolescents often impacts how they manage their energy, emotions, ambitions, and risk taking behaviors. Parents of middle grade students must recalibrate their role from the parent of a child to a parent of an early adolescent to ensure communication that builds trust and respect. Parents must convey their values through their own health actions and willingness to discuss sensitive topics such as alcohol and drug use, sexuality, dating, violence, and curfew. Communities also contain resources that provide experiences and adult role models through community service, recreation, and career options.

Health Promotion for Faculty and Staff. Schools, like any organization or business, need to take care of their employee's health and well-being. Teaching can be a stressful occupation, and teaching early adolescents can be even more demanding because of the energy and challenges they bring to school. Staff can also have personal and family crises that require support and mental health services from counselors and nurses working in a middle grade school. Many schools provide in-house health promotion programs like Weight Watchers, exercise groups, health screenings, health fairs, and educational brown bag lunches where staff learn about health issues and obtain group support for behavior change.

LEADERSHIP THROUGH ASSESSMENT OF CHSPs

The competition for time and attention in schools makes it critical that CSHPs have the support and leadership of the administrators, teachers, and community stakeholders. Middle grade schools can sustain CSHP efforts by creating a Health Council that is responsible for oversight and effects of the CSHP. How a particular component is working can only be determined through continuous quality improvement and outcome evaluation. To that end, Health Council must ensure the process and outcome evaluation of the CSHP is part of the overall school improvement plan.

Several CSHP assessment tools are available for middle grade schools. The CDC developed the *School Health Index: Self-Assessment and Planning Guide* that assesses and provides annual feedback on the strengths and challenges of the eight CSHP areas (Centers for Disease Control and Prevention, 2004). To monitor outcomes, CDC's Youth Risk Behavior Survey (YRBS) is available to assess multiple health behaviors and risk factors (Centers for Disease Control and Prevention, 2005c). These data can establish a baseline of health behaviors and assess implementation and impact of CSHP. These data should be used for program improvement and to adapt programs and polices.

SUMMARY

Middle grade schools are dynamic places where early adolescents begin their intrepid journey between childhood and adulthood. Effective CSHPs can facilitate healthy learning, responsible choices, appropriate norms, and behaviors for students and teachers. Health is particularly salient to early adolescents as they are enter puberty where they face opportunities and choices regarding high-risk behaviors. Middle grade schools must be healthy resources for early adolescents and their families by providing positive role models, accurate, and timely information, a healthy school environment and consistent expectations for health and well-being.

REFERENCES

Allensworth, D., Lawson, E., Nicholson, L., & Wyche, J. (Eds.). (1997). *Schools and health: Our nation's investment.* Committee on Comprehensive School Health Programs in Grades K-12, Institute of Medicine. Washington DC: National Academy Press.

Carnegie Council on Adolescent Development. (1989). *Turning Points: Preparing American youth for the 21st century.* New York: Carnegie Corporation.

Centers for Disease Control and Prevention. (2004). *School health index: A self-assessment and planning guide. Middle school/high school version.* Retrieved June 20, 2005, from http://apps.nccd.cdc.gov/SHI/HealthyYouth/pdf/Middle%20High%20School%20text.pdf

Centers for Disease Control and Prevention. (2005a). *Healthy youth: Coordinated school health programs.* Retrieved June 20, 2005, from http://www.cdc.gov/HealthyYouth/CSHP/index.htm

Centers for Disease Control and Prevention. (2005b). *Registries of programs effective in reducing youth risk behaviors.* Retrieved June 20, 2005, from http://www.cdc.gov/HealthyYouth/publications/registries.htm

Centers for Disease Control and Prevention. (2005c). *YRBBS: Youth risk behavior surveillance system.* Retrieved June 27, 2005, from http://www.cdc.gov/HealthyYouth/yrbs/index.htm

Collaborative for Academic, Social and Emotional Learning. (2003). *Safe and sound: An educational leader's guide to evidence-based social and emotional learning (SEL) programs.* Philadelphia: Mid-Atlantic Regional Education Laboratory for Student Success.

Flay, B. R., Allred, C. G., & Ordway, N. (2001). Effects of the positive action program on achievement and discipline: Two matched-control comparisons. *Prevention Science, 2*(2), 71-89.

Goleman, D. (1994). *Emotional intelligence: Why it can matter more than IQ.* New York: Bantam.

Hawkins, D., Catalano, R. C. & Miller, J. Y. (1992). Risk and protective factors for alcohol and other drug problems in adolescence and early adulthood: Implications for substance abuse prevention. *Psychological Bulletin, 11*(1), 64-105.

Jackson, A. W., & Davis, G. A. (2000). *Turning Points 2000: Educating adolescents in the 21st century.* New York: Teachers College Press.

Luther, S. L. (2003). A culture of affluence: Psychological costs of material wealth. *Child Development, 74*(6), 1581-1593.

Morbidity and Mortality Weekly Report. (1996). *Guidelines for school and community programs to promote lifelong healthy eating.* Retrieved June 25, 2005, from http://www.cdc.gov/mmwr/PDF/RR/RR4509.pdf

Morbidity and Mortality Weekly Report. (1997). *Guidelines for school and community programs to promote lifelong physical activity among young people.* Retrieved June 25, 2005, from http://www.cdc.gov/mmwr/PDF/RR/RR4606.pdf

National Institute on Drug Abuse. (2003). *Preventing drug abuse among children and adolescents: A Research-based guide for parents, educators and community leaders* (2nd ed.). Retrieved June 24, 2005, from: http://www.drugabuse.gov/pdf/prevention/RedBook.pdf

Resnick, M. D., Bearman, P. S., Blum, R. W., Bauman, K. E., Harris, K. M, Jones, J, et al. (1997). Protecting youth from harm: Findings from the National Longitudinal Study on Adolescent Health. *Journal of American Medical Association, 278*, 823-832.

Reddy, R., Rhodes, J. E., & Mulhall, P. F. (2003). The influence of teachers support on student adjustment in middle school years: A latent growth curve study. *Development and Psychopathology, 15*(1), 119-138.

Substance Abuse and Mental Health Services Administration. (2002a). *2002 National Survey on Drug Use & Health* [Detailed tables]. Retrieved June 20, 2005, from http://www.oas.samhsa.gov/nhsda/2k2nsduh/html/Sect4seTabs1to76.htm - tab4.16

Substance Abuse and Mental Health Services Administration. (2002b). *SAMHSA model programs: Effective substance abuse and mental health programs for every community.* Retrieved June 20, 2005, from http://www.modelprograms.samhsa.gov/template_cf.cfm?page=model_list

Substance Abuse and Mental Health Services Administration. (2003). *Substance abuse and mental health data archive: List of available quick tables for the National Survey of Drug Use and Health, 2002.* Retrieved June 20, 2005, from http://webapp.icpsr.umich.edu/quicktables/quickconfig.do?nsduh02_druguse

Tubman, J., Gil, A. G., & Wagner, E. F. (2004). Co-occurring substance use and delinquent behavior during early adolescence. *Criminal Justice and Behavior, 31*(4), 463-488.

U.S. Department of Health and Human Services. (1999). *Mental health: A report of the Surgeon General.* Retrieved June 27, 2005, from http://www.surgeongeneral.gov/library/mentalhealth/home.html

U.S. Department of Health and Human Services. (2003). *Summary health statistics for U.S. children: National Interview Survey, 2000.* Retrieved June 27, 2005, from http://www.cdc.gov/nchs/data/series/sr_10/sr10_213.pdf#search='Summary%20health%20statistics%20for%20U.S.%20children:%20National%20Interview%20Survey,%202000'

Walrath, C. M., Bruns, E. J., Anderson, K. L., Glass-Siegel, M., & Weist, M. D. (2004). Understanding expanded school mental health services in Baltimore City. *Behavior Modification, 28*(4), 472-490.

—Peter F. Mulhall
CPRD, University of Illinois

HEALTH: MENTAL HEALTH AND YOUNG ADOLESCENTS

Early adolescence is seen to be a crucial time for identity development, yet it is also a critical time in the development and diagnosis of mental illness. Studies from the National Institute of Mental Health (1999) indicate that mental illness is the fourth leading cause of disability in young people. The National Mental Health Information Center (2002) estimates that between 14 and 20% percent of U.S. children ages 9 to 17 have a diagnosable mental or addictive disorder associated with at least minimum impairment. For those in early adolescence, mental illness can have devastating effects on relationships, school performance, and physical and emotional well-being.

MENTAL HEALTH IN SCHOOLS

In 1999 the White House conference on mental health revealed the Surgeon General's report on mental health that urged the integration of mental health services into all systems serving youth and children (U.S. Public Health Service, 2000). Through interactions with young adolescents diagnosed with mental illness, school personnel are an integral part of serving those students with mental health concerns. Teachers, who often see young people in high-stress situations, have reported working with children exhibiting signs of depression, distractibility, and self-destructive behavior. Though it is not the role of to school personnel to diagnose mental illness, teachers and administrators are responsible for modifying instruction and creating optimal learning environments for those diagnosed.

Until recently those students requiring special services or an Individual Education Plan (IEP) have mostly been students with physical disabilities or severe cognitive and/or emotional needs. Since its inception in 1975, revisions of the Individuals with Disabilities Education Act (IDEA) have created a legal mandate for special education and individualized services (U.S. Office of Special Education Programs, 2005). As a result, more students diagnosed with mental illnesses than ever before are receiving IEPs and 504 plans, having a direct impact on classroom teachers who may or may not be knowledgeable of particular mental illnesses. Even with the increased awareness of mental health issues and modifications for those diagnosed, drop out and suicide rates among young people continue to escalate, and many students go undiagnosed and untreated.

COMMON DSM IV-TR DIAGNOSES FOR EARLY ADOLESCENTS

Diagnosis of a mental disorder usually takes place under the direction of a licensed psychologist or psychiatrist, though social workers and general physicians are also an integral part of this process. Mental health practitioners in the United States use the *Diagnostic and Statistical Manual of Mental Disorders* (American Psychological Association, 2000) as a diagnostic reference manual. As the knowledge of mental health and neuroscience has grown, this manual has undergone major revisions since it was first published in 1952. Norm-based diagnostic tools such as the *Beck Depression Inventory* (Beck, Steer, & Brown, 1996), the *Miller Multiphasic Personality Inventory—Adolescent* (Butcher et al., 1992), or the *Diagnostic Interview Schedule for Children* (Shaffer & Fisher, 1997) also inform diagnoses.

Doctors, counselors, parents, and teachers become primary sources of information and education about a young person's particular disorder(s). Therefore, those working with young people need to be aware of what these particular diagnoses mean in terms of their affect on social, emotional, and cognitive domains. The next section briefly describes some of the most common mental disorders seen in early adolescents in mainstreamed or inclusion classrooms, including depression, manic depression, anxiety disorders, attention deficit disorders, and learning and communication disorders. Common treatment approaches and implications for those who work with middle school students follows.

DEPRESSION

Large-scale research studies have reported that up to 3% of children and up to 8% of adolescents in the United States suffer from depression, a serious mental disorder unlike normal or passing states of sadness (APA, 2000). Symptoms of depression are extreme and persistent and can interfere significantly with the ability to function at home and/or at school. There is evidence that depression emerging early in life often recurs and continues into adulthood and may predict more severe illness in adult life (APA, 2000).

Depressive disorders in adolescents are characterized by a depressed mood and irritability throughout most of the day. Other indicators of depression include diminished pleasure in daily activities, weight loss or gain, feelings of worthlessness and guilt, and lack of concentration. Behaviors include changes in sleeping patterns, complaining of a loss of energy, and/or exhibiting physical agitation or delayed reaction observable by others for a period of 2 weeks or longer. Depression may also bring about recurrent thoughts of death. Depression is termed "dysthymia" when it is chronic. Those with dysthymic disorder are depressed more often than they are not, either by their own account or from another's report.

MANIC DEPRESSIVE ILLNESS

According to one study, 1% of adolescents ages 14-18 were found to have met criteria for manic-depressive illness in their lifetime (APA, 2000). Also known as bipolar disorder, manic depression is characterized by an "abnormally and persistently elevated, expansive, or irritable mood" (APA, 2000, p. 357). Recent research revealed that many young people who are mistakenly diagnosed with ADHD are actually in the early stages of bipolar disorder, perhaps because the indicators are so similar. Symptoms of mania include inflated self-esteem and feelings of grandiosity, decreased need for sleep, incessant talking or pressured speech, racing thoughts and ideas, distractibility, increased goal-directed activity (including excessive planning, hypersexuality, and hyperreligiosity), physical agitation, and high risk behavior. A manic episode is diagnosed if elevated mood occurs with three or more of the other symptoms for 1 week or longer.

Sometimes, severe episodes of mania or depression include symptoms of psychosis with hallucinations and delusions. In some people symptoms of mania and depression may occur together in what is called a mixed bipolar state, which often include agitation, trouble sleeping, significant change in appetite, psychosis, and suicidal thinking. A person may have a very sad, hopeless mood while at the same time feeling extremely energized. A mild to moderate level of mania is called hypomania during which the person who experiences it may feel good, have increased functioning, and enhanced productivity. Thus, even when family and friends learn to recognize the mood swings as possible bipolar disorder, the person may deny that anything is wrong. Without proper treatment, however, hypomania can become severe mania in some people or can switch into depression.

ANXIETY DISORDERS

Anxiety disorders are the most common mental health problems that occur in children and adolescents (Costello et al., 1996). According to one large-scale study of 9- to 17-year-olds, as many as 13% of young people had an anxiety disorder in a year (National Institute of Mental Health, 1999). Several types of anxiety disorders can be diagnosed. Symptoms of Generalized Anxiety Disorder include exaggerated worry and tension over everyday events that persist for over 6 months. At least one third of all adult cases of Obsessive Compulsive Disorder (OCD) begin in childhood. The disorder is characterized by intrusive, unwanted, repetitive thoughts and rituals performed out of a need to neutralize the anxiety. Obsessions, unlike worries of everyday life that most people experience, manifest as persistent thoughts that often center around contamination, repeated doubts, sequencing and ordering, and aggressive or horrific images. Compulsions are the repetitive behaviors, such as washing and cleaning, counting, checking, that become excessive and anxiety-producing. Though most adult sufferers of OCD can see the behaviors as irrational, children, however, often do not have the knowledge that what they are doing is not logical or unnecessary.

Panic attacks are characterized by feelings of extreme fear and dread that strike unexpectedly and repeatedly for no apparent reason. These unexpected attacks are accompanied by intense physical symptoms, including chest pain, pounding heart, shortness of breath, dizziness, or abdominal distress. People experiencing panic attacks often describe a fear of losing control, dying, or "going crazy" along with a feeling of unreality and detachment.

Post Traumatic Stress Disorder (PTSD) is a common co-occurring disorder with depression. PTSD shows up in young people who have had exposure to a terrifying event such as child abuse, war, natural disasters, or murders. It is most often characterized by the repeated re-experience of the ordeal in the form of frightening, intrusive memories, and brings on hyper vigilance and deadening of normal emotions. Adolescents suffering from PTSD may engage in traumatic reenactment, in which they incorporate aspects of the trauma into their daily lives. In addition, adolescents are more likely than younger children or adults to exhibit impulsive and aggressive behaviors.

Social Anxiety Disorder consists of extreme fear of embarrassment or being scrutinized. Avoidance behaviors are practiced by those with social phobia, which for adolescents often leads to truancy problems. Specific phobias such as excessive fear of an object or situation, such as dogs, heights, loud sounds, flying, costumed characters, or enclosed spaces also impact daily functioning. As in the case of OCD, young people are less like to realize the illogical nature of their phobias. Other anxiety disorders including separation anxiety, and selective mutism can directly impact young people's social and academic performance.

ATTENTION DEFICIT AND BEHAVIORAL DISORDERS

Attention deficit disorders are the most commonly diagnosed psychiatric disorders of childhood and are estimated to affect 3 to 5% of school-aged children (APA, 2000). There are three subtypes of Attention Deficit/Hyperactivity Disorder (ADHD): Combined Type, Predominantly Inattentive Type, and Predominantly Hyperactive Type. The diagnosis is most often given in late childhood to early adolescence, and features of the disorder vary with age and environment. In adolescents, ADHD often manifests in outbursts, low frustration tolerance, bossiness, excessive insistence that demands be met, distractibility, and impulsivity. Children with ADHD usually have trouble with peer and adult relationships; however, those diagnosed with these disorders often do not manifest symptoms in all arenas of life. Those with ADHD, Predominantly Inattentive Type seem to have the most difficulty in schools; whereas, those diagnosed as ADHD, Primarily Hyperactive Types have more trouble with social-emotional development. By early adolescence hyperactivity symptoms may be confined to inner feelings of jitteriness, fidgeting, or pervasive restlessness.

Oppositional Defiance Disorder (ODD) is a common co-occurring disorder with a diagnosis of ADHD. This disorder is characterized by short tempers, lack of compliance with adult requests, deliberately annoying behavior, assigning blame for own mistakes to others, and angry and vindictive thoughts and acts. As several of the indicators for ODD typically occur in preteens and adolescents, mental health professionals are urged to consider criterion as significant only if occurs more frequently and for at least a 6 month period of time.

LEARNING AND COMMUNICATION DISORDERS

An estimated 2 to 10% of children in U.S. public schools are identified as having a Learning Disorder (APA, 2000). Learning disorders are identified and subsequently diagnosed when an individual's achievement on standardized tests falls significantly below that expected by peers. Dropout rates for these students are particularly high, nearly 1.5 times the average (APA, 2000). Learning disorders are differen-

tiated from normal variations in academic attainment brought about by lack of opportunity, poor education, and/or cultural factors. Common learning disorders teachers see in the classroom are Reading Disorders, including dyslexia; Mathematics Disorders, including dyscalculia; Disorders of Written Expression, including dysgraphia, and Expressive Language Disorders, including aphasia. Often Learning Disorders are the result of genetic predisposition, a general medical condition, or a head trauma; therefore, learning disorders can appear at any stage in a young person's development.

TREATMENT AND EDUCATION

For many parents and guardians learning their child has a mental illness is confusing and intimidating. Parents often blame themselves or are paralyzed from taking action due to the stigma surrounding the disorders. The World Health Organization (2001) suggests that the intersection of biological, social, and psychological factors converge in the development of mental disorders. Mental illnesses that have been identified as neurologically-based and are often treated with medications. Though the medications are often an essential part of the treatment of mental disorders, they can also have residual side effects that interfere with learning and interaction. Individual and group psychotherapy are also treatment options used separately or in combination with medications. For specific mental and learning disorders, particular pedagogical approaches are found to more successful than others in helping individual students.

The Internet is an excellent source for people desiring to educate themselves on mental illness. Several national mental health organizations including the National Institute for Mental Health (2004a, 2004b,) and the National Alliance for the Mentally Ill (2004) offer online booklets on a range of mental illnesses. Dr. Leslie Packer (2004) has created a web site called "Tourette Syndrome Plus" (www.tourettesyndrome.net/index.htm) that serves as a clearinghouse of information for parents and educators on a host of issues surrounding mental health and education, particularly legal rights related to IEPs for mental health diagnoses. On-line support groups and chat rooms also assist those seeking knowledge and support for mental disorders. Even among the massive amount of misinformation, the goal of increased understanding and knowledge through the web is being reached (NIMH, 2003).

Parental and teacher involvement has resulted in more accommodations for students with mental health diagnoses. When coming together to create an

IEP or less formal learning plan for these students, both the adults and the young people are better served if they are knowledgeable of the specifics of the disorders involved. Common accommodations allowed by most states include individual or small group test administration, in-depth explanations of instructions, extended time on tests and assignments, computer and machine assisted instruction, and read-alouds on tests. Though these accommodations appear often in IEPs and on 504 plans, they are not one-size-fits-all. For example, students with mental health issues that lead to decreased sleep may need to have shorter school days that start later. An adolescent with ADHD may do better in a classroom with teachers who use less lecture and more hands-on activities. Someone with Social Anxiety Disorder may need smaller class sizes or to complete some course work in an on-line environment.

With the number of early adolescents diagnosed with mental disorders on the rise, school personnel cannot afford to turn their back on these students. IEPs that traditionally served those with severe cognitive functioning now must be created to fit those who might otherwise dropout or be overlooked. The first step for classroom teachers and administrators is education on mental illness common to young people. Another essential part of helping those who have differences in mind is communication among the home, mental health organizations, and school. The junctures of mental health, adolescent identity development, and academic performance involves many people. Being attentive to what young people need to successfully navigate these difficult times requires a multisystemic approach that addressed the whole child rather than the label or diagnosis.

References

American Psychiatric Association. (2000). *Diagnostic and statistical manual of mental disorders* (4th ed.). Washington, DC: Author.

Beck, A. T., Steer, R. A., & Brown, G. K. (1996). *Beck Depression Inventory®-II, (BDI®-II)*. San Antonio, TX: Harcourt Assessment.

Butcher, J. N., Williams, C. L., Graham, J. R., Archer, R. P., Tellegen, A., Ben-Porath, Y. S., et al. (1992). *Minnesota Multiphasic Personality Inventory™-Adolescent, MMPI™-A*. Minneapolis: The University of Minnesota Press.

Costello, E. J., Angold, A., Burns, B. J., Stangl, D. K., Tweed, D. L., Erkanli, A., et al. (1996). The Great Smoky Mountains Study of Youth. Goals, design, methods, and the prevalence of DSM-III-R disorders. *Archives of General Psychiatry, 53*(12), 1129–1136.

National Alliance for the Mentally Ill. (2004). *Understanding bipolar disorder: What you need to know about this medical illness*. National Alliance for the Mentally Ill. Retrieved May 21, 2004, from http://www.nami.org/Content/ ContentGroups/Helpline1/UnderstandingBipolar Disorder-r.pdf

National Institute of Mental Health. (1999). Children and mental health. In *Mental health: A report of the surgeon general*. Retrieved May 25, 1999, from http://www. surgeongeneral.gov/library/mentalhealth/pdfs/c3.pdf

National Institute of Mental Health. (2003). *Breaking ground, breaking through: The strategic plan for mood disorders research of the National Institute of Mental Health*. Retrieved May 21, 2004 from: http://www.nimh.nih.gov/strategic/ mooddisorders.pdf

National Institute of Mental Health. (2004a, April). *Bipolar disorder*. National Institute of Mental Health. Retrieved May 21, 2004, from: http://www.nimh.nih.gov/publicat/ bipolar.cfm

National Institute of Mental Health. (2004b). *Depression*. National Institute of Mental Health. Retrieved May 21, 2004, from http://www.nimh.nih.gov/HealthInformation/ Depressionmenu.cfm

National Mental Health Information Center. (2002). *The myth of the bad kid*. Retrieved June 29, 2005, from: http:// www.mentalhealth.org/publications/allpubs/Ca-0021/ default.asp

Packer, L. (2004). *Welcome to Tourette Syndrome "Plus."* Retrieved May 21, 2004, from http://www.tourettesyndrome.net/index.htm

Shaffer, D., & Fisher, P. (1997). *NIMH—Diagnostic interview schedule for children*. New York: New York State Psychiatric Institute.

U.S. Office of Special Education Programs. (2005). *Federal Register 70*(103).

U.S. Public Health Service. (2000). *Report of the Surgeon General's Conference on Children's Mental Health: A national action agenda*. Retrieved June 30, 2005, from: http:// www.surgeongeneral.gov/topics/cmh/childreport.htm

World Health Organization. (2001). *The World Heath report 2001, mental health: New understanding, new hope*. Retreived June 30, 2005, from: http://www.who.int/whr/ 2001/en/

—Leslie S. Cook
The University of North Carolina, Charlotte

INCLUSION

Inclusion is a philosophy that promotes educating children and youth with and without disabilities in the same classrooms, and providing *all* students equal access to and opportunities for participation in cocurricular and extracurricular activities. The goal is to create communities of learners in schools that meet the needs of all learners by respecting and learning from each other's differences (Salend & Duhaney, 1999). Inclusion implies that students with disabilities are full members of the general education community. This principle is consistent with current middle level practices which call for reliable, close relationships, a sense of belonging in a group, a core of common knowledge for all, and assuring success for all (Jackson & Davis, 2000). Proponents of inclusion call for reform of practices that segregate and exclude students with disabilities (Lewis & Doorlag, 2003). Such theorists see pull-out and self-contained programs for students with special needs as discriminatory and segregationist, that is, separation is not equal.

Inclusion is not a law, nor is the term "inclusion" included in any of the public laws regulating special education services. The IDEA (Individuals with Disabilities Education Act), starting in 1975 and continuing until today, mandates that children and youth with disabilities be educated in "the least restrictive environment," which is determined on an individual basis. Schools are held accountable for offering a full continuum of educational services that include full and partial inclusion, as well as alternative day treatment and/or home hospital programs that address the unique medical and mental health needs of some students. The full continuum of services safeguards against a "one-size-fits-all" approach to education.

The most recent Reauthorization of IDEA (1997) stressed the need for all educators to share in the responsibility for educating all students, including those with disabilities, and requires that general education teachers participate in the Individualized Educational Plan (IEP) process (IEP is the coordinated educational "game plan" for a student with special needs).

There is usually little debate about whether students with special needs should be included to some extent in school activities; the debate centers around how much, when and where. Most special education students receive at least part of their education in the general education classroom. The debate tends to focus on whether they should receive their special education services in the general education classroom, or in a separate classroom for part of the day, or in other words, via an inclusion or mainstreaming approach.

In *full inclusion*, students who are eligible to receive special education services receive assistance in the general education classroom. Their assistance is a result of collaboration between general and special education teachers who jointly determine the learning characteristics and teaching strategies for each student in the IEP process (Lewis & Doorlag, 2003). Class and school activities may be modified and adapted to make it possible for all students to fully participate in the academic and social culture of the school. With inclusion, students with disabilities are members of the general education community and receive services as a member of that community, rather than being separate, peripheral members of their school.

In *mainstreaming*, students who receive special educational services (those with an IEP) spend some part of a school day with their general education peers engaging in instructional and social activities (Lewis & Doorlag, 2003). The amount of time spent in general education activities varies from student to student. It may include integration in academic or social activities or both. Typically, elective courses are selected for this purpose (art, music, physical and vocational education), while IEP students receive their academic core courses in segregated classes with other students with disabilities. More recently the term "partial inclusion" has been substituted for mainstreaming and refers to students with disabilities participating in some (but not all) classes and activities with their peers who do not have identified disabilities. For example, "Jerome is *included* part of the day. He is *included* for basic practical arts and music." Students who are mainstreamed or partially included are still very much a part of the special education department, with a special education teacher responsible for their grading and academic accommodations. Students who are mainstreamed are clearly a "separate" group who encounter separate educational experiences and opportunities. The big difference between mainstreaming and inclusion is that with mainstreaming the student is going "out" from special education to experience partial participation in the full school community, rather than being a full participating member of an inclusive school community.

SOCIAL BENEFITS OF INCLUSION

Inclusion as a philosophy highlights the importance of schools as social institutions in our society. The best way to promote acceptance of diversity in society is to start with schools that promote acceptance of everyone's different strengths and weaknesses. Inclusion celebrates the diversity of humans and acknowledges that the greatest commonality among all humans is a need to feel of a sense of belonging and acceptance. Diversity is a hallmark of early adolescence, as is the need to belong. Unfortunately, research (e.g., Reid & Button, 1995) has found students in special education classrooms to feel anger and frustration resulting from being isolated from their classmates.

Children with and without disabilities benefit from the experience of getting to know each other and develop relationships. To investigate middle school students' perspectives of diversity and inclusion, Capper and Pickett (1994) conducted focus group interviews with 46 school students from a traditionally structured school, and 46 students from an inclusive school. Students at the inclusion-based school showed an increased acceptance, understanding, and tolerance of individual differences. In contrast, students attending the traditionally structured school were more likely to engage in stereotyping and held more negative perceptions of diversity and students with disabilities. In another study, 181 middle school students without disabilities reported that inclusion resulted in positive outcomes, particularly in terms of social and interpersonal skills, for their peers with disabilities; and more realistic and positive perspectives for themselves concerning their classmates with disabilities (York, Vandercook, Macdonald, Heise-Neff, & Caughey, 1992).

Hendrickson, Shokoohi-Yekta, Hamre-Nietupski, and Gable (1996) surveyed 1,137 middle and high school students without disabilities regarding friendships with peers who experienced disabilities. These students reported that inclusion facilitated the development of friendships between themselves and their peers with disabilities. These students suggested using cooperative grouping arrangements, sharing information about disabilities, and implementing social activities to promote interactions between students.

ACADEMIC BENEFITS OF INCLUSION

A national study on inclusion reported fewer incomplete assignments, more positive interactions with peers, and improved attitudes toward school and learning for students with disabilities participating in full inclusion (National Center for Educational Restructuring and Inclusion, 1995). Additionally, they found that placement in inclusion programs led to academic gains for students with disabilities, including improved performance on standardized tests, mastery of Individualized Education Program (IEP) goals, grades, on-task behavior, and motivation to learn. Jones and Carlier (1995) reported that middle school students without disabilities shared tasks and adapted jobs so the students with disabilities were participants rather than just observers.

Staub and Peck (1995) investigated the effects of inclusion on students without disabilities and found: (a) instructional time was not lost, (b) academic progress was not decelerated, (c) growth in social cognition and self-concept was experienced, (d) more acceptance and appreciation of diversity was experienced, and (e) "many nondisabled students experienced a growth in their commitment to personal moral and ethical principles as a result of their relationship with students with disabilities" (p. 36).

INSTRUCTION, NOT PLACEMENT, IS THE KEY

Much of the research on inclusion has emphasized placement in the general education versus special education classroom rather than what happens in those classrooms (Hocutt, 1996). To date, there is no compelling evidence that placement, rather than instruction, is the critical factor in student academic or social success. Academic and social benefits are possible from inclusion, but instruction is the key variable.

Middle school instructional practices such as cooperative grouping, interdisciplinary units, developmentally appropriate curricula attending to the unique physical, cognitive and social/emotional needs of each individual, active and meaningful curricula, differentiated curricula, and appreciation of the diverse learning needs of all adolescents are practices that support academic and social gains for all students as a result of inclusion.

In summary, the inclusion is applied quite inconsistently, with implementation varying greatly from district to district and school to school (Hines, 2001). It must be noted that special education is not a place—it is a set of services provided to students to help them achieve success in school. Therefore, services and supports may be brought to students in the general education classroom as needed. For the inclusion philosophy to be transformed into effective educational practice, there must be a shared vision by all at the school—including administrators, staff, support personnel (cafeteria, maintenance and custodial workers), teachers, parents, and students. The structure of most middle school programs facilitates the professional collaboration needed to make inclusion work.

REFERENCES

Capper, C. A., & Pickett, R. S. (1994). The relationship between school structure and culture and student views of diversity and inclusive education. *The Special Education Leadership Review, 2,* 102-122.

Hendrickson, J. M., Shokoohi-Yekta, M., Hamre-Nietupski, S., & Gable, R. A. (1996). Middle and high school students' perceptions on being friends with peers with severe disabilities. *Exceptional Children, 63,* 19-28.

Hines, R. A. (2001). *Inclusion in middle schools.* Champaign, IL. (ERIC 459000).

Hocutt, A. M. (1996). Effectiveness of special education: Is placement the critical factor? *Future of Children, 6*(1), 77-102

Jackson, A. W., & Davis, G. A. (2000). *Turning points 2000: Educating adolescents in the 21st century.* New York: Teachers College Press.

Jones, M. M., & Carlier, L. L. (1995). Creating inclusionary opportunities for learners with multiple disabilities: A team-teaching approach. *Teaching Exceptional Children, 27*(3), 23-27.

Lewis, R. B., & Doorlag, D. H. (2003). *Teaching special students in general education classrooms* (6th ed.). Upper Saddle River, NJ: Merrill Prentice Hall.

National Center for Educational Restructuring and Inclusion. (1995). *National study of inclusion.* New York: Author.

Reid, D. K., & Button, L. J. (1995). Anna's story: Narratives of personal experience about being labeled learning disabled. *Journal of Learning Disabilities, 28,* 602-614.

Salend, S. J., & Duhaney, L. M. G. (1999). The impact of inclusion on students with and without disabilities and their educators. *Remedial and Special Education, 20*(2), 114-126.

Staub, D., & Peck, C. A. (1995). What are the outcomes for nondisabled students? *Educational Leadership, 52*(4), 36-40.

York, J., Vandercook, T., Macdonald, C., Heise-Neff, C., & Caughey, E. (1992). Feedback about integrating middle-school students with severe disabilities in general education classes. *Exceptional Children, 58,* 244-258.

—Rhonda Black
—Paul Deering
University of Hawaii, Manoa

INCLUSION: COMPREHENSIVE INCLUSION

Comprehensive inclusion is a cultural construct denoting that stakeholders from all explicit or implicit groups at a school consistently have positive opportunities to interact with one another, and with each other's values and ideas (Deering, 1998). Explicit, or officially recognized groups, include students designated for special education, limited English proficiency and gifted and talented services, those of both genders, and all races, ethnicities, religions, and socioeconomic groups. Implicit groups include informal cultural groups, like jocks, nerds, goths, townies, and so forth. Also included are persons of gay, lesbian, bisexual and transgender sexual identity, regardless of how explicit or implicit this identity might be.

Comprehensive inclusion calls for a school's stakeholders—educators, parents, students, community—to seek to understand all the explicit and implicit groups present and to consistently provide all with equal opportunities for full participation in all social and academic activities. This means that the people of various groups, as well as their values, ideas and beliefs are included in any and all school-related contexts. Comprehensive inclusion is in concert with the middle school (Erb, 2001; Jackson & Davis, 2000; National Middle School Association, 1998) and multicultural education literature (Banks & Banks, 1995; Gallego, Cole, & Laboratory of Comparative Human

Cognition, 2001), and can support early adolescents' development of identity by promoting acceptance of self and others.

Comprehensive inclusion necessitates coordination and scaffolding. Coordination entails policies and practices at all levels of the school consistently supporting comprehensive inclusion (Deering, 1998). Scaffolding is providing "just enough" assistance for a learner to succeed at a task (Vygotsky, 1978), in this case, for students and other stakeholders to establish positive relationships with members of all other groups.

A school policy placing students with special needs in regular educational settings is a good start as it provides the opportunity for widespread intergroup contact. However, coordination is essential to ensure that such opportunities are not undermined. For example, programs that involve select groups of students can have a "ripple effect" through the schedule that limits opportunities for diverse intergroup interactions; examples would be a band program that involves a large number of higher achieving students, or placement of all students with special needs on a single middle level team. In addition, "inclusion classrooms" can be re-segregated if teachers frequently employ homogenous groups within them.

At a face-to-face level, comprehensive inclusion requires that adults scaffold students' academic and social relationships. Differentiated (Tomlinson, 1999) and multiple intelligences (Gardner & Hatch, 1989) curriculum can help students of diverse abilities and interests to succeed in the same classroom while supporting inter-group interactions. Small group learning can also scaffold the development of very productive academic and social relationships (Cohen, 1994; Slavin, 1991; Webb, 1989); choice of group members can vary, with the students deciding some of the time, in which case they will likely tend toward homogeneity (Deering, 1996), while sometimes by the teacher should choose in order to promote heterogeneity. Peer tutoring can also provide opportunities for intergroup interaction, with positive academic and social benefits for both the tutor and tutee (Logan, Diaz, Piperno, Rankin, MacFarland, & Borganian, 1995; Staub & Peck, 1995). Additionally, teaching and reinforcing social and inclusion skills can help students to establish relations outside their typical affiliation groups (Gibbs, 2001). All these scaffolded intergroup interactions can then carry over to nonclassroom settings such as the lunch room, hallways, social events, and so forth. (Deering, 1996, 1998).

A further aspect of comprehensive inclusion calls for the values and material culture of all groups to be a part of the mainstream culture of the school. Thus, the language, history, art, etc., of each stakeholder group should, at least be studied and accepted, and ideally, celebrated.

Assessment of comprehensive inclusion calls for first, inquiring into and identifying all the possible explicit and implicit stakeholder groups at a school and the various contexts where they might interact. If members of the various groups regularly interact with, and encounter the values and material culture of all others, then the school is doing well at comprehensive inclusion.

REFERENCES

Banks, J. A., & Banks, C. A. M. (Eds.). (1995). *Handbook of research on multicultural education.* New York: MacMillan.

Cohen, E. G. (1994). *Designing groupwork* (2nd ed.). New York: Teachers College Press.

Deering, P. D. (1996). An ethnographic study of norms of inclusion and cooperation in a multiethnic middle school. *Urban Review, 28*(1), 21-39.

Deering, P. D. (1998). Making comprehensive inclusion of special needs students work in a middle school. *Middle School Journal, 29*(3) 12-19.

Erb, T. O. (Ed.). (2001). *This we believe: And now we must act.* Westerville, OH: National Middle School Association.

Gallego, M. A., Cole, M., & Laboratory of Comparative Human Cognition. (2001). Classroom cultures and cultures in the classroom. In V. Richardson (Ed.), *Handbook of research on teaching* (4th ed., pp. 951-997). Washington, DC: American Educational Research Association.

Gardner, H., & Hatch, T. (1989). Multiple intelligences go to school: Educational implications of the theory of multiple intelligences. *Educational Researcher, 18*(8), 4-10.

Gibbs, J. (2001). *Discovering gifts in middle school: Learning in a caring culture called Tribes.* Windsor, CA: Center Source Systems.

Jackson, A. W., & Davis, G. A. (2000). *Turning points 2000: Educating adolescents in the 21st century.* New York: Teachers College Press.

Logan, K. R., Diaz, E., Piperno, M., Rankin, D., MacFarland, A. D., & Borganian, K. (1995). How inclusion built a community of learners. *Educational Leadership, 52*(4), 42-44.

National Middle School Association. (1998). *NMSA research summary #14: What is the impact of inclusion on students and staff in the middle school setting?* Retrieved March 17, 2001, from http://www.nmsa.org/research/ressum14.htm

Slavin, R. E. (1991). Synthesis of research on cooperative learning. *Educational Leadership, 48*(5), 71-77.

Staub, D., & Peck, C. (1995) What are the outcomes for nondisabled students? *Educational Leadership, 52*(4), 36-41.

Tomlinson, C. A. (1999). *The differentiated classroom: Responding to the needs of all learners.* Alexandria, VA: Association for Supervision and Curriculum Development.

Vygotsky, L. S. (1978). *Mind in society: The development of higher psychological processes* (M. Cole, V. John-Steiner, S. Scribner, & E. Souberman, Trans.). Cambridge, MA: Harvard University Press.

Webb, N. M. (1989). Peer interaction and learning in small groups. *International Journal of Educational Research, 13*, 21-40.

—Paul Deering
—Rhonda Black
University of Hawaii at Manoa

INCLUSION: INCLUDING STUDENTS WITH DISABILITIES IN THE MIDDLE GRADES

In 1975 the original special education legislation, P.L. 94-142, established the education of children with disabilities in general education schools and classrooms as a key goal. Over the subsequent decades, more and more students with disabilities are participating in general education classrooms, however, there is still much debate concerning how students are to be included as well as the effects and even what it means to be "included" (Hines, 2001).

THE LEGAL BASIS FOR INCLUSION

The legal foundation for inclusion is the Least Restrictive Environments (LRE) provision in the Individuals with Disabilities Education Act (IDEA) (formerly P.L. 94-142) which requires that that states have procedures in place assuring that,

1. to the maximum extent appropriate, children with disabilities, including children in public or private institutions or other care facilities, are educated with children who are not disabled, and

2. special classes, separate schooling, or other removal of children with disabilities from the regular educational environment occurs only when the nature or severity of the disability is such that education in regular classes with the use of supplementary aids and services cannot be achieved satisfactorily (IDEA Regulations, 34 C.F. R. § 300.550 (b)).

However, determining LRE for an individual student must be based on an Individualized Education Program (IEP) which is developed by a team including the child's parents and which specifies the special education and other services the child needs to benefit from education. Under the law, the IEP team is to first determine what constitutes an appropriate education for the child and to then determine the environment(s) in which the education will be provided.

In 1997 Congress amended the IDEA and placed even more emphasis on educating students in general education classrooms by requiring that each child's IEP include statements regarding, "the involvement and progress of each child with a disability in the general education curriculum including the unique needs that arise out of the child's disability" (Sec. 300.347(a)). In addition, the IDEA regulations required that IEP teams include regular education teachers who are familiar with the general education curriculum and that the team specifies the supports that will be necessary for a child to be educated in general education classrooms (Yell & Drasgow, 1999). In December, 2004 the IDEA was again reauthorized and further reinforced the national commitment to provide each eligible student with a disability a free, appropriate public education but also reinforced the need to end the isolation of students with disabilities by requiring that they be educated with their nondisabled peers.

Determining the LRE for an individual student can be a difficult task for teachers, administrators and parents and can sometimes result in disagreements and disputes (Yell, 1999). Over the years, some of these disputes have involved the courts which have resulted in decisions that provide current legal standards for determining LRE. In particular, four federal court cases have established a set of principles that IEP teams are to use to decide the LRE for any individual student. The first of these cases, *Roncker v. Walter* (1983), established the principle of "portability" which requires that IEP teams determine why the special education and services that a child may require cannot be provided in general education classrooms (Yell & Drasgow, 1999). In other words, IEP teams cannot determine where a child is to be educated solely because a school happens to have a program or services in a particular site. The services should follow the child.

In a later case, *Daniel R. R. v. State Board of Education* (1989), the court ruled in favor of the school district and concluded that schools were not obligated to provide inclusive settings in every instance nor are teachers required to spend most of their time with one student. Furthermore, the court noted that modifications to the curriculum are required to accommodate children with disabilities but there are two factors to be considered when determining if a school has made an appropriate effort to educate a children with disabilities in a regular classroom: (1) will the child be provided with an adequate education in a regular classroom, even with supplementary aids and services; and (2) if not, and the school removes the child from the regular classroom setting, is the school making an effort to include the student to the maximum extent possible?

A third case, the *Sacramento City Unified School District v. Rachel H.* (1994) case added two additional factors that may be considered by IEP teams in addition to those specified in *Daniel R.* These include the effects of the student's presence on the educational environment and the cost of including the student in the general education setting. Also, the courts noted that the educational benefits of inclusion may include social as well as academic skills. Finally, the *Hartmann v. Loudon County Board of Education* (1997) decision firmly established that when schools make decisions about including a child in a general education classroom, the major obligation is to first determine what constitutes the most appropriate special education and related services for the child and then to determine the environment in which those services can best be provided. In this and the other LRE cases, the courts have consistently looked first at whether the child is benefiting educationally and then determining where that education is provided (Yell & Drasgow, 1999).

In summary, neither federal law nor judicial decisions have established an absolute right to inclusion. Instead, what is required is to make a case-by-case decision. However, the courts and the IDEA have indicated that the first preference is to educate a child with a disability in a general education classroom and that a good faith effort must be made to determine if the special education and related services can be provided in that setting before moving to a more segregated environment (Vitello, 1998).

How Many Students are "Included"

Data relative to LRE and students with disabilities is reported by States to the federal government annually. Data are reported on the numbers of students with disabilities by age group and disability category that are receiving special education in general education classrooms for a proportion of each data. Data are also reported on students with disabilities being educated in special schools and other settings outside of the regular school. State-reported data for the 1999-2000 school year (U.S. Department of Education, 2002) indicates that 96% of students with disabilities were being educated in regular school buildings. Moreover, 47% of all students with disabilities were being educated in regular education classrooms 80% of the day

or more, which represents a 16% increase over a 10 year period.

Despite the overall increase in the proportions of children being included, there are substantial variations by age group, state and disability category. For example, New Hampshire educates 74% of its students with disabilities in regular education classrooms 80% or more of the day, while in Georgia, the percentage is only 19. In addition, among students with multiple disabilities, there has been only a 4% increase over the past decade in the numbers of those students educated in general education classroom 80% or more of the day, while inclusion of students with specific learning disabilities rose from 20 to 45% (U.S. Department of Education, 2002).

Furthermore, elementary-aged children are more likely to be served in regular classrooms than older students. During the 1999-2000, approximately 56% of students ages 6 through 11 were educated in the regular classroom for at least 80% of the school day, while for students ages 12 through 17 and 18 through 21 the percentage was 39 and 33, respectively (U.S. Department of Education, 2002).

What Does the Research Say about Inclusion?

Research on the effects of inclusion is somewhat limited and interpretation is complicated by the definition (e.g., proportion of time spent in general education) and nature of the children's disabilities. Little research has been conducted in academic achievement and social outcomes for middle grade students with disabilities (Rea, McLaughlin, & Walther-Thomas, 2002). Moore (1998) summarized the research on educating students with disabilities in general education classrooms and found some evidence that communication, social, and behavioral skill acquisition among students with disabilities is somewhat improved in inclusive classes or schools, although findings do not apply generally across all ages or disability groups. Several researchers have documented positive social and academic outcomes (Helmstetter, Curry, Brennan, & Sampson-Saul, 1998; Kishi & Meyer, 1994; Snell, 1998). In a meta-analysis of the impact of setting on learning, Baker, Wang, and Walberg (1995) found a "small-to-moderate beneficial effect of inclusive education on the academic and social outcomes of special needs students" (p. 34). A small number of studies have validated the negative impact of placement in regular education when individualized supports are not provided (York & Wycoff, 1999; Zigmond & Baker, 1995).

To date, no studies have documented the negative impact of inclusive practices on students without disabilities and proponents assert that if academic performance is at least as good in inclusive classrooms as those without students with disabilities, there is no legitimate academic argument against inclusion.

In summary, research involving children with more severe disabilities appears to indicate benefits in social and communication skills, the research focusing on the effects of including students with other disabilities is inconclusive (Hines, 2001; Snell, 1998). This is due in large part to the inconsistencies in variables including the nature of the students' educational needs, the type and amount of supports provided in the general classroom, the amount of time spent in general education, and the intended outcomes.

A number of authors have identified key factors that appear to influence whether inclusion is successful. Eight of the more frequently cited factors include: (1) schools/classrooms value and support inclusion and diversity; (2) positive teacher attitudes; (3) parent and family support; (4) teachers plan together through collaborative teaming; (5) classrooms facilitate both social and instructional inclusion; (6) teachers use adaptations so students can learn in general education classes; (7) peer support; and (8) paraprofessionals facilitate, not prevent, peer interactions (McGregor & Vogelsberg, 1998).

Researchers have also identified a number of organizational, knowledge and attitudinal barriers to including children with disabilities in regular classroom settings (Hines, 2001). Teacher attitudes and beliefs about learning, learners and teaching are considered strong predictors of their practices and, in turn, relate to student motivation and achievement (King, 2003). Attitudes about inclusion and providing students with disabilities the opportunities to participate in general education settings vary among educators and administrators. For example, although teachers agree in principle with the goals of inclusion, many do not feel prepared to teach and work in inclusive settings (Hines, 2001; Praisner, 2003). Furthermore, many feel that they have received only minimal training to be able to properly serve diverse student groups that include students with various types of disabilities (Praisner, 2003). Student's views and preferences of inclusion also vary. While some feel comfortable and confident with fully being included in regular academic settings, others prefer the "pull-out" model (Klinger, Vaughn, Schumm, Cohen, & Forgan, 1998). Parents and families also have different perceptions regarding inclusion, although a constant theme for parents is whether their child will be teased or not

be accepted in the classroom (Soodak, Podell, & Lehman, 1998).

INCLUSION IN MIDDLE SCHOOLS

Middle schools can provide an optimal milieu for inclusion due to practices such as use of interdisciplinary teaching teams and shared planning (Hines, 2001). However, all schools differ in how they approach inclusion. In part the differences can be due staffing patterns or lack of training (King, 2003). Two recent studies of inclusion in middle and high school schools (Morocco & Aguilar, 2002; Wallace, Anderson, & Bartholomay, 2002) cited the importance of collaborative teaching between general and special education teachers. In particular, co-teaching, involving two qualified teachers, usually a special educator and a general educator, share instructional responsibility for a diverse group of students, including children with disabilities (Council for Exceptional Children, 1994) has been found to result in improved academic achievement in several studies involving middle schools (Murawski & Swanson, 2001; Walther-Thomas, 1997). This arrangement allows each of the teachers to provide more individualized instruction to each student in the classroom and appears to be particularly effective in the reading and language arts area (Murawski & Swanson, 2001).

CONCLUSIONS AND FUTURE TRENDS

This brief overview of inclusive practices has demonstrated some of the dilemmas that have faced schools as they have implemented inclusion of students with disabilities. While enormous progress has been made, it is likely that more and more children with disabilities will be educated in general education classrooms with the increased accountability for student achievement required under Title 1 of the No Child Left Behind Act of 2001. With new demands for improving the performance of all students on challenging state standards, the students who receive special education will have to access the general education curriculum and be taught by teachers who are qualified to teach that curriculum. Inevitably, the number of students with disabilities educated in general education classrooms alongside their non-disabled peers will increase. Thus, it will be imperative that special and general education teachers work collaboratively and share responsibility for ensuring that every student has an equal opportunity to attain higher levels of learning.

REFERENCES

Baker, E. T., Wang, M. C., & Walberg, H. J. (1995). The effects of inclusion on learning. *Educational Leadership, 52*(4), 33-35.

Council for Exceptional Children. (1994, October). *Thinking about inclusion and learning disabilities: A teacher's guide.* Retrieved July 30, 2004, from http://www.cec.sped.org/

Daniel R. R. v. State Board of Education, 874 F.2d 1036 (5th Cir. 1989).

Hartmann v. Loudon County Board of Education, (4th Cir. 1997). Retrieved June 21, 2005, from http://www.law.emory.edu/4circuit/july97/962809.p.html

Helmstetter, E., Curry, C. A., Brennan, M., & Sampson-Saul, M. (1998). Comparison of general and special education classrooms of students with severe disabilities. *Education and Training in Mental Retardation and Developmental Disabilities, 33*(3), 216-27.

Hines, R. A. (2001). *Inclusion in middle schools.* Champaign, IL: Clearinghouse on Elementary and Early Childhood Education. (ERIC ED459000).

Individuals with Disabilities Education Act (IDEA), 20 U.S.C. Sec. 1401-1485.

King, I. C. (2003). Examining middle school inclusion through the lens of learner-centered principles. *Theory into Practice, 42*(2), 151-158.

Kishi, G. S., & Meyer, L. H. (1994). What children report and remember: A six-year follow-up of the effects of the social contact between peers with and without disabilities. *Journal of the Association for Persons with Severe Handicaps, 19*(2), 277-89.

Klingner, J. K., Vaughn, S., Schumm, P. C., & Forgan, J. W. (1998). Inclusion or pull-out: Which do students prefer? *Journal of Learning Disabilities, 31*, 148-158.

McGregor, G., & Vogelsberg, R. T. (1998). *Inclusive school practices. Pedagogical and research foundations. A synthesis of the literature that informs best practices about inclusive schooling.* Pittsburg, PA: Allegheny University of the Health Sciences.

Moore, C. (1998). *Educating students with disabilities in general education classrooms: A summary of the research.* Eugene: University of Oregon, Western Regional Resource Center.

Morocco, C. C., & Aguilar, C. M. (2002). Coteaching for content understanding: A schoolwide model. *Journal of Educational Psychological Consultation, 13*(4), 315-348.

Murawski, W. W., & Swanson, L. H. (2001). A meta-analysis of co-teaching research: Where are the data? *Remedial and Special Education, 22*(5), 258-267.

Praisner, C. (2003). Attitudes of elementary school principals towards the inclusion of students with disabilities. *Council for Exceptional Children, 69*, 135-145.

Rea, P. J., MacLaughlin, V. L., & Walther-Thomas, C. (2002). Outcomes for students with disabilities in inclusive and pullout programs. *Exceptional Children, 68*(2), 203-222.

Roncker v. Walter, 700 F.2d 1058 (6th Cir. 1983).

Sacramento City Unified School District v. Rachel H., 14 F.3d 1398 (9th Cir. 1994).

Snell, M. E. (1998). Characteristics of elementary school classrooms where children with moderate and severe disabilities are included: A compilation of findings. In S. J. Vitello & D. E. Mithaug (Eds.), *Inclusive schooling: National and international perspectives* (pp. 76-97). Mahwah, NJ: Erlbaum.

Soodak, L. C., Podell D. M., & Lehman, L. R. (1998). Teacher, student and school attributes as predictors of teachers' responses to inclusion. *Journal of Special Education, 31*(4), 480-497.

U.S. Department of Education. (2002). *Twenty-third annual report to Congress.* Retrieved July 30, 2004, from http://www.ed.gov

Vitello, S. J. (1998). The law on inclusion. In S. J. Vitello & D. E. Mithaug (Eds.), *Inclusive schooling: National and international perspectives* (pp. 24-53). Mahwah, NJ: Erlbaum.

Wallace, T. Anderson, A. R., & Bartholomay, T. (2002). Collaboration: An element associated with the success of four inclusive high schools. *Journal of Educational Psychological Consultation, 13*(4), 315-348.

Walther-Thomas, C. (1997). Co-teaching experiences. *Journal of Learning Disabilities, 30*(4), 395-407.

Yell, M. L. (1999). Education and the law. *Preventing School Failure, 43*(2), 84-90.

Yell, M. L., & Drasgow, E. (1999). A legal analysis of inclusion. *Preventing School Failure, 43*(3), 118-125.

York, A. C., & Wycoff, H. E. (1999). Integration in the secondary school of students with mild or moderate disabilities. In M. J. Coutinho & A. C. Repp (Eds.), *Inclusion: The integration of students with disabilities* (pp. 312-331). Belmont, CA: Wadsworth.

Zigmond, N., & Baker, J. M. (1995). Concluding comments: Current and future practices in inclusive education. *Journal of Special Education, 29*(2), 245-50.

—Margaret J. McLaughlin
Universit of Maryland

——Glenda Y. Hernández
Montgomery College, Maryland

INDUCTION AND MENTORING

Educational equity is the heart and soul of current concern for induction and mentoring opportunities for new teachers. As citizens of the United States, we are linked to a legacy of commitment to ensure that all children have equal access to a quality education. With the passing of The No Child Left Behind Act, the federal government directly associated student achievement with teacher quality and proclaimed that every class be taught by a "highly qualified teacher."

Fiscal responsibility also contributes to sustained interest in induction and mentoring options. In a recent report from the Alliance for Excellent Education (2004), induction was cited as the most significant strategy to turn the tide of a rapidly increasing rate of teacher attrition. Currently, American schools are spending over $2.5 billion every year replacing teachers who drop out of the profession. In addition to this extraordinary financial drain, Smith and Ingersoll (2004) report, "High rates of teacher turnover can inhibit the development and maintenance of a learning community; in turn, lack of community in a school may have a negative impact on teacher retention, thus creating a vicious cycle" (pp. 686-687). On a more hopeful note, Smith and Ingersoll also document that beginning teachers who participated in induction activities are more likely to stay, although, this finding did not hold true for beginning teachers in middle schools.

Despite burgeoning support for induction and mentoring as key concepts and constructs in the effort to address student achievement and keep quality teachers teaching, there is clearly more to be learned about the relationship between induction and mentoring and workplace development. A brief, critical review of the positioning of these approaches in our efforts to sustain and keep new teachers will allow us to speculate about possible next steps.

PERCEPTIONS OF INDUCTION AND MENTORING

Teacher induction is viewed in the literature as describing one of three situations: (a) the first year of a teacher's career in the classroom, (b) a period of transition where novices are socialized into the culture of teaching, and (c) a specific program, either formal or informal, often mandated by a legislative or governing body (Feiman-Nemser, Schwill, Carver, & Yusko, 1999). Huling-Austin (1990) defined induction to one year, while Fideler and Haselkorn's (1999) definition a decade later used 3 years. Both definitions delineate between evaluation and induction. They also connote a wide variety of scaffolding activities as part of induction, but require that induction must be systematic and sustained: more than simply orientation meetings that focus solely on district-mandated paperwork and insurance plans.

PROGRAMMATIC WAVES

The national shortage of teachers in the late 1950s prompted the Ford Foundation to offer grants to institutions of higher education that would create fifth-year programs to increase the number of teachers—alternative certification in its infancy. Master of Arts in teaching (MAT) programs were born as was The Teacher Corps (Serpell, 2000). These programs were not designed to ease entry into teaching; rather they were dedicated to providing warm bodies to teach children. Combined with wage increases, these programs were successful in almost obliterating the teacher shortage. However, the cancellation of most of these recruitment incentives in the 1980s led to renewed shortages when student populations again soared (Darling-Hammond, 1996).

Induction programs, although many not labeled as such, existed prior to 1980 but were subject to the prevailing winds of budget cutting and legislative unresponsiveness. Three waves have existed (prior to 1986, 1986-1989, 1990-1996), and a fourth wave is in process (Fideler & Haselkorn, 1999). The educational reforms of the 1980s produced a plethora of beginning teacher induction programs legislated by state lawmakers and developed by state education agencies. The induction programs were crafted to help novices acquire teaching competence more comprehensively and be socialized into school district and specific school cultures more quickly (Darling-Hammond, 1995; Gold, 1996). Either overtly or covertly, these programs also sought to increase teacher satisfaction, thus aiming to increase teacher retention especially in the first 5 years (Arends & Rigazio-DiGilio, 2000). In 1992, 46 states had enacted specific programs for beginning teachers and three states were considering programs. Some states labeled their work as induction programs, and others did not because the programs may have included a component of evaluating novice teachers (Serpell, 2000). This statistic was soon antiquated as funding for programs dissipated, leaving induction programs, whether or not they evaluated novice teachers, unfunded. The landscape is still a "crazy quilt" (Fideler & Haselkorn, 1999) of activity because of the extreme variation in requirements and policies.

NEGOTIATING STANDARDS

As early as 1981, researchers were encouraging induction program developers to acknowledge the personal nature of teaching and individualize induction programs (Gold, 1996; Grant & Zeichner, 1981; Huling-Austin, 1990). When Educational Testing Services introduced *Pathwise®: A Framework for Teaching*, a prepackaged induction program, Huling-Austin, Putman, and Galvez-Hjornevik (1986) argued, "a 'canned' program determined in advance will not be flexible enough" (pp. 52-53).

However, successful induction programs that use standards are not necessarily "canned." Connecticut and California have implemented statewide plans that are built on standards that their particular state has developed. The partnership between the University of New Mexico and the Albuquerque Public Schools have successfully used standards since 1983 and has altered them to align with the National Board for Professional Teaching Standards (NBPTS) (Fideler & Haselkorn, 1999). The Interstate New Teacher Assessment and Support Consortium (INTASC) licensing standards and assessments are widely-used documents.

The Georgia Systemic Teacher Education Project (GSTEP) has used multiple sets of standards as heterogeneous groups of educators jointly crafted the Principles and Framework for Accomplished Teaching and Learning in order to bring coherence to teacher preparation and induction. Three institutions of higher education, over 15 school districts, and three Regional Educational Service Agencies jointly crafted the work. This project has begun to reformulate teacher education, creating a seamless experience from the first year of college through the second year of full-time teaching by recasting university curriculum, developing early community-based educational experiences, and supporting multiple induction programs. Initiatives such as NBPTS, INTASC, and GSTEP view teaching as a complex process—dependent on decisions to support particular students at particular times.

EDUCATIVE MENTORING

These experiences can be realized through the process of educative mentoring, coined by Feiman-Nemser (2001) and built on Dewey's (1934/1958) notion of educative experiences. In this view, growth depends upon the presence of difficulty to be overcome by the exercise of intelligence. "Educative mentoring rests on an explicit vision of good teaching" (Feiman-Nemser, 2001). Like effective teachers, educative mentors attend to pressing issues and concerns without losing sight of long-term goals. Mentors interact with novices that encourage inquiry in and through their practice. Most importantly, they use their own knowledge and expertise to assess the direction novices are heading in order to create opportunities for teacher learning that positively benefit the quest for student learning.

Mentors, or mentorship, can play a powerful role in the experiences of novice teachers. Most often, however, realistic pictures of mentoring often portray experienced teachers, with or without specific training about mentoring, assigned to multiple novices geographically distanced in the building without any release time in their academic schedules to support their protégés.

Wang and Odell (2002) note that novice teachers most often expect mentors to offer emotional and technical support rather than contributing to their professional learning. Concurrently, mentors' expec-

tations for this role do not include "engaging novice teachers in developing a deeper understanding of subject matter and connecting that knowledge to a diverse student population" (p. 512). Ultimately, Wang and Odell conclude, "Novice teachers need to be nudged to examine their beliefs about teaching and learning to teach, to construct reform-minded images of teaching, and to develop relevant dispositions for learning to teach" (p. 513).

Traditional mentor pairings are still often used. The novice teachers in Johnson and Birkeland's (2003) work shared that mentors did not equate with worth. "Although on the surface this design makes sense, it seldom delivers what most new teachers imagine it will—personal encouragement, assistance in curriculum development, advice about lesson plans, and feedback about teaching" (p. 608). They also concluded that despite the fact that the majority of their respondents were assigned paid mentors, these pairings seldom "clicked" and often were inappropriate in terms of subjects, grades, and location.

WHAT NEXT

Traditional professional learning, characterized by short-term, decontextualized direct instruction, has been shown over and over again to be inadequate to the task of helping practitioners make deep and lasting changes in their practice (Lieberman, 1995; Little, 1993; Lord, 1994). These skill-based programs deify their foundational studies, touting them as incontrovertible (Hargreaves & Fullan, 1992).

Two camps of professional learning, then called "staff development," began their paths in the 1980s. Training became the buzzword, fueled by process-product research (Gage, 1963; Rosenshine, 1971). School districts across America hired educational consultants to design and provide training opportunities on topics ranging from peer coaching to phonemic awareness. Training was widely accepted as the most cost-effective way to reach and teach a teacher. Evolving concurrently with the training camp was a group of researchers with a less patronizing perspective dedicated to providing inquiry-based professional development. Loucks-Horsley, Hewson, Love, and Stiles (1998) offer that teachers are intelligent, have legitimate expertise, want to search for data to answer questions and develop new meanings. Teacher action research was also beginning to be reflected in the writings of educational researchers (Glatthorn, 1987; Glickman, 1985; Hovda & Kyle, 1984; Zeichner, 1983). Many teacher education programs have identified with this camp of researchers, creating inquiry-oriented programs and numerous opportunities for action research.

Now researchers, policymakers, seemingly all stakeholders, are demanding changes. The National Commission on Teaching and America's Future set six goals for the year 2006. This group, realizing that long-term engagements are required, has set lofty aims, one of which is especially pertinent here: "All teachers will have access to high-quality professional development, and they will have regularly scheduled time for collegial work and planning" (Darling-Hammond, 1996, p. 198). The National Staff Development Council's revised standards urge staff developers to organize adults into learning communities and provide educators with the knowledge and skills to collaborate (NSDC, 2001).

Educational theorists call for fostering teacher learning communities (Barth, 1990; McLaughlin & Talbert, 1993). The "learning" component of a teacher learning community identifies its inquiry stance that engages teachers in critical reflection that challenges implicit assumptions of teaching and schooling practices (Achinstein & Meyer, 1997). Challenging ideas, theories, and societal "givens" are commonplace in teacher education programs. It is remarkably missing when novices are experiencing the larger sphere surrounding these issues (Johnson & Birkeland, 2003).

Support is required for realizing the flexibility that standards-based instruction actually affords. Leaving the comfort of routine behind and looking beyond initial attempts to implement a program or policy is a first step toward engaging in true professional learning—developing as a professional interdependent on other professionals. Only then can colleagues assume a critical stance and open the conversation for shared meanings and productive disequilibrium (Lord, 1994). Lord's (1994) concept of "critical colleagueship" supports teachers in their efforts in making sense of standards, like INTASC and NBPTS, and also content-specific standards that are influenced by the constructivist approaches so richly described in these standards documents. Teachers' questions are honored and deemed legitimate (Rosenholtz, 1989) as groups of individuals struggle with creating learning environments that positively affect student achievement. The value of technical training is not ignored; rather it is contextualized in classroom-specific teaching practices. Only through this questioning and wrestling with standards can teachers articulate their own assumptions about teaching and learning and determine what their practice looks like in light of the standards.

These programs also align themselves with the shared agenda of school restructuring and teacher preparation. Creating learner-centered classrooms while not participating in learning-centered teaching experiences is paradoxical. It is problematic when graduates from university programs that tout themselves as progressive and claim to prepare teachers who will co-construct meaning with their students enter school district induction programs that view the novice teachers as recipients of knowledge rather than the generators of knowledge. Teachers teach in the way they have learned (Brooks & Brooks, 1996); therefore teachers need to experience what learning is like in constructivist classrooms. Darling-Hammond and Sclan (1996) insist that induction programs must engage and empower novice teachers to own, use, and develop knowledge about teaching and learning.

Zeichner and Gore (1990) call for research that examines how novice teachers reconstruct the existing structures they are being socialized into. Hollingsworth's (1992) collaboration with novice teachers heeded that call by offering opportunities for novices to clarify their own beliefs and to "recognize they were not wrong for holding other than standard school beliefs" (p. 400). Although not presented as a form of induction support, Hollingsworth's work offers a key finding for induction specialists. The novice teachers began to see themselves as knowledgeable for critiquing structures and content that were either supporting or hindering their work as teachers and learners. It took a learning community and a facilitator to offer this space in which these understandings could develop.

Teacher induction is a significant element in a broad reform agenda that focuses on recruitment, retention, student achievement, professional development, licensure, and preservice teacher education. There is work waiting to be done by new teachers with experienced teachers in shared professional dialogue in practicing learning communities.

REFERENCES

Achinstein, B., & Meyer, T. (1997, March). *The uneasy marriage between friendship and critique: Dilemmas of fostering critical friendship in a novice teacher learning community.* Paper presented at the annual meeting of the American Educational Research Association, Chicago, IL.

Alliance for Excellent Education. (2004). *Pending federal legislation related to the Alliance's teacher and principal quality initiative: Helping communities recruit and retain highly qualified teachers.* Retrieved June 30, 2005 from http://www.all4ed.org/publications/TeacherLegislativePolicyBrief.pdf

Arends, R. I., & Rigazio-DiGilio, A. J. (2000, July). *Beginning teacher induction: Research and examples of contemporary practice.* Paper presented to the Japan-United States Teacher Education Consortium.

Barth, R. S. (1990). *Improving schools from within: Teachers, parents, and principals can make a difference.* San Francisco: Jossey-Bass.

Brooks, M. G., & Brooks, J. G. (1996). Constructivism and school reform. In M. W. McLaughlin & I. Oberman (Eds.), *Teacher learning: New policies, new practices* (pp. 30-38). New York: Teachers College Press.

Darling-Hammond, L. (1995). Changing conceptions of teaching and teacher development. *Teacher Education Quarterly, 22*(4), 9-26.

Darling-Hammond, L. (1996). What matters most: A competent teacher for every child. *Phi Delta Kappan, 78*(3), 193-200.

Darling-Hammond, L., & Sclan, E. M. (1996). Who teaches and why: Dilemmas of building a profession for twenty-first century schools. In J. Sikula, T. J. Buttery, & E. Guyton (Eds.), *Handbook of Research on Teacher Education* (2nd ed., pp. 67-101). New York: Macmillan.

Dewey, J. (1934/1958). *Art as experience.* New York: Capricorn.

Feiman-Nemser, S. (2001). Helping novices learn to teach: Lessons from an exemplary support teacher. *Journal of Teacher Education, 52*(1), 17-30.

Feiman-Nemser, S., Schwille, S., Carver, C., & Yusko, B. (1999). *A conceptual review of literature on new teacher induction.* Washington, DC: National Partnership for Excellence and Accountability in Teaching.

Fideler, E. F., & Haselkorn, D. (1999). *Learning the ropes: Urban teacher induction programs and practices in the United States.* Belmont, MA: Recruiting New Teachers.

Gage, N. L. (Ed.). (1963). *Handbook of research on teaching.* Chicago: Rand McNally. Georgia Systemic Teacher Education Program. Retrieved June 30, 2005 from http://www.teachersbridge.org

Glatthorn, A. A. (1987). Cooperative professional development: Peer-centered options for teacher growth. *Educational Leadership, 45*(3), 31-35.

Glickman, C. (1985). *Supervision of instruction: A developmental approach.* Boston: Allyn & Bacon.

Gold, Y. (1996). Beginning teacher support: Attrition, mentoring, and induction. In J. Sikula, T. Buttery, & E. Guyton (Eds.), *Handbook of research on teacher education* (2nd ed., pp. 548-594). New York: Macmillan.

Grant, C., & Zeichner, K. (1981). Inservice support for first-year teachers: The state of the scene. *Journal of Research and Development in Education, 14*(2), 99-111.

Hargreaves, A., & Fullan, M. G. (1992). *Understanding teacher development.* New York: Teachers College Press.

Hollingsworth, S. (1992). Learning to teach through collaborative conversation: A feminist approach. *American Educational Research Journal, 29*(2), 373-404.

Hovda, R., & Kyle, D. (1984). A strategy for helping teachers integrate research into teaching. *Middle School Journal, 15*(3), 21-23.

Huling-Austin, L. (1990). Teacher induction programs and internships. In W. R. Houston (Ed.), *Handbook on research on teacher education* (pp. 535-548). New York: Macmillan.

Huling-Austin, L., Putman, S., & Galvez-Hjornevik, C. (1986). *Model teacher induction project study findings* (Report No. 7212). Austin: University of Texas at Austin, R & D Center for Teacher Education.

Johnson, S. M., & Birkeland, S. E. (2003). Perusing a "sense of success": New teachers explain their career decisions. *American Educational Research Journal, 40*(3), 581-617.

Lieberman, A. (Ed.). (1995). *The work of restructuring schools: Building from the ground up.* New York: Teachers College Press.

Little, J. W. (1993). Teachers' professional development in a climate of educational reform. *Educational Evaluation and Policy Analysis, 15*(2), 129-151.

Lord, B. (1994). Teachers' professional development: Critical colleagueship and the role of professional communities. In N. Cobb (Ed.), *The future of education: Perspectives on national standards in America.* New York: College Entrance Examination Board.

Loucks-Horsley, S., Hewson, P. W., Love, N., & Stiles, K. E. (1998). *Designing professional development for teachers of science and mathematics.* Thousand Oaks, CA: Corwin Press.

McLaughlin, M. W., & Talbert, J. E. (1993). *Contexts that matter for teaching and learning.* Palo Alto, CA: Center for Research on the Context of Secondary School Teaching, Stanford University.

National Staff Development Council. (2001). *Standards for staff development.* Retrieved June 30, 2005, from http://www.nsdc.org/standards/learningcommunities.cfm

Rosenholtz, S. J. (1989). Workplace conditions that affect teacher quality and commitment: Implications for teacher induction programs. *The Elementary School Journal, 89*(4), 421-439.

Rosenshine, B. V. (1971). *Teaching behaviours and student achievement.* Windsor, Berkshire, United Kingdom: National Foundation for Educational Research.

Serpell, Z. (2000). *Beginning teacher induction: A review of the literature.* Washington, DC: American Association of Colleges for Teacher Education.

Smith, T., & Ingersoll, R. (2004). What are the effects of induction and mentoring on beginning teacher turnover? *American Educational Research Journal, 41*(3), 681-714.

Wang, J., & Odell, S. (2002). Mentored learning to teach according to standards-based reform: A critical review. *Review of Educational Research, 72*(3), 481-546.

Zeichner, K. M. (1983). Alternative paradigms of teacher education. *Journal of Teacher Education, 34*(3), 3-9.

Zeichner, K. M., & Gore, J. M. (1990). Teacher socialization. In W. R. Houston (Ed.), *Handbook of research on teacher education* (pp. 329-348). New York: Macmillan.

—Thomas M. Van Soelen
City Schools of Decatur, Georgia

—Betty Shockley Bisplinghoff
The University of Georgia

INSTRUCTIONAL METHODS/ STRATEGIES

A strategy is a plan of action in pursuit of a particular goal. Teachers and students select strategies based on their purposes. There are scores of strategies available in dozens of books and on Internet Web sites. The National Middle School Association Web page (www.nmsa.org) and the Association for Supervision and Curriculum Development Web page (www.ascd.org) offer excellent strategy resources for middle level educators. Using the key words "instructional strategies" or "learning strategies" on Google or Yahoo will produce dozens more resources. Strategies included here are just a small part of the volume of strategies that work well for middle school students and with most school subjects.

Middle school students are beginning to think in abstract ways, seek autonomy, prefer active over passive learning, prefer to work in groups rather than alone, and want to take part in making decisions affecting their learning (Eccles & Wigfield, 1997; Jackson & Davis, 2000; Lipsitz, 1990; National Middle School Association, 2003; Pate, Homestead, & McGinnis, 1997). Teachers should consider strategies that take these characteristics of their students into account. Strategies that provide opportunities for students to solve mysteries or puzzles, take charge, make decisions, be active, and work with peers are particularly appropriate for middle school students. Strategies can help students be more successful in their schooling by building vocabulary (Pressley & Lysynchuk, 1995) ; making decisions (Beane, 1993; Homestead & Pate, 2000) ; assessing understanding and misunderstanding (Wiggins & McTighe, 1998); and organizing, sharing, remembering, and discussing information (Marzano, Pickering, & Pollock, 2001).

VOCABULARY BUILDING

Success in school is closely related to a student's ability to learn subject-related vocabulary. Vocabulary-building strategies can help students remember, understand, and correctly use new words. Using a combination of strategies is more effective than using just one.

Word Wall. As new words are introduced they are put on the classroom wall. Words can stand alone or be accompanied by definition, picture, or sentence. The word wall can be built by students and teachers. Since words are always within sight, word walls provide unlimited opportunities for review.

Semantic Mapping. A semantic map is a graphic organizer or web developed around one word. The process begins when the teacher introduces a new vocabulary word. Students and teacher brainstorm everything they can think of related to the term, organize the brainstormed list into categories, and put these lists into a web with the vocabulary word at the center. Semantic-mapping generates a deep, conceptual understanding that is not possible with just a definition.

Student-Created Definitions. When students create their own definition, they generate their own meaning. The definition rendered makes more sense to the student than does a dictionary or glossary definition. This strategy helps teachers see student understandings and misunderstandings.

MAKING DECISIONS

Consensus Building. When teachers and students are making decisions regarding classroom rules, what they will learn, how they will learn, or how learning will be assessed building consensus is required. Consensus means that each student and each teacher agrees to abide by the group's decisions. With consensus building you do not create winners and losers that occur when decisions are determined by majority vote. Consensus building also teaches students valuable negotiation skills. The process begins when students are asked to individually brainstorm solutions to a class problem or issue (e.g., developing classroom rules). The next step is to have students get into pairs and share their ideas. They must negotiate their two lists into one. Next, the pairs get together in groups of four and repeat the process. This continues until the class is in two large groups. At this point, the teacher becomes the facilitator and helps negotiate the two lists into one class list. To determine agreement, a vote is taken. If students are enthusiastic about the results, they raise hands with all five fingers showing. If they are okay with the results, they show three fingers. If they hate the results, they raise their hands with thumbs down. If anyone has a thumb down, the issue is revisited. No action is taken until everyone agrees.

Design Down. When teachers and students collaborate to develop the curriculum, students take ownership of and become more engaged in their learning. The "design down" or "backward design" process is a great strategy for student-teacher curriculum collaboration. The process begins when teacher and students identify what will be learned (i.e., important concepts in the content standards). Teacher and students then brainstorm what essential questions must be answered in order for students to understand the concepts. The next step is to identify what evidence of student understanding will be required (i.e., performance tasks, tests, quizzes, observations). Learning activities are then planned so that students will uncover the necessary content knowledge and skills necessary to answer the essential questions in order for them to understand the concepts. Resources are identified, located, and gathered. A timeline is then generated for how long the unit will take. Students come to class each day knowing what they will be doing and why.

ASSESSING UNDERSTANDING AND MISUNDERSTANDING

Reflection. When students reflect on their work they have opportunities to identify understandings and misunderstandings through self-assessment. Self-assessment helps students become independent learners. Student reflections can also provide teachers feedback on their teaching. Journaling and teacher prompts are good ways for students to reflect.

Rubrics. Rubrics are used to evaluate student performances (e.g., oral presentations, writings, and experiments). A rubric identifies what critical attributes will be assessed and then describes these attributes from novice or beginner to sophisticated or accomplished. A rubric given to students before work begins helps guide their work (process), it also evaluates the results (product). Students can use rubrics to judge the quality their work (self-assess). Rubrics help take the subjectivity out of evaluating student performances.

Grade-Your-Own. The assignment to be graded is placed on the student's desk. No writing utensils are permitted. The teacher then passes out colored pencils or pens. As the correct answers are given, students cross out their incorrect answers replacing them with correct answers. The student puts the grade on the paper and turns it in. To encourage honesty and accuracy in grading, when the teacher grades the paper she counts off double the points for each incorrect answer left uncorrected. Since students grade their own work they get the immediate feedback not possible for a teacher-graded assignment. Before incorrect answers become embedded, they are replaced with correct answers in the student's mind. Another benefit of grade-your-own is that it is respectful of students' dignity and privacy where the often used exchange-papers-and-grade is not.

ORGANIZING AND SHARING INFORMATION

Data Retrieval Chart. Data Retrieval Chart is a strategy for helping students identify, collect, and use information. To begin, the teacher and students identify what question or questions need to be answered. For example, In what ways was the founding of the Southern colonies different from the rest of the 13 colonies? Next they develop a chart that will organize the data collected from their research. For example, the left side of the chart lists all 13 colonies; the top of the chart lists the categories of information such as date founded, who founded, why founded, and where located. Students are then equipped to, independently, locate, and record the information needed to answer the question.

Story Board. Students like to make videos or use computer-generated programs, like PowerPoint, to create slide shows for classroom presentations. Often these presentations are more "bells and whistles" than substance. The story-board strategy helps students generate logical, comprehensive, and visually pleasing presentations. The strategy begins when teacher and students decide on what information needs to be included and in what order. For a slide show, the following format could be used: Slide one-title and student's first and last name; Slide two-table of contents; Slide three-the first topic on your table of contents written in the who, what, where, when, why format; and so on. After all information is recorded, then students go back and pencil in where pictures, audio, background, borders, and such will be added. All "slides" must be completed on paper before going to the computer lab.

Venn Diagram. Venn diagram is a way to visually organize information so students can easily compare and contrast. Two or three topics can be examined at one time. When considering two topics, two overlapping circles are drawn. Information that the topics have in common are written in the overlapping area, all other information is written outside the overlapping area. Students are now ready to write about or discuss similarities and differences.

REMEMBERING INFORMATION

Teams-Games-Tournament. When a test requires that students remember a large amount of information, Teams-Games-Tournament (T-G-T) is helpful. Robert Slavin created T-G-T to ensure that students are highly motivated and engaged when reviewing information for a test. When students are highly motivated and engaged, they are more likely to remember the information. To begin the process the teacher organizes "home teams" composed of one high, one, low, and two average students. The task for the home team is to make sure that everyone on the team learns the required information. The hook is, that the home team earning the most points during the games will get points added to their test scores. This creates a win-win situation for each student. After a review period, students are then organized into groups of three or four. High students compete with high students, average with average, and low with low. This ensures that all students have a chance to win points for their home team. No student competes with a member of his home team. During the game, students answer questions that will be on the test; one correct answer is worth one point. When all questions are answered, the points are tallied for that "game" is tallied. Students and teacher decide how many games will be played in the tournament. Middle school students love competition and games; this strategy has both.

DISCUSSING INFORMATION

Chalktalk. A strategy for organizing whole-class discussions is Chalktalk. The teacher begins by writing a question on the board. Three pieces of chalk (or white board markers) are placed on the chalk tray. Three students at a time come to the board and write their reactions to the question. To question a student's comment, a line is drawn from the comment and a question mark written. The student who wrote the comment under question comes back to the board and adds more information. If a student wants to expand on to a comment already made, she draws a line from it and adds her own comments. Strengths of this strategy is that it is quiet and orderly; students have time to think before contributing their ideas; and since there are no "put-downs," students who may not be willing to take part in verbal class discussions are willing to contribute their ideas in a Chalktalk discussion

Quality Circle. Another strategy for conducting whole-class discussions is Quality Circle. The class sits in a circle. The teacher explains the topic for discussion. Going clock-wise, students comment and raise questions. If a student does not wish to speak he can say "pass." If a student questions another student's comments the question cannot be answered until the student whose comment has been questioned has her turn. There is no cross-talk allowed. The structure of Quality Circle assures that students listen to one another, do not talk over each other, and each student gets a chance to be heard.

TEACHING STRATEGIES TO STUDENTS

Scaffolding. A strategy for teaching strategies to students is Scaffolding. Steps in scaffolding are model, coach, fade, and transfer. The teacher begins by modeling the strategy for the students. The teacher explains what the strategy is, how it is used, and then takes the students through the strategy, step-by-step. The teacher then coaches students as they use the strategy. As students become proficient using the strategy, teacher-help gradually fades. When students take ownership of the strategy they transfer, or use the strategy in new and different situations. Depending on the difficulty of the strategy, more or less modeling and coaching may be needed.

CONCLUSION

Middle school students need a repertoire of strategies and need to know when and how to use them. Teachers must provide students with multiple opportunities to use a variety of strategies. It is perfectly fine for students to invent, combine, or change strategies. The most important thing to remember is that students need to make strategies their own.

REFERENCES

Beane, J. A. (1993). *A middle school curriculum: From rhetoric to reality* (2nd ed.). Columbus, OH: National Middle School Association.

Eccles, J. S., & Wigfield, A. (1997). Young adolescent development. In J. L. Irvin (Ed.), *What current research says to the middle level practitioner* (pp. 15-29). Columbus, OH: National Middle School Association.

Homestead, E. R., & Pate, P. E. (2000). The enemy of understanding is coverage. In T. R. Koballa, Jr. & D. J. Tippins (Eds.), *Cases in middle and secondary science education: The promise and dilemmas* (pp. 67-70). Columbus, OH: Merrill.

Jackson, A. W., & Davis, G. A. (2000). *Turning points 2000: Educating adolescents in the 21st century.* New York: Teachers College Press.

Lipsitz, J. (1990). *Successful schools for young adolescents.* New Brunswick, N. J.: Transaction Books.

Marzano, R. J., Pickering, D. J., & Pollock, J. E., (2001). *Classroom instruction that works: Research-based strategies for increasing student achievement.* Alexandria, VA: Association for Supervision and Curriculum Development.

National Middle School Association (2003). *This we believe: Successful schools for young adolescents.* Westerville, OH: Author.

Pate, P. E., Homestead, E. R., & McGinnis, K., (1997). *Making integrated curriculum work: Teachers, students, and the quest for coherent curriculum.* New York: Teachers College Press.

Pressley, M., & Lysynchuk, L. (1995). Vocabulary. In M. Pressley & V. Woloshyn (Eds.), *Cognitive strategy instruction that really improves children's academic performance* (pp. 101-115). Cambridge, MA: Brookline Books.

Wiggins, G., & McTighe, J. (1998). *Understanding by design.* Alexandria, VA: Association for Supervision and Curriculum Development.

—Elaine R. Homestead
McConnell Middle School, Grayson, GA

INSTRUCTIONAL METHODS: DIFFERENTIATED INSTRUCTION

Differentiated instruction is a way of thinking about teaching. It is not new, but rather is reflected in writings as old as those of Confucius. It was certainly practiced in one-room-schoolhouses across the United States and is evident in many high quality classrooms today (Tomlinson, 1999, 2003). In fact, it may be argued that what we call differentiation is simply excellent educational practice (Stronge, 2002).

What is Differentiated Instruction?

Differentiated instruction is "responsive instruction." A teacher who differentiates instruction attends to the learning needs of varied students, just as he or she attends to the requirements of the curriculum. Differentiation is rooted in a belief that each student should have the opportunity to make sense of important ideas and powerful skills. To provide that opportunity, teachers must develop learning environments that are safe, affirming, challenging, and supportive for each student, and address students' varied learning needs within those environments (Tomlinson, 2003).

Students vary in at least three important ways—in their readiness to learn, their interests, and their learning profiles. Each of those elements can have a potent impact on how a student learns (Tomlinson, 1999, 2001).

Why Respond to Student Readiness?

Readiness can be shaped by ability, experience, language, economics, and a constellation of other factors. Given any particular learning objective or set of learning objectives, some students in a classroom will likely have gaps in knowledge and/or misunderstandings that cause the learning objective to be currently out of reach for those learners. Teachers can either attend to the gaps by helping the student build bridges to the goals—or they can move ahead in "covering the curriculum" without providing a way for students to gain the competencies necessary to progress. Some students in a classroom are likely to have mastered goals before a teacher sets out to teach them. Once again, a teacher has the option of helping the student grow from his or her point of readiness—or assuming that as long as the teacher has "covered the curriculum," the student has been well served. It is a reality that individuals learn only when tasks are a little to demanding for the individual and there is a support system to help the learner overcome the difficulty to become independent with the knowledge, understanding, and/or skill reflected in the goal. Then it becomes the teacher's job to craft a next task at a degree of difficulty a bit too great for a student—and again to provide support systems to enable growth.

Why Respond to Student Interest?

Interest is highly personal. While some students find a particular subject, topic, book, question, and so forth. to be intriguing, other students will likely find the same catalyst to be dull or irrelevant. Interest is a gateway to motivation to learn. We learn more eagerly and with more commitment those things we find to be interesting (Collins & Amabile, 1999). While teachers have a responsibility to help students succeed with a prescribed curricular goals, teachers also have the opportunity link those goals with ideas, experiences, questions that enlist student interest. Though tapping into existing student interests and helping students develop new interests, teachers cultivate more motivated—and thus likely more successful—learners.

Why Respond to Student Learning Profile?

Learning profile refers to ways in which a person will learn most efficiently. Learning profile is shaped by culture, gender, intelligence preference, and learning style.

While it is certainly not the case that all males or all females learn in the same way, it is the case that there are modes of learning more likely to be preferred by males (Gurian, 2001)—or by females (Gilligan, 1982). Similarly, it is not the case that all students from a given culture learn alike. Nonetheless, there are patterns of learning that may be stronger in some cultures than others (Lasley & Matczynski, 1997).

In regard to what experts like Howard Gardner (e.g., 1993) and Robert Sternberg (e.g., 1985) refer to as "intelligence preference," it appears that most people learn more readily in some modes than in others. These preferences seem to have a basis in our "neurological wiring."

Finally, all of us respond to a greater or lesser degree to learning environment factors such as light/darkness, quiet/sound, stillness/movement, auditory input/visual input and so on. When learners have the opportunity to work in circumstances that work for them, they generally learn better (Sullivan, 1993).

The role of the teacher in regard to learning profile is to provide as wide an array of options as possible for how students encounter the curriculum, how they make sense of it, and how they express their learning. There will not be a perfect match of every opportunity to every student, but when a teacher systematically provides a generous array of learning options, school will be a better fit for more learners.

WHY IS DIFFERENTIATION IMPORTANT IN THE MIDDLE GRADES?

There are at least two reasons why differentiation or responsive teaching is particularly important in the middle grades. The first has to do with the nature of early adolescents. The second has to do with middle grades philosophy.

There may be no more developmentally diverse group of learners than early adolescents. They range from very concrete thinkers to those who think comfortably with multiple abstractions. They include students who are emotionally fragile and those who are emotionally mature beyond their years. They are students who are physically immature and those whose physical maturity is almost complete. In addition, of course, early adolescence is a part of the journey of students for whom school is natural and those for whom school is painful. Early adolescents are speakers of English and students who struggle to learn English. They are students of privilege and students whose lives know little of privilege. They are students who are reflective and impulsive, auditory and visual, dreamers and devoid of dreams. There is likely no such thing as a "typical" early adolescent in terms of development.

To effectively guide the growth of such a diverse student population would seem to call for teachers who are flexible with use of time, materials, student groupings, degrees, and kinds of scaffolding, and so on. In other words, differentiated instruction seems particularly well suited to the great variability among learners in the middle years (Tomlinson & Eidson, 2004).

A second reason for the "fit" of differentiation and middle school relates to the beliefs upon which middle schools develop. Middle school philosophy advocates maximum use of heterogeneity in assignment of students to classes. It is core to middle school belief that all students should have access to high quality curriculum with maximum support for success (Jackson & Davis, 2000). Strict ability grouping and tracking often result in some students consistently working with low expectations curriculum based on drill and practice of low level skills and knowledge in teacher-centered settings. Other students work with more complex, problem-oriented curriculum with an emphasis on student-centered approaches. It may be particularly dangerous to make assumptions about the capacity of early adolescents both because of the substantial changes these students undergo and because, for many of them, middle grade learning opportunities will determine the shape of the future.

In order to ensure maximum learning opportunity and maximum support for success for each middle school student, it is important to advocate for high quality, rich curriculum in all classrooms, with scaffolding that ensures each student can move forward with full support from his or her point of entry, with connections to personal interest, and with opportunities to learn in preferred ways.

On the other hand, proponents of tracking propose that segregating students by perceived ability is a preferred way to deal with students differences. They also suggest that differentiation is too difficult for teachers to implement.

HOW CAN TEACHERS RESPOND TO VARIANCE IN STUDENT READINESS?

There are many ways teachers can support the growth of students at various readiness levels. There is no single, right way to do so. Following are a few of many ways middle level teachers can help students of differing readiness levels succeed.

1. Make preassessment a regular part of the teaching cycle. Preassessments are not graded, but rather help the teacher develop a clearer sense of the knowledge, understanding, and skill with which each learner is entering a new unit of study.

2. Practice on-going assessment. Use a variety of means to monitor students' developing understanding and skill as a unit progresses so that you can make adjustments necessary to help students span gaps in their proficiency or move ahead in their thinking, as appropriate.

3. Make small-group teaching a regular part of your classroom routines. Having the opportunity to meet with small groups of students enables you to target instruction more efficiently to the changing needs of learners.

4. Accumulate a range of materials at different reading levels on key topics. Media specialists can be very helpful in acquiring materials at different levels of complexity. In addition, teachers themselves can, over time, amass an impressive array of materials on important areas of study. The internet can also be a valuable source of resource materials that can address varied reading needs.

5. Incorporate into your teaching routines strategies that help students become more focused, aware, and effective readers. Among such strategies are Read-Alouds, Close Reads, multiple entry journals, graphic organizers, and peer reading partners.

6. Use tiering at key points in a unit. Tiering is an instructional strategy teachers can use to have all students work with the same important knowledge, understanding, and skill, but at levels of challenge appropriate to particular students' readiness needs.

7. Assign targeted homework. There are times when it makes sense for students to have different homework assignments based on particular strengths and weaknesses which are evident to the teacher through on-going assessment of student growth.

HOW CAN TEACHERS RESPOND TO STUDENT INTEREST?

Teachers can help students establish new interests and build on existing interests as ways of increasing student motivation to learn. There are many ways teachers can tap and expand student interest, including the following.

1. Share personal interests in topics of study. Help students see your own enthusiasm for and experience with key ideas. Take time to share your own stories.

2. Use interest surveys or checklists through the year to help students reflect their interests. Then use what you learn to help shape some parts of your instruction.

3. Encourage students to share their interests in things you study. They can do this by sharing experiences, materials, applications, hobbies, and so on.

4. Provide high interest supplementary materials on key topics and opportunity for students to use them. Interest centers, Jigsaw activities, and anchor activities (work students do when they complete an assigned task) are just a few

strategies to invite students to explore ideas further than the text or class presentations allow.

5. Use strategies like learning contracts that allow for student choice.

6. Invite students to apply key ideas and skills to learning about people, places, hobbies, etc. in which they have a high interest. Key principles and skills of virtually every subject can be transferred to subjects in which students have strong personal interests.

HOW CAN TEACHERS RESPOND TO STUDENTS' LEARNING PROFILES?

Understanding all the nuances of learning profile requires time and study. Nonetheless, any time teachers can make their classrooms more flexible, it's likely that more students will find room for themselves in learning. Among the many ways teachers can respond to students' varied learning preferences are the following.

1. Increase your presentation repertoire. As you develop the habit of presenting in words, images or graphics, metaphors, illustrations, and models, more and more students will likely make sense of important ideas.

2. Provide options for how students express their learning. For example, students might express key insights and skills related to a science unit through designing an information brochure for younger learners, developing a position statement, or creating storyboards for a television public service announcement.

3. Use analytical (school-like), practical (real world application), and creative (imaginative, problem solving) approaches to teaching and learning.

4. Invite students to work alone or with peers whenever possible.

5. Use whole to part as well as part to whole explanations on a regular basis.

6. Study your students' cultures. As you understand various culture-based approaches to learning, incorporate them into your plans. Work to understand the role that race plays in learning for many early adolescents.

DIFFERENTIATION PROVIDES WHAT IT TAKES TO ENSURE LEARNING FOR EACH STUDENT

Differentiated instruction is not a particular strategy. Rather, it is a teacher's mindset that the classroom has to work for each student, and that much of the teacher's responsibility is to develop a repertoire of approaches supportive of that goal. Differentiation suggests that we seldom teach well when teach with little regard to the array of differences inevitably reflected in our students. This approach also proposes that the best teachers do whatever it takes to make school work for each learner.

REFERENCES

Collins, M., & Amabile, T. (1999). Motivation and creativity. In R. J. Sternberg (Ed.), *Handbook of Creativity* (pp. 297-312). New York: Cambridge University Press.

Gardner, H. (1993). *Multiple intelligences: The theory into practice*. New York: Basic Books.

Gilligan, C. (1982). *In a different voice: Psychological theory and women's development*. Cambridge, MA: Harvard University Press.

Gurian, M. (2001). *Boys and girls learn differently*. San Francisco: Jossey-Bass.

Jackson, A., & Davis, G. (2000). *Turning points 2000: Educating adolescents in the 21st century*. New York: Teachers College Press.

Lasley, T., & Matczynski, T. (1997). *Strategies for teaching in a diverse society: Instructional models*. Belmont, CA: Wadsworth.

Sternberg, R. (1989). *The triarchic mind: A new theory of human intelligence*. New York: Penguin.

Stronge, J. (2002). *Qualities of effective teachers*. Alexandria, VA: Association for Supervision and Curriculum Development.

Sullivan, M. (1993). *A meta-analysis of experimental research studies based on the Dunn and Dunn learning styles model and its relationship to academic achievement and performance*. Unpublished doctoral dissertation, St. John's University, Jamaica, NY.

Tomlinson, C. (1999). *The differentiated classroom: Responding to the needs of all learners*. Alexandria, VA: Association for Supervision and Curriculum Development.

Tomlinson, C. (2001). *How to differentiate instruction in mixed ability classrooms* (2nd ed.). Alexandria, VA: Association for Supervision and Curriculum Development.

Tomlinson, C. (2003). *Fulfilling the promise of the differentiated classroom: Strategies and tools for responsive teaching*. Alexandria, VA: Association for Supervision and Curriculum Development.

Tomlinson, C., & Eidson, C. (2004). *Differentiation in practice: A resource guide for differentiating curriculum, Grades 5-9*. Alexandria, VA: Association for Supervision and Curriculum Development.

—Carol Ann Tomlinson
University of Virginia

INTERDISCIPLINARY TEAM ORGANIZATION

INTERDISCIPLINARY TEAMING DEFINED

Interdisciplinary team organization offers students a transition between the self-contained, more student-centered elementary school classroom and the departmentalized, subject-centered structure of the high school. It is a "way of organizing the faculty so that a group of teachers share: (1) the same group of students; (2) the responsibility for planning, teaching, and evaluating curriculum and instruction in more than one academic area; (3) the same schedule; and (4) the same area of the building" (George & Alexander, 2003, p. 305). *Turning points 2000: Educating adolescents in the 21st century*, a widely-influential policy statement, calls for middle schools that "Organize relationships for learning to create a climate of intellectual development and a caring community of shared educational purpose … with teams of teachers and students as its underlying organizational structure" (Jackson & Davis, 2000, p. 24).

Interdisciplinary teaming is not synonymous with "team teaching." The latter refers to two or more teachers who collaborate in teaching, for example, the same unit or lesson, but who do not necessarily share the same students or room for the rest of the day. However, interdisciplinary teaming lends itself to team teaching.

When middle level educators are asked to identify the signature practice of middle level schools, the consensus is that interdisciplinary teams are associated with the overall success of the middle school program (Clark & Clark, 1994; Hackmann, Petzko, Valentine, Clark, Nori, & Lucas, 2002; National Middle School Association, 2003; Strahan, Bowles, Richardson, & Hanawald, 1997). While it is important to understand that any particular practice is part of a larger system, and that all parts of the system need to work together in order to be successful in accomplishing its goals, it is worthwhile to examine the history, trends, types, outcomes, obstacles, and critiques of this practice, as well as its implications for the education of teachers for its contribution to the overall success of middle level schools.

THEORETICAL CONTEXT

Two competing theories about what matters most in school for students' academic achievement and engagement frame much of the research and practice in educational reform. One theory, related to academic press, emerged in the early 1980's, "a decade characterized by an emphasis on individualism and instrumental motivation" (Phillips, 1997, p. 634). Out of this came the effective schools research which claims that high expectations for student achievement, clear achievement-oriented goals, the amount of time spent on instruction, and the amount of homework assigned to students, would make all of the difference for student learning.

The second theory, built on Dewey's ideas about democracy in education, re-emerged in the late 80s and early 90s. This communitarian approach emphasized community, democracy, and "an ethic of caring (Noddings, 1988, p. 215) and assumes that satisfying teachers' and students' personal and social needs for attachment, care, and so forth, is a prerequisite to students' academic achievement. The communal model emphasizes "shared responsibility for work, shared commitment to a common set of goals, lateral communication and power in decision making, and expectations and behavior framed by greater personalization and individual discretion" (Lee & Smith, 1995, p. 243).

The question of which approach, academic press or communitarian, is most successful in promoting student academic achievement and engagement, is taken up most recently by the middle level policy group, the National Forum to Accelerate Middle Grades Reform. Its vision statement argues that high performing schools with middle grades need to be academically challenging, developmentally responsiveness, and socially equitable (National Forum to Accelerate Middle-Grades Reform, n.d.). These are three interrelated goals and emphasizing one at the expense of the others will not result in the quality of education that middle level educators want.

TRENDS IN THE USE OF INTERDISCIPLINARY TEAMING

Four large-scale surveys examined the incidence of teaming in middle level schools (Alexander & McEwin, 1989; Epstein & MacIver, 1990; Valentine, Clark, Hackmann, & Petzko, 2002; Valentine, Clark, Irvin, Keefe, & Melton, 1993). According to these studies, interdisciplinary team organization has increased from 33% (1989) to 42% (1990) to 57% (1992) to 79% (2002). According to the Valentine et al. 1993 study, teaming was most commonly used in Grades 6-7-8 schools (87%) and least likely used in schools with 7-8-9 grade pattern (66%). The return rate on surveys is often small and it is difficult to make generalizations to the total population of middle grades schools in the United States.

PRINCIPLES FOR ORGANIZING EFFECTIVE TEAMS

Erb and Stevenson (1999) outline principles for organizing effective teams:

1. *Keep teams small in number of teachers and students.* Teams range in size from two person teams with 40-60 students to six person teams with 150-190 students. Jackson and Davis (2000) recommend no more than five teachers and 125 students. The advantage of smaller teams is that they carry out more teaming practices (Flowers, Mertens, & Mulhall, 1999) such as coordinating curriculum and student assignments. Teachers develop closer relationships between teachers and students but often take on a greater workload. Larger teams often include special education teachers, music/art/ technology teachers, as well as teachers with subject area specialization. With fewer subjects to plan for, teachers potentially have the time to differentiate curriculum. With a wider range of expertise, teachers potentially have the skills and knowledge to meet the needs of individual students.

2. *Provide sufficient individual and team planning time for teachers.* Flowers, Mertens, and Mulhall (1999) found that teams with at least four meetings per week, with each meeting lasting at least 30 minutes, engage in a greater number of teaming practices than teams with less common planning time. Teaming practices reported in this study include curriculum coordination, coordination of student assignments, assessments, and feedback, parent contact and involvement, and contact with other resource staff.

3. *Allow teams to design their students' daily schedule.* "Because teachers are closest to the instructional program they are in the best position for establishing instructional priorities and judging the most appropriate way to apportion time (George, Stevenson, Thomason, & Bean, 1992, p. 72). The greater degree of teacher autonomy for making decisions about their team and their students, the greater the degree of teacher creativity, variety of instructional practices, and ability to identify and address student needs (Steffes & Valentine, 1995). Teachers who design their students' schedules have the potential to flexibly use time for in-depth studies, labs, field trips, speakers, etc.

4. *Assign teams to their own area of the building.* Proximity allows for opportunity for faculty and students to collaborate. Ideally, teachers

have a space for team meetings and a room large enough to accommodate all students for team meetings. The downside of this is that teams often become isolated from the rest of the school, thus inhibiting the development of a school community. Administrators and teacher can overcome this by transferring the positive aspects of team relationships into the working relationships of faculty and staff within the wider school community (Kruse & Louis, 1997).

5. *Allow teams to work together for multiple years.* Teachers need three or more years to develop into a strong team (Arnold & Stevenson, 1998). They progress through stages, from wondering why they are together, to asking how they can learn together. Students staying together with their teachers for more than one year in a practice called "looping" creates the conditions in which teacher-student relationships can flourish and teachers are less likely to "write off" difficult students because teachers know they will be working with those students again for another year (Arhar, 1992; George & Alexander, 2003).

CHARACTERISTICS OF HIGHLY EFFECTIVE TEAMS

What are the specific conditions, features, and dynamics of team work that enhance team effectiveness in improving teaching and learning? Conley, Fauske, & Ponder's (2004) review of work group effectiveness and middle school interdisciplinary teams indicate the following: Teachers need time to collaborate, autonomy in decision-making, knowledge of other curricular areas and instructional strategies, feedback from the work itself and from others, knowledge of students and contribution to students' total educational experience, and interdependence with others. The composition of teacher teams ideally includes a high degree of diverse professional experience and at least a moderate to high degree of interpersonal skills, including effective coordination and communication.

George and Alexander (2003) include the following characteristics of highly effective teams: student-centered focus, strong commitment to academic achievement, collaborative policies, and accountability system, strong sense of team community, regular communication with parents, a proactive approach, and teachers who work professionally and collaboratively.

The most problematic interpersonal issues include coordination problems, an imbalance in participation, and uneven commitment of members. If teachers prefer the departmental structure rather than the team structure because of the importance of their disciplinary background to their professional identify, the lack of commitment to collaboration will jeopardize team work (Lee & Smith, 1993). Other obstacles include teachers' sense of classroom autonomy and independence that frames a culture of individual rather than collective work. If working as a team "costs" members more than they benefit (Galvin, 1998), collaboration will not likely sustain itself.

ADVANTAGES OF INTERDISCIPLINARY TEAMING

Outcomes for Teachers

Collaboration among teachers has been positively related to teachers' feeling of efficacy (Arhar, Johnston, & Markle, 1989; Rosenholtz, 1989; Lee, Dedrick, & Smith, 1991; Raudenbush, Rowan, & Cheong, 1992; Erb & Stevenson, 1999; Warren & Payne, 1997). Working together to solve complex problems of teaching enables teachers to feel more professionally accomplished because of the belief that they can help even the most challenging students learn.

Other benefits of teaming include increased professional satisfaction with teaching due to less personal isolation (Mills, Powell, & Pollack, 1992), reduced stress (Gatewood, Cline, Green, & Harris, 1992), new leadership roles (Polite, 1992), and increased confidence about ability to teach together (Hart, Pate, Mizell, & Reeves, 1992).

OUTCOMES FOR STUDENTS

Achievement

The increased feelings of efficacy and professional satisfaction that frequently accompany teamwork have been associated with increased student achievement (Ashton & Webb, 1986; Rosenholtz, 1989). Lee and Smith (1993) found that students in restructured middle schools (less departmentalization, more heterogeneous grouping, more team teaching, and other restructuring factors) scored significantly higher on achievement and engagement than students in non-restructured schools. Other studies (Felner, Jackson, Kasak, Mulhall, Brand, & Flowers, 1997) indicate that this outcome is related to the level of implementation of middle school practices. Mertens, Flowers, and Mulhall (1998) found that higher percentages of students in Middle Start Initiative schools that had implemented interdisciplinary teaming at a high level with common planning time achieved a "satisfactory" performance level on the statewide achievement test than did students in schools with low levels or no implementation. These studies are not without problems and more research is needed, but they represent major efforts to make the link between very complex processes.

PSYCHO-SOCIAL-BEHAVIORAL OUTCOMES

An increased sense of belonging, particularly for students in low-income schools (Arhar, Johnston, & Markle, 1989; Arhar, 1992, 1997) may be the result of stronger relationships with teachers and a decreased sense of alienation produced when teachers know students well. Reduced discipline problems (Felner et al., 1997) may be due to a more consistent discipline plan when teachers work together to solve student problems. Increased sense of self-esteem, a more positive attitude toward school, greater feeling of safety and health are also associated with interdisciplinary teaming (Felner et al., 1997; Reiser, 1999).

CRITIQUES OF INTERDISCIPLINARY TEAMING

Interdisciplinary teaming is not without its critics. There are some who are concerned that because teachers gain greater knowledge about students' personal, social, and academic lives, they may use "affectional ties" to control students (Lesko, 1994). Those who advocate for a more discipline-based approach to curriculum wonder if teaming is worth all of the effort it takes for teachers to collaborate. Teaming has some "costs" associated with providing teachers common planning time in addition to individual planning time and in hard economic times, common planning time may have to be eliminated.

REFLECTIONS

Interdisciplinary teaming, if implemented in a thoughtful way with ample professional development, common planning time and careful selection of team members has a research base that supports its use. Teacher education programs are guided to prepare teachers to become members of interdisciplinary teams so that new generations of teachers have the skills and knowledge to collaborate for student learning.

REFERENCES

Alexander, W. M., & Mc Ewin, C. K. (1989). *Schools in the middle: Status and progress.* Columbus, OH: National Middle School Association.

Arhar, J. M. (1992). Interdisciplinary teaming and the social bonding of middle level students. In J. L. Irvin (Ed.), *Transforming middle level education: Perspectives and possibilities* (pp. 139-161). Boston: Allyn & Bacon.

Arhar, J. M. (1997). The effects of interdisciplinary teaming on teacher and students. In J. L. Irvin (Ed). *What current research says to the middle level practitioner* (pp. 49-55). Columbus, OH: National Middle School Association.

Arhar, J. M., Johnston, J. H., & Markle, G. C. (1989). The effects of teaming on students. *Middle School Journal, 20*(3), 21-27.

Ashton, P. T., & Webb, R. B. (1986). *Making a difference: Teachers' sense of efficacy and student achievement.* New York: Longman.

Arnold, J., & Stevenson, C. (1998). *Teachers' teaming handbook: A middle level planning guide.* Orlando, FL: Harcourt Brace.

Clark, S. N., & Clark, D. C. (1994). *Restructuring the middle level school: Implications for school leaders.* Albany: State University of New York Press.

Conley, S., Fauske, J., & Pounder, D. G. (2004). Teacher work group effectiveness. *Educational Administration Quarterly, 40*(5), 663-703.

Epstein, J. L., & Mac Iver, D. J. (1990). *Education in the middle grades: National practices and trends.* Columbus, OH: National Middle School Association.

Erb, T. O., & Stevenson, C. (1999). From faith to facts: Turning points in action—What difference does teaming make? *Middle School Journal, 30*(3), 47-50.

Felner, R. D., Jackson, A. W., Kasak, D., Mulhull, P., Brand, S., & Flowers, N. (1997). The impact of school reform for the middle years: Longitudinal study of a network engaged in Turning Points-based comprehensive school transformation. *Phi Delta Kappan, 78*(7), 528-550.

Flowers, N., Mertens, S. B., & Mulhall, P. F. (1999). The impact of teaming: Five research-based outcomes of teaming. *Middle School Journal, 31*(2), 57-60.

Galvin, P. F. (1998). The organizational economics of interagency collaboration. In D. G. Pounder (Ed.), *Restructuring schools for collaboration: Promises and pitfalls* (pp. 43-64). Albany, NY: State University of New York Press.

Gatewood, T. E., Cline, G., Green, G., & Harris, S. E. (1992). Middle school interdisciplinary team organization and its relationship to teacher stress. *Research in Middle Level Education, 15*(2), 27-40.

George, P. S., & Alexander, W. M. (2003). *The exemplary middle school* (3rd ed.). Belmont, CA: Thomson/Wadsworth.

George, P. S., Stevenson, C., Thomason, J., & Beane, J. (1992). *The middle school—and beyond.* Alexandria, VA: Association for Supervision and Curriculum Development.

Hackmann, D. G., Petzko, V. N., Valentine, J. W., Clark, D. C., Nori, J. R., & Lucas, S. E. (2002). Beyond interdisciplinary teaming: Findings and implications of the NASSP National Middle Level Study. *NASSP Bulletin, 86*(32), 33-47.

Hart, L. E., Pate, P. E., Mizelle, N. B., & Reeves, J. L. (1992). Interdisciplinary team development in the middle school: A study of the Delta Project. *Research in Middle Level Education, 16*(1), 79-98.

Jackson, A. W., & Davis, G. A. (2000). *Turning points 2000: Educating adolescents in the 21st century*. New York: Teachers College.

Kruse, S. D., & Louis, K. S. (1997). Teacher teaming in middle schools: Dilemmas for a schoolwide community. *Educational Administration Quarterly, 33*, 261-89.

Lee, V. E., Dedrick, R. F., & Smith, J. B. (1991). The effects of the social organization of schools on teachers' efficacy and satisfaction. *Sociology of Education, 64*, 190-208.

Lee, V. E., & Smith, J. B. (1993). Effects of school restructuring on the achievement and engagement of middle-grade students. *Sociology of Education, 66*(3), 164-187.

Lee, V. E., & Smith, J. B. (1995). Effects of high school restructuring and size on early gains in achievement and engagement. *Sociology of Education, 68*, 241-270.

Lesko, N. (1994). Back to the future: Middle schools and the Turning Points Report. *Theory into Practice, 33*(3), 143-148.

Mertens, S. B., Flowers, N., & Mulhall, P. (1998). *The middle start initiative, phase I: A longitudinal analysis of michigan middle-level schools*. Center for Prevention Research and Development, University of Illinois.

Mills, R. A., Powell, R. R., & Pollack, J. P. (1992). The influence of interdisciplinary teaming on teacher isolation: A case study. *Research in Middle Level Education, 12*(2), 9-26.

National Forum to Accelerate Middle-Grades Reform. (n.d.). *Our vision statement*. Retrieved May 28, 2005, from http://www.mgforum.org/about/vision.asp

National Middle School Association. (2003). *This we believe: Successful schools for young adolescents*. Westerville, OH: Author.

Noddings, N. (1988). An ethic of caring and its implications for instructional arrangements. *American Journal of Education, 96*, 215-231.

Phillips, M. (1997). What makes schools effectives? A comparison of the relationships of communitatian climate and academic climate to mathematics achievement and attendance during middle school. *American Educational Research Journal, 34*(4), 633-662.

Polite, M. M. (1992). Team negotiation and decision-making: Linking leadership to curricular and instructional innovation. *Research in Middle Level Education, 18*(1), 65-81.

Raudenbush, S. W., Rowan, B., & Cheong, Y. F. (1992). Contextual effects on the self-perceived efficacy of high school teachers. *Sociology of Education, 65*, 150-167.

Reiser, R. A. (1999). Project TEAMS final report. Retrieved May 5, 2005, from http://www.ifsi.org/TEAMS%20final%20report.htm

Rosenholtz, S. (1989). *Teacher's workplace: The social organization of schools*. New York: Longman.

Steffes, R., & Valentine, J. (1995). *Organizational characteristics and expected outcomes of interdisciplinary teaming*. Paper presented at the annual meeting of the National Association of Secondary School Principals, San Antonio, TX.

Strahan, D., Bowles, N. Richardson, V., & Hanawald, S. (1997). Research on teaming: Insights from selected studies. In T. S. Dickinson & T. O. Erb (Eds.), *We gain more than we give: Teaming in middle schools* (pp. 359-384). Columbus, OH: National Middle School Association.

Valentine, J. W., Clark, D. C., Irvin, J. L. Keefe, J. W., & Melton, G. (1993). *Leadership in middle level education, Volume 1: A national survey of middle level leaders and schools*. Reston, VA: National Association of Secondary School Principals.

Valentine, J. W., Clark, D. C. Hackmann, D. G., & Petzko, V. N. (2002). *A national study of leadership in middle level schools, Volume I*. Reston, VA: National Association of Secondary School Principals.

Warren, L. L., & Payne, B. D. (1997). Impact of middle grades" organization on teacher efficacy and environmental perceptions. *Journal of Educational Research, 90*, 301-308.

—Joanne M. Arhar
Kent State University

JOHNSTON, J. HOWARD

A researcher, writer, and teacher, J. Howard Johnston is an expert on effective schooling for young adolescents. His interests include school achievement and productive behavior of learners, the diversity of the American population and the need to structure schools for success, and the effective use of technology in challenging environments.

J. Howard Johnston began his education career in 1969 as a junior and senior high school English teacher in New York and Wyoming. He earned his masters and doctorate degrees while serving as a demonstration teacher. He served on the faculty of the University of Cincinnati for 16 years as professor, department chair, associate dean for graduate studies, and acting dean. In 1990 Dr. Johnston moved to the University of South Florida as full professor.

Dr. Johnston's work extends beyond teaching in university classrooms. He is a prolific writer and a well-know speaker. He has worked with educators throughout the United States and across the globe. He has maintained a consistent commitment to research and in 1979 initiated the column in *Middle School Journal* entitled "What Research Says to the Middle Level Practitioner." He was the lead author of *An Agenda for Excellence at the Middle Level* (1984), published by the Middle Level Council of the National Association of Secondary School Principals (NASSP). Among his more than 100 publications on middle grades education, are the books *New American Family and the Schools (1990), Effective Schooling for Economically Disadvantaged Students: School-Based Strategies for Diverse Student Populations* (1992) and, *What Research Says to the Middle Level Practitioner* (1986). Dr. Johnston's articles have appeared in the *NASSP Bulletin, Middle School Journal,*

Phi Delta Kappan, School Administrators, American School Boards Journal, and *Schools in the Middle.*

Dr. Johnston has developed and maintained strong working relationships with various education and reform organizations. He has served as a member of the NMSA Board of Trustees, and the Council on Middle Level Education for NASSP. He is a charter member of the National Forum to Accelerate Middle Grades Reform and a Lead Team Consultant for the High School Principals' Partnership, sponsored by Union Pacific.

Among Dr. Johnston's awards are the NASSP Distinguished Service Award, the NMSA Presidential Award for Excellence, the Gruhn-Long Award for lifetime service to middle-level education, and NMSA's John Lounsbury Award.

REFERENCES

Johnston, J. H. (1990). *New American family and the schools*: Columbus, OH: National Middle School Association.

Johnston, J. H., & Borman, K. M. (1992). *Effective schooling for economically disadvantaged students: School-based strategies for diverse student populations.* Norwood, NJ: Ablex.

Johnston, J. H., & Markel, G. C. (1986). *What research says to the middle level practitioner.* Columbus, OH: National Middle School Association.

NASSP Council on Middle Level Education. (1984). *An agenda for excellence at the middle level.* Reston, VA: National Association of Secondary School Principals.

—Mary Henton
National Middle School Association

JOURNAL OF ADOLESCENT RESEARCH

The *Journal of Adolescent Research* (http://www.sage-pub.com/journal.aspx?pid=135) is a bimonthly source for current analysis on how adolescents develop, behave, and are influenced by societal and cultural factors. It uses an interdisciplinary approach to present peer-reviewed articles on topics from diverse fields, including: psychology, sociology, education, public health, family studies, criminology, social work, communication, counseling, and health care. Members of the editorial board represent over 30 different disciplines and bring a broad perspective to this publication.

Articles in the *Journal of Adolescent Research* present empirical, theoretical, and social policy research. They include topics concerning adolescents such as: sexual behavior, drug and alcohol abuse, affect and emotion, adolescent pregnancy, adolescent medicine, delinquency, identity formation, rites of passage, and parenting styles. These articles aspire to increase understanding of individuals in adolescents and in transition of adulthood.

—Alison Buehler
The University of Tennessee

JOURNAL OF EARLY ADOLESCENCE

The *Journal of Early Adolescence* publishes articles designed to increase understanding of individuals in early adolescence. It provides information on the development of early adolescents to researchers and practitioners in areas such as criminology, developmental psychology, education, human development and family studies, psychology, psychiatry, public health, and sociology. The journal, published 4 times each year, features the developmental period of children aged 10 to 14 in empirical studies, literature reviews, and theoretical writings. These articles and reviews, which are peer-reviewed by a multidisciplinary panel of experts, explain, and examine:

significant advances and issues from diverse developmental contexts (peer, family, and community), such as education motivation and achievement, identity development (self-esteem and self-concept), problem behaviors (health risks, reactions to stress), sexuality, the importance of culture, as well as in-depth discus-sions on research design and methodology. (http://www.sagepub.com/journal.aspx?pid=125, ¶ 2)

Features of the *Journal of Early Adolescence* include articles, reviews, guest editorials, and themed issues on a variety of current topics. Subjects covered in the journal include: academic competence, depression, delinquency, ethnic and racial issues, gender issues, program evaluations, parenting and family processes, self-esteem and worth, and prosocial behaviors. These topics cover the care, development, and education particular to early adolescents.

—Alison Buehler
The University of Tennessee

JOURNAL OF RESEARCH ON ADOLESCENCE

The *Journal of Research on Adolescence* (http://www.blackwellpublishing.com/journal.asp?ref=1050-8392) is the official journal of the Society for Research on Adolescence. It publishes original research and reviews on a broad spectrum of themes related to the developmental period of adolescence. The journal presents qualitative, quantitative, cross-national, and cross-cultural studies that foster understanding of adolescent growth and maturation. This quarterly journal focuses on normative developmental patterns and individual differences concerning "cognitive, physical, emotional, and social development and behavior" of adolescents.

—Alison Buehler
The University of Tennessee

THE JUNIOR HIGH SCHOOL

In its essence the junior high school is a device of democracy whereby nurture may cooperate with nature to secure the best results possible for each individual adolescent as well as for society at large. (Briggs, 1920, p. 327)

T. H. Briggs is considered one of the founders of the junior high school movement. When he wrote *The Junior High School* (1920), Briggs drew from his experiences as the educational advisor to the Speyer Experimental Junior High School in New York, his observations from visits to 60 junior high schools across the United States, surveys from junior high schools, correspondence with reportedly hundreds of administrators and teachers, conferences, and "all available literature on the subject of reorganization."

In *The Junior High School*, Briggs focuses on two main topics. First, Briggs critiques the traditional school eight-four organization, elementary school for 8 years and secondary school for 4 years, and emphasizes school reorganization. Briggs advocates for the establishment of junior high school as a necessary institution between elementary and secondary education. Second, he surveyed 68 junior high school administrators and using this feedback created a "composite definition of the junior high school."

Briggs discusses the Junior High School movement's theoretical and implementation advances since the turn of the twentieth century. He claims that the "most remarkable change in the history of education is now well underway" (p. vii). At the time that he wrote *The Junior High School*, the educational concerns and conditions in the United States were changing. More students continued their education past elementary grades and it was widely accepted that adolescents had unique educational and social needs that were not being met with the "eight-four" structure of traditional elementary and secondary school split. Briggs asserts that the educational theories regarding, merits of, and justifications for junior high schools as transitional institutions had finally been widely accepted—"the long discussion of proposals for reorganization of our secondary schools has now passed into concrete action" (p. vii).

Briggs criticizes the disconnectedness and the "indefiniteness of function and of purpose" of elementary and high schools and stresses that the traditional formation does not address adolescents' educational and adjustment needs. He asserts that the need for an intermediate period between elementary and high school that (1) integrates the education of the elementary and secondary education; (2) ascertains and attempts to satisfy students' immediate and future needs; (3) explores students' interests, aptitudes and capacities; (4) reveals the possibilities in all major fields of learning (i.e., vocational possibilities) and; (5) directs students to a career via exploratory courses that suit each student.

Although Briggs concedes that advancements had been made toward reorganizing schools, he also asserts that much of the junior high school wisdom was not universally understood and applied. He collated the definitions and components of junior high schools enumerated in the literature of the day and then asked 68 education professionals to determine the validity of, rank the importance of, and ultimately, cull the "essential items" or components from numerous junior high school classifications. Briggs used his research to present a more uniform and honed theoretical and practical definition of the junior high school.

REFERENCE

Briggs, T. H. (1920). *The junior high school*. Boston: Houghton Mifflin.

—Cody Stephens
CPRD, University of Illinois

THE JUNIOR HIGH SCHOOL

In Leonard Koos' book, *The Junior High School* (1927) (an enlarged edition of his 1920 book also entitled *The Junior High School*), he investigates both the theoretical and practical demonstrations of junior high schools and attempts to encapsulate the "multifarious forms of the institution." During the first half of the twentieth century, junior high schools were instituted, developed, and studied. The junior high school movement was fueled by the burgeoning understanding that adolescents had distinct educational and developmental needs that were not addressed by either elementary or secondary schools. Koos' book added to the collective knowledge of the junior high school and its evolution by evaluating the various functions and features that comprised many junior high schools and examining the convergence of theory and practice. Like other junior high school proponents of the time, Koos advocated for the reorganization of traditional education institutions to address the unique needs of adolescents but asserted that there were still many divergent junior high school practices and purposes.

To gather information for the book, Koos surveyed high schools educators and asked them to prioritize the educational objectives established by the Commission of the Reorganization of Secondary Education (1918). In addition to surveys, he examined public school documents and statements of the aims, advantages, or functions of the junior high schools made by other educational leaders in articles and editorials. Koos classified his findings into categories relevant to the various and often overlapping theoretical and practical functions of the junior high school: (1) retention of pupils; (2) economy of time; (3) educational and vocational guidance and exploration; (4) vocational education; (5) recognizing the nature of the child; (6) providing the conditions for better teaching; (7) securing superior scholarship; (8) improving the disciplinary situation and socializing opportunities; (9) effecting financial economy; (10) relieving the building situation; (11) continuing the influence of the home; (12) hastening the reform in grades above and below; and (13) normalizing the size of classes.

> its roots must always lie, as do those of the present statement of purposes, in the minds of many rather than one. (p. 113)

At the heart of the *Junior High School*, Koos stresses that theory and opinion of what junior high schools ought to be was crystallizing but that this theoretical stability and understanding needed to be uniformly implemented and collectively pursued. Koos calls for a working statement or plan to overhaul the divergent junior high school practices. He says that it is not enough to conceptualize the purpose of junior high schools but the uniform application of reorganization also needs to be an integral part of the discourse and practice. He expresses the importance of the pervasive school reform buy-in, in particular junior high school reorganization and insists that reforms must be conceived and then championed by many because they will never stick if they are the cause of an individual.

REFERENCES

Commission on the Reorganization of Secondary Education. (1918). *Cardinal principles of secondary education*. Bulletin 1918, No. 35. Washington, DC: U.S. Department of Interior, Bureau of Education.

Koos, L. V. (1927). *The junior high school*. Chicago: Ginn.

—Cody Stephens
CRPD, University of Illinois

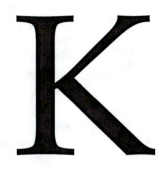

KILPATRICK, WILLIAM HEARD

William Heard Kilpatrick, next to John Dewey, was the most renowned of the progressive educational philosopher active in the first half of the last century. In many respects, Kilpatrick was more influential than Dewey, for he was a superior teacher directly impacting thousands upon thousands of classroom teachers through his lectures at home and abroad. He has been called the Dean of American Education, America's greatest teacher, the million dollar professor, and, to critics, a liberal, social activist.

The son of a Baptist minister, Kilpatrick entered Mercer University in 1888. He showed his brilliance early in mathematics. Following graduation he went to Johns Hopkins, intending to return to Mercer to assist an older professor. Much stimulated by the intellectual life at this mecca, he decided he wanted to teach.

When the assistantship at Mercer did not materialize, he accepted a teaching position in Blakely, Georgia, serving as coprincipal and teacher in Grades 7 through 10. He immersed himself in the literature of education reading Spencer, Froebel, Pestalozzi, and others and began implementing newer educational practices. Kilpatrick had a genuine interest in his students, and people appreciated his personal charm and penetrating mind. As one historian would later comment, "In the summer of 1892, Kilpatrick arrived in Blakely as a college mathematician, and three years later he departed as a progressive educator" (Beineke, 1998, p. 21).

He returned to Johns Hopkins; but this time the study in mathematics was disappointing, and he returned to Georgia, accepting the principalship of an elementary school in Savannah, where in addition to supervising nine teachers and over 400 students, he taught seventh grade. Kilpatrick eliminated report cards and corporal punishment and introduced group work to assist with classes of over 50. Out of a sense of duty and family tradition, Kilpatrick returned to Mercer as a professor of mathematics. His personality and openness to ideas made him especially attractive in that rather staid and closed environment. Although only 29, he was elected Mercer's vice-president.

During his years at Mercer, his views and educational philosophy crystallized. He rejected the theory of formal discipline, which held that the study of math trained the mind much as the exercise of the body produces greater muscles. In 1898 at a summer school, one of his professors was John Dewey. Kilpatrick now turned his back on mathematics as a new calling, education, beckoned him.

In 1907 he accepted a graduate assistantship at Teachers College. Dewey would later claim that Kilpatrick was "the best student I ever had." Upon completing his doctorate in January 1911, he was appointed an assistant professor. Word of Kilpatrick's excellence as a teacher spread, and he became a much sought after teacher and lecturer, gaining a national platform from which to share his maturing ideas about student-centered, democratic education. This charismatic southerner's meteoric rise was due to his ability to communicate the often hard to grasp ideas of Dewey and his ability to enthrall classes that often numbered in the hundreds. Kilpatrick, Dewey, Thorndike, and others at Teachers College were challenging conventional schooling practices as the progressive education movement got underway. In 1918, Kilpatrick published an 18-page article, "The Project Method: The Use of the Purposeful Act in the Educational Process," which applied his educational philosophy to classroom teaching. Extremely well received, it brought Kilpatrick enduring fame. The key to the significance of the project was purpose.

> In the case where no purpose is present, there the weak and foolish teacher has often in times past cajoled, promised and sugar coated, and this we all despise. Purpose, then–its presence or its absence— exactly distinguishes the desirable interest from the mushy type of anything-to-keep-the-dear-things-interested or amused. It is purpose then that we want, worthy purposes urgently sought; get these, and the interest will take care of itself. (Beineke, 1998, p. 102)

Kilpatrick believed that education should stress the development of character and personality, not just the acquisition of bookish information. He wanted children to interact with peers, parents, and society at large and saw the inculcation of self-reliance, initiative, cooperation, and even joy as important concomitants in the learning process. He argued for the "extended acquaintance" between teacher and student, against the compartmentalized-by-subject curriculum, and supported the 6-3-3 proposal. Kilpatrick's broad view of education is apparent in this statement:

Education must aim at developing in the individual the best possible insight into life's problems as they successfully present themselves before him; at helping him to make ever finer distinctions in what he does, to take more and more considerations ever better into account, and finally to bring the best social-moral attitudes to bear on each decisions as made and enacted. For the only proper aim of education is fullness of living through fully developed character. (Beineke, 1998, p. 314)

The central educational concept that came to be associated with Kilpatrick was, "We learn what we live," He often elaborated on this idea in such ways as: "We learn what we live and then live what we learned."

Kilpatrick retired in 1937 but remained very active until a few years before his death in 1975 at age 93. The views of Kilpatrick and other progressives so parallel the middle school concept that some have seen the middle school movement as the rebirth of progressive education.

REFERENCE

Beineke, J. (1998). *And there were giants in the land: The life of William Heard Kilpatrick.* New York: Peter Lang.

—John H. Lounsbury
Georgia College and State University

LEARNING STYLES

Individuals make sense of new ideas in unique ways. Their preferences, or learning styles, vary with the tasks at hand and with the resources available to them. Modifying instruction to accommodate these differences in skills, interests, and abilities invites young adolescents to participate in the middle school classroom with self-confidence. Respecting the differences among people enriches the learning environment and fosters respect for diverse cultural perspectives within a community. Teachers and students use the understanding of their learning styles as tools to develop appropriate curriculum and instruction in the classroom.

Generally, learning styles refers to three primary modes: (1) visual, (2) verbal, and (3) motor or kinesthetic. Some researchers include a fourth, the sense of touch, or a tactile mode and a fifth focused on emotions or feelings (Dunn & Dunn, 1993). Several inventories of learning style exist in the research but the results are often not conclusive. People are likely to use more than one mode for learning and may benefit from engaging in other approaches.

Closely related to learning styles is cognitive ability or intelligence. Gardner (1993) identified nine multiple intelligences that provide further insight into the design of appropriate and relevant instruction. The roots of designing learning experiences according to the way people learn come from John Dewey and the progressive education movement. Their insights offer the middle school a rich foundation for developing varied learning experiences and support the National Middle School Association (NMSA) guidelines for successful school curriculum as relevant, challenging, integrative, and exploratory.

Another area of study that informs learning styles is current brain research that affirms the importance of active learning with manipulative materials, projects, field trips, and real-life investigations. Learning is a complex process and requires the activation of multiple areas of the brain. Recognizing many avenues for engaging the adolescent encourages meaningful involvement in the whole educational process.

Applying the knowledge from research to meet the needs of various adolescents' learning styles is made easier by expanded use of technology for instruction. One such feature is the text-to-speech capabilities found on many computers. No longer is it necessary for a teacher to read aloud text material for a student with visual impairments or with low reading skills. The technology is available to modify the curriculum for that student's learning style within the regular lesson development. With these tools, a school can establish a safe and respectful environment that generates interest in learning and encourages student success across many layers of diversity in the classroom (Tomlinson, 2004).

The National Middle School Association (2003), in recognizing successful schools, also recognizes the wide range of characteristics of young adolescents.

The differences in learning styles is one response to the needs of all learners and offers each student equitable opportunities to academic success in the school environment. Within a typical middle school classroom are students with learning disabilities, giftedness, limited English proficiency, visual and hearing impairments, and academic skills ranging from second grade reading skills to college level skills. Curriculum that is designed with opportunities for expression through the arts, second language learning, and skills classes offer students avenues for academic success and personal growth.

LEARNING PREFERENCES

Learning style inventories can be used to identify preferred learning styles, but they may be unavailable, or unwieldy in informal classroom situations. Self-reflection with young adolescents heightens their investment in understanding how they learn. For those with a strong preference for verbal learning, they identify the value of hearing about concepts prior to applying them to projects; for visual learners, seeing a diagram or picture or web of a concept activates their learning processes more effectively. For others an inquiry method of instruction stimulates their learning because they can physically move around to see alternate perspectives and can touch and feel the artifacts that form the basis of the subject knowledge.

Identifying their own strengths gives students ownership of their learning and respect for the differences among peers. Within the learning community, students develop tolerance for the verbal style of the student who dominates discussion and for the diagrams another visual learner creates for organizing new information. The self-reflection aspect of this method of identifying learning preferences is in keeping with the goals of the NMSA for curriculum that is relevant and exploratory in the lives of young adolescents.

To see how this works, consider a challenging task you learned on your own recently. In one group of adults the list included landscaping a patio walkway,

replacing bathroom tiles, writing a resume, painting with watercolors, designing a contemporary worship, exploring a new city, finding an appropriate preschool. Each selected one task and examined their own processes of learning to identify particular learning preferences. Several chose landscaping a patio and walkway and shared their experiences. Some toured patios to get a picture of ways they might create an inviting setting. Others gathered reading materials about patios and water gardens or studied landscape design blueprints. Another group bought some of the materials and laid them out in the setting as the first step in the process. As the project continued, many described how they integrated multiple modes of learning. When they finished, their self-analysis helped them identify their learning preferences. They transferred the self-knowledge into study strategies at a community college.

MULTIPLE INTELLIGENCES

Another dimension of learning styles comes from research on multiple intelligences. Howard Gardner (1983) initially identified seven intelligences based on individual cognitive strengths and have been used to recognize the diversity among ways learners access new knowledge (Table 1). He continued to study intelligences (1993, 1999) and, over time, added two more. Perhaps researchers will find reasons to add others in the future.

In the past, teachers used a one dimensional strategy for instruction. It included a teacher's lecture followed by students reading the text and turning in written answers to questions. Students who learned

Table 1.   List of multiple intelligences

(1) Linguistic or verbal	Using written and spoken language for learning and thinking.
(2) Logical mathematical	Using mathematics, computing, analyzing, and problem-solving.
(3) Spatial	Visualizing through art and design, locating self in spatial environment.
(4) Musical	Thinking and learning with the sounds and rhythm of music.
(5) Bodily—kinesthetic	Using the physical body and movement to understand ideas and concepts.
(6) Interpersonal	Developing relationships with others to think and learn.
(7) Intrapersonal	Understanding the world by engaging in introspection and heightened self awareness.
(8) Naturalistic	Sensitivity to the natural environment.
(9) Existential	A dimension of spiritual intelligence in thinking about the universe and the meaning of life.

by listening, reading, and writing absorbed the new knowledge. Others were unsuccessful in school. Integrating these intelligences into the classroom offers students multiple avenues to explore new knowledge that is both relevant and challenging. For example, some linked traditional poetry with the music in the pop culture world of adolescents as a modification of the curriculum.

ROOTS IN PROGRESSIVE EDUCATION

John Dewey and the progressive education movement challenged the traditional classroom at the beginning of the twentieth century. He observed the structured lecture and recitation format and he also observed children. Dewey recognized the importance of children relating learning to their own experiences and established a Laboratory School at the University of Chicago to develop his ideas. Through a long career as an educator, his philosophy and writings influenced curriculum in schools. His works included *Child and the Curriculum* (1902/1983), *How We Think* (1933/1981), *Democracy in Education* (1916/1983). For the progressives the task of the school was to provide activities for children to investigate their environment and create products to demonstrate their understanding of concepts. Education was a process of integrating knowledge from multiple sources and applying it to new situations. This education addressed different learning styles and tapped into what Gardner would identify as multiple intelligences.

BRAIN RESEARCH

The processes involved in learning rely on the complex system within the brain. The brain receives data from all the senses and sorts the sensory data through a variety of individualized transfers. The greater the variety of experiences available to the brain, the more opportunities a person has to assimilate new knowledge. Students can focus on lecture material for short periods of time. Then the brain needs time to elaborate on the concept and encode the new learning into larger patterns of knowledge.

In the brain are neurological connections related to the learning process. Activity in the brain strengthens the synapses between nerve cells. Increased brain activity using manipulatives, real-life projects, and other forms of active-learning strengthen the synapses between nerve cells. Engaging emotions in learning is another tool of the brain. Lessons that include students in storytelling, debate, and celebration combine logic and emotion in an active brain. The movement of the body further activates the complex brain functions to enhance learn-

ing. Some suggest natural movement and its development into smooth patterns of movement contribute to overall enhancement of self concept. The work of brain research and learning continues to inform teaching and learning decisions (D'Arcangelo, 1998; Tomlinson & Kalbfleisch, 1998; Wolfe & Brandt, 1998).

TECHNOLOGY

Technology is another tool of learning styles. The use of projects in the classroom addresses multiple styles of learning and appeals to different intelligences. Students demonstrate their knowledge by making choices about the products they create. With expanded technology students integrate content, narrative, imagery, music, and interactive programs into the classroom. Using digital text, a lesson can use the features of text-speech to integrate verbal and visual learning. Following text as it is read overcomes issues of students with limitations in reading ability (Curry, 2002). Not only for students with visual or hearing impairments, these attributes of the digital material enhance learning for all students.

Digital format also encourages students to share their own written material enhanced with imported images and video clips. Handwritten notes from groups no longer are undecipherable scribbles but presented to peers as typed text. The challenge of selecting and publishing quality materials brings the global learning community into the adolescent world. Portfolios, drama, artwork, oral presentations, and narratives measure learning in addition to traditional multiple choice tests and programmed learning modules.

CRITICS OF LEARNING STYLES

Critics of learning styles as a strategy for organizing instruction question the research on learning styles. They say the data does not predict which students learn better when taught with particular learning styles (Curry, 1990; Kavale & Forness, 1987), but much of this research attempted to predict the learning preferences for particular groups of students such as gifted students or Native American students (Burns, Johnson, & Gable, 1998). The prediction, based on a several different inventories of learning styles, was not conclusive.

What was valid, however, was the modification of instruction for individual students and way they perceived and processed information. When elementary teachers identified their own preferences, often a visual learning style, (Sloan, Daane, & Giesen, 2004) and then intentionally integrated more spoken language, more movement, more handling of materials, and more learning experiences for expressing feelings, their multiple strategies of instruction improved student achievement and attitudes.

Critics pointed to sample curriculum units (Klein, 2003). Lessons did show evidence of misplaced emphasis on learning styles. In the examples, the lessons were so focused on activities for each learning style that the modes become the goal of the unit rather than the content of the learning. Dropping a question card into a bucket is not kinesthetic learning. The criticisms are important to consider.

Limiting students to one mode of learning misunderstands the value learning styles and the application of multiple intelligence theory. Multiple perspectives are needed in the learning process. The richness of teaching and learning increases as people share ideas and experiences with one another and bring their strengths to understanding the wholeness of a concept. Students may have preference for a particular mode but not to the exclusion of other means of learning. As teachers and students explore other ways of knowing, their interaction increases understanding and new inquiries emerge. The point is that learning style theory and multiple intelligence theory is only one of many teaching and learning methods. The process of educating people is complex.

Conclusions

Different teaching and learning styles are one aspect of the diversity in the classroom. Modifying curriculum and instruction for the preferences of students shows a respect for differences within the learning environment. It enriches the whole learning process and gives value to other ways of learning, thinking, and understanding.

An awareness of multiple approaches of instruction increases the opportunities for access to learning. Further understanding of multiple intelligences provides teachers with a framework to broaden the curriculum to be more inclusive of students with accelerated academic achievement, multilingual communication, or visual/hearing impairments.

Exceptional abilities in athletics, music, leadership, or self-understanding contribute to a richer learning community. Knowing these skills are valued in their learning community, young adolescents are encouraged to explore new fields. At the same time, teachers introduce new curriculum and instructional strategies into the learning process to meet the needs of the diverse middle school population. The successful schools for young adolescents, as the NMSA says,

have curriculum that is relevant, challenging, interactive, and exploratory.

References

Burns, D. E., Johnson, S. E., & Gable, R. K. (1998). Can we generalize about the learning style characteristics of high academic achievers? *Roeper Review, 20*(4), 276-281.

Curry, L. (1990). A critique of the research on learning styles. *Educational Researcher, 48*(2), 50-52.

Curry, D. L. (2002). Adapting technology for all students. *Creative Classroom, 16*(5), 64-65

D'Arcangelo, M. (1998). The brains behind the brains. *Educational Leadership, 56*(3), 20-25.

Dewey, J. (1981). *How we think.* In J. Boydston (Ed.), *John Dewey: 1925-1952 later works.* Carbondale, IL: Southern Illinois University Press. (Original work published in 1933)

Dewey, J. (1983). *Child and the curriculum.* In J. Boydston (Ed.), *John Dewey: 1899-1924 middle works.* Carbondale, IL: Southern Illinois University Press. (Original work published in 1902)

Dewey, J. (1983). *Democracy in education.* In J. Boydston (Ed.), *John Dewey: 1899-1924 middle works.* Carbondale, IL: Southern Illinois University Press. (Original work published in 1916)

Dunn, R. S., & Dunn, K. (1993). *Teaching secondary students through individual learning styles: Practical approaches for grades 7-12.* Boston: Allyn & Bacon.

Gardner, H. (1983). *Frames of mind: Theory of multiple intelligences.* New York: Basic Books.

Gardner, H. (1993). *Multiple intelligences: The theory in practice.* New York: Basic Books.

Gardner, H. (1999). *Intelligence reframed: Multiple intelligences for the 21st century.* New York: Basic Books.

Kavale, K. A., & Forness, S. R. (1987). Substance over style: Assessing the efficacy of modality testing and teaching. *Exceptional Children, 54,* 228-239.

Klein, P. D. (2003). Rethinking the multiplicity of cognitive resources and curricular representations: Alternatives to learning styles and multiple intelligences. *Journal of Curriculum Studies, 35*(1), 45-81.

National Middle School Association. (2003). *This we believe: Successful schools for young adolescents.* Westerville, OH: Author.

Sloan, T., Daane, C. J., & Giesen, J. (2004). Learning styles of elementary preservce teachers. *College Student Journal, 38*(3), 494-500.

Tomlinson, C. A. (2004). *Differentiation for gifted and talented students.* Thousand Oaks, CA: Sage.

Tomlinson, C. A., & Kalbfleisch, M. L. (1998). Teach me, teach my brain: A call for differentiated classrooms. *Educational Leadership, 56*(3), 52-55.

Wolfe, P., & Brandt, R. (1998). What do we know from brain research? *Educational Leadership, 56*(3), 8-12.

—Reese H. Todd
Texas Tech University

LILLY ENDOWMENT INC.

Lilly Endowment, Inc. is an Indianapolis-based private philanthropic foundation created in 1937 by three members of the Lilly family—J. K. Lilly Sr. and sons J. K. Jr. and Eli—through gifts of stock in their pharmaceutical business. In keeping with the wishes of the three founders, Lilly Endowment exists to support the causes of education, community development, and religion. The Lilly family's foremost priority was to help the people of their city and state build a better life, and the Endowment remains primarily committed to the Lilly family's hometown, Indianapolis, and home state, Indiana.

In 1986, Lilly Endowment chose to concentrate a substantial portion of its K-12 education efforts on developing more effective and responsive middle-grades schools. By targeting this age, when young adolescents are forming their sense of self and aspirations for the future, the Endowment hoped to make a positive impact on the number of students who graduate from high school and enroll in college.

The first major initiative, the Middle-Grades School Recognition Project, publicly recognized and rewarded with $1,000 recognition grants the self-improvement efforts of 30 middle-grades schools. Awards were based on demonstrated improvements in their instructional programs in the prior 5 years. The Endowment then invited the 30 recognized schools to submit proposals for $20,000 grants to extend their improvement efforts, and 15 grants subsequently were awarded. This program was administered by the Academy for Educational Development. It planned and conducted a statewide conference on middle-grades school improvement.

In 1987, the Endowment issued an invitation to Indiana's major urban school districts to participate in the Middle Grades Improvement Program (MGIP), resulting in grants to 16 Indiana school districts.

The Endowment also worked to strengthen the state's affiliate of the National Middle School Association, known at that time as the Indiana Middle School Association (IMSA). In 1988, IMSA had a membership of about 40. Through rejuvenated leadership and vision of the organization and with the help of targeted Endowment grants to encourage especially rural schools to participate in IMSA's annual conferences, the membership grew to more than 500 by 1991, and it changed its name to the Indiana Middle-Level Education Association (IMLEA). In 1992, nearly $450,000 was awarded to IMLEA to support a two-tier program of staff development for middle-grades educators, including graduate-level seminars, workshops and summer institutes.

The Endowment also began in 1988 to work with the Education Development Center (EDC) in Newton, MA, when EDC coordinated technical assistance efforts for MGIP. EDC, a nonprofit research and development firm with 30 years of experience in school reform work, helped improve curriculum and instruction in the MGIP sites. Between 1988 and 1995, the Endowment awarded grants to EDC to coordinate technical assistance, strengthen curriculum and instruction, and to support a book by Nancy Ames and Edward Miller that presented four portraits of MGIP schools, *Changing Middle Schools* (Ames & Miller, 1994).

In 1989, a grant was made to Education Writers Association (Washington, DC) to underwrite an Indiana middle-grades newsletter for distribution to MGIP teams, community-based youth-serving agencies, education reporters and policy-makers. This grant also resulted in a monograph relating to middle-grades improvement (Mancini, 1993).

The Endowment was an early contributor (1990) to the efforts of the National Board for Professional Teaching Standards, underwriting the development of certification standards for middle-grades teachers (Early Adolescence Generalist and Early Adolescence English and/Language Arts). This effort was significant because it centered attention on teachers in middle-level schools, which served students who presented a distinct, but usually unacknowledged, teaching challenge.

Lilly Endowment also directed resources to support programs that encouraged students to enhance their reading skills and, at the same time, acquire a lifelong love of books. Beginning in 1987, the Endowment began its work in reading improvement by providing funding for Reading Excitement and Paperbacks (REAP), administered by the Indiana Department of Education. Students in 40 public schools, Grades 4 to 6, served on selections teams that chose a collection of recreational books from more than 500 that were brought in the school by caravan. By 1990, the Endowment funded an "explosion" of reading grants, "seeding" school and community reading programs for students, teachers, and parents. Grants included an expansion of REAP, student-run bookshops, teacher reading groups, school and public librarian partnerships, programs to encourage parents' reading habits, access to recreational reading materials, curriculum (Developmental Studies Center, Oakland, CA), and assessments. The Middle Grades Reading Network, an umbrella program for these broad-based, middle-grades reading efforts, was established in 1992 at the University of Evansville. Its central goal is to make the entire state of Indiana a Community of Readers. More information about the Network is available at http://www2.evansville.edu/mgrnweb, including the *Reading Bill of Rights for Indiana's Young Adolescents*, *Reading Blueprint for the State of Indiana*, and articles from its newsletter, *NetWords*. The Middle Grades Reading Network remains at the University of Evansville and operates with Lilly Endowment funding.

The Endowment's emphasis on middle-grades education culminated in 1995, capped by the publication of an article in *Kappan*, "Speaking with One Voice" (Lipsitz, Mizell, Jackson, & Austin, 1997). Spurred by that publication, and by a series of what was termed "Continuing Conversations" (for which the Endowment and other foundations provided modest support) among the Endowment and other foundations, intermediary organizations, and researchers, the National Forum to Accelerate Middle Grades Reform (www.mgforum.org) was formed in 1997.

While the Endowment no longer specifically targets middle-grades school-improvement efforts, it continues to recognize the importance of middle grades as an important stage at which to encourage students to consider and prepare for higher education. An example of its work is the career and guidance counseling project called "C3," administered by the Indiana Youth Institute (IYI) (www.iyi.org). C3 is a new web-based project that initially will target Indiana middle school students and their parents by providing information and encouragement about college and career opportunities. The genesis for C3 was the 1994 Lilly Endowment-funded study, "High Hopes, Long Odds," that was disseminated by IYI. Among that study's findings was that Indiana middle school students had bold aspirations, including college, but many lacked the information about what they had to do to prepare to achieve their dreams.

More recently, Endowment education efforts have encouraged Indiana colleges and universities to make connections with K-12 schools across the state to raise the level of educational attainment of Indiana residents. Finally, through many of Indiana's community foundations, the Endowment's CAPE (Community Alliances to Promote Education) initiative has touched, directly, and indirectly, many middle-grades students in the state.

REFERENCES

Ames, N. L., & Miller, E. (1994). *Changing middle schools*. San Francisco: Jossey-Bass.

Lipsitz, J., Mizell, M. H., Jackson, A. W., & Austin, L. M. (1997, March). Speaking with one voice. *Phi Delta Kappan, 78*, 533-540.

Mancini, G. H. (1993). *Gentle ambitions: Indiana's thoughtful middle grades movement*. Washington, DC: Education Writers Association.

—Gretchen Wolfram
Lilly Endowment Inc.

LIMITED ENGLISH PROFICIENCY

LIMITED ENGLISH PROFICIENCY AND ENGLISH LANGUAGE LEARNERS (ELL)

Drastic demographic shifts in the later half of the twentieth century have resulted in the influx of many students into American schools whose native language is not English. According to Ovando (1998), students who speak one language in the home and may have some English proficiency but are still more fluent in their home language have historically been referred to as Limited English Proficient (LEP) students. Criticized for the implications of the term "limited," however, the term English Language Learner (ELL) has been used to more equitably describe this group of students. This term implies that the student is in the process of learning the English language without a negative connotation.

Many students might be described as English Language Learners. Some of these students come from families of indigenous minorities with long histories in the United States while others are more recent immigrants. Houk (2005) defined this group of students as those who are frequently first generation children raised to speak a language other than English. Typically, the parents of these students are also beginning to learn English. On the other hand, families may have had a variety of formal literacy experiences, some being highly educated and literate in a first language with the children also having pre-literacy skills. Others may not have had formal literacy experiences in their native language which may have left the children without formal introductory literacy skills as well.

Early adolescent English Language Learners may face particular challenges as they adjust to the demands of the middle school. Multiple teachers rather than one may result in the needs of these students being overlooked. It is critical that middle level educators become sensitive to the variety of language, program, cultural, and social needs of ELL students (Van Ness & Platt, 1997).

FIRST AND SECOND LANGUAGE ACQUISITION

Research supports that first language acquisition is a natural, innate, developmental process that occurs throughout the lifespan. From birth, children are predisposed to learning language subconsciously through use, not formal instruction. This process is universal in children from all cultures and backgrounds who are exposed to language input (Chomsky, 1965; Berko Gleason, 1993). Ovando (1998) explained that children, by age five, demonstrate knowledge of first language phonology, vocabulary, grammar, semantics, and contextual use. From ages 6-12, children develop knowledge of complex grammar rules, phonological distinctions, expanded vocabulary, semantics, discourse, and more complex contextual usage (Berko Gleason, 1993; Goodluck, 1991). Knowledge of written language is introduced in school and continues the development of the first language throughout the years of formal instruction. By adolescence, students understand language at a fairly complex level although development continues to occur throughout a lifetime (Ovando, 1998).

Second language acquisition is also a developmental process and occurs in stages according to Krashen (1985). The first stage, preproduction, is characterized by minimal comprehension and no verbal production. A silent stage may occur while students are beginning to internalize a new language and verbal speech should not be forced during this time. Self-consciousness around peers, cultural socialization norms, or previous background experiences might encourage students to remain in a silent stage (Van Ness & Platt, 1997). The second stage, early production, involves limited comprehension and one or two word responses. Speech emergence is the third stage where students demonstrate increased comprehension, simple sentences, and basic errors in speech. Reading is limited to what has been learned by ear, and writing is limited to brief responses. The fourth stage, intermediate fluency, is characterized by good comprehension, the use of more complex sentences, fewer errors in speech, increased reading comprehension, and emerging cultural knowledge. Not all language learners progress through each stage at the same pace and movement from one stage to the next should not be forced (Krashen, 1982, 1985).

Wong Fillmore (1991) claimed that critical to the language learning process are … learners who realize that they need to learn the target language and are motivated to do so; speakers of the target language who know it well enough to provide the learners with access to the language and the help they need for learning it; and a social setting which brings learners and target language speakers into frequent enough contact to make language learning possible. (pp. 52-53)

Fillmore insisted that all three components must be present for language development to occur. Without all three, language development would be difficult, if not impossible. Researchers also agree that culture plays a pivotal role in language acquisition. (See Berko Gleason, 1993; Ovando, 1998; Nieto, 2000; and Houk, 2005)

TEACHING APPROACHES FOR ENGLISH LANGUAGE LEARNERS

Traditional approaches to teaching second languages to nonnative speakers have been teacher centered and controlled, highly structured, sequenced by grammar structures in discrete units of language taught part to whole, focused mostly on producing correct form, less focused on language used for meaningful communicative purposes, and taught in isolation of integrated contexts. The grammar-translation, audiolingual, and direct methods are examples of traditional approaches (Ovando, 1998). Transitional methods that embody a variety of techniques and have been widely used are Total Physical Response (Asher, 1982) and the Natural Approach (Krashen & Terrell, 1983).

Methods that have replaced traditional models reflect a whole language philosophy which emphasizes the natural developmental process of language acquisition. The whole language approach is humanistic and student centered. The use of language for a variety of purposes, language learned in meaningful contexts, frequent writing from an early stage, exposure to quality literature, and student choice of reading material are all aspects of the whole language approach.

The Cognitive Academic Language Learning Approach (CALLA) trains teachers to focus on students' acquisition of learning strategies as language is being taught through content. According to O'Malley & Chamot (1990),

a common reaction to the less than fluent English of a student is to teach content from a lower grade level and to expect from LEP students only lower-level cognitive skills such as simple recall. CALLA demands the opposite. LEP students need to learn content appropriate to their developmental level and previous educational experience; higher-level thinking skills are as much to be expected from them as from any other student. Instead of watering down content for LEP student, CALLA teachers make challenging content comprehensible by providing additional contextual support in the form of demonstrations, visuals, and hands-on experiences, and by teaching students how to apply learning strategies to understand and remember the content presented. When asking LEP students higher-order questions, CALLA teachers evaluate responses on the basis of the ideas expressed rather than on the correctness of the language used. (p. 194)

O'Malley & Chamot recommend this method for content area instruction with adolescents especially in the areas of science and math.

BILINGUAL EDUCATION AND ENGLISH AS A SECOND LANGUAGE

In terms of organizational structures, programs are essentially either Bilingual or English only (Van Ness & Platt, 1997). Bilingual instruction involves teaching in two languages by teachers, aides, and/or peers. Students in this setting may speak a variety of languages and may be served by education professionals that represent a range of languages spoken. As defined by the California Department of Education (1981) bilingual education programs include "the continued development of the student's primary language, acquisition of the second language, which for many language minority students is English, and instruction in the content areas utilizing both the primary and second languages" (p. 215). One of problems inherent in bilingual education programs is that there are often insufficient numbers of education professionals who can speak all of the primary languages represented in the classroom.

> English as a second language (ESL) is a component of bilingual education programs.

Allen (1991) explained that

> transitional bilingual programs are ones in which children's first language is used as a medium of instruction until they become fluent enough to receive all their instruction in English. ESL is a part of such programs. It is expected that the amount of instruction offered in the child's native language will decrease as the child's ability to use English increases. (p. 360)

If too few primary language speakers are available, students might attend ESL content classes part of the day and all English mainstream classes the rest of the time.

Teachers of English to Speakers of Other Languages (TESOL) is the professional organization that advocates for the bilingual education of English Language Learners. In the TESOL Statement on the Education of K-12 Language Minority Students in the United States (1992), the following are recommended for meeting the needs of English Language Learners:

1. Comprehensive English as a second language instruction for linguistically diverse students that prepares tem to handle content area material in English.
2. Instruction in the content areas that is not only academically challenging, but also tailored to the linguistic proficiency, educational background, and academic needs of students.
3. Opportunities for students to further develop and/or use their first language to promote academic and social development.
4. Professional development for both ESOL (English to Speakers of Other Languages) and other classroom teachers that prepares them to facilitate the language and academic growth of linguistically and culturally different children. (p. 12)

The inclusion model involves the full time mainstreaming of English Language Learners in the English speaking content classroom. In this setting, teachers instruct students in English using a number of ESL strategies. At times, a bilingual instructor might also work in the classroom along side the mainstream content teacher. This approach requires a great deal of time devoted to planning and coordinating the different instructional needs of the students.

Some reject the idea of bilingual education altogether and believe in linguistic assimilation, especially in schools. For a balance of perspectives concerning the issues surrounding bilingual education and the English-only movement, see Unz (1999), Nieto (2000), and Houk (2005).

PRINCIPALS FOR TEACHING ENGLISH LANGUAGE LEARNERS

Several suggestions have been proposed for working with English Language Learners. Early (1990) noted that capitalizing on the prior experiences of learners recognizes student values and culture. Furthermore, language learning should permeate all areas of the curriculum including the academic, social, and affective domains. This is very important for adolescents in the middle school where the focus is on educating the whole child. Activities that encourage children to use language for a variety of purposes and include exposure to a number of text types are beneficial. Multimedia approaches allow for clearer communication and reduce barriers for language learners. Finally, encouraging parental participation in student learning not only supports academic growth, but also fosters social development.

Dixon (1976) found that activities benefiting members of a whole group may be more successful than activities that benefit only individuals. Cooperative learning and activities within both the classroom and the school context are more advantageous than those that foster competition. This is also in keeping with the middle grades philosophy of education. Additionally, language learners should have ample opportunity to participate in leadership roles in the classroom and the school and should be afforded occasions to interact in peer teaching relationships. This may strengthen academic growth as well as the reinforcement of cultural knowledge.

Norton (1997), who wrote extensively on teaching the language arts, referred to de Felix's (1982) five step approach for working with ESL students: (a) develop comprehension; (b) select and analyze for vocabulary, grammar, and linguistic function; (c) plan activities to meet students' needs; (d) present lessons by proceeding from the known to the unknown; and (e) integrate and affirm skills in various contexts. Norton also asserted that many of the techniques and strategies used in working with ESL students are also useful for all populations. For further suggestions on specific classroom activities and techniques for assessment of English language proficiency, see Cummins (1981) and Houk (2005).

REFERENCES

Allen, V. (1991). Teaching bilingual and ESL children. In J. Flood, J. Jensen, D. Lapp, & J. Squire (Eds.), *Handbook of research on teaching the English language arts* (pp. 356-364). New York: Macmillan.

Asher, J. (1982). *Learning another language through actions: The complete teachers guide book* (2nd ed.). Los Gatos, CA: Sky Oaks.

Berko Gleason, J. (1993). *The development of language* (3rd ed.). New York: Macmillan.

California Department of Education. (1981). *Schooling and language minority students: A theoretical framework.* Los Angeles: Evaluation, Dissemination, and Assessment Center, California State University.

Chomsky, N. (1965). *Aspects of the theory of syntax.* Cambridge, MA: MIT Press.

Cummins, J. (1981). The role of primary language development in promoting educational success for language minority students. In *Schooling and language minority students: A theoretical framework.* Los Angeles, CA: Evaluation, Dissemination, and Assessment Center, California State University.

de Felix, J. W. (1982). Steps to second language development in the regular classroom. In C. Carter, (Ed.), *Non-native and non-standard dialect students: Classroom practices in teaching English, 1982-1983.* Urbana, IL: National Council of Teachers of English.

Dixon, C. N. (1976). Teaching strategies for the Mexican American child. *The Reading Teacher, 30,* 141-145.

Early, M. (1990). Enabling first and second language learners in the classroom. *Language Arts, 67,* 567-575.

Houk, F. A. (2005). *Supporting English language learners.* Portsmouth, NH: Heinemann.

Goodluck, H. (1991). *Language acquisition.* Oxford, England: Blackwell.

Krashen, S. D. (1982). *Principles and practices in second language acquisition.* Oxford, England: Pergamon.

Krashen, S. D. (1985). *The input hypotheses: Issues and implications.* New York: Longman.

Krashen, S. D., & Terrell, T. D. (1983). *The natural approach: Language acquisition in the classroom.* Oxford, England: Pergamon.

Nieto, S. (2000). *Affirming diversity: The sociopolitical context of multicultural education* (3rd ed.). New York: Longman.

Norton, D. E. (1997). *The effective teaching of language arts,* (5th ed.). Upper Saddle River, NJ: Merrill.

O'Malley, J. M., & Chamot, A. U. (1990). *Learning strategies in second language acquisition.* Cambridge, England: Cambridge University Press.

Ovando, C. J. (1998). *Bilingual and ESL classrooms: Teaching in multicultural contexts.* Boston: McGraw-Hill.

Teachers of English for Speakers of Other Languages. (1992) TESOL statement on the education of K-12 language minority students in the United States. In *TESOL resource packet: Is your school helping its language minority students meet the national education goals?* Alexandria, VA: Teachers of English for Speakers of Other Languages.

Unz, R. (1999). *California and the end of white America.* Retrieved June 29, 2005, from http://www.onenation.org/9911/110199.html

Van Ness, J., & Platt, E. (1997). A multifaceted approach to teaching limited English proficient students. In J. L. Irvin (Ed.), *What current research says to the middle level practitioner* (pp. 121-135). Westerville, OH: National Middle School Association.

Wong Fillmore, L. (1991). Second language learning in children: A model of language learning in social context. In E. Bialystok (Ed.), *Language processing in bilingual children* (pp. 49-69). Cambridge, England: Cambridge University Press.

—Lynne M. Bailey
The University of North Carolina, Charlotte

LIPSITZ, JOAN

Among the contributions to middle grades education for which Joan Lipsitz is credited are her authorship of *Growing up Forgotten: A Review of Research and Programs Concerning Early Adolescence* (1980) and *Successful Schools for Young Adolescents* (1984); establishment of the Center for Early Adolescence, the first national center to focus on early adolescence as a critical period of human development; and the development and implementation of the Middle Grades Improvement Program, the first major foundation foray into middle grades school reform.

The first step in Lipsitz's professional career was as a language arts teacher at the high school, then the middle school level, between 1960 and 1972. Lipsitz found the transition from teaching high school to middle school difficult, as undergraduate coursework and senior high school teaching experience were insufficient in providing knowledge and skills to best teach young adolescents. Attempting to locate support, information, and research about young adolescents, she recognized the serious lack of such resources. Her career focus on research and policy crystallized as the Civil Rights movement and the assassination of Dr. Martin Luther King, Jr. fired her passion for social justice and equity.

Between 1972 and 1978, Lipsitz was Program Associate at the Learning Institute of North Carolina, where she began her work on public school reform. *Growing up Forgotten*, written during this time, documented the struggles of adolescent growth. Lipsitz soon became founding director of the Center for Early Adolescence, a position she held until 1986 when she moved to Indianapolis to develop and direct a 17-school, middle grades reform initiative funded by the Lilly Endowment for the next 9 years.

Throughout her career Lipsitz has advised foundations and other nonprofit organizations concerned with school improvement and youth development. In 2000 Lipsitz became a senior fellow at MDC (Making Difference in Communities in the South) in Chapel Hill, NC. She is a founding member of the National Forum to Accelerate Middle-Grades Reform and serves on the governing boards of the Hershey Trust Company and the Milton Hershey School. She is on the boards of the North Carolina Child Advocacy Institute, DonorsChoose/North Carolina, and the Family Support Network. She has been a member of the College Board's Commission on Precollegiate Guidance and Counseling, a research associate at the National Institute of Education, and a consultant to the Pillsbury Company, the Carnegie Corporation, the National Science Foundation, the U.S. Department of Education, and the Foundation for the Mid South, among others. Among her honors is her 1995 designation as a Sagamore of the Wabash (Indiana's highest citizen award), the Ken McEwin Award for Service to Middle Level Education (NC), the American Orthopsychiatric Association Leadership Award, and a Phi Delta Kappa Award for Outstanding Research.

REFERENCES

Lipsitz, J. (1980). *Growing up forgotten: A review of research and programs concerning early adolescence.* New Brunswick, NJ: Transaction Books.

Lipsitz, J. (1984). *Successful schools for young adolescents.* New Brunswick, NJ: Transaction Books.

—Mary Henton
National Middle School Association

LITERACY

Literacy development in the middle school is a multifaceted concept. In this context, the scope of development crosses traditional content area lines and is addressed in all content areas as well as in all aspects of the school culture (National Middle School Association, NMSA, 2003). Literacy programs at this level are purposefully student centered and focused on individual development. "The needs of the students drive the school schedule, curriculum, and instruction; students are treated with respect and are rewarded for their achievements. Literacy is celebrated in an exemplary middle school" (Strauss & Irvin, 2000, p. 59) The following will outline some of the more specific aspects of literacy development in middle level education.

HOW DO STUDENTS LEARN?

Two areas of research that have informed educators' notions of how learners create meaning through reading, writing, speaking, and listening are information processing and schema networks. Individuals who process information effectively use general and specific knowledge they already possess along with strategic knowledge in order to complete tasks. The more that is known about a topic or idea already, the more likely a learner will be able to process new or more complex information (Carr, 2002).

A second theory explaining how learners create meaning involves the existence of schemes of knowledge based on previous direct and indirect experiences (Rumelhart, 1977). Categories of information comprise a knowledge network, or schema. As learners integrate new knowledge and experience into existing schemas, new networks are constructed. The philosophy of constructivism is, in part, based on this theory. For more on constructivism, see Fuhler (2003).

Effective processors of information are aware of their ability to link prior knowledge to new knowledge and can effectively monitor when comprehension breaks down. These learners are also able to apply the necessary strategies to encourage meaning making. This process is referred to as metacognition (Pressley, 2002). Typically, early adolescents may not be strong metacongnitive learners. The responsibility rests with teachers to help students access prior knowledge, to learn to construct new meanings, and to apply strategies that will help them learn when they encounter difficulties.

There are several approaches to helping students activate prior knowledge before new ideas are introduced. One of these techniques is the use of advance organizers (Carr, 2002). Advance organizers are narratives that provide concrete examples of ideas to students so they can begin to identify connections between the concepts. These connections help students organize new information.

Graphic organizers have been used prolifically to help students activate prior knowledge and to create new understandings. These picture, or graphic, representations of information are especially helpful to middle school learners who are beginning to encounter ever growing amounts of expository text. Buehl (2001) demonstrated the use of concept definition maps to activate prior knowledge and to introduce new key vocabulary. The strategy identifies key concepts, the definitions of concepts, and examples of the concepts.

Brainstorming is another strategy that has been employed extensively in a variety of settings, school and otherwise, to help introduce new information to learners. The K-W-L strategy (Carr & Ogle, 1987) has been used to ask learners (a) what they already know about a topic or idea, (b) what they think they know about the topic or idea, and after reading or instruction, (c) what they learned about the topic or idea. The responses may be written on individual student charts or on the board for the whole class to compose together. This strategy may also be modified and used to help students make predictions about what they think they might learn.

STRATEGIES FOR READING IN THE CONTENT AREAS

Proficient readers are strategic readers. They are able to use a variety of strategies and techniques to process information and repair breakdowns in comprehension. Many middle school students, however, are not necessarily well trained in such skills. For this reason, teachers must instruct students directly in how to apply learning and reading strategies (Pearson & Fielding, 1991). Many content area teachers are not fully aware of the critical importance of such instruction and underestimate the difficulties students will encounter in reading tasks. Additionally, the introduction of increasing amounts of factual and expository information places particular demands on students who are struggling readers or whose native language is something other than English.

Pressley (2002) found that a think aloud technique can be taught to students to help them recognize the thinking processes that occur as they create meaning from what they read. Proficient readers who use this strategy were found to do the following (Carr, 2002):

1. Set a purpose or a goal for the learning activity. Proficient readers decide what their reading stance will be, that is, they know how and why they are approaching the text. In classrooms, the goals may be locating information, learning the material to recall on a test, or gathering information for a character analysis.... Skimming also lets the reader know if this piece of text is relevant to the goal to be achieved and which sections of text are important to the goal.

2. Activate prior knowledge and experience.

3. Ask questions of themselves, the authors, and the texts, before, during, and after reading. Questions relate to speculations about the text to be read. They also serve to clarify the meaning of individual vocabulary and of large chunks of texts (Palincsar & Brown, 1984).

4. Create visual and other sensory images from text. [Effective readers] create mental images to facilitate their understanding. Graphic representations have been found to be very useful for both information storage and easy access to that information.

5. Retell or synthesize information in the text. Students who paraphrase or summarize, discover the main idea and attempt to put ideas together to form an integrated synopsis have greater overall understanding of textual information and greater ability to recall the information in the future (Pressley, 2002).

6. Use a variety of fix-up strategies to repair comprehension when it breaks down (pp. 24-26).

One of the goals of the teacher should be to gradually enable readers to function on their own. Careful modeling of literacy behaviors including the use of think aloud techniques, followed by guided and student independent practice are two steps in this process. The teacher must also provide timely and specific feedback as students attempt to internalize new reading behaviors. Finally, students will benefit from self-reflection on their successes and struggles (Duke & Pearson, 2002; Garner, 1994).

ADDRESSING THE NEEDS OF STRUGGLING READERS AND ENGLISH LANGUAGE LEARNERS

Struggling readers require not only strategic reading instruction, but also require efforts to help them actively engage in literacy behaviors. Based on their research, Ivey and Broadus (2001) suggested that (a) teachers read interesting books and articles aloud to the class, (b) teachers maintain a variety of high interest reading material in the class, both fiction and nonfiction, (c) teachers offer opportunities for students to choose what they want to read, and (d) provide silent reading time in class. These suggestions will actually enable all readers to become actively engaged in reading.

Teachers can also assist their students in becoming more reflective thinkers. Meier (1995) said that teachers can encourage their students to ask the following questions about what they learn:

1. Connections: Where do these ideas come from? Is this idea connected to other things?
2. Perspective: From whose point of view is the information being presented?
3. Evidence? How do you know what you know? What is the proof for what you are considering?
4. Supposition: What if things were different?
5. Significance: Why do these ideas matter? To whom do they matter? Why are we considering them?

English language learners face special challenges in the middle school. Not only are they attempting to learn a new language, but they are also attempting to appreciate new social and cultural expectations. Houk (2005) relied heavily on the research of Brian Cambourne (1988) to design balanced literacy environments for English language learners. Similarly, Allen (1995) also based her work with struggling adolescents largely on Cambourne's research. His findings are based on the premise that if all children, regardless of background, can successfully master oral communication, then there may be inherent learning conditions upon which other forms of literacy may be developed.

According to Cambourne's "learning conditions,"

Learners are immersed in all kinds of text, they are exposed to continuous demonstrations of how to negotiate text successfully, there are many authentic purposes to which they are expected to apply their knowledge, they have some freedom to direct their own literacy acquisition, the atmosphere allows children many opportunities to practice new learning without risk of failure or embarrassment, and there is regular positive feedback to guide children's performance. (Houk, 2005, pp. 111-112)

Following from these conditions, Cambourne claimed, are several components that may be included in a balanced literacy program and may be implemented with all groups of students.

A number of researchers have found success applying practices that are in keeping with Cambourne's (1988) work. In the area of reading, activities include: (a) read-alouds (where the teacher reads to the students), (b) shared reading (where students have copies of the text being read), (c) guided reading (where strategies are incorporated to help students build fluency and comprehension), and (d) independent reading (where students read on their own). Independent reading may occur when the teacher chooses, but should be sustained and uninterrupted time. Students should also be allowed to choose what they wish to read from a wide variety of texts. Finally, the key feature in independent reading time is meaningful engagement in reading, not recordkeeping or assessment.

Writing activities include: (a) shared writing (where the teacher and the students compose together while the teacher writes for the class), (b) interactive writing (where students participate in writing for the class), (c) guided writing (where the teacher provides direct instruction in writing skills), and (d) independent writing (where students write on their own for their own purposes) (Houk, 2005; Goodman, 1984).

ASSESSING LITERACY DEVELOPMENT

In keeping with the middle school philosophy of nurturing the development of the early adolescent, assessing literacy skills in the middle grades is an ongoing process that requires teachers to analyze writing in terms of its strengths and weaknesses rather than for its errors (NMSA, 2003). Students should not fear the process of having their work evaluated. They should be encouraged to look upon the opportunity as one in which to receive individual attention and support from the teacher in becoming better readers and writers. Feedback from the teacher might include praise for what is done well, and suggestions for improvement.

Portfolios lend themselves naturally and well to this approach to writing assessment (Goodman, 1984). Student work is collected in a file, or portfolio, and is examined by the teacher with the student during individual conferences. Teachers act as guides, allowing students to analyze and reflect on their progress. Teachers can also assist students in forming new writing goals. Other forms of alternative assessment in a balanced literacy program might include the use of rubrics or checklists.

REFERENCES

Allen, J. (1995). *It's never too late: Leading adolescents to lifelong literacy.* Portsmouth, NH: Heinemann.

Buehl, D. (2001). *Classroom strategies for interactive learning* (2nd ed.). Newark, DE: International Reading Association.

Cambourne, B. (1988) *The whole story: Natural learning and the acquisition of literacy in the classroom.* Auckland, NZ: Ashton Scholastic.

Carr, M. S. (2002). *Inquiring minds: Learning and literacy in early adolescence. Creating communities of learning & excellence.* Portland, OR: Northwest Regional Educational Lab.

Carr, E., & Ogle, D. (1987). K-W-L Plus: A strategy for comprehension and summarization. *Journal of Reading, 30*(7), 626-631.

Duke, N. K., & Pearson, P. D. (2002). Effective practices for developing reading comprehension. In A. E. Farstrup & S. J. Samuels (Eds.), *What research has to say about reading instruction* (3rd ed., pp. 205-242). Newark, DE: International Reading Association.

Fuhler, C. (2003). Joining theory and best practice to drive classroom instruction. *Middle School Journal, 34*(5), 23-30.

Garner, R. (1994). Metacognition and executive control. In R. B. Ruddell, M. R. Ruddell, & H. Singer (Eds.), *Theoretical models and processes of reading* (4th ed., pp. 715-732). Newark, DE: International Reading Association.

Goodman, Y. (1984). The development of initial literacy. In H. Goelman, A. Oberg, & F. Smith (Eds.), *Awakening to literacy: The University of Victoria symposium on children's response to a literate environment. Literacy before schooling* (pp. 102-109). Portsmouth, NH: Heinemann.

Houk, F. A. (2005). *Supporting English language learners: A guide for teachers and administrators.* Portsmouth, NH: Heinemann.

Ivey, G., & Broadus, K. (2001). Just plain reading: A survey of what makes students want to read in middle school classrooms. *Reading Research Quarterly, 36*(4), 350-377.

Meier, D. (1995). *The power of their ideas: Lessons for America from a small school in Harlem.* Boston, MA: Beacon Press.

National Middle School Association. (2003). *This we believe: successful schools for young adolescents.* Westerville, OH: National Middle School Association.

Palincsar, A. S., & Brown, A. L. (1984). Reciprocal teaching of comprehension-fostering and comprehension-monitoring activities. *Cognition and Instruction, 1*(2), 117-175.

Pearson, P. D., & Fielding, L. (1991) Comprehension instruction. In R. Barr, M. L. Kamil, P. B. Mosenthal, & P. D. Pearson (Eds.), *Handbook of reading research* (Vol. 2, pp. 815-860). New York: Longman.

Pressley, M. (2002). Metacognition and self-regulated comprehension. In A. E. Farstrup & S. J. Samuels (Eds.), *What research has to say about reading instruction* (3rd ed., pp. 291-309).

Rumelhart, D. E. (1977). Toward an interactive model of reading. In S. Dornic (Ed.), *Attention and performance* (Vol. 6, pp. 573-603). Hillsdale, NJ: Erlbaum.

Strauss, S. E., & Irvin, J. L. (2000). Exemplary literacy learning programs: What research says. *Middle School Journal 32*(1), 56-59.

—Lynne M. Bailey
The University of North Carolina, Charlotte

LOUNSBURY, JOHN H.

Called the "Conscience of the Middle School Movement" (Johnston, 1992, p. 45) and recognized as one of its founders, as well as NMSA's foremost editor, John H. Lounsbury has shaped much of the thought and language of middle grades education for over 40 years.

John Lounsbury attended public schools in Plainfield, New Jersey, where he was active in student government and athletics. After completing his freshman and sophomore years at Tusculum College (TN) as biology major, he enlisted in the U.S. Army in 1943. First assigned to the infantry then the Signal Corps, he completed his service in Okinawa in 1946. Lounsbury finished his undergraduate studies at John B. Stetson University (FL) where a history of education course sparked his interest in teaching. Lounsbury earned his masters at George Peabody College for Teachers and began his educational career in 1948 in Wilmington, North Carolina, as a junior/senior high school social studies teacher. He earned his doctorate at Peabody in 1954.

Lounsbury's career is characterized by teaching, writing, editing, and considerable professional service. He was Chairman of the Division of Education at Berry College (GA) from 1954-1956, then Associate Professor of Education at the University of Florida from 1956-1960. He moved to Georgia College in 1960, first as Director of the Division of Teacher Education, and Director of Graduate Studies, then as Dean of the School of Education. Lounsbury retired from Georgia College in 1983 in order to devote full time to his editing for the National Middle School Association (NMSA) and related middle school interests. He edited the fledgling *Middle School Journal* from 1976 to 1990, building it into a major professional journal and then assumed the post of publications editor for NMSA in 1990, directing NMSA's entry into the publication of books. He was named Consulting Editor in 2002.

Grounded in the integrity of his personal values and principles, as well as the tenets of progressive education, two themes emanate from Lounsbury's work. First is his conviction that a free, universal, and democratic education is the birthright of every citizen and necessary for the welfare of a democratic society. Lounsbury believes that the school itself should be a democratic institution faithfully organized and functioning as such. Second, Lounsbury vigilantly upholds the belief that "the school must be child-centered in all that it does" (Johnston, 1992). The structures, curriculum, organizations of school must first and foremost fit the student.

Lounsbury has authored or coauthored more than 130 articles, two college textbooks, five national research reports, numerous chapters, and other publications. He has written forewords for more than 40 books, and edited, designed, and produced more than 100 professional publications for NMSA. He has served on numerous committees, boards, and task forces, including the Administrative Committee of the National Study of School Evaluation (1969-1976), the Secondary Commission of the Southern Association of Colleges and Schools (1963-1969), the Task Force on Teacher Education for the State of Georgia (1982-1983), and the Middle Level Council of the National Association of Secondary School Principals (1983-1990). Lounsbury also founded the Professors of Middle Level Education in 1989. Among the numerous honors he has received are three yearbook dedications and the designation, in 1997, of the School of Education at Georgia College and State University as the John H. Lounsbury School of Education.

REFERENCE

Johnston, J. H. (1992). John H. Lounsbury: Conscience of the middle school movement. *The Middle School Journal, 24*(2), 45-50.

—Mary Henton
National Middle School Association

MAKING MIDDLE GRADES WORK

In 1997 the Southern Regional Education Board (SREB) (www.sreb.org) and 14 states launched a comprehensive, middle-grades improvement effort, Making Middle Grades Work (MMGW). MMGW began with extensive research on the status of middle grades education in the southern region (Cooney, 1998a, 1998b, 1998c, 1999). MMGW has a very clear goal of raising student achievement based on a framework of research-based key practices and conditions, continuous improvement through data collection and analysis, and membership in a network of schools supporting improvement. SREB and states provide professional development services, materials and ongoing support.

The MMGW design for comprehensive improvement in middle grades education requires changes in the school's mission; what is taught; how students are taught; what is expected of students; how the school is organized; how teachers relate to students, to each other and to parents; how students are supported; how the school uses data; how teachers are prepared, selected and supported; and how leaders motivate and manage school improvement.

The MMGW comprehensive improvement design works in all kinds of schools. The 52 original MMGW schools included rural and urban schools ranging in size from fewer than 100 students to more than 1,300 students. Minority student populations ranged from zero to 90%, and students eligible for free or reduced-price lunches totaled between 14% and 88%.

Schools in the MMGW network prepare students for college-preparatory work in high school by using proven activities that raise achievement. Students who take part in these activities perform at signifi-cantly higher levels—regardless of race, ethnicity, or economic status. In schools where eighth graders made the most improvement in three areas (reading, mathematics, and science), more students reported intensive literacy experiences. Eighth graders who reported intensive numeracy experiences achieved at or near the proficiency level in mathematics (Cooney & Bottoms, 2003).

Other factors also make a difference: The most-improved MMGW schools have teachers with content majors who use engaging activities to increase the rigor of academic courses. Eighth-graders who have access to extra help are more likely to perform at a higher level. Three other factors also contribute to higher achievement: (1) giving students an adult at school who acts as a personal adviser, (2) encouraging students to take hard courses like Algebra I, and (3) involving parents in helping students plan for high school success.

MMGW recommends that states, districts and schools act together to improve middle grades education by:

- Agreeing that the middle grades mission is to prepare students for challenging high school studies.
- Stating clearly what students need to know and be able to do to succeed in high school studies.
- Setting reasonable performance standards to determine if students are ready for challenging high school work.
- Making a commitment to provide extra time and high-quality extra help for students who need it.
- Planning smooth transitions between schools that help students meet higher expectations.
- Employing only teachers who have content knowledge and instructional skills.

- Preparing leaders who can manage change and improve curriculum, instruction and student achievement.

REFERENCES

Cooney, S. (1998a). *Education's weak link: Student performance in the middle grades.* Atlanta, GA: Southern Regional Education Board.

Cooney, S. (1998b). *Raising the bar in the middle grades: Readiness for success.* Atlanta, GA: Southern Regional Education Board.

Cooney, S. (1998c). *Improving teaching in the middle grades: Higher standards for students aren't enough.* Atlanta, GA: Southern Regional Education Board.

Cooney, S. (1999). *Leading the way: State actions to improve student achievement in the middle grades.* Atlanta, GA: Southern Regional Education Board.

Cooney, S., & Bottoms, G. (2003). *What works to improve student achievement in the middle grades.* Atlanta, GA: Southern Regional Education Board.

—Sondra S. Cooney
Southern Regional Education Board

McEWIN, C. KENNETH

Middle grades teacher preparation and licensure owes much to the extensive research, writing, teaching, and advocacy of C. Kenneth McEwin. While McEwin's contributions to middle grades education have been far reaching and substantial, McEwin has focused the greatest part of his professional energies to research regarding preservice preparation and licensure.

A native of Texas, McEwin earned his undergraduate and master's degrees from East Texas State University and his doctorate from North Texas State University. After 7 years in the public school, first as a sixth grade teacher, then as elementary school principal, McEwin began to address the preparation of new teachers for the middle grades. He assumed the positions of assistant professor and coordinator of middle grades teacher education at Appalachian State University, Boone, NC in 1973. Over the course of the next 17 years, he moved through the ranks of associate professor to professor and the coordinator or middle grades education at Appalachian State.

McEwin has served middle grades education at both the state and national level. He was one of the founders of North Carolina Middle School Association (NCMSA) and served as its first executive director and editor of its journal (*Journal of the North Carolina League of Middle/Junior High Schools*) from 1979-1988. He has consulted extensively throughout the state of North Carolina as well as across the United States.

McEwin has provided expertise and leadership at the national level in several capacities. He served as president of NMSA in 1982; consulting editor of the *Journal of Early Adolescence* (1981-1993); Regional Association or ERIC Clearinghouse on Teacher Education (1984-1986); member of the National Board for Professional Teaching Standards (1992-1998). McEwin has been a member of the National Forum to Accelerate Middle-Grades Reform since 1997. A member and former chair of NMSA's Professional Preparation Committee and NMSA liaison to the National Council for Accreditation of Teacher Education (NCATE) McEwin has played a vital role in the development of guidelines for middle level licensure, which were subsequently adopted by NCATE. Other activity on this front includes membership in the New Professional Teacher Standards Development Project, membership on the Board of Examiners of NCATE and NMSA Program Review Coordinator for NCATE.

A prolific writer, McEwin has authored or co-authored over 100 journal articles, books, book chapters, monographs, and reports. While the bulk of these published works is on teacher preparation, there is a significant selection devoted to the topics of adolescents and sports, and middle school practices and programs.

McEwin counts among his mentors, middle school pioneers William Alexander and John Lounsbury. He also credits middle school experts such as Paul George, John Swaim, and Tom Dickinson as providing him opportunities to learn and grow professionally.

McEwin is the recipient of numerous awards. NCMSA awarded him a Founders Award (1980) and its first Annual Distinguished Service Award from the North Carolina Middle School Association (1988), which it subsequently renamed the C. Kenneth McEwin Distinguished Service Award. McEwin is also a recipient of the Distinguished Scholar Award, Reich College of Education, Appalachian State University (1988); NMSA's Past-President's Award (1983) and NMSA's President's Award (1977).

—Tracey W. Smith
Appalachian State University

MELTON, GEORGE

With 30 years in public education, first as a classroom teacher, and then a junior high school principal, George Melton's contributions to middle grades education were well-grounded. He put into practice the concepts of middle level education long before the language to describe middle school had developed, and then in 1985, coined the term "middle level" to dissolve the philosophical arguments between those who advocated for reformed junior high schools and those who advocated for middle schools.

Melton was born and raised in central Illinois. He completed his undergraduate work at Illinois Wesleyan. He earned his graduate degree from Columbia Teacher's College, in the early 1950s, where he studied under Ruth Strang. As a principal, first in Bloomington, IL, then in Shaker Heights, OH, Melton earned stature among his peers, and was selected president of the State Principals' Associations first in Illinois, then in Ohio, and then for the National Association of Secondary School Principals (NASSP).

During his tenure as deputy executive director of NASSP, beginning in 1980, Melton initiated the publication of *Schools in the Middle* and established the Middle Level Council. The council led sponsored institutes, conferences, conducted research, and published documents that influenced middle school principals and their schools. Melton conceived of the idea to celebrate National Middle Level Education Week, which was initiated in 1987.

In suggesting the term "middle level," Melton attempted to build a bridge between the two prevailing views about appropriate educational practices for young adolescents. Advocates of reformed approaches to the education of young adolescents tended to perceive the issues surrounding the education of young adolescents as either a complete break from junior high schools or as a healthy evolution of practice. Those who argued for middle school faulted junior high schools as barely reconfigured high schools with departmentalized curriculum and a focus on content mastery. On the other side of the argument were educators who saw the emerging middle school as an organic, albeit, newly evolved outgrowth of the earlier junior high school.

Three fundamental premises shaped Melton's contributions to middle level education. The first was his conviction that a school's vision and mission statement are its key consensus-building tools, and that these tools influence and inform choices regarding curriculum and instructional methodology. This is outlined in the 1987 monograph, *Developing a Mission Statement for the Middle Level School* (Council of Middle Level Education, 1987) which Melton cowrote.

The second theme is that curriculum and methodology are the means, not the ends, of a child's education. Melton cautioned educators against becoming so entrenched in the strategies and methodologies of education that they lose sight of the student and the process of learning. Finally, Melton advocated for the support of what he called the "magic" of learning, and the "magical nature" of young adolescents (Harycki, 2004). For Melton, the word "magic" captured the process whereby information becomes knowledge and part of the student's personal experience and understanding.

Melton was the recipient of the first William Gruhn-Forrest Long Award from the National Council of Junior/Middle School Administrators, the President's Award from NMSA, and the Distinguished Service Award from several different state education associations. The George Melton Middle Level Education Award is the highest recognition in Nebraska for middle level educators.

REFERENCES

Council of Middle Level Education. (1987). *Developing a mission statement for the middle level school.* Reston, VA: National Association of Secondary School Principals.

Harycki, D. B (2002). *Curious George Melton: The caring curmudgeon.* Retrieved July 15, 2004, from http://www.mhtc.net/~dharycki/Melton.html

—Mary Henton
National Middle School Association

MIDDLE GRADE SCHOOL STATE POLICY INITIATIVE

The Middle Grade School State Policy Initiative (MGSSPI) was developed in 1990 by the Carnegie Corporation to stimulate widespread middle grade reform. The MGSSPI project used the comprehensive framework of middle grades reform that was laid out in the landmark 1989 report, *Turning Points, Preparing American Youth for the 21st Century* (Carnegie Council on Adolescent Development, 1989) as the basis of this national initiative. The Carnegie Corporation awarded MGSSPI grants to 15 states in order to stimulate statewide changes in the policy and practice of middle grades education especially among schools serving youth from low income families.

The MGSSPI initially provided $60,000 planning grants to 27 states. Then, from 1991 to 1999, the initiative focused its support on 15 states with a series of 2-year grants ranging from $50,000 to $360,000 (Jackson & Davis, 2000). The 15 states involved in this initiative included: Arkansas, California, Colorado, Connecticut, Delaware, Illinois, Maryland, Massachusetts, New Mexico, New York, North Dakota, Rhode Island, South Carolina, Texas, and Vermont. In addition to the monetary award, the initiative also provided states with technical assistance via the Council of Chief State School Officers and a data collection component where schools in the initiative gathered survey data for use in a self assessment and data-based decision making.

In the beginning of the MGSSPI, states focused on developing awareness of middle grades student and school needs by highlighting the promising practices in *Turning Points* like small learning communities, interdisciplinary instruction, expert teachers and administrators, family and community involvement, and linkages to health services. Most states also developed policy statements about their middle grades reform efforts. As the initiative matured, states established networks of schools that became involved in this systemic change. Over the course of the initiative, more than 225 schools across the country were involved (Jackson & Davis, 2000). States supported the network schools with summer institutes, seminars, coaching, and knowledge exchange.

The MGSSPI was successful at stimulating systemic national change as well as fostering improvements in curricula, instruction, and assessment in middle grades schools across the country. Many of the lessons learned from the MGSSPI initiative are discussed in *Turning Points 2000: Educating Adolescents in the 21st Century* (Jackson & Davis, 2000). Further, the work of MGSSPI continues with the Turning Points National Network at the Center for Collaborative Education (CCE) in Boston. CCE developed the Turning Points principles into a comprehensive middle grades school reform design and has established regional centers across the country work who with middle grades schools to improve education for young adolescents.

REFERENCES

Carnegie Council on Adolescent Development. (1989). *Turning points: Preparing American youth for the 21st century* (The Report of the Task Force on Education of Young Adolescents). New York: Carnegie Corporation of New York.

Jackson, A. W., & Davis, G. A. (2000). *Turning Points 2000: Educating adolescents in the 21st century.* New York: Teachers College Press.

—Nancy Flowers
CPRD, University of Illinois

MIDDLE GRADES IMPROVEMENT PROGRAM

Funded by the Lilly Endowment, the Middle Grades Improvement Program (MGIP) was started in 1987 in 16 urban school districts in Indiana: Indianapolis Public Schools and seven of the surrounding townships, Anderson, East Chicago, Evansville, Fort Wayne, Hammond, Muncie, South Bend, and Terre Haute. These districts included some of the poorest, most populous, and most racially diverse public education systems in the state. MGIP was derived from and driven by a clearly defined set of values—equity, excellence, fairness, and developmental responsiveness—related to the necessity for schools to help young people grow to be caring, contributing members of a diverse democracy. MGIP sought districtwide reform, helping districts to rethink middle-level schools to (1) establish a warmer, more adolescent-centered environment; (2) support sustainable communities of learners marked by high student achievement and creativity; (3) reduce disparities caused by race and class; (4) achieve developmentally responsive and academically excellent curriculum and instruction; and (5) engage parents and community organizations in the work of the school.

The program began with 6-month planning grants during which districts could design their own improvement plans, concentrating on two or more of the following areas: (1) school-based self-assessment and institutional reform, (2) the development of instructional leadership, (3) reading improvement, (4) dropout prevention and increased access to post-secondary education, and (5) building public support for school improvement. The planning process was followed by the first round of 3-year grants of $150,000 per school district. During the first implementation phase, the endowment fielded a team of skilled and knowledgeable consultants to go into the districts as "critical friends" and confidantes. Strong relationships were formed in this early phase of MGIP, many of which lasted throughout and beyond the entire MGIP experience. At the same time, the endowment began awarding small grants to groups of teachers, providing an incentive for interdisciplinary teams to create innovative curriculum units. In different rounds of funding, teachers were asked to integrate reading with language arts, social studies with the arts, and science with mathematics and technology.

In 1990, a second round of MGIP grants ($100,000 per school district) challenged districts to establish more focused priorities and to concentrate either on improved curriculum and instruction or on parent/ community involvement. In the third and final set of implementation grants in 1994, three districts were awarded funding for a comprehensive scenario, focusing on classroom change, parent/community involvement, and transitions from elementary to middle and from middle to high school (Lipsitz, 1997). At the same time, individual schools (rather than districts) received recognition grants to honor and extend their improvement efforts, sometimes despite ineffective or inhospitable district contexts.

The endowment commissioned a documentation effort of MGIP undertaken by Education Resources Group and the University of Pittsburgh's Learning Research and Development Center, resulting in a monograph (Clark, Bickel, & Lacey, 1993).

To buttress the work of the districts, a series of grants (1988–1995) to the Education Development Center (Newton, MA) was awarded to design and implement staff development and technical assistance to MGIP districts. The endowment also established the MGIP Network, a self-governing body of key representatives of the 16 school districts. The purpose of the network (1990–1997) was to form a lasting structure to continue the work of MGIP after formal funding was completed.

In 1993, the endowment awarded a grant to the Center for Prevention Research and Development (CPRD) of the University of Illinois to support work that focused on the impact that various middle-grades reform efforts have on teachers, students, administrators and parents of students. Indiana's MGIP schools were added to the growing database of schools across the country, and the schools were encouraged to use the CPRD Self-Study instrument and results to improve school and classroom practice.

REFERENCES

Clark, T. A., Bickel, W. E., & Lacey, R. A. (1993). *Transforming education for young adolescents*. New York: Education Resources Group.

Lipsitz, J. (1997). Middle Grades Improvement Program. *Phi Delta Kappan, 78,* 554-555.

—Gretchen Wolfram
Lilly Endowment Inc.

MIDDLE LEVEL EDUCATION RESEARCH SPECIAL INTEREST GROUP

Middle Level Education Research (MLER) is a Special Interest Group (SIG) of the American Educational Research Association (AERA). The primary responsibility of MLER to AERA is to maintain a professional support system for its membership consistent with the purpose of the Association as a whole. The formation of the SIG, originally known as Research in Middle Level Education (RMLE), was approved by AERA in 1991. At that time officers were elected and a constitution and bylaws were articulated. The bylaws of the SIG are subject to the bylaws and constitution of AERA. AERA places financial responsibility on SIGs to partially reimburse the association for expenditures incurred in the support of the SIGs.

The purpose of MLER SIG is to improve, promote, and disseminate educational research reflecting early adolescence and middle-level education. MLER SIG employs a variety of methods in carrying out its work:

- the publication of research in the SIG book series, *The Handbook of Research in Middle Level Education;*
- distribution of the SIG's newsletter, *The Chronicle of Research in Middle Level Education;*
- creation of the SIG Web site available at http:// www.rmle.pdx.edu/index.html;
- documentation of the SIG's history;
- development of a strategic plan;
- policy briefs developed by members of the MLER SIG—*High Stakes Testing* and *Middle Level Principal Preparation and Licensure* endorsed in April 2004; and
- presence of members on the NMSA Research Committee.

As noted, the MLER SIG is guided by a constitution and bylaws, which were revised and amended in August 2002. Membership in the MLER SIG, including the right to vote and hold office, is open to any person whose AERA and SIG dues have been paid for the current year. Members may be nominated and hold elective office. The elected officers of the SIG include: immediate past president, president, president-elect/program chair, vice president, secretary, and treasurer. Additionally, seven members of the organization are elected to the SIG Association Council—the legislative and policy making body of the association—for a term of 2 years. The officers serve on the executive committee of the SIG. Every 2 years the president becomes the immediate past president, the president-elect assumes the office of the president, and the vice president becomes the president-elect/program chair. All officers hold office for 2 years. Since its establishment, nine members have served as president of the MLER SIG: Richard Lipka (1992-1993), Lynn Wallich (1993-1994), P. Elizabeth Pate (1994-1995), Nathalie Gehrke (1995-1996), Janet McDaniel (1996-1997), Rebecca Mills (1998-2000), Barbara Whinery (2000-2002), Vincent A. Anfara, Jr. (2002-2004), and Kimberly Hartman (2004-2005). Future presidents include Kathleen Roney (2005-2007) and Micki Caskey (2007-2009).

MLER SIG members meet twice a year—once in the fall at the National Middle School Association (NMSA) Annual Conference and Exhibit, and again in the spring at the AERA Annual Meeting. Presentations of research findings targeted to improve the quality of schooling for young adolescents are also offered by members during these two annual conferences.

—Kathleen Roney
The University of North Carolina, Wilmington

MIDDLE LEVEL LEADERSHIP CENTER

The Middle Level Leadership Center (MLLC) was established in the fall of 1997 as a research and service center in the Department of Educational Leadership and Policy Analysis, College of Education, University of Missouri-Columbia. The overall mission of the center is to positively impact the quality of school leadership and thus the quality of schooling for middle school students. To impact middle level leadership, the MLLC director and staff develop and disseminate knowledge about effective leadership and educational practices at the middle level. The specific goals of the center are to (a) identify, design, and conduct research about critical issues in middle level leadership, (b) disseminate current knowledge about middle level leadership to practicing school-site leaders, university faculty, and leaders of professional organizations and educational agencies, (c) work with middle level leaders and school faculty to translate existing knowledge into effective school practices, and (d) collaborate with other professional organizations committed to middle level education.

MLLC staff develop and implement research projects designed to add to the knowledge about best practices in school leadership and educational programs at the middle level. Grants and contracts with professional organizations and agencies support the Center's research and service projects. One noteworthy grant/contract was the design and implementation of the National Association of Secondary School Principals' "decade" study of middle level leaders and program, a national study from 2000-2003 that resulted in two books distributed to more than 10,000 middle level principals. Another contract with NASSP prepared a series of monographs for the National Alliance of Middle Level Schools professional development project. Another contract was for the coordination and preparation of "Research Summaries" for the National Middle School Association's Web site. In addition to contracts with external agencies, the center's Web-based research capabilities are used regularly to implement studies pertinent to middle level leadership. Doctoral students employed by the center develop research, writing, service, and presentation skills, thus the center contributes to current research and the development of future middle level researchers.

The center's Web site (www.mllc.org) is the primary tool for disseminating the work of the center. The site provides research reports and copies of presentations made by center staff at national and international professional meetings.

The primary service project of the center is Project ASSIST. ASSIST stands for Achieving Success through School Improvement Site Teams. ASSIST is a comprehensive, systemic school improvement process designed by the center's director in 1996. The multiyear process is based on the concept of developing the capacity to lead change among a nucleus of faculty leaders. Center staff members work with the ASSIST team of teachers and the principal on a monthly basis. They study best practices in (a) change processes, (b) middle level education, (c) curriculum, instruction, and assessment, (d) leadership, and (e) organizational structures. School culture, climate, empowerment, leadership, curriculum alignment and articulation, instructional practices, assessment methods, student achievement, and student achievement are assessed and analyzed for formative and summative decision making. The MLLC Web site provides detailed information about the ASSIST process and examples of the evaluation tools used in the project.

—Jerry Valentine
University of Missouri

THE MIDDLE SCHOOL

The Middle School documents Donald Eichhorn's (1966) dissertation research on applying system theory to construct a sociopsychological model of a functioning middle school. In this model, the mental, emotional, physical, and cultural relationships that existed among middle school students were interconnected and interdependent within the school setting. This work was seminal in that Eichhorn proposed a formal response to the inadequate traditional junior high school models of mid-twentieth century education for a not yet fully defined group of young people.

Eichhorn coined the term *transescence* to describe the stage of development that is today commonly referred to as early adolescence. He claimed that at the time of his study there was no adequate term to refer to that group of individuals aged 9-14 that included prepubescents, early adolescents, and adolescents. Students in the middle school included individuals at all of these phases (p. 3). What is of particular interest in Eichhorn's discussion of the physical, sexual, emotional, and intellectual growth of the transescent is the abundant reference made to research in these areas from the first half of the twentieth century. Early studies that documented the more rapid, sooner occurring physical and sexual growth are cited as well as research supporting the possibly cyclic nature of the variables affecting transescent maturation. In addition, the adjustment of transescents to experiences of rapid growth was found to be dependent on the quality of their relationships with adults, peers and cultural expectations.

Eichhorn concluded that this research implied that educators must focus primarily on the child's growth needs and that schools should design programs that supported the developing child's emergent self-knowledge (p. 23). Eichhorn acknowledged earlier efforts to move away from the graded 6-3-3 structure of school organization to a more developmentally appropriate 6, 7, 8 grade configuration. Noting the greater differences in physical, psychological, and social development between seventh and ninth grade students, it was suggested that the sixth grade might have more in common developmentally with the eighth grade. Delaying the transition to a departmentalized program for students in grades 7 and 8 might also prove to be more appropriate (pp. 2-3).

These views encouraged Eichhorn's emerging support for a 5-3-4 organization with grade 12 perhaps serving as the first year of junior college. The curriculum of his sociopsychological model is explained in terms of how it would reflect and interrelate with the characteristics of transescents. The two branches of this model included (1) an analytical curriculum containing areas of language, mathematics, science, and social studies, and (2) a physical-cultural curriculum that included fine arts, physical education, practical arts, and cultural studies. Ultimately, study in each of these areas would demonstrate the interconnectedness and interrelationships among concepts (pp. 66-67). *The Middle School* is important to the middle school movement in that Eichhorn articulated a model that reflected focused attention to the developmental needs of the early adolescent, the relationship between the early adolescent, culture, and its subsequent implications for education, the middle school environment, the middle school program with its guidance and support services, and the role of administration in the middle school. Much of what is evident in middle level education of the early twenty-first century was explored by Eichhorn in this research.

REFERENCE

Eichhorn, D. H. (1966). *The middle school*. New York: The Center for Applied Research in Education.

—Lynne M. Bailey
The University of North Carolina, Charlotte

THE MIDDLE SCHOOL CONCEPT

Interdisciplinary teams, young adolescents, advisory programs, exploratories, cooperative learning, intramurals, integrated curriculum, activity periods, hands-on learning—while these represent some of the most common elements or practices associated with the middle school concept, they are only some of the many programs or practices that are parts of the middle school concept. Individually or even collectively they are not the middle school concept itself, for it also includes a philosophy or undergirding set of beliefs that holds the parts together and gives them meaning.

Sometimes mistakenly regarded as a set of grades, usually 5-8 or 6-8, and a set of common practices, the middle school concept really refers to a vision for middle grades education that "guide the decisions of those responsible for shaping educational programs that are committed to improving both learning and learners" (National Middle School Association, 2003, p. 1). Jackson and Davis (2000) also note the importance of a vision when establishing middle level education, not merely adhering to a set of practices or programs. "The movement to establish a distinctive form of education for young adolescents—the middle school movement—reflects the grassroots genius of American educators. It is the response of visionary and caring teachers, administrators, and parents to the unique mix of evolving capacities and emerging needs that epitomizes middle grades students" (p. 1).

Deceptively simple in theory, and surprisingly complex in reality, the middle school concept is seen as a "consistent collection of ideas about what constitutes a good middle school" (Anfara, 2004, p. 5). This body of knowledge—including research and best practices—describes what excellent schools for 10 to 15-year-olds should be like. Today, when we talk about the middle school concept, we mean to answer the question, "What is the best educational plan for *every* young adolescent, ages 10-15" not just students in a named "middle school" or a school with some combination of Grades 5-8. While it is noteworthy that the middle school movement began by distancing itself from some of the practices of the junior high school, the junior high school versus middle school debate of the 1970s and 1980s was never valid, and early middle schools were still very "junior high" in actual practice. It is this focus on the evolving capacities and emerging needs of young adolescents that has been the guiding light of the middle school movement since William Alexander first proposed the middle idea (1998).

While some critics point to the lack of implementation of the core beliefs that comprise the middle school concept as an indication that the concept is somehow undefined or faulty (Dickinson, 2001), that is not the case. It would be unrealistic to have only one statement to represent the middle school concept. The varied explanations, all espouse the same essential ideas, and lend credibility to the middle school concept. Its beliefs and practices have been expressed most notably in the position statement of National Middle School Association, *This We Believe: Successful Schools for Young Adolescents* (2003) and its earlier versions in 1982 and 1995. *This We Believe* is the most widely read document, and for many schools, boards, and faculties, has defined middle level education. Another influential report, *Turning Points: Preparing American Youth for the 21st Century* (Carnegie Council on Adolescent Development, 1989) and its follow-up volume, *Turning Points 2000: Educating Adolescents in the 21st Century* (Jackson & Davis, 2000), provide another excellent perspective, albeit consistent with the precepts set forth in *This We Believe*. The seven recommendations of *Turning Points 2000*, outline what middle level schools should do—and be—with great specificity and clarity.

FROM CONCEPT TO MOVEMENT

Eager acceptance of the middle school idea soon led to what has been called the "middle school movement," as successful practices were disseminated, more schools became engaged in this work, and the literature grew with examples of exemplary programs (Eichhorn, 1966; George & Oldaker, 1985; Grooms, 1967). In spite of the current controversy about how effective middle level schools are, the changes that have occurred in the movement are really remarkable for their clarity, distinctiveness, adherence to the developmental needs of young adolescents, and consistency over the years (Jackson & Davis, 2000). And while there are a number of strong professional reasons for the development of middle level schools—to meet the unique needs of the age group, primarily—it is also fair to recognize that in a great many instances, middle schools began for a plethora of non-educational reasons as well—crowded elementary and high schools, unhappiness with various junior high school practices, and the need for a "quick-fix" for the problems in the middle (Melton, 1984).

WHAT CONSTITUTES THE MIDDLE SCHOOL CONCEPT?

The middle school concept is grounded in a solid understanding of the special characteristics of young adolescents and their unique educational needs and goals. Translating these needs and goals into practice for middle level schools includes three underlying beliefs:

- The concern for young adolescents as a distinct age group and the recognition that the 10 to 15-year-old time is a critical developmental period for learning. Until Joan Lipsitz's call for more attention to the 10-15-year-old age group in *Growing Up Forgotten* (1980), attention in education and other facets of life had been on children and older adolescents, and not young adolescents.
- Young adolescents' personal-social development and intellectual development are inseparable and work hand-in-hand.
- There are organizational structures—ways of grouping and organizing students—and curricular and instructional approaches that respond to the unique nature and needs of young adolescents.

It is important to note that in the early days, middle schools began to put into practice educational ideas for which there was little, if any, empirical evidence. Now, however, supportive research evidence has become available in the last 15 years.

There are many specific practices that reflect and demonstrate these beliefs, but most seem to cluster around the following three areas. The 14 characteristics of *This We Believe* and the seven recommendations of *Turning Points 2000*, as well as many other descriptions of middle school characteristics, emphasize these essential areas:

- *Curriculum, Instruction, and Assessment.* The curriculum of the middle level school should be "relevant, challenging, integrative, and exploratory." It is also standards-based, yet actively engages students, giving them many opportunities to pose and answer questions about themselves and the world. This type of middle level curriculum looks very different from the traditional teacher-directed curriculum. Instructionally, successful middle level teachers employ a wide array of teaching and learning strategies with emphasis on hands-on and inquiry approaches. Of great importance are those teachers who set high expectations for their students while helping them to learn to monitor and be responsible for their own learning. Assessment in such schools is continuous and authentic and never depends on a single measure, such as a standardized, high-stakes state test or teacher made paper and pencil tests. Rather, students learn to set personal and academic goals, reflect on their learning, and become full partners in learning and assessing their learning.
- *School Culture.* The school culture is set initially by the professional staff of teachers and administrators who are prepared to teach in a middle level school and want to do so. They understand the subtleties of youth culture, the learning process, and the many options open to them in teaching young adolescents. In addition to a shared vision that guides all decisions made about the school, an inviting, supportive, and safe environment is maintained. One of the most critical attributes of successful middle level schools is that every young adolescent has an adult advocate, at least one adult who helps foster the academic and personal growth of her students.
- *Leadership and Organization.* Middle level schools may be organized in many different ways: looping, multiage grouping, traditional grade level groups, interdisciplinary teams, both horizontal and vertical teams, smaller partner teams, and more. What-

ever organization is used the structures themselves must support effective learning and positive student-teacher relationships. Organization should come after the other basic decisions about curriculum, instruction, and assessment are made. While leadership begins with the principal, a larger leadership team, comprised of representatives from the various teams and groups in the school, allows much greater opportunity for success when it advocates for change at the school level.

CONTROVERSY, CAVEATS, AND CONCERNS

In spite of the positive influence of the middle school concept on thousands of middle level schools and millions of young adolescents over the past decades, there is still much controversy and concern surrounding middle schools. Myths and stereotypes have hounded the middle school concept, since its beginning, causing it to mean everything to everyone. The litany often goes something like, "We track at our school because that is what the middle school concept says we should do." Or, "we let our sixth-eighth grade students decide what electives to take because that is the middle school concept." Or, "middle school is a time to prepare our students for the reality of the high school; that is the middle school concept." Hearing such statements means the ones voicing them just don't understand the middle school concept as they should.

The most common myths about the middle school concept, however, center around the following (Lounsbury & Brazee, 2004, p. 38-39): middle school as a "feel-good" school; middle school exists to prepare students for high school; middle school is "fun time, and; middle level schools have failed. Each of these refers to the perception by critics of the middle school concept that it is often more a holding pen for students until they get to the serious work at the high school; that the middle level school is not academically "rigorous"—with too much concern given to students' fragile self-esteem.

The current irony is that at the same time that middle level schools are under fire for trying to implement the middle school concept, the American high school, in a time of reform, is installing these middle school practices and embracing them, as if they were right out of the box! As high schools are moving ahead with these essential concepts, because they work with adolescents, the middle school is being asked to stop doing these same things.

The reality remains that in spite of the persistent advocacy for middle level education in the last 30 years, there are still fewer middle schools that actually do what the middle school concept suggests, than there are schools that have faithfully and consistently adopted middle school philosophy and practices (McEwin, Dickinson, & Jenkins, 2003).

If we have learned anything in the last 3 decades, it is that the middle school concept is not a set of discrete characteristics that schools may choose to implement. Rather, it is a system of beliefs, best practices, and common sense that work closely together, each one dependent on the other.

REFERENCES

Alexander, W. (1998). The junior high school: A changing view. In R. David (Ed.), *Moving forward from the past—Early writings and current reflections of middle school founders* (pp. 3-13). Columbus, OH: National Middle School Association.

Anfara, V. A., Jr. (2004). Creating high-performance middle schools—Recommendations from research. In C. S. Thompson (Ed.), *Reforming middle level education: Considerations for policymakers* (pp. 1-18). Greenwich, CT: Information Age.

Carnegie Council on Adolescent Development. (1989). *Turning points: Preparing American youth for the 21st century* (The Report of the Task Force on Education of Young Adolescents). New York: Carnegie Corporation of New York.

Dickinson, T. (2001). *Reinventing the middle school.* New York: RoutledgeFalmer.

Eichhorn, D. (1966). *The middle school.* New York: The Center for Applied Research in Education.

George, P. S., & Oldaker, L. L. (1985). *Evidence for the middle school.* Columbus, OH: National Middle School Association.

Grooms, M. (1967). *Perspectives on the middle school.* Columbus, OH: Merrill.

Jackson, A. W., & Davis, G. A. (2000). *Turning points 2000: Educating adolescents in the 21st century.* New York: Teachers College Press.

Lipsitz, J. (1980). *Growing up forgotten: A review of programs and research concerning early adolescence.* New Brunswick, NJ: Transaction Books.

Lounsbury, J., & Brazee, E. (2004). *Understanding and implementing This we believe—First steps.* Westerville, OH: National Middle School Association.

McEwin, K., Dickinson, T, & Jenkins, D. (2003). *America's middle school in the new century: Status and progress.* Westerville, OH: National Middle School Association.

Melton, G. E. (1984). The junior high school—Successes and failures. In J. H. Lounsbury (Ed.), *Perspectives: Middle school education, 1964-1984* (pp. 5-13). Columbus, OH: National Middle School Association.

National Middle School Association. (2003). *This we believe: Successful schools for young adolescents.* Westerville, OH: Author.

—Edward N. Brazee
University of Maine

A MIDDLE SCHOOL CURRICULUM: FROM RHETORIC TO REALITY

In 1990, James Beane published the first edition of his text which explains his proposed curriculum for young adolescents. Beane was writing to fill a perceived need opened by the call for reform in middle level education issued by *Turning Points* (Carnegie Council on Adolescent Development, 1989). Immediate changes were being made to the organization of middle schools, the interdisciplinary team was taking the place of the junior high school's subject area teachers. In the wake of the reform, Beane's question rang forth, "What should be the curriculum of the middle school?" (Beane, 1993, p. 5).

Beane's text begins with a discussion of the question of middle school curriculum and the various pressures that have come to bear on curriculum development. He suggests guidelines that may be used in addressing curriculum development. Guidelines he raises include a focus on general education, exploration of self, respect for early adolescents, grounded in democracy, aware of diversity, "lifelike and lively," and addressing the knowledge and skill of the students. Beane does not present "the" curriculum guidelines, but opens the discussion that guidelines need to be identified and used in the curriculum design process. From there, he takes a chronological look at the many curricula designed for the middle level. He traces the movements and theories that stand behind his call for a distinctly middle school curriculum.

Based on theory and research, Beane proposes his own answer to the question of what the curriculum should be in the middle school. In his model, the curriculum is organized around thematic units "drawn from the intersecting concerns of early adolescents and issues in the larger world" (p. 68). That intersection is made up of the social, personal and technical content and skills of "traditional" curricula, social concerns and personal concerns of young adolescents, and broad concepts such as democracy, dignity and diversity. While not determining the specific curriculum themes at the centerpiece of the model, Beane, nonetheless, proposes that his model become "the curriculum of the middle school" (p. 71). The goal of curriculum development is to design "a coherent, unified, and complete curriculum" (p. 71) around those issues, subjects, skills and concepts which may be different for different groups of young adolescents. The actual planning would thus draw on young adolescents themselves, their unique needs and development.

In concluding his proposal, Beane acknowledges the many aspects necessary to implement his curriculum in schools, where more is involved than the content alone. Teaching the units calls for facilitators invested in the process, for heterogeneous groupings, and scheduling that allows for small and large groups both inside and outside the school itself. Like the *Turning Points* report, he also calls for input from parents and community. The epilogue in the 1993 second edition reminds readers that real reform in the middle level has yet to address reformation of the curriculum and that it should: "After all, it is the curriculum, rather than grade level reorganization or teaming, that defines the value of schools for early adolescents" (p. 107).

REFERENCES

Beane, J. A. (1993). *A middle school curriculum: From rhetoric to reality* (2nd ed.). Columbus, OH: National Middle School Association.

Carnegie Council on Adolescent Development. (1989). *Turning points: Preparing American youth for the 21st century* (The Report of the Task Force on Education of Young Adolescents). New York: Carnegie Corporation of New York.

—Janis D. Flint-Ferguson
Gordon College

MIDDLE SCHOOL JOURNAL

First published as the *Midwest Middle School Journal* in 1970, the *Middle School Journal*, published today by the National Middle School Association (NMSA), is for many educators the most accessible source of scholarship on middle school education. The *Middle School Journal* publishes descriptions of practice grounded in middle school literature as well as the findings of research with implications for middle level practice. Also included among the articles are grounded conceptual pieces related to middle grades policy.

Edited since 1994 by Tom Erb the *Middle School Journal* is distributed to nearly 35,000 readers five times a year from September to May. The 64-page format permits about 30 unsolicited articles to be published each year along with 18 regular column articles. The four recurring columns focus on research ("What Research Says," "Research into Practice," and "Research on Middle School Renewal") and leadership ("Middle Level Leadership"). The first two departments date from John Lounsbury's tenure as editor (1976-1990).

"What Research Says to the Middle Level Practitioner," which first appeared in May 1979, was originally edited by J. Howard Johnston and Glenn Markle. For the past decade Judith Irvin has edited this column. Karen Wood initially edited "Research into Practice" in 1987 and continues today in that capacity. The latter two columns were begun under the tenure of Tom Erb. The team of Steve Mertens, Nancy Flowers, and Peter Mulhall has continuously edited "Research on Middle School Renewal" since May 1999. "Middle Level Leadership" has been edited since November 2001 by Sally and Don Clark.

Over the years a number of other columns have been published: "Teacher to Teacher" (Nancy Doda, Jeanneine Jones, & Greg Hart), "For Love of Books" (Jane Vossler), "This We Believe and Now We Must Act" (Authors of the 1995 version of *This We Believe*), and "Journal into Action" (Jerome Belaire & Paul Freeman). The latter column, begun in March 2000 as a feature published in the Journal, has morphed into a feature of the NMSA Web site (www.nmsa.org). This feature, now titled "Using *Middle School Journal* for Professional Development," appears online along with a copy of the lead article of each issue of the *Journal*.

Since the editorship of Tom Dickinson (1990-1993) the Journal has used an independent panel of between 50 and 60 reviewers who carry out blind reviews of submitted manuscripts. In recent years approximately 15% to 20% of submitted manuscripts have been accepted for publication. Themes that have dominated from the late 1990s into the 2000s include "Challenging, Relevant, Integrated Curriculum," "Teaching Diverse Learners," "Student Achievement Broadly Conceived," "Promoting Literacy," "Hiring and Keeping Highly Qualified Teachers," and "Responsive, Equitable Curriculum."

From its inception in 1970 through 1972 the *Midwest Middle School Journal* was the official publication of the Midwest Middle School Association whose membership was concentrated in Indiana, Ohio, and Michigan. Tom Gatewood and Ron Maertens edited it during its 3-year existence. Gatewood would continue as editor of the *Middle School Journal* until he ascended to the presidency of the Association in 1976.

At the founding of the National Association in 1973, Glenn Maynard and Gordon Vars undertook to reedit the three volumes of the *Midwest Journal* into the first three volumes bearing the name *Middle School Journal*. Maynard, president of the newly formed NMSA in 1974-1975, served as managing editor of the *Middle School Journal* during the last 3 years of Gatewood's editorship. The *Midwest Journal* was mimeographed on school duplicating machines. The first issue of the new *Middle School Journal* (Volume IV, number 1, dated

Spring 1973) contained just two articles, one written by Conrad Toepfer and the second by Ronald Tyrell, along with some association news, in its 12-page format.

In 1976 when John Lounsbury assumed the editorship of the journal, a position he would hold for the next 14 years and 61 issues, the journal was upgraded to be printed on a "hot lead" linotype machine. Lounsbury's first issue in March 1976 had a press run of 800 copies. It spanned 20 pages cover-to-cover and contained six articles plus an editor's column and some "Research Notes." The lead article that spring of 1976 was written by Lounsbury and addressed middle school curriculum. During the late 1970s and early 1980s, publications represented the greatest area of growth for NMSA. The journal expanded to 32 pages and a press run of 2,000. The quality improved so that by 1980 the Educational Press Association proclaimed it "a stalwart professional publication." Lounsbury began receiving compensation for his editing responsibilities in 1981. The publications committee of the association served as referees for the ever-increasing number of submissions.

As the demands of editing the *Middle School Journal* continued to grow along with the monograph publishing that NMSA had undertaken, Lounsbury found that he could no longer edit the journal, the monographs, and continue to serve as dean of education at Georgia College. He retired from his college position in 1983 to devote full attention to NMSA's publications. By 1990 he felt he could no longer continue to edit the journal and the expanding monograph/book operation. The last issue of the journal edited by Lounsbury was a 56-page issue that reprised earlier elements of the Gatewood and early Lounsbury eras. The May 1990 issue of *MSJ* contained another article by Conrad Toepfer and a lead article on curriculum, this one by James Beane. This issue contained 15 articles averaging two to four pages in length that were circulated to 12,000 readers.

With the arrival of Tom Dickinson in the fall of 1990, the editorship of the journal moved into NMSA headquarters in Columbus, Ohio. Working with the newly recruited review panel, Dickinson added several new features including the Founder's Series, which celebrated five key figures in the founding of the middle school movement: John Lounsbury, William Alexander, Don Eichhorn, Conrad Toepfer, and Gordon Vars. In the 3 years that Dickinson edited the journal, he instituted several practices that characterize the journal to this day. He elevated the journal to a new level of respectability among scholarly journals in education. He did this at a time in which the association itself was going through a period of transition that led to Dickinson's decision to return to an aca-

demic position in the fall of 1993. He left behind an 80-page journal with a circulation of 20,000.

After an interim period in the 1993-1994 academic year that saw Tom Erb and Ed Brazee serve as guest editors, Erb assumed the editorship in the fall of 1994. With Erb's arrival, the editorship once again moved out of headquarters, as he remained half time on the faculty at the University of Kansas. The role of the *Middle School Journal* took a new turn in the late 1990s with the addition of *Middle Ground* to the pantheon of NMSA publications. Since its inception in the early 1970s, *Middle School Journal* had been both the scholarly journal and the news magazine for the association. With the publication of *Middle Ground* as the news magazine of middle level education in the alternative months to *Middle School Journal*, the latter assumed a clearer role as the scholarly journal of record for middle level education in the United States and worldwide.

Author's Note: Much of the information in this article came directly from back issues of the *Middle School Journal* and the personal knowledge of the author. However, four sources (Lounsbury, 1994; National Middle School Association, 1998; Parker et al., 2003; Pickett, 1984) were relied on for information, especially of the early history of the journal.

REFERENCES

Lounsbury, J. H. (1994). As an era ends. *Middle School Journal, 25*(3), 2.

National Middle School Association. (Ed.). (1998). From hot-lead to zip disk: The story of our publications. In *Because we believed: A quarter-century of service to young adolescents* (pp. 23-24). Columbus, OH: Author.

Parker, A. K., Bickmore, D. L., Fiske, A. G., Altman Lowe, C. L., Mullen, T. M., Paisley, W. L., et al. (2003). Changes in *Middle School Journal* over 30 years. *Middle School Journal, 35*(2), 23-29.

Pickett, W. (1984). The development of the National Middle School Association. In J. H. Lounsbury (Ed.), *Perspectives: Middle school education, 1964-1984* (pp. 157-175). Columbus, OH: National Middle School Association.

—Thomas O. Erb
DePauw University

MIDDLE START

Middle Start is a comprehensive improvement initiative for middle grades schools. Through the Middle Start National Center at the Academy for Educational Development and its regional collaborators, Middle Start (1) provides school-site professional development to teachers and administrators to improve teaching and learning; and (2) organizes regional networks of schools, districts, universities, and advocacy organizations to provide support and accountability. The combination of on-site and regional support is intended to spread and sustain successful practices.

Middle Start assists schools in undertaking reflective review and self-assessment; establishing small learning communities; aligning instruction and assessment with rigorous curricula; and sharing leadership and engaging staff, families, and community organizations in supporting students. Each area of work is based on critical practices highlighted in the research on middle-grades education and school improvement.

Reflective review and self-assessment are advocated by proponents of internal accountability as drivers of sustainable, student-centered school improvement (Ancess, 1996, Little, 1999; McLaughlin & Zarrow, 2001; Stokes, 2001; Sykes 1999). Effective small learning communities promote positive relationships between teachers and students, and enable interdisciplinary and differentiated approaches to teaching and learning (Dufour & Eaker, 1994; Kruse & Louis, 1997). Research has shown positive correlations between small learning communities and student achievement (Flowers, Mertens, & Mulhall, 1999).

Rigorous curriculum, instruction and assessment are based on practices such as integrative curriculum, project-based learning, cooperative learning, differentiated instruction, student-led conferencing and mastery learning (Jackson & Davis, 2000; National Forum to Accelerate Middle-Grades Reform, n.d.). Distributed leadership and sustainable partnerships are evolving concepts in the research that promote alliances of teachers, administrators, families and communities in improving schools. Distributed leadership is a capacity-building strategy that promotes instructional leadership in schools (Elmore, 2000; Spillane, Halverson, & Diamond, 1999;). Engaging families and communities in school improvement ensures that reforms are meaningful to students and their families and will outlive administrative transitions (Henderson & Mapp, 2002).

Research on Middle Start indicates the program has been effective in urban and rural schools serving low-income and low-performing students. For example:

Students in Middle Start schools in Michigan and Louisiana demonstrated greater gains in reading and mathematics achievement than students in comparable non-Middle Start schools (Center for Prevention Research and Development, 2001, 2004).

- Students in Middle Start schools in Michigan, Mississippi, Louisiana, and Alabama exhibited greater engagement in academics and reported a greater sense of belonging and safety (Gopalan, 2001; Williams & Mitchell, 2003).
- Teachers in Middle Start schools demonstrated consistent improvements in classroom practices, as compared with similar schools (Center for Prevention Research and Development, 2001). Administrators and staff collaborated on schoolwide reform, became more focused on student learning, and undertook more effective professional development (Gopalan, 2001; Williams& Mitchell, 2003).
- Middle Start staff and collaborators also created partnerships in Michigan and the Mid South that established teacher networks among participating schools, strengthened professional development and leadership programs, and influenced policies affecting middle-grades education.

Middle Start has been recognized as a research-based program in the *Catalog of School Reform Models* (Northwest Regional Educational Laboratory, n.d.), and is among the top 30 of 357 programs undertaken by schools receiving CSR funds, according to the Southwest Educational Development Laboratory (n.d.). Recently, a RAND Corporation report *Focus on the Wonder Years* (Juvonen, Le, Kaganoff, Augustine, & Constant, 2004), cited Middle Start as a promising school improvement intervention for the middle grades.

REFERENCES

Ancess, J. (1996) *Outside/inside, inside/outside.* New York: National Center for Restructuring Education, Schools and Teaching, Teachers College.

Center for Prevention Research and Development. (2001). *An evaluation of Michigan Middle Start schools from 1994 to 2001.* Unpublished manuscript. Champaign: University of Illinois.

Center for Prevention Research and Development. (2004). [Analysis of 2001-02 and 2002-03 Louisiana achievement data (LEAP21) for Mid South Middle Start and the Foundation for the Mid South.] University of Illinois, Institute of Government and Public Affairs. Unpublished data.

DuFour, R. F., & Eaker, R. (1998). *Professional learning communities at work: Best practices for enhancing student achievement.* Bloomington, IN: National Educational Service.

Elmore, R. F. (2000) *Building a new structure for school leadership.* Washington, DC: The Albert Shanker Institute.

Flowers, N., Mertens, S. B., & Mulhall, P. (1999). The impact of teaming: Five research-based outcomes of teaming. *Middle School Journal, 31*(2), 57-60.

Gopalan, P. (2001). *Lake middle school: A case study.* New York: Academy for Educational Development.

Henderson, A. T., & Mapp, K. L. (2002). *A new wave of evidence: the impact of school, family and community connections on student achievement.* Austin, TX: Southwest Educational Development Laboratory.

Jackson, A. W., & Davis, G. A. (2000). *Turning points 2000: Educating adolescents in the 21st century.* New York: Teachers College Press.

Juvonen, J., Le, V., Kaganoff, T., Augustine, C., & Constant, L. (2004). *Focus on the wonder years: Challenges facing the American middle school.* Santa Monica, CA: Rand Corporation.

Kruse, S. D., & Louis, K. S. (1997). Teacher teaming in middle schools: Dilemmas for a schoolwide community. *Educational Administration Quarterly, 33*(3), 261-289.

Little, J. W. (1999). Organizing schools for teacher learning. In L. Darling-Hammond & G. Sykes (Eds.), *Teaching as the learning profession: Handbook of policy and practice* (pp. 233-262). San Francisco: Jossey-Bass.

McLaughlin, M. W., & Zarrow, J. (2001). Teachers engaged in evidence-based reform: Trajectories of teacher's inquiry, analysis and action. In A. Lieberman and L. Miller (Eds.), *Teachers caught in the action: Professional development that matters* (pp. 79-101). New York: Teachers College Press.

National Forum to Accelerate Middle-Grades Reform. (n.d.). *Schools to watch criteria.* Retrieved June 23, 2004, from http://www.mgforum.org/Improvingschools/STW/STWcriteria.asp.

Northwest Regional Educational Laboratory. (n.d) *The catalog of school reform models.* Retrieved June 30, 2004, from http://www.nwrel.org/scpd/catalog/index.shtml

Southwest Educational Development Laboratory. (n.d.). *CSR awards database.* Retrieved June 30, 2004, from http://www.sedl.org/csr/summary.html

Spillane, J. P., Halverson, R., & Diamond, J. B. (1999, April). *Distributed leadership: Toward a theory of school leadership practice.* Paper presented at the annual meeting of the American Educational Research Association, Montréal, Canada.

Stokes, L. (2001). Lessons from an inquiring school: Forms of inquiry and conditions for teacher learning. In A. Lieberman & L. Miller, (Eds.), *Teachers caught in the action: Professional development that matters* (pp. 141-158). New York: Teachers College Press.

Sykes, G. (1999). Teaching as the learning profession. In L. Darling-Hammond & G. Sykes (Eds.), *Teaching as the learning profession: Handbook of policy and practice* (pp. xv-xxiv). San Francisco: Jossey-Bass.

Williams, L., & Mitchell V. (2003). *Voices from Mid South Middle Start: Developing learning communities.* New York: Academy for Educational Development.

—Patrick Montesano
Academy for Educational Development

MOTIVATION

Teachers are challenged daily by students who don't seem interested in learning. Teachers struggle with discipline issues, and with meeting the needs of students at widely differing ability/achievement levels. One of the most persistent questions facing individual teachers is, "How do I motivate *all* children to learn?" The real problem facing educators is helping all students achieve optimal learning (conceptual understanding and the ability to apply knowledge to new problems, learning, and creations) with high quality content (from the students' own interests, from state and local curricula, and national standards).

Because the studies included under the umbrella of "motivation" are so broad and varied, and have evolved over time, it is impossible to provide a review of the literature that would satisfy all the theories and traditions. Therefore, this section will focus on Muir's (2001) motivation model of Meaningful Engaged Learning. There are four key components: the learning environment, experience, motivation, and meaning making.

THE LEARNING ENVIRONMENT

Environment is the first critical factor for meaningful, engaged learning. Students will not learn from teachers they think do not like them (Muir, 2001). Students need to feel safe and respected before they will learn. "Significant adult relationships have been found to be a major contributor to the resiliency of at-risk youth" (Dowty, 1997, p. 1). Students want their teachers to know them well and have a positive attitude, including being fun and humorous. Further, an environment that is not emotionally or physically safe can shut down higher cognitive processes, including learning (Caine & Caine, 1991, 1997).

Whitmore (1980) advocates for supportive strategies that help a student feel more like they are in a "family" than a "factory." All the subjects in Emerick's (1992) study of underachieving gifted students who reversed their underachieving behaviors agreed that it was "the actions of and respect for a particular teacher that had the greatest positive impact" (p. 144). The influencing teacher displayed five characteristics: he/she cared for and sincerely liked the student as an individual, was willing to communicate with the student as a peer, was perceived to be enthusiastic and knowledgeable about the topic taught, and demonstrated a personal desire to learn more, was perceived as not being "mechanical" in methods of instruction, and was perceived as having high but realistic expectations for the student.

How teachers make students feel about themselves and their abilities will also impact achievement. Students' beliefs about their abilities determine how they feel, think, and behave (Bandura, 1993; Schunk, 1989; Weiner, 1984, 1985). Students who have experienced trauma often lack confidence in their abilities and generally have a low degree of self-efficacy (Bandura, 1997). Self-efficacy, the individual's beliefs about his or her abilities, is often a better predictor of achievement than actual ability (Bandura, 1993; Schunk, 1989), and is often affected by how the student attributes the success or failure. "People who regard themselves as highly efficacious ascribe their failures to insufficient effort: those who regard themselves as inefficacious attribute their failures to low ability" (Bandura, 1993, p. 128). Whether students attribute their successes or failures to their effort (changeable) or ability (unchangeable) will impact their achievement (Weiner, 1984, 1985).

What can teachers do? Teachers' instructional practices and daily interactions with students can communicate their expectations for students, as well as whether student ability is fixed or modifiable (Graham, 1990). Bandura (1993) reports, for example, that "[p]erformance feedback that focuses on achieved progress underscores personal capabilities. Feedback that focuses on shortfalls highlights personal deficiencies" (p. 125). Teachers can retrain student perception by helping students attribute failure to insufficient effort instead of low ability. Also, modeling can lead to higher levels of student success than didactic instruction (Schunk, 1989). Further, Schunk points out that efficacy cues from teachers about how well students are learning can be used by students to appraise their own self-efficacy for continued learning. "Being told that one can achieve better results through harder work can motivate one to do so and convey that one possesses the necessary capability to succeed" (p. 31).

EXPERIENCE

Experience is the second component of meaningful, engaged learning. Ellis and Fouts (1993, p. 153) point out, "experience is the key to meaningful learning, not someone else's experience abstracted and condensed into textbook form, but one's own direct experience." Experience provides students with rich sensory data, furnishing multiple cues for memory and recall (Bruning, Schraw, & Ronning, 1995; Rumelhart, 1980). Educators should remember that most learning is finding patterns in experiences (Schank & Cleary, 1995). These patterns become schema and

help define how a person perceives and understands her world. Experience provides students with rich sensory data, furnishing multiple cues for memory and recall (Bruning et al., 1995; Rumelhart, 1980). Teachers should use active teaching strategies, especially those providing hands-on work or involving experiential learning.

People perceive and process experiences differently (Fairhurst & Fairhurst, 1995; Gardner, 1983; Papert, 1996; Sternberg, 1997). As Gardner says (ABC News, 1993), it is no longer "How smart are you?" but "How are you smart?" Different theorists classify these abilities differently. Some learning style inventories break abilities into verbal, auditory, and tactile. Jungian personality types are classified around our preferences within four scales: (1) extroversion/introversion (source of energy), (2) sensing/feeling (what is observed), (3) thinking/feeling (evaluation style), and (4) judging/perceiving (energy direction and flow) (Fairhurst & Fairhurst, 1995). Gardner (1983, 1998, 1999) proposes eight different kinds of intelligence: logical/mathematical, verbal/linguistic, bodily kinesthetic, musical, visual/spatial, interpersonal, intrapersonal, and natural/environmental. Each person has all eight but they are each of various strengths. Sternberg's (1997) categories include the analytical, practical, and creative aspects of intelligence.

Mismatch between learning styles and teaching styles can result in confusion, frustration, and underachievement for gifted minority students (Ford, 1996), and Papert (1996) asserts that most failure to learn is a result of instruction not matching the individual's learning style. Teachers can meet students' diverse needs by using a variety of teaching strategies from learning style or Multiple Intelligence theories. Teachers can also provide assignments, such as projects, that are flexible enough that different students can complete the task in different ways.

INTRINSIC AND EXTRINSIC MOTIVATION

Motivation is the next key factor. Many motivation theories distinguish between internal and external motivating factors. A student who is *intrinsically* motivated undertakes an activity for its own sake, for the enjoyment it provides, the learning it permits, or the feelings of accomplishment it evokes (Lepper, 1988). An *extrinsically* motivated student performs in order to obtain some reward or avoid some punishment external to the activity itself, such as grades, stickers, or teacher approval (Lumsden, 1994).

Many motivational researchers have concluded that people learn best when intrinsically motivated (Alkin, 1992; Kohn, 1994; Lepper, Greene, & Nisbett,

1973). "Perception is goal directed. We do not passively wait for some stimuli to arrive and then at the late date attempt an interpretation. Instead, we actively seek information relevant to our current needs and goals" (Rumelhart, 1980, p. 51). Further, "human beings innately organize their thinking and perception around what they regard to be important" (Caine & Caine, 1997, p. 112). Wurman (1989) simply refers to learning as remembering what you are interested in. Schank and Cleary (1995) describe learning as pursuing answers to questions that grow from our goals and interests. "It is important to recognize that it is internally generated questions that drive memory and hence drive learning" (p. 42). They go on to explain: "memory is obsessive enough to fail to pay attention to information provided that is not an answer to any question it may have, thus making learning of information it is not seeking fairly difficult" (p. 42).

Changes in how teachers deliver the curriculum can help mediate this problem (Deci, Vallerand, Pelletier, & Ryan, 1991). Educators can better match content and instruction to students' interests and goals. Teachers can work either to build on student curiosity and interests or to capture their imaginations by making content interesting through conundrums, contradictions, or any other strategy that gets students asking questions. Davis (1972) reported, for example, that junior high students will not act up in a class that is interesting. Lepper and Hodell (1989) recommend trying to enhance children's intrinsic motivation through challenge, curiosity, control, and fantasy. Teachers can also better connect content and classroom experiences and activities with students' personal goals. Keller (1987) recommends presenting the objectives and useful purpose of the instruction and specific methods for successful achievement (e.g., the teacher explains the objectives of the lesson) and matching objectives to student needs and motives.

Teachers can do many things to try to make learning more intrinsically motivating for students, but it is not possible to do this for every child all the time. How can educators motivate students to learn when they are not intrinsically interested in learning? The work people do in the real world is often regulated by both intrinsic and extrinsic factors. People need to learn and do things that they may not find interesting or aligned with their goals. Under what conditions will students learn when they are not intrinsically motivated?

A focus on punishments and rewards can be counterproductive to learning (Kohn, 1993, 1994). Teachers may rely on extrinsic motivators with underachieving students (either as a carrot or a stick) precisely because teachers are challenged to find a way to help these students learn. Autonomous supportive strategies (such as providing students choices and giving them opportunities for decision making, planning, designing, and creating), on the other hand, can make extrinsically required learning as powerful as intrinsically motivated learning (Deci & Ryan, 1985; Deci, Spiegel, Ryan, Koestner, & Kauffman, 1982; Deci et al., 1991).

MEANING MAKING

Meaning is the fourth component. Students do not compile knowledge in some objective data retrieval system. Memory works primarily to make meaning of experience and functions as a connection machine, making associations between different memories, facts, skills, and attitudes (Anderson, Reynolds, Schallert, & Goetz, 1977; Anderson, Spiro, & Anderson, 1978; Bruning et al., 1995; Rumelhart, 1980; Schank & Cleary, 1995).

Richness in experience allows students to make multiple connections to new information, maximizing their ability to make meaning to integrate into their knowledge base. "Imagine a section from a geography text about an unfamiliar nation. An adult would bring to bear an elaborate nation schema, which would point to subschemata representing generic knowledge about political systems, economics, geography, and climate" (Anderson et al., 1978, p. 439). This would certainly frame the information about the new nation in a way qualitatively different from how someone without the depth of knowledge about political systems, economics, geography, and climate (such as a middle level student) would understand it.

Rich contexts and connections are vital for recall, as well. "[T]hese same schemata guide our *information seeking*. Not only do schemata tell us *what to see*, but they also tell us *where to see it*." (Rumelhart 1980, p. 51). For example, many people find it easier to remember the words to a song when the music for it is playing.

Students' memories do not function like tape recorders or videotape machines; they cannot simply replay events at their choosing. Instead, retrieval depends on the cues they have available to call forth memory. Further, the context of a remembering event determines what will be remembered. A rich context providing multiple cues for retrieval will lead to good memory performance. A poor context with few or no retrieval cues is apt to give us a poor indication of what students really do have in memory. (Bruning et al., 1995, p. 113)

Rote learning rarely helps to provide those additional cues for children. When students memorize facts out of context, they limit how the information can be retrieved. Because rote memory is used to store unrelated facts, it is not designed to transfer learning to other contexts. If something is learned out of context, it can generally only be recalled out of context. This is why students can do well on a test, but then not be able to use the information later.

> The reason why schoolbook knowledge fails to come to mind when it's needed is that it is not well indexed in memory. When students learn, they are often not encouraged to try out the new knowledge on problems they face or relate that knowledge to what they already know. So the schoolbook learning forms isolated islands of structures in their memories. They know how to apply these islands to the schoolbook problems they face because that is the context in which they learned it. But the knowledge does not come to mind when they are faced with a problem in a different context. (Schank & Cleary 1995, pp. 59-60)

By providing contexts for learning and mental frameworks for new knowledge, teachers can help students learn material better by helping them develop associations, connections, and contexts for understanding and meaning making. Teachers need to find ways to relate learning to student's lives, whether that is showing how new knowledge and skills are useful to them or by connecting it to their own lives. Involving students in work for an audience beyond the teacher and other students, giving them real world work to complete, or using metaphors while presenting new information are strategies that help students make meaning of what they are learning.

SUMMARY

In summary, what specifically motivates a student is dependent on the individual. There are, however, broad categories of motivation that have been shown to positively impact most students. These are the learning environment, experience, intrinsic and extrinsic motivation, and meaning making.

REFERENCES

ABC News. (1993). *Common miracles: The American revolution in learning.* [Television broadcast].

Alkin, M. C. (Ed.). (1992). Motivation. In *Encyclopedia of educational research* (pp. 860-865). New York: Macmillan.

Anderson, R., Reynolds, R., Schallert, D., & Goetz, E. (1977). Frameworks for comprehending discourse. *American Education Research Journal, 14,* 367-381.

Anderson, R., Spiro, R., & Anderson, M. (1978). Schemata as scaffolding for the representation of information in connected discourse. *American Education Research Journal, 15,* 433-440.

Bandura, A. (1993). Perceived self-efficacy in cognitive development and functioning. *Educational Psychologist, 28,* 117-148.

Bandura, A. (1997). *Self-efficacy: The exercise of control.* New York: W. H. Freeman.

Bruning, R. H., Schraw, G. J., & Ronning, R. R. (1995). *Cognitive psychology and instruction.* Englewood Cliffs, NJ: Merrill.

Caine, R. N., & Caine, G. (1991). *Making connections: Teaching and the human brain.* Alexandria, VA: Association for Supervision and Curriculum Development.

Caine, R. N., & Caine, G. (1997). *Education on the edge of possibility.* Alexandria, VA: Association for Supervision and Curriculum Development.

Davis, J. (1972). Teachers, kids, and conflict: Ethnography of a junior high school. In J. P. Spradley & D. W. McCurdy (Eds.), *The cultural experience: Ethnography in complex society* (pp. 103-119). Chicago: Science Research Associates.

Deci, E. L., & Ryan, R. M. (1985). *Intrinsic motivation and self-determination in human behavior.* New York: Plenum.

Deci, E. L., Spiegel, N. H., Ryan, R. M., Koestner, R., & Kauffman, M. (1982). The effects of performance standards on teaching styles: The behavior of controlling teachers. *Journal of Educational Psychology, 74,* 852-859.

Deci, E., Vallerand, R., Pelletier, L., & Ryan, R. (1991). Motivation and education: The self-determination perspective. *Educational Psychologist, 26*(3 & 4), 325-346.

Dowty, G. (1997). *The development of at-risk children's self-efficacy for social functioning and interpersonal relationships: A review of the literature and implications for residential interventions.* Unpublished paper.

Ellis, A., & Fouts, J. (1993). *Research on educational innovations.* Princeton Junction, NJ: Eye On Education.

Emerick, L. J. (1992). Academic underachievement among the gifted: Students' perceptions of factors that reverse the pattern. *Gifted Child Quarterly, 36*(3), 140-146.

Fairhurst, A., & Fairhurst, L. (1995). *Effective teaching effective learning: Making the personality connection in your classroom.* Palo Alto, CA: Davies-Black.

Ford, D. Y. (1996). *Reversing underachievement among gifted black students: promising practices and programs.* New York: Teachers College Press.

Gardner, H. (1983). *Frames of mind.* New York: Basic Books.

Gardner, H. (1998). A multiplicity of intelligences [Special issue on exploring intelligence]. *Scientific American, 9*(4), 18-23.

Gardner, H. (1999). *The disciplined mind.* New York: Simon & Schuster.

Graham, S. (1990). Communicating low ability in the classroom: Bad things good teachers sometimes do. In S. Graham & V. Folkes (Eds.), *Attribution theory: Applications to achievement, mental health, and interpersonal conflict* (pp. 17-36). Hillsdale, NJ: Erlbaum.

Keller, J. M. (1987). Strategies for stimulating the motivation to learn. *Performance and Instruction, 26*(8), 1-7.

Kohn, A. (1993). *Punished by rewards: The trouble with gold stars, incentive plans, A's, praise, and other bribes.* Boston: Houghton Mifflin.

Kohn, A. (1994). The risks of rewards. *ERIC digest.* Urbana, IL: ERIC Clearinghouse on Elementary and Early Childhood Education. (ERIC ED376990)

Lepper, M. R. (1988). Motivational considerations in the study of instruction. *Cognition and Instruction.* 5(4), 289-309.

Lepper, M. R., & Hodell, M. (1989). Intrinsic motivation in the classroom. In R. Ames & C. Ames (Eds.), *Research on motivation in education: Goals and cognitions* (Vol. 3, pp. 73-105). San Diego, CA: Academic Press.

Lepper, M. R., Greene, D., & Nisbett, R. (1973). Undermining children's intrinsic interest with extrinsic reward: A test of the "over-justification" hypothesis. *Journal of Personality and Social Psychology, 28,* 129-137.

Lumsden, L. (1994). Student motivation to learn. Retrieved June 24, 2005, from http://eric.uoregon.edu/publications/digests/digest092.html (ERIC ED370200).

Muir, M. (2001). What engages underachieving middle school students in learning? *Middle School Journal, 33(2),* 37-43.

Papert, S. (1996). *The connected family: Bridging the digital generation gap.* Marietta, GA: Longstreet Press.

Rumelhart, D. (1980). Schemata: The building blocks of cognition. In R. Spiro, B. Bruce, & W. Brewer (Eds.), *Theoretical issues in reading comprehension* (pp. 33-58). Hillsdale, NJ: Erlbaum.

Schank, R., & Cleary, C. (1995). *Engines for education.* Hillsdale, NJ: Erlbaum.

Schunk, D. H. (1989). Self-efficacy and cognitive skill learning. In R. Ames & C. Ames (Eds.), *Research on motivation in education: Goals and cognitions* (Vol. 3, pp. 13-43). San Diego, CA: Academic Press.

Sternberg, R. (1997). What does it mean to be smart? *Educational Leadership, 54(6),* 20-24.

Weiner, B. (1984). Principles for a theory of student motivation and their application within an attributional framework. In C. Ames & R. Ames (Eds.), *Research on motivation in education: Student motivation* (Vol. 1, pp. 15-38). San Diego, CA: Academic Press.

Weiner, B. (1985). An attributional theory of achievement motivation and emotion. *Psychologyical Review, 92(4),* 548-573.

Whitmore, J. F. (1980). *Giftedness, conflict and underachievement.* Boston: Allyn & Bacon.

Wurman, R. S. (1989) *Information anxiety.* New York: Doubleday.

—Mike Muir
University of Maine, Farmington

MOTIVATION: EXTRINSIC

Motivation is extrinsic when it originates from outside the student. That can include having to meet requirements that others impose (e.g., completing classroom assignments, or meeting state or national standards). Also, a student who performs "in order to obtain some reward or avoid some punishment external to the activity itself" (Lepper, 1988), such as grades, stickers, or teacher approval, is extrinsically motivated. Extrinsic motivation can either shut down learning or improve it, depending on the type.

Counterproductive extrinsic motivation occurs when there is a focus on punishments or rewards. The concern is that although those strategies may get students to participate in classroom activities, when students perform for grades or other rewards simply do not perform as well as those who expect nothing (Kohn, 1993). According to Kohn (1994), this effect is evident for young children, older children, and adults; for males and females; for rewards of all kinds; and for tasks ranging from memorizing facts to designing collages to solving problems. Further, Kohn (1993) indicates that people offered a reward generally choose the easiest possible task. In the absence of rewards, by contrast, children are inclined to pick tasks that are just beyond their current levels of ability. Grades in particular have been found to have a detrimental effect on creative thinking, long-term retention, interest in learning, and preference for challenging tasks (Butler & Nisan, 1986; Grolnick & Ryan, 1987). Lepper, Greene, and Nisbett (1973) found that an overreliance on extrinsic rewards can damage the quality of work, impede the ability to be creative or to accomplish non-routine tasks, squelch any pre-existing intrinsic interest, and diminish interest in doing the activity once the rewards are removed.

Self-determination theory (Deci & Ryan, 1985; Deci, Vallerand, Pelletier, & Ryan, 1991) adds to the discussion of extrinsic motivation that there are different differing types. Counterproductive extrinsic motivation (like Kohn writes about) interferes with learning since it is perceived by the learner as controlling. Productive extrinsic motivation, on the other hand, occurs when students have autonomy (e.g., having choices and opportunities for decision making, planning, designing, and creating). Deci et al. (1991) link students who had more self-determined forms of motivation with remaining in school, positive academic performance, greater conceptual understanding, better memory, more positive emotions in the classroom, more enjoyment of academic work, more satisfaction with school, less anxiety, and better coping with failure. Further, students in classrooms with autonomy-supportive teachers displayed more intrinsic motivation, and more perceived competence and self-esteem than did students in classrooms with controlling teachers.

Proponents of self-determination theory maintain that productive extrinsic motivation can be achieved through a variety of strategies, including allowing students to share in the decision-making and authority within the classroom. They may negotiate the curriculum with the teacher, or help the teacher decide how they will learn the curriculum. Project-based learning, for example, allows students numerous choices around what form their finished product will take, while learning valuable content determined by the teacher, district, or state. The key is to make sure students have choices about their learning.

REFERENCES

Butler, R., & Nisan, M. (1986). Effects of no feedback, task-related comments, and grades on intrinsic motivation and performance. *Journal of Educational Psychology, 78*(3), 210-216.

Deci, E. L., & R. M. Ryan. (1985). *Intrinsic motivation and self-determination in human behavior.* New York: Plenum.

Deci, E., Vallerand, R., Pelletier, L., & Ryan, R. (1991). Motivation and education: The self-determination perspective. *Educational Psychologist, 26*(3 & 4), 325-346.

Grolnick, W. S., & Ryan, R. M. (1987). Autonomy in children's learning: An experimental and individual difference investigation. *Journal of Personality and Social Psychology, 52,* 890-898.

Kohn, A. (1993). *Punished by rewards: The trouble with gold stars, incentive plans, A's, praise, and other bribes.* Boston: Houghton Mifflin.

Kohn, A. (1994). The risks of rewards. *ERIC digest.* Urbana, IL: ERIC Clearinghouse on Elementary and Early Childhood Education. (ERIC ED376990)

Lepper, M. R. (1988). Motivational considerations in the study of instruction. *Cognition and Instruction, 5*(4), 289-309.

Lepper, M. R., Greene, D., & Nisbett, R. (1973). Undermining children's intrinsic interest with extrinsic reward: A test of the "over-justification" hypothesis. *Journal of Personality and Social Psychology, 28,* 129-137.

—Mike Muir
University of Maine, Farmington

MULTIPLE INTELLIGENCES

MULTIPLE INTELLIGENCE THEORY

In what ways are students smart? In the early 1900s, many traditional psychologists defined intelligence solely based on how well students performed on verbal-language and/or mathematical tasks. An individual's general intelligence was typically defined by results on mental tests or IQ (Intelligence Quotient) scores. This view assumed that all human problem solving is regulated by a single underlying mental ability or general intelligence. However, in his 1983 book, *Frames of Mind: The Theory of Multiple Intelligences* (Gardner, 1983), Harvard psychologist Howard Gardner challenged this unitary concept of general intelligence by proposing that intelligence should be viewed as individuals' abilities to solve problems in real life, create new problems to solve, or offer something valuable in a culture or community (Gardner, 1999).

Based on his research in the arts, developmental psychology, and neuropsychology at Project Zero (the research group at Harvard's Graduate School of Education), Gardner (1983) presented his theory of multiple intelligence (MI) revealing that rather than explaining all human intelligence narrowly in terms of a general score on a standardized test, intelligence comes in a variety of forms, may be localized to certain areas of the brain, and is developed and expressed in differing social and cultural contexts. In 1983, Gardner initially formulated seven types of intelligences. However, after conducting further research and reflection, Gardner (1999) proposed that most students possess at least eight distinct types of intelligences but to varying degrees. Subsequently, he added naturalistic intelligence to the original seven intelligences. In order for something to be categorized as an "intelligence," it had to satisfy a range of criteria that Gardner established after reviewing a diverse range of literature that varied from developmental psychology and neuropsychology to anthropology and evolutionary biology. The criteria included the following:

- The intelligence could potentially be isolated in brain-damaged individuals.
- It could be seen in idiots-savants, prodigies and other exceptional people.
- It should demonstrate an identifiable core, information-processing operation meaning that there is almost an automatic mental process that handles information related to the intelligence.

- There exists a distinctive developmental history. For instance, growing from infancy to adulthood, different intelligences develop at different rates and can be defined by a set of observable and measurable performances.
- It should exhibit a plausible evolutionary history that can be seen in other mammals and that has helped human ancestors survive.
- It is supported by experimental psychological tasks.
- It is supported by traditional psychometric tests of intelligence.
- It could be captured by a symbolic system. For example, information that draws on the intelligence may be transmitted through music, notations in mathematics, language, spatial relations, etc. (Gardner, 1983, p. 62-69)

DESCRIPTION OF THE INTELLIGENCES

Gardner (Checkley, 1997) identified the following eight intelligences:

Linguistic intelligence ("word smart") refers to the capacity to communicate, think and use language to express ideas and understand other people. People possessing this strong language sense in both written and spoken form include authors, poets, writers, journalists, public speakers, lawyers, and newscasters.

Logical-mathematical intelligence ("number/reasoning smart") allows individuals to use, calculate, quantify, analyze abstract relationships and to solve complex mathematical operations. Often seen in mathematical reasoning and science experimentation, individuals who demonstrate this include scientists, accountants, mathematicians, engineers, computer programmers and logicians.

Spatial intelligence ("picture smart") is evident in individuals who have the ability to think in three-dimensional ways that allow them to transform information from the visual world to their minds. Individuals such as chess champion players, sculptors, pilots, surgeons, architects, sailors and artists are able to perceive external and internal images, to recreate images from memory, transform or manipulate images, to navigate themselves and objects through space and to skillfully decode or develop graphic information.

Musical intelligence ("music smart") enables individuals to create, communicate and understand through sound. These people are sensitive to pitch, melody, rhythm, tone and have the ability to think in musical terms. Musicians, composers, acoustic engineers, music critics, and conductors can recognize and hear patterns and are able to remember and manipulate music.

Bodily-kinesthetic intelligence ("body smart") consists of the capacity to use parts of or their entire bodies to manipulate and create objects and solve problems. Kinesthetically-gifted people demonstrate keen physical skills and are able to coordinate bodily movements and conduct advanced forms of problem solving and creativity. These abilities are seen in athletes, rock climbers, surgeons, dancers, choreographers, and jewelers.

Interpersonal intelligence ("people smart") refers to the capacity to interact and understand people and relationships. Individuals with this ability are able to recognize, connect and understand other people's feelings, desires, and intentions and are able use these in problem solving. It allows individuals to work effectively with others. For example, successful politicians, actors, teachers, therapists, salespeople, religious leaders, and social workers exhibit strong interpersonal intelligence.

Intrapersonal intelligence ("self smart") allows individuals to possess and construct accurate self-knowledge. They are able to use this knowledge to plan and direct their decision making and behavior. Because individuals high in this ability have a strong understanding of their feelings, fears and motivations, they tend to make sound choices in their lives and know what they can and cannot do or know where to seek help if needed. Examples include psychologists, philosophers, theologians, and autobiographers.

Naturalist intelligence ("nature smart") enables people to discriminate among, identify, classify and use features of the natural world to solve problems. They are able to understand natural and human-made systems and can categorize different kinds of plants and animals and are keenly sensitive to the other features of the natural world such as weather, clouds, rock configurations, and so forth. Architects, archeologists, and hunters make keen observations about natural changes, interconnections and patterns.

ADDITIONAL INTELLIGENCES?

Rather than viewing intelligence as a general ability, Gardner argues that each individual possesses at least eight relatively independent intelligences and that each individual has a unique blend of these intelligences. However, Gardner also explains that with more investigations, many more types of intelligences may be potentially identified in the future. In *Intelligence Reframed* (1999), Gardner discussed potential inclusion of new intelligences such as existential intelligence, moral intelligence, and spiritual intelligence. However, each of these intelligences is complex and requires additional empirical evidence to substantiate its clear existence. For instance, existential intelligence allows individuals to philosophize about the meaning of life and death but since Gardner is not able to detect its brain origins, it cannot be defined as an intelligence yet. Similarly, moral intelligence entails making value judgments and since intelligence is considered value-free, this capacity is not yet established as an intelligence. Likewise, spiritual intelligence is the ability to construe cosmic and transcendent truths but it is heavily dependent on ill-defined realms of attitudes, emotions and values. As noted, Gardner has broadened our view of human intelligence and with more research; other types of intelligence may be established in the future.

APPLICATION IN THE CLASSROOM

Although not all academic psychologists readily accept Gardner's theory of multiple intelligences, it has changed the perception and understanding of human intelligences among many educators. In general, all individuals possess all of the intelligences but each intelligence appears to emerge at different rates and different times in life. Additionally, each intelligence seems to have its own developmental sequence. Because of this, students differ in the relative degree of strengths and weaknesses for each intelligence. For instance, even though Einstein was gifted in mathematics and science, he did not demonstrate equal giftedness in linguistic, kinesthetic and interpersonal capacities. Typically, students are able to show strengths in one or two intelligence areas.

Because each student combines and uses these types of "smartness" in highly personal ways, limiting educational experiences only to the traditional academic ways of learning that focuses primarily on linguistic and mathematical intelligences really lessens the importance of others ways of learning and knowing for students. Consequently, Gardner's theory has been embraced by many educational theorists, teachers, and administrators and has generated countless new ideas and practices in the education field (Chen, Krechevsky, & Viens, 1998; Kornhaber, 1999; Kornhaber, Fierros, & Veenema, 2004).

Numerous North American schools have adopted a MI-based curricula that encompass a broad range of disciplines which not only attend to reading, writing and mathematics but also go beyond these areas. Gardner designed the Entry Points Framework (a tool for curriculum development) to help teachers that complemented MI (a tool for understanding students' cognitive abilities). Entry Points Framework offered teachers different instructional approaches by providing students with multiple entry points to study topics and allowed students to express their understanding through diverse methods such as writing, dramatizations, and music.

WHAT MULTIPLE INTELLIGENCE RESEARCH SAYS

Research studies (Kornhaber, 1994; Kornhaber & Krechevsky, 1995) reported that educators adopted MI for several distinct reasons:

the theory validates educator's everyday experience: students think and learn in many different ways. It also provides educators with a conceptual framework for organizing and reflecting on curriculum assessment and pedagogical practices. In turn, this reflection has lead many educators to develop new approaches that might better meet the needs of the range of learners in their classrooms. (Kornhaber, 2001, p. 276)

Although the MI theory has stimulated alternative ways to think and teach, critics have pointed to the shortcomings and problems around how Gardner conceptualized multiple intelligences. These issues include questions about the adequacy surrounding Gardner's individual criteria for the qualification and establishment of an "intelligence." For instance, how were the criteria applied and why are these criteria especially relevant? (White, 1998). Other issues relate to the problems in substantiating and validating the theory a whole (Chen, 2004). For instance, rather than using traditional scientific educational research methods to generate the theory, Gardner conceived the theory based more on his own intuitions and reasoning. To date, there is not a clearly defined set of tests to identify and measure the different intelligences. Although the specific aspects of the MI theory are left open for debate and further investigations, current available research on brain functions tend to generally support the existence of multiple intelligences.

In addition, although there are still serious unanswered questions and issues about the MI theory, many classroom teachers have attested to the benefits and usefulness of the theory in producing positive student and school outcomes, especially at the elementary and middle school levels. Kornhaber and her colleagues, who also worked in Project Zero, conducted a study called Project SUMIT (Schools Using Multiple Intelligences Theory) and identified positive MI implementation outcomes that included increased standardized tests scores, improved student behavior, increased parental participation and increased learning, effort, motivation and social adjustments among students with learning disabilities (Kornhaber, Fierros & Veenema, 2004). Moreover, these researchers identified six organization practices called "Compass Point Practices" that helped guide teacher practice and track MI implementation progress. These were derived and characterized from schools successful in MI implementation:

- *Culture*: schools supported diverse learners and hard work among teachers and students.
- *Readiness*: schools gradually prepared and introduced teachers and staff to MI reform teaching practices over 12 to 18 months.
- *Collaboration*: teachers collaborated informally and formally to share and exchange ideas that provided richer student learning experiences.
- *Choice*: students were offered choices in how they wanted to attain and display their knowledge and skills.
- *Tool*: MI was used as a tool to support and promote high quality student learning rather than using the theory as an end in and of itself.
- *Arts*: integration of the arts played a critical role in developing students' skills and knowledge within and across disciplines.

REFERENCES

Checkley, K. (1977). The first seven and the eighth. *Educational Leadership, 55*(1), 8-13.

Chen, J. Q. (2004). Theory of multiple intelligences: Is it a scientific theory? *Teachers College Record, 106*(1), 17-23.

Chen, J. Q., Krechevsky, M., & Viens, J. (1998). *Building on children's strengths: The experience of Project Spectrum.* New York: Teachers College Press.

Gardner, H. (1983). *Frames of mind: The theory of multiple intelligences.* New York: Basic Books.

Gardner, H. (1999). *Intelligence reframed multiple intelligences for the 21st century.* New York: Basic Books.

Kornhaber, M. L. (1994). *The theory of multiple intelligences: Why and how schools ut it.* Unpublished manuscript, Harvard Graduate School of Education, Cambridge, MA.

Kornhaber, M. L. (1999). Multiple intelligences theory in practice. In J. H. Block, S. T. Everson, & T. R. Guskey (Eds.), *Comprehensive school reform: A program perspective* (pp. 179-191). Dubuque, IA: Kendall/Hunt.

Kornhaber, M. L. (2001). Howard Gardner. In J. A. Palmer (Ed.), *Fifty modern thinkers on education. From Piaget to the present* (pp. 272-279). London: Routledge.

Kornhaber, M. L., & Krechevsky, M. (1995). Expanding definitions of teaching and learning: Notes from the MI underground. In P. Cookson & B. Schneider (Eds.), *Transforming schools* (pp. 120-149). New York: Garland Press.

Kornhaber, M. L., Fierros, & E., Veenema, S. (2004). *Multiple intelligences: Best ideas from research and practice.* Boston: Allyn & Bacon.

White, J. (1998). *Do Howard Gardner's multiple intelligences add up?* London: Institute of Education, University of London.

—Emily Lin
University of Nevada, Las Vegas

NATIONAL ADOLESCENT LITERACY COALITION

The National Adolescent Literacy Coalition was formed in the fall of 2003 because of the urgent need for effective reading and writing instruction for adolescents. The coalition, whose members are educators, researchers, and policymakers, represent several agencies doing substantive work in adolescent literacy. The purpose of the coalition is to serve as a single, powerful voice that advocates and shapes policy for adolescent literacy and serves as a clearinghouse for resources, current research, and effective programs to meet the needs of adolescents.

This sense of urgency that underlies the coalition's work is predicated on the fact that the majority of students to be tested under No Child Left Behind (NCLB) will soon be in the upper grade levels, currently these students fare poorly on all measures of literacy. For example, the latest results on the National Assessment of Education Progress (NAEP) indicate that only one in four students tested cannot comprehend even simple texts, and only one in three can apply higher order and critical reading skills to interpret and analyze different types of text. The level of comprehension and percentage of students at below basic is even greater among nonwhites and low-income students.

Research provides conclusive evidence that activities to promote adolescent literacy at the secondary level should be a major priority of the nation's policy makers and educators. The value of explicit literacy instruction by highly skilled teachers, while often overlooked is the essential ingredient for supporting adolescent literacy. While the National Adolescent Literacy Coalition does not advocate one "best" program to meet the needs of all adolescents, it has agreed on some essential elements that need to be at the core of any effective literacy program. These elements include, but are not limited to:

- High expectations and access to rigorous curriculum and instruction for all students.
- Committed, collaborative leadership, working to implement a well-defined literacy program.
- Research-based instructional strategies in literacy, taught across the content areas.
- Multiple forms of assessment to identify strengths and weaknesses of student's literacy competencies, instructional strategies, and professional development activities.
- Accelerated intervention plans for individual students based on the results of reliable diagnostic measures.
- Research-based, job-embedded, and on-going professional development opportunities that provide school faculty with instructional strategies that support literacy across the content areas.
- Expert teachers (content teachers and literacy coaches) who know how to model explicit strategies to support the professional learning needs of other teachers.
- Literacy strategies that take into account the cultural and linguistic diversity of students.
- Access to a variety of engaging literacy materials to support the multiple reading levels and interests of students.
- Special attention to the transition years (e.g., sixth and ninth grade), with accelerated courses in academic literacy to significantly boost academic achievement.

- Adolescent literacy instruction that fosters active engagement of the family and community in their children's education.

—Peggy H. Burke
Central Michigan University

NATIONAL ASSESSMENT OF EDUCATIONAL PROGRESS

NAEP, the National Assessment of Educational Progress is also known as the "Nation's Report Card" (National Assessment of Educational Progress, n.d.). Since 1969, NAEP has assessed various subject areas. The Commissioner of Education Statistics in the United States Department of Education is legally responsible for the NAEP project. Since its inception NAEP has had two major goals: (1) to compare student achievement, and (2) to track changes over time in achievement of fourth, eighth, and 12th graders in mathematics, reading, writing, science, and other content areas. Currently, long-term assessments are conducted only in math and reading. NAEP is developing assessments in world history, economics, and foreign language. Since eighth grade math and reading are assessed, these results are often used by middle grade teachers in assessing their own students in comparison to other eighth graders in the United States.

The reports NAEP generates are based on subject achievement, instructional expertise, and certain populations (e.g., fourth, eighth, and 12th graders). Scores for subgroups are reported as well. National NAEP data are reported for samples of public and nonpublic schools. NAEP collects information about contextual and background variables from students, teachers, and principals using questionnaires. If a state chooses not to participate in NAEP, samples of schools and students are selected for the national sample. Participating states receive assessment results for students in that state. Long-term trend assessments, administered in Grades 4, 8, and 12 provide data on the changes in math and reading. NAEP results are reported with the state accountability results required by No Child Left Behind (NCLB). NEAP results were not intended to enhance student learning. They were designed to show what students know and can do. However, NCLB provides incentives for schools to participate in NAEP since any school that receives Title 1 grant money must participate in fourth and eighth grade assessments in reading and math.

Validity and reliability are important since NAEP findings impact the public's understanding of student academic achievement. Thus, subject related committees and NCES and the National Assessment Governing Board (NAGB) staff regularly conduct reviews and evaluations. Fewer students score at or above grade level on NAEP tests than they score on state administered tests. (Popham, 2005). In 2003, 53 states or jurisdictions participated in math and reading assessments, and 51 states or jurisdiction participated in the writing assessment. These assessments are conducted biennially.

NAEP reports are available to educators and the general public, but schools cannot get individual information about their own students. The reports include state, regional, and national results. The only exceptions to this are the results from large urban districts. NAEP began reporting district data on a trial basis in 2002 (Trial Urban District Assessments); these districts include Atlanta, Boston, Charlotte, Chicago, Cleveland, Houston, Los Angeles, New York City, San Diego, and the District of Columbia. Individual student data is not available on these reports.

Occasionally, NAEP coordinates special educational studies related to assessment. Examples include the Technology Based Assessment and the High School Transcript Assessment. The Oral Reading Study was designed for fourth graders. Other specialty assessments include the National Indian Educational Study and the report on America's Schools.

REFERENCES

National Assessment of Educational Progress. (n.d.). *The nation's report card.* Retrieved May 31, 2005, from http://nces.ed.gov/nationsreportcard/

Popham, J. (2005). NEAP: Gold Standards or fool's gold? *Educational Leadership, 65,* 79-81.

—Kimberly J. Hartman
The University of North Carolina, Charlotte

NATIONAL ASSOCIATION OF ELEMENTARY SCHOOL PRINCIPALS

The National Association of Elementary School Principals (NAESP) (www.naesp.org), founded in 1921, is a professional organization serving over 28,500 elementary and middle school principals and other educators in the United States, in Canada, and from overseas. NAESP operates through a network of affiliated associations in every state and the District of Columbia.

The association's demonstrated belief is that the development of quality education in each elementary and middle school depends on the expertise, dedication, and leadership of the principal. As a result, NAESP actively pursues the development and dissemination of programs, activities, and resources to promote high standards and to enhance the leadership capacity of principals at the elementary and middle school levels. The organization is currently engaged in a nationwide campaign to heighten public awareness of elementary and middle school education as the foundation for all future academic achievement.

Among the association's many services are the award-winning *Principal* magazine and *Communicator* newsletter, seven other publications per year that address the specific needs of practicing school administrators, an annual convention, an assessment center, and a variety of professional development programs for principals and school leadership teams. Services for students are offered through NAESP's American Student Council Association.

Recognizing that our middle school members face unique challenges and issues, NAESP offers a variety of activities and services designed exclusively for the middle school principal. A newsletter, *Middle Matters*, is published three times a year in cooperation with the National Middle School Association (NMSA), and is also available online at www.naesp.org by selecting the Middle Grades/Schools topic heading. This section of the NAESP Web site also highlights news of special interest to middle grades principals, including information on the activities and services of NMSA and the National Forum to Accelerate Middle Grades Reform, and provides links to other organizations whose work focuses on the middle grades.

The NAESP Leadership Academy offers targeted professional development opportunities for middle grades principals at our national convention, including preconvention workshops, concurrent sessions, and an annual Middle Grades Luncheon cosponsored with the National Middle School Association. The academy has developed several full-day workshops available for sponsorship by state associations and school districts, and sponsors a series of Web casts during the school year that enable principals to provide economical, site-based staff development.

—Cheryl Riggins
National Association of Elementary School Principals

NATIONAL ASSOCIATION OF PROFESSORS OF MIDDLE LEVEL EDUCATION

The National Association of Professors of Middle Level Education (NAPOMLE) was chartered on October 28, 1997 as the 55th affiliate of the National Middle School Association (NMSA). The charter was signed by 56 middle level professors from across the nation, and listed the following as charter institutional members: Clark Atlanta University, Georgia Southwestern University, Clayton State University (GA), Valdosta State University, Miami University (OH), Georgia College and State University, University of Wisconsin at Platteville, Phillips University, the University of Cincinnati, the College of Charleston, Southeast Missouri State University, Bridgewater State College (MA), Northeastern Illinois University (Chicago), State University of West Georgia, and Georgia Southern University. John Lounsbury was the first to sign, and added the signature of William Alexander (deceased) in remembrance of one of the other founders of the middle school movement.

While the creation of NAPOMLE occurred as a result of collaboration among a group of middle level professors from across the nation, it evolved from an association that existed more than a decade before in Georgia, the Georgia Professors of Middle Level Education, established by John Lounsbury, Jay Hertzog, and others. Both organizations were established to provide a forum for middle level educators to share information and ideas, and to network with one another to the benefit of the middle grades movement. A steering committee was formed which developed a constitution and bylaws based on a model provided by NMSA, and application was made for affiliate status. Upon approval of the charter in 1997, John Myers of the State University of West Georgia was elected as first president of the association. The purposes of the organization are to:

- Provide a professional network to enhance the exchange of information and ideas, as well as, to encourage the discussion of topics related to the preparation of middle level educators,
- Contribute to the development of an expanded middle level research base, and provide additional means for sharing and disseminating current research and ideas among those interested in middle level education,
- Serve actively as advocates for the middle school movement, especially in terms of promoting middle level concepts among various publics com-

monly dealt with in the preparation of middle level educators, and

• Share in the advocacy for the middle school movement by supporting the stated purposes and goals of the National Middle School Association.

NAPOMLE also publishes a journal, *Current Issues in Middle Level Education*. John Lounsbury designed the cover for the debut issue, and recognized leaders in the middle school movement contributed articles. Articles in the journal regularly focus on best teaching practices in colleges and universities, school-university partnerships, and other topics of interest to faculty.

—John Myers
State University of West Georgia

—Barbara R. Blackburn
Winthrop University

NATIONAL ASSOCIATION OF SECONDARY SCHOOL PRINCIPALS

Founded in 1916, the National Association of Secondary School Principals (NASSP) (www.nassp.org) is the nation's largest school leadership organization, with over 32,000 high school and middle level principals, assistant principals, aspiring principals and other school leaders. The mission of NASSP is to promote excellence in school leadership. NASSP serves its members by offering products and services through publications, conferences and workshops.

Middle Level education has been a long-time interest of the association. In fact, since the 1980s the association has published a once-a-decade study of leadership in middle level education. During the summer of 2004, *Leadership for Highly Successful Middle Level Schools (A National Study of Leadership in Middle Level Schools, Volume II)* was released.

NASSP co-published *Turning Points 2000* with the National Middle School Association and Teachers' College Press. *Turning Points 2000 Study Guide* was written with extensive input from a group of active middle level NASSP members and published in 2002.

In 1981 NASSP began the publication of a monthly middle level newsletter that became a magazine entitled *Schools in the Middle*. In 2000 the name of the magazine changed to, *Principal Leadership, Middle Level Edition*. We also publish numerous middle level articles in *Bulletin* and *NewsLeader* and in our bimonthly, *NASSP News*. As an active member organization of

the National Forum to Accelerate Middle Grades Reform since its inception, we participate in advocacy efforts on behalf of middle level education and provide information on best practices at the middle level.

From 2002 to 2004 the NASSP National Middle Level Task Force was charged with creating a database of effective middle level practices and serving as a sounding board for the board of directors and staff in matters concerning middle level education. Middle level concerns and issues will also be at the forefront of three task forces currently being formed by the board of directors.

OTHER MIDDLE LEVEL ACTIVITIES

• Middle Level Long Conference: a yearly conference focused on various middle level topics
• Gruhn-Long-Melton Award: given since 1983 to a middle level educator who has exhibited outstanding service and leadership in the field
• Middle Level General Assembly & Ice Cream Social: features a middle level presentation of high interest to practitioners
• Middle Level Dissertation Award: recognizes an outstanding middle level doctoral student's work
• National Middle Level Education Month: a celebration of middle level schools and their programs
• State and National Middle Level Principal of the Year program: recognizes 52 "state" winners and three national finalists yearly
• Literacy Leaders Institute: Sponsored by: Scholastic/NASSP/NMSA/NCTE each summer

—John Nori
National Association of Secondary School Principals

NATIONAL BOARD FOR PROFESSIONAL TEACHING STANDARDS

The National Board for Professional Teaching Standards (NBPTS) (www.nbpts.org) was formed in 1987 to establish a national system of advanced certification for teachers. It is an independent, nonprofit organization governed by a board of directors of whom the majority are active classroom teachers. To earn certification, teachers must demonstrate that their practice exemplifies the five core propositions established by the NBPTS: (1) Teachers are committed to students and their learning, (2) Teachers know the subjects they teach and how to teach those subjects to students, (3) Teachers are responsible for managing and monitoring student learning, (4) Teachers think systematically about their practice and learn from experience, and (5) Teachers are members of learning communities. National Board certification is a performance-based assessment, requiring teachers to demonstrate their knowledge and ability by the submission of a portfolio containing videotapes of their teaching, student work samples, and reflective analysis of their teaching and their students' learning and by their performance at an assessment center.

National Board certification is available to teachers with a baccalaureate degree, a valid state teaching license, and a minimum of 3 years teaching experience in public or private schools. Certification is organized by content area and developmental level of a teacher's students. Certificates are available in the content areas of generalist, art, career and technical education, English as a new language, English language arts, exceptional needs specialist, library media, literacy: reading-language arts, mathematics, music, physical education, school counseling, science, social studies-history, and world languages other than English. Developmental levels are early childhood (ages 3-8), middle childhood (ages 7-12), early adolescence (ages 11-15), adolescence and young adulthood (ages 14-18+), with some certificates spanning multiple age groups. Certification is awarded for a 10-year period with renewal available. One hundred and seventy-seven teachers earned National Board certification in 1993-1994; as of 2004, over 40,200 teachers have earned National Board Teacher certification.

Critics of National Board Teacher Certification express concerns about the ability of any assessment process to effectively capture the complexities of teaching, the establishment of one vision of teaching excellence to the exclusion of other models, the possibility of creating a competitive atmosphere and a hierarchy among teachers, the lower percentages of African American teachers achieving certification, and the cost of achieving National Board Certification (Serafini, 2002).

Supporters view National Board Teacher Certification as a means to increase the professionalism of teachers while benefiting both teachers and students. As of 2005, 32 states recognize National Board Certification as meeting their state certification requirements, and 30 states provide salary bonuses or increases up to $6,000/year or 12% of a teacher's salary. There is evidence that students taught by National Board Certified Teachers have higher academic achievement (Center on Reinventing Public Education, 2004; CNA Corporation, 2004; Vandevoort, Amrein-Beardsley, & Berliner, 2004). The American

Federation of Teachers, Council for American Private Education, Council of Great City Schools, National Alliance of Black School Educators, National Conference of State Legislatures, National Education Association, and the National School Boards Association have supported and endorsed the National Board for Professional Teaching Standards.

REFERENCES

Center on Reinventing Public Education. (2004). *National Board certification successfully identifies effective teachers.* Retrieved May 24, 2005, from http://www.crpe.org/workingpapers/pdf/NBPTSquality_brief.pdf

CNA Corporation. (2004). *New CNAC study finds National Board Certification is effective indicator of teacher quality.* Retrieved May 24, 2005, from: http://cna.org/news/releases/041118.aspx?fromsearch=1

Serafini, F. (2002). Possibilities and challenges: The National Board for Professional Teaching Standards. *Journal of Teacher Education, 53,* 316-37.

Vandevoort, L. G., Amrein-Beardsley, A. & Berliner, D. C. (2004). National board certified teachers and their students' achievement. *Education Policy Analysis Archives, 12*(46). Retrieved May 24, 2005 from: http://epaa.asu.edu/epaa/v12n46/

—Shari L. Britner
Bradley University

NATIONAL CLEARINGHOUSE FOR COMPREHENSIVE SCHOOL REFORM

The mission of National Clearinghouse for Comprehensive School Reform (NCCSR) is to collect and disseminate information that builds the capacity of schools to raise the academic achievement of all students. The expansion of schoolwide reform programs during the last decade created a need for a central source of information on planning, implementing, and evaluating reform programs. Understanding that practitioners need information on assessing needs, developing reform programs, and documenting the impact of reforms, the U.S. Department of Education established the National Clearinghouse for Comprehensive School Reform (NCCSR) in 1999 to disseminate information through a web site, reference and retrieval services, outreach, and publications.

The clearinghouse is a partnership of The George Washington University and the Institute for Educational Leadership. Together, these organizations have expertise in school reform, providing technical assistance, and preparing educational leaders at the local, state, and national levels. NCCSR draws on the expertise and wisdom of its partners as well as Technical Working Group (TWG), a diverse group of education professionals who represent practitioners, researchers, policymakers, clearinghouse experts, and academics. The TWG provides NCCSR with guidance stemming from their varied perspectives.

NCCSR provides a variety of products and services designed to ensure easy access to the best resources for planning, implementing, and evaluating CSR. NCCSR's Web site (www.csrclearinghouse.org/) is the gateway to good information on CSR. Web resources include, the CSR library, Step by Step, The Catalog of School Reform Models, Issue and Research Briefs, Newsletters, Reference and Referrals, and a resource directory.

NCCSR makes efforts to ensure that research on school reform is disseminated to practitioners and that researchers are aware of the concerns of school-based practitioners. One way in which NCCSR keeps apprised of current CSR research is by maintaining contacts with researchers in the field. NCCSR has developed a Network of CSR Researchers to foster discussion among education researchers around the topic of school improvement and to build the knowledge base of researchers, practitioners, and policymakers. The network includes national and district-level researchers engaged in large-scale CSR studies and representatives of national organizations.

NCCSR engages in proactive outreach activities are to raise awareness of comprehensive school reform (CSR), introduce NCCSR resources, and connect practitioners and policymakers with the tools they need for successful implementation and support of school-wide improvement. NCCSR works to fulfill these goals by making presentations and conducting workshops at national and regional meetings; sponsoring an annual conference; building relationships and networks, and disseminating publications and information to targeted audiences.

—Monica Martinez
KnowledgeWorks Foundation

NATIONAL FORUM TO ACCELERATE MIDDLE-GRADES REFORM

The National Forum to Accelerate Middle-Grades Reform (the Forum) was established in 1997 amid a flurry of descending test scores, increasing reports of school violence, and heated debates about the nature and purpose of middle-grades education. Seeded through grants from the Edna McConnell Clark and W. K. Kellogg Foundations, members committed to a common goal: accelerating the academic performance and healthy development of every young adolescent in the nation.

The Forum unites over 60 of the most prominent leaders in middle-grades reform including state and local administrators, researchers, technical-assistance providers, executives of professional associations, parent advocates, comprehensive school reform model providers, and foundation program officers.

Members believe that students in the middle grades are capable of learning and achieving at high levels. They share a sense of urgency that high-performing schools with middle grades become the norm, not the exception. The Forum crafted a vision statement and a set of criteria for high-performing middle-grades schools focused on the interrelated areas of academic excellence, developmental responsiveness, and social equity. The criteria also describe needed organizational structures and supports.

The Forum's members work together and mobilize others to improve students' academic and developmental outcomes. The Forum functions in two-ways:

- as a "think tank," researching and disseminating policies and practices that advance high-performance. Twice a year, it convenes the best minds in the field to explore critical issues affecting middle-grades education and to strive for consensus to speak with one voice about their shared point-of-view.

- as a collective committed to working in the field to make its vision a reality. Members identify priority areas then develop and carry-out high-leverage strategies that produce results.

The Forum adds value to the ongoing work by targeting three primary goals:

1. *Improve school and classroom practice* to help educators accelerate their students' learning and healthy development. The Forum initiated the Schools to Watch Program in 1999. Since 2001, states replicate the STW program identifying schools that meet the Forum's rigorous, research-based criteria. These schools serve as beacons of excellence and assist others as they work to implement improved practices (www.schoolstowatch.org).

2. *Engage key stakeholders in middle-grades reform.* The Forum speaks with a unified voice and informs key stakeholders at the federal, state

and local levels about appropriate policies, research, programs and instructional practices that support middle-grades education. It develops and disseminates policy statements and communicates its position through multiple media outlets.

3. *Enhance the capacity middle-grades leaders* to accelerate reform, so they can better support their respective networks, affiliates, and the field as a whole in the pursuit of more effective middle-grades education. The Forum's strategies for capacity building have included the creation of a regional affiliate (Southern Forum to Accelerate Middle-Grade Reform), a city-based affiliate (New York City Forum to Accelerate Middle-Grades Reform), and a leadership training curriculum.

To learn more about the National Forum and its mission to improve middle-grades education, visit www.mgforum.org.

—Deborah Kasak
National Forum to Accelerate Middle-Grades Reform

NATIONAL MIDDLE SCHOOL ASSOCIATION

The National Middle School Association (NMSA) (www.nmsa.org), a professional education association, is dedicated to improving the educational experiences of young adolescents by providing vision, knowledge, and resources to all who serve them in order to develop healthy, productive, and ethical citizens. To fulfill this mission, NMSA develops and provides professional development, print and electronic publications, research, advocacy support, and network opportunities for professionals and non-professionals who work with young adolescents (ages 10-15).

From its beginnings as the Midwest Middle School Association in 1973 with fewer than 100 members, to the present day membership of 30,000, NMSA remains the only national education association exclusively focused on middle grades and young adolescents. An open-member association, NMSA counts principals, teachers, central office personnel, professors, college students, parents, community leaders, and educational consultants among its membership, and provides resources and services to anyone interested in the health and education of young adolescents.

The need for a model of education for young adolescents appropriate to their developmental needs had begun to gain attention during the 1960s. Discussion about teacher preparation for middle grades education and the need for a middle school organization gained momentum during a meeting of Michigan and Ohio school administrators and education professors in October 1970. More than 100 educators from Michigan, Ohio, and Indiana attended the next year's conference, October 28-29, 1971, and the Midwest Middle School Association (MWMSA) came into being.

Attendance at the 1972 MWMSA annual meeting doubled and represented a wider spread of states, including Wisconsin, Georgia, New York, Wyoming, and Missouri. Recognizing the growing interest, MWMSA contemplated redefining itself as a national organization. At the 1973 conference in Indianapolis, Conrad Toepfer presented a motion that was seconded, and passed to rename the association the National Middle School Association. Three hundred people attended NMSA's first annual conference the next year in Columbus, OH.

For several years, all association work was done voluntarily. As NMSA's first director, Hal Gaddis conducted association work from his office at Wright State University (OH) where he was professor. By 1976, NMSA headquarters had moved to Fairborn, OH, and membership exceeded 1000. Six years later the headquarters established itself in Columbus, OH, first at a small house, then to leased office on Evanswood Drive. Attendance at the annual conference had already exceeded 2000, and a paid staff now numbered one part-time and four full-time positions. After several renovations, additions to staff and positions, the association moved to a professional complex at Corporate Exchange Drive in 1994. Just 5 years later, further growth demanded another move to NMSA's current location on Executive Parkway in Westerville, OH, just outside the Columbus city limits.

Twenty-eight full-time staff currently serve over 30,000 members and 58 affiliates. Annual conference attendance ranges between 8,500 and 10,000. The association's professional development services include topic-focused workshops and conferences, technology-enabled instruction, on-site professional development, and print and media for site-managed staff development.

NMSA has been an active publisher of middle level education materials since its beginning. *The Middle School Journal* began as the *Midwest Middle School Journal* in 1970. In 1973 its name changed coincided with the appointment of its first paid editor, John

Lounsbury, who held that position for fourteen years. NMSA quickly expanded its publishing efforts to monographs and research. It released its first book, *The Middle School: A Look Ahead* in 1977, the same year that the first volume of *The Middle School Research Annual* appeared. *Middle Ground* joined the library of NMSA publications in 1985. NMSA's output averages ten new book titles per year, along with research briefs, policy statements, electronic publications, staff instructional materials.

Since its beginning, NMSA has been actively involved in research and middle grades teacher preparation. NMSA official research journal is *Research in Middle Level Education* which has developed from a quarterly to an annual journal, and now exists as an online publication. Committees devoted to these areas have been in existence since 1973. The work of these committees has influenced both the association and the larger arena of middle grades education.

Notable among the association's contributions to education is its work defining the needs for and characteristics of education specific to ten- to fifteen-year olds. Prior to 1980, the field lacked a comprehensive statement about middle level education. John Swaim, association president that year, appointed a committee to develop a position paper that outlined the rationale for and characteristics of education specific to young adolescents. In 1982, NMSA Board of Trustees approved and released *This We Believe*, which became the most widely cited document about middle level education over the next ten years. In the mid-1990's, a second committee was convened to review and revise the position statement. *This We Believe: Developmentally Responsive Middle Schools*, released in 1995, reflected the expanded knowledge and increased research data of the preceding decade along with the expectations about education for the twenty-first century.

In 2001 the NMSA Board again authorized a review of the foundation piece. With input from 250 educators and researchers and the entire association membership, the review committee developed the third edition of *This We Believe*. *This We Believe: Successful Schools for Young Adolescents* was released in 2003 along with a companion document, *Research and Resources in Support of This We Believe* (Anfara et al. 2003).

REFERENCES

Anfara, V. A., Andrews, P. G., Hough, D. L., Mertens, S. B., Mizelle, N. B., & White, G. P. (2003). *Research and resources in support of This We Believe*. Westerville, OH: National Middle School Association.

National Middle School Association. (1977). *The Middle School: A Look Ahead*. Columbus, OH: Author.

National Middle School Association. (1982). *This we believe*. Columbus, OH: Author.

National Middle School Association. (1995). *This we believe: Developmentally responsive middle schools*. Columbus, OH: Author.

National Middle School Association. (2003). *This we believe: Successful schools for young adolescents*. Westerville, OH: Author.

—Mary Henton
National Middle School Association

NATIONAL STAFF DEVELOPMENT COUNCIL

The National Staff Development Council (NSDC) is an 11,000-member organization working toward the goal of all teachers in all schools experiencing high quality professional learning as part of their daily work. Members of NSDC include school and district administrators, teachers, staff developers at both the school and central office levels, other educators, consultants, and others. A representative of NSDC has been an active participant in the National Forum to Accelerate Middle Grades Reform since that organization's founding. In recent years, NSDC's annual conference has frequently included presentations relating to professional development at the middle level.

In 1999, NSDC published *What Works in the Middle: Results-Based Staff Development* (Killion, 1999). This ground-breaking report described 27 discipline-specific staff development programs with credible evidence that they had helped improve student achievement. Seven were staff development programs in language arts, seven were in mathematics, five were in science, three were in social studies, and four were in interdisciplinary programs. However, to identify these programs NSDC researchers had to review more than 500 staff development programs, most of which had little or no data demonstrating that the programs had an effect on student performance.

To obtain more information about NSDC, visit their Web site at: www.nsdc.org.

REFERENCE

Killion, J. (1999). *What works in the middle: Results-based staff development*. Oxford, OH: National Staff Development Council.

—Hayes Mizell
National Staff Development Council

NEW AMERICAN SCHOOLS

As part of an unprecedented partnership formed to strengthen middle-grades schooling in 2002, the W. K. Kellogg Foundation awarded a $3 million grant to New American Schools (NAS), the business-led education nonprofit that promotes the quality, scale and sustainability of service providers such as Middle Start, a middle-grades school improvement program.

The 3-year award recognized New American Schools' strong record in assisting promising education programs in having widespread impact on schools and students and becoming financially sustainable. The award also recognized the foundation's confidence in Middle Start, which was developed by the foundation, the Academy for Educational Development, and several other Michigan- and Mid-South-based partners, on its journey toward self-sufficiency.

Under the grant, NAS provided assistance in the areas of model refinement and business planning as well as in the area of external relations so that the program can maintain a high level of quality as it continues to be implemented in schools on a wider scale.

As part of the grant, New American Schools also provided public relations guidance to the National Forum to Accelerate Middle-Grades Reform, an alliance of educators, researchers, national associations, officers of professional organizations, and foundations dedicated to improving education in the middle grades. The outreach work included targeted communications to policymakers, arming them with up-to-date information needed to make decisions on behalf of middle-grades students.

"Innovative partnerships of this kind are required for deep and lasting improvement in our middle grades," said Mary Anne Schmitt, President of NAS. "When like-minded organizations come together to leverage their skills and experience, the pay-off for students is significant, helping them meet high standards and face the increasingly complex demands of the competitive twenty-first century job market and the global economy."

Middle Start, a comprehensive school improvement program for the middle grades, is dedicated to building strong local, state, and regional support for middle-grades schools and students across the country. The program combines on-site coaching, professional development, and the resources of regional partners to strengthen student achievement in schools with middle grades. Guided by current research and practice emphasizing the developmental needs of young adolescents, Middle Start upholds the three goals that form broad student achievement—

academic excellence, developmental responsiveness, and social equity in middle-grades education—and it does so through small learning communities; team structure; student-focused instruction; meaningful student assessment; reflective review and self-study; as well as sustainable and meaningful partnerships.

NAS is uniquely positioned to assist education organizations such as Middle Start in moving to a sustainable, national platform, bridging the gap between the initial research and development phase and mature operations. New American Schools (NAS) is a leading nonprofit provider of professional services and investment in K-12 education. The mission of NAS is to help all students succeed by shaping, supporting and sustaining system-wide innovation and improvement in learning. NAS provides support to state departments of education, school districts, charter authorizers, and foundations, offering key stakeholders the tools and assistance needed to facilitate and sustain student learning. Effective in January 2005, NAS will merge with the American Institutes for Research, bridging high-quality educational research and improved K-12 system performance.

—Louise Kennelly
New American Schools

NEW YORK CITY FORUM TO ACCELERATE MIDDLE-GRADES REFORM

As elsewhere around the country, the middle grades in New York City have been "tested and found sorely wanting" (New York State United Teachers, 2002). Although the continued low performance of eighth graders on state and city tests has made numerous headlines over the years in the *New York Times* and elsewhere, New York City schools with middle grades have yet to receive the sustained resources and focused attention needed to make lasting improvements in the educational experience of young adolescents.

To address this need, in spring 2000, a number of organizations, many of which were involved in the New York City Middle School Initiative (1995-2000), formed a partnership with the New York State Department of Education and the then New York City Board of Education. The group's goal was to advocate for and help bring about better outcomes for young adolescents in the middle grades, beginning with developing awareness among educators in the city about the academic and social needs of young adolescents and the changes in schooling originally proposed by the Carnegie Corporation's *Turning Points* report (Carnegie Council on Adolescent Development, 1989). The resulting New York City Forum to Accelerate Middle-Grades Reform (NYC Forum) is made up of representatives from the city and state departments of education, intermediary education organizations, universities, and unions.

The NYC Forum was also inspired by the work and mission of the National Forum to Accelerate Middle-Grades Reform (www.mgforum.org) and by the idea that a partnership of committed organizations and individuals representing a broad constituency of education stakeholders could be more effective advocating collectively for the middle-grades improvement needed to stimulate and sustain reform over time. As of 2003, the NYC Forum formally affiliated with the National Forum and now participates in its semiannual meetings and subcommittees.

Since its formation, the NYC Forum, a volunteer-run organization, has achieved a number of significant accomplishments, including two citywide conferences focused on closing the racial gap in student achievement; broad distribution of a NYC Forum newsletter; and testimonials at state and city public hearings on middle-level education. Most recently, the NYC Forum was invited by the New York City Department of Education to cosponsor a symposium on middle-grades in September 2004.

Among the NYC Forum's priorities for future work in New York City are:

- Developing and disseminating a clear vision of effective middle-grades practices among educators, parents, and the public;
- Developing a partnership among key education stakeholders to move forward a middle-grades improvement agenda;
- Linking the work of improving the middle grades in the city to state policies, national research, and exemplary practices regarding such critical issues as equity, standards, and professional development;
- Making visible exemplary and promising middle-grade practices within districts and individual schools; help school leaders and regional supervisors learn from and adapt these good practices; and encourage and support data-based inquiry;
- Advocating for policies that will support the continual improvement of middle-grades education through public engagement campaigns and discussions with influential policy makers at all levels of the educational and political systems.

BELIEFS, PURPOSE, AND GOALS

The New York City Forum to Accelerate Middle-Grades Reform shares the belief of the National Forum to Accelerate Middle-Grades Reform that youth in the middle-grades are capable of learning and achieving at high levels in schools that are:

- *Academically excellent.* Such schools challenge all students to use their minds well, providing them with the curriculum, instruction, assessment, support, and time they need to meet rigorous academic standards.
- *Developmentally responsive.* Such schools create small learning communities of adults and students in which stable, close, and mutually respectful relationships support all students' intellectual, ethical, and social growth.
- *Socially equitable.* Such schools work to educate every child well and to overcome systematic variation in resources and outcomes related to race, class, gender, and ability.

The overarching purpose of the New York City Forum is to improve education for all NYC students in the middle-grades. To do this we propose to create and sustain a systemic support network for middle-grade educators, families, community members, policy-makers, and others interested in and concerned about teaching, learning, and achievement in the middle grades.

REFERENCES

Carnegie Council on Adolescent Development. (1989). *Turning points: preparing American youth for the 21st century* (The Report of the Task Force on Education of Young Adolescents). New York: Carnegie Corporation of New York.

New York State United Teachers. (2002). *Caught in the middle: Helping students avoid the middle-school trap.* Latham, New York: Author.

—Maud Abeel
Academy for Educational Development

NO CHILD LEFT BEHIND ACT OF 2001

The No Child Left Behind Act (NCLB) of 2001 reauthorized and significantly expanded the Elementary and Secondary Education Act, first enacted in 1965. Its most important title, Title I, has focused federal government attention and money on students in high poverty schools for 40 years. Congress made significant changes to the law in 1994, and the most recent changes of 2001 build on them dramatically. Congress also provided very large funding increases for the first 3 years of NCLB, though critics argue that NCLB funding remains inadequate. NCLB was the result of bipartisan leadership among five political leaders—President Bush, Senators Kennedy and Gregg and Representatives Boehner and Miller–and a large majority of the U.S. Congress who were clearly frustrated with inadequate learning among the groups of students that federal programs are supposed to help the most.

NCLB contains 10 titles and authorizes numerous programs both old and new. Most of the large NCLB programs target high poverty schools and are administered by state education agencies.

The titles and major parts of NCLB are as follows:

Title I: Improving the Academic Achievement of the Disadvantaged

Part A: Improving Basic Programs Operated by Local Education Agencies

Part B: Student Reading Skills Improvement Grants

Subpart 1:   Reading First

Subpart 2:   Early Reading First

Subpart 3:   William F. Goodling Even Start Literacy Programs

Subpart 4:   Improving Literacy Through School Libraries

Part C: Education of Migratory Children

Part D: Prevention and Intervention Programs For Children and Youth Who Are Neglected, Delinquent or At-Risk

Part F: Comprehensive School Reform

Title II: Preparing, Training, and Recruiting High Quality Teachers and Principals

Part A: Teacher and Principal Training and Recruiting Fund

Part B: Mathematics and Science Partnerships

Part D: Enhancing Education through Technology

Title III: Language Instruction for Limited English Proficient and Immigrant Students

Title IV: 21st Century Schools

Part A: Safe And Drug-Free Schools and Communities

Part B: 21st Century Community Learning Centers

Title V: Promoting Informed Parental Choice and Innovative Programs

Part A: Innovative Programs

Part B: Public Charter Schools

Subpart 1:   Charter School Programs

Subpart 2:   Credit Enhancement Initiatives To Assist Charter School Facility Acquisition, Construction, And Renovation

Subpart 3:   Voluntary Public School Choice Programs

Part C: Magnet Schools Assistance

Part D: Fund for the Improvement of Education (Numerous small appropriations)

Title VI: Flexibility and Accountability

Part A: Improving Academic Achievement

Subpart 1:   Accountability (Grants for State Assessment)

Part B: Rural Education Initiative

Title VII: Indian, Native Hawaiian, and Alaska Native Education

Title VIII: Impact Aid

Title IX: General Provisions

Federal funds for all these programs are available to states, districts, and schools only if they meet certain requirements. In other words, "strings are attached" to federal money. The federal government uses a "take it or leave it" approach that says "if you want our money, you must meet our requirements."

NCLB builds on the standards-based reforms that Congress enacted into both Goals 2000 and the Elementary and Secondary Education Act in 1994. It endorses the belief that all students can learn at high levels if they receive high-quality instruction and have access to a strong curriculum. The Act establishes a goal of proficiency for all students in core content areas (reading, math, and science) within 12 years, by 2014. NCLB assumes that the 1994 requirements have been met, i.e., state and local educators and community members have reached consensus on "what students should know and be able to do;" developed a set of specific and challenging academic content and student academic achievement standards, and put in place a rigorous curriculum, aligned with the standards, for *all* students.

The standards framework calls upon all those responsible for delivering public education--teachers, schools and district administrators, and state officials—to be held accountable for reaching a measurable level of performance and accomplishment. The NCLB toughens previous accountability as well as program design requirements. Following is a description of the major new requirements of the No Child Left Behind Act of 2001.

QUALITY PROGRAMS

Throughout NCLB there are calls for program activities based on "scientifically based research" and for "explanation[s] of why the activities are expected to improve student academic achievement." Educators must spend these federal dollars on strategies and implementing activities with demonstrable evidence of success. In various places, NCLB specifies the program approaches and activities that Congress believes are most likely to result in improved academic achievement for students in low performing schools. While they are not mandates, federal officials are likely to examine state and local plans with the expectation of finding several of them in use.

SCHOOL AND DISTRICT ACCOUNTABILITY FOR STUDENT PERFORMANCE

NCLB aspires to close achievement gaps by requiring that subgroups of racial/ethnic minorities, low-income students, students with disabilities, and students with limited English proficiency each achieve proficiency by 2014. It requires state testing in grades three through eight by the 2005-2006 school year, defines more precisely than previously the measure of "adequate yearly progress" for schools and districts, and sets forth required consequences for schools and districts identified as needing improvement.

HIGH QUALITY TEACHERS AND PARAPROFESSIONALS

The NCLB Act puts states, districts, and schools on notice to end the common practice of hiring and assigning the least qualified teachers and the weakest paraprofessionals to high poverty and minority schools. State plans must spell out affirmative steps to ensure that poor and minority students are "not taught at higher rates than other children by inexperienced, unqualified, or out-of field teachers" as well as the measures they will use to evaluate and publicly report progress with these steps.

Beginning with the 2002-2003 school year, all newly hired teachers in Title I schools had to be highly quali-

fied. By the end of the 2005-2006 school year, states must assure that in *every* school all teachers in core academic subjects are highly qualified. States must establish annual measurable objectives for district gains in the percentages of teachers who are highly qualified and participating in high quality professional development and must report on their progress. The NCLB Act defines what high quality teachers are. It defines a *high quality middle school teacher,* in part, as one who "holds at least a bachelor's degree and has demonstrated a high level of competency in each of the academic subjects in which the teacher teaches by" a rigorous state academic subject test or completing specific college study or credentialing in the subject.

As of January 2002, NCLB required that new paraprofessionals in Title I schools meet higher education standards. High school diplomas alone are insufficient. Paraprofessionals need at least two years of postsecondary education or must pass a rigorous state or local academic assessment of their knowledge and ability to assist with instruction of reading, writing, or math or readiness for these subjects. Current paraprofessionals must meet these requirements by 2006. Paraprofessionals who work as translators or with parental involvement are exempted. Acceptable assignments for Title I paraprofessionals are also spelled out in legislation for the first time. Principals must annually report in writing their school's compliance with this provision.

PROFESSIONAL DEVELOPMENT

NCLB redesigned the previous Title II Eisenhower program and the Class Size Reduction program to focus entirely on improving the quality of teaching in core content areas. Districts must direct their Title II funds to schools with the lowest proportion of highly qualified teachers, largest class sizes, or those identified as in need of improvement under Title I. No specific grade span or core academic subject gets priority. With the involvement of teachers, the district must conduct an assessment of needs for professional development and hiring. It must then outline what activities, from a long list of allowable ones, it will undertake and describe how they are based on scientifically based research, explain why and how they are expected to improve student academic achievement, and how they will help eliminate the achievement gap that separates low income and minority students from other students. They may enter into partnerships with nonprofit or for-profit organizations to help them.

The NCLB Act includes a one and one-half page definition of professional development which can be supported under this law. It says, among other things, that it is "high quality, sustained, intensive, and classroom-focused" and is "not 1-day or short-term workshops or conferences."

Finally, Title I also strengthens the focus on professional development by requiring a funding set-aside. Districts and schools identified as in need of improvement must use 10% of Title I funds on high quality professional development. The remaining Title I districts must use between 5% and 10% on such efforts.

PUBLIC REPORTING

States and districts must publish reports cards annually with information on each school. Disaggregated data on student achievement in each district and school must be publicly reported by race, ethnicity, gender, disability status, migrant status, English proficiency and poverty status. States and districts may report additional information as well.

NCLB requires every state to participate in the National Assessment of Educational Progress (NAEP), a random sample achievement test which is administered every 2 years in math and reading for Grades 4 and 8. Consequently, progress on state NAEP tests can be compared across the country.

States also must report publicly on the quality of teachers. Specifically, they have to report on the professional qualifications of teachers, the percentage of teachers on emergency or provisional credentials, and the percentage of classes not taught by highly qualified teachers, disaggregated by schools in the lowest and highest quartiles of poverty. Both states and districts must also report their progress in meeting measurable objectives to improve the percentage of high quality teachers and the percentage of teachers receiving high quality professional development.

REPORTS TO PARENTS

Title I schools must inform parents about their child's level of achievement on state tests in interpretive, descriptive, and diagnostic reports. They also must give timely notice to parents if their child has been assigned or taught for four or more consecutive weeks by a teacher who is not highly qualified.

Districts must notify parents that they may also request information about whether their child's classroom teachers have met state licensure standards or have emergency or provisional certification, the baccalaureate degree major and field of discipline of their graduate degree or certification, and whether their

child receives services from, and if so the qualifications of, paraprofessionals.

PARENT CHOICES

NCLB added two new accountability provisions that expand federal funding for parent choice. The first requires school districts to offer students who attend schools identified for improvement a choice to transfer, with free transportation, to another public school in the district that is not deemed low performing. The second is the provision of supplemental educational services, that is, free tutoring, by state-approved providers for low-income students in low performing schools.

HELP FOR LOW PERFORMING SCHOOLS

NCLB strengthens the obligation of states and districts to help Title I schools in need of improvement and provides additional money for such schools. States must set up systems of intensive and sustained assistance that use very knowledgeable school support teams and distinguished, successful educators and that give priority to the lowest performing schools. Districts must also help schoolwide Title I programs and schools in need of improvement.

BILINGUAL EDUCATION

NCLB redesigned Title III so that bilingual education and related funds are sent to states and districts based on their numbers of second language learners and immigrant students. No longer are they distributed by competitive grants from the federal level. Districts can decide for themselves the methods of instruction they want to use as long as they are tied to scientifically based research on teaching limited English proficient children and have been demonstrated to be effective. School officials must inform parents when their child needs special language instruction, offer them choices among programs, and allow them to remove their child from such programs.

AFTER SCHOOL PROGRAMS

NCLB renewed the 21st Century Learning Communities Program to support extended learning programs before and after school and during weekends and summers.

States operate a competitive grant program for local districts and community based applicants. They may choose to require local matching funds. Programs that receive funding must serve students, or their families, who primarily attend high poverty schools. Grants may be for 3 to 5 years, may support a wide variety of activities to improve academic performance, and must meet principles of effectiveness, that is, be based on objective data, performance measures, and scientifically based research.

—Cynthia G. Brown
Center for American Progress

P

PARENTS FOR PUBLIC SCHOOLS

Parents for Public Schools (PPS) began in the late 1980s with the efforts of 20 parents in Jackson, Mississippi, to recruit families to stay in or come back to public schools in the aftermath of desegregation. When the undertaking grew and 800 parents led the passage of the first local bond issue in 20 years, PPS received nationwide attention. As parents in other cities joined the work, the national Parents for Public Schools organization was formed in 1991.

PPS has become a network of local chapters working to create good public schools for all children in urban, mid-sized, and rural districts across the country. PPS engages parents as leaders in school improvement and builds support for parent involvement as a school improvement strategy. Chapters have no formal connection to the school district but are autonomous, community-based agents for systemic change. PPS encourages membership in and is compatible with the campus-focused work of parent-teacher associations and other such organizations.

The national office provides support for chapters and advocates for an approach to parent involvement based on leadership, action, and decision making. Technical assistance is provided to grassroots parents and chapter leaders through toll free telephone access, site visits for strategic planning, access to the national clearinghouse, website resources, and regional and national convenings. Chapters, in turn, provide a local framework for parents to collaborate across traditional dividing lines of race, class, neighborhood, language, and special interests. The national office also works in partnership with other influential organizations, creating a powerful presence to preserve public education and improve public schools.

Parents, the largest group of stakeholders in the public schools, do not have the same collective resources that teacher unions, school boards, business alliances, and others have to advocate for their interests. Often parent voices are not welcomed, and sometimes they are pitted against each other. PPS chapters harness the potential of parents by developing their capacity to speak with powerful voices, identify themselves as owners of public schools, and act as agents for change.

Through a variety of initiatives, PPS chapters take responsibility for being equal partners in the education process, hold schools accountable for educating every student well, and reinvent relationships between schools and families by building skills of both parents and educators. This type of parent involvement is critical to achieving a public education system with equitably distributed resources and opportunities, and where all students have equal access to quality education.

PPS parents come to the decision-making table—without waiting to be asked—with authority, talents, and a resolve for proactive problem solving. Parents of different races, income levels, and interests work together to identify district-wide problems, put these issues on the community's agenda, and work constructively as empowered peers with educators, policymakers, and community members to find solutions.

PPS understands that healthy public schools are necessary for a healthy community and recognizes public education as vital to a strong democracy. Parents for Public Schools acts because public schools must be good enough for every child, not just our own.

—Kris Kaiser Olson
Parents for Public Schools

R^3 = RESEARCH, RHETORIC, AND REALITY: A STUDY OF STUDIES

R^3=*Research, Rhetoric, and Reality: A Study of Studies* (Hough, 2003) is an important publication that identifies, examines, and classifies research studies conducted in the field of middle grades education over the past 12 years. This is an excellent resource for middle grades educators and scholars interested in a thorough review of available published research on issues related to the middle grades and the middle school concept.

The book begins with a preface by the author who explains that the book is designed to document what middle grades topics are being studied by researchers, where the research is being disseminated, when studies have been published, what types of research designs are being used, and what is the quality of the research. The author explains in chapter 1 that the methodology for studying the published middle grades research for the book was to examine all studies from 1991 to 2002 that address the research needs and suggested agenda laid out in *A 21st Century Research Agenda: Issues, Topics & Questions Guiding Inquiry Into Middle Level Theory and Practice* (National Middle School Association, 1997) and *This We Believe* (National Middle School Association, 1995).

The subsequent chapters of the book identify and classify the 3,717 studies that were found to examine middle grades topics per the methodology. Detailed tables and figures depict the scope of the studies, where they were published, and the type of research design they employed. In the summary of findings chapter, the author notes that a tremendous body of research on middle level topics is evident from this study. Other key findings are that the studies were primarily published in 13 different distribution types/sources, dissertations account for the largest portion of the research, and two-thirds of all the studies employ a qualitative methodology. The author identifies the areas of middle level education that have not been adequately addressed in research studies to include topics related to flexible schedules, adult advocates for students, school climate, health/wellness, and the impact of middle level education on student outcomes.

REFERENCES

Hough, D. L. (2003). R^3 = *Research, rhetoric, and reality: A study of studies*. Westerville, OH: National Middle School Association.

National Middle School Association. (1995). *This we believe: Developmentally responsive middle level schools*. Columbus, OH: Author.

National Middle School Association. (1997). *A 21st century research agenda: Issues, topics & questions guiding inquiry into middle level theory and practice*. Columbus, OH: Author.

—Nancy Flowers
CPRD, University of Illinois

RESEARCH AND RESOURCES IN SUPPORT OF THIS WE BELIEVE

Research and Resources in Support of This We Believe (Anfara et al., 2003) is an important and informative text for those interested in the education of young adolescents. This unique book addresses research and resources in a highly useful and organized manner. It is an invaluable and practical source for practitioners, researchers, and policy makers who need evidence to champion the programs and practices of middle level schools.

The book begins with a foreword by Sue Swaim who characterizes the book as a companion to the National Middle School Association's position statement, *This We Believe: Successful Schools for Young Adolescents* (NMSA, 2003). The authors specify the tool-like nature of the book and describe its organization. The book consists of five parts including (1) an introduction that sets the stage for the book; (2) research that concentrates on the middle school concept; (3) research that addresses programmatic components of *This We Believe*; (4) research that examines teachers and administrators; and (5) recommendations for future research.

Parts 1 and 2 establish a contextual framework for research in general and middle level research specifically. First, the "Introduction" offers an operational definition of research, provide an overview of recent middle level research, and call for additional research. Next, the authors summarize four of the seminal research studies on middle grades reform in Part 2, "Research that Looks at the Middle School Concept as an Integrated Reform Model." Following a brief description, the authors communicate the salient findings of each study.

The most expansive portion, "Research on This We Believe Programmatic Components," addresses research on the programmatic components of *This We Believe: Successful Schools for Young Adolescents* (NMSA, 2003). After identifying the components that successful schools provide for the education of young adolescents, the authors developed a section for each component. The programmatic components are (1) curriculum that is relevant, challenging, integrative, and exploratory; (2) multiple learning and teaching approaches that respond to their diversity; (3) assessment and evaluation programs that promote quality learning; (4) organizational structures that support meaningful relationship and learning; (5) school-wide efforts and policies that foster health, wellness, and safety; and (6) multifaceted guidance and support services. Each section includes a research summary, cited references, a set of annotated references, and a list of recommended resources. As a result, readers can locate the relevant research and resources for a specific programmatic component. Teachers and administrators, local and national policy makers, and researchers of middle level education should find Part 3 to be most useful.

"Courageous Leadership: Teachers and Administrators", the fourth part of the book, follows the orga-

nizational pattern of Part 3. Notably, Part 4 highlights the need for specialized preparation for educators before they begin work in middle level classrooms and schools. Professional preparation programs and state departments of education need to review these recent research findings and associated resources.

Research and Resources in Support of This We Believe concludes with "Directions for Future Research." The authors recommend large-scale longitudinal research, mixed-methods studies, research that examines multiple components, replication studies, experimental research, and the development of a national database. In summary, this book identifies key research and resources in support of middle level philosophy and practice.

REFERENCES

Anfara, V. A., Andrews, P. G., Hough, D. L., Mertens, S. B., Mizelle, N. B., & White, G. P. (2003). *Research and resources in support of This We Believe*. Westerville, OH: National Middle School Association.

National Middle School Association. (2003). *This we believe: Successful schools for young adolescents*. Westerville, OH: Author.

—Micki M. Caskey
Portland State University

RESEARCH IN MIDDLE LEVEL EDUCATION

Research in Middle Level Education Online (RMLE) is the National Middle School Association's official research journal. Currently published semi-annually by NMSA, RMLE is an international, peer-reviewed journal that accepts research syntheses, integrative reviews and interpretations of research literature, case studies, action-research, and data-based qualitative and quantitative studies. The readership includes middle level education professionals who work in schools, school districts, colleges, universities, foundations, agencies, and research centers throughout the United States and other countries. RMLE is acknowledged by the Middle Level Education Research (MLER) Special Interest Group (SIG) of the American Educational Research Association (AERA) as a preferred outlet for publication of middle level education research. RMLE is indexed and annotated by the ERIC Clearinghouse on Elementary and Early Childhood Education for the ERIC database and *Current Index to Journals in Education* Research.

NMSA's Research Committee serves as an advisory board for RMLE, and 57 college, university, and public, private, and parochial educators from across the United State, Canada, New Zealand, and countries in Europe review manuscripts submitted for consideration of publication. Approximately 95% of all manuscripts submitted are unsolicited; invited theme issues account for the remaining 5%. Contributors may be aware of and choose RMLE for consideration by reading various "calls" published twice a year in AERA's *Educational Researcher*. Organizations such as AERA, NASSP, NAESP, and the ERIC Clearinghouse are also sources of information for potential contributors. The review process requires that three fully "blinded" manuscripts be examined and rated by reviewers after an initial screening by the editor. The current acceptance rate is approximately 17%.

The first attempt to publish a research journal specifically targeted for middle school research occurred in 1977 when J. Howard Johnston and Glenn Markle coedited *The Middle School Research Annual*, published by the University of Wyoming. In 1980 NMSA began publishing a research annual, and in 1991 this became a semi-annual with a new name: *Research in Middle Level Education* (RMLE). The year 1994 marked a significant turning point for the publication of research that addressed middle school topics, issues, and questions. Three issues a year were published from 1994 to 1997 when RMLE then became a quarterly until 1999 (National Middle School Association, 1998). Beginning in 2000, the NMSA Board of Directors approved the publication of RMLE as an online journal to produce one or two issues per year.

As documented in $R^3 = Research, Rhetoric, and Reality: A Study of Studies$ (Hough, 2003), the RMLE editorial office in Springfield, Missouri, received 462 manuscripts for review from 1994 to 2002. Of these 116 were published, yielding a 25% acceptance rate. RMLE's contribution to middle level education research can, perhaps, best be examined by giving close scrutiny to the types of studies submitted for review, as well as those ultimately making their way to publication.

Research studies addressing teaching and learning approaches as detailed in NMSA's *21st Century Research* Agenda (NMSA, 1997), account for over 22% of all the submissions and 28% of published manuscripts. With almost 52% of all submissions being qualitative studies, approximately 37% quantitative, and 11% of mixed design, one can readily acknowledge a distribution of research orientations that mirrors educational research in general. The trend since 1997 has been for middle school researchers to utilize qualitative approaches at a significantly greater rate than quantitative and/or mixed designs, and this phenomenon is reflected in RMLE's publications. Qualitative studies published in RMLE have increased by almost 30% from 1994 to 2004. The research design of choice has been descriptive 51.5%, with action research accounting for 20.3%, correlational 14.9%, and historical 13.2%. Survey research accounts for 28.6% of all the research, and "scholarship" represents 17.5%, followed by case studies (14.5%), interviews (14.1%), unobtrusive methods (8.9%), observations (7.8%), focus groups (6.5%), and meta analysis (2.2%). Most RMLE submissions have been applied research (42.2%); another 19.7% can be classified as theoretical or synthesized works. These latter types of research published in RMLE have increased by over 42% from 1994 to 2004. Research and development accounts for 16.2%, evaluations (14.3%), and basic research (7.6%). Just over 9% of all the research studies submitted and published utilized experimental or quasi-experimental designs; approximately 91% were non-experimental (Hough, 2003).

In sum, RMLE's contribution to middle school research has been significant. From 1996 to 1999, well over 100 manuscripts were submitted for review, and these were among the most sophisticated in terms of design, methodology, data analysis, and contribution to the field's existing body of knowledge. The year 1997 was the "high water" mark for RMLE, as the journal's quarterly publication was most widely recognized as the premier publication for middle school research. RMLE continues to be an important outlet for peer reviewed research and continues to support NMSA's research agenda by promoting high quality research validated by scholars in the field who carefully review each study submitted. For research to of value, it must be widely disseminated, carefully critiqued, and (when appropriate) put into practice. RMLE strives to be the foremost mechanism to achieve these goals.

REFERENCES

Hough, D. (2003). $R^3 = Research, rhetoric, and reality: A study of studies$. Westerville, OH: National Middle School Association.

National Middle School Association. (1998). *Because we believed: A quarter-century of service to young adolescents 1973-1998*. Columbus, OH: Author.

National Middle School Association. (1997). *A 21st century research agenda: Issues, topics & questions guiding inquiry into middle level theory & practice*. Columbus, OH: Author.

—David Hough
Missouri State University

RURAL MIDDLE SCHOOLS

Middle level schools in rural America face many of the same challenges that confront their counterparts in inner-city, urban, and suburban schools. The No Child Left Behind Act of 2001 does not discriminate among school types, geographic location, grade span configurations, names and labels, shibboleth, or any other characteristic peculiar to any specific school. Even so, many middle school programs, policies, and practices that have evolved over the past 2 decades or so have taken on a different complexion, have been implemented differently, (and in a different context) and have developed into noticeably different components than those in middle level schools located in more urban areas of the country. While recognizing that some commonalities exist among all middle level schools such as similar goals and accountability mechanisms (not to mention the young adolescent learner whose developmental characteristics transcend all other demographic variables), one will also discover that rural middle schools often share more in common among themselves than they do with inner-city, urban, and suburban schools in terms of structures, organization, and curriculum.

Researchers have documented perceived cultural differences that separate rural and urban schools and, even more specifically, those that typify rural middle level schools and the relationship between economic and social issues as these schools move from community-based to consolidated school systems (e.g., De Young, Howley, & Theobald, 1995a, 1995b; Pardini, 2002). In addition, the relationship between middle level programs, policies, and practices and student achievement specific to rural communities has been compared and found to account for some differences across different types of rural middle level schools (Hough & Sills-Briegel, 1997). However, few have attempted to quantify these differences in terms of direct relationships between rural middle level education and other variables. Those who (most recently) have tackled this issue have accessed one of the national data bases established and maintained by the United States Department of Education's National Center for Educational Statistics (nces.ed.gov/). The National Assessment of Educational Progress (NAEP), National Educational Longitudinal Study (NELS), and Schools and Staffing Survey (SASS) data bases allow for a number of important questions to be examined, including rural versus urban demographics, grade spans, and student outcomes (Juvonen, Le, Kaganoff, Augustine, & Constant, 2004). High on the list of current comparisons is the relationship between academic achievement and varying types of middle level school grade span configurations across different geographic locations, including those in rural, urban, and suburban settings. While the Lee and Smith (1993) study has been frequently cited for their analyses of the NELS data in which they report no definitive conclusions, more recently researchers have applied regression techniques, structural equation models, and hierarchical linear models to the NELS and NAEP data sets to examine variables such as socioeconomic status, gender, ethnicity, and school settings/community populations and their relationships to middle level schooling factors. Wenglinsky (2004), for example, found statistically significant differences in mathematics achievement as measured by NAEP across different types of "middle schools." Unfortunately, the USDE national data bases utilize different samples and cannot be linked for aggregated cross-comparisons. Moreover, they do not identify a common (or uncommon) definition of "middle school" nor a middle school curriculum that would allow for the type of extensive examination needed to produce valid and reliable comparisons across rural and urban middle level schools, so their usefulness is limited.

In addition to information on rural middle level schools contained in the USDE national data bases, a number of individual data collection efforts have been undertaken to examine specific school structures and programmatic/curricular questions. These inquiries often examine more narrowly defined questions, such as the relationship between school size and achievement or the number of vertical transitions from one school to the next (see for example, Alspaugh, 1998a, 1998b, 1999, 2000; Wren, 2003). Other issues common to the study of middle level education often focus on educators' commitment to young adolescents, assessment/evaluation, and classroom practice (varied teaching and learning approaches and curricular issues); and approximately 3%-6% of all research on middle level education is experimental or quasi-experimental (Hough, 2003a, 2003b). In addition, only infrequently do researchers disaggregate the data in these studies by school setting and focus on rural issues. The *Journal of Research in Rural Education* is, perhaps, the foremost outlet for studies that focus attention in this area.

Prior to the last decade of the last millennium, a few individual data collection efforts (many at the state level) were made, and findings were aggregated with national data from the United States Department of Education (USDE) National Center for Education Statistics (NCES) Common Core of Data (CCD) to examine levels of middle school program implemen-

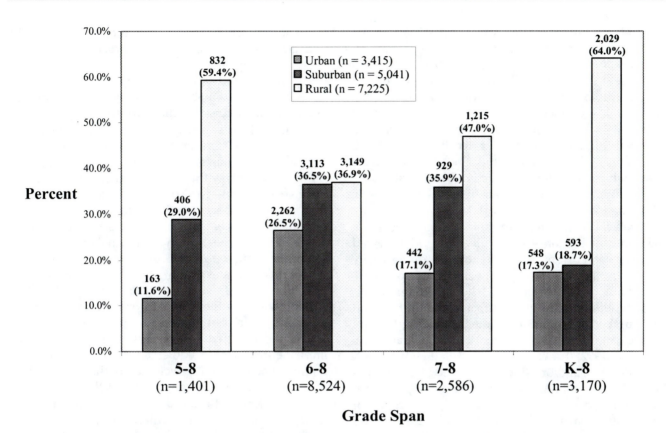

Figure 1.   Number and (percent) of middle level schools by grade span and location (*n* = 15,681) (Source: National Center for Education Statistics, Common Core of Data, 2002-03).

tation across different grade span configurations (e.g., Hough, 1991a, 1991b). Figure 1 shows these national data from the USDE NCES CCD as of December 2003, reflecting the number and percent of middle level schools by four different grade span configurations by school setting (i.e., urban, suburban, and rural).

Of the 27,000+ schools across the United States that contain a seventh grade, for instance, roughly 60% can be found in schools with grade spans of K-8, 5-8, 6-8, and 7-8 (Juvonen et al., 2004). Add 7-9 and 7-12 to these and another 15% can be identified (National Center for Education Statistics, 2003). One quarter of the rest of the seventh grades can be found in any one of over 50 different grade span configurations (National Center for Education Statistics, 2003). Rural schools account for the greatest percentage of K-8 and 5-8 schools in the United States, 64% and 59.4%, respectively. Middle level schools configured as Grades 6-8 are more common in urban and suburban settings. These differences are somewhat less dramatic, however, when one considers that rural middle level schools, in general, outnumber their urban counterparts by more than two to one and include almost a third more schools than are found in subur-

ban settings (National Center for Education Statistics, 2003).

Counting the number of schools across the county that have changed their grade span configurations (and, sometimes, names) has been an ongoing effort for many scholars of the middle school education movement since the mid 1960s (see Alexander & McEwin, 1989; Hough, 1991a, 1991b; McEwin, Dickinson, & Jenkins, 1996; Juvonen et al., 2004; Valentine, Clark, Irvin, Keefe, & Melton, 1993; Valentine, Clark, Nickerson, & Keefe, 1981). These studies demonstrate rapid growth in the number of 6-8 middle schools "benchmarked" circa 1966, then again in the mid-1980s. The number of K-8 schools dwindled significantly during this period as did K-6, 7-8, and 7-9 schools, while 6-8 schools grew significantly, especially throughout the last half of the 1980s, many in rural areas throughout the United States. Some attribute these changes in grade span configurations to the NMSA philosophy and position paper first published in 1982 under the title *This We Believe* and then refashioned and reprinted in 1995 under the title *This We Believe: Developmentally Responsive Middle Level Schools*. Any impact these position papers had on middle level schooling, including those in rural America, is purely speculation, however. The last half of the 1990s has seen a renewed interest in the K-8 school structure, surprisingly, not just in rural America but in urban settings as well (Connolly, Yakimowski-Srebnick, & Russo, 2002; Education World, 2004a, 2004b). Look (2001) identified a number of large, urban school districts, including Baltimore, Boston, Cincinnati, Cleveland, Denver, Detroit, Harrisburg, Hartford, Palm Beach, Philadelphia, and Phoenix, that have either returned to the K-8 structure or were studying the feasibility of doing so in an effort to improve schooling for young adolescents.

While an accelerated interest in comparative grade span studies has once again given rise to renewed inquiry, the current focus is now more narrowly defined as the relationship between grade span configurations in a variety of school settings (most broadly defined as rural and urban communities) and any number of student outcomes, including but not limited to student achievement. Wihry, Coladarci, and Meadow (1992), for example, found that eighth graders in K-8, K-9, and/or 3-8 schools scored higher on the Maine Educational Assessment than did eighth graders attending schools configured as 6-8 schools or other grade spans. Tucker and Andrada (1997) found similar results at the sixth-grade level on the Connecticut Mastery Test. These studies do not disaggregate data by rural and urban settings, however, and as Paglin and Fager (1997) note, school size accounts for much of this variance, and school size, ipso facto, is quite often related to grade configurations that are often related to geographic location tied to student populations.

The recent return to K-8 grade spans in both rural and urban settings is an apparent irony that lends credence to the current middle school philosophy as articulated in *This We Believe: Successful Schools for Young Adolescents* (NMSA, 2003; Hough, 2003b). That is, when middle school programs, policies, and practices are implemented at high levels in Grades 6-8 or 5-8 within the K-8 grade configuration, what I labeled "elemiddle" schools back in 1991 (Hough, 1991a, 1991b), a number of positive student outcomes, including but not limited to academic achievement, are often found. Many of these elemiddle schools are located in rural America (Hough & Sills-Briegel, 1997), and urban schools that are striving to improve student outcomes such as academic achievement and searching for programs, policies, and practices believed to achieve these goals are now turning to elemiddles as examples from which implementation strategies that undergird the middle school philosophy can be drawn. Still, researchers struggle to determine whether the "causal" variable is grade span,

curriculum, school size, community/parent/family engagement, location, demographics, or some combination. Clearly, not all rural middle level schools (regardless of grade span configuration) are achieving the same results, many with similar demographics and other distinguishing characteristics per the above.

Even so, in many respects, some rural elemiddle schools are now leading the way in terms of creating smaller communities of learners, sometimes organized as "schools within schools" in an effort to effect positive outcomes for students. Research indicates that middle level schools (both rural and urban) that provide for fewer and more effective transitions across school types, often with smaller class sizes, sometimes subsequently experience lower high school dropout rates and higher achievement in post-transition years (Alspaugh, 1998a, 1998b, 1999, 2000; Alspaugh & Harding, 1995). In prior research, similar schools in rural settings had been found to contain teachers committed to "promising pedagogy" and implementing young adolescent middle school programs, practices and policies at higher levels than other school types (Hough, 1991a, 1991b).

Middle level education in rural America may be taking a more proactive direction in the future. Because the federal mandate of No Child Left Behind requires every school system to continually assess student learning and reach high academic standards, cultural preferences in rural communities may necessarily yield to whatever programs, policies, and practices are found to produce desired, in fact "required," outcome(s). This may bode well for the middle school philosophy (NMSA, 2003; Hough, 2003b) that promotes effective programs, polices, and practices to achieve these goals, regardless of specific school types or settings. While the future can only be speculation, one could conclude that rural middle level schools might soon lead the way in terms of exemplifying positive student outcomes that can be achieved through high levels of implementation of the middle school philosophy.

References

Alexander, W., & McEwin, K. (1989). *Schools in the middle: Status and progress.* Columbus, OH: National Middle School Association.

Alspaugh, J. W. (1998a). Achievement loss associated with the transition to middle school and high school. *Journal of Educational Research, 92*(1), 20-25.

Alspaugh, J. W. (1998b). The relationship of school-to-school transitions and school size to high school dropout rates. *High School Journal, 81*(3), 154-160.

Alspaugh, J. W. (1999, April). *The interaction effect of transition grade to high school with gender and grade level upon dropout rates.* Paper presented at the annual meeting of the American Educational Research Association, Montréal, Canada. (ERIC ED431066)

Alspaugh, J. W. (2000). The effect of transition grade to high school, gender, and grade level upon dropout rates. *American Secondary Education, 29*(1), 2-9.

Alspaugh, J. W., & Harting, R. D. (1995). The transition effect of school grade-level organization on student achievement. *Journal of Research and Development in Education, 28*(3), 145-149.

Connolly, F., Yakimowski-Srebnick, M. E., & Russo, C. V. (2002). An examination of K-5, 6-8 versus K-8 grade configurations. *Educational Research Service Spectrum, Spring,* 28-37.

De Young, A. J., Howley, C., & Theobald, P. (1995a). The cultural contradictions of middle schooling for rural community survival. *Journal of Research in Rural Education, 11,* 24-35.

De Young, A. J., Howley, C., & Theobald, P. (1995 b) Revisiting and extending the argument: A rejoinder to Wiles and Lipsitz. *Journal of Research in Rural Education, 11,*130-133.

Education World. (2004a). Is the time right for "elemiddles"? Retrieved January 7, 2004, from http://www. education-world.com/a_admin/admin/admin324.shtml

Education World. (2004b). K-8 schools: an idea for the new millennium? Retrieved January 7, 2004, from http://www.education-world.com/a_admin/admin/admin115.shtml

Hough, D. L. (1991a). *Middle level organization: A curriculum policy analysis.* Paper presented at the annual meeting of the National Association of Secondary School Principals, Orlando, FL. (ERIC ED331157)

Hough, D. L. (1991b, April). *A review of middle level organization.* Paper presented at the annual meeting of the American Educational Research Association, Chicago, IL.

Hough, D. L. (2003a). R^3 = *research, rhetoric, and reality: A study of studies.* Westerville, OH: National Middle School Association.

Hough, D. L. (2003b, Winter). The case for the elemiddle school. *Middle Matters,* 1-3.

Hough, D. L., & Sills-Briegel, T. (1997). Student achievement and middle level programs, policies, and practices in rural America: The case of community-based versus consolidated organizations. *Journal of Research in Rural Education, 13,* 64-70.

Juvonen, J., Le, V., Kaganoff, T. Augustine, C., & Constant, L. (2004). *Focus on the wonder years: Challenges facing the American middle school.* Santa Monica, CA: RAND.

Lee, V. E., & Smith, J. B. (1993). The effects of school restructuring on the achievement and engagement of middle-grade students. *Sociology in Education, 66*(3), 164-187.

Look, K. (2001). *The great K-8 debate. Philadelphia public schools notebook.* Retrieved June 10, 2004, from http://www.philaedfund.org/notebook/TheGreatK8Debate.htm

McEwin, C. K., Dickinson, T. S., & Jenkins, D. M. (1996). *America's middle schools: Practices and progress-a 25 year per-*

spective. Columbus, OH: National Middle School Association.

National Center for Education Statistics, Common Core Data. (2003). *Public Elementary/Secondary School Universe Survey Data, 2002-03* [Data file]. Available from Core of Common Data Web site, http://nces.ed.gov/ccd/

National Middle School Association. (1982). *This we believe.* Columbus, OH: Author.

National Middle School Association. (1995). *This we believe: Developmentally responsive middle schools.* Columbus, OH: Author.

National Middle School Association. (2003). *This we believe: Successful schools for young adolescents.* Westerville, OH: Author.

Paglin, C., & Fager J. (1997). *Grade configuration: Who goes where?* Retrieved January 10, 2004, from: http://www.nwrel.org/request/july97/grade.pdf

Pardini, P. (2002). Research on K-8: Limited and inconclusive. *School Administrator* web edition, Retrieved January 7, 2004, from http://www.aasa.org/publications/sa/2002_03/pardini_research.htm

Tucker, C. G., & Andrada, G. N. (1997, April). *Accountability works: Analysis of performance by grade span of school.* Paper presented at the annual meeting of the American Educational Research Association, Chicago, IL. (ERIC ED411278)

Valentine, J. W., Clark, D. C., Nickerson, N. C., & Keefe, J. W. (1981). *The middle level principalship: A survey of middle level principals and programs* (Vol. 1). Reston, VA: National Association of Secondary School Principals.

Valentine, J. W., Clark, D. C., Irvin, J. L., Keefe, J. W., & Melton, G. (1993). *Leadership in middle level education: Vol. I. A national survey of middle level leaders and schools.* Reston, VA: National Association of Secondary School Principals.

Wenglinsky, H. (2004). The link between instructional practice and the racial achievement gap in middle schools. *Research in Middle Level Online, 28*(1). Retrieved June 23, 2005, from http://www.nmsa.org/research/rmle/summer04/pdf/link_between_1204.pdf

Wihry, D. F., Coladarci, T., & Meadow, C. (1992). Grade span and eighth-grade academic achievement: Evidence from a predominantly rural state. *Journal of Research in Rural Education, 8*(2), 58-70.

Wren, S. D. (2003). *The effect of grade span configuration and school-to-school transition on student achievement.* Michigan Educational Assessment Program Report. (ERIC ED479332)

—David L. Hough
—Katherine B. Harmon
—Bethany K. Black
Missouri State University

—Vicki L. Schmitt
University of Kansas

S

SCHEDULING: FLEXIBLE INTERDISCIPLINARY BLOCK SCHEDULES

The organizational structure of the school day reflects what a school values most. It is the configuration of the schedule that allows a school to fulfill its mission, programmatic goals, and purpose. Historically, a typical junior high or high school day was 45-minute periods for 180 days totaling 120 hours, with six-, seven-, or eight-period days. This schedule reflected one of the key roles of education at the turn of the century, which was to prepare workers for the compartmentalized factory model. While there were brief attempts to reorganize the school day in the late 1960s and early 1970s, the most significant cracking of the rigid 45-minute schedule prescribed by the Carnegie Unit began at the middle school in the mid 1990s. Based on research regarding teaching and learning to meet the development needs of young adolescents a case was made for longer blocks of flexible teaching time (George & Alexander, 1993). Flexible block scheduling facilitates the transition for young adolescents from the self-contained elementary school structure to the traditional departmentalized structure of the high school and supports the programmatic structures that most effectively meet the developmental needs of young adolescents.

Decades of research on the ideal middle level principles and practices such as adult advocates for every student, small learning communities, interdisciplinary or integrated teaching, exploratory courses, and common planning time for teachers is most effectively supported in the middle school by flexible scheduling patterns (Viadero, 1996). According to Hackmann and Valentine, "the schedule must support the assignment of both students and teachers into team structures that promote the delivery of an interdisciplinary curriculum" (1998, p. 3).

The concept of "flexible scheduling" (Alexander, 1987; George & Alexander, 1993; George, Stevenson, Thomason, & Beane, 1992; Jackson & Davis, 2000; Lipsitz, 1984; Wiles & Bondi, 1993) is a core component of a true middle school. It determines how many students are in each class and how many teachers each student sees in a day/term/year. The schedule contributes to a positive learning environment as it determines how often students and teachers change classes; how fragmented or cohesive the school day is; or how much flexibility teachers have to meet the needs of each student.

A "flexible organizational structure" as advocated by the National Middle School Association (2003) provides teachers and students with extended periods of time to engage in inquiry-based integrated learning and to create caring relationships that allow young adolescents to feel connected and significant. A flexible schedule also supports a variation in schedules to specifically meet every student's learning needs and interests and provides opportunities for teachers to plan and work together.

Before making decisions about the structure of the school day, the school community must examine their beliefs about numerous issues:

- number of students in a class;
- number of students a teacher can know well in a term/year;
- students' abilities to cope developmentally with multiple teachers;
- number of teachers on an interdisciplinary team;
- number of specialized teachers;

- types of encore and/or exploratory classes and the rotation of such classes; and
- how time and monetary resources should be allocated

There are an infinite variety of scheduling formats, which a school can adapt to meet its needs. However, most schedules begin from one of four basic designs (Rettig & Canady, 2000). These four designs include: a modular schedule, an alternate-day schedule, the four-block schedule, and the five-block schedule. Whichever scheduling format a school chooses and adapts should be assessed by whether it meets the beliefs held by the school community and meets the developmental needs of young adolescents. For example, does the schedule provide a core teacher-student ratio between 50 to 120 students depending on whether teams are two, three, four, or five person teams (Jackson & Davis, 2000); does approximately 75% of a student's day focus on core subjects (Rettig & Canady, 2000); does each student feel connected to an adult and part of a small community of learners? "Flexibility through the use of block scheduling may, therefore, address one of the basic premises of instruction; we do not all learn in the same way or in the same amount of time" (Wunderlich, Robertson, & Valentine, 2000, p. 4)

MODULAR SCHEDULING

A modular schedule is built from small increments of time, usually 20 or 30-minute blocks. The shortest period of time used during the day defines the length of time for each module. Frequently, lunch or an advisory period is the shortest segment of time. If the advisor/advisee period is 20 minutes, then the entire day may be built using 20 minute segments. Once the length of a module is determined, then the total number of minutes in the school day is divided by the number of minutes in the module to determine the number of modules available. In a school day with 420 minutes there are 20, 20-minute modules. Figure 1 shows a possible format for a 420-minute school day built on 20-minute modules in a school with two teams at each of three grade levels. School begins at 7:30 and the first lunch begins at 10:10 a.m. Students have 10 minutes before advisories to go to their lockers and 10 minutes are distributed during the day for passing time and going to lockers at the end of the day.

Similar formats can be created with 30 minute blocks. Lunches for each grade are assigned first and physical education, electives and exploratories are added second. These teachers are frequently itiner-

ants and their schedules must coordinate with other schools. This format allows the elective time to also be used for extended time for students that may need additional time to master specific skills. How the "Core Time" is used is determined by the interdisciplinary team.

ALTERNATE DAY

The alternate-day schedule provides another plan for large blocks of time with students responsible for only two or three core subjects each day. The schedule is based on a traditional six-, seven-, or eight-period day. Each period is doubled and scheduled on alternate days. This pattern is frequently referred to as an A/B or Odd/Even plan. Figure 2 illustrates a six-period format for an A/B plan at a school with two teams at each of two grade levels. The school day is 330 minutes long with 20 minutes for lunch and 10 minutes for passing distributed throughout the day.

In this variation of the alternate-day plan the following week will begin on B day. Another variation of this plan is to alternate days Monday through Thursday with all classes meeting on Friday for shorter periods. By teaching all classes on one day of the week, there is less likelihood that a three or four-day weekend will cause some subjects to have a long gap between classes. One period is usually split in half to allow for physical education and electives or math and language arts may be taught four of the five days with each having one day with an extended period of time. Because most schools do not have sufficient cafeteria space for all students one grade usually will have a split block with lunch in the middle.

There are several benefits from this model. There are fewer class changes and time normally used for passing is added to instructional time. Because students spend less time passing, behavior problems are reduced. Teachers have extended blocks of time that support instructional strategies such as readers' and writers' workshop, science labs, or Socratic seminars. Students are able to concentrate on fewer core subjects per day and are less likely to have multiple tests or projects due on the same day. Itinerant teachers' schedules may be simplified so that they may be at one school for an entire day. Students miss fewer classes when they miss a day and they have fewer teachers to see about make-up work (Rettig & Canady, 2000).

FOUR-BLOCK SCHEDULE

Administratively, the four-block schedule, which assigns three blocks to core academic subjects, language arts/reading, mathematics, science or social

Team	6-A	6-B	7-A	7-B	8-A	8-B	Phys Ed /Explore	Electives
Module (20 min)								
1	Advisor/Advisee (20 Minutes)							
2	Core Time	Core Time	Core Time	Core Time	Core Time	Core Time	Plan	Plan
3								
4								
5								
6			Electives	Electives	Team Plan Phys Ed/ Explore	Team Plan Phys Ed/ Explore	Teams 8A & 8B	Teams 7A & 7B
7								
8	Electives	Electives	Core Time	Core Time				Teams 6A & 6B
9								
10	Lunch	Lunch			Core Time	Core Time	Lunch	Plan
11								
12	Core Time	Core Time	Lunch	Lunch			Plan	Lunch
13								
14			Team Plan Phys Ed/ Explore	Team Plan Phys Ed/ Explore	Lunch	Lunch	Teams 7A & 7B	Plan
15								
16					Core Time	Core Time		
17								
18	Team Plan Phys Ed/ Explore	Team Plan Phys Ed/ Explore	Core Time	Core Time			Teams 6A & 6B	
19								
20					Electives	Electives		Teams 8A & 8B
21								

Figure 1.

Days		A (Monday)				B (Tuesday)				A (Wednesday)				B(Thursday)				A (Friday)			
		7-1	7-2	8-1	8-2	7-1	7-2	8-1	8-2	7-1	7-2	8-1	8-2	7-1	7-2	8-1	8-2	7-1	7-2	8-1	8-2
B	I	1	2	1	2	2	1	2	1	1	2	1	2	2	1	2	1	1	2	1	2
L	II	3	4	3	4	4	3	4	3	3	4	3	4	4	3	4	3	3	4	3	4
O																						
C								Lunch														
K	III	5	6	5	6	6	5	6	5	5	6	5	6	6	5	6	5	5	6	5	6
S																						

Figure 2.

studies, and the fourth block to physical education and electives, is the most basic design. In a four-block schedule at the middle level, science is frequently taught one semester and social studies the other semester. However, with the increase in yearly standardized testing, many districts are alternating science and social studies in an alternate-day structure or teaching both daily for shorter periods of time. The four-block is also known as a 4x4, four period day, or Block 4 (Rettig & Canady, 2000).

A typical schedule for one student at a school with 420 minutes per day might begin with 90 minutes of language arts, followed by 90 minutes of mathematics, 30 minutes for lunch, 20 minutes for advisory, then a 100-minute block for electives that is divided into 50 minutes for physical education and 50 minutes for music, followed by another 90 minutes for science/ social studies.

The four-block schedule will work for a variety of team configurations. On a two-person team with 50-60 students, one teacher may teach a block of humanities and the other teacher will be responsible for math and science. However, it also is easy for a two-person team to adjust their time to fit the needs of students and demands of the curriculum. Teachers on a three-person team are each responsible for three blocks. One teacher may teach science and social studies, which allows the teacher to configure the best strategy for rotating and/or integrating the two content areas. Figure 3 illustrates a design for a four-person team who share the same 120 students. The school day is 420 minutes.

In this plan each class will miss one core subject every day. This design allows students to engage in all core subjects for a full year and also allows students to be responsible for only three subjects per day. An alternative model might be for teachers C & D to each

Blocks	Teacher A Language Arts	Teacher B Math	Teacher C Social Studies	Teacher D Science	Phys Ed /Electives
Advisory 7:30-7:50					Plan time/ Serve other
Block I 7:50-9:20	Class 1	Class 2	Class 3	Class 4	grades or
Block II 9:20-10:50	Class 2	Class 3	Class 4	Class 1	teams
Lunch (30 minutes)					
Block III 11:20-1:00	Phys Ed/ Electives	Electives/ Phys Ed	Phys Ed/ Electives	Electives/ Phys Ed	Core Teachers team and individual planning time
Block IV 1:00-2:30	Class 3	Class 4	Class 1	Class 2	

Student classes for each teacher are designated a 1, 2, 3, 4

Figure 3.

teach two classes one semester and then switch the second semester.

FIVE-BLOCK SCHEDULE

The five-block schedule is similar to the four-block but offers more flexibility and is ideal in a middle school that offers foreign language or wants to offer more extended learning. In the five–block format, each class period is usually seventy minutes long. For teachers that have not taught in a large block of time before, the shorter 70 minutes is an easier to manage. The drawback is that teachers and students are responsible for more classes all year.

CONCLUSION

Scheduling is an important tool that facilitates the implementation of the principles and practices that meet the developmental needs of every adolescent. The schedule, "promotes a particular philosophy about the way teachers and students interact, and either creates opportunity for improved service to students or creates hurdles that inhibit the instructional program" (Wunderlich et al., 2000, p. 3). A flexible block schedule serves the instructional needs of young adolescents, planning time for teachers, and sufficient time to engage in integrated learning experiences.

REFERENCES

Alexander, W. M. (1987). Toward school in the middle: Progress and problems. *Journal of Curriculum and Supervision, 2*(4), 314-329.

George, P. S., & Alexander, W. M. (1993). *The exemplary middle school* (2nd ed.) Fort Worth, TX: Harcourt Brace.

George, P. S., Stevenson, C., Thomason, J., & Beane, J. (1992). *The middle school—and beyond.* Alexandria, VA: Association for Curriculum Development and Supervision.

Hackmann, D. G., & Valentine, J. W. (1998) Designing and effective middle level schedule. *Middle School Journal, 29*(5), 3-13.

Jackson, A. W., & Davis, G. A. (2000). *Turning points 2000: Educating adolescents in the 21st century.* New York: Teachers College Press.

Lipsitz, J. (1984). *Successful schools for young adolescents.* New Brunswick, NJ: Transaction Books.

National Middle School Association. (2003). *This we believe: Successful schools for young adolescents.* Westerville, OH: Author.

Rettig, M. D., & Canady, R. L., (2000). *Scheduling strategies for middle schools.* Larchmont, NY: Eye on Education.

Viadero, D. (1996, May 29). Middle school gains over 25 years chronicled. *Education Week,* 1.

Wiles, J., & Bondi, J. (Eds.) (1993). *The essential middle school* (2nd ed.). New York: Macmillan.

Wunderlich, K., Robertson, T., & Valentine, J. (2000). *What types of block schedule benefit middle school students?* Summary 17. Retrieved May 26, 2005, from http://www.nmsa.org/research/ressum17.htm

—Peggy H. Burke
Central Michigan University

SCHOOL CULTURE

DEFINING SCHOOL CULTURE

School culture is a complex term, which has been commonly equated with "climate," "ethos," and "saga" (Deal & Peterson, 1999). As Prosser (1999) aptly states, it is not surprising that there is no agreement on the definition or meaning of the terms associated with school culture—it is a term too often assumed as needing little explanation.

The roots of the idea of "school culture" stem from numerous sources, some conflicting, over the past 30 or more years. Some educational experts say the notion of schools having a culture derives from the corporate workplace, which provided a model for schools to create a more efficient and stable learning environment (Stolp, 1994). Other experts see the notion of school culture as deriving from different theoretical camps, such as organizational theory, anthropology, sociology, and various methodological branches like ethnography and holistic studies.

As many experts have stated, "Culture is the integrated pattern of human behavior that includes thought, speech, action, artifacts, and depends on man's capacity for learning and transmitting knowledge to succeeding generations" (Deal, 1993, p. 6, quoting Webster's Dictionary). A noted philosopher, Clifford Geertz (1973) defined "culture" as "historically transmitted patterns of meaning" (as cited in Stolp, 1994, p. 1)

Notions of schools having these "historically transmitted patterns" are not recent. As early as 1932, Waller noted the "complex rituals of personal relationships," within a school and described school culture as:

[A] set of folkways, mores, and irrational sanctions, a moral code based upon them. There are games [or politics], which are sublimated wars, teams, and an elaborate set of ceremonies concerning them. (p. 96)

More recently, school culture lies in the "commonly held beliefs of teachers, students and principals" (Heckman, 1993, p. 266), while Deal and Peterson (1990) described school culture as reflecting "deep themes and patterns of core values, common beliefs, and regular traditions that develop over time" (p. 7).

IMPLICIT AND EXPLICIT ASPECTS OF SCHOOL CULTURE

Several experts agree with the notion of school culture as having what Prosser (1999) describes as both "concrete" and "theoretical" aspects—or what Stolp (1994) describes as "implicit" and "explicit" aspects. According to Prosser (1999):

On a theoretical level, school culture is an unseen and unobservable force behind school activities, a unifying theme that provides meaning, direction, and mobilization for school members ... in its concrete form, school culture is sustained through artifacts, human behavior, language, and action. (p.14)

Similarly, Deal and Peterson (1990) describe school culture as the "stable, underlying social meanings" often existing "outside conscious awareness and underneath everyday life" that shape "everything inside the school" (p. 7).

In brief, school culture can be defined as encompassing all aspects of the school environment—the symbols, customs, values, morals, beliefs, rituals, language and knowledge of the people within the school—teachers, administrators, other staff, and students, as well as the families and community adults connected to the school in some way.

WHO SHAPES A SCHOOL'S CULTURE?

The above-mentioned groups— teachers, administrators, other staff, and students, as well as families and other community members—all have a role in shaping a school's culture. Webb and Vulliamy (1996) put it succinctly: "Cultures lie within the control of those who participate in the system. [For example], leaders and the members together make their own school" (p. 456).

In this scenario, the principal can be seen as the main actor, with the role of reinforcing and molding school values through his/her behavior and promotion of routine activities. However, the principal does not act alone:

Principals cannot manipulate or reshape culture through sheer force or intimidation. A culture must be transformed through incremental steps that reinforce new values and new beliefs about quality and excellence. (Deal & Peterson, 1990, p. 91)

SCHOOL CULTURE IS MEASURABLE

However varied the notions of school culture, there is agreement that school culture has a number of measurable, concrete dimensions. These include relationships within the school community; perception of school goals and ideology; school organizational structure; academic challenges; curriculum and instructional practice; and decision making structure, etc. Studies have shown that school culture can have a direct relationship with teacher attitudes and student outcomes. For instance, Yin Cheong Cheng (1993) found schools with stronger school cultures had better motivated teachers. Stolp (1994) reasoned that implementation of a clear mission statement, shared vision and schoolwide goals would promote increased student achievement; and one study of tenth graders from 820 public schools in Chicago determined that students in schools with stronger cultures were more motivated to learn (Fyans & Maehr, 1990).

However, while there are many measurable aspects of a school's culture, it is, on the whole, very difficult to change because, as Prosser (1999) points out, a school's culture is shaped by values that are "deeply embedded and taken-for-granted" (p. 9). Waller (1932) put it bluntly, maintaining that in any school, 'There are traditions, and traditionalists waging their world-old battle against innovators" (p. 103). Most people would probably agree that a school culture can only be effectively changed when a clear vision is in place and buy-in has occurred among all/most of the actors.

REFERENCES

Cheng, Y. C. (1993). Profiles of organizational culture and effective schools. *School Effectiveness and School Improvement*, 4(2), 85-110.

Deal, T. E. (1993). The culture of schools. In M. Sashkin & H. J. Walberg (Eds.), *Educational leadership and school culture* (pp. 3-18). Berkeley, CA: McCutchan.

Deal, T. E., & Kennedy, A. (1982). *Corporate cultures: the rites and rituals of corporate life*. Reading, MA: Addison-Wesley.

Deal, T. E., & Peterson, K. D. (1990). *The principal's role in shaping school culture*. Washington, DC: Office of Educational Research and Improvement.

Fyans, L. J., Jr., & Maehr, M. (1990). *School culture, student ethnicity, and motivation*. Urbana, IL: The National Center for School Leadership.

Geertz, C. (1973). *The interpretation of cultures*. New York: Basic Books.

Hargreaves, D. H. (1995). School culture, school effectiveness and school improvement. *School Effectiveness and School Improvement, 6*(1), 23-46.

Heckman, P. E. (1993). School restructuring in practice: Reckoning with the culture of school. *International Journal of Educational Reform, 2*(3), 263-71.

Hoy, W. K., & Feldman, J. A. (1999). Organizational health profiles for high schools. In H. Jerome Freiberg (Ed.), *School climate: Measuring, improving and sustaining healthy learning environments* (pp. 84-102). Philadelphia, PA: Falmer Press.

Meyer, J., & Rowan, B. (1983). The structure of educational organizations. In J. V. Baldridge & T. E. Deal. (Eds.), *The dynamics of organizational change in education* (pp. 60-87). Berkeley, CA: McCutchan.

Owens, R. (1987). *Organizational behavior in education* (3rd ed.). Upper Saddle River, NJ: Prentice Hall.

Prosser, J. (1999). The evolution of school culture research. In J. Prosser (Ed.), *School culture* (pp. 1-14). London: Paul Chapman.

Stolp, S. (1994). *Leadership for school culture*. Eric Digest. Retrieved June 29, 2004, from the Clearinghouse on Educational Policy and Management. College of Education, University of Oregon.

Waller, W. (1932). *The sociology of teaching*. New York: Wiley.

Webb, R., & Vulliamy, G. (1996). Impact on ERA on primary school management. *British Educational Research Journal, 22*(4), 441-458.

—Lea Williams Rose
Academy for Educational Development

SCHOOL SIZE

Ever since 1647 when the Massachusetts legislative body passed the landmark Old Deluder Satan Act, school size has been a consideration in American education. To ensure sufficient literacy among the population, that most famous educational act required towns of 50 or more households to start what, in effect, was a public elementary school, while towns of 100 families were required to establish a grammar (high) school that would prepare youth for the university (Mayer, 1964). As communities in New England worked to provide schools, the size problem was limited to gathering enough pupils to constitute a school. The one-room school soon became the symbol of public education.

By 1900 educators saw the need to merge small districts in order to provide adequate facilities and faculty for schools. The major consolidation movement was soon underway, and by mid-century the number of school districts had decreased markedly while the size of schools increased proportionately. Soon the yellow school bus replaced the one-room school as the common symbol of American commitment to universal public education.

School size has varied with population shifts and other factors unrelated to educational advocacy. Rarely are schools planned and built to fulfill someone's belief in what is the best size, educationally speaking. Existing buildings, demography, costs, and other factors usually determine school size. Consolidation made it possible for junior and senior high schools to be large enough to offer more extensive courses, group students to meet varied needs, provide special facilities such as science labs, offer student activities and sports, and stock a library. Schools in the booming cities and suburbs, however, were becoming very large and impersonal, a condition that has plagued middle level and high schools in recent decades.

As schools became more impersonal and anonymous because of their size, the gap between adults and youth in their out of school time widened. Parents and other adults spend less and less time in the company of youth. Family homes and the neighborhood no longer provide a safe haven where young people can spend afternoon and early evening hours. Young adolescents, to an alarming degree, are on their own for several hours every weekday in a world full of dangerous and readily available temptations. No previous generation of adolescents has had so little supervision and guidance from adults or been influenced more by their peers. While not sought, the resulting need for the middle school to serve "in loco parentis" cannot be denied.

Middle level educators question the ability of large middle schools to be developmentally responsive. Can schools of over 1,000 be the protective cocoon these emerging butterflies need? Can the desired sense of family be maintained in an institution that size? Can the personal-social needs of young adolescents be met in such an atmosphere? Although educators recognize fully that the overall quality of schools is more closely related to the program offered, the leadership, and the organizational plan, the size of a school is still a factor to be considered.

RECOMMENDED SIZES OF MIDDLE LEVEL SCHOOLS

In the literature, there have been several recommendations on the right size for middle level schools. In 1962 a NASSP position statement on junior high school education stated, "Enrollments of approximately 750 to 1,000 pupils provide satisfactory departmentalization and specialist teachers and class groups which challenge the varying levels of ability and exploratory interests" (p. 5). The justifications given may no longer be seen as best for middle schools, but an advocacy for fairly large schools was typical for that time. However, in the book *Modern Education for the Junior High School Years* (1961), Van Til, Vars, and Lounsbury took this position:

> Schools housing the junior high school years should be large enough to provide special facilities and services, but not so large as to destroy the students' sense of identification with a group. Schools with an enrollment of much over 600 might well experiment with the "little school" plan in which a number of homeroom groups are assigned to a particular wing of the building. The students have most of their classes with teachers in that area; they come to know their teachers and fellow little school students more intimately. (p. 504)

Thirty-two years later a NASSP study (Valentine Clark, Irvin, Keefe, & Melton, 1993) reported the opinions of administrators on the optimum size for a middle level school. "Forty-one percent of the middle level administrators in this study indicated that optimal enrollment for a middle level school was in the range of 400-599 students, and 27 percent preferred a school of 600-799 pupils" (pp. 76-77).

In the highly regarded *Turning Points 2000* Jackson and Davis (2000) made these assertions: "At the middle grades level, we believe from our observations over the past decade that no school should exceed 600 students; ideally, a school should serve an even smaller number of young adolescents" (p. 123).

Following their report on a national survey, McEwin, Dickinson, and Jenkins (2003) offered this recommendation: "When possible the school populations of middle schools should be kept in the 400-800 range. When larger schools are unavoidable, great care should be taken to establish "schools within a school" plans to ensure that young adolescents are not placed in schools that are impersonal and ineffective" (p. 47).

ACTUAL SIZES OF MIDDLE LEVEL SCHOOLS

Reports on the sizes of middle level schools, while limited, reveal considerable consensus with recommended sizes. In 1968, 45% of the schools reporting in the earliest status study of middle schools fell in the 401-800 range. Thirty-nine percent reported enrollments of less than 400 with only 16% exceeding 800. The next national survey conducted in 1988 revealed some but not marked shifting in the percentages over the 20-year period. Schools of less than 400 dropped to 34% while schools in the 401-800 range increased to

52%, but somewhat surprisingly schools of over 800 dropped from 16% to 14%. Then, just 5 years later, a 1993 national survey using the same enrollment ranges as in the previous studies found the number of over 800 middle schools had jumped from 14% to 30 percent with middle schools of less than 400 dropping from 34% to 22% (McEwin, Dickinson, & Jenkins, 1996, pp. 15-16). The size of middle schools reflect America's burgeoning population, and very big middle schools have become a fact of life.

SMALLER IS BETTER

As a generalization, it is hard to argue with this one relative to school size—*smaller is better*. Although most of the research has been conducted at the elementary and high school levels, a growing body of research points to the benefits of smallness in the middle school. What research says largely confirms what logic and common sense would conclude about the advantages of having smaller schools. Commonly cited benefits include these:

- Improved student achievement
- Higher rates of attendance
- Students are known as individuals better
- School climate is improved
- Increased parental involvement
- Greater participation by students in activities and clubs
- Reduced discipline problems and tardiness
- Improved attitudes about school
- Higher faculty morale
- Greater degree of teacher collaboration
- Safer

Such benefits have led to major efforts to break down large schools in several of our biggest cities. Deborah Meier (1996), a key figure in such reformings in New York City, in touting the importance of having small schools made this claim:

> Small schools come as close to being a panacea for America's educational ills as we're likely to get. Smallness is a prerequisite for the climate and culture that we need to develop the habits of the heart and the mind essential to a democracy. Such a culture emerges from the authentic relationships built on face-to-face conversations by people engaged in common work and common work standards. (p. 12)

Studies also indicate the positive effects of smallness are greatest on minorities and students lower in socio-economic status (Farber, 1998; Galletti, 1998; George & Lounsbury, 2000).

The National Forum to Accelerate Middle-Grades Reform (2004) in a policy statement makes a strong case for small learning communities and small schools. Tying the low level of student achievement that has been so frequently reported in the media to the fact that too many middle grades students attend large, impersonal schools, where they are not purposefully engaged in learning and lack meaningful relationships with adults, the Forum details several advantages and cites supporting research. The paper recommends creation of small middle grades schools, but when that is not feasible, large middle grade schools should be broken down into smaller schools and learning communities.

The few negatives of smallness pale in comparison to the positives. Those who seek to have honors or Advanced Placement sections and several levels of math offerings would see smallness as a limitation. But when it comes to the middle school concept with its emphasis on student-teacher relationships and the individualization of instruction, there is little doubt that, where possible, middle schools of 600 or less are preferable.

THE MIDDLE SCHOOL'S RESPONSE TO BIG SCHOOLS

The middle school concept supports, and indeed has pioneered a number of strategies or organizational structures that can alleviate the effects of bigness. First, of course, is the signature component of middle schools—*teaming.* By assigning to a small group of teachers a contingent of students they teach in common and for whom they assume other responsibilities, teams can be small learning communities. Second, the concept of *advisory* helps to counter bigness by providing an advisor for 12 or so pupils who are scheduled to meet together on some regular basis. Third, the *schools-within-a-school* notion, an old idea, is gaining prominence in middle schools. Used successfully in many middle schools for decades, it provides a continuity of caring and a sense of smallness in large middle schools. Fourth, *looping,* often practiced in elementary schools, has now become common at the middle level. This proven student-teacher progression plan keeps a team of students and teachers together for more than one year. Five, *multiage grouping* has proven to be especially effective at the middle level. All of these successful strategies are detailed in this encyclopedia in separate entries. Their importance in the movement warrants examination.

CONCLUSION

Across the history of American education school size has been a factor in determining a school's ability to fulfill accepted educational objectives. From early concerns about having enough pupils to employ teachers and mount an adequate program to more recent concerns about the negative effects of schools growing too big, educators have recognized that size does, indeed, matter. Particularly at the middle level, because of the many responsibilities that fall on the middle level school, largeness has become a growing concern. In response, middle schools have employed strategies to ensure meaningful long-term student-teacher relationships and the desired sense of belongingness.

REFERENCES

Committee on Junior High School Education. (1962). What do we believe about grades, desirable size, appropriate location, and facilities? *NASSP Bulletin, 46*(276), 67-84.

Farber, P. (1998, March/April). Small schools work best for disadvantaged students. *The Harvard Education Letter,* 6-8.

Galletti, S. (1998, September/October). Small schools create communities with results. *Schools in the Middle, 8*(1), 24-27.

George, P., & Lounsbury, J. (2000). *Making big schools feel small: Multiage grouping, looping, and schools-within-a-school.* Westerville, OH: National Middle School Association.

Jackson, A., & Davis, G. (2000). *Turning points 2000: Educating adolescents in the 21st century.* New York: Teachers College Press.

Mayer, F. (1964). *American ideas and education.* Columbus, OH: Charles E. Merrill Books.

McEwin, C. K., Dickinson, T., & Jenkins, D. (1996). *America's middle schools: Practices and Progress. A 25 year perspective.* Columbus, OH: National Middle School Association.

McEwin, C. K., Dickinson, T., & Jenkins, D. (2003). *America's middle schools in the new century: Status and progress.* Westerville, OH: National Middle School Association.

Meier, D. (1996). The big benefits of smallness. *Educational Leadership, 51*(1), 12-15.

National Forum to Accelerate Middle-Grades Reform. (2004, June). *Small schools and small learning communities, Policy Statement,* Issue 4.

Valentine, J., Clark, D., Irvin, J., Keefe, J., & Melton, G. (1993). *Leadership in middle level education: Vol. I. A national survey.* Reston, VA: National Association of Secondary School Principals.

Van Til, W., Vars, G., & Lounsbury, J. (1961). *Modern education for the junior high school years.* Indianapolis, IN: Bobbs-Merrill.

—John H. Lounsbury
Georgia College and State University

SCHOOLS TO WATCH

Recognizing the importance of accelerating middle grades reform at the school and classroom level, the National Forum to Accelerate Middle-Grades Reform (the Forum) established a Schools to Watch Committee in 1998. The Forum was aware that there are many schools across the country providing students a curriculum that stresses academic rigor while also meeting the needs of young adolescents. Schools to Watch has provided a vehicle for recognizing and honoring schools on a sustained trajectory of growth and improvement, and for providing a wide range of models from which other schools can learn. The members of the National Forum understand that academic excellence, developmental responsiveness, and social equity must ALL be present and in balance to have a truly effective, high performing middle level school for all students. The Forum found many schools where academic excellence was at the forefront, and test scores were high; however, when these scores were disaggregated, there was often another tale. Many schools with high test scores also had high achievement gaps between groups of students. Schools to Watch have learned that the highest level of achievement occurs when all students are challenged with a rigorous curriculum in an environment that supports their growth and development.

The National Forum developed 37 criteria in the key areas of academic excellence, developmental responsiveness, social equity, and organizational support, and began a pilot program to identify "Schools to Watch." After an exhaustive national search, four schools—one in Kentucky, two in Illinois, and one in Texas were identified in 1999 and 2000. The practices, programs, and policies at these schools were carefully documented and used to further develop the program.

To infuse the criteria into schools and classrooms around the country, impact middle grades education policy, and accelerate the rate of middle-grades reform, the members of the National Forum expanded the program to the state level. In 2002, three states—California, Georgia, and North Carolina—were selected as the first Schools to Watch states. Each state had a long history of successful middle grades reform, and brought to the program an established partnership of middle-grades stakeholders—including departments of education, middle school associations, principal and curriculum leadership groups, and educators and administrators from both the middle grades and university level. These experts became state-level Schools to Watch teams, who came together to screen applications submitted

by schools. Schools had to provide a wealth of supporting detail to show that they were indeed meeting the criteria in a consistent manner. Schools that appeared to be on a sustained trajectory of improvement in all areas were selected by the state teams for rigorous site visits to ascertain if they were, in fact, truly meeting the criteria. In 2003, the first 10 Schools to Watch were identified in these states.

Following a successful roll-out, the call went out to bring more states into the fold. Colorado, Illinois, Kentucky, and Virginia joined in 2003. During the 2003-2004 school year, 26 more schools were recognized in the seven states—bringing the total to 40 nationwide. By 2004, New York and Ohio had also become Schools to Watch states.

Through the interest generated by each of the state's programs, thousands of school leaders, teachers, parents, and community members have learned about the criteria and seen the impact that schools have when addressing high performance in terms of not just academic excellence, but also in terms of meeting students' needs and of social equity. Many schools have used the criteria to assess their performance in a broad way. These schools have reported that using the criteria to examine their practices and as part of their professional development plan has led to many rich and fruitful conversations about school improvement, and, more importantly, these conversations have led to action.

The Schools to Watch project continues to grow and gather momentum. Through public awareness created by the attendance of thousands at local Schools to Watch celebrations, television, radio, newspaper, and Internet coverage of recognized schools, and attendance at presentations made at state and national conferences, the program has helped shape the middle grades conversation at the local, state and national level.

Schools that have been identified as "Schools to Watch" are all very different places. Some are urban and others are rural. Some have several thousand students, while some have several hundred. Some are in high-wealth areas; others are in high-poverty areas. Some are from very homogeneous communities; others have great racial, ethnic, and socioeconomic diversity. While many are middle schools containing grades 6-8, there are a number of grade configurations among the schools based upon the needs of the individual communities and their students. Despite their differences, Schools to Watch share in common the fact that they are meeting the challenges of middle grades education in ways that foster a community where academic excellence, developmental responsiveness, and social equity thrive. Information about the individual Schools to watch can be found on the Forum's Web site, www.mgforum.org .

THE SCHOOLS TO WATCH CRITERIA

Academic Excellence: High-performing schools with middle grades are academically excellent. They challenge all students to use their minds well.

1. All students are expected to meet high academic standards. Teachers supply students with exemplars of high quality work that meets the performance standard. Students revise their work based on feedback until they meet or exceed the performance standard.
2. Curriculum, instruction, and assessment are aligned with high standards. They provide a coherent vision for what students should know and be able to do. The curriculum is rigorous and non-repetitive; it moves forward substantially as students' progress through the middle grades.
3. The curriculum emphasizes deep understanding of important concepts, development of essential skills, and the ability to apply what one has learned to real-world problems. By making connections across the disciplines, the curriculum helps reinforce important concepts.
4. Instructional strategies include a variety of challenging and engaging activities that are clearly related to the concepts and skills being taught.
5. Teachers use a variety of methods to assess student performance (e.g., exhibitions, projects, performance tasks) and maintain a collection of student work. Students learn how to assess their own and others' work against the performance standards.
6. The school provides students time to meet rigorous academic standards. Flexible scheduling enables students to engage in extended projects, hands-on experiences, and inquiry-based learning. Most class time is devoted to learning and applying knowledge or skills rather than classroom management and discipline.
7. Students have the supports they need to meet rigorous academic standards. They have multiple opportunities to succeed and extra help as needed.
8. The adults in the school have opportunities to plan, select, and engage in professional development aligned with nationally recognized standards. They have regular opportunities to work with their colleagues to deepen their knowledge and improve their practice. They collaborate in making decisions about rigorous curriculum and effective instructional methods. They discuss student work as a means of enhancing their own practice.

Developmental Responsiveness: High-performing schools with middle grades are sensitive to the unique developmental challenges of early adolescence.

1. The school creates a personalized environment that supports each student's intellectual, ethical, social, and physical development. The school groups adults and students in small learning communities characterized by stable, close, and mutually respectful relationships.
2. The school provides access to comprehensive services to foster healthy physical, social, emotional, and intellectual development.
3. Teachers use a wide variety of instructional strategies to foster curiosity, exploration, creativity, and the development of social skills.
4. The curriculum is both socially significant and relevant to the personal interests of young adolescents.
5. Teachers make connections across disciplines to help reinforce important concepts and address real-world problems.
6. The school provides multiple opportunities for students to explore a rich variety of topics and interests in order to develop their identity, discover and demonstrate their own competence, and plan for their future.
7. Students have opportunities for voice—posing questions, reflecting on experiences, developing rubrics, and participating in decisions.
8. The school develops alliances with families to enhance and support the well-being of their children. It involves families as partners in their children's education, keeping them informed, involving them in their children's learning, and assuring participation in decision-making.
9. The school provides students with opportunities to develop citizenship skills, uses the community as a classroom, and engages the community in providing resources and support.
10. The school provides age-appropriate co-curricular activities.

Social Equity: High-performing schools with middle grades are socially equitable, democratic, and fair. They provide every student with high-quality teachers, resources, learning opportunities, and supports. They keep positive options open for all students.

1. Faculty and administrators expect high-quality work from all students and are committed to helping each student produce it. Evidence of this commitment includes tutoring, mentoring, special adaptations, and other supports.
2. Students may use many and varied approaches to achieve and demonstrate competence and mastery of standards.
3. The school continually adapts curriculum, instruction, assessment, and scheduling to meet its students' diverse and changing needs.
4. All students have equal access to valued knowledge in all school classes and activities.
5. Students have on-going opportunities to learn about and appreciate their own and others' cultures. The school values knowledge from the diverse cultures represented in the school and our nation.
6. Each child's voice is heard, acknowledged, and respected.
7. The school welcomes and encourages the active participation of all its families.
8. The school's reward system demonstrates that it values diversity, civility, service, and democratic citizenship.
9. The faculty is culturally and linguistically diverse.
10. The school's suspension rate is low and reflects the diversity of the student population.

Organizational Structures and Processes: High-performing schools with middle grades are learning organizations that establish norms, structures, and organizational arrangements to support and sustain their trajectory toward excellence.

1. A shared vision of what a high-performing school is and does drives every facet of school change. Shared and sustained leadership propels the school forward and preserves its institutional memory and purpose.
2. Someone in the school has the responsibility and authority to hold the school-improvement enterprise together, including day-to-day know-how, coordination, strategic planning, and communication.
3. The school is a community of practice in which learning, experimentation, and reflection are the norm. Expectations of continuous improvement permeate the school. The school devotes resources to ensure that teachers have time and opportunity to reflect on their classroom practice and learn from one another. At school everyone's job is to learn.

4. The school devotes resources to content-rich professional development, which is connected to reaching and sustaining the school vision. Professional development is intensive, of high quality, and ongoing.
5. The school is not an island unto itself. It draws upon others' experience, research, and wisdom; it enters into relationships such as networks and community partnerships that benefit students' and teachers' development and learning.
6. The school holds itself accountable for its students' success rather than blaming others for its shortcomings. The school collects, analyzes, and uses data as a basis for making decisions. The school grapples with school-generated evaluation data to identify areas for more extensive and intensive improvement. It delineates benchmarks, and insists upon evidence and results. The school intentionally and explicitly reconsiders its vision and practices when data call them into question.
7. Key people possess and cultivate the collective will to persevere and overcome barriers, believing it is their business to produce increased achievement and enhanced development for all students.
8. The school works with colleges and universities to recruit, prepare, and mentor novice and experienced teachers. It insists on having teachers who promote young adolescents' intellectual, social, emotional, physical, and ethical growth. It recruits a faculty that is culturally and linguistically diverse.
9. The school includes families and community members in setting and supporting the school's trajectory toward high performance. The school informs families and community members about its goals for students and students' responsibility for meeting them. It engages all stakeholders in ongoing and reflective conversation, consensus building, and decision making about governance to promote school improvement

—John A. Harrison
Southern Forum to Accelerate Middle-Grades Reform

—Joan S. Lipsitz
MDC, Inc.

Barbara S. DeHart
Lilly Endowment Inc.

SCHOOL-WITHIN-SCHOOL ORGANIZATION

WHAT IS THE SCHOOL-WITHIN-SCHOOL ORGANIZATION?

An illustrative example. Creekland Middle School (CMS), in suburban Atlanta, Georgia, is one of America's largest middle schools, with 3,200 students, 274 staff members, 38 portables, 70 busses, and 141 students on Ritalin! With that many students in Grades 6-8 housed in one place, it might also have been one of the most unproductive situations in all of middle level education. Founding principal Joan Akin, however, engineered a successful effort to make this big school feel small. Using the school–within-school (SWS) process, Akin organized CMS into five smaller schools within the school, called learning communities at CMS, of 600-650 students, each with an equal share of sixth, seventh, and eighth graders. Each SWS (or community, or house) has its own assistant principal, counselor, and clerk in that area of the building; each house has its own computer lab.

In each house at CMS, teachers and students are organized into interdisciplinary teams: small teams or two teachers in the sixth grade, two, three, and four teacher teams in the seventh, and four-teacher teams in the eighth grades. Each house, and classes within each house, is grouped heterogeneously; gifted students are not all placed in one house or team within a house. Even siblings are placed in the same house, for family convenience, and for the family feeling it brings to the house. A long block schedule of 80-minute periods facilitates the sort of instruction that helps students feel known by their teachers. The combination of these organizational factors (houses, small teams, heterogeneous grouping, block schedule) makes CMS feel much, much smaller that it is. The SWS process is a key element.

A definition. In the SWS process, traditional grade level wings, or departmentalized areas, are replaced. In SWS, the larger school is, instead, divided into sub-units of the school often called houses, villages, pods, communities, or neighborhoods, each containing interdisciplinary teams from each grade level in the school.

Unlike looping situations where students and teachers move together from one year to the next, in a SWS organization each team of students moves to a new team of teachers, within their house, each year. Teachers maintain their grade level team membership within the house, and often teach the same subject at the same grade level each year. Teachers on the sixth grade team in a house, for example, would continue to be the sixth grade team in that house year after year, working with a new group of students each year. But (and this is an important distinction) instead of having their students move with all the school's other rising seventh graders to a seventh grade wing, in SWS, each part of the building is a microcosm of the school as a whole.

WAKULLA MIDDLE SCHOOL: A PRIME EXAMPLE

Wakulla Middle School (WMS), in Crawfordville, Florida, is an exemplary illustration of the SWS process, especially since the school's record of academic achievement places it among the most highly achieving schools in the state. Educators at WMS have been grouping students and teachers this way, as of 2004, for just about 30 years. Figure One, a diagram of the floor plan, illustrates how the student population of approximately 750 students in Grades 6-8 is deployed for teaching and learning. C House contains teams of teachers and students in each of the sixth, seventh, and eighth grades; so do A, T, and S houses. Students spend 3 years in one house, but not with just one set of teachers. Each house has all three grade levels, in smaller teams that would have been the case if the teachers and students had simply been placed in grade levels wings, one for each grade.

The placement of teams in houses, as it is done at Wakulla, means that incoming sixth graders quickly learn not only who their teachers are for the current year, but also who they will be for the next year and the next. Knowing this, do the sixth graders in S House (for example) pay closer attention to what the seventh and eighth grader teachers in that house say to them about their behavior? They certainly do. Do the seventh graders in a house care what sixth and eighth grade teachers think? Yes they do, because they had them last year or will have them next year. Students move within the house, from one year to the next.

Teachers can, likewise, accurately forecast who will be in their classes one or two years hence. Teachers in a house also see, daily, students they taught last year, and/or students they will teach next year. Teachers on sixth and seventh grade teams care about the behavior of eighth graders. Sixth grade teachers care what eighth grade teachers, in their house, have to say about student behavior in the hallways. Eighth grade students care what their former sixth grade teachers think of them. Seventh graders have to look both ways on everything. It is a 3-year positive structure without either the intensity or the complexity of the looping process.

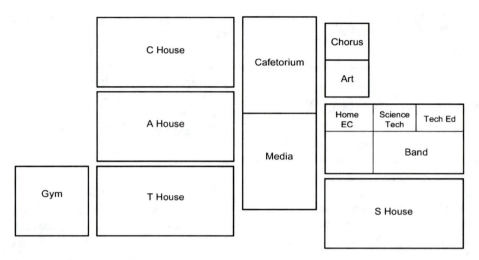

Figure 1. Wakulla Middle School.

WHY ARE MANY MIDDLE SCHOOLS ORGANIZED THIS WAY?

All of the reasons for the popularity of the SWS process relate to the power of long term relationships in human lives, in every institution in our society. Schools serving young adolescents are no different: Middle school students profit from high quality, enduring, relationships with teachers as a means of providing social support for the learning process. High academic achievement, the school's primary purpose, is more effectively attained when a balance is achieved between two essential factors: "academic press" and "school social support" (Lee & Smith, 1999). One effective method for enhancing both academic press and the school social support that students need, middle school educators have learned, is through the use of the SWS process.

Keeping the above examples in mind, here are some of the ways in which the factors of academic press and social support are enhanced in a SWS format:

1. *Sense of community.* As the old poster says, "True friendship is a plant of slow growth." When teachers and students can stay together in the same house for 2, 3, or more years, even though teams change from year to year, the opportunity for the development of a robust sense of community grows rapidly. While passing through some of the most turbulent years of their lives, young adolescents require stable, strong relationships with teachers, and with their peers, relationships that are enhanced by the multiple years the SWS provides.

2. *Behavior management and classroom discipline.* Effective classroom management depends on the quality of the relationships between teachers and their students. Classroom management is also more positive in circumstances where the relationships between teachers and parents are positive and prolonged. When parents, students, and teachers are connected, even loosely over a period of years, classroom discipline problems decline.

3. *Peer relationships.* Experience suggests that positive peer modeling and peer teaching are more likely to occur in school settings where several ages and grade levels are combined in the SWS process. Cross-age friendships may develop more readily. Harassment of younger students, ironically, seems to be less of a problem when students from several grade levels interact regularly than when they encounter each other only on the bus going to and from school.

4. *Parental involvement.* In an SWS setting, parents know, on the first day of their child's sixth grade year, where their student will be for three years, and who the child's teachers will be for the whole time they are at the middle school. In a sense, the school is "downsized" by two-thirds, and with it the potential intimidation that can be present when parents interact with professionals with masters degrees. A SWS organization can present a much more human scale for parents, especially nonprofessional parents, to deal with.

5. *Teacher individualized perception of students.* In SWS, teachers no longer face the prospect of (in the worst scenarios) of dealing with 150 students per day, 300 a year, and up to 900 over a period of three years. In such circumstances, the chances of a teacher being able to see students

as individuals may be slight. Instead, teachers interact with a very small subgroup of the school, sometimes only 50 to 75 per year on two-teacher and three-teacher teams. In an SWS program, teachers may interact with as few a 150 students over a period of 3 years, instead of 900. With such reductions in human numbers, teachers are more likely to get to know students, and their needs, in individual ways.

6. *Synergism.* One of the most important advantages of the alternative grouping strategies, like SWS, is that they act in a synergistic fashion, strengthening the other programs with which they interact. Advisor-advisee programs and the interdisciplinary team are both much more effective, for example, in combination with a grouping plan that extends the life of the team or the advisory group. When teacher and students remain in the same house for two, three, or four years, all of the goals of the teacher advisory process become much more realizable. The interdisciplinary team, and all of the advantages connected with it, can be significantly enhanced when teachers from different grade levels, but in the same house, work together over a period of three years. Without this built-in increase in supportive interpersonal structure, these programs achieve significantly less than they might with the multiplier effect of the SWS process utilized.

7. *Curriculum alignment.* In a period of standards-based reform, attention to the scope and sequence of the curriculum assumes a vital importance. Teachers must know the "map" of their curriculum, paying attention to issues like content duplication or instances where content, for one reason or another, may be getting much less attention than desired. Curriculum pacing, difficult to map in a large school, can be done much more readily in each house, where teachers from the same content area interact even on a daily basis, without being in a departmentalized framework. In the SWS system, curriculum alignment becomes much less difficult, "downsized" in the same way other procedures can be.

8. *Teacher investment in students.* Everyone wants teachers to treat students in personal ways; we want teachers to be willing to "go the extra mile" and "bend over backwards" for their students. When relationships last longer than one year, as in SWS, teachers are encouraged to feel like all of the students in the house are "ours." The teachers' willingness to invest extra time and energy to ensure the success of students rises when their relationships with those students last for more than 1 year.

9. *Diagnosis and prescription.* In an SWS setting, only one-third of the students are totally new each year. Within a house, teachers can share mountains of information and suggestions that can improve learning of whole groups of students. At the end of an academic year, and again at the beginning of a new one, seventh grade teachers can easily and frequently confer with the team of teachers in their house who taught the incoming students as sixth graders the previous year. Review of previous work can be much more efficient. Planning for remediation can be much more accurate. Enrichment can involve less duplication. The curriculum and the needs of teams of students can be much more effectively matched.

10. *Continuous progress.* In a house, records of student progress can be kept in common planning areas for all teams. Counselors can serve the same students, in one house, year after year, instead of assigning students alphabetically or by grade level. Students can begin their middle school studies at whatever point their academic achievement indicates and continue virtually uninterrupted for the next 3 years.

11. *Ease of implementation.* Unlike other alternatives to traditional organization, like looping and multiage grouping, the SWS process has few, if any, real disadvantages. This makes the SWS strategy appealing to virtually everyone involved—parents, students, and teachers. Teachers can teach what they have always taught, the way they have always taught it, if it meets the needs of students to do so. Parents are not apprehensive about too frequent interaction between older and younger students, and do not fear their children having a poor teacher for more than one year. All it really takes to change from grade level wings to the house format; everything else can stay the same. Few innovations deliver as many positives at so little "cost."

REFERENCE

Lee, V., & Smith, J. (1999). Social support and achievement for young adolescents in Chicago: The role of school academic press. *American Educational Research Journal, 36*(4), 907-945.

—Paul S. George
The University of Florida

SELF-ESTEEM/SELF-CONCEPT

INTRODUCTION

Cognitive learning is hard-won by someone whose life is in affective disarray. At the very heart of those affective concerns is the development of clear self-concept and positive self-esteem. These dimensions of self represent the central feature of the human personality, which in the case of young adolescents unifies the physical, social and cognitive characteristics into a sense of identity, competence and affirmation. From an understanding of self springs a host of other variables such as behavior, motivation and the perception of others. Understanding that self brings us closer to understanding the early adolescent. Attending to the self in school brings us closer to developing the kind of middle school early adolescents need and deserve (Lipka, 1997, p. 31).

SELF-CONCEPT AND SELF-ESTEEM DEFINED

Self-concept is the description an individual attaches to himself or herself, as a function of the roles one plays or attributes one possesses. In response to the question tell me about yourself an individual might respond, "I am an eighth grader with few friends." Each of these responses is descriptive in nature, and whether true or false, it is perceived to be true by the individual and thus part of the personal self-concept. Self-concept is the content or cognitive part of the personal self-perception (Beane & Lipka, 1986, 2000; Hamachek, 1995).

Self-esteem on the other hand refers to the assessment or evaluation one makes of the self-concept description. The eighth-grader who has few friends and is unhappy about this has presented us with a judgment, an indication of the sense of self-worth. Self-esteem is the affective dimension of self-perception, thus in addition to having ideas about our self we also have feelings about who we are (Beane & Lipka, 1986, 2000; Hamachek, 1995).

THE STUDY OF SELF-PERCEPTIONS: PAST AND PRESENT

The history of self is the history of man. Cave drawings were an example of self-expression and world views. Each successive generation has had its artists, composers, and authors who used their work as self-expression, as a revelation of personal feelings, values and world views. In recent time the study of self-perceptions has become the purview of such disciplines as philosophy, psychology, and sociology.

Current interest in self-perceptions can be traced to the work of William James (1890) who postulated that an individual knows and thinks about many things including himself or herself. Cooley's (1902) addition to our thinking was the concept of the "looking glass" self; that is what we know about ourselves is a function of the feedback, verbal and nonverbal that we receive from others. We say something, we do something, and then we look to others for their reactions and use these reactions to make judgments of ourselves. Mead (1934) refined Cooley's concept with the contribution that self-perceptions are multidimensional, consisting of perceptions of the roles we play and the attributes we possess. Further, these dimensions are hierarchical in that some of these dimensions are more important to us than others. Sullivan's (1953) examination of the "feedback from others" literature led him to advance the idea that individuals placed more importance on the feedback from some persons rather than others and thus the concept of "significant others" was introduced into our literature.

We continue to stand upon the shoulders of others as we advance the field of self-perceptions. From Wylie (1967, 1979), Kelley (1962), Coopersmith (1967), Gergen (1971), Jourard (1971), and Epstein (1973) we have gained the following fairly consistent ideas about self-perceptions:

- The concept of self has a central place in personality, acting as a source of unity and as a guide to behavior.
- Self-perceptions are multidimensional and hierarchical, although at one level they tend to blend into a general sense of self.
- Self-perceptions tend to seek stability, consistency and enhancement.
- Self-perceptions may be based upon roles played by the individual, as well as attributes and beliefs he or she possesses.
- While the self may be an "initiator," self-perceptions arise mainly in a social context, influenced largely by feedback from "significant others." (Beane & Lipka, 1986, p. 4)

With this information as a backdrop it is time to examine early adolescence, a developmental stage characterized by rich and complex developments in self as process and content.

SELF IN EARLY ADOLESCENCE

Casting our thinking within a developmental framework and keeping the work of Havighurst (1972) in mind, the task of early adolescent self development will require the prerequisite success with the tasks of middle childhood—especially the following two tasks (see Shirk & Renouf, 1992 for a more complete treatment of this topic): "the first task of development of the self in middle childhood involves anchoring the process of self evaluation in reality—rather than fantasy or wish" (Shirk & Renouf , 1992, p. 56). This task is a natural for the use of pupil-teacher planning, integrative curriculum and authentic assessment in our middle school settings. "A second task of development of the self in middle childhood involves the coordination of one's sense of self worth with one's emerging sense of competence" (Shirk & Renouf, 1992, p. 56).

Competence goes "hand in glove" with authenticity for middle school students. Students must believe that what they are working on will make a difference in their lives and in the lives of those around them. One of the clearest ways to build authenticity is to provide our students with the opportunity to learn and apply the temporally rich set of skills we associate with "problem solving."

The first step in this rich process is *problem finding*. Within this step, the individual must identify an issue that has personal validity. Such problems may range from getting along with persons of the opposite sex, to water pollution in an area creek, to acquainting the local citizenry with the issues involved in global warming. The second step is *problem distillation*—that is, making the issue manageable in terms of the resources (and time is clearly a potent resource) that can be brought to bear for the solution of the problem. The third step is the actual *problem solving*, the resolution of the issue at hand. A fourth and a most important step is the *communication of the findings* of the process to all of the stakeholders that have the potential to be impacted by the results of the process.

Completion of this rich process engenders the competence required in this developmental task. Successful resolution of these tasks of middle childhood positions the young person to undertake the central task of early adolescence: "identify formation" (Shirk & Renouf, 1992). Identity formation for this age group really becomes an amalgam of the two subtasks of conservation of self and the maintenance of self-esteem as a function of developmental transitions and the vicissitudes of life (Shirk & Renouf, 1992, p. 76).

Conservation of self is the ability to promote continuity by linking change to existing self-structures. The linkage process is enhanced by the early adolescents' emerging cognitive ability to create a present self through the consideration of the past and possible future selves as the young person literally begins to develop an awareness of his or her own self- awareness. External observers of the conservation process are mislead by not understanding the differences between barometric and baseline self (Rosenberg, 1985) "the barometric self-concept refers to moment to moment fluctuations, and clearly early adolescence has the widest array of peaks and valleys of any age period. Baseline self, on the other hand, refers to a underlying self-concept that changes slowly over an extended period of time, and is focused upon striving towards healthy self-development" (Lipka, 1997, p. 33).

The maintenance of self-esteem looms large for the early adolescent given the numerous biological, social and cognitive transitions. In addition to the number of transitions the timing of the transitions becomes critical in the construction of self. Perhaps the key timing issue is the onset of puberty, as being "early" or "late" in relation to ones peers can have profound effects upon self-esteem (Lipka, Hurford, & Litten, 1992).

The social transitions involve three new domains for competence: job/tasks competence, romantic appeal and close friendships (Lipka, 1997; Shirk & Renouf, 1992). These three domains suggest a need for the acquisition and coordination of new skills within an educational environment that clearly understands that the process of growing up is the process of making mistakes and that having support, time and other resources to learn from their mistakes is critical to self-development. Add the vicissitudes of life e.g. illness, divorce of parents, loss of family income and geographical moves that make salient issues of race, gender, religion to the mix and the maintenance of self becomes a daunting task requiring the assistance of our most able teachers.

Given the centrality of "identity formation" within this age group and our requirements as educators to promote positive academic identity formation, what must our middle schools look like and be about in day-to-day functioning? The desired outcomes of school achievement, school completion and healthy attitudes towards self and others will be those environments where our early adolescents receive positive, affirming responses to the following questions within the following categories (Roeser & Lau, 2002):

Need for Competence

- What are the teacher's goals? (I am clear on what I am expected to do and how to proceed)
- Does this work challenge my abilities?
- How am I progressing?
- What kind of feedback am I getting on how well I am doing in the class?

Support of Autonomy

- Can I express my opinions in this class?
- Do our teachers really care about what students think?
- How does what I am learning relate to my own values, interests and experiences?

Quality of Relationships

- Do I feel cared for and respected as a person by classmates, teachers and administrators?
- Do I view my teachers as role models?
- Do I feel that I can go to them in times of need?
- Are students respectful of one another?
- Am I given opportunities to work with students in productive ways here?

Answering these questions will require middle grades schools that create motivating and supportive environments for teachers and students alike. Roeser and Lau note:

> By helping adolescents frame culturally meaningful academic and social goals and develop the strategies for realizing them; by providing them with challenging and meaningful activities; by giving them formative feedback on how well they are doing in relation to personally and socially valued goals; and by providing support and care as they progress towards "attaining" such goals, educators and other adults do a great deal to assist adolescents in developing healthy senses of themselves as students, as future members of society, and as whole individuals who can envision and attain productive and fulfilling lives. (2002, p. 124)

In Sum

- "Confusion in deciding between kids or mature young adults."
- "Our parents treating us our age."
- "Different parts of our body are beginning to change into men and women."
- "We are starting to have emotional and physical attraction for the opposite sex."
- "We are beginning to understand what we must do in life and who we want to be."
- "We've started to understand how quickly time passes."
- "We also understand that you don't live forever"
- "We are beginning to have more respect for our elders, but by the same token we want to rebel."

- "We no longer have all the answers therefore we always feel like we're missing something."

The quotes above represent the views of seventh graders who were asked the question: What are the changes you are going through at this time in your life? (Beane & Lipka, 2000). Such quotes prove false the "fans" of middle grades education who use terms like "range of the strange" and "hormones with feet" to describe our young adolescents. Clear self-concept and self-esteem is serious work requiring our complete attention.

REFERENCES

Beane, J. A., & Lipka, R. P. (2000). *When the kids come first: Enhancing self-esteem.* Troy, New York: Educator's International Press.

Beane, J. A., & Lipka, R. P. (1986). *Self-concept and self-esteem and the curriculum.* New York: Teachers College Press.

Cooley, C. H. (1902). *Human nature and the social order.* New York: Charles Scribner's.

Coopersmith, S. (1967). *The antecedents of self-esteem.* San Francisco: Freeman.

Epstein, S. (1973). The self-concept revisited: Or a theory of a theory. *American Psychologist, 28,* 404-416.

Gergen, K. J. (1971). *The concept of self.* New York: Holt, Reinhart and Winston.

Hamachek, D. E. (1995). *Psychology in teaching learning and growth.* Boston: Allyn & Bacon.

Hamachek, D. E. (1978). *Encounters with the self* (2nd ed.). New York: Holt, Rinehart, and Winston.

Havighurst, R. J. (1972). *Developmental tasks and education* (3rd ed.) New York: Longman.

James, W. (1890). *Principles of psychology* (Vols.1-2). Magnolia, MA: Peter Smith.

Jourard, S. M. (1971). *The transparent self.* New York: D. Van-Nostrand.

Kelley, E. C. (1962). The fully functioning self. In A.W. Combs (Ed.), *Perceiving, behaving, becoming: A new focus for education* (pp. 9-20). Washington, DC: Association for Supervision and Curriculum Development.

Lipka, R. P. (1997). Enhancing self-concept/ self-esteem in young adolescents. In J. H. Irvin (Ed.), *What current research says to the middle level practiner* (pp 31-39). Columbus, OH: National Middle School Association.

Lipka, R. P., Hurford, D. P., & Litten, M. J. (1992). Self in school: Age and school experience effects. In R. P. Lipka & T. M. Brinthaupt (Eds.), *Self-perspective across the lifespan* (pp. 93-115). Albany: State University of New York Press.

Mead, G. H. (1934). *Mind, self and society.* Chicago: University of Chicago Press.

Roeser, R. W., & Lau, S. (2002). On academic identity formation in middle school settings during early adolescence. In T. M. Brinthaujst & R. P. Lipka (Eds), *Understanding early adolescent self and identity: Applications and interven-*

tions (pp. 91-131). Albany: State University of New York Press.

Rosenberg, M. (1985). Self-concept and psychological well-being in adolescence. In R. Leahy (Ed.), *The Development of the self* (pp. 135-162). New York: Academic Press.

Rosenberg, M. (1979). *Conceiving the self*. New York: Basic Books.

Shirk, S. R., & Renouf, A. G. (1992). The tasks of self-development in middle childhood and early adolescence. In R. P. Lipka & T. M. Brinthaupt (Eds.), *Self-perspective across the life span* (pp. 53-90). Albany: State University of New York Press.

Sullivan, H. S. (1953). *The interpersonal theory of psychiatry.* New York: Norton.

Wylie, R.C. (1961, 1979). *The self-concept* (Vols. 1-2). Lincoln, NE: University of Nebraska Press.

—Richard P. Lipka
Pittsburg State University

SERVICE LEARNING

Service-learning is a philosophy and methodology involving the application of academic skills to addressing or solving real-life needs or problems in the community. Service-learning focuses on problems of life experience as well as mastering content from the subjects involved. Students become active participants in service projects that aim to respond to communities while simultaneously furthering their academics (Kahne & Westheimer, 1996, p. 593). A community is a group having similar interests, locale, commonalities, or identities. Thinking broadly, a community can be the classroom, school, town, state, world, or virtual, as in the Internet.

Service-learning is different from volunteerism and community service. Volunteerism is the engagement of students in activities where some service or good work is performed. Community service is also the engagement of students in activities where some service or good work is performed; however, students also learn how their service makes a difference in the lives of the service recipients. With volunteerism and community service there is little, if any, reciprocity (mutual or cooperative exchange of ideas) between those doing the service and those being served; little, if any, reflection (review and analysis of learning throughout and at the culmination of the experience with respect to oneself, collaborators, and community). Service, for both volunteerism and community service, is the focus with motivation based on civic duty, religious conviction, or altruism (concern for the welfare of others).

Service-learning is the engagement of students in activities designed to address or meet a community need, where students learn how their service makes a difference in themselves and in the lives of the service recipients, and where learning is intentionally linked to academics. In service-learning, there is intentional reciprocity between those doing the service and those being served; formative (throughout experience) and summative (culmination of experience) reflection is critical to the process; and learning and service are the foci with motivation based on addressing or meeting a community need. While volunteerism and community service are worthwhile aspects of middle grades education, service-learning is especially important for young adolescents because it provides an opportunity for students to learn and to do something of consequence with that learning. Service-learning is congruent with academic and other educational outcomes; service-learning should become a central strategy for teaching and learning in schools; and all students should be afforded the opportunity to participate in service-learning projects (National Commission on Service-Learning, 2005).

SERVICE-LEARNING METHODOLOGY

Service-learning projects can be teacher-directed—where teachers are primary decision makers—or democratic in nature—where students, teachers, and participants make decisions collaboratively. In either case, in conjunction with learning state-mandated content and curriculum, students engage in collaborative inquiry and action research. They frame guiding questions, develop research agendas, collect and record and analyze data, interpret findings and offer conclusions, and reflect. They use this information as they make decisions about the type and appropriateness of their service. Generally, the amount of time spent on the service aspect of service-learning is less than the time spent on learning.

Components of a well-planned and executed service-learning project include: (a) need (lack of something required or desirable) or problem (question or situation that presents uncertainty, perplexity, or difficulty); (b) learning (acquired wisdom, knowledge, or skill); (c) collaborators (all participants in the project); (d) service (work done to address a need or address or solve a problem); (e) reflection (a review and analysis of learning throughout and at the culmination of the experience with respect to oneself, collaborators, and community); (f) evaluation (systematic way to reflect upon service-learning activities that involves all participants); and, (g) publicity (act or process of disseminating project information). Service-learning projects are interdisciplinary in nature, naturally cutting across concepts and content areas. Service-learning, as a philosophy and methodology, is a natural fit for the middle grades.

SERVICE-LEARNING PROJECTS

Young adolescents want to make a difference (National Middle School Association, 2003; Scales & Blyth, 1997). In the democratic service-learning project *Walk through the Watershed*, 104 seventh grade science students and their teacher (Melissa Keyes) spent time learning about the environment and identifying issues and needs related to watersheds (all of the land area that drains into a given stream or river). Pairs of students chose watershed topics to research with a five-paragraph essay and a PowerPoint presentation as the culminating activity/evaluation. Learning objectives addressed included life science, Earth science, physical science, language arts, social science, and basic math objectives. Based on their new knowledge of watershed issues, students identified issues and needs that existed in their own watershed. Using a consensus-building strategy, they decided to address the need for public information and education about watersheds. Each class came up with different projects to implement. One class chose to demonstrate an environmentally friendly car wash. Others chose to use multiple forms of media to get information out to the community, such as brochures, flyers, newspaper articles, letters to public officials (mayor and the governor), and a comic book. Other projects included surveying participants at a local environmental event about their concerns and placing trash containers near local streams. Students reflected periodically throughout the project and at the end of the project regarding what they learned in the content areas, about themselves and their role in society.

Young adolescents want to know the relevance of their learning—relevance beyond the test and high school. In the teacher-directed service-learning project *Will We Ever Really Use Quadratic Equations?*, 24 gifted/high achieving eighth grade algebra students and their teacher (Jeannine Crowe) felt that a large number of their peers had a difficult time learning quadratic equations (e.g., $ax^2 + bx + c$) because of the complexity of the concept and the perceived lack of irrelevancy in daily living. They wanted to help struggling Algebra I and II students (and teachers) understand the mechanics of solving quadratic equations and have access to application problems that demonstrate their relevancy. The students learned: different methods of factoring and solving equations through a

continuum of learning from concrete (e.g., algebra tiles) to abstract (e.g., F.O.I.L.); how to graph quadratic equations using input/output tables and by using x-intercepts and the vertex of the parabola; basic computer and software skills; reasons behind learning complex mathematical ideas; relevance of quadratic equations in daily living; appropriate use of visual aids; pride in work and responsibility for learning; self-monitoring skills; personal strengths and weaknesses; written and oral communication skills; and, "most importantly, how to use what we know and understand to help those that are struggling and in need of help." For their service, the students created an electronic book on a compact disc using Microsoft PowerPoint. The CD contained step-by-step instructions on how to use various methods to factor expressions and solve quadratic equations as well as real-life application-based problems. As publicity, the students presented their work to high school teachers and administrators.

Young adolescents are beginning to make life-long decisions; they want to offer advice; they want to be supportive. Thirty eighth-grade students and their language arts teacher (Cindy Hensley) chose their service-learning project by first exploring issues of personal concern. Their brainstormed list contained the issues of pollution, time management, sexual activity (abortion), relationships (divorce), abuse, drugs, poverty/hunger/homelessness, care of old, and living beyond your means. The class discussed each issue and then reached a consensus. They wanted to work on a project that would address both "living beyond your dreams" and "homelessness." The following was their rationale: *Every year more and more people declare bankruptcy and some even become homeless. Most of these people never expected to end up in this situation. Proper money management could have alleviated the problem. We need to educate ourselves and others about guidelines for sound money management.* They decided to write a financial planning book. Their project, *Money Management: Dollar Sense for Young Adolescents*, addressed the need for sound money management skills. Dubbed Future Investors in Training (FIT), the students researched financial planning programs to identify best practices regarding spending, credit, checking and savings accounts, taxes, insurance, and interest. They authored a 50-page financial planning workbook specifically targeted for teenagers. In the introduction the FIT students wrote:

By the time you finish this workbook, we hope that you will:

• Be able to set short term, middle term, and long term financial goals;

- Understand the importance of having good credit and know how to establish it;
- Understand how to shop for insurance and the factors that affect rates;
- Understand how to shop for a loan and the importance of making timely payments;
- Understand how to open a checking account, write checks, and keep an accurate balance; and,
- Understand how to read your earnings statement and know what deductions will be subtracted from your gross earnings.

Language arts skills gained by FIT students included: writing, grammar, listening, reading, interviewing, public-speaking, following directions, organization, sequencing, and spelling. Financial skills gained included: balancing, planning, goal-setting, personal responsibility, savings/spending, income producing, debit and credit, and management.

Young adolescents are constantly exploring, changing, growing, and learning (National Middle School Association, 2003). In the teacher-directed service-learning project, *Discovering Different Perspectives of the Atomic Bombing of Hiroshima and Nagasaki in World War II*, 53 sixth-grade social studies students, their teacher (Janet Davis) and guest teacher (Masato Ogawa), and retired military personnel explored varying historical views, personal perspectives, and textbook treatment of World War II. The students listened to and interviewed guest speakers from Japan and the United States. They read entries from state-adopted U.S. textbooks and Japanese textbooks. They searched for answers to the following questions: Who made the atomic bomb and how was it tested?, Why did the United States drop the bombs?, What was the Soviet role in dropping the atomic bombs?, How many people died or were injured by the atomic bombing?, and What was the aftermath of the bombs? Students used data retrieval charts (DRC) to document their findings and discussed, compared, and contrasted information and perspectives. They engaged in dialogue, debate, problem solving, decision making, and analysis. Students synthesized their learning, employed moral reasoning and critical thinking, and acquired perspective-taking skills. As their service, students started a letter writing campaign. They wrote to publishers suggesting the need to present accurate information and address varying perspectives in textbooks.

SERVICE-LEARNING AND YOUNG ADOLESCENTS

Service-learning responds to the diversity of young adolescents (Anfara, Andrews, Hough, Mertens, Mizelle, & White, 2003). Service-learning offers young adolescents the venue for them to become active citizens while making contributions to society (Billig & Conrad, 1997). It combines the "need to know" with the application of learning—relevance that is real and now. Service-learning is exploratory—exploration of self, community, standards and content, and so forth—and advisory—safe, supportive, and so forth. Engagement in service-learning facilitates change and growth. Among the changes and growth resulting from service-learning are: improved attitude toward school and academic learning (Billig & Conrad, 1997; Duckenfield & Swanson, 1992; Eyler & Giles, 1999; Scales, Blyth, Berkas, & Kielsmeier, 2000); increased motivation, sense of responsibility, and ownership in learning; heightened respect, empathy and acceptance for and tolerance of others (Berkas, 1997; Melchior, 1999; Stephens, 1995), growth in personal and interpersonal development (Eyler & Giles, 1999); enhanced problem solving, higher-order thinking, and teamwork skills; and increased level of self-confidence, and self-worth.

REFERENCES

Anfara, V. A., Jr., Andrews, P. G., Hough, D. L., Mertens, S. B., Mizelle, N. B., & White, G. P. (2003). *Research and resources in support of This We Believe*. Westerville, OH: National Middle School Association.

Berkas, T. (1997, February). *Strategic review of the W. K. Kellogg Foundation's service-learning projects, 1990-1996*. Battle Creek, MI: W. K. Kellogg Foundation.

Billig, S., & Conrad, J. (1997). *An evaluation of the New Hampshire Service-Learning and Educational Reform Project*. Denver, CO: RMC Research.

Duckenfield, M., & Swanson, L. (1992). *Service-learning: Meeting the needs of youth at risk*. Clemson, SC: National Dropout Prevention Center.

Eyler, J., & Giles, D. E., Jr. (1999). *Where's the learning in service learning?* San Francisco: Jossey-Bass.

Kahne, J., & Westheimer, J. (1996). In the service of what? The politics of service learning. *Phi Delta Kappan, 77*(9), 593.

Melchior, A. (1999). *Summary report: National evaluation of Learn and Serve America*. Waltham, MA: Center for Human Resources, Brandeis University.

National Commission on Service-Learning. (n.d.). *National Commission on Service-Learning*. Retrieved June 30, 2005, from http://www.learningindeed.org/slcommission

National Middle School Association. (2003). *This we believe: Successful schools for young adolescents*. Westerville, OH: National Middle School Association.

Scales, P., & Blyth, D. (1997, Winter). Effects of service-learning on youth: What we know and what we need to know. *Generator*, 6-9.

Scales, P., Blyth, D., Berkas, T., & Kielsmeier, J. (2000). The effects of service learning on middle school students' social responsibility and academic success. *Journal of Early Adolescence, 20*(3), 331-358.

Stephens, L. (1995). *The complete guide to learning through community service, Grades K-9*. Boston: Allyn & Bacon.

—P. Elizabeth Pate
The University of Texas, San Antonio

SHOOTING FOR THE SUN: THE MESSAGE FOR MIDDLE SCHOOL REFORM

Shooting for the Sun: The Message of Middle School Reform (Mizell, 2002) is a collection of inspiring speeches given by M. Hayes Mizell on the topics of middle school reform, school improvement, academic standards, and accountability. The speeches were delivered at variety of venues including conferences, annual meetings, gatherings of middle level educators and local, state, and national level administrators, representatives of various community organizations, and the Edna McConnell Clark Foundation grantee organizations.

This compilation starts with a forward by Michael Bailin, president of the Edna McConnell Clark Foundation, who introduces Mizell and describes his speeches as optimistic, applied, aspirations for the education system and educators. The speeches that ensue are organized into four sections: (1) The Challenge of Middle School Reform, (2) Getting it Done, (3) Academic Standards and Accountability, and (4) Conclusion—Where We Are Now.

In the first collection of speeches, Mizell discusses the challenges facing middle schools and proposes a range of solutions in order to impel change. He describes a "new kind of principal;" a principal whose activities and goals are grounded in a holistic approach focused on achievement and high standards. His speeches in this section accuse middle schools of complacency in the face of needed reforms. He urges educators to strive to achieve high standards and demand accountability both for themselves, their students, and schools. The section ends with a speech that outlines the characteristics of middle schools that are truly focused on student achievement and the steps to toward creating such a school. "Students matter more than anyone or anything in public education. How students' perform is a barometer of a school's effectiveness" (p. 121).

Mizell uses superhero, hiking, running, mountain climbing, and wrestling analogies in the speeches in Part 2 (Getting it Done) to insist and reiterate that the key to reform is an unwavering commitment to helping students learn despite hurdles and challenges. Each speech is a rallying call to persist with reform efforts and put student learning and achieving performance standards above all other priorities. He details various challenges and ways to counter them; he assesses how far the reform movement has come and where it can improve or should continue to focus. These speeches stress that student learning must come above all other things and that schools need to prioritize student learning and facilitate learning at a higher level for *all* students. Mizell says that the way to improving students' performance is by unwaveringly adhering to standards and not accepting sub par outcomes. He insists that schools use standards as both goals and means to improving student achievement. Throughout these speeches he stresses the importance of staff development; he insists that teachers, principals and administrators performance is fundamentally linked to students' performance, the more educators learn from each other, their own trials and errors, and other professional development experiences the better off they are to serve students and help them learn.

In Part 3 (Academic Standards and Accountability) Mizell's speeches focus on three key and reciprocal components to successful middle school reform: (1) improving the abilities of teachers to teach effectively via valid and applicable professional development opportunities; (2) tracking student and staff progress using academic standards as tools to foster academic success and; (3) external and internal accountability. Mizell insists that "standards are about much more than scores on tests" (p. 175) and that high quality standards can be an impetus for school reform and they should not be discredited. He concedes that there are shortcomings to some arbitrary state and national standards but he poses the question, what would happen in the absence of external pressures for schools to perform? Mizell asserts that establishing credible but challenging academic standards and goals that students and school staff are ardently expected to reach is the foundation of accountability and the resulting academic success.

Shooting for the Sun concludes with an overview of the lessons learned from the past decade of middle school reform. Mizell is passionate about middle school reform and it resonates in all his words. At the core of all his rhetoric, Mizell provokes all people in the education field to "be resolute, be brave, be determined, be tenacious in creating school systems that serve *all* children *well*" (p. 145).

REFERENCE

Mizell, M. H. (2002). *Shooting for the sun: the message of middle school reform*. New York: The Edna McConnell Clark Foundation.

—Cody Stephens
CPRD, University of Illinois

SOCIETY FOR RESEARCH ON ADOLESCENCE

The Society for Research on Adolescence (SRA), established in 1984 with 20 charter members, is an international, multidisciplinary society that, according to its Web site (http://www.s-r-a.org/), "focuses on theoretical, empirical, and policy research issues" related to adolescence. SRA, which has a membership of over 1,100 scholars from 25 countries, including the leading researchers in the field of adolescent research, is dedicated to promoting "the understanding of adolescence through research and dissemination." The society held its first research conference in Madison, Wisconsin, in 1986, under the leadership of its founding president, Hershel D. Thornburg, and invites promising and distinguished scholars to submit their research for possible presentation at its biennial spring conference.

The biennial conference, which meets for the 11th time in San Francisco in March, 2006, attracts highly respected and experienced researchers and policy analysts, as well as graduate students and other promising scholars in the field of adolescent development. SRA also sponsors several special interest groups (SIGs), including Adolescents in Schools and Minority Adolescents, which sponsor pre-conference sessions. Researchers may submit proposals for papers, posters, symposia, and special topic discussions for possible inclusion in the meeting program.

The *Journal of Research on Adolescence*, a leading peer-reviewed multidisciplinary publication, is the official journal of SRA and is published four times per year (http://www.blackwellpublishing.com/journal.asp?ref=1050-8392). SRA members receive a subscription to the journal. The journal includes studies that are both quantitative and qualitative in nature that relate to cognitive, physical, emotional, and social development and behavior of adolescents. Cross-cultural and longitudinal research studies are encouraged.

—L. Mickey Fenzel
Loyola College, Maryland

SOUTHERN FORUM TO ACCELERATE MIDDLE-GRADES REFORM

The National Forum to Accelerate Middle Grades Reform (see National Forum) formed the Southern Forum in 1999 to stimulate middle grades school improvement throughout the South. The Forum recognized that by forming a group of middle level stakeholders at the state and regional level, the rate of improvement would be accelerated and brought closer to the classroom. The South was chosen as the first regional Forum because there was already a strong nucleus of support, leadership, and infrastructure throughout the region, and because of the strong need to address gaps in achievement and test scores.

Key leaders from ten southeastern states were identified and invited to apply for membership in the Southern Forum. The ten states originally comprising the Forum included Alabama, Arkansas, Florida, Georgia, Kentucky, Louisiana, Mississippi, North Carolina, South Carolina, and Tennessee (Ricks, 2000). Virginia was added as the eleventh Southern Forum state in 2003. During 2003, the Southern Forum selected an executive director, Dr. John Harrison, became incorporated, and gained nonprofit 501 (c)(3) status. During the first 4 years of its existence, the Southern Forum developed a set of goals and purposes, and formed state-level Forums. Each state has five representatives to the Southern Forum who are members of their states' various stakeholder groups. Included on the Forum are superintendents, principals, teachers, parents, business/civic leaders, state department personnel, and professors. Each of a state's five Southern Forum representatives is also a member of his or her state-level Forum, which is comprised of school, district, and state-level stakeholders.

The vision statement of the National Forum to Accelerate Middle Grades Reform provides a framework for the goal of the Southern Forum, which is "to provide assistance in the development of middle level school programs, practices, and personnel, which will positively impact the trajectory of middle grades reform in the South" (Bylaws, 2003). Members of the Southern Forum then added four specific purposes to guide activities of the Forum:

1. Strengthen the capacity of the Southern Forum to improve middle-grades education throughout the region.
2. Identify and develop the next generation of leaders.
3. Create and support state-level forums where members can work collaboratively to bring

about improvements in middle-grades education.

4. Disseminate ideas and materials to middle-grades educators, parents, and other stakeholders. (Bylaws, 2003)

During the early years of the Southern Forum, members field-tested leadership modules created by the National Forum to provide both leadership training to members and important feedback for revision of the modules. After publication of the modules, members of the Forum shifted their focus to supporting and strengthening state-level forums in a combined effort with the National Forum to drive reform to the school and classroom level. State Forums offer leadership training to middle-grades educators using the National Forum modules, conduct their own Schools to Watch programs (see Schools to Watch) and/or advocate supportive middle-grades policies at the state level. They also cultivate networks among member and non-member organizations that have assets to contribute to the academic success and personal development of middle grades students.

REFERENCES

Southern Forum to Accelerate Middle Grades Reform. (2003, July). *Bylaws*. Presented at the semi-annual meeting of the Southern Forum, Nashville, TN.

Ricks, S. (2000). *The history of the Southern Forum to Accelerate Middle Grades Reform*. (Available from the Southern Forum to Accelerate Middle Grades Reform, PO Box 5216, Pinehurst, NC 28374)

—Barbara R. Blackburn
Winthrop University

—John A. Harrison
Southern Forum to Accelerate Middle-Grades Reform

SOUTHERN REGIONAL EDUCATION BOARD

The Southern Regional Education Board (SREB), the nation's first interstate education compact, was created in 1948. SREB was founded to help states share resources and multiply benefits while dividing costs. Government and education leaders work cooperatively to advance education as a way to improve the social and economic life of the region. SREB is governed by a board that consists of the governor of each of the 16 member states and four other individuals

from each state appointed by the governor, including at least one state legislator and one educator. SREB's member states are: Alabama, Arkansas, Delaware, Florida, Georgia, Kentucky, Louisiana, Maryland, Mississippi, North Carolina, Oklahoma, South Carolina, Tennessee, Texas, Virginia, and West Virginia.

SREB maintains an extensive database about education in all 16 states. It publishes many informative publications ranging from short, timely reports on legislative actions in each state to a comprehensive fact book on higher education that is updated regularly. SREB-sponsored meetings enable policy-makers and educators to share information within their states and across state lines.

SREB services are designed to meet states' demands for improved education. Policymakers in the region set goals for education that are monitored and reported on regularly by SREB. The current goals, known as *Challenge to Lead*, reflect the aspiration of SREB states to lead the nation in educational progress. The 12 goals focus state educational reform on helping students make smooth transitions from grade level to grade level; on closing gaps in the performance of ethnically diverse groups of boys and girls, and of students who live in urban, suburban, and rural areas; and, on creating an education system of schools, colleges and universities that works together to promote student achievement.

The middle grades goal is to bring all students to national averages and to close achievement gaps. It fits a middle grades mission to prepare students for a rigorous high school curriculum. It is intended to keep our sights on the middle grades and student achievement until all students are ready for high school.

To achieve the goal, SREB has built an initiative to improve schools in the middle grades—*Making Middle Grades Work* (MMGW). MMGW has 200 schools in 19 states. Data are available from about 15,000 eighth-grade students on their achievement and perceptions of their school experiences; other data on curriculum, instruction and assessment from about 5,000 teachers and principals in *MMGW* schools complement the student data. The network provides a rich environment for research on both policy and practice.

Schools in the *MMGW* network for at least three years made more progress between 2000 and 2002 in reading and mathematics on reducing the percentage of students who score below the basic performance level than the nation made over longer time periods (Cooney, 2003). Every SREB state posted higher percentages of eighth-grade students scoring at or above the National Assessment of Educational Progress basic achievement level in reading in 2002 than they posted for fourth-grade students in 1998 (SREB, 2004).

REFERENCES

Cooney, S., & Bottoms, G. (2003). *What works to improve student achievement in the middle grades*. Atlanta, GA: Southern Regional Education Board.

Southern Regional Education Board. (2004). *Getting the mission right in the middle grades*. Atlanta, GA: Author.

—Sondra S. Cooney
Southern Regional Education Board

SPORTS IN MIDDLE SCHOOLS

Efforts to create and sustain developmentally responsive middle schools that meet the educational needs of young adolescents have been continuous since the 1960s. Although many developmentally responsive programs and practices have been successfully implemented in the nation's middle schools (McEwin, Dickinson, & Jenkins, 2003), middle school interscholastic (interschool) sports programs have been resistant to change and reform. Typically, middle school interscholastic sports programs more accurately resemble highly competitive programs designed for high school students and adults than developmentally responsive models that are more appropriate for young adolescents. Too often, the desires and interests of adults—family members, coaches, fans, the press—rather than what is best for young adolescents receive priority when decisions are being made about the nature of middle school sports programs (Swaim & McEwin, in press a)

The American culture has embraced competitive sports at unprecedented levels in recent years. It is estimated that more than 30 million children and teens under the age of 18 participate in some form of organized sports. The context in which sports are played, especially by children and young adolescents, has also changed from spontaneous, fun oriented, youth organized activities to highly structured competitions organized by adults. This change in emphasis has resulted in children as young as five participating in organized sports competitions, children as young as nine or ten specializing in one sport and playing that sport on a year round basis, and in other practices that often have negative effects on the young participants (Engh, 2002; Metzl & Shookhoff, 2002; Murphy, 1999; Patel, 2001).

Middle schools have not escaped the pressures associated with the popularity of competitive sports. The percentage of middle schools with interscholastic sports programs has increased from 50% in 1968, to 77% in 1993, to 96% in 2001. The number and variety of sports offered to both boys and girls has also dramatically increased during this time period (McEwin et al., 2003; Swaim & McEwin, in press b). Along with the widespread establishment of these middle school sports programs have come some controversial issues and debates regarding the value and appropriateness of highly competitive sports programs for young adolescents (McEwin & Dickinson, 1997). Some of these issues are discussed below (e.g., injury rates, psychological considerations, attrition).

PHYSICAL INJURY

High rates of physical injuries have plagued competitive sports programs for children and young adolescents since the beginnings of organized competitive sports. Young adolescents, usually defined as 10- to 14-year-olds, are especially susceptible to injury due to the softness of their growing bones and the relative tightness of their ligaments, tendons, and muscles. The high level of the incidence of these injuries is easily discernable by examination of injury statistics. For example, a nationwide analysis of visits to hospital emergency departments conducted by the Centers for Disease Prevention found that 4.3 million nonfatal sports and recreation-related injuries were treated in emergency rooms in a 12 month period ending June 2001. Although injury rates varied by age and sex, they were highest for boys ages 10-14. Almost 2 million youth, ages 10 to 14, were treated in emergency rooms for sports and recreation injuries during the twelve month period. This number is higher than the number of youth receiving medial attention for automobile accidents and makes sports injuries a major public health concern (Centers for Disease Control, 2002; Noonan, 2003).

The statistics just discussed represent both organized sports and recreation injuries. Therefore, questions arise regarding how many of these injuries occurred in organized sports versus other recreational activities, and what percentage of these injuries resulted from school-sponsored sports. Data dividing these statistics into school-sponsored versus community sports are not available. However, the numbers of 10-14-year-olds receiving injuries serious enough to require visits to emergency care reveal that sports traditionally sponsored by schools constitute a major percentage of these injuries. For example, during the 1-year period just discussed, 144,907 10-14-year-olds were treated in emergency care for football injuries, 170,937 for basketball injuries, and 57,186 for soccer injuries (Centers for Disease Control, 2002).

These statistics represent only injuries serious enough for emergency care and do not include visits to physicians in other settings. It is estimated that 3.5 million youth under the age of 15 require medical treatment each year for sports injuries (*USA Today*, 2002). Although it is not known what percentage of these injuries result from school sponsored sports, approximately 20 percent of children and adolescents that participate in organized sports play on school sponsored teams (Patel, 2003).

PSYCHOLOGICAL CONSIDERATIONS

Even though the psychological effects of sports are difficult to determine, young adolescents' psychological well being should be a priority in developing middle level sports programs (McEwin & Dickinson, 1997; Patel, 2001). Historically, sports literature has touted the benefits of participation in promoting socialization skills, building character, enhancing personality development, and as "preparation for adult life" (Coakley, 1987; Darst & Pangrazi, 2002; National Association for Sport and Physical Education, 2002; Seefeldt, Ewing, & Walk, 1993). There is little doubt that, at least to some extent, many of these claims are based on reality. However, some question the psychological readiness of children and young adolescents to cope with becoming instant successes and failures in very public ways while competing in sports activities. Involving young adolescents in highly competitive sports before they are psychologically ready for the pressures associated with this participation can eliminate the enjoyment of sports participation because of regimented practices, pressures to always perform at high levels, and the all too often prevalent attitude of "winning at all costs" (Metzl & Shookhoff, 2002).

The "cut policies" employed by many sports teams also have implications for the psychological and emotional readiness of young adolescents for competitive sports competition. The processes typically utilized to select some individuals and eliminate others from sports teams are based on factors that are beyond the control of those wishing to participate (e.g., maturational differences, the capricious nature of coaches' judgments). Cutting young adolescents from sports teams denies them the opportunities to learn new skills and build confidence in their own abilities. Those cut from teams often feel that they have failed to meet the expectations of their peers as well as the adults that are influential in their lives. One result of being cut from sports teams is the decision made by

many young adolescents to drop out of sports altogether (McEwin & Dickinson, 1998; Ogilvie, 1988). For these and other reasons, the National Association for Sport and Physical Activity (2002) has recommended that a "no cut" policy should be in place so that young adolescents are not eliminated from participation.

ATTRITION IN SPORTS

Despite the popularity of sports in American culture, the number of youth participating in organized sports competition has declined in recent years. Although the number of youth ages 6 to 17 increased by more than seven million between 1990 and 2002, some of the most popular team sports have lost significant numbers of players. For example, the number of youth in this age group playing organized basketball has decreased from 22 to 18 million since 1998. Soccer, after gaining in popularity from 1990 to 1998, has decreased by one million players since that time. Softball and baseball have also experienced decreases. The declines in participation in softball and baseball between 1990 and 2002 were 6 million and 3 million respectively (Cary, 2004, p. 48).

These decreases are not surprising considering approximately 70% of youth who participate in non-school organized sports drop out by age 13 (Engh, 2002). Although information regarding attrition rates for middle school-sponsored organized sports is not available, it seems safe to conclude that attrition is also a problem for these sports programs. While there are multiple reasons for these youth dropping out of organized sport including the development of new interest, other reasons include: (a) lack of playing time; (b) the way practices are conducted; (c) interactions with teammates; (d) dislike of coaches; (e) a feeling of unworthiness; (f) not having fun; and, (g) needing additional time to study. These reasons apply to all sports, but the largest numbers of dropouts are in basketball, football, soccer, and track and field (Engh, 2002; Ewing & Seefelt, 1989; Holm, 1996; Rotella, Hanson, & Coop, 1991; Seefeldt, Ewing, & Walk, 1993).

Young adolescents who are typically eliminated or drop out of organized sports are the ones who are poor performers (e.g., later maturing boys, those who do not show enough aggression). However, gifted athletes are also sometimes negatively effected when they are forced to specialize in one sport in which they have demonstrated talent or are placed under excessively high expectations by coaches, peers, and others (Engh, 2002; Murphy, 1999). When these youth are continually pushed to be more competitive and to participate in intense practices, they begin to "burn-out" and sometimes decide to leave sports.

ASPIRATIONS FOR SCHOLARSHIPS AND PROFESSIONAL SPORTS CONTRACTS

Middle level educators, parents, and other adults should be realistic in their own expectations about the extremely small changes of individual young adolescents obtaining college scholarships or playing on professional sports teams. Young adolescents should be encouraged to reach their full potential in athletics, but they should also understand that they are very unlikely to ever play college level or professional sports. According to estimates from the National Center for Educational Statistics, less than 1% of youth playing on organized sports teams receive any type of college scholarship (Ferguson, 1999). Of the one-million high school varsity football players that play each year, fewer than 6% college teams (5.6%). This percentage includes those who play without receiving scholarships.

According to the National Collegiate Athletics Association, a high school senior playing football has less than a one in 1,000 chance of being drafted by a professional sports team (Metzl & Shookhoff, 2002) In basketball, approximately 475,000 fourth graders play on organized sports teams. Eighteen percent of those participating make high school teams, only .009 percent receive college scholarships, and approximately 30 will play for professional teams (.00006). The odds are even longer in soccer because many colleges recruit players from other nations (Cary, 2004). A key message inherent in the statistical realities regarding the chances of young adolescents receiving college scholarships and playing professional sports is the importance of helping them, and the adults that are influential in their lives, comprehend that although sports participation has many potential benefits to offer, one's future should not be predicated on the possibility of becoming a college and/or a professional athlete.

OTHER MIDDLE SCHOOL SPORTS ISSUES

There are other important issues that accompany discussions of middle school interscholastic sports. The quality of coaching is often questioned at the middle school level since many coaches are not physical educators and have had little or no preparation for coaching young adolescents. There is also concern about the inappropriate behavior of parents and other fans at sports events, the high cost of interscholastic sports, the loss of instructional time due to sports activities (e.g., travel time, pep rallies), and the prefer-

ential treatment sometimes given to successful athletes. Concern has arisen about the increasing number of lawsuits against schools, coaches, and sports equipment (Kralovec, 2003; Mac, 1998; McEwin & Dickinson, 1998).

RECOMMENDATIONS

Despite the problems that are evident in middle school sports, it is important to understand that many benefits that can be gained from developmentally responsive middle school sports programs (e.g., physical activity; lessons about fair play, cooperation and competition; leadership opportunities). However, much remains to be accomplished if middle school sports programs are going to be developmentally responsive and serve young adolescents safely and well.

Some examples of steps that can be taken to accomplish the goal of safe and effective middle school sports include (Swaim & McEwin, in press a): (a) Middle school sports programs should have clearly stated philosophies and guidelines that provide direction for the programs; (b) coaches should be carefully selected based on their knowledge of young adolescent development, knowledge of the sports being coached, and their dispositions toward the purposes of middle school sports; (c) all young adolescents should have the opportunity to participate in at least one sport that is available at their grade level; (d) precautions should be taken to reduce the number of injuries; (e) emphasis should be placed on enhancing self-esteem and developing social skills as well as physical ability; (f) priority should be placed on developing skills rather than *winning at all costs*; (g) there should be a willingness to modify rules in some sports to make them safer for the age group; (h) a balanced approach to physical education, intramural sports, and interscholastic sports should be established; and (i) relationships between academic and interscholastic sports programs should be examined on a continuing basis to ensure that the academic programs are the top priority.

REFERENCES

Cary, P. (2004, June 7). Fixing kid's sports. *U. S. News and World Report, 136*(20), 44-53.

Centers for Disease Control. (2002, August 23). *Nonfatal sports and recreation-related injuries treated in emergency departments: United States July 2000 to June 2001.* Retrieved July 24, 2004, from http://www.cdc.gov/mmwr/preview/mmwrhtml/mm5133a2.htm

Coakley, J. J. (1987). Children and the sport socialization process. In D. Could & M. R. Weiss (Eds). *Advances in pediatric sport sciences: Behavioral issues* (pp. 89-125). Champaign, IL: Human Kinetics.

Darst, P. W., & Pangrazi, R. P. (2002). *Dynamic physical education for secondary school students*. San Francisco: Benjamin Cummings.

Engh, F. (2002). *Why Johnny hates sports: Why organized youth sports are failing our children and what we can do about it*. New York: Square One.

Ewing, M. E., & Seefeldt, V. (1989). *Participation and attrition patterns in American agency-sponsored and interscholastic sports: An executive summary*. North Palm Beach, FL: Sporting Goods Manufacturer's Association.

Ferguson, A. (1999, July 12). Inside the crazy culture of kids sports. *Time, 154*(2), 52-60.

Holm, H. L. (1996). Sport participation and withdrawal: A developmental motivational commentary. *Research in Middle Level Education Quarterly, 19*(3), 41-61.

Kralovec, E. (2003). *Schools that do too much*. Boston: Beacon Press.

Mac, M. R. (1998, November). Managing the risks of school sports. *The School Administrator*. Retrieved July 5, 2004, from http://www.aasa.org/publications/sa/1998_11/Mac. htm

McEwin, C. K., & Dickinson, T. S. (1997). Interscholastic sports: A battle not fought. *Schools in the Middle: Theory into Practice*, 17-23.

McEwin, C. K., & Dickinson, T. S. (1998). What role for middle school sports? *The School Administrator, 10*(55), 56-56.

McEwin, C. K., Dickinson, T. S., & Jenkins, D. M. (2003). *America's middle schools in the new century: Status and progress*. Westerville, OH: National Middle School Association.

Metzl, J. D., & Shookhoff, C. (2002). *The young athlete: A sports doctor's guide for parents*. New York: Little Brown.

Murphy, S. (1999). *The cheers and the tears: A healthy alternative to the dark side of sports today*. San Francisco: Jossey-Bass.

National Association for Sport and Physical Education. (2002). *Co-curricular physical activity and sport programs for middle school students: A position statement of National Association for Sport and Physical Education Council*. Retrieved July 30, 2004, from http://www.nmsa.org/mssports.htm

Noonan, D. (2003, September 22). When safety is the name of the game. *Newsweek, 142*(64), 64-66.

Ogilvie, B. C. (1988). The role of pediatric sports medicine specialists in youth sports. In J. A. Sullivan & W. A. Grana (Eds.), *The pediatric athlete* (pp. 34-57). Rosemont, IL: American Academy of Orthopedic Surgeons.

Patel, D. R. (2001, March). Youth sports: More than sprains and strains. *Contemporary Pediatrics*. Retrieved July 24, 2004, from http://www.aap.org/advocacy/releases/sportsinjury.htm

Rotella, J., Hanson, T., & Coop, R. H. (1991). Burnout in youth sports, *The Elementary School Journal, 91*(5), 421-428.

Seefeldt, V., Ewing, M, & Walk, S. (1993). *Overview of youth sports programs in the United States*. NY: Carnegie Council on Adolescent Development.

Swaim, J. H., & McEwin, C. K. (in press a). *Middle school sports programs*. Westerville, OH: National Middle School Association.

Swaim, J. H., & McEwin, C. K. (in press b). The status of middle school sports: Results from a national survey. *Middle Ground*.

USA Today (2002, October 18-20). Retrieved July 24, 2004, from http://www.aap.org/advocacy/releases/sportsinjury.htm

—John H. Swaim
Otterbein College

—C. Kenneth McEwin
Appalachian State University

STEVENSON, CHRISTOPHER

"Wondering about the lives of young adolescents" (Bergstrom, Bishop, & Carr, 2001) is the core of Chris Stevenson's work. The profound insight that comes from this wondering and countless hours of conversation with young adolescents is the mark of Chris Stevenson's contributions to the field of middle grades education. Dr. Stevenson's knowledge, understanding, and insight about young adolescents is grounded in his 16 years as a teacher and administrator of schools with young adolescents in South Carolina, New York City, Atlanta, and Cambridge, MA. Even after he became a college professor at the age of 42, Dr. Stevenson remained directly connected to young adolescents, visiting and working in schools, spending countless hours talking with, listening to, and recording conversations with them as they talk about their lives and their schools. Stevenson's fundamental assertion is that curriculum begins with students, and the emphasis of schools must be helping kids develop and become better people.

One of Stevenson's most influential teaching experiences was his time as headmaster and team leader at Fayerweather School, Cambridge, MA, an experimental school designed around the integrated day, progressive school design. "The school was a model of democratic, student-focused learning, with nongraded family groups, learning centers, integration of experiential learning, interdisciplinary/thematic inquiry, group projects, and problem-solving [initiatives]"(Bergstrom, Bishop, & Carr, 2001). Stevenson was at Fayerweather for seven years, during which time the school obtained considerable success and acclaim.

Stevenson joined the faculty of the University of Vermont (UVM) as a member of the elementary education department in 1982. He soon became the influential link between the emerging, yet isolated pockets of interest in middle schools and effective education for young adolescents within the state. Stevenson taught UVM's first course on middle schools in 1984. He provided guidance and expertise to an informal support group of teachers and principals interested in improving middle grades education. In 1985 he offered the first middle grades summer institute in Vermont. That same year he sponsored the state's first middle level conference. Originally expected to be a gathering of fifty, the numbers swelled to 300. In 1986 Steven became a member of the statewide Certification Review Board and laid the groundwork to establish a separate middle level certification. A culminating event of these numerous activities was the formation of the Vermont Association for Middle Level Education in 1987.

While Stevenson played a significant role in the professional development of middle school educators, his equally profound impact has been in bringing the voices of young adolescents to the conversation. Stevenson has been keenly interested in understanding young adolescents from their own stories, experiences, and perspectives. An influential result of this commitment is the Five Basics of Personal Efficacy for Young Adolescents, a framework for understanding students from their own perspective. While he did not publish this framework until 1994, Stevenson had been formulating the concept for many years prior.

Among Stevenson's most influential books are *Teaching Ten to Fourteen Year Olds* (first published 1992, 3rd edition, 2001); *Integrated Studies in the Middle Grades: Dancing Through Walls* (1993); and *Teachers as Inquirers: Strategies for Learning With and About Early Adolescents* (1986).

Prior to his retirement, Stevenson led an initiative to collect and house NMSA archives at the Research Collections Department of Bailey-Howe Library at the University of Vermont. He is the recipient of the Distinguished Service Award from the New England League of Middle Schools and the Distinguished Service Award from the Connecticut Association of Schools.

REFERENCE

Bergstrom, K., Bishop, P., & Carr, J. (2001). *Living and learning in the middle grades: The dance continues.* Westerville, OH: National Middle School Association.

Stevenson, C. (1986). *Teachers as inquirers: Strategies for learning with and about early adolescents.* Columbus, OH: National Middle School Association.

Stevenson, C. (1993). *Integrated studies in the middle grades: Dancing through walls.* New York: Teachers College Press.

Stevenson, C. (2001). *Teaching ten to fourteen year olds* (3rd ed.). New York: Longman.

—Mary Henton
National Middle School Association

SUCCESS FOR ALL MIDDLE SCHOOL

Success for All Middle School, a program of the Success for All Foundation (SFAF), is a comprehensive model for accelerating the achievement of students in the middle grades. It is based on the widely used and extensively evaluated Success for All elementary model (Slavin & Madden, 2001), but designed to meet the developmental needs of young adolescents. Cooperative learning, reading, conflict resolution, social skills, and family involvement comprise the core of this program. Schools may also choose to implement SFA's middle school curriculum in humanities (language arts and social studies) and science.

SFAF's experience and research substantiate the idea that improved literacy skills can empower young adolescents, not only by making them critical thinkers better able to negotiate the many choices that confront them at this pivotal stage in their development, by also by giving them access to the most challenging curricula in the content areas. To fill any gaps and build on strengths, Success for All Middle School provides every student with instruction in reading at his or her instructional level. Students are assessed regularly and moved to a higher level as soon as they are ready. This approach motivates students to achieve by making them aware of their gains, and what they still need to learn to succeed.

Success for All Middle School provides well-structured instructional guides and materials for teachers and students, as well as extensive professional development, follow-up support from SFA coaches, and opportunities for teachers to work together to reach school goals. SFA provides a "critical friend" for school and district leaders to guide them through a goal-focused process of continuous improvement in classroom instruction and student achievement.

Sixty-two schools in urban, rural, and small city locations used the program in the 2003/2004 school year. Data from schools implementing Success for All Middle School show promising effects on state assessments. A third party evaluator, the National Opinion Research Center (NORC) at the University of Chicago, is collecting student-level data from state assessments to evaluate the program. The subjects of NORC's research are students in grades 6-8 in seven pairs of middle schools located in six districts. Each pair consists of a Success for All Middle School and a matched control site. Based on school level data, SFA middle schools gained 7.5 percentage points on their state reading tests, while matched controls gained 3.9 points. Gains in the schools' respective states averaged 3.3 percentage points. For more information

Table 1

Gains in Percent of Students Passing State Reading Tests in
Success for All and Control Middle Schools, 2001 to 2003

School (State)	Measure	Grades Tested	Gains in Percent Passing		
			SFA	Control	State
Washington-1	WASL	7	+22.2	+6.0	+8.1
Missouri-1	MAP	7	+29.2	+10.7	−1.8
Indiana-1	ISTEP	6, 8	+9.0	+0.5	+6.5
Indiana-2	ISTEP	6, 8	+14.5	+4.0	+6.5
Mississippi	MCT	6, 7	+2.9	−2.1	+6.5
Arizona-1	AIMS	8	−15.0	+3.0	−1.0
Colorado-1	CSAP	7	−10.0	+5.0	−2.0
Means*			+7.5	+3.9	+3.3

*Means across different state assessments should be interpreted cautiously.

about the program, the research, or participating schools, please visit the SFA Web site at www.success-forall.net

REFERENCE

Slavin, R.E., & Madden, N.A. (Eds.) (2001). *One million children: Success for all.* Thousand Oaks, CA: Corwin.

—Cecelia P. Daniels
Success for All Foundation, Inc.

SUCCESSFUL SCHOOLS FOR YOUNG ADOLESCENTS

Joan Lipsitz's book, *Successful Schools for Young Adolescents* (1984), is a compilation of four case studies documenting success stories of middle grades schools, those schools serving young adolescents, ages 10-14. Through the case studies, Lipsitz seeks to better characterize "developmentally appropriate" schools within the context of different settings such as urban and rural, to identify practices of effective schools, to explore the characteristics of positive learning environments, and to build an awareness of successful schools beyond the educational community (Lipsitz, 1984).

At the time of the book's publication, many policymakers and the public were calling for a revamping of the nation's public schools after the release of *A Nation at Risk: The Imperative for Educational Reform.* (The Commission on Excellence in Education, 1983).

Lipsitz, who was working as a research associate at the National Institute of Education, sought out middle grades schools that were academically successful and effective, while meeting the developmental needs of students. Her research focused on answering questions such as "What constitutes an effective middle grades school?" and "Does schooling have to be standardized everywhere for all students to achieve?"

Lipsitz invited researchers and practitioners familiar with the nature and needs of young adolescents to nominate effective middle grades schools. From the twelve nominated sites, she selected four schools based on initial school visits, needs criteria established by the Center for Early Adolescence's Middle Grades Assessment Program, school and community location, criteria found in effective schools literature, and the personalities of the schools (Lipsitz, 1984). Selected schools were Western Middle School in Alamance County, North Carolina; Region 7 Middle School in Detroit, Michigan; Samuel V. Noe Middle School in Louisville, Kentucky; and The Shoreham-Wading River Middle School in Shoreham, New York.

In each school, Lipsitz conducted observations for seven days. The case studies developed from those observations included several basic elements such as the school's climate, curriculum, and leadership. She also conducted interviews with key internal and external stakeholders such as teachers, students, administrators, and parents.

Lipsitz concluded that the four schools were responsive to students' social, emotional, cognitive, physical, and moral needs. Each school was unique in its approach to school improvement, given each school's attention to the nature of the community and families the school served (Lipsitz, 1984). All four schools had a clear purpose and vision, emphasizing the importance of knowing the students they teach. Principals played a crucial role in all four schools. Positive school climate was evident and essential to school success. School organization focused on meeting the developmental needs of students (Lipsitz, 1984). From this study, Lipsitz projected that the barriers America's public schools face—such as social and political pressures, economic disparities, and diversity—should not keep middle grades schools from being effective, successful, and developmentally responsive.

REFERENCES

Lipsitz, J. (1984). *Successful schools for young adolescents.* New Brunswick, NJ: Transaction.

The Commission on Excellence in Education. (1983). *A nation at risk: The imperative for educational reform.* Retrieved September 24, 2003, from http://www.ed.gov/pubs/NatAtRisk/index.html

—Angela G. Fiske
The University of Georgia

SWAIM, JOHN H.

John Swaim has been a pioneer in advancing the field of middle grades teacher education. His career has been focused on new and aspiring middle grades teachers and the preparation by which they become highly qualified professionals.

Born and raised in Kansas, Swaim was successful both as a student and as an athlete. He earned his bachelors degree in 1967, then his masters the next year, both at Emporia State University (KS). After a year as social studies teacher at the Kansas State Teachers College Lab School, he moved to Colorado where he earned his doctorate at the University of Northern Colorado (UNC). While serving as a social studies teacher and coach at the university's Lab School, he was active in the developing work of middle grades education. Swaim served as an officer in the Colorado Middle School/Junior High School Association and was a founder of the Western Regional

Middle School Consortium. During these years Swaim was a driving force in efforts to establish a middle level certificate in Colorado.

The Colorado Association of Middle Level Education came into existence in 1976 as a direct result of Swaim's leadership. He served as chair of the founding committee, then as the association's first president from 1976-1977. He cochaired the 1977 NMSA annual conference in Denver. The first NMSA conference to be held in the western part of the United States, where there were few members, the conference was an enormous success, due, in large part, to Swaim's leadership.

As professor at UNC (1976-1994), Swaim assumed numerous responsibilities, including coordinator of early childhood, elementary, and middle school programs, and coordinator of middle school external degree program. Deeply committed to the education and experiences of aspiring middle school teachers, Swaim initiated a campus student group at UNC which set the stage for the establishment of the Collegiate Middle Level Association, of which he was founding faculty sponsor (1990).

In 1980, he was elected president of NMSA. During this tenure, he established a committee to prepare a position paper which ultimately became the landmark publication, *This We Believe.* Swaim's leadership brought national prominence to the association's work in middle level teacher preparation. As a member of the association's Professional Preparation Committee, he helped write the standards that the National Council for the Accreditation of Teacher Education (NCATE) adopted. He was then appointed a member of NCATE's Special Studies Board in 1987, served as chair of that board in 1995-1996, and served as a member of NCATE's Executive Board in 1998-2001.

Swaim has shared his commitment to and expertise in middle level education through the years by teaching at various institutes; presenting at over 100 state, national, and international conferences; consulting with over 90 schools and school districts; writing numerous articles; and contributing to and coauthoring numerous books.

—Mary Henton
National Middle School Association

TAKING CENTER STAGE

In March 2001, the California Department of Education published *Taking Center Stage: A Commitment to Standards-Based Education for California's Middle Grade Students* (2001) as a sequel to the earlier report *Caught in the Middle* (1987).

Taking Center Stage makes the case that student-focused, developmentally responsive schools are the most effective means for bringing all middle grade students to the rigorous achievement levels defined by California's Content Standards. Authentic middle school philosophy, rigorous standards, assessment, and accountability are a complementary ensemble. The document provides practical guidance for teachers and principals.

Taking Center Stage included 14 chapters:

1. California's Middle Schools: Poised for World-Class Performance
2. Standards-Based Education Takes Center Stage: Content and Performance Standards
3. Assessment Takes Center Stage
4. Accountability Takes Center Stage
5. Middle School Philosophy Takes Center Stage: Defining and Affirming Authentic Middle Schools
6. Creating a School Culture to Sustain Standards-Based Education
7. Team Teaching: Made to Order for Standards-Based Middle Schools
8. Instructional Significance of Research on How Students Learn
9. Providing Time for Standards-Based Education
10. Academic Literacy: Key to Equal Access and High Standards of Achievement
11. Social Promotion and Grade Retention: Issues and Challenges
12. Creating High Quality After-Hours Academic Programs in Middle Schools
13. Health, Safety, Resilience, and Civility: Correlates of High Academic Achievement
14. Standards-Based Professional Development at the School Site

In addition, *Taking Center Stage* presented sixteen recommendations for action developed by the Superintendent's Middle Grades Task Force. Table 1 organizes these recommendations by "key elements."

REFERENCES

California Department of Education. (1987). *Caught in the middle: Educational reform for young adolescents in California's public schools.* Sacramento, CA: CDE Press.

California Department of Education. (2001). *Taking center stage: A commitment to standards-based education for California's middle grades students.* Sacramento, CA: CDE Press.

—Jim Miller
California Department of Education

TALENT DEVELOPMENT MIDDLE SCHOOLS

Talent Development Middle Schools implement a comprehensive whole-school reform model developed at Johns Hopkins University. The model was created especially for middle schools that serve many students living in poverty. It assists these schools to

Table 1
Key Elements of *Taking Center Stage*

Key Element	Recommendation of Task Force
I. Rigorous Academic Content and Performance Standards	1. Implement rigorous and consistent standards while maintaining a dynamic student-centered culture.
	2. Provide sustaining resources and support for standards-based education.
II. Curriculum and Instruction	3. Demonstrate commitment to essential elements of the middle grades philosophy.
	4. Align curriculum, instruction, and assessment practices with the California content and performance standards.
	5. Connect the contributions of California's diverse multicultural population as standards are implemented.
	6. Use technology as a tool to improve and increase student academic achievement.
	7. Examine the use of time to provide students and teachers opportunities to plan, integrate, teach, and learn.
	8. Work with feeder elementary schools and destination high schools to provide consistent expectations and seamless transitions.
III. Assessment and Accountability	9. Relate performance standards to content standards to define levels of academic excellence and proficiency.
	10. Develop classroom and local assessment data systems that are used to determine appropriate instructional practices.
	11. Hold all stakeholders accountable for high academic and behavioral expectations.
IV. Student Interventions	12. Provide appropriate accelerated interventions based on the results of relevant assessment instruments.
V. Professional Development	13. Provide relevant and appropriate school-based, comprehensive, ongoing, professional development.
VI. Parent and Community Partnerships	14. Engage families and the community to support student achievement.
VII. Health and Safety	15. Create and sustain safe school environments.
	16. Provide access to health and social services to maximize student well-being.

narrow the huge achievement gap between high-poverty schools and wealthier schools.

The Talent Development Middle School Model (TDMS) is designed to strengthen the supports provided to teachers and administrators and the learning opportunities provided to students while simultaneously facilitating more productive relationships and a less chaotic, demoralized, unsafe or dysfunctional climate in the school (Balfanz, Ruby, & Mac Iver, 2002). Schools who choose to implement TDMS contract with TDMS's nonprofit implementation center to receive assistance. This assistance includes help in selecting and implementing standards-based and research-based instructional programs in reading/English/language arts, math, science, and U.S. history and in providing each teacher with a 2- or 3-year course of study of hands-on training and in-classroom coaching focused on these instructional programs. The hands-on training includes monthly professional development sessions that are grade- and curriculum-specific. These sessions are used to preview and model upcoming lessons, units, and activities; high-

light key or difficult sections; go over critical content knowledge; demonstrate the instructional strategies that will be used; and provide teachers with an opportunity to learn from each other. The professional development sessions are accompanied by weekly classroom implementation coaching from a respected nonjudgmental peer. The coaching ranges from modeling and coteaching to customizing and troubleshooting to making sure the teacher has all the necessary materials and tools to implement the instructional program. To help ensure that the instructional reforms are sustained, "emergent leaders" in each school in each subject are given additional training to equip them to provide timely professional development and support to new teachers as they enter the school.

TDMS's implementation center personnel also assist schools in establishing labs that provide extra academic help to students during regular school hours (Mac Iver, Balfanz, & Plank, 1998; Sion & Garriott, 2002) in judiciously using communal organization structures that give teachers the opportunity to work with smaller groups of students for longer periods of time (Balfanz, Ruby, & Mac Iver, 2002), in creating a schoolwide climate program that addresses lateness, acting out in the classroom, bullying and other troubled or disruptive student behavior (Sorrell, 2003), and in developing effective school, family and community partnerships (Epstein, Sanders, Simon, Salinas, Jansorn, & Van Voorhis, 2002). These interventions work together to create a "no excuses" credo: a faith shown by action that all students can succeed with a challenging, standards-based curriculum, and that it is the collective responsibility of the adults and students in the school to overcome obstacles to this success (Mac Iver & Balfanz, 2001; Wilson & Corbett, 2001).

TDMS's instructional programs are being used in over two dozen schools in six states. Several quasi-experimental longitudinal evaluation studies have been conducted to estimate the impact of these programs on student achievement (e.g., Balfanz & Byrnes, in press; Balfanz, Mac Iver, & Byrnes, in press; Balfanz et al., 2002; Mac Iver, Ruby, Balfanz, & Byrnes, 2003; Mac Iver, Balfanz, Ruby, Byrnes, Lorentz, & Jones, 2004; Plank & Young, in press; Ruby, 2004). These studies show that schools using these programs significantly and substantially outgain control schools in achievement. These superior gains are not limited to one type of student: most student subgroups measurably benefit from a richer and more demanding curriculum, better trained and supported teachers, and an improved teaching and learning environment. Finally, the results also suggest that schools that adopt comprehensive reforms do better than those choosing narrower reforms (e.g. reforms that focus just on academic excellence) because improved classroom instruction and assessment must be combined with improved relationships, support systems, effort, behavior, and attendance to obtain the highest gains in student achievement.

REFERENCES

Balfanz, R., & Byrnes, V. (in press). Closing the mathematics achievement gap in high poverty middle schools: Enablers and constraints. *Journal of Education for Students Placed At Risk*.

Balfanz, R., Mac Iver, D. J., & Byrnes, V. (in press). The implementation and impact of evidence based mathematics reforms in high poverty middle schools: A multi-school, multi-year study. *Journal of Research in Mathematics Education*.

Balfanz, R., Mac Iver, D. J., & Ryan, D. (2002). Enabling "algebra for all" with a facilitated instructional program: A case study of a Talent Development Middle School. In

V. Anfara (Ed.), *Middle school curriculum, instruction, and assessment: Vol. 2. The handbook of research in middle level education* (pp. 181-212). Greenwich, CT: Information Age.

Balfanz, R., Ruby, A., & Mac Iver, D. (2002). Essential components and next steps for comprehensive whole-school reform in high-poverty middle schools. In S. Stringfield & D. Land (Eds.), *Educating at-risk students: One hundred-first yearbook of the National Society for the Study of Education, Part II* (pp. 128-147). Chicago, IL: NSSE.

Epstein, J. L., Sanders, M. G., Simon, B. S., Salinas, K. C., Jansorn, N. R., & Van Voorhis, F. L. (2002). *School, family, and community partnerships: Your handbook for action* (2nd ed.) Thousand Oaks, CA: Corwin Press.

Mac Iver, D.J., & Balfanz, R. (2001, February). No excuses: Committing to high performance. *Principal Leadership, 1*(8), 36-40.

Mac Iver, D. J. Balfanz, R., & Plank, S. B. (1998). An 'elective replacement' approach to providing extra help in math: The Talent Development Middle Schools' Computer- and Team-Assisted Mathematics Acceleration (CATAMA) Program. *Research in Middle Level Education Quarterly, 22*(2), 1-23.

Mac Iver, D. J., Ruby, A., Balfanz, R., & Byrnes, V. (2003). Removed from the list: A comparative longitudinal case study of a reconstitution-eligible school. *Journal of Curriculum and Supervision, 18*(3), 259-289.

Mac Iver, D. J., Balfanz, R., Ruby, A., Byrnes, V., Lorentz, S., & Jones, L. (2004). Developing adolescent literacy in high poverty middle schools: The impact of Talent Development's reforms across multiple years and sites. In P. R. Pintrich & M. L. Maehr (Eds.), *Advances in Motivation and achievement: Vol. 13. Motivating students, improving schools: The legacy of Carol Midgley* (pp. 185-207). Oxford, United Kingdom.: Elsevier.

Plank, S., & Young, E. (in press). In pursuit of school improvement: Evaluations of reading comprehension in the Talent Development Middle School. *School Effectiveness and School Improvement*.

Ruby, A. (2004). *Science reform within whole school reform.* [Manuscript submitted for publication.]

Sion, F., & Garriott, M. (2002). *Computer and Team-Assisted Reading Acceleration (CATARA) handbook.* Baltimore, MD: Talent Development Middle School Program, The Center for the Social Organization of Schools, Johns Hopkins University.

Sorrell, A. (2003, March). *School-wide applications: Talent Development Middle Schools Climate Program.* Paper presented at the First International Conference on Positive Behavior Support, Orlando, Florida.

Wilson, B. L., & Corbett, H. D. (2001). *Listening to urban kids: School reform and the teachers they want.* Albany: State University of New York Press.

—Douglas J. Mac Iver
—Robert Balfanz
—Allen Ruby
Talent Development Middle Schools

TEACHERS: PRESERVICE PREPARATION

For more than 80 years, advocates of young adolescents, who are between the ages of 10 and 15, have called for the specialized preparation of teachers of young adolescents (McEwin, Smith, & Dickinson, 2003). Young adolescents need teachers with specific training who can understand and appreciate the intense emotional, social, moral, and physical changes experienced during this period. Adolescence is bursting with change. Young adolescents experience growth and development at a rapid rate; in fact, this development is more rapid in adolescence than in any other developmental stage except for infancy (Jackson & Davis, 2000). A discussion of the components of middle level teacher preparation programs—experiences that develop a deep and multifaceted understanding of the nature and needs of young adolescents, knowledge of the middle school curricula and philosophy, selection of two areas of specialization, early and continuous field experiences—as well as the current status of middle level teacher preparation follow.

Educators, professional organizations, policymakers, foundations, and other individuals have come to consensus and identified the essential components of middle level teacher preparation programs (Jackson & Davis, 2000; McEwin et al., 2003; National Forum to Accelerate Middle-Grades Reform, 2002; National Middle School Association, 2001). Relevant, authentic academic experiences for middle grades preservice teachers include enlisting in coursework that develops a deep and multifaceted understanding of the nature and needs of young adolescents, emphasizes the philosophy and organization of the middle school, and focuses on the unique aspects of the middle level curricula. In addition, selecting academic specializations in two content areas as well as engaging in early and extended field experiences is essential to the successful preparation of middle level teachers (Jackson & Davis, 2000; McEwin & Alexander, 1986; McEwin & Dickinson, 1995; McEwin et al., 2003). The fundamental elements of middle level teacher preparation focus on the uniqueness of young adolescents and middle schools (Jackson & Davis, 2000).

Coursework that develops a deep and multifaceted understanding of the nature and needs of young adolescents lays the foundation on which all other components build (McEwin & Alexander, 1986; McEwin & Dickinson, 1995). Preservice teachers must understand young adolescents before preparing to teach and interact with them. Muth and Alverman (1999)

state, "Early adolescent transition is a distinct phase requiring special understanding of the conjunction of changes that a young person is undergoing and that have a bearing on learning" (p. 9). Because of the tremendous changes young adolescents' experience, middle school teachers must understand the cognitive, emotional, physical, and social needs of young adolescents and translate that understanding into their practice. Knowing that the needs of young adolescents differ greatly from students of other ages, preservice teachers learn to employ developmentally appropriate learning activities and practices (McEwin et al., 2003).

By engaging in coursework that focuses on the philosophy and organization of middle schools, prospective teachers gain an understanding of the structures within which they will work (Jackson & Davis, 2000; McEwin & Alexander, 1986; McEwin & Dickinson, 1995; McEwin et al., 2003). Preservice teachers must learn about the components of the middle school concept. The components—which include but are not limited to, flexible scheduling, which allows teachers to develop a schedule that best meets the needs of students; integrated curriculum, in which teaching and learning cross traditional subject boundaries; and interdisciplinary teaming, which organizes teachers and students in middle school into teams—usually no more than 5 teachers and 120 students per team (George & Alexander, 2003; Jackson & Davis, 2000; Muth & Alverman, 1999; Stevenson, 2002) must be understood by preservice teachers so their teaching reflects the practices specific to the middle school. Further, preservice teachers must use the particular components of the middle school to foster the growth and development of young adolescents.

By recognizing that middle schools and young adolescents are unique, teachers of young adolescents know that their methods of teaching are also unique (George & Alexander, 2003). Interdisciplinary and integrated instructional methods connect students' interests and concerns about themselves and the world to the curriculum and mandated content standards (Jackson & Davis, 2000; McEwin et al., 2003; National Middle School Association, n.d.). Curriculum in a middle school not only focuses on content knowledge, but also on the interests and needs of the students. Meeting students' needs—such as social, emotional, and intellectual—lies at the heart of middle level curriculum.

Planning, teaching, and assessing student work requires a comprehensive understanding of young adolescent development and content knowledge (McEwin et al., 2003). Preservice teachers need many opportunities to engage in meaningful instructional activities. These activities should be in both the university classroom and the middle school classroom (McEwin et al., 2003). Development of a wide repertoire of planning skills and instructional strategies enables preservice teachers to engage students in purposeful learning activities.

The majority of middle level teacher preparation programs prepare preservice teachers in two academic areas, i.e., math, science, language arts, and social studies (McEwin & Alexander, 1986; McEwin & Dickinson, 1995; McEwin et al., 2003). Preparation in multiple academic areas will enable preservice teachers to "function as effective learning resources in one or more subject areas" (George & Alexander, 2003, p. 57). It is imperative that middle level teachers hold licenses to teach in both areas of specialization and have a vast academic background on which to draw. McEwin and Alexander (1986) state, "This gives preservice candidates more academic specialization than elementary teachers but not as narrow a specialization as that required of secondary teachers" (p. 6). Having knowledge of other content areas enables middle level teachers to be able to make smoother interdisciplinary connections between their content area and others. In addition, using the interdisciplinary connections will serve as a model for students who are seeking ways to connect their learning across subject areas, to themselves, and to the "real world."

Field experiences provide crucial opportunities for preservice teachers to apply knowledge gained in the university classroom and work with students. Field experiences in exemplary middle schools occur early and extend throughout the entire teacher preparation program (Butler, Davies, & Dickinson, 1991; McEwin & Alexander, 1986; McEwin & Dickinson, 1995; McEwin et al., 2003). Early field experiences allow preservice teachers to witness young adolescents in action and gain first-hand knowledge and understandings about young adolescent behavior. Extended field experiences, such as student teaching, provide practice in the real world of teaching and learning (Jackson & Davis, 2000; McEwin et al., 2003). Early and continuous field experiences are critical in middle level education—preservice teachers must understand the population in which they are preparing to teach.

"Advocacy for specialized middle level teacher preparation and licensure has reached unprecedented levels in recent years" (McEwin et al., 2003, p. 11). In 2000, 44 states had some type of middle level licensure, which is a drastic increase from 2 states in 1969 (McEwin et al., 2003). However, only 21 of the 44 states actually require licensing to teach in middle schools. Organizational support (e.g., National Middle School Association), foundations (e.g., Carnegie Corporation of New York), special alliances (National Forum to Accelerate Middle-Grades Reform), and several state departments of education support middle level education and continue to advocate for the special preparation of middle level teachers.

The number of states offering some type of licensure for middle level education is on the rise. Teacher educators and policymakers have come to consensus regarding the essential elements of middle level teacher preparation. Nonetheless, the struggle for support continues. Until teachers who desire to work with young adolescent receive specialized training to teach all young adolescents, advocacy for middle level education and young adolescents must continue.

REFERENCES

Butler, D., Davies, M., & Dickinson, T. (1991). *On site: Preparing middle level teachers through field experiences.* Columbus, OH: National Middle School Association.

George, P. S., & Alexander, W. M. (2003). *The exemplary middle school* (3rd ed.). Belmont, CA: Wadsworth/Thomson Learning.

Jackson, A. W., & Davis, G. A. (2000). *Turning points 2000: Educating adolescents in the 21st century.* New York: Teachers College Press.

McEwin, C. K., & Alexander, W. M. (1986). *Professional certification and preparation for the middle level: A position paper of the National Middle School Association.* Columbus, OH: National Middle School Association.

McEwin, C. K., & Dickinson, T. S. (1995). *The professional preparation of middle level teachers: Profiles of success.* Columbus, OH: National Middle School Association.

McEwin, C. K., Smith, T. W., & Dickinson, T. S. (2003). Middle level teacher preparation: Status, progress and challenges. In P.G. Andrews & V. A. Anfara (Eds.), *Leaders for a movement: Professional preparation and development of middle level teachers and administrators* (pp. 3-26). Greenwich, CT: Information Age.

Muth, K. D., & Alvermann, D. E. (1999). *Teaching and learning in the middle grades* (2nd ed.). Boston: Allyn & Bacon.

National Forum to Accelerate Middle-Grades Reform. (2002). *National forum policy statement: Teacher preparation, licensure, and recruitment.* Retrieved May 14, 2003, from http://www.mgforum.org

National Middle School Association. (2001). *Middle level teacher preparation standards.* Columbus, OH: Author. Retrieved July 15, 2003, from: http://www.nmsa.org

National Middle School Association. (n.d.). *National middle school association's position on professional preparation of middle levelTeachers.* Retrieved July 15, 2003, from http://www.nmsa.org/news/middlelevelteachers.htm

Stevenson, C. (2002). *Teaching ten to fourteen year olds* (3rd ed.). Boston: Allyn & Bacon.

—Nicole L. Thompson
Mississippi State University

TEACHER PROFESSIONAL DEVELOPMENT

INTRODUCTION

According to the National Staff Development Council the term "professional development" is used by educators "to describe the continuing education of teachers, administrators, and other school employees" (2004, para. 1). Since the professional preparation of middle level teachers is situated in a political reality that has traditionally allowed both elementary and secondary certified teachers to teach in middle grades the desirability of professional development programs for teachers of young adolescents is all the more critical.

Currently 21 of 44 states require teachers to acquire a middle level license in order to teach in middle grades schools (Gaskill, 2002). Yet calls for specialized preparation and development programs have been included in the literature for over 80 years and date back to the days of the junior high (see Dickinson & Butler, 1994; Douglas, 1920; Elliot, 1949; Floyd, 1932; Van Til, Lounsbury, & Vars, 1967). Reflecting on the junior high experience, Vars pointed out, "After 60 years in existence, the junior high is still largely a 'school without teachers'—that is without teachers prepared specifically to work at this level" (1969, p.172). In his article, "Must Middle Grades Education Consist of Cast-Offs?," Toepfer (1973) reflected that middle level staffing practices had followed the "retread" approach by staffing middle grades schools with teachers prepared to teacher other age groups at other levels of schooling. Van Til, Lounsbury, and Vars observed, "Perhaps the most serious obstacle to the educational development of the junior high school has been the lack of teachers specifically prepared to work at this level" (p. 49). They further noted that this obstacle had elicited labels such as "the forgotten teaching area."

MIDDLE SCHOOL TEACHERS

The middle school movement, which began in the 1960s primarily as a reform of the junior high movement, inherited many of the same problems that plagued the junior high schools. Pioneers of the middle school movement like William M. Alexander and Donald H. Eichhorn strongly supported the idea of specialized preparation of middle grades teachers. One response to the lack of higher education programs for middle school teacher preparation was presented by the Southern Association of Colleges and Secondary Schools stating, "Because the preparation of teachers, principals and other professional personnel needed to staff our junior high schools has been neglected by most teacher education institutions, development of skills needed at this level must for the present take place in large measure through in-service education" (1958, p. 93).

The Carnegie Council on Adolescent Development took the lead in shaping the agenda for middle level educators with its publication of *Turning Points: Preparing American Youth for the 21st Century* (1989). With regard to the call for ensuring student success by restructuring the tracking system in middle schools, the Carnegie Council emphasized the need for "significant pre- and in-service staff development in alternative instructional practices geared to student diversity" (p. 12). Nevertheless, in their follow up to the original report, Jackson and Davis (2000) admitted, "*Turning Points* paid little attention to middle grades educators' need for effective professional development opportunities" (p. 110).

In January 2002 educators became focused on No Child Left Behind (NCLB). National reports found that one in four classes was taught by a teacher teaching a subject for which s/he had not received a baccalaureate degree, with the ratio climbing to one in two in middle schools (Jerald, 2002). This comprehensive educational reform package guaranteed a highly qualified teacher in every classroom, renewing a focus on subject matter expertise. Certainly the advice of Flowers, Mertens and Mulhall (2002) on teacher professional development during a reform effort applies here: "Schools need to take a proactive approach to teacher professional development that involves a careful examination of current skills and interests as well as an assessment of what needs to be developed through professional development and training" (para. 1). When adopting such an approach, Flowers et al. hold that priority must be given to:

- Assessing teacher skill levels and interests,
- Determining professional development needs,
- Creating a plan for providing teachers with the resources and skills they need to implement new programs and practices in their classrooms. (para. 3)

A BALANCED APPROACH

Supporting new and experienced teachers, the National Staff Development Council's (NSDC) revised Standards for Staff Development reflect what NSDC and the broader staff development community have learned about professional learning since the creation of the original standards in 1995. Staff development that improves the learning of all students:

- Organizes adults into learning communities whose goals are aligned with those of the school and district. (Learning Communities)
- Requires skillful school and district leaders who guide continuous instructional improvement. (Leadership);Requires resources to support adult learning and collaboration. (Resources)
- Uses disaggregated student data to determine adult learning priorities, monitor progress, and help sustain continuous improvement. (Data-Driven)
- Uses multiple sources of information to guide improvement and demonstrate its impact. (Evaluation)
- Prepares educators to apply research to decision making. (Research-Based)
- Uses learning strategies appropriate to the intended goal. (Design)
- Applies knowledge about human learning and change. (Learning)
- Provides educators with the knowledge and skills to collaborate. (Collaboration)
- Prepares educators to understand and appreciate all students, create safe, orderly, and supportive learning environments, and hold high expectations for their academic achievement. (Equity)
- Deepens educators' content knowledge, provides them with research-based instructional strategies to assist students in meeting rigorous academic standards, and prepares them to use various types of classroom assessments appropriately. (Quality Teaching)
- Provides educators with knowledge and skills to involve families and other stakeholders appropriately. (Family Involvement) (National Staff Development Center, 2001)

Drawing upon the theory espoused by NSDC, Sue Swaim, Executive Director of the National Middle School Association advises, "The best way to increase the effectiveness of middle grades teachers is through targeted, ongoing, job-embedded professional development that helps them address the unique needs of their 10- to 15-year-old students" (2004, p. 1). Dickinson, Butler, and Pittard (2003) add that the constructivist approach is the paradigm directing teacher learning and professional development today.

As more is learned about the process of learning to teach and the ways in which teachers hold knowledge about pedagogy and content, professional development has moved in new directions that empower teachers and enable them to construct new knowledge and to renew their commitment to teaching. Professional development has become increasingly important given that the diverse context of schooling becomes more challenging and demanding by the minute. Specific to middle level education, increased research and resulting knowledge of early adolescent development, combined with the impact of the middle school movement, have contributed to changes in professional development programs in middle schools. (pp. 108-109)

The "bottom line" for Jackson and Davis (2000) is a professional development plan that is embedded in the daily work lives of middle level teachers. According to Pate and Thompson (2003), change is the key to effective professional development: "Teachers taking new knowledge about young adolescents, parents, community members, content, curriculum, instruction, assessment, and so on, and using that information to make a difference in the lives of their students" (p. 126). Results of their study of 8,300 teachers from 294 middle grades schools, led Flowers and Mertens (2003) to conclude that one size does not fit all when it comes to designing professional development activities. In addressing the same topic, Mullen and Andrews (2003) take a stronger position stating, "The National Board's certification process is superior to traditional methods of professional development in one crucial way: It requires ownership" (p. 173). All agree that professional development of teachers is available in many forms and should be based on input from both teachers and administrators. The following forms warrant attention.

UNDERGRADUATE AND GRADUATE STUDIES

There is consensus regarding the appropriate nature of specialized middle level teacher preparation and professional development (McEwin & Dickinson, 1996; National Forum to Accelerate Middle-Grades Reform, 2002). As reflected in the performance-based National Middle School Association (NMSA/National Council for Accreditation of Teacher Education [NCATE]) Middle Level Teacher Preparation Standards (2001), candidates are required to demonstrate their knowledge of middle level curriculum and competence in applying developmentally appropriate instructional practices to meet the diverse needs of middle level students.

LEARNING COMMUNITIES

From his perspective as former elementary school administrator in three schools, Barth (1990) found success in "promoting the growth of teachers by rearranging the conditions and structures under which teachers work" (p. 59). By instituting three new practices, Barth suggests that schools can become communities of learners. The common theme was giving teachers access to one another's classrooms.

1. Faculty meetings were held each time in a different teacher's classroom. The meetings began with the host teacher giving a description of what characterized the classroom at the time.
2. Placement of pupils was based upon the answers to two questions: "Under what instructional conditions does each child in a class seem to work best? And which of next year's teachers comes closest to providing those conditions?" (p. 60).
3. Schoolwide responsibilities were shared among committees of teachers with full autonomy to make decisions (excerpted from Barth, pp. 59-62).

EVALUATION AND ASSESSMENT

The National Association of Elementary School Principals recommends that principals develop a teacher evaluation plan. Based on the assumption that evaluations are meant "to build on the foundation of skills that teachers already possess" (1988, p. 1), teachers are afforded information and feedback on where and how to improve their teaching. In so doing, teachers are able to become more effective.

Research conducted by Wise, Darling-Hammond, McLaughlin, and Bernstein (1984) reveals two purposes for evaluation of individual teachers: improvement (development assessment) and/or accountability (personal rating). A teacher is given a personal rating when administrative decisions need to be made regarding tenure, salary, contracts, promotions, etc. Until recently, the rating scale recommended by the Research-Based Teacher Evaluation (RBTE) was widely used. Critics of this scale questioned its validity with regard to teacher as moral agent (Greene, 1985), and teaching as a dichotomous activity (Doyle, 1985; Popham, 1987). In response to the critics, the National Board for Professional Teaching Standards developed other approaches to teacher evaluation inclusive of written tests of knowledge and portfolios (Shulman, 1988).

CLINICAL SUPERVISION

The second purpose of assessment is development and improvement. The most common form of developmental assessment is the clinical supervision cycle pioneered by Goldhammer (1969) and Cogan (1973). Though current models adapt to particular circumstances, the stages that generally occur in clinical supervision are: (a) planning, (b) observing, (c) analyzing, (d) conferring, and (e) reflecting/evaluating (see also Acheson & Gall, 1987). The process of clinical supervision requires extensive classroom observation.

In her synthesis of 32 studies on the effects of clinical supervision, Pavan (1985) revealed that teacher attitudes were positive toward supervision of this type. At that time, however, Pavan found little evidence to support the process of clinical supervision as a means for teacher improvement. Subsequently, Pavan (1993) introduced a diagnostic tool developed for examining current levels of clinical supervision practice, which promises to serve as a set of standards to determine degrees of implementation. *Turning Points* (Carnegie Council on Adolescent Development, 1989, p. 60) describes a teacher selection procedure based on classroom observation and portfolio evaluation which could naturally flow into the developmental assessment process of clinical supervision.

TEACHER AS RESEARCHER

"Research with practitioners, and often *by* practitioners, who want to improve their own situation and discover and solve problems is called action research" (Marshall & Rossman, 1999, p. 160). Action research is based upon the inquiry model (teacher inquiry, collaborative inquiry, teacher-as-researcher) and typically involves practitioners who engage in research to improve their practice. The researcher's role is that of facilitator who expands the questions through knowledge of existing literature.

PDS

The appearance of Professional Development Schools/System (PDS) resulted from an understanding that concurrent reforms in teacher preparation and school transformation can best be brought about when schools and universities work together in partnerships. PDS improves the quality of teacher preparation and performance through application experiences such as site-based seminars and classroom- and school-level research.

CONCLUSION

The NMSA Research Committee (2003) recently offered directions for future research in middle level education. Top on the list of six recommendations is the need for more large-scale, longitudinal studies focused on the link between the middle school model and student achievement. To that end, Dickinson, Butler and Pittard (2003) add: "While the implications abound for support of the relationship between teacher professional development and student achievement, the field currently lacks a corpus of literature and research specifically explaining that relationship. At the middle level, we need to move in the direction of exploring that relationship" (p. 117).

REFERENCES

Acheson, K., & Gall, M. (1987). *Techniques in the clinical supervision of teachers: Preservice and inservice applications* (2nd ed.). New York: Longman.

Barth, R. (1990). *Improving schools from within: Teachers, parents, and principals can make the difference.* San Francisco: Jossey-Bass.

Carnegie Council on Adolescent Development. (1989). *Turning points: PreparingAmerican youth for the 21st century* (The Report of the Task Force on Education of Young Adolescents). New York: Carnegie Corporation of New York.

Cogan, M. (1973). *Clinical supervision.* Boston: Houghton Mifflin.

Dickinson, T. S., & Butler, D. (1994). The journey to the other side of the desk: The education of middle school teachers. In F. M. Smith & C. O. Hausafus (Eds.), *The education of early adolescents: Home economics in the middle school, Yearbook of the American Home Economics Association* (pp. 183-191). Peoria, IL: Macmillan/McGraw-Hill.

Dickinson, T. S., Butler, D. A., & Pittard, W. M. (2003). Professional development and the middle level school: Tangled threads. In P. G. Andrews & V. A. Anfara, Jr. (Eds.) *Leaders for a movement: Professional preparation and development of middle level teachers and administrators* (pp. 99-122). Greenwich, CT: Information Age.

Douglas, A. (1920). *The junior high school.* Bloomington, IL: National Study of Education.

Doyle, W. (1985). Effective teaching and the concept of the master teacher. *Elementary School Journal, 86*(1), 27-34.

Elliot, L. H. (1949). The junior high school: A school without teachers. *Education, 70*, 186-190.

Flowers, N., Mertens, S. B., & Mulhall, P. F. (2002, May). Four important lessons about teacher professional development. *Middle School Journal Research Articles.* Retrieved June 8, 2004, from http://www.nmsa.org/research/articles/res_articles_may2002c.htm

Flowers, N., & Mertens, S. B. (2003). Professional development for middle grades teachers: Does one size fit all? In P. G. Andrews & V. A. Anfara, Jr. (Eds.) *Leaders for a movement: Professional preparation and development of middle level teachers and administrators* (pp. 145-162). Greenwich, CT: Information Age.

Floyd, O. R. (1932). *The preparation of junior high school teachers.* U. S. Office of Education Bulletin, No. 20, Washington, DC: U. S. Government Printing Office.

Gaskill, P. E. (2002). Progress in the certification of middle level personnel. *Middle School Journal, 33*(5), 33-40.

Goldhammer, R. (1969). *Clinical supervision: Special methods for the supervision ofteachers.* New York: Holt, Rinehart, & Winston.

Greene, M. (1985). A philosophic look at merit and mastery in teaching. *Elementary School Journal, 86*(1), 17-26.

Jackson, A.W., & Davis, G. A. (2000). *Turning points 2000: Educating adolescents in the 21st century.* New York: Teachers College Press.

Jerald, C. D. The Education Trust. (2002). All talk, no action: Putting an end to out-of-field teaching. Retrieved August 28, 2002, from http://www2.edtrust.org/NR/rdonlyres/8DE64524-592E-4C83-A13A-6B1DF1CF8D3E/AllTalk.pdf

Marshall, C., & Rossman, G. (1995). *Designing qualitative research* (2nd ed.). ThousandOaks, CA: Sage.

McEwin, C. K., & Dickinson, T. S. (1995). *The professional preparation of middle level teachers: Profiles of successful programs.* Westerville, OH: National Middle School Association.

Mullen, T. M., & Andrews, P. G. (2003). National board certification as staff development: A teacher's perspective. In P. G. Andrews & V. A. Anfara, Jr. (Eds.) *Leaders for a movement: Professional preparation and development of middle level teachers and administrators* (pp.163-176). Greenwich, CT: Information Age.

National Association of Elementary School Principals. (1988). *Effective teachers: Effective evaluation in America's elementary and middle schools.* Alexandria, VA: Author.

National Forum to Accelerate Middle-Grades Reform. (2002). *Policy statement: Teacher preparation, licensure, and recruitment.* Newton, MA: Education Development Center.

National Middle School Association. (2001). *Middle level teacher preparation standards.* Columbus, OH: Author. Retrieved June 10, 2004, from http://www.nmsa.org.

NMSA Research Committee. (2003). *Research and resources in support of This We Believe.* Westerville, OH: National Middle School Association.

National Staff Development Council. (2001). *NSDC standards for staff development.* Retrieved June 13, 2004, from http://www.nsdc.org/standards/index.cfm

Pate, P. E., & Thompson, K. F. (2003). Effective professional development: What is it? In P. Gayle Andrews & Vincent A. Anfara, Jr. (Eds.) *Leaders for a movement: Professional preparation and development of middle level teachers and administrators* (pp.123-143). Greenwich, CT: Information Age Publishing.

Pavan, B. (1985). *Clinical supervision: Research in schools utilizing comparative measures.* Paper presented at annual meeting of the American Educational Research Association. (ERIC Document Reproduction Service No. 255 516)

Pavan, B. (1993). Examining clinical supervision practice. In R. Anderson & K. Snyder (Eds.) *Clinical supervision: Coaching for higher performance* (pp. 135-153). Lancaster, PA: Technomic.

Popham, W. (1987). The shortcomings of champagne teacher evaluations. *Journal ofPersonnel Evaluation in Education, 1*(2), 25-28.

Shulman, L. (1988). A union of insufficiencies: Strategies for teacher assessment in a period of educational reform. *Educational Leadership, 46*(3), 36-40.

Southern Association of Colleges and Secondary Schools. (1958). *The junior high school program.* Atlanta, GA: Author.

Swaim, S. (2004). Letter available on Nmsa Web site.

Toepfer, C. F. (1973). Must middle grades education consist of "cast offs"? *Educational Leadership, 30,* 211-213.

Van Til, W., Vars, G. F., & Lounsbury, J. H. (1967). *Modern education for the junior high school.* New York: Bobbs-Merrill.

Vars, G. F. (1969). Teacher preparation for the middle schools. *High School Journal,* 172-177.

Wise, A., Darling-Hammond, L., McLaughlin, M., & Bernstein, H. (1984). *Teacher evaluation: A study of effective practices.* Santa Monica, CA: RAND.

—Kathleen Roney
The University of North Carolina, Wilmington

TECHNOLOGY INTEGRATION

Whether educators are ready or not, technology is already changing education (Shank, 2000). Many view students as needing to be technologically savvy if they are going to live in our wired world. Technology is here and changing how students and teachers interact with each other, how they access information, and how they do their work.

Significant resources have been expended to place computers in the schools. Those expenditures seem to be growing almost exponentially. According to a study by the Educational Testing Service, the total cost of technology in U.S. schools by the late 1990s was about $3 billion (Coley, Cradler, & Engal, 1998) and the Milken Family Foundation reports that in 1999 schools spent nearly $5.4 billion dollars on educational technology. The U.S. Department of Education has responded to the growing infusion of educational technology with National Educational Technology Goals, including the need to use research and evaluation to "improve the next generation of technology applications for teaching and learning." As plans are made for the increased use of technology, it is important for policymakers, educators, and researchers to understand how teachers and children relate to this technology (Martin, Heller, & Mahmoud, 1992).

EDUCATION TECHNOLOGY AND ACHIEVEMENT

"Does it work? Is it effective?" are legitimate questions about educational technology. Bracewell, Breuleux, Laferriere, Beniot, and Abdous (1998) assert that the integration of educational technology into the classroom, in conjunction with supportive pedagogy, typically leads to increased student interest and motivation in learning, more student-centered classroom environments, and increased real-life or authentic learning opportunities. Davis (1997) agrees that technology integration has led to student-centered classrooms, which increased student self-esteem "The Impact of Educational Technology on Student Achievement" (Schacter, 1995) reflects the analysis of more than 700 studies and concludes that students who had access to educational technology showed positive gains in academic achievement.

According to "Technology in American Schools: Seven Dimensions for Gauging Progress" (Lemke & Coughlin, 1998), while further research studies are needed, emerging trends indicate that under the right conditions technology:

- Accelerates, enriches, and deepens basic skills.
- Motivates and engages students in learning.
- Helps relate academics to the practices of today's work force.
- Increases economic viability of tomorrow's workers.
- Strengthens teaching.
- Contributes to change in schools
- Connects schools to the world.

After reviewing the available research, the National Association of School Boards of Education Study Group on e-Learning (NASBE, 2001) concluded "e-Learning will improve American education in valuable ways and should be universally implemented as soon as possible" (p. 4).

WHAT CRITICS SAY

Not all the research paints a rosy picture of technology in schools. Some show no academic improvement; no pay off for costly investments (Mathews, 2000). And some stories in the press from communities, like Henrico County in Virginia, that have invested heavily in technology only to have equipment broken and stolen and students accessing inappropriate web sites, scare parents and teachers alike. Some critics see technology hindering learning for children. Healy (1999) and Oppenheimer (1997) believe that funds invested in technology take funding away from other resources and programs that may be more beneficial to students. A report issued by The Alliance for Childhood (2000) states that an over-reliance on technology can rob from children opportunities to express creativity, build human relationships, or experience hands-on learning.

Some of these studies that show no positive effect from the introduction of technology into schools indicate deeper problems with the implementation. Many schools for example, have technology sitting idle, or only allow students to use it infrequently. Other schools conduct almost no training for their teachers or provide teachers with technology based curriculum materials. Under such circumstances, no one would expect there to be increases in student achievement.

Other studies with negative results indicate that the initiatives themselves focused on hardware and software, or teachers taught about the technology instead of using the technology to enhance learning experiences. Analyzing over 700 studies, Schacter (1995) concludes that technology initiatives have to focus on teaching and learning, not the technology, in order to be successful: "One of the enduring difficulties about technology and education is that a lot of people think about the technology first and the education later" (Schacter, 1995, p. 11). Educators are starting to recognize it is more important to use technology for learning than it is to learn how to use technology.

It is clear that when researchers try to evaluate the educational uses of technology, what they are really evaluating are the broader pedagogical practices being used. The question is becoming what kinds of technology are being used, under what context, and in what ways (Fulton, 1998; Software and Information Industry Association, 2000; Wenglinsky, 1998).

> People who recommend more computers for the schools are like doctors who prescribe more medicine. What medicine? How much medicine? For what reason? The same questions apply to computers. (Tapscott, 1998, p. 135)

The "automation" approach to educational computing (sometimes called "Type I"; Maddux, Johnson, & Willis, 2001)) uses computers to mimic the same behaviors and procedures that teachers do without the technology. That would include using technology to create worksheets and keep track of grades, to create PowerPoint presentations instead of using the blackboard or overheads, to post coursework and content online, to practice skills or learn new information through educational software, or to have online discussions.

> Much of our early educational software, for example, was really direct textbook automation—we called it computer-assisted instruction. Later on came computer literacy, the computer-as-a-tool movement, and distance learning - which also repeated the basic prac-

tice of schools. Teachers still instruct in the same manner as before the technological innovation, delivering a content-based curriculum. (November, 1990)

Automation, ease of access, ease of modification, and looking good: these are real advantages of Type I computing. There are lots of times that it is appropriate to simply automate conventional practices. The problem, however, is that educational technologists do not generally feel that automation (Type I) tasks alone are a cost-effective use of technology.

> Type I applications by themselves, no matter how well applied, cannot justify educational computing to media critics, other educators, school board members, legislators, or the public at large. Type I uses are insufficient because educational computing is too expensive to devote entirely to relatively trivial problems. (Maddux et al., 2001, p. 96)

In some places, Type I computing is equated with the educational use of technology, and it is not surprising, therefore, that, under those circumstances (e.g. Oppenheimer, 1997), technology integration has met with a great deal of criticism.

NEW TEACHING MODELS

Educational visionaries are often frustrated with how technology has mostly been used only to automate traditional education. They see the various ways technology will be used to revolutionize education through learning by doing (Papert, 1996;) and through the kinds of collaborative communities young people are creating through technology (Tapscott, 1998). Further, "[c]omputer based technology has been called an essential ingredient in restructuring because it can provide the diversity in instructional methods necessary to reach all school children," according to Polin (1991, p. 6). Papert sees the important role technology can play in learning.

> I am convinced that a large proportion (though certainly not all) of cases of learning difficulty are produced by imposing on children ways of learning that go against their personal styles. Over and over again I have seen children shake off their apparent disabilities when given the opportunity to learn in a way that comes naturally to them. What I see as the real contribution of digital media to education is a flexibility that could allow every individual to find personal paths to learning. (Papert, 1996, p. 16)

The real gains which come from new technologies are not from Type I applications, but from Type II applications (Maddux et al., 2001). Type II applications represent innovation in teaching and learning. Within education, Type II applications make available new and better ways of teaching. Muir (2001) points out that Type II uses of educational technology involve empowering students to do work they could not do before (or do as easily). Innovation often involves looking beyond how teachers can use technology for their teaching, to how students can use technology for their learning. There is often a focus on the process of learning content, not just how to make content available to students.

Papert advocates allowing students to construct their own knowledge by creating products to teach others. Tapscott explains Papert's view this way: "He explains that an instructionalist might make a game to teach the multiplication tables. A constructionist presents students with the challenge of inventing and creating the game" (Tapscott, 1998, p. 144).

> Teresa M., a teacher at Bellevue Elementary School near Seattle, gave her fourth-grade class this assignment. The students were to organize themselves into groups of four, each of which would act as an educational software company for the semester. By the end of the semester, each company would produce an "educational software package" containing software, a user's manual, a teacher's manual, advertising and whatever else the company decided to include. Each company could choose the educational content of its package…. Idit Harel [found] that when the students were asked to make educational software about a subject they found boring—in this case it was fractions—they developed an interest in the subject and increased their test scores. (Papert, 1996, pp. 21-22)

One approach, for example, shown to engage students in learning is the use of computers driving multimedia and hypermedia tools (Gooden, 1996; International Society for Technology in Education, 1990; Jensen, 1991; Muir, 1993; Ray, 1991). Lehrer (1993) found that multimedia tends to have long term effects on understanding and retention. In a study of eighth graders using a hypertext/multimedia tool to design their own lessons about the American Civil War, the scores of students using the multimedia tool did not differ from the scores of the control group on a test given at the completion of the lesson. However, when tested one year later by an independent interviewer, the multimedia group displayed elaborate concepts and ideas that they had extended to other areas of history. In contrast, the control group of students remembered almost nothing about the historical content of the Civil War lesson.

Other examples of Type II computing include the following:

Fast ForWord, a CD-ROM training program focused on auditory processing and oral language, can enable children with dyslexia to learn to read, helping them learn to process and interpret the very rapid sequence of sounds within words and sentences by exaggerating and slowing them down. Various and vast were the improvements as a result of this program (Temple et al., 2003).

Seventh, eighth, and ninth grade physics students used software (ThinkerTools) that enabled them to be aware of where they were in the inquiry process and to reflect upon their own and other student's inquiries. These students were better able to apply principles of Newtonian mechanics to real-world situations than were eleventh and twelfth grade students who had not used the software (White & Frederiksen, 1998).

Boster, Meyer, Roberto, and Inge (2002) studied instruction involving video clips offered by a company called Unitedsteaming. One group of eighth graders were shown clips related to state learning standards related to social studies and science and the control group covered similar content but without exposure to the video clips. The experimental group showed significant improvements in social studies over the control group.

TECHNOLOGY INTEGRATION PROMOTES EFFECTIVE PEDAGOGY

Technology may not simply offer teachers new instructional opportunities. It also promotes that shift in teaching paradigms from whole class instruction to small group learning environments, as well as, a change from passive learning to more engaged learning (Pelgrum & Anderson, 1999; Roblyer & Edwards, 2000; Voogt & Odenthal, 1999). Means and Olson (1997) found that technology helps teachers in that it allows an increase in their technology and pedagogical skills, fosters greater collaboration, greater contact and collaboration with external school reform and research organizations, and more involvement in training and professional conferences. Another study (Barrett, 2002) showed that the technology extended ways of teaching, and accommodated different learning styles. Yang's (2002) study revealed that the strategies the teacher used with laptops in the classroom including problem-based learning, project-based learning, collaborative learning, hands-on activities, and having students use laptops as cognitive tools. In summary, technology has the potential to improve teaching and learning, but it depends heavily on the teachers' purposes in using the technology, under which contexts they use it, and in which ways it is used.

REFERENCES

Alliance for Childhood. (2000). *Fool's gold: A critical look at computers in childhood.* College Park, MD: Author. Retrieved January 20, 2005, from http://www. allianceforchildhood.net/projects/computers/ computers_reports_fools_gold_contents.htm

Barrett, J. (2002, September). Four years of portability: Perspectives on a laptop program. *MultiMedia Schools,* 46-49.

Boster, F. J., Meyer, G. S., Roberto, A. J., & Inge, C. C. (2002). *A report on the effect of the unitedstreaming (TM) application on educational performance.* Farmville, VA: Longwood University.

Bracewell, R., Breuleux, A., Laferriere, T., Beniot, J., & Abdous, M. (1998). *The emerging contribution of online resources and tools to classroom learning and teaching.* Montreal, Québec, Canada: Universite Laval. Retrieved March 19, 2002, from http://www.tact.fse.ulaval.ca/ang/html/ review98.html

Coley, R. J., Cradler, J., & Engal, P.K. (1998). *Computers and classrooms: The status of technology in U.S. schools* (Policy Information Report). Princeton, NJ: Policy Information Center, Educational Testing Service.

Davis, S. (1997, November) How matering technology can transform math class. *Educational Journal,* 49-51.

Fulton, K. (1998). *Kathleen Fulton on evaluating the effectiveness of educational technology.* Academy for Educational Development. Retrieved January 20, 2005, from http:// millennium.aed.org/fulton.shtml

Gooden, A. R. (1996). *Computers in the classroom: How teachers and students are using technology to transform learning.* San Francisco: Apple Press/Jossey-Bass.

Healy, J. M. (1999). The mad dash to compute. In K. Ryan & J. M. Cooper (Eds.), *Kaleidoscope* (pp. 414-418). Boston: Houghton Mifflin.

International Society for Technology in Education. (1990). *Vision: TEST (Technologically Enriched Schools of Tomorrow).* Eugene, OR: Author.

Jensen, E. (1991). HyperCard and AppleShare help at-risk students. *The Computing Teacher, 18*(6), 26-29.

Lehrer, R. (1993). Authors of knowledge: Patterns of hypermedia design. In S. P. Lajoie & S. J. Derry (Eds.), *Computers as cognitive tools* (pp. 197-227). Hillsdale, NJ: Erlbaum.

Lemke, C., & Coughlin, E. C. (1998). *Technology in American schools: seven dimensions for gauging progress. a policymaker's guide.* The Milken Exchange on Educational Technology. Retrieved January 20, 2005, from http://www.mff. org/publications/publications.taf?page=158

Maddux, C., Johnson, D., & Willis, J. (2001). *Educational computing: Learning with tomorrow's technologies.* Needham Heights, MA: Allyn & Bacon.

Martin, C. D., Heller, R. S., & Mahmoud, E. (1992). American and Soviet children's attitudes toward computers. *Journal of Educational Computing Research, 8*(2), 155-185.

Mathews, J. (2000, May 2). High-tech heretics: Group of skeptical educators questions the usefulness of computers in the classroom. *The Washington Post,* p. A11.

Means, B., & Olson, K. (1997). Technology and education reform. Office of Educational Research and Improvement, Contract No. RP91-172010. Washington, DC: U.S. Department of Education. Retrieved February 3, 2003, from http://www.ed.gov/pubs/SER/Technology/title. html.

Muir, M. (1993). *Kindling the fire: A classroom guide to curriculum-driven HyperCard projects.* Eugene, OR: International Society for Technology in Education.

Muir, M. (2001). What engages underachieving middle school students in learning? *Middle School Journal, 33*(2), 37-43.

National Association of School Boards of Education Study Group on e-Learning (NASBE). (2001). *Any time, any place, any path, any pace: Taking the lead on e-learning policy.* Retrieved September 25, 2005, from http://www.nasbe. org/Organization_Information/e_learning.pdf

November, A. (1990). *Moving beyond automation.* Retrieved January 20, 2005, from http://www.anovember.com/ articles/automation.html).

Oppenheimer, T. (1997, July). The computer delusion. *Atlantic Monthly.* Retrieved January 20, 2005, from http:// www2.theAtlantic.com/issues/97jul/computer.htm

Papert, S. (1996). *The connected family: Bridging the digital generation gap.* Marietta, GA: Longstreet Press.

Pelgrum, W. J., & Anderson R. E. (1999). *ICT and the emerging paradigm for life long learning: A worldwide assessment of infrastructure, goals and practices.* Amsterdam: International Association for the Evaluation of Educational Achievement.

Polin, L. (1991). Research windows: School restructuring and technology. *The Computing Teacher, 18*(6), 6-7.

Ray, D. (1991). Technology and restructuring part I: New educational directions. *The Computing Teacher, 18*(6), 9-20.

Roblyer, M. D., & Edwards, J. (2000). *Integrating educational technology into teaching* (2nd ed). Upper Saddle River, NJ: Prentice Hall.

Schacter, J. (1995). The impact of educational technology on student achievement. The Milken Exchange on Educational Technology. Retrieved January 20, 2005, from http: //www.mff.org/publications/publications.taf?page=161

Shank, R. C. (2000, January). A vision of education in the 21st century. *Technology Horizons in Education (T.H.E.) Journal,* 42-45.

Software and Information Industry Association. (2000). *2000 research report on the effectiveness of technology in schools: Executive summary.* Washington, DC: Author.

Tapscott, D. (1998). *Growing up digital: The rise of the net generation.* New York: McGraw-Hill.

Temple, E., Deutsch, G., Poldrack, R., Miller, S., Tallal, P., Merzenich, M., & Gabrieli, J. (2003). Neural deficits in children with dyslexia ameliorated by behavioral remediation: Evidence from functional MRI. *Proceedings from the National Academy of Sciences,* PNAS, March 4, 2003, Vol. 100, No. 5, pp. 2860-2865. Retrieved May 12, 2003, from http://www.pnas.org/cgi/doi/10.1073/pnas.0030098100

Voogt, J. M., & Odenthal, L. E. (1999). Met het oog op de toekomst. Een studie naar innovatief gebruik van ICT in het onderwijs [With a view to the future. A study on innovative use of ICT in education]. Enschede: University of Twente.

Wenglinsky, H. (1998). *Does it compute? The relationship between educational technology and student achievement in mathematics*. Princeton, NJ: Educational Testing Service. Retrieved March 6, 2002, from ftp://ftp.ets.org/pub/res/technolog.pdf

White, B. Y., & Frederiksen, J. R. (1998). Inquiry, modeling, and metacognition: Making science accessible to all students. *Cognition and Instruction, 16*(1), 3-188.

Yang, C. (2002, June). *Integration of laptops into a k-12 learning environment: A case study of a science teacher in the middle school*. ED-MEDIA 2002 World Conference on Educational Multimedia, Hypermedia & Telecommunications. Proceedings.

—Mike Muir
—Nick Scott
—Holly Wess
University of Maine, Farmington

TESTING

The most common testing situation students encounter is in the regular classroom setting when their teacher decides it is time to see what they have learned. Sometimes students face tests written by the textbook author, and sometimes the teacher creates the test. Most students in middle school see these types of tests every week, but that is not what the majority of educators mean when they use the word "testing." For educators, testing usually refers to a state or federal test that is used to measure student achievement. People in general like to use numbers. Numbers are unemotional, easy to compare, and give the feeling of something scientific and indisputable. The desire to put a number on students' achievement has become a driving force for much of our educational system.

Intelligence and knowledge are not something we can measure as accurately as someone's height or weight. The U.S. Army, however, popularized the idea of using a number to represent their soldiers' intelligence. IQ tests were first used in World War I to determine what assignments were best for different soldiers. IQ tests provided a way to attach a number to intelligence and allowed people's intelligence levels, at least in theory, to be compared as easily as their heights.

Testing is now used to attach an array of numbers to students, classes, schools, districts, states, and nations. Teachers want to know what their students missed in the previous grade. Administrators want a way to divide their students into classes or tracks, and compare how the teachers are doing. School boards want to know which schools are performing better than others in their district so they can reallocate funds. Parents want to know if their kid is smarter than the next-door neighbor's kid. The state wants to know which schools should be rewarded or punished for this year. Researchers want to know which curricula, reforms, teaching styles, grouping strategies, and assessment methods work best. Everyone from the federal government on down wants to know what is best for educating children, and testing is where we tend to look for answers.

Middle schools are not immune to the testing epidemic. The National Middle School Association (NMSA) has said that the eighth grade is the most tested of all the grades. The test scores, however, show that the middle school is apparently lagging behind. Bradley (1998), referring to the Third International Mathematics and Science Study, stated, "On the international study, 13-year-olds perform less well as a group than 9-year-olds" (p. 39). Some critics of the "middle school concept" use studies that report any kind of negative result as evidence that middle schools do not work. We as educators need to be aware of the significance attached to test results.. We also need to understand the different types of testing and the vocabulary associated with testing.

The following sections summarize some key testing terminology including criterion-referenced and norm-referenced testing, achievement testing, and standardized testing. What makes testing terminology even more difficult is that a single test may have a number of different terms attached to it, such as, "standardized, norm-referenced, achievement test." However, a test that is criterion-referenced cannot also be norm-referenced at the same time, so the testing terminology summary will begin there.

CRITERION-REFERENCED TESTING

The main differences between criterion-referenced and norm-referenced testing relate to how the test-takers are scored and how they will be compared to other test-takers. Criterion-referenced tests assign a score to each student that reflects how well the student did on the test. The scores of other test-takers have no effect on the scoring. An example of a criterion-referenced test would be a chapter test on the levels of government in a sixth grade social studies class. The teacher gives the test then assigns a score to each student based on his or her answers. It is possible for every student to make a 100%. It is also possible for every student to fail, but there is normally a spread of scores ranging from 0-100%. A well-developed test has questions that are moderately difficult and are designed to test the specific knowledge or skills that the students should have learned prior to the assessment. This way the students who did learn the material will score well and the ones that need more instruction can be identified. Many states are now administering their own criterion-referenced tests to their students to measure their mastery of the grade level curriculum. Using guidelines from the No Child Left Behind Act of 2001, the states typically take students' scores and assign them to one of three categories: does not meet expectations, meets expectations, or exceeds expectations. Since the tests are criterion-referenced, no set number of students shows up in each category. In theory, every student could make the exact same score. This outcome, of course, is highly unlikely, but the goal for the states is to have every student score in the meets or exceeds expectations categories.

NORM-REFERENCED TESTING

Norm-referenced tests are more difficult to create, score, and explain to parents, but these are the type of tests that schools have used most in the past. When students take a norm-referenced test, they are compared to all the other students in the country who have taken the same test. Students are given a score known as a percentile ranking. This is a percent score that ranges from 1-99%. It tells where on a normal range the students would be. For example, Morgan takes the Iowa Test of Basic Skills (ITBS) in sixth grade. When his test scores come in, he receives a percentile ranking of 75% in math. This score means that he did better than 75% of all the sixth graders in the nation that took the test. It also means that 25% did better than Morgan. The average score is 50%. When the tests are scored, half of the test-takers score above 50% and half score below 50%. Since Morgan's score was higher than 50%, he could be considered above average. His 75% does not tell us how many questions he answered correctly. He may have answered 95% correctly and still received a percentile ranking of 75%, if 25% of the nation's sixth-graders answered more than 95% of the questions correctly.

When a test has been "normed," its test questions contain a wide range of difficulty. The test-makers intentionally have some items that are easy, some that are difficult, and some that are in-between. This allows them to give the percentile rankings more accurately. If all of the test items were so simple that every student answered all of them correctly, how could we tell which students outperformed other students? Many of the scores would be similar. In order to ensure a wider range of scores, the tests are normed and contain a range of difficulty; so we can decide who is best, second best, and so on.

STANDARDIZED TESTING

Often, the tests administered state-wide or nation-wide are standardized. This simply means that the test is administered in the same fashion for every student. All students have the same instructions read to them, and they are all given the same amount of time to complete the test. This standardization is extremely important when giving a norm-referenced test. It would not be appropriate to compare student scores if some students were allowed 60 minutes for a test and others were only allowed 25 minutes.

Each test has its own definition for what is standardized. For example, some tests allow students to use calculators for certain sections of the math test. Their answer sheets include a place to mark whether or not the students used calculators. The test-makers then take that into account when assigning the rankings. Most tests that teachers give in their classroom during the normal business of schooling are not standardized. The teacher may read a word or a sentence for a student who has trouble with a question. If the teacher does not read the same words for everyone, the test is not considered standardized. Norm-referenced and criterion-referenced tests are often standardized so that they are considered appropriate for everyone.

ACHIEVEMENT TESTING

Achievement tests are tests given to students to see if they have achieved an understanding of a concept. Most often teachers administer achievement tests to their students after the class has received some instruction in class. These are the types of tests that are used in education quite frequently. The social studies test, mentioned in the criterion-referenced testing section, would probably not have been given until the teacher had taught the chapter about the levels of government. The teacher would use the test to see if the class understood the levels and why they are used. If the class did not do well, then the teacher would reteach the material that the class missed.

Even though they are not used as often as classroom tests, state-wide and nation-wide tests are what come to most people's minds when achievement tests are mentioned. These large scale tests may be norm-referenced, like the Iowa Test of Basic Skills (ITBS) or they may be criterion-referenced like Georgia's Criterion Referenced Competency Test (CRCT).

TESTING CONUNDRUMS

Hopefully, now it's clear what it means when someone says the ITBS is a norm-referenced standardized achievement test. You won't look bewildered when the assistant principal says, "this is standardized so only read the instructions once to the whole group." But how do you use this information? Does knowing this make you a better teacher? That depends on how you use your new-found knowledge. You might teach your students these terms so they understand why you can't help them on the Stanford Achievement Test when you have helped them on all the other tests you have given them this year. You may need to use this when an irate parent wants to know why their child has made 100% on every math test this year but only scored an 85% on the ITBS. You could even see how this year's students did on the statewide criterion-referenced test last year to identify their weaknesses and teach more in those areas.

Some teachers look at testing as an intrusion upon their classroom teaching time. They feel that it is an evil procedure handed down from the state. Others see it as an opportunity to improve their teaching and their school. The way you look at testing and what you do with the results is entirely up to you.

REFERENCES

Bradley, A. (1998). Muddle in the middle. *Education Week, 17*(31), 38-42.

No Child Left Behind Act of 2001, 20 U.S.C. 6301 et seq. (2001).

—Merritt M. Arnold
The University of Georgia

TESTING: HIGH STAKES

THE PREMISE FOR CREATING HIGH STAKES STANDARDIZED TESTS—A BRIEF HISTORY

"Life may have less mystery but it will also have less disillusionment and disappointment. Hope will not be a lost source of strength but it will be kept within reasonable bounds" (Nairn & Associates, 1980 p. 1). These were the 1950 comments of Henry Chauncey, former dean of Harvard, offered up to guide the philosophy of a new Corporation-Educational Testing Service. A corporation designed to serve American education by providing tests and testing related services.

As uneasy as the aforementioned quote should make you feel, it is even more contentious when you unearth the conversations amongst the ETS staff and their consultants. Chauncey saw industrial applications for their data analyses as it would empirically validate "the ability difference between men and women, and the trends of employment as between the sexes" (Nairn & Associates, 1980, p. 3). In addition to gender commentary, racial superiority populated the early testing literature. Professor Carl Campbell Brigham considered by many to be the inventor of ETS testing went on record as saying: "The intellectual superiority of our Nordic group over the Alpine, Mediterranean, and Negro groups has been demonstrated " (Nairn & Associates, 1980, p. 179).

The present day rhetoric when overlaid with the historical literature resonates in the observation of Alan Nairn: Although the basic mental measurement technique (the mass administration of multiple-choice tests and the application of correlation statistics to the results) has remained intact for eighty years, the claims about what the tests measure have gone through several phases of dramatic fluctuation. Yet, throughout the odyssey of the testing profession's scientific verdicts, there have been at least two constants. First, there is the consistent finding that the working class, the poor, and the most oppressed minorities of a particular historical era have relatively little "intelligence," "aptitude," or whatever the profession is purporting to measure at the time. And, second, one consistently finds an institutional arrangement whereby the professionals who construct these tests and report these findings are backed and employed by the nation's richest and most powerful institutions; they persistently report and interpret their findings with confidence in their authority to direct the course of people's lives and thoughts (Nairn & Associates, 1980, pp. 162-163).

USES/ABUSES OF HIGH STAKES STANDARDIZED TESTS

The concept of standardized testing is built upon an assumption of quicksand- that is, that everything related to the particular "testing" experience is "standardized." To come close to that reality an "affirmative" response would be necessary for each of the following questions:

1. Is the emotional environment (climate) of each and every school in which the test is given identical?
2. Is the physical environment of each and every classroom used for testing identical?
3. Is the demeanor of every individual providing the directions and monitoring the test identical?
4. Is the racial and gender composition of each group taking the test identical? (Readers are encouraged to examine the research on social comparison theory and salience of self for the power of this question.)

If we could validate this "standardized" assumption—and we can't, we could then move forward with the uses of said instruments.

1. One of the predominate uses involves the monitoring/accountability function predicated upon the unspoken assumption that the judgments of teachers are subjective while testing is objective. How about answering the following objective test item: Which of the following does not belong with the others? Circle the correct response.

   Football
   Baseball
   Bowling Ball
   Croquet Ball
   Ping-pong Ball

An item similar to this appeared in a British newspaper and over a 2-week period letters to the editor provided skillful and sometimes humorous explanations of why each option was correct.

2. Standardized test as diagnostic tool-with the right scoring services this is a possible benefit to standardized tests. However, given the usual district print out it's a bit like a thermometer. Your temperature may be above normal but you do not know what is wrong or how to go about the healing process (Bracey, 1998)
3. Standardized test as a tool for teacher accountability-predicated upon the "curriculum as vaccine" model. The teacher's role is to provide a knowledge injection in the students arm or buttock depending upon the climate of the school. Teaching to the test negates pupil-teacher planning and generally narrows pedagogy to a didactic approach. High stakes testing can lead to issues of malpractice such as a

pretest and post-test design where spring test norms are used for both times of testing.
4. Standardized tests as a tool for student accountability i.e. promotion and retention. A lack of well-controlled experiments continues to promote the myth of retention. Such singular actions fly in the face of the concepts of multiple measures and triangulation of measurement. Recently AERA, APA, and NCME have written position papers indicating that use of test scores alone for issues of promotion, retention and graduation represent grave ethical problems (Bracey, 1998).
5. Standardized test as a tool for selection decisions. Perhaps the most pernicious of all uses. This usage is predicted upon the faulty assumption that intellect is a scarcity phenomenon like oil or clean water or to literally paraphrase Gould (1996) the promotion of the argument that achievement can be meaningfully abstracted as a single number capable of ranking all people in a linear scale of intrinsic and unalterable mental worth, (p. 20). Our job is not to sort and screen to justify a class driven society; rather, our goal as middle level educators is to help all individuals develop their full potential.

Even if it were possible to address all of these abuses we would be left with the fact that from birth to age 18, schooling accounts for about 9% of ones life experience. (Bracey, 1998). Put another way, schooling accounts for about 9% of the variance on standardized achievement tests, what accounts for the other 91% of the variance? The answer resides in such variables as family income, educational level of parents, poverty (as in the setting in which the school is situated), motivation, personal hygiene, and cultural factors. In short, the aforementioned list may become moderating/confounding variables in any sort of an attempt to create a one to one correspondence between instruction in school and the reported results of standardized high stakes test.

PSYCHOLOGICAL CONSEQUENCES OF HIGH STAKES TESTS WITH MIDDLE GRADE STUDENTS

The seminal review and interpretation of this literature was the manuscript by Paris, Lawton, Turner and Roth in 1991. As Developmental Psychologists they were keenly concerned about the impact of high stakes testing upon the developmental stage of early adolescence. What follows is a brief review of their findings. All middle school teachers could share antidotes "about students who cannot mark their answer sheets properly, who become anxious or ill during testing, who quit in the middle of the test, who struggle with the language and format of the items, who cheat, or who cannot sit still for the entire test. (Jervis, 1989 as cited in Paris et al., 1991, p. 14) These are teacher observations, how about the students' view of high stakes achievement tests? Young children adopt an optimistic view of their own ability and count their own efforts as evidence of success in schools. By middle school however, these same young people begin to make decisions about their own self worth and domains of competence by relying more on comparative information derived from test scores, tracking and grades. What was once attributed to personal effort shifts to luck, ability or other people, factors that they view as being beyond their control. "When students feel that external forces such as test scores rather than their own efforts control success, they show less interest in academic work, demonstrate less persistence, and are more inclined to take shortcuts or adopt maladaptive strategies" (Paris et al., 1991, p. 14). Clearly, high stakes testing is hazardous to the psychological health of our middle grade students and may represent one area of agreement for educators to undertake action in the larger political arena.

REFERENCES

Bracey, G. W. (1998). *Put to the test: An educators and consumers guide to standardized testing.* Bloomington, IN: Phi Delta Kappa International.

Gould, S. G. (1996). *The mismeasure of man.* New York: N.W. Norton.

Nairn, A., & Associates. (1980). *The reign of ETS: The corporation that makes up minds.* The Ralph Nader Report on the Educational Testing Service.

Paris, S. G., Lawton, T. A., Turner, J. C., & Roth J. L. (1991). A developmental perspective on standardized achievement testing. *Educational Researcher, 20*(5), 12-20.

—Richard P. Lipka
Pittsburg State University

THEMATIC UNITS

"Thematic units" are curricular approaches that seek to unify subject areas, knowledge, and learning activities around a central theme that is either a content-based topic (e.g., "Colonial Life"), a social issue (e.g., "The Environment"), a personal issue (e.g., "Who Am I?"), or a broader concept (e.g., "Conflict"). How thematic units are planned, implemented, and assessed depends on the approach to curriculum that is being utilized.

Through an interdisciplinary approach, units are organized around a teacher-identified theme, and subject areas, knowledge, and learning activities are arranged in interdisciplinary ways. In planning a thematic unit using an interdisciplinary approach, a team of teachers chooses a theme that young adolescents may find meaningful, challenging, and relevant to their concerns (Caskey, 2002; Jackson & Davis, 2000; Knowles & Brown, 2000; Manning & Bucher, 2005; Nesin & Lounsbury, 1999; Powell, 2005; Stevenson, 2002; Stevenson & Carr, 1993; Wood, 2005). Beane (1993) described seven criteria that themes should meet (see p. 75, *A Middle School Curriculum: From Rhetoric to Reality,* 2nd edition). Themes in an interdisciplinary unit may often be subject-bound and are either content-based (e.g., "Colonial Life") or concept-based (e.g., "Conflict"); however, middle level teachers should strive for concepts, rather than content-based topics, because topics tend to be less fundamental, universal, relevant, and substantive than concepts (Jackson & Davis, 2000; Tomlinson, 1998). Teachers decide how identifiable disciplinary content can be interconnected to contribute to the theme (Drake, 1998; Knowles & Brown, 2000; Manning & Bucher, 2005; Nesin & Lounsbury, 1999; Stevenson & Carr, 1993). Often, the approach to developing a thematic, interdisciplinary unit involves using a graphic organizer such as webbing (Fogarty, 1991; Stevenson, 2002; Stevenson & Carr, 1993; Wood, 2005); a thematic web using an interdisciplinary approach may appear as follows:

Social Studies   Math

THEME
(e.g., The Civil War)

Science   Language Arts

Fine Arts   PE

Teachers plan learning activities that allow young adolescents to explore the theme in each of the content areas by determining "essential questions" (Brough, 2003; Jacobs, 1989; Kurtzberg, Mineo, & O'Reilly, 1998) or "big ideas" (Powell, 2005) about the theme. Learning activities in a thematic, interdisciplinary unit are student-centered, constructivist, and experiential (Alexander, 1995; Stevenson & Carr, 1993; Wood, 2005) and are sequenced from an introductory or launching lesson to a culminating event (Knowles & Brown, 2000; Kurtzberg, Mineo, & O'Reilly, 1998; Stevenson & Carr, 1993; Wood, 2005). Formative and summative assessments occur throughout the implementation of the unit in experiential, authentic ways such as portfolios, performances, presentations, or outings (Alexander, 1995; Brough, 2003; Powell, 2005; Stevenson & Carr, 1993; Thompson, 2002). A final evaluation of the thematic, interdisciplinary unit allows for students' reflective input as well as others (e.g., guest speakers) who participated in the unit (Brough, 2003; Powell, 2005; Stevenson & Carr, 1993).

An integrated approach to thematic units is focused upon unifying the social and personal concerns of young adolescents and larger social issues. An integrated theme emerges from the interests of young adolescents and their social worlds and engages the curriculum in a dynamic manner, rather than being imposed from a specific content area (e.g., "The Civil War") or decided upon by teachers. Young adolescents and teachers work together in democratic, collaborative ways to decide upon questions that young adolescents have about their social worlds (Beane, 1993, 1997; Brazee & Capelluti, 1995; Knowles & Brown, 2000). Once their personal concerns are identified, young adolescents directly participate in finding ways that their personal concerns are linked to broader global issues, and a conceptual theme, which integrates these two concerns, emerges. That the theme is conceptual is a distinctive hallmark of an integrated thematic unit. Conceptual themes are broad and inclusive of various domains of social life and are issue-oriented (rather than interest-oriented or content-based) (Tomlinson, 1998); for example, "a theme such as 'Conflict' might emerge from concerns about family and neighborhood crime and violence along with concerns about global violence and terrorism" (Beane, 1997, p. 49). Conceptual themes integrate what Beane (1997) wrote are "four kinds of knowledge:" personal knowledge that attends to ways of knowing about the self; social knowledge that focuses on local and global issues; explanatory knowledge that utilizes both content and common-sense knowledge to make sense of the theme; and technical knowledge that is skills-based (p. 49-50). Therefore, an integrative theme unifies more than subject areas; in fact, distinct disciplinary boundaries are disregarded. In an integrated thematic unit, a conceptual theme unifies personal needs/concerns/questions, social/global issues, multiple fields of knowledge, and relevant skills (Beane, 1993, 1997; Brazee & Capelluti, 1995; Knowles & Brown, 2000; Stevenson & Carr, 1993).

Democratic participation and collaborative planning between teachers and young adolescents is another distinguishing feature of integrated thematic units (Beane, 1993, 1997; Brazee & Capelluti, 1995; Knowles & Brown, 2000; Nesin & Lounsbury, 1999). This integrative planning process contextualizes young adolescents' knowledge, experiences; utilizes their perceptions about how they best learn; and guarantees direct experience with the integrative nature of knowledge and experience (Beane, 1993, 1997; Stevenson & Carr, 1993). To begin planning an integrated thematic unit, teachers and young adolescents work together to make lists of "self questions" and "world questions" that they have, and then they identify themes that unify these questions (Beane, 1997, 1998; Drake, 1998). Next, the whole group votes on a theme to study, followed by a brainstorming session during which they develop activities that will lead to investigations regarding the theme and decide upon assessments that will demonstrate the application of their knowledge (Beane, 1997; Brazee & Capelluti, 1995; Stevenson & Carr, 1993). Finally, the whole group develops a final plan to implement the theme.

The learning goals for thematic units, interdisciplinary or integrated, include adolescents' (1) growing in their confidence as participatory learners (Alexander, 1995; Pate, 2001; Stevenson & Carr, 1993), (2) recognizing the importance of cooperative learning (Drake, 1998; Kurtzberg, Mineo, & O'Reilly, 1998; Stevenson & Carr, 1993), (3) developing personal empowerment and responsibility (Alexander, 1995; Drake, 1998; Knowles & Brown, 2000; Stevenson & Carr, 1993), and (4) increasing their cognitive skills (Brazee & Capelluti, 1995; Drake, 1998; Knowles & Brown, 2000; Stevenson & Carr, 1993).

REFERENCES

Alexander, W. M. (1995). *Student-oriented curriculum: Asking the right questions.* Columbus, OH: National Middle School Association.

Beane, J. A. (1993). *A middle school curriculum: From rhetoric to reality* (2nd ed.). Columbus, OH: NMSA.

Beane, J. A. (1997). *Curriculum integration: Designing the core of democratic education.* New York: Teachers College Press.

Beane, J. A. (1998). A process for collaborative teacher-student planning. *The core teacher, 48*(3), 3-4.

Brazee, E. N., & Capelluti, J. (1995). *Dissolving boundaries: Toward an integrative curriculum.* Columbus, OH: National Middle School Association.

Brough, J. A. (2003). Designing effective and meaningful integrated units. *Middle Ground, 7*(1), 27-28.

Caskey, M. M. (2002). Authentic curriculum: Strengthening middle level education. In V. A. Anfara, Jr. & S. Stacki, Eds., *Middle school curriculum, instruction, and assessment* (pp. 103-118). Greenwich, CT: Information Age.

Drake, S. M. (1998). *Creating integrated curriculum: Proven ways to increase student learning.* Thousand Oaks, CA: Corwin Press.

Fogarty, R. (1991). *The mindful school: How to integrate the curricula.* Palatine, IL: Skylight.

Jackson, A. W., & Davis, G. A. (2000). *Turning points 2000: Educating adolescents in the 21st century*. New York: Teachers College Press.

Jacobs, H. H. (1989). *Interdisciplinary curriculum: Design and implementation*. Alexandria, VA: Association of Supervision and Curriculum Development.

Knowles, T., & Brown, D. F. (2000). *What every middle school teacher should know*. Portsmouth, NH: Heinemann.

Kurtzberg, R. L., Mineo, D., & O'Reilly, A. D. (1998). Bringing history to life with an interdisciplinary unit: The Hessian. *Middle School Journal, 29*(4), 42-49.

Manning, M. L., & Bucher, K. T. (2005). *Teaching in the middle school* (2nd ed.). Upper Saddle River, NJ: Pearson Education.

Nesin, G. & Lounsbury, J. (1999). *Curriculum integration: Twenty questions—with answers*. Atlanta: Georgia Middle School Association.

Pate, P. E. (2001). Standards, students, and exploration: Creating a curriculum intersection of excellence. In T. S. Dickinson (Ed.), *Reinventing the middle school* (pp. 79-95). New York: RoutledgeFalmer.

Powell, S. D. (2005). *Introduction to middle school*. Upper Saddle River, NJ: Pearson Education.

Stevenson, C. (2002). *Teaching ten to fourteen year olds* (3rd ed.). Boston: Allyn & Bacon.

Stevenson, C., & Carr, J. F. (Eds.). (1993). *Integrated studies in the middle grades: Dancing through walls*. New York: Teachers College Press.

Thompson, S. (2002). Reculturing middle schools to use cross-curricular portfolios to support integrated learning. In V. A. Anfara, Jr. & S. Stacki (Eds.), *Middle school curriculum, instruction, and assessment* (pp. 157-179). Greenwich, CT: Information Age.

Tomlinson, C. A. (1998). For integration and differentiation choose concepts over topics. *Middle School Journal, 30*(2), 3-8.

Wood, K. E. (2005). *Interdisciplinary instruction: A practical guide for elementary and middle school teachers*. Upper Saddle River, NJ: Pearson Education.

—Alecia Youngblood Jackson
Appalachian State University

THIRD INTERNATIONAL MATHEMATICS AND SCIENCE STUDY

The Third International Mathematics and Science Study (TIMSS) is the largest international education study ever undertaken with data from approximately 500,000 students from 45 different nations. Data were collected in more than 30 different languages. Conducted in 1995-1996 under the direction of the International Association for the Evaluation of Educational Achievement (IEA), it has been characterized as one of the most rigorous and comprehensive international studies. The IEA has conducted a series of international comparative studies since its inception in 1959 for the expressed purpose of providing policymakers, educators, researchers, and practitioners with information about educational achievement and learning contexts.

TIMSS compares the mathematics and science scores of students at three junctures in the educational system—fourth, eighth, and twelfth grades. In the United States over 40,000 students in more than 500 schools participated. As well as content assessments, there were curriculum analyses, teacher surveys, and a video study of teaching in three countries.

TIMSS offers findings in three key areas: student achievement, curriculum, and teaching. In the area of student achievement America students were the only students with above average scores in fourth grade to lose ground in the eighth grade, and then do worse again in the 12th grade. By the time our students moved through the education system, they were among the lowest scoring students in the study. In middle school our students were above average in science, but were below average in mathematics. American middle grades students were outperformed in science by nine nations; performed similarly to 17 nations; and outperformed 15 nations. Twenty nations outperformed American students in eighth grade mathematics; 14 performed at the same level; and seven nations fell below our students. The United States was one of 11 TIMSS nations in which there was no significant gender gap in eighth grade math and science achievement.

In relation to curriculum, there are no required national curriculum standards in the United States/ Curriculum standards are developed and maintained at various levels of government—local, state, and national. The TIMSS curriculum studies were conducted by researchers at Michigan State University. It appears that U.S. mathematics and science curricula lack the coherence, focus, and rigor of the curricula taught in other countries that participated in TIMSS. Most state curriculum frameworks emphasize breadth over depth. Mathematics and science textbooks in the United States were found to be substantially longer than the international average and to express the incoherence, fragmentation, and lack of rigor noted in the curriculum. The content taught in U. S. eighth grade mathematics classrooms is at a seventh grade level in comparison to other countries.

The third area focused on teaching. The eighth grade mathematics videotape classroom study conducted in the United States, Germany, and Japan found American and German lessons, unlike Japanese lessons, to focus primarily on the acquisition and application of skills rather than problem solving and thinking. While 62% of the Japanese and 21% of the German mathematics lessons included deductive reasoning, no American lessons did. The lessons plans from each country were blindly judged by an independent group of American college mathematics teachers. Eighty-nine percent of American lessons were judged to be of low quality and none were judged to be of high quality. In comparison, 11% of Japanese lessons and 34% of German lessons were found to be of low quality, and 39 % of Japanese lessons and 28% of German lessons were judged to be of high quality.

The findings from TIMSS challenge us to view our educational system in a different way, challenge what we have taken for granted, and force us to reevaluate our cultural assumptions about educational excellence. While we give our students a good start, we must ask why student lose the lead as they are presented more complex mathematics and science content after grade four. In relation to middle grades education, the release of the TIMSS report provided the fuel to ignite dissatisfaction with America's middle schools.

Following the release of this report, many indictments, citing TIMSS, were levied against the middle school. *Education Week* published two articles attacking middle schools. One was titled "A Crack in the Middle" (March 1998) and the other was "Muddle in the Middle" (April 1998). The Southern Regional Education Board (Cooney, 1998) concluded that middle schools are the "weak link" in the K-12 education chain. Also, in 1998 Tucker and Codding of the National Center on Education and the Economy wrote the book, *Standards for Our Schools: How to Sell Them, Measure Them, and Reach Them*, in which they characterized the middle school as the "wasteland" of our primary and secondary educational landscape. Bradley (1998) reported on the disillusionment with the middle schools in a Maryland school district and noted:

> Overemphasis on the social, emotional, and physical needs of the middle school student has led to neglect of academic competencies. The result is a school system with vague academic expectations and complacency in the middle school years. (p. 39)

Silver (1998) found "a pervasive and intolerable mediocrity in mathematics teaching and learning in the middle grades" (p. 1). Whitmire (1998), voicing a similar opinion, wrote: "U.S. students stagnate in seventh and eighth grades, leaving them unprepared and unmotivated for the stiff high school … classes looming ahead" (p. A-1).

CONCLUSION

With the current emphasis on academic achievement due in large part to the No Child Left Behind legislation, we are currently faced with a number of urban school systems that have concluded that 6-8 schools no longer work for them. These districts include, among others, Cincinnati, Cleveland, Milwaukee, New York, Philadelphia, Baltimore, New Orleans, Boston, Harrisburg, Phoenix, Denver, Oklahoma City, and Trenton. Whether or not the TIMSS study contributed to the current state of affairs is not as important as realizing that the middle grades school could be following in the footsteps of its predecessor, the junior high.

REFERENCES

Bradley, A. (1998). Muddle in the middle. *Education Week,* 17(31), 38-42.

Cooney, S. (1998, March). *Education's weak link: Student performance in the middle grades.* Atlanta, GA: Southern Regional Education Board.

Silver, E. (1998). *Improving mathematics in middle school: lessons from TIMSS and related research.* Washington, DC: U.S. Department of Education, office of Educational Research and Improvement.

Tucker, M., & Codding, J. B. (1998). *Standards for our schools: How to set them, measure them, and reach them.* San Francisco: Jossey-Bass.

Whitmire, R. (1998, March). Middle schools targeted as weak link in education chain. *The Reporter,* pp. A1, A4.

—Vincent A. Anfara, Jr.
The University of Tennessee

THIS WE BELIEVE

This We Believe is the position statement of the National Middle School Association (NMSA) concerning the education of young adolescents. Originally published in 1982, *This We Believe* has been revised twice, once in 1995 and again in 2003. It has been one of the most popular and widely cited documents about middle level education.

The 1982 version of *This We Believe* examined the rationale for the middle school and provided a descriptive definition of a middle school. John Swaim, a past president of NMSA states in the Foreword of *This We Believe*, "Because the middle school concept has been implemented in a variety of different ways across the nation, the [National Middle School] Association felt that a clear and relatively complete statement was needed which would reflect the consensus views of the Association regarding the essential elements of middle school education" (NMSA, 1982, p. 1). Ten essential elements of a "true" middle school are also described and discussed.

In 1992, due to popular demand, NMSA re-released *This We Believe*. The 1992 version is nearly identical to the 1982 version with two notable exceptions. First, the 1992 version replaced the term "transecents" with "young adolescents." Second, the 1992 version included a set of resolutions concerning the education of young adolescents adopted by the National Middle School Association. The introduction of the resolutions signaled the transition of the position statement into a position paper.

Fifteen years after the original publication, NMSA's Board of Trustees unanimously approved the second edition of the position paper, *This We Believe: Developmentally Responsive Middle Schools* in September 1995. The Introduction of the 1995 version cites the need for the revision as, "Developments in education and in the practice of middle level education in particular have been so extensive since its [*This We Believe*] release that the Association [NMSA] recognized the need to assemble a group to revisit that position paper" (NMSA, 1995, p. 2). Based on the expanded knowledge and increased research data of the preceding decade along with the expectations about education for the twenty-first century, this version of the position paper introduced six characteristics of developmentally responsive middle level schools:

1. Educators committed to young adolescents;
2. A shared vision;
3. High expectations for all;
4. An adult advocate for every student;
5. Family and community partnerships; and
6. A positive school climate (NMSA, 1995, p. 11).

Given the above characteristics, developmentally responsive middle level schools will therefore provide the following programmatic components:

1. Curriculum that is challenging, integrative, and exploratory;
2. Varied teaching and learning approaches;
3. Assessment and evaluation that promote learning;
4. Flexible organizational structures;
5. Programs and policies that foster health, wellness, and safety; and

6. Comprehensive guidance and support services (NMSA, 1995, p. 11).

The third and most recent edition of the position paper was released in 2003. "The positions stated or inferred in *This We Believe: Successful Schools for Young Adolescents* are supported by a burgeoning research base about young adolescent growth and development and successful practices in curriculum, organization, and indeed every aspect of middle level schools" (NMSA, 2003, p. xi). In this edition, the characteristics of successful schools for young adolescents have been revised and expanded. In addition to the six characteristics introduced in the second edition, two new characteristics were added: (1) courageous, collaborative leadership, and (2) students and teachers engaged in active learning (NMSA, 2003, p. 7). The six programmatic components remained the same.

In addition to the release of the new edition in 2003, NMSA decided to release a companion document, *Research and Resources in Support of This We Believe*, which "brings together research studies and related resources that support sound educational practices for young adolescents" (Anfara, Andrews, Hough, Mertens, Mizelle, & White, 2003, p. iii).

REFERENCES

Anfara, V. A., Andrews, P. G., Hough, D. L., Mertens, S. B., Mizelle, N. B., & White, G. P. (2003). *Research and resources in support of* This We Believe. Westerville, OH: National Middle School Association.

National Middle School Association. (1982). *This we believe.* Columbus, OH: Author.

National Middle School Association. (1995). *This we believe: Developmentally responsive middle schools.* Columbus, OH: Author.

National Middle School Association. (2003). *This we believe: Successful schools for young adolescents.* Westerville, OH: Author.

—Steven B. Mertens
CPRD, University of Illinois

THIS WE BELIEVE … AND NOW WE MUST ACT

Following the publications of the seminal works *This We Believe* (1982), *Turning Points: Preparing American Youth for the 21st Century* (1989), and *This We Believe: Developmentally Responsive Middle Level Schools* (1992/ re-issued 1995), *This We Believe … And Now We Must*

Act (2001) sought to clarify and expand on the 12 characteristics and components of the model middle school as outlined by the National Middle School Association. The work originated as a 12 part series published in the Middle School Journal beginning in September 1996. Contributors to *This We Believe ... And Now We Must Act* included some of the most influential professionals in middle level education. Among them was Gordon Vars, who helped draft the original position paper of the National Middle School Association, *This We Believe*, in 1982. This book is important to the middle school movement in that the authors who contributed intended to further explain the applicability of the middle school concept and what one would actually see and experience in practice in such settings. The first four chapters in the book outlined the similarities between *Turning Points 2000* and *This We Believe*, discussed what is meant by teachers who are truly committed to young adolescents, explored the critical importance of developing and implementing a shared vision, and what it meant to have high expectations for all students. The nature of the advisory component in the middle grades, the importance of community, school, and family partnerships, the cultivation of a positive school climate, and the need for varied teaching and learning approaches were discussed in chapters five through nine. The concluding chapters, 10-12, addressed aspects of assessment and evaluation that promote learning, flexible organizational structures, and programs and policies that support health, wellness, and safety in middle level schools. Considered to be a key piece of literature in middle grades education, the book presented guidelines for educators and policy makers who wished to embrace the complete middle school concept and philosophy.

REFERENCES

Carnegie Council on Adolescent Development. (1989). *Turning points: Preparing American youth for the 21st century*. New York: The Carnegie Corporation.

Erb, T. O. (Ed.). (2001). *This we believe...And now we must act*. Westerville, OH: National Middle School Association.

Jackson, A. W., & Davis, G. A. (2000). *Turning points 2000: Educating adolescents in the 21st century*. New York: Teachers College Press.

National Middle School Association. (1982). *This we believe*. Columbus, OH: Author.

National Middle School Association. (1992). *This we believe: Developmentally responsive middle level schools*. Columbus, OH: Author.

—Lynne M. Bailey
The University of North Carolina, Charlotte

TOEPFER, JR., CONRAD F.

Human rights, equity, diversity, and democracy are the themes that run through Conrad Toepfer's life personally and professionally. Toepfer earned his undergraduate and masters degrees in English, with the expectation of teaching high school English literature. However, his first teaching position was at the junior high school level, and Toepfer's work remained with young adolescents from that point on.

The 1950s was a time of Toepfer's growing interest in early adolescence. He became convinced that these years were pivotal for young people, and that school and educational practices needed to respond to the interests and needs of these students. Various forums enabled Toepfer to pursue issues of equity and democracy as related to young adolescents, including his own doctoral work, the Association for Supervision and Curriculum Development (ASCD), the National Core Conference, and the Long Conference (a forum for junior high school principals to engage in dialogue).

Dr. Toepfer published his first article, "The Historical Development of Curricular Patterns of Junior High School Organization in America" in 1962. Also during this time, he took an active role in organizing the original Emergent Adolescent Learner Council of ASCD. Over the next decade, he was editor of several publications, including New York ASCD's quarterly journal, *Impact on Instructional Improvement*; *Transescence: The Journal on Emerging Adolescent Education*; and *Dissemination Services on the Middle Grades*.

Toepfer served as president of National Middle School Association (NMSA), 1987-1988, during which time he established three standing committees and a task force: Cultural, Ethnic, and Racial Diversity; Negotiations; and Parent Issues; Urban Middle Level Task Force. In the role as advocate, one of Toepfer's messages is "that education's greatest goal is to continually extend the opportunity and freedom for all to learn."

As an activist, Toepfer has played important roles in various organizations. He assisted in the establishment of the European League of Middle Schools, served as advisory board member of NMSA's Urban Middle Level Initiatives and the National Resource Center for Middle Grades Education. His awards include a distinguished Service to Middle Level Education Award from National Association of Secondary School Principals (NASSP), the Service to Youth Throughout the World award from New York State Middle School Association, the Louis E. Raths Award from New York's ASCD, and the Outstanding Educator Award for Middle Level Research from the Alpha Nu Chapter of Pi Lambda Theta Educational Honor Society.

—Mary Henton
National Middle School Association

TRANSITIONS

The effects of the transition from elementary school to a middle level school have been the focus of considerable interest and research for several decades now. The early work of Roberta Simmons and her colleagues in Baltimore and Milwaukee in the early 1970s (see Simmons & Blyth, 1987) called attention to the possibility that the transition to junior high or middle school may be difficult for many young adolescents. This research raised concerns about the possible effects of multiple school transitions for those students who made one transition to a middle level school and another to high school two or three years later. Studies of the effects of such transitions on the quality of students' subsequent adjustment to a new school setting continue to the present day and the research has helped school personnel design prevention activities to ease the transition for young adolescents.

Studies on the transition to a middle level school generally show that the transition tends to be more difficult for girls than boys (or, alternatively, more beneficial for boys than for girls) and for young people who move to large urban middle level schools that bring together students from several elementary schools. When these transitions have been difficult they have been evidenced in declines in students' school performance and perceptions of self-worth and increases in their feelings of anonymity and other psychological symptoms, such as anxiety.

Research findings related to middle school transitions that did not prove difficult for young people showed that transitions are eased when schools prepare the transitioning students well for the new school experience beginning when they are in the last few months of their elementary school experience. Students also experience a less stressful transition when their middle school programs provide adequate support in an environment that is conducive to meeting students' social and cognitive developmental needs. Such an environment is characterized by smaller learning environments wherein schools are organized into houses or teams within which students interact with teachers and other students more

often than once each day and teachers are given the opportunity to compare notes with each other on the progress of each of their students. Team organization helps to meet young adolescents' needs for greater intimacy with peers and adults by reducing the size of their reference group. Also, students' cognitive developmental needs are met when middle schools provide academic learning activities commensurate with students' emerging formal operational thinking abilities, rather than assign repetitious busy work. Cooperative learning activities that also challenge students and enable them to exercise adequate autonomy and decision making can provide a good *fit* for students' social and cognitive developmental needs and help ease the transition to a middle level school.

The perspective I have used in my examinations of the transition to middle school has focused on the changes in students' roles and the nature of the strains that can accompany the exercise of those roles (see Fenzel, 1989, 2000). The role of student undergoes several changes as a child moves from elementary to secondary school that are reflected in changing expectations of teachers, parents, and peers associated with the new larger and more complex school structure. More specifically, the transition to middle school is characterized by the challenge of making new friends, moving from being among the oldest to the youngest in school, meeting the expectations of a larger number of teachers, encountering a more diverse student body with its own sets of cultural and behavioral expectations, and entering a larger school in which teachers and administrators may exert more control over student behavior than did elementary school staff and fail to meet early adolescents' developmental needs for autonomy and self-management. The more the experience of being a middle school student differs from that of being an elementary school student, the more the young person will experience strain in the exercise of the student role, especially if teachers and parents fail to adequately prepare the student for the transition and provide support during the process. This experience of strain can then lead young people to perform less well academically and perceive themselves as less worthwhile than they did prior to the transition.

Transitions, of course, can provide important developmental benefits, and the transition from elementary to a middle level school is no exception. Although middle schools replaced junior high schools for a number of reasons, one important reason was that they could be designed to be more developmentally appropriate for young people in grades six through eight (or, in some cases, Grades 5 through 8). The transition to middle school can be a very beneficial right of passage for a young adolescent who leaves behind the elementary school of his or her childhood and enters the world of adolescence. An effective transition to adolescence involves helping the young person become more of an independent learner who takes more personal responsibility for that learning under the guidance of a teacher who also serves as the student's advisor and mentor. It also involves providing the middle school student with more opportunities to make informed choices and solve worthwhile problems. The middle school program must also provide challenge as well as support to the young person who is in the midst of an important developmental period.

In my longitudinal study of the transition from elementary to a 6-8 middle school in a small upstate New York city, the transition was found to be generally stress-free for most students, with boys showing an even better transition than did girls. For boys, stressors tended to decline more and their perceptions of self-worth improved more as compared to those of girls. Reasons for the positive transition for all students were related, I believe, to the way in which middle school and elementary school staff worked together to orient the students to the new building during fifth grade, the structuring of the first day of middle school such that only sixth graders were present, the minimal contact sixth graders had with older students in the halls between classes because of the way the school building was organized, and the organization of the middle school program into teams of either 75 or 125 students each with very skilled and supportive teachers. In addition, students from only three elementary schools attended the middle school, giving the students a higher concentration of familiar faces than if they had been in a larger school. The advantage for boys over girls suggests that the middle school, while continuing to be supportive to all children, by having male teachers on both teams who could serve as role models and advisors for boys, provided an environment with which boys could feel more comfortable than in the elementary schools that had a much smaller percentage of male teachers.

Research findings suggest strongly that, during the transition to middle school, young adolescents benefit from a middle school environment that feels small and personal to them and relationships with middle school teachers that are conducive to students' developing sense of identity. Sensitive and skilled middle school teachers are also needed who will take the time to get to know the academic and interpersonal strengths and weaknesses of each of their students and construct the kinds of learning activities and environments that will be flexible enough to move forward from each student's unique starting point and that will take advantage of students' individual strengths and talents. Some researchers and educators have advocated the use of student "buddies" for each incoming student who will provide initial and ongoing individual support and the scheduling of individual or group counseling or advisory sessions to help students receive any help they may need but find it difficult to seek out on their own.

As the research shows, considerable attention must be directed to larger middle schools, especially those in urban areas, where students experience elevated levels of anonymity and fear for their safety and where many enter the school achieving behind grade level and lacking organizational and study skills. In some of these schools, students become disengaged from the learning process early on and are at risk for school failure and dropping out. Clearly, these schools require a restructuring and a well-trained and committed staff that enables students to get off to a successful start and to grow throughout the middle school experience.

Middle school students generally look forward to the more "grown up" nature of middle school with lockers in the hall, changing classes and teachers, and the opportunity to make new friends, although these new experiences can be sources of stress as well. A transition in which students feel welcome, safe, supported, challenged, and respected from the start can be a springboard toward positive growth. Parents can play a role in facilitating the transition as well, especially when their efforts are coordinated with those of the schools.

REFERENCES

Akos, P., & Galassi, J. P. (2004). Middle and high school transitions as viewed by students, parents, and teachers. *Professional School Counseling, 7*, 212-221.

Eccles J. S., & Midgley, C. (1989). Stage environment fit: Developmentally appropriate classrooms for young adolescents. In R. E. Ames & C. Ames (Eds.), *Research in motivation in education* (Vol. 3, pp. 139-186). New York: Academic Press.

Elias, M. J. (2002). Transitioning to middle school. *The Education Digest, 67*(8), 41-43.

Fenzel, L. M. (1989). Role strains and the transition to middle school: Longitudinal trends and sex differences. *Journal of Early Adolescence, 9*, 211-226.

Fenzel, L. M. (2000). Prospective study of changes in global self-worth and strain during the transition to middle school. Journal of Early Adolescence, 20, 93-116.

George, P. S., & Alexander, W. M. (1993). *The exemplary middle school* (2nd ed.). Fort Worth, TX: Harcourt Brace Jovanovich.

Hirsch, B. J., & Rapkin, B. D. (1987). The transition to junior high school: A longitudinal study of self-esteem, psychological symptomatology, school life, and social support. *Child Development, 58*, 1235-1243.

Simmons, R. G., & Blyth, D. A. (1987). *Moving into adolescence: The impact of pubertal change and school context.* New York: Aldine.

—L. Mickey Fenzel
Loyola College, Maryland

TRANSITION PROGRAMS

Reports describing the risks associated with the transition to middle school have prompted many to create programs designed to facilitate student articulation. Concerns about dropout rates and the large interpersonal nature of high schools have also prompted reform (e.g., smaller learning communities) and a focus on programs to facilitate a successful transition out of middle school. The current research documents several negative outcomes (e.g., declines in academic achievement and motivation, increased psychological distress) associated with school transitions as well as qualitative reports of students' needs, concerns, and excitement about transition. Unlike many of the unexpected challenges (e.g., parent divorce, illness) middle school students face, school transitions are normative and preplanned. These transitions, therefore, create an opportunity for middle school personnel to promote optimal developmental pathways. Transition programs range from a single event (e.g., middle school tour, orientation) to extensive, school-wide programs that begin the year before the transition and continue through the fall of the transition year. The published findings of previous research on transition programs are highlighted and recommendations for transition programming are provided.

RESEARCH ON TRANSITION PROGRAMS

Elementary to middle school. The three primary areas often cited for transition programming are organizational, academic, and personal/social needs. Anderson, Jacobs, Schramm, and Splittgerber (2000) suggest that preparedness (e.g., academic skills, coping mechanisms) and support (e.g., home environments, teachers, peers, and information) can combine into a comprehensive program that helps students negotiate the transition between levels. Research has also suggested that common activities for the transition to middle school include students visiting the next level of schooling (e.g., tours), administrators meeting on articulation and programs, and school counselors meeting across levels (Mac Iver & Epstein, 1991). This research also discovered that high socioeconomic and high achieving schools have more extensive articulation programs, and that an articulation program that uses three or more transition activities increased the likelihood that students would succeed in the first year of school (Mac Iver & Epstein, 1991).

In one of the few studies which evaluated a preparedness program prior to making the transition to middle school, Ferguson and Bulach (1994) investigated the social adjustment levels of fifth grade students who "shadowed" sixth graders for one school day. Students who participated in the program scored higher on social adjustment and teachers perceived that the program was effective. Most often, transition programming is planned for students' arrival in middle school. Leland-Jones (1998) investigated an 8-month peer counselor-mentor and tutor program for students new to middle school. Compared to students the previous year, the intervention year cohort saw a decrease in referrals, absences, and help forms, along with a slight increase in grades and ability to articulate and resolve transition issues for peers. Walsh-Bowers (1992) utilized a creative drama group program for students new to middle school. The program led to enhanced social skills and more positive teacher and parent reports. Akos, Masina, and Creamer (2004) demonstrated strong teacher and parent support, and student satisfaction, as a result of a 3-week orientation program at the start of middle school. Several others have built transition interventions around coping or problem solving skills with moderate success (Elias, Gara, & Urbinco, 1985; Snow, Gilchrist, Schilling, & Schinke, 1986). Using more stringent experimental design, Greene and Ollendick (1993) targeted students who were struggling in their academic transition to middle school. The students were divided into three groups, including a control group, a group that received additional support from block teachers, and one that received a counseling group and increased teacher and parent support. The results indicated that the most intensive support strategy had the greatest effect and improvement in grade point average.

Middle to High School. Less outcome research has investigated middle school to high school transition programming. Mac Iver (1990) advocates for transition programs to include information, social support, and collaboration on curriculum and requirements between middle and high school personnel. Most of the attention for the transition to high school examines high school reform that seeks to engage students to prevent drop out.

Mizelle (1995) found that cooperative and experiential learning for a cohort of students who stayed together in sixth through eighth grade was more successful in the transition to ninth grade than a noncohort comparison group. The STEP program, articulated by Felner and his colleagues (1993), demonstrated that restructuring the ninth grade ecology led to higher grades, less absences, lower drop out rates, and better student perceptions. Primary in the intervention were subgroups of students with similar schedules in close proximity that included a homeroom period with an adult. Finally, the Smaller Learning Communities (SLC) initiatives by the U.S. Department of Education (2001) reflect a movement to better serve students in large, interpersonal high school environments. This movement seeks to increase opportunities for students to develop personal relationships with teachers and other students in smaller school structures such as academies, house plans, schools-within-schools, and magnet schools. In particular, freshmen are placed in these structures for extra support from adults and may also receive mentoring from older students and career exploration classes designed to engage students in high school curricula. SLC also advocates for looping, block scheduling, adult advocate systems or advisory, and academic teams that most middle schools are quite familiar with.

While most of the literature about the transition to high school lists the importance of collaboration and preparation at the middle school level, contemporary published preparation programs at the middle level are difficult to find. The lack of research on high school preparation programs is particularly puzzling due to the importance of educational and career planning in registering for high school, the often cited lack of academic readiness of ninth grade students, and that parent involvement in the transition relates to better achievement and lower drop out rates (Paulson, 1994).

Part of the difficulty in articulating and researching transition programs are cross level relationships and clear delineation of duties. With multiple feeder patterns, collaboration is often needed across levels and in various schools, and leadership in transition programs is ambiguous at best. Additionally, because transitions are multidimensional, the responsibility for programming needs to be adequately distributed among staff (e.g., school counselors, teachers, administrators).

Previous transition and transition program research provide useful guides and considerations for schools and districts in planning context specific programming. Even so, more extensive, longitudinal, and multifaceted outcome research is needed to guide practice. While this research indicates several positive aspects of transition programming, there are also methodological cautions. The investigations cited above often utilized self-designed measures, questionable comparison samples, and served one specific school. This is significant because few transition programs are stringently evaluated and as a whole, very little outcome data exist about effective ways to promote a successful transition to and from middle school.

RECOMMENDATIONS FOR TRANSITION PROGRAMS

Transition teams in the school. It is unrealistic and less effective to have one person responsible for an entire transition program. Transition team composition should minimally include school counselors at both feeder and receiving schools, as well as teachers from both transition years. It would also be useful to include administrators at each level, special needs instructors (e.g., special education, ESL), club and extracurricular coordinators, parents of students in transition, and students from transition year grades. Vertical teaming, or teacher and curricular collaboration across school levels, should accompany similar communication processes that occur between school counselors and administration. Vertical teams of teachers can focus on curriculum articulation, classroom management and discipline, homework and grading procedures, parent-teacher meetings, and a variety of topics related to the classroom.

Needs assessment. It is important to understand the needs of students, parents, and school staff for the transition. Research has demonstrated that different school cultures and contexts relate to distinct transitional needs. Moreover, a transition from one elementary to one middle school would differ markedly from a transition from three elementary schools into one middle school. Students moving with an intact peer group may be less concerned about new social structures at the new school than students being combined with multiple elementary schools. In addition, students from a high performing district may be more concerned about the academic demands of the new school, whereas a school district with high levels of violence may be more concerned about safety and academic demands in the new school. Since needs vary considerably depending on the location and demographics of the school, a thorough needs assessment is essential and can be done at each level (both before and after transition).

Facilitate and sequence organizational, personal/social, and academic needs. There is emerging evidence that these are temporal needs, or that there may be an appropriate sequence to addressing these needs (Akos & Galassi, 2004b). For example, tours, scavenger hunts, rule and information (e.g., bus routes, school nurse) reviews, and "practice" days are relatively short term interventions that help students negotiate the organizational aspect of school transition. These needs are mentioned by nearly all students and are most intense right before a transition and at the start of a new school year. Furthermore, study and time management skills, tutoring, increased communication of expectations (e.g., websites, homework hotlines), and vertical teaming may be useful interventions for the academic transition. Finally, small group activities, team building, extracurricular participation, and cooperative learning may be ways to increase students' ability to network with peers.

Written and disseminated yearlong district transition plan. Beginning in January of the fifth or eight grade year and ending in December of the sixth or ninth grade year, a comprehensive program for the transition can be cultivated based on national research, local needs, and school resources. A transition year gives feeder schools the responsibility to prepare students for transition and receiving schools the responsibility to help students connect and adjust to the new school. In feeder schools, a number of interventions can target preparedness of students. Common interventions to be implemented in the spring semester may include presentations to feeder schools, parent involvement opportunities, transition group counseling (Akos & Martin, 2002), coping skills curriculum (Snow et al., 1986), school tours, and teacher and student shadowing among others.

In the fall semester, the concepts of adjustment and support (Anderson et al., 2000) become important. Koizumi (2000) termed formal and informal support structures as anchor points, where students may identify personal links to the new environment. Orientation programs are the most common intervention choice of receiving schools. These programs are offered to all students and focus most on the organizational or procedural changes in the transition. Orientation programs can be 1-day events or last 3 to 4 weeks at the start of the school year. Transition orientation activities may include lunch and PE orientation, introduction of staff and school rules/policies, team building, social events, locker relay races, and orientation to school events and extracurricular opportunities. Orientation experiences are important to build a sense of community and belonging (Anderson) that should lead to more student engagement in school. Additional fall activities may include peer ambassador or mentor programs or a new student web link or portal that organizes information (e.g., contacts, policies, virtual tour, clubs and organizations, registration forms).

As the transition program is created, it is essential that the program be clear, replicable, and documented. The document should propose the specific activities, responsibilities of people involved, costs, provide dates and sequence of activities, and evaluation plans for each activity. The transition plan should be approved at the central office level and be disseminated among all schools and school staff. The dissemination across schools is especially necessary in larger school districts with multiple feeder and receiving schools. With consensus and a clearly articulated transition plan; students, parents, teachers, and school staff have reduced anxiety and clear focus on using the transition as an intervention to promote success.

Special needs and multiple system programming. Transition programs are not often tailored to special needs students or to parents. Low achieving students may need summer enrichment or additional academic intervention (e.g., tutoring, mentoring) to help with adjustment to the new school. Similarly, special education students require transitional plans, where special education teachers discuss useful techniques and revisions to IEP plans in the transition to the new school. Another example of special consideration includes limited English proficient (LEP) students. Research has demonstrated that, during times of school transition, Latino students have greater concerns and suffer greater GPA declines than their peers (Akos & Galassi, 2004a; Wampler, Munsch, & Adams, 2002). In this context, it may be useful to include Latino events, where extended family and bilingual presentations help prepare students for the transition prior to coming to middle school.

Although students are often the main focus, it is well documented that parent participation both positively influences student achievement and drops off significantly as students move beyond elementary school. Students do report parents as significant sources of help in the transition, although the same research suggests parents most often provide negative information about middle and high school. Parent newsletters and PTA or PTO meetings that originate at middle and high school should include parents of feeder schools in the spring prior to the transition year. By engaging parents prior to the transition, parents will have more open communication and feel more invested in the receiving school. Additional parent programming may include parent mentors for new sixth and ninth grade parents, additional orientation to procedures and policies at the receiving schools, and increased parent outreach (e.g., positive calls or emails, invite to school events).

Research, evaluate, and document transition program effectiveness. The specific type and duration of transition intervention vary markedly and depend on district configurations, feeder systems, particular needs of students and parents, school culture and climate, and a variety of other factors. While existing and emerging research will help answer these questions, designing evaluation and research on local transition programs is needed. As well researched transition programs are made more available in the literature, schools and school personnel have greater opportunity to positively influence students' developmental pathways and achievement.

REFERENCES

Akos, P., & Galassi, J. (2004a). Gender and race as factors in psychosocial adjustment to middle and high school. *The Journal of Educational Research, 98*(2), 102-108.

Akos, P., & Galassi, J. (2004b). Middle and high school transitions as viewed by students, parents, and teachers. *Professional School Counseling, 7*(4), 212-221.

Akos, P., & Martin, M. (2003). Transition groups for preparing students for middle school. *The Journal for Specialists in Group Work, 28*(2), 139-154.

Akos, P., Masina, P., & Creamer, V. (2004). Promoting connectedness and belonging in middle school orientation. *Middle School Journal, 36*(1), 43-50.

Anderson, L., Jacobs, J., Schramm, S., & Splittgerber, F. (2000). School transitions: Beginning of the end or a new beginning? *International Journal of Educational Research, 33,* 325-339.

Elias, M., Gara, M., & Urbinco, M. (1985). Sources of stress and support in children's transition to middle school: An empirical analysis. *Journal of Clinical Child Psychology, 14*(2), 112-118.

Felner, R., Brand, S., Adan, A., Mulhall, P., Flowers, N., Sartain, B., & Dubois, D. (1993). Restructuring the ecology of the school as an approach to prevention during school transitions: Longitudinal follow-ups and extensions of the School Transition Environment Project (STEP). *Prevention in Human Services, 10, 103-136.*

Ferguson, J., & Bulach, C. (1994). The effect of the "Shadow" transition program on the social adjustment of middle school students. *Research in Middle Level Education Quarterly, 20*(2), 1-21.

Greene, R., & Ollendick, T. (1993). Evaluation of a multidimensional program for sixth-graders in transition from elementary to middle school. *Journal of Community Psychology, 21,* 162-176.

Koizumi, R. (2000). Anchor points in transitions to a new school environment. *Journal of Primary Prevention, 20*(3), 175-187.

Leland-Jones, P. J. (1998). Improving the transition of sixth-grade students during the first year of middle school through a peer counselor mentor and tutoring program. Elementary and Early Childhood Education (ED424911).

Mac Iver, D. (1990). Meeting the needs of young adolescents: Advisory groups, interdisciplinary teams, and school transition programs. *Phi Delta Kappan, 71*(6), 458-464.

Mac Iver, D. J., & Epstein, J. L. (1991). Responsive practices in the middle grades: Teacher teams, advisory groups, remedial instruction, and school transition programs. *American Journal of Education 99,* 587-622.

Mizelle, N. (1995, April). *Transition from middle school into high school: The student perspective.* Paper presented at the Annual Meeting of the American Educational Research Association, San Francisco.

Paulson, S. (1994). Relationships of parenting styles and parent involvement with ninth *Psychology, 14,* 112-118.

Snow, W., Gilchrist, L., Schilling, R., & Schinke, S. (1986). Preparing for junior high school: A transition training program. *Social Work in Education, 9*(1), 33-43.

U. S. Department of Education. (2001). *An Overview of student learning communities in high school. Office of Elementary and Secondary Education.* Retrieved January 20, 2005, from www.ed.gov/offices/OESE/SLCP

Walsh-Bowers, R. T. (1992). A creative drama prevention program for easing early adjustment of whitewater middle school students. *The Journal of Primary Prevention, 13*(2), 131-147.

Wampler, R., Munsch, J., & Adams, M. (2002). Ethic differences in grade trajectories during the transition to junior high. *Journal of School Psychology, 40,* 213-237.

—Patrick Akos
The University of North Carolina, Chapel Hill

TURNING POINTS: PREPARING AMERICAN YOUTH FOR THE 21ST CENTURY

In the history of the middle school reform movement, the 1989 report, *Turning Points: Preparing American Youth for the 21st Century,* stands as a milestone in the transformation of educational policy and practices and is recognized as a catalyzing force for establishing a comprehensive research agenda in middle level education across America (Jackson & Davis, 2000). Prepared by the Carnegie Corporation's Council on Adolescent Development, *Turning Points* was originally developed as a blueprint for reform in middle level education in the United States (Carnegie Council on Adolescent Development [CCAD], 1989).

Recognizing widespread failure of middle schools in adequately preparing young adolescents for academic success, in 1986, the Carnegie Corporation of

New York established the Task Force on Education of Young Adolescents to examine the conditions in the education of students between the ages of 10 and 15 years of age and to identify best practices for promoting healthy and optimal intellectual development (CCAD, 1989). *Turning Points* called attention to the opportunities and risks associated with early adolescence, a growth period of rapid physical, intellectual, and social change characterized within a context of discovery, experimentation, and transition often accompanied by stress and declining achievement. The authors of *Turning Points* argued that providing high quality middle level education to every young adolescent in America was not only a matter of social justice but also a matter of national economic self-interest for protecting America's future within a global economy.

The core values of intellectual development and equity for all students are reflected in eight fundamental principles that were derived from research on middle level education, and which form the essence of the blueprint for improving middle level education. The eight principles are:

- Divide large middle grades schools into smaller learning communities.
- Teach a core of common knowledge to all students.
- Organize middle schools to ensure student success for all.
- Share leadership and decision-making among principals and teachers in middle schools.
- Staff middle schools with teachers who are experts at teaching young adolescence.
- Promote good health for all.
- Form alliances among families and school staff by facilitating respect, trust, and communication.
- Form school-community partnerships.

Addressing these principles, *Turning Points* provides recommendations that focus upon improvement in curriculum, instruction and assessment, teacher preparation and development, school environment, and the role of parents and educational partners in improving teaching and learning in the middle grades. The National Forum to Accelerate Middle Grades Reform reinforces and further articulates these principles with a six-point process for achieving high performing middle schools that are academically excellent, developmentally responsive, inclusive, and socially just.

Utilizing a systems approach, *Turning Points'* (1989) recommendations are offered as non-linear suggestions for middle level reform. In other words, each element in the system is interactive and dependent on other elements, so that a change in one element requires and mediates changes in other elements, which, in turn, may cause other changes to occur. The result is ongoing, systemic change that by design, will lead to continual self-improvement within middle schools.

REFERENCES

Carnegie Council on Adolescent Development. (1989). *Turning points: Preparing American youth for the 21st century.* New York: Carnegie Corporation of New York.

Center for Collaborative Education. *Turning points principles and practices.* Retrieved May 25, 2005, from http://www.turningpoints.org/principle.htm

Jackson, A. W., & Davis, G. A. (2000). *Turning points 2000: Educating adolescents in the 21st century.* New York: Teachers College Press.

Texas Youth Commission. *Turning points: Preparing American youth for the 21st century.* Retrieved May 25, 2005, from http://www.tyc.state.tx.us/prevention/turning.htm

The National Forum to Accelerate Middle Grades Reform. *Our vision statement.* Retrieved May 25, 2005, from http://www.mgforum.org/about/vision

—Karen Embry Jenlink
St. Edward's University

TURNING POINTS: SCHOOL REFORM DESIGN

Turning Points is a comprehensive middle school change design developed and coordinated by the Center for Collaborative Education in Boston, Massachusetts. The design is based on the Turning Points report issued by the Carnegie Corporation in 1989, which concentrated on the considerable risks that young adolescents face as they reach the "turning point" between childhood and adulthood.

Turning Points seeks to create high-performing schools, especially those serving high percentages of low-income students and students of color. The model includes support through on-site coaching, networking, professional development, and an accountability process. Turning Points schools engage in the following six practices:

- *Improving Learning, Teaching, and Assessment for All Students:* Faculty use local and state standards to develop curriculum with a focus on literacy and numeracy, select instructional strategies to meet the needs of all students, and develop effective assessments.

- *Building Leadership Capacity and a Professional Collaborative Culture:* Faculty create a democratic school community, establish a leadership team and teacher study groups, examine student and teacher work, and engage in other ongoing professional learning.
- *Data-Based Inquiry and Decision Making:* Faculty and students examine a range of data about the school's and students' progress. They use it to identify strengths and gaps, and develop solutions for improving learning.
- *Creating a School Culture to Support High Achievement and Personal Development:* Schools create small learning communities, eliminate rigid ability grouping, create longer blocks of learning time, and build family and community partnerships.
- *Networking with Like-Minded Schools:* Schools engage in a supportive professional network, participating in a range of school-year and summer network activities.
- *Developing District Capacity to Support School Change:* Districts partner with schools to provide them with increased flexibility and autonomy.

IMPLEMENTATION ASSISTANCE

- **Initial Training:** Onsite and offsite meetings and workshops help faculty to examine the Turning Points design, the needs of the school, and what implementation would look like. Before a school adopts Turning Points, a faculty vote is taken—80% approval is required for joining Turning Points.
- **On-Site Coaching:** A Turning Points coach supports teachers' professional development and builds shared leadership, meeting regularly with the leadership team, principal and teacher leaders, teacher teams, study groups, and the full faculty to assist the school in implementation.
- **Networking:** Opportunities include several network meetings each school year, a national four-day summer institute, a regional summer institute for teacher teams, and a national conference. Turning Points publishes a national newsletter and guides to the Turning Points practices, and hosts an interactive Web site (www.turningpts.org).
- **Accountability Process:** Turning Points schools use the Turning Points Benchmarks to measure progress in an annual assessment and goal-setting process, and in a more intensive School Quality Review every 3 to 4 years. In addition, most schools choose to complete the Self-Study Survey developed by the Center for Prevention Research and Development every two years. The survey pro-

vides comprehensive data on a wide range of measures including teaching and learning, teaming, climate, and student adjustment.

REFERENCE

Carnegie Council on Adolescent Development. (1989). *Turning points: Preparing American youth for the 21st century* (Report of the Task Force on Education for Young Adults). Washington, DC: Carnegie Council on Adolescent Development.

—Leah Rugen
Center for Collaborative Education

TURNING POINTS 2000: EDUCATING ADOLESCENTS IN THE 21ST CENTURY

Turning Points: Preparing American Youth for the 21st Century, a 1989 groundbreaking report from the Carnegie Corporation of New York, offered specific recommendations for improving the education of young adolescents. Capturing the attention of numerous educators, a flurry of middle grades research continued and reform models flourished. The following decade led hundreds of middle schools to implement the document's recommendations while others espoused similar measures. In order to further examine and analyze the documented progress, Anthony W. Jackson, a principal author of *Turning Points,* and Gayle A. Davis, one of the main leaders in implementing its principles, advanced a new understanding of effective measures in the realm of modern young adolescent education. By embellishing the original report with the credible research and best practice, Jackson and Davis published *Turning Points 2000: Educating Adolescents in the 21st Century.*

Following a foreword from Dr. David A. Hamburg of the Carnegie Foundation, the book blends practical suggestions and an overarching vision for the middle grades. *Turning Points 2000* documents the most salient lessons from those educators who attempted reform in the previous decade. Within its pages, the practitioner is offered translations of the most substantive research, solutions for critical issues like tracking and teacher licensure, and perspectives on effective structural changes needed in both classrooms and schools.

Like its predecessor, *Turning Points 2000* builds on the essential understandings of various aspects of middle grades as tenets of a system that encourages success for every student. In an effort to capture the findings of the 1990s, this volume aspires to mold the twenty-first century by recommending that middle grades should:

- Teach a curriculum grounded in rigorous, public academic standards for what students should know and be able to do, relevant to the concerns of adolescents and based on how students learn best.

Use instructional methods designed to prepare all students to achieve higher standards and become life-long learners.

- Staff middle grades schools with expert teachers specializing in educating young adolescents, and engage those educators in ongoing, targeted professional development opportunities.
- Organize relationships for learning (teams) in order to create a climate of intellectual development and a nurturing, educational community.
- Govern democratically, through of all school staff members, the adults who know the students best.
- Provide a safe and healthy school environment as an integral part of improving academic performance and developing caring and ethical citizens.

- Involve parents and communities in supporting student learning and healthy development.

Resonating from the epicenter of *Turning Points 2000*, its authors inform and appeal to parents, educators, policy makers, and community members to upgrade learning, teaching, and assessment for every American young adolescent so that each child may reach his/her highest potential and succeed. According to the document itself, "As we enter the 21st century, we see no more important goal in American education."

REFERENCES

Carnegie Council on Adolescent Development. (1989). *Turning points: Preparing American youth for the 21st century* (The Report of the Task Force on Education of Young Adolescents). New York: Carnegie Corporation of New York.

Jackson, A. W., & Davis, G. A. (2000). *Turning points 2000: Educating adolescents in the 21st century.* New York: Teachers College Press.

—Gena Bramlett-Guignon
Association of Illinois Middle-Level Schools

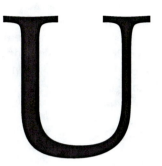

UNDERACHIEVEMENT: CHARACTERISTICS, CAUSES, AND REVERSAL

CHARACTERISTICS OF UNDERACHIEVING STUDENTS

Forty years of research have helped educators understand underachieving students. They can be characterized by attributes such as disorganization, lack of concentration, perfectionism, low self-esteem, unwillingness to conform, anxiety, vulnerability to peer pressure, and a sense of external locus of control (Coleman, Campbell, Hobson, McPartland, Mood, Weinfeld, & York, 1966; Ford, 1992, 1996; Whitmore, 1980). Much of what has been written about underachievement has been written about underachieving gifted students. In fact, the gifted underachiever has been described as "one of the greatest social wastes of our culture" (Gowan, 1955, p. 247). Of course, any student who is unable to reach his or her academic potential in school deserves the kind of attention that gifted students receive.

Rimm (1986, 1988) is interested in all underachieving students and developed the Achievement Identification Measure (AIM) that describes five dimensions, or classes, of indicators for identifying underachieving students: competition, responsibility, self-control, achievement communication, and respect. In comparing Rimm's list of indicators of underachievement to other lists of characteristics for underachieving gifted students (see Ford, 1996), it becomes evident that, in general, underachievers share many of the same characteristics: the student does not participate in school activities, the need for acceptance outweighs his or her academic concerns about school and achievement, home life is stressful, the student's family is of low socioeconomic status, the student feels alienated, the student has a negative attitude toward school, the student cannot tolerate structured and/or passive activities, the student has low self-esteem or self-concept, the student exerts little effort on school tasks as reflected in standardized test scores or grades, and the student bores easily and is disruptive.

CAUSES OF UNDERACHIEVEMENT

Educators attribute students' lack of motivation, engagement, and achievement to a long list of contributing factors such as psychological problems, emotional problems, poor study habits, low self-esteem, withdrawal, aggression, social isolation, conflicts at home, unsupportive parents, over-expectations or under-expectations of parents, physical or medical causes, poverty, social/class differences and expectations, conflicts with teachers, lack of academic readiness and preparation, learning disabilities, previous traumatic experience, and low self-confidence.

The Carnegie Council on Adolescent Development (1996) recognized that "[m]any problem behaviors in adolescence have common antecedents in childhood experience. One is academic difficulty; another is the absence of strong and sustained guidance from caring adults" (p. 5). Ford (1992) points to psychological, social, and cultural factors contributing to underachievement. Scales (1996) points to 40 "developmental assets" that help students develop socially, intellectually, and academically. He organizes these assets into eight categories: support, empowerment, boundaries, and expectations, constructive use of time, educational commitment, values, social competencies, and positive identity. Without access to a critical mass of these assets, students are more likely to have social, intellectual, and academic difficulties.

Some of the thinking on underachievement lays the blame on factors outside the school's influence, such as poverty, home life, and students' academic motivation. The implication is that since schools have little control over these factors, then schools have little control over improving achievement.

The National Educational Research Policy and Priorities Board (1997) acknowledges that "[l]earning does not take place in isolation. Students bring to the learning setting what they have experienced and the values they have been taught at home and in their neighborhoods." However, they also note that research shows "[s]tudents who take more courses and at higher levels learn more. All students, regardless of race, gender, or ethnic background, can learn to higher levels." *Turning Points: Preparing American Youth for the 21st Century* (Carnegie Council on Adolescent Development, 1989) concluded that studies of adolescent development did not provide persuasive evidence that young adolescents were unable to engage in critical thinking or meaningful learning.

Nieto (1994) highlights several studies that demonstrate schools can have an impact on challenged students:

> Thus, poverty, single-parent households, and even homelessness, while they may be tremendous hardships, do not in and of themselves doom children to academic failure (see, among others, Clark, 1983; Lucas, Henze, & Donato, 1990; Mehan & Villanueva, 1993; Moll, 1992; Taylor & Dorsey-Gaines, 1988). These and similar studies point out that schools that have made up their minds that their students deserve the chance to learn do find the ways to educate them successfully in spite of what may seem to be overwhelming odds. (p. 2)

Certainly factors beyond the control of educators contribute to the challenges of educating underachievers, but school itself may also contribute to the problem of underachieving and disengaged students. Emerick (1992) reports, for example, that the level of achievement occurring outside the classroom indicated that school was frequently the only place academic and creative achievement were not taking place. If this is so, then educators must closely examine the roles played by schools and teachers in developing underachievement patterns.

The concern that some school practices interfered with students' learning to their potential dates back to the first half of the twentieth century. In 1930, the Commission on the Relation of School and College examined secondary school performance (Aikin,

1942). Although the Commission was fully aware of the achievements of America's then fairly new high schools, their study revealed numerous areas needing improvement. Among other things, the study noted little connection between teaching practices and what was then known about learning:

> *Schools failed to create conditions necessary for effective learning.* In spite of greater understanding of the ways in which human beings learn, teachers persisted in the discredited practice of assigning tasks meaningless to most pupils and of listening to recitations. The work was all laid out to be done. The teacher's job was to see that the pupil learned what he was supposed to learn. The student's purposes were not enlisted and his concerns were not taken into account. All this was in violation of what had been discovered about the learning process. The classroom was formal and completely dominated by the teacher. Rarely did students and teacher work together upon problems of genuine significance. Seldom did students strive ahead under their own power at tasks which really meant something to them. (Aikin, 1942, pp. 5-6)

Dewey also warned about the important role school plays in whether a student achieves or not:

> If the pupil left it [the class, instruction] instead of taking it, if he engaged in physical truancy, or in the mental truancy of mind-wandering and finally built up an emotional revulsion against the subject, he was held to be at fault. No question was raised as to whether the trouble might not lie in the subject-matter or in the way in which it was offered. The principle of interaction makes it clear that failure of adaptation of material to needs and capacities of individuals may cause an experience to be non-educative quite as much as failure of an individual to adapt himself to the material. (Dewey, 1938, pp. 46-47)

Today, there continues to be evidence that school practices (or the lack of effective school practices) interfere with some students' learning. For example, in a study of gifted African-American achievers and underachievers (Ford, 1995), those underachievers reported (a) less positive teacher-student relations, (b) too little time to understand the material, (c) a less supportive classroom climate, and (d) a lack of motivation and interest in school. Testimony provided before Carnegie Corporation of New York's Quality Education for Minorities Project National Resource Group (McKenzie, 1993) indicated that the following factors contributed to minorities dropping out of school: differential tracking, lack of identification with counselors and teachers, poor attitudes and low expectations from teachers, feelings of failure, and curriculum that does not include minority perspectives.

Rimm (1986) identifies structure, competition, labeling, negative attention, boredom, and conformity (versus individualization) as school causes of underachievement. Wheelock and Dorman (1988) report that the choice to drop out of school may be the result of alienating practices in middle grades schools. They listed several factors contributing to students' decisions to drop out of school, including retention in grade, tracking and ability grouping, discrimination based upon standardized tests, boredom with standardized curriculum and instruction, punitive practices, suspension and expulsion practices, school climate and rules, and fragmented school organization.

REVERSAL OF UNDERACHIEVEMENT PATTERNS

Reversing the pattern of underachievement requires identifying effective techniques for enhancing instructional design, improving classroom management, and meeting the needs of diverse student populations (Wlodkowski, 1981). Stories of successful classrooms describe what teaching and learning can look like when educators and students engage in reflection, focus on content drawn from student questions and concerns, incorporate student choices and decision-making, and integrate real-life connections and problem-based learning (Alexander, 1995; Beane, 1993; Brodhagen, Weilbacher, & Beane, 1992; Delisle, 1997; Muir, 1994; Muir, 1998; Pate, Homestead, & McGinnis, 1997; Nagel, 1996; Wigginton, 1985).

Reversal of underachievement patterns is unique to each child (Emerick, 1992; Rimm, 1986; Whitmore, 1980). Ford (1992) points out that underachievement is "complex and perplexing" and requires moving away from traditional theories, including those that allege underachievement results only from a lack of student motivation to achieve. Her work also suggests that underachievement, as perceived by the African-American students sampled, is influenced most by psychological variables rather than by social and cultural variables. Ford also says that this is consistent with some studies and inconsistent with others that show social forces have a significant impact. Whitmore (1980) recommends the use of three kinds of strategies: supportive strategies (students feel like part of a family, not a factory), intrinsic strategies (engender positive attitudes, encourage attempts, seek student input, and offer opportunities for self-evaluation), and remedial strategies (recognize student strengths, weaknesses and needs; provide a safe environment and plenty of opportunities to excel and learn new strategies).

According to Emerick (1992), gifted underachievers who became achievers, without direct parental or teacher intervention, reported the following six factors in their upturn: out-of-school interests/activities, parents, the class, goals associated with grades, the teacher, or self. Most importantly, "a significant change in the individual's concept of self was viewed as necessary for the reversal of the underachievement pattern. In particular, each student believed he or she had undergone such a change and that without this change, the other factors would have had little or no personal impact" (Emerick, 1992, p. 144). For example, the student developed more self-confidence and a positive attitude toward the achievement situation, began to perceive academic success in school as a source of personal satisfaction and a matter of personal responsibility, and believed he or she had gained the ability to reflect on and understand factors that may have contributed to the underachievement pattern.

In summary, underachieving students share a set of common characteristics. Although underachievement patterns can be caused by factors beyond the school's control, some classroom practices (such as ability grouping and a focus on rewards) can also cause underachievement. Underachievement patterns are not fixed and can be reversed, but doing so is complex and unique to the individual student.

REFERENCES

Aikin, W. (1942). *The story of the 8-year study*. New York: Harper & Brothers.

Alexander, W. (1995). *Student-oriented curriculum: Asking the right questions*. Columbus, OH: National Middle School Association.

Beane, J. (1993). *A middle school curriculum: From rhetoric to reality*. (2nd ed.). Columbus, OH: National Middle School Association.

Brodhagen, B., Weilbacher, G., & Beane, J. (1992, June). Living in the future: An experiment with an integrative curriculum. *Dissemination Services in the Middle Grades, 23*(9), 1-7.

Carnegie Council on Adolescent Development. (1989). *Turning points: Preparing American youth for the 21st century. The Report of the Task Force on Education of Young Adolescents*. New York: Carnegie Corporation of New York.

Carnegie Council on Adolescent Development. (1996). *Great transitions: Preparing adolescents for a new century. Concluding Report*. New York: Carnegie Corporation of New York.

Clark, R. M. (1983). *Family life and school achievement: Why poor black children succeed or fail*. Chicago: University of Chicago Press.

Coleman, J., Campbell, E., Hobson, C., McPartland, J., Mood, A., Weinfeld, F., & York, R. (1966). *Equality of educationl opportunity*. Washington, DC: U.S. Government Printing Office.

Delisle, R. (1997). *How to use problem-based learning in the classroom*. Alexandria, VA: Association for Supervision and Curriculum Development.

Dewey, J. (1938). *Experience and education*. New York: Collier Books.

Emerick, L. J. (1992). Academic underachievement among the gifted: Students' perceptions of factors that reverse the pattern. *Gifted Child Quarterly, 36*(3), 140-146.

Ford, D. Y. (1992). Determinants of underachievement as perceived by gifted, above-average, and average black students. *Roeper Review, 14*(3), 130-136.

Ford, D. Y. (1995). *A study of achievement and underachievement among gifted, potentially gifted, and regular education black students*. Storrs, CT: The University of Connecticut, National Research Center on the Gifted and Talented.

Ford, D. Y. (1996). *Reversing underachievement among gifted black students: Promising practices and programs*. New York: Teachers College Press.

Gowan, J. C. (1955). The underachieving child: A problem for everyone. *Exceptional Children, 21*, 247-249, 270-271.

Lucas, T., Henze, R., & Donato, R. (1990). Promoting the success of Latino language-minority students: An exploratory study of six high schools. *Harvard Educational Review, 60*(3), 315-340.

McKenzie, F. D. (1993). Equity: A call to action. In G. Cawelti (Ed.), *Challenges and achievements of American education* (pp. 9-18). Alexandria, VA: Association for Supervision and Curriculum Development.

Mehan, H., & Villanueva, I. (1993). Untracking low achieving students: Academic and social consequences. *Focus on diversity* (Newsletter available from the National Center for Research on Cultural Diversity and Second Language Learning, 399 Kerr Hall, University of California, Santa Cruz, CA 95064).

Moll, L. (1992). Bilingual classroom studies and community analysis: Some recent trends. *Educational Researcher, 21*(2), 20-24.

Muir, M. (1994, April). Putting computer projects at the heart of the curriculum. *Educational Leadership, 51*(7), 30-32.

Muir, M. (1998). Planning integrative curriculum with skeptical students. *Middle School Journal, 30*(2), 9-17.

Nagel, N. (1996). *Learning through real-world problem solving: The power of integrative teaching*. Thousand Oaks, CA: Corwin Press.

National Educational Research Policy and Priorities Board. (1997). Building knowledge for a nation of learners: A framework for education research. Office of Educational Research and Improvement. Retrieved January 20, 2005, from http://www.ed.gov/offices/OERI/RschPriority/plan/

Nieto, S. (1994, Winter). Lessons from students on creating a chance to dream [Electronic version]. *Harvard Educational Review, 64*(4). Retrieved January 20, 2005, from http://www.edreview.org/issues/harvard94/1994/wi94/w94nieto

Pate, P. E., Homestead, E. R., & McGinnis, K. L. (1997). *Making integrated curriculum work: Teachers, students, and the quest for coherent curriculum*. New York: Teachers College Press.

Rimm, S. (1986). *Underachievement syndrome: Causes and cures*. Watertown, WI: Apple.

Rimm, S. (1988). Identifying underachievement: The characteristics approach. *Gifted Child Today, 11*(1), 50-56.

Scales, P. (1996). *Boxed in and bored: How middle schools continue to fail young adolescents—and what good middle schools do right*. Minneapolis, MN: Search Institute.

Taylor, D., & Dorsey-Gaines, C. (1988). *Growing up literate: Learning from inner-city families*. Portsmouth, NH: Heinemann.

Wheelock, A., & Dorman, G. (1988). *Before it's too late: Dropout prevention in the middle grades*. A Report by the Massachusetts Advocacy Center and the Center for Early Adolescence. Boston, MA and Carrboro, NC: Massachusetts Advocacy Center and Center for Early Adolescence.

Whitmore, J. F. (1980). *Giftedness, conflict, and underachievement*. Boston: Allyn and Bacon.

Wigginton, E. (1985). *Sometimes a shining moment: The foxfire experience*. Garden City, NY: Anchor Books.

Wlodkowski, R. J. (1981). Making sense of our motivation: A systematic model to consolidate motivational constructs across theories. *Educational Psychologist, 16*(2), 101-110.

—Mike Muir
University of Maine, Farmington

URBAN MIDDLE SCHOOLS

Regardless of geographic location, the characteristics of high-performing middle grades schools are the same. As described in *Turning Points 2000: Educating Adolescents in the 21st Century* (Jackson & Davis, 2000), *This We Believe: Successful Schools for Young Adolescents* (National Middle School Association, NMSA, 2003), and the vision statement of the National Forum to Accelerate Middle-Grades Reform (1998), high-performing middle grades schools are academically excellent, developmentally responsive and socially equitable.

Geographic location has often been used to determine if a school is labeled as urban, suburban, or rural. However, the term "urban" has come to mean a geographical space occupied by children of poverty and children of color. Social scientists, researchers, and educators often describe schools as "urban" when the schools serve significant numbers of children from low-income families or communities and minority (children of color), regardless of whether the schools are located in inner city, metropolitan, or even suburban geographic areas (Eubanks & Parish, 1992). This definition of urban will guide the discussion of urban middle grades schools in this entry.

Although many families within the urban environment live above the poverty level and have stable relationships within the family, the other side of the story is that many students' parents struggle every day to provide the barest necessities for their children. In addition to the challenges facing many urban middle grades students because of the poverty in which they live, deficit thinking about the concept of "urban spaces" further complicates their education. Some educators view these spaces as dangerous places where students have to be controlled and managed and where learning is not the primary focus of schooling.

It is extremely important that urban middle grades educators understand the historical, social, political, and economic contexts of students living in neighborhoods that are oftentimes impoverished. According to Sanders (1999), "Poverty has the most devastating impact on children" (p. xi).

Recent trends in student demographics suggest that urban middle grades schools are becoming more racially segregated. Davis and Thompson (in press) state, "Because of recent Supreme Court decisions, housing patterns, white flight, and other economic factors, schools in many urban cores have resegregated themselves." Urban middle grades schools, consequently, are often *de facto* segregated schools. Many urban middle grades schools are mono-racial in nature, including urban middle schools that serve a substantial number of white students who live in the urban area. One factor that ties all these students together is their socioeconomic level, which is often low.

SUPPORTING LEARNING IN URBAN MIDDLE GRADES SCHOOLS

By maintaining high expectations for students' learning and achievement and providing opportunities for students to use their minds well, educators who work in urban middle grades schools challenge the assumptions of the deficit model that depicts urban schools as abnormal and disordered spaces and urban students as objectified subjects.

For example, standards must be linked to the students' own social, ethnic, and cultural lives. According to Lee (2003), the knowledge a student must learn in school cannot exist apart from the learner's current mental schemata, motivations, and life experiences. Because the urban student often does not have the cultural capital to navigate through a curriculum based on the lived experiences of the majority culture,

it is extremely important to allow students in urban middle grades schools to create their own meaning and understanding of the content they are being taught. Lee argues that "A culture of quality based on high expectations requires that students be treated as intelligent beings who are capable of doing challenging work. This means they are placed in demanding, long-term intellectual environments that support an effort-based view of ability" (2003, p. 449).

In addition to the challenges facing students of poverty, many urban middle grades schools are staffed by teachers with less than three years of experience. According to Brown (2002), "The teacher turnover rate in the urban schools is much higher than in the suburban schools.... The result is that urban schools, especially those in the inner cities, are often staffed largely by newly hired or uncertified teachers. These teachers, who were trained to teach students from middle class families and who often come from middle class families themselves, now find themselves engulfed by minority students, immigrants, and other students from low income families – students whose values and experiences are very different from their own" (p. 1).

Middle school principals can either give up on these teachers or start aggressive professional development programs that focus on academics and, perhaps just as importantly, on helping all teachers get to know and understand the students in the school. Teachers can either view their students as deprived or culturally different; failing and low achieving or unrecognized and untapped; unmotivated or engaged/self-motivated; and at-risk or resilient (Williams, 1996). According to Davis and Thompson (in press), cultural stereotyping must be challenged, and urban middle grades schools must create cultures of possibilities.

Urban middle grades educators face many challenges, but research shows that these challenges can be overcome with the consistent implementation of the recommendations outlined in *Turning Points: Preparing American Youth for the 21st Century* (Carnegie Council on Adolescent Development, 1989) and the updated recommendations from *Turning Points 2000* (Jackson & Davis, 2000). Jackson and Davis state, "Along with intellectual development, at the heart of our definition of 'middle grades education' is the requirement for equity in outcomes for all groups of students, regardless of their race, ethnicity, gender, family income, or linguistic background" (2000, p. 11). They further state that "Schools grounded in the *Turning Points* design are dedicated to excellence and equity and to being responsive to the developmental needs of young adolescents" (p. 11).

The National Forum to Accelerate Middle-Grades Reform's three-part vision statement includes the belief that youth in the middle grades are capable of learning and achieving at high levels. Urban middle grades educators must look at their students through a lens of possibilities rather than a lens of deficits. These educators must question their own and others' beliefs and attitudes about the urban student in order to change the learning environments of low-performing, high-poverty middle grades schools. Urban middle grades educators must challenge the status quo and the social-deficit theory that contends that students from impoverished communities cannot be successful in school because of "inferior" home and community life (Sanders, 1999).

Urban middle grades educators also should embrace student culture. Although their lived experiences are often very different from those of their students, teachers in urban middle grades schools must honor their students' histories and cultures. These urban educators have the responsibility to overcome systematic variations in resources and outcomes related to race, class, gender, and ability. They must recognize the untapped potential and often unrecognized abilities of their students (Williams, 1996).

According to the National Forum, in order for middle schools to be socially equitable, middle school educators must have high expectations for their students and work diligently to keep their students' future options open. They must be sure that the work students produce is of high quality, and middle grades school leaders must ensure that students' teachers are expertly prepared. Urban middle grades educators can and must create a culture that provides for the cognitive-intellectual development, the psychological development, the social-emotional development, and the physical development of the young adolescents entrusted to their care by delivering educational programs that reflect the recommendations of *Turning Points 2000* (Jackson & Davis, 2000), meet the standards set by the National Forum to Accelerate Middle-Grades Reform (1998), and support the goals of the National Middle School Association's *This We Believe: Successful Schools for Young Adolescents* (2003).

REFERENCES

Brown, D. (2002). *Becoming a successful urban teacher.* Portsmouth, NH.: Heinemann.

Carnegie Council on Adolescent Development. (1989). *Turning points: Preparing American youth for the 21st century.* The Report of the Task Force on Education of Young Adolescents. New York: Carnegie Corporation of New York.

Davis, D., & Thompson, S. (in press). The importance of creating high-performing middle schools in segregated settings: Brown v. the Board of Education—50 years later. *Middle School Journal.*

Eubanks, E., & Parish, R. (1992). Leadership that promotes instability: A hope for at-risk students. In H. Waxman, J. de Felix, J. Anderson, & H. Baptiste, Jr. (Eds.), *Students at risk in at-risk schools: Improving environments forlearning* (pp. 143-159). Newbury Park, CA: Corwin Press.

Jackson, A. W., & Davis, G. A. (2000). *Turning points 2000: Educating adolescents in the 21st century.* New York: Teachers College Press.

Lee, J. (2003). Standards, testing, and urban schools—implementing highstandards in urban schools: Problems and solutions. *Phi Delta Kappan, 84*(6), 449-460.

National Forum to Accelerate Middle-Grades Reform. (1998). *Vision statement of the National Forum to Accelerate Middle-Grades Reform.* Newton, MA: Education Development Center.

National Forum to Accelerate Middle-Grades Reform. (2002). National Forum Leadership Training: A Leadership Curriculum for Advancing Middle-Grades Reform. Newton, MA: Education Development Center.

National Middle School Association. (2003). *This we believe: Successful schools for young adolescents.* Westerville, OH: Author.

Sanders, E. (1999). *Urban school leadership: Issues and strategies.* Larchmont, NY: Eye on Education.

Williams, B. (Ed.). (1996). *Closing the achievement gap: A vision for changing beliefs and practices.* Alexandria, VA: Association for Supervision and Curriculum Development.

—Sue C. Thompson
—Loyce Caruthers
The University of Missouri, Kansas City

VARS, GORDON F.

Cofounder and first president of the Midwest Middle School Association, precursor of National Middle School Association, Gordon Vars has been a proponent of core curriculum since his first education course as an undergraduate at Antioch College. His career has been devoted to teaching about and advocating for core curriculum—a person-centered, democratic approach to education.

Vars entered Antioch College in 1941 only to have his undergraduate studies interrupted by World War II. He served the U.S. Infantry in Germany, then returned to Antioch and completed his undergraduate degree in 1948.

Vars credits Hilda Wallace Hughes, an education professor at Antioch, for introducing him to the principles of core and interdisciplinary curriculum (Dyer, 1993). Taking advantage of the Antioch College fifth-year program, Vars researched the Progressive Education Association's Eight-Year Study (1933-1941), which fueled an emerging passion for core curriculum (see Lipka, Lounsbury, Toepfer, Vars, Alessi, & Kridel, 1998).

After completing his masters at Ohio State in 1949, Vars took his first teaching position in Bel Air, Maryland, as an eighth-grade core teacher. Three years later, he joined the Peabody Demonstration School in Tennessee to teach English, social studies, science, and mathematics and direct the outdoor education program. Vars began his doctoral studies at the George Peabody College of Education at Vanderbilt University with William Van Til as his mentor. Four years later, Vars moved to Plattsburgh, New York as associate professor of education at the State University Teachers College. Upon completion of his dissertation,

Methods and Materials in the Core Curriculum: Some Suggestions for Teachers, in 1958, Vars joined the Junior High School Project at Cornell University as associate professor of Secondary Education.

In 1966 Vars moved to Kent State University in two roles: professor of education in the Department of Teaching, Leadership, and Curriculum Studies; and coordinator of the Middle School Division of the Kent State University School of Education. In 1975 he became coordinator of the Kent State University Junior High/Middle School Staff Development Program, a field-based graduate concentration to assist current classroom-based educators to improve their middle grades teaching practices. He remained in this position until his retirement in 1993.

Staying in direct contact with young adolescents has been vital to Vars. While associate professor at State University Teachers College, Plattsburgh, Vars taught ninth grade at the campus school. During his 10 years as coordinator of the Kent State Middle School Division, he taught English, social studies, health, and personal development to students in grades six through nine. Until 1997 he taught a weekly Sunday school class of middle grades students.

Among his written contributions to the field are *Modern Education for the Junior High School Years*, with John Lounsbury and William Van Til (1961/1967); *A Curriculum for the Middle School Years* (1978), with John Lounsbury; and *Interdisciplinary Teaching: Why and How* (1987/1993). Vars was editor of *Common Learnings: Core and Interdisciplinary Team Approaches* and the author of numerous articles, book chapters, and monographs. Vars played a significant role in the formation of the National Association for Core Curriculum, founded in 1954, and has served as editor of its newsletter, *The Core Teacher*, since 1961.

Vars was recipient of the 1980 Ohio Middle School Educator of the Year and in 1987 he received National Middle School Association's (NMSA) highest honor, the John H. Lounsbury Award for Distinguished Service. In 1993 NMSA further honored him by dedicating its 20th annual conference to him.

REFERENCES

Dyer, D. (1993). Gordon F. Vars: The heart and soul of core curriculum. *Middle SchoolJournal, 24*(3), 31-38.

Lipka, R., Lounsbury, J., Toepfer, C., Vars, G., Alessi, S., & Kridel, C. (1998). *The eight-year study revisited: Lessons from the past for the present.* Columbus, OH: National Middle School Association.

Lounsbury, J. H., & Vars, G. F. (1978). *A curriculum for the middle school years.* New York: Harper.

Van Til, W., Vars, G. F., & Lounsbury, J. (1967). *Modern education for the junior high school years.* New York: Bobbs-Merrill. (Original work published in 1961)

Vars, G. (1958). *Methods and materials in the core curriculum: Some suggestions for teachers.* Unpublished doctoral dissertation, George Peabody College of Education, Vanderbilt University, TN.

Vars, G. (1993). *Interdisciplinary teaching: Why and how.* Columbus, OH: National Middle School Association. (Original work published in 1987)

—Mary Henton
National Middle School Association

W

WE GAIN MORE THAN WE GIVE: TEAMING IN MIDDLE SCHOOLS

We Gain More Than We Give: Teaming in Middle Schools (Dickinson & Erb, 1997) presents a comprehensive analysis of the dynamics of interdisciplinary teaming at the middle level. The text begins by examining why teaming is central to the middle school concept. A series of vignettes demonstrate what it means to be a member of a team, how teamwork can nurture teachers as well as students, and how teamwork requires personal commitment. A review of historical factors documents the tensions inherent in shifting from teaching as "cellular" toward teaching as collaborative. These introductory chapters provide a conceptual framework for those that follow, characterizing teaming as "means" toward the "ends" of student success, a dynamic that simultaneously links giving and gaining.

In the section that follows, four authors offer rich "team portraits" that bring these dynamics to life. These cases share the voices of teachers as they form teams, face issues that arise in their schools, and experience moments of intense learning. The third section, examines specific aspects of practice: sharing experiences, starting a new team, maturing as a team, working with administrators, affirming students' voices, and collaborating with parents. The next segment offers syntheses of research: trends in interdisciplinary organization, team teaching, team philosophy, and impact on students. The following section addresses six perennial issues related to teaming: teaming with elective teachers, leadership, decision making, curriculum development, language learning, and inclusion.

In the final chapter, Erb and Dickinson bring these strands together, concluding that "Interdisciplinary teaming is the hallmark of reformed middle schools," noting that teaming is both an "organizational structure" and a dynamic personal process that "goes to the heart of middle school teaching and learning" (p. 525). Citing a series of studies that document the power of teaming to increase academic and affective achievement among students, Erb and Dickinson insist that "So long as schools continue to be the main means of educating youth in the 21st century, teaming's place seems secure, particularly if information age organizations continue to revolve around teams.

In the 8 years since its publication, the insights in this text have grown even more important. While teaming has flourished in some locations, team planning, time, interdisciplinary units, and collaborative teaching have withered elsewhere as teachers and administrators have de-emphasized teaming in favor of departmental structures. In this context, this book is especially relevant. For new teachers, it offers enough practical advice to understand the basics of teaming. For experienced teachers, administrators, and policy makers, its chapters provide compelling evidence that teaming is not just nice, but necessary for the well-being of students and teachers.

As this encyclopedia went to press, the National Middle School Association circulated a flyer advertising a "best of the best" package of eight books that "provide the inspiration and information you need to improve your middle grades program." *We Gain More Than We Give: Teaming in Middle Schools* was one of those books. For middle level educators who want to understand the inner workings of teaming as an essential element of good schooling, it will continue to hold that status for some time to come.

REFERENCES

Dickinson, T. S., & Erb, T. O. (Eds.). (1997). *We gain more than we give: Teaming in middle schools*. Columbus, OH: National Middle School Association.

—David Strahan
Western Carolina University

YOUNG ADOLESCENT DEVELOPMENT

Since its inception, National Middle School Association (NMSA) has maintained that "to succeed with young adolescents, schools must be responsive to their developmental needs" (Lipsitz, 1984, p. 6). The most recent articulation of its position statement, *This We Believe: Successful Schools for Young Adolescents* (NMSA, 2003) identifies five interrelated areas of young adolescent development. In the following sections, the reader will gain insight into what researchers say about the physical, intellectual, psychological, social, and moral development of young adolescents.

PHYSICAL DEVELOPMENT

Developmental researchers have painted a comprehensive portrait of the young adolescent (Craig, 1976; George & Alexander, 1993; Simmons & Blyth, 1987). Growth spurts, the onset of puberty, and the development of primary and secondary sex characteristics mark this phase of human development. Physically, girls generally develop earlier than boys, reaching sexual maturity between 11 and 12 years of age. Boys lag behind by about 18 months, reaching sexual maturity between 12 and 14 years of age. Other insights from these researchers include the following:

1. Concern over and preoccupation with body image may cause young adolescents to avoid physical activities. For boys the concern is with athletic prowess and maturing muscles; for girls, it is breast development and menstruation. Both may lead to any excuse to avoid undressing in front of or showering with classmates (Milgram, 1992).

2. Advancements in the quality of medical care coupled with an increase in nutritional awareness contribute to earlier maturation trends. Results are sometimes realized in early sexual activity and teenage pregnancies (Bullough, 1981; Coleman, 1980; Tanner, 1978).

3. Mood swings result from hormonal changes; excitable and lethargic behavior can be the results of changes in basal metabolism. Physiological factors, however, are not the only contributors to the emotional state and behavior of young adolescents. Middle grades boys who develop early get a jump start on self-confidence whereas the late bloomers lag in feelings of competence (George & Alexander, 1993; Lawton, 1993). White females who develop early actually have lower self-esteem and more difficulty with the transition from elementary school to the middle grades, though African-American females who develop early do not show a similarly negative pattern (Eccles, Lord, Roeser, Barber, & Jozefowicz, 1996).

4. Worry, fragile self-esteem, feelings of inadequacy and self-consciousness often characterize the young adolescent. Preoccupation with physical appearance and thoughts of imperfections frequently are foremost on their minds. (Milgram, 1992)

Bearing in mind the physical developmental characteristics of the middle school student, George and Alexander (1993) offer the following advice to middle school educators:

Middle school students need frequent opportunities for physical movement and for rest and change of activity. They also need help in diet, nutrition, personal hygiene, and coping with such physical factors as menstruation, growing beards, changing voices, and outgrowing clothes. The opportunity for personal counseling on such matters is unparalleled. (p. 7)

Manning (1993) concurs and adds that middle school educators need to respond appropriately by examining "practices and expectations that ignore variability in maturation, such as chronological age or ability groups for all activities" (p. 16).

INTELLECTUAL DEVELOPMENT

Educators have long relied on the theories of Jean Piaget to understand the cognitive stages of human development. Piaget (1977) described four major periods of cognitive development: the sensorimotor functioning of infancy (0-2 years), the preoperational stage of early childhood (2-7 years), the concrete operational logic of middle and later childhood (7-11 years), and the formal operational logic of adolescence into adulthood (12+ years). Keating (1980) submits that much of the Piagetian legacy "benefits current work on adolescent cognition. The emphasis on adolescence as a transitional period in cognitive development remains justifiably influential" (p. 59).

Due in large part to the work of Piaget, middle level educators have placed great emphasis on the middle school student's ability to complete complex intellectual tasks. Recent research shows that brain development "not only expands during adolescence, it goes through one of its biggest growth spurts in puberty, particularly in the areas of the brain responsible for such functions as problem solving, reasoning, and organization" (Jackson, Andrews, Holland, & Pardini, 2004, p. 17).

Although young adolescents are in the early stages of formal reasoning and can tackle complex tasks, "most young adolescents continue to think in concrete terms" (Manning & Bucher, 2005, p. 51). While many are capable of using the power of mental reasoning, young adolescents are not typically "cognitive risk takers" (Milgram, 1992, p. 24). Their feelings of awkwardness in abstract thinking can result in complex, inappropriate solutions to simple problems. It follows, then, that their awkwardness and inexperience with higher-order thinking may cause undue frustration and lower self-esteem (Elkind, 1978; George & Alexander, 1993).

Research on brain functioning has significant implications for middle grades educators. Keating

(1980) contends that schools can influence cognitive development by focusing on meaningful content, actively supporting young adolescents in using higher order thinking skills, and incorporating the use of critical thinking into everyday learning tasks. In *Turning Points 2000: Educating Adolescents in the 21st Century*, Jackson and Davis (2000) call for curriculum standards that are "Developmental. Standards should be appropriate to the developmental capacity of students as they age, with the knowledge and skills that standards require growing in sophistication to match students' increase in capacity" (p. 37).

The research on cognitive development summarized in *How People Learn: Brain, Mind, Experience, and School* (Bransford, Brown, & Cocking, 1999) supports organizing curriculum around important concepts, the big ideas that form the foundation of understanding. In contrast to this suggestion for best practice, Bransford et al point out, "Many approaches to curriculum design make it difficult for students to organize knowledge meaningfully. Often there is only superficial coverage of facts before moving on to the next topic; there is little time to develop important organizing ideas" (p. 30).

The Carnegie Council on Adolescent Development (1989) argues that middle grades educators should be facilitators of learning: "Teachers will be called upon to promote a spirit of inquiry and to stimulate students to think about and communicate ideas. Far greater reliance will be placed on learning techniques that allow students to participate actively in discovering and creating new solutions to problems" (p. 43).

Research in gender role and sex differences reveals that a gender gap exists, especially in the mathematical and verbal performance of girls and boys. With regard to mathematics, Gober and Mewborn (2001) found that girls' motivation and achievement in mathematics are lower than boys'. Terwilliger and Titus (1995) discovered that boys, in addition to demonstrating higher levels of achievement and motivation, also had more confidence and interest in mathematics classes. With regard to reading, however, the American Association of University Women (1992) points out that on a national survey of eighth-grade girls mean scores for girls are higher than for boys on reading tests. In fact, "Girls were less likely to score below 'basic' and more likely to be rated as 'advanced' when compared to boys" (p. 23).

PSYCHOLOGICAL DEVELOPMENT

Milgram (1992) reminds those working with middle grades students that young adolescents "do a good job of hiding their fragility as they make the transition from childhood to adolescence" (p. 23). Lawton (1993) adds that during this period of transition young adolescents develop a self-identity, including role and sex identification. They also begin to more fully form their opinions about others, and may express concern for oppressed groups.

In fact, young adolescence is a time for moving from an egocentric view to a sociocentric view of the self in the world. George and Lawrence (1982) submit that this phase engenders a series of conflicts in the young adolescent. For example, they face a conflict between wanting to be unique and wanting to conform to peer-group standards. Tension surfaces within the young adolescent psyche when ties to family and ties to friends conflict. Likewise, young adolescents tend to move from idealism to realism in dealing with the world and their experiences in it.

SOCIAL DEVELOPMENT

The benefits of friendships in the social development of young adolescents have been well documented (Blum, McNeely, & Rinehart, 2002; Brendgen, Markiewicz, Doyle, & Bukowski, 2001; Crockett, Losoff, & Peterson, 1984). Manning (1993) summarizes the benefits as follows:

1. Relationships and conversation between friends can boost young people's self-esteem and reduce anxiety as trust and respect develop,
2. friends help young adolescents develop their sense of identity, and
3. friendships contribute to the development of interpersonal skills important for future intimate relationships. (p. 17)

Simmons and Blyth (1987) concur and add that adolescent girls are more concerned about being liked by their own sex and rate being popular and well liked as more important than being competent or independent. Boys, on the other hand, rank independence and competence as more important.

MORAL DEVELOPMENT

Classic studies such as those conducted by Piaget (1977), Kohlberg (1981), and Gilligan (1982) offer insight into stages of moral development. Expounding upon Piaget's work, specifically his explanation of the concrete operational stage of middle and later childhood (7-11 years), Kohlberg articulated three levels and six stages of moral reasoning from middle childhood through adulthood. Stage three, interpersonal conformity, is the stage at which the middle grades student is customarily found. According to

Kohlberg's framework, young adolescents are reconciling their understanding of what is expected of them by the people who care about them with their own self-centeredness. The reason to be "good" for young adolescents stems from feelings of social approval as well as those of self-esteem. Although Gilligan challenged Kohlberg on his study's sample (boys) in studying the moral reasoning employed by young adolescents and adults, her study of girls resulted in similar conclusions.

CONCLUSION

As active leaders of the movement to improve middle grades schooling, Doda, George, and McEwin (1987) reflected on 25 years of addressing young adolescents' developmental needs: "What works today has less to do with modern technology and sophisticated curriculum plans than it does with the person of the teacher and how students experience that teacher on a daily basis" (p. 5). From their experience and research, they offered ten "truths" about effective middle schools. The second five of the ten truths address what effective middle level teachers do when working with young adolescents.

- "Effective middle level teachers do not sit down while they teach" (p. 5). A standing, roving teacher has more opportunity to monitor student behavior. As well, the teacher models an active involvement in teaching and learning.
- "Effective middle level teachers work to create lessons that bring students as close to the real thing as possible" (p. 5). Young adolescents are concrete thinkers and need concrete symbols to help them enter into the lesson.
- "Effective middle level teachers have a sense of humor" (p. 5). Middle level teachers keep the affect light when faced with the choice to laugh or scream.
- "Effective middle level teachers think big but teach small" (p. 5). With middle school students this is the option for quality versus quantity.

- "Effective middle school teachers work to weasel their way into the hearts of the young adolescents they teach" (p. 5). Middle school teachers do not underestimate the value of affection in creating bonds with their students.

Jackson and Davis (2000) suffice it to say that "Middle grades teachers must be well grounded in the development and needs of young adolescents if they are to be successful" (p. 100).

Table 1
Center for Early Adolescence's Seven Needs of Young Adolescents

Need	Appropriate Practices
1. The need for diversity	Different opportunities for learning and different relationships with a variety of people; different opportunities to refine thinking skills
2. The need for self-exploration and self-definition	Opportunities to establish positive self-concept and a sense of identity
3. The need for meaningful participation in school and community	Opportunities to become independent and to have a role in making the rules affecting them
4. The need for positive social interaction with both peers and adults	Opportunities for association, companionship, and criticism regarding new social roles
5. The need for physical activity	Opportunities for physical exercise to avoid energy levels that are too high and opportunities for proper rest to avoid fatigue
6. The need for competence and achievement	Opportunities to try out new physical, psychosocial, and cognitive abilities
7. The need for structure and clear limits	Opportunities for increased independence and self-direction yet with clear limits

Source: Dorman (1984, pp. 6-8; Copyright 1984 by the Center for Early Adolescence. Reprinted with permission of the author).

Developed for the *Middle Grades Assessment Program* (Dorman, 1984), Table 1 outlines seven basic needs of the young adolescent. Developmentally responsive middle grades educators make curricular and co-curricular decisions with these needs in mind (see section on "Developmental Responsiveness").

REFERENCES

American Association of University Women. (1992). *How schools shortchange girls.* Washington, DC: Author.

Blum, R. W., McNeely, C., & Rinehart, P. M. (2002). *Improving the odds: The untapped power of schools to improve the health of teens.* Minneapolis, MN: Center for Adolescent Health and Development, University of Minnesota.

Bransford, J. D., Brown, A. L., & Cocking, R. R. (Eds.). (1999). *How people learn: Brain, mind, experience, and school.* Washington, DC: National Academy Press.

Brendgen, M., Markiewicz, D., Doyle, A. B., & Bukowski, W. M. (2001). The relations between friendship quality, ranked-friendship preference, and adolescents' behavior with their friends. *Merrill-Palmer Quarterly, 47*(3), 395-415.

Bullough, V. (1981). Age of menarche: A misunderstanding. *Science, 213*(4505), 365-366.

Carnegie Council on Adolescent Development. (1989). *Turning points: Preparing American youth for the 21st century.* The Report of the Task Force on Education of Young Adolescents. New York: Carnegie Corporation of New York.

Coleman, J. (1980). *The nature of adolescence.* London: Meuthuen.

Craig, G. (1976). *Human development.* Englewood Cliffs, NJ: Prentice-Hall.

Crockett, L., Losoff, M., & Peterson, A. (1984). Perceptions of the peer group and friendship in early adolescence. *Journal of Early Adolescence, 4*(2), 155-181.

Doda, N., George, P., & McEwin, C. K. (1987). Ten current truths about effective schools. *Middle School Journal, 18*(3), 3-5.

Dorman, G. (1984). *Middle grades assessment program: User's Manual* (2nd ed.). Carrboro, NC: Center for Early Adolescence.

Eccles, J. S., Lord, S. E., Roeser, R. W., Barber, B. L., & Jozefowicz, D. M. H. (1996). The association of school transitions in early adolescence with developmental trajectories through high school. In J. Schulenberg, J. Maggs, & K. Hurrelmann, (Eds.), *Health risks and developmental transitions during adolescence* (pp. 283-320). New York: Cambridge University Press.

Elkind, D. (1978). *The child's reality: Three developmental themes.* Hillsdale, NJ: Erlbaum.

George, P., & Alexander, W. (1993). *The exemplary middle school* (2nd ed.). New York: Holt, Reinhart, and Winston.

George, P., & Lawrence, G. (1982). *Handbook for middle school teaching.* Glenview, IL: Scott, Foresman.

Gilligan, C. (1982). *In a different voice: Psychological theory and women's development.* Cambridge, MA: Harvard University Press.

Gober, D. A., & Mewborn, D. S. (2001). Promoting equity in mathematics classrooms. *Middle School Journal, 32*(3), 31-35.

Jackson, A. W., Andrews, P. G., Holland, H., & Pardini, P. (2004). *Making the most of middle school: A field guide for parents and others.* New York: Teachers College Press.

Jackson, A. W., & Davis, G. A. (2000). *Turning points 2000: Educating adolescents in the 21st century.* New York: Teachers College Press.

Keating, D. (1980). Thinking processes in the adolescent. In J. Adelson (Ed.), *Handbook of adolescent psychology* (pp. 211-246). New York: Wiley.

Kohlberg, L. (1981). *The philosophy of moral development.* New York: Harper & Row.

Lawton, E. (1993). *The effective middle level teacher.* Reston, VA: National Association of Secondary School Principals.

Lipsitz, J. (1984). *Successful schools for young adolescents.* New Brunswick, NJ: Transaction Books.

Lounsbury, J., & Vars, G. (1978). *A curriculum for the middle school years.* New York: Harper & Row.

Manning, M. (1993). *Developmentally appropriate middle level schools.* Wheaton, MD: Association for Childhood Education International.

Manning, M. L., & Bucher, K. T. (2005). *Teaching in the middle school* (2nd ed.). Upper Saddle River, NJ: Pearson Prentice Hall.

Milgram, J. (1992). A portrait of diversity: The middle level student. In J. Irvin (Ed.), *Transforming middle level educa-tion: Perspectives and possibilities* (pp. 16-27).Needham Heights, MA: Allyn and Bacon.

National Middle School Association. (2003). *This we believe: Successful schools for young adolescents.* Westerville, OH: Author.

Piaget, J. (1977). *The essential Piaget.* New York: Basic Books.

Simmons, R., & Blyth, D. (1987). *Moving into adolescence: The impact of pubertal change and the school context.* New York: Aldine de Gruyter Press.

Stevenson, C. (1992). *Teaching ten to fourteen year olds.* New York: Longman.

Tanner, J. (1978). *Fetus into man: Physical growth from conception to maturity.* Cambridge, MA: Harvard University Press.

Terwilliger, J. S., & Titus, J. C. (1995). Gender differences in attitudes and attitude changes among mathematically talented youth. *Gifted Child Quarterly, 39*(1), 29-35.

—Kathleen Roney
The University of North Carolina, Wilmington

Index